Theos, Anthropos, Christos

American University Studies

Series VII
Theology and Religion

Vol. 208

PETER LANG
New York • Washington, D.C./Baltimore • Boston • Bern
Frankfurt am Main • Berlin • Brussels • Vienna • Oxford

Theos, Anthropos, Christos

A Compendium of Modern Philosophical Theology

EDITED BY

Roy Abraham Varghese

PETER LANG
New York • Washington, D.C./Baltimore • Boston • Bern
Frankfurt am Main • Berlin • Brussels • Vienna • Oxford

BT
40
.T4
2000

Library of Congress Cataloging-in-Publication Data

Theos, anthropos, Christos: a compendium of modern
philosophical theology / edited by Roy Abraham Varghese.
p. cm. — (American university studies.
Series VII, Theology and religion; vol. 208)
Includes bibliographical references.
1. Philosophical theology. I. Varghese, Roy Abraham. II. Series.
BT40.T4   210—dc21   98-27379
ISBN 0-8204-4175-9
ISSN 0740-0446

Die Deutsche Bibliothek-CIP-Einheitsaufnahme

Theos, anthropos, Christos: a compendium of modern
philosophical theology / ed. by Roy Abraham Varghese.
–New York; Washington, D.C./Baltimore; Boston; Bern;
Frankfurt am Main; Berlin; Brussels, Vienna; Oxford: Lang.
(American university studies: Ser. 7,
Theology and religion; Vol. 208)
ISBN 0-8204-4175-9

The paper in this book meets the guidelines for permanence and durability
of the Committee on Production Guidelines for Book Longevity
of the Council of Library Resources.

Printed in the United States of America

Dedication

For my wife Anila
In gratitude and appreciation for our union in the Christos
Who is Theos and Anthropos

Acknowledgment

The Case for Dualism by John Foster is reprinted here with the permission of the author and the University Press of Virginia.

Table of Contents

Section II: Anthropos

Section III: Christos

Introduction

From Skepticism to the Rediscovery of Reality

Roy Abraham Varghese

"Perhaps what is inexpressible (what I find mysterious and am not able to express) is the background against which whatever I could express has its meaning."—Ludwig Wittgenstein, *Culture and Value*

The greatest superstition of the twentieth century is the widespread idea that the conscious thinking experienced by all human beings at every waking moment was produced entirely from and by mindless matter and is in fact reducible purely and simply to matter. We have lost our minds in more senses than one!

Theos, Anthropos, Christos: A Compendium of Modern Philosophical Theology is an anthology of twenty one essays by noted thinkers who address this and similar superstitions by rigorously deploying the tools of modern thought to re-examine and restate the central insights of classical philosophy. In natural theology, the contributors address the challenge of influential varieties of skepticism while developing a cogent and coherent framework of thought to defend the existence and the simplicity, immutability, goodness and infinity of God. In philosophy of mind, they counter modern materialisms with an extensive defense of the existence of a mental reality that is radically non-physical. In moral philosophy, the contributors consider the contradictions of relativism and the application of rationally defensible norms to contemporary ethical debates. The final section comprises a phenomenological analysis of the Jesus of the New Testament and a critique of syncretism in comparative religion.

From Conscious Awareness to Infinite Intelligence

The full absurdity and indefensibility of the thesis that there is no such thing as thinking should be self-evident if we just stop to think about it—and thinking, in this context, would mean a clear consideration of the issue on its own terms without diving into conceptual foxholes designed to keep out the hard facts of everyday experience.

The data of our daily experience may be summarized thus: We are conscious and aware that we are conscious; we perceive, conceive, remember, imagine, sense, feel, plan, intend, choose. Our experience is not only qualitatively subjective in nature (consciousness) but also experienced as our experience (the self) and experienced by us (intention); we can describe and discuss things that go beyond anything that we directly experience (intellect); moreover, experience itself is known to us as irreducibly different from all that is physical in nature.

Could these fundamental features of the human condition of which we are directly and constantly aware—and aware of as intrinsically immaterial—have arisen from lifeless, purposeless mass-energy given not just a few billion years but an infinite period of time? It is almost as if we were to say that given an infinite amount of time, a pen and a paper, without any external intervention, would somehow give rise to the concepts embodied in the Gettysburg Address: we are not speaking of the words that constitute the Address but the concepts represented by the words: concepts as such are so radically different in nature from the physical objects used to represent them that it is simply nonsensical to suppose that the latter could "produce" the former.

We think and our thinking is so obviously distinct from the physical realm that we cannot conceive of it as having risen from the physical: certainly we cannot give any credence to the idea that a certain bundle of mass-energy that just happened to exist (without beginning or end) then evolved without any direction or guidance over time into THOUGHT. We cannot seriously believe that intellect sprang out of mindless mass-energy, consciousness out of lifeless matter, intelligence out of blind force fields. Once we truly recognize that we are conscious thinking agents, we can never again conceive of our coming to be from anything less than a conscious thinking agent. Only Mind can beget mind; only an infinite Intelligence, an intelligence that has no limitation of any kind, can create beings with any kind of intelligence. Descartes said, "I think therefore I am". It would have been more correct to say: "I think and therefore know that I cannot as a thinking being have come into existence from non-thinking matter." I think: therefore God exists.

Let us be clear that the issue here is not the question of the precise neuronal activity associated with consciousness and thought-processes or the mode in which Natural Selection is said to have driven evolution or the difference between animals and humans or whether or not there is a life after death. Nor do arguments about the reality of the self, of intention and freewill and the precise relationship between universals and particulars, sense-data and concepts have any direct bearing here. Rather, the fundamental facts are: we think; we know that our thinking is radically different from all physical reality (our thought of justice has no size or shape or any other sensory correlate); and it is self-evident that this activity of thinking that we experience everyday could not have arisen out of mindless matter, just as a rock cannot give rise to a thought, even over an infinite period of time. To be conscious that we are thinking is to know that God exists.

Once we arrive at this fundamental insight, all the other facts of our everyday experience as conscious thinking agents make sense: consciousness, which is inexplicable on a purely physical level, is seen to be qualitatively incorporeal in character; concepts and universals, as well as language, testify to the intrinsically immaterial nature of thought; the self that continues through all our experiences is not an illusion but an independently existing reality; the intentions and free actions that characterize most of our daily activities are not simply and solely the pre-determined applications of the laws of physics. But the bedrock on which these other insights rest is our immediate and irreducible awareness of ourselves as conscious thinking agents and the simultaneous perception that "conscious thinking" could never be the product of mindless matter and blind physical forces but could only originate from Something that is Itself Conscious and Thinking. Likewise, a self cannot come from non-self or intentional activity from a non-intentional template. The argument as it stands is not dependent on additional explication of the ontological standing of the contents of our conscious awareness. Nevertheless we will consider the relevance of our experience of consciousness, intellect and language and of the self, freewill and intention to the fundamental insight outlined here.

Consciousness and Intellect

Of this we are all certain: we are conscious and aware that we are conscious. The data of our consciousness ranges from sensations that reach us through one or more of the five senses; memories that "relive" sensory experiences of the past; images that we form in our imagination by extrapolating from our sensory experience; concepts that do not have any correlation with our sensory experience such as the notion of liberty or mathematical entities and theories; intentions that we form and execute such as planning to go for a walk or a vacation; and choices that we make ranging from giving up our lives for our country to telling the truth in a conversation. Some of the data of our consciousness are directly related to the physical world, for instance the objects perceived by the five senses or objects that we imagine from our previous sensory experience, whereas others are simply pure acts of the intellect, for instance the acts of understanding, judging and reasoning.

We perceive and we conceive—these are the two primary and distinct activities of the mind, one sensory in nature and the other intellective (although the activity of sense-perception often requires intellective analysis as well). The activity of the intellect is especially apparent in the classification of our experience under universal concepts: the mind works on the data of our immediate experience to see what is similar between different objects and to separate these similar elements into universal concepts (the concept of dog from our experience of particular dogs): but the universals have no separate existence apart from the instances in which they are embodied. Also not all concepts are directly related to sensory data: the concept of God, for instance, explains the existence of the world of sense-data but is not itself a part of sensory experience.

Concepts are a particularly thorny problem for materialists. "Our concepts transcend material configurations in space-time," writes the philosopher J.J. Haldane in a debate on theism and atheism with J.J.C. Smart, "For any naturally individuated object or property there are indefinitely many non-equivalent ways of thinking about it. That is to say, the structure of the conceptual order, which is expressed in judgements and actions, is richer and more abstract than that of the natural order, and the character of this difference makes it difficult to see how the materialist could explain the former as arising out of the latter."[1] In *The Mind-Maker*, a paper in this volume, Thomas Sullivan and Russell Pannier argue that the existence of universals, the intentional awareness of instantiable characteristics, cannot be explained in a naturalistic framework.

The higher animals share some of our abilities of sense-perception but not of intellection. The experiments with chimpanzees and other animals have shown that they respond to certain perceptual objects when these are displayed—but there is no evidence that the animals are capable of pure conceptual thought particularly when there is no perceptual component to the activity. Certainly, there is no evidence that animals can deal with concepts that lie outside sensory experience. Moreover, the fact that computers process information just like the intellect does not establish any identity between them since the computer is not conscious or aware of itself doing the processing as we are when we think; nor does it have insights and intuitions as we do or understand the meaning of the symbols it processes; and finally, the computer only performs the activities it was programmed to do by its human creator.

Not only are we conscious and aware of being conscious but we are just as clearly conscious that our consciousness is dramatically different from anything material or physical. It has a reality of its own that cannot be perceived as being physical in any relevant sense of the term. When we perceive a neural firing in the brain we perceive a physical process not that which we experience "on the inside" as a thought. The argument that the thought and the neural firing are identical although they "look and feel" different quite clearly flies in the face of the only empirical evidence that will ever be available to us, namely, what we can know about the physiological workings of the brain and the sensation or thought of which we are directly and immediately conscious. Consciousness, as we experience it, is irreducibly non-physical although it interacts constantly with the physical. But interaction between the mind and the brain does not by any means imply that the brain and the mind are the same thing—just as the conductor is not identical with the orchestra. Damage to the brain obviously affects the functioning of the mind since in its present state the mind works with the brain. When its batteries run out, the radio can no longer transmit the messages it used to pick up—but the physical components of the radio are by no means identical with the messages let alone with the person or persons from whom the messages originate.

The materialists, physicalists, determinists, mechanists, behaviorists and functionalists have scurried from one argument to another as even they eventually disavow each new attempt to deny the obvious and try to come up with yet another argument in favor of the idea that mind is just matter. The very fact that they have to keep inventing new arguments—all of them based on unverifiable speculation—is an argument against the overall soundness of their futile enterprise since materialism seems to be in a state of perpetual retreat. C.D. Broad said a long time ago, about Behaviorism that it is one of "the numerous class of theories which are so preposterously silly that only very learned men could have thought of them. But such theories are frequently countenanced by the naive since they are put forward in highly technical terms by learned persons who are themselves too confused to know exactly what they mean."[2] The leading proponent of Logical Positivism in the English-speaking world, Sir Alfred Ayer, said in an interview with me for *Great Thinkers on Great Questions* (as he has in some of his writings) that the mental is clearly distinct from the material and there is no ground for identifying the one with the other. John Searle, himself a materialist, said in his *The Rediscovery of the Mind* that "no sane person can deny its [consciousness'] existence, though many pretend to do so."[3]

At the present time, materialist philosophers like Donald Davidson, W.V.O. Quine, Daniel Dennett and Paul and Patricia Churchland have rejected the old arguments for materialism only to come back with even more implausible alternatives that are addressed in this volume. But in becoming more sophisticated, today's materialists have admitted all that we need or require, in the current context, for evoking the insight that God exists. For once they accept, as they do, that our experience of consciousness is real, then our next question to them is not what tortured physicalist explanation can there be for this very real non-physical experience, but how (setting aside the issue of how one entity can at one and the same time be truly mental and truly material) a purely physical universe can give rise at random to something that we experience intentionally as qualitatively non-physical. The contention of this essay is that it is simply incoherent to assert that a universe of pure matter—with no purpose, no intellect, no consciousness, no will whatsoever—can give rise to conscious, thinking, willing agents. Once we admit that we are conscious of being conscious then we are on the way to a recognition of the inevitability of an infinite Intelligence that grounds all mental experience.

Language

Syntactical language is unique to human beings—found even in ancient civilizations and instinctively mastered by children at a very young age. Although animals communicate through various sounds, we know that they are incapable of forming verbal or grammatical structures. Chimpanzees tutored by humans learn visual signals and then use these signals to get things. But this "learning" is really a process of being conditioned to perform certain actions in response to given stimuli—something that is qualitatively different from such innate human capacities as seeking explanations and deducing causal relationships. Nor can the chimps manipulate the symbols they "learn" to give new meanings as children do. Furthermore, the words that they "learn" are all derived from their direct perceptual experience of the object designated by the word. Human children, with their power of conceptual thought, do not have to learn the meanings of words simply from perceptual experience but can be told what something means just by explaining it in terms of something with which they are already familiar (once they know what animals are they can understand the notion of a place where animals are kept without having to actually visit a zoo).

Scientists cannot explain the origin of language or the jump from primitive to syntactical language (*Scientific American* April 1991, October 1994). The linguist Noam Chomsky holds that the capacity for language and especially the complexities of syntax can only be explained as innate in humans. Moreover, as David Braine has shown, the process of linguistic understanding does not have any neural correlate and is not the activity of a specific bodily organ.

Words are symbols or codes signifying something—and the coding and decoding activities required in using language presuppose an entity that can endow and perceive meaning in symbols. Can a material object perceive meaning? By its very nature, the act of comprehending the meaning of something is non-physical. Moreover many words we commonly use designate things that either have not been perceived (e.g., quarks) or cannot be perceived by the senses (e.g., angels)—but they have meaning. The acts of giving meaning or seeing meaning is again irreducibly immaterial and are carried on all the time as illustrated by our use of language.

The Self

What is it that perceives and conceives, feels and thinks, judges and chooses? It is the self, the center of our consciousness, the unitary unifier of our experiences—that which gives us the identity of being the same person throughout our lives although the physical components of our bodies change constantly. Obviously, each person changes in response to different experiences, develops habits as he or she keeps performing certain acts, and so on, but there is no question it is one single person to whom these changes occur. Although we are not conscious of the self separate from its acts, we are conscious of it as the ground that pervades and unifies our acts, the entity that thinks, wills and feels. When Descartes said, "I think therefore I am" he already assumed that his self existed: it is *I* who think: the thinker cannot be separated from the thought. It has sometimes been said that Descartes regarded human persons as disembodied egos and we cannot emphasize enough the fact that our experience of the self is of an embodied self: the self is a unity of mind and body: all of our sense-data comes from the body and the mind is required to process the sense-data. Nevertheless the mind goes beyond sensory data, beyond sensation and imagination, to think thoughts and form concepts that have no sensory correlate. In principle there is no reason why the mind cannot exist separately from the body since thinking and willing are not physical in nature—but the separation of mind from body is truly a dissolution of human nature as such and a disembodied self exists in an unnatural state. Be that as it may, the recognition of the self is devastating for materialism for the material world in itself—and materialism tells us that this is the only world that exists—has no "centers" and cannot recognize a perspective of "I", of the first person. But this "I" is that which is most obvious in our experience: it is I whom am conscious, I who chooses and intends. The self, like its acts, cannot be reduced to the physical.

Freewill

That we think we make free choices (whether it is a question of eating out this evening or of responding positively to a request for a donation) all the time is undeniable. The only question is whether these choices are truly free as we believe them to be. If materialism is true—if matter is all that exists—then there is no freewill. But our experience of freewill, on its own, is a sufficient disproof of materialism if we attend to it on its own terms without trying to advance extraneous metaphysical agendas. We know that we are faced with alternate courses of action all the time and we know that we choose between these alternates sometimes after deliberation and sometimes with very little or no thought. The determinist tells us that even those choices we made after much deliberation were not made on the basis of our weighing of reasons pro and con but were the inevitable results of physical states of affairs going back to the very origin of the universe. But this "explanation", it has often been pointed out, cuts both ways: if there are no reasons that ground any choice or decision, then there are no reasons that ground determinism. Thus the argument for determinism (like the argument for materialism as a whole) collapses into a metaphysical mud-slinging match: physical causes on the one side and reasons on the other.

The fact of the matter is that our actions can quite clearly be explained in terms of reasons and purposes—not simply in terms of our brain states. Heredity and environment certainly have a part to play in the kind of decisions we make but these are not the whole story in all of our decisions. There are choices and decisions we make after weighing attractive alternatives—and we make right and wrong decisions sometimes "against our wills." Some philosophers turn to determinism because they believe that the alternative is to attribute all actions in the world to purely arbitrary factors or to chance—in other words the actions are uncaused. But the choice is not simply between predetermination by physical processes and total arbitrariness. There is a third option: reason, the exercise of the will under the influence of the intellect (of course there is a use and an abuse of reason). Human beings cause their own actions—their actions are not simply arbitrary—but their causing of these actions does not originate in a physical event.

The old determinism assumed that all physical events in the universe were in principle predictable. Quantum physics has shown us that at least at the subatomic level there can be no exact predictions—only statistical ones. But this does not of itself show the reality of freewill: the kind of causal indeterminacy we find in freewill is different from the causal indeterminacy of quantum theory. Likewise Godel's Theorem, especially as expounded by J.R. Lucas, has shown the inadequacy of the mechanist model when applied to the human mind and to freewill. But the ultimate basis of freewill is our experience of being agents who make up our minds on various matters and make decisions for which we are responsible.

Responsibility is especially relevant here because if we have no freewill then we are not responsible for any of our actions. Murderers and embezzlers cannot be punished and heroes and altruists cannot be praised because all of their actions were caused by purely physical factors over which they had no control. The whole fabric of society would collapse if we acted as if determinism were true not to speak of the trivialization of such moral outrages as the Holocaust. This does not prove the truth of freewill but it certainly indicates that determinism can only be preached, not practiced. Only in recognizing a non-physical center of all our willing can we make sense of our experience—and also of the basis of our responsibility. All acts of the will are non-physical in nature, although some of them require the cooperation of our bodies; these acts are not uncaused but have reasons and purposes rather than physical processes as their driving force; and all acts of the will are acts of a person. Freewill does not introduce arbitrariness and uncaused events into nature. Freewill instead shows that there are mental causes for mental events and that (as we already know) we are truly responsible for our choices.

Purpose and Intention

Closely related to freewill is the reality of intention—another non-physical activity—in our lives. Now purposive behavior—which is lethal for full-blooded materialism—is evident at all levels of life. Naturalists may deny that the eye in its current state exists for a particular purpose: to see. Likewise they will deny that reproductive systems exist in order to enable the replication of a species (we note here that no satisfactory account has been given of the qualitative transition from non-replicating entities to a reproducing species; more important the very idea of reproductive systems is incorrigibly teleological[4]). These implausible denials are primarily intended to frustrate any introduction of "purpose" or "design" in natural phenomena which in turn could lead to recognition of the existence of a Purposer. It must be confessed that much of the fear of teleology derives from anthropomorphic ideas of God held as much on the one side by David Hume and the Darwinists as on the other by William Paley and the Creationists. The infinite Intelligence of traditional theism is neither a god-of-the-gaps nor a deistic watchmaker but the Supreme Source of life, consciousness and intellect (which by their very nature will always be beyond the reach of quantitative methodologies) Who is also the transcendent Creator and Conserver of all existent being.

The manifestation of purpose in the world reaches its summit in the intentional behavior of human persons. Every person is aware of pursuing goals, of intending to act in certain ways and then carrying out the intention. Such intention cannot be a purely physical process since the very act of intending something implies a deliberation that is intellectual and a deliberation that is performed by a self. Intention is not restricted to abstract planning sessions but covers the most trivial everyday activities (for instance, intending to bend down and tie one's shoelaces). But, in observing intentional acts that require thought and deliberation, we recognize that these acts are non-physical in nature since they involve acts of the intellect, conceptual thinking as opposed to simple responses to sensory experience, acts indeed of a personal consciousness. As with the denial of other irreducibly immaterial phenomena, any attempt to deny purpose and intention has a boomerang effect. A.N. Whitehead's summation is particularly apt: "Those who devote themselves to the purpose of proving that there is no purpose constitute an interesting object of study."[5]

From Skepticism and Relativism to the Discovery of Theos, Anthropos, Christos

It is a truism that philosophers disagree on almost everything. It is equally plain that skepticism and relativism represent the orthodox position in modern thought. And to those who are intellectually intimidated by the spectacle of scholars trotting out seemingly conclusive arguments on both (or multiple) sides of most issues, skepticism and relativism offer the paths of least resistance.

Historically, skepticism, here understood as the rejection of belief in supernatural agents and interventions and in an after-life, began in the Western world with such Greek thinkers as Epicurus (341–270 B.C.) and Lucretius (94–55

B.C.) and remained an intellectual force until about 450 A.D. The skepticism of this era was not necessarily a reaction to religious belief and co-existed with various other world-views. From 500 A.D. until the sixteenth century, monotheism was dominant in the West. It was in the late sixteenth century that skeptical views again returned to prominence. Initially, the skeptics rediscovered the works of the Greek skeptics and rejected, either directly or indirectly, the Christian religion while remaining deists (although some of the French skeptics rejected even deism). Their skepticism was at least in part a reaction to Christianity. By the nineteenth century, skeptics no longer held on to deism and sought to explain religious belief in secular (psychological, sociological, economic) terms. In the twentieth century, skeptics turned to full-blown atheism without reference to the demands of religious belief-systems. Today, in fact, skepticism is the mainstream, establishment position of modern academia in most parts of the world.

The intellectual foundation of skepticism, understood as a rejection of belief in the supernatural, is a doctrine or ideology of materialism. So much so the whole enterprise of modern skepticism depends on the viability of materialism as a cogent and compelling belief-system. But, to be intellectually viable, materialism must address and explain two primordial "brute facts" of human experience. One is our experience of experience—and we have seen earlier how this leads ineluctably to the recognition and affirmation of an infinite Intelligence that grounds life, consciousness and intellect. The other "brute fact" is the human mind's inability to remain at the level of brute facts. We seek explanations for everything and it is the quest for explanation that drives and underlies most human enterprises including the natural and social sciences.

Materialism asserts that the material world is all that exists. But this assertion, which is offered as an explanation in our inquiry into reality, cannot function as an explanatory ultimate for we immediately face two new questions: where did this material world come from and why is there a material world at all? To say that the material world exists eternally is to make a statement that can never be empirically proved, a statement that if accepted leads to another question: how do you explain and account for the phenomenon of an eternally existing material world? The only viable explanation for the existence of any one of the entities or all of the entities that make up the material world would be the existence of an ultimate uncaused being, a being that did not receive existence from anyone or anything else and can completely explain its own existence. This self-explanatory being that we call "God" is the explanatory ultimate demanded by all non-self-explanatory entities from subatomic particles to galaxies (an infinite series of non-self-explanatory entities still cannot explain the existence of even one of these entities just as an infinite series of mail-carriers cannot explain the existence of one letter).

A common error made in considering the ontological origin of material reality is to look for answers in contemporary cosmology. This is an error primarily because our quest for explanation as it pertains to the ultimate origin of material reality goes beyond empirical and quantifiable causes as such since we are here concerned with the transition from nothing to something. Nothing is absolute nothingness: no laws, no vacuums, no fields, no physical entities. Science can only get to work once something exists. Consequently the transition from nothingness to something lies forever beyond the purview of scientific methodology.

Many of the currently popular cosmological theories (Stephen Hawking, Roger Penrose, Andrei Linde) agree on the idea of a Big Bang origin of the Universe and on standard models of the development of the Universe after the first fraction of a second following the Big Bang. Radical differences come into play in speculation about the parameters that constitute the initial conditions in Big Bang theory. It has been said that these differences owe as much to aesthetic preferences as they do to scientific considerations but the fact remains that influential cosmologists have very different views on ultimate origination. These differences depend on postulates that cannot be empirically confirmed and so it is unlikely that any resolution will or can be reached. At any rate, the philosophical questions at issue cannot be settled by cosmological speculation of this kind. If the speculative scientist postulates certain ultimate laws of nature or mathematical models, the follow-up question is how did these laws and models come to exist and how is it that they were instantiated in reality. The existence of material reality with all its regularities and laws is ultimately unintelligible if we do not recognize the existence of an absolutely transcendent and infinitely perfect Creator of the cosmos.

The recognition of the existence of an infinitely perfect Being that always existed represents the fulfillment of human rationality since it makes sense of all levels of our experience. But it also heightens our awareness of the mystery of existence: we ask how it is that God always existed. To recognize that our existence is unintelligible if it is not grounded in a self-existent God is also to recognize (without knowing how this is possible) that God exists always and that His Existence is free of all limitations.

The essays in this volume testify to the mystery of existence, to the mystery of our existence as conscious, thinking agents. It is our apprehension of this mystery that helps us uncover the fallacies of skepticism and materialism and fortify the foundations of rational theism.

In the first chapter, F.F. Centore gives a brief overview of the history of modern unbelief—with particular emphasis on the turn to the subjective begun by Descartes and his separation of the God of science from the God of religion—and then develops an argument for God's existence that avoids traditional objections. Centore notes that William Paley's watchmaker argument had already been preempted by David Hume because, at best, it could prove the existence of a finite designer. Furthermore, Charles Darwin seemed to have eliminated this argument decisively. Centore holds, however, that Darwin's version of the theory of evolution has yet to come up with satisfactory evidence for his account of speciation. The lack of fossil evidence coupled with the short time frame that natural selection had available to operate, he says, makes the Darwinian model untenable.

Centore's argument is centered on the existential dependency here and now of every sensible thing and of all sensible things taken together on an existentially independent Being. Anything whose nature or essence does not include its own existence is something dependent upon some other, already extramentally existing, thing external to itself for its existence. Whatever is true of the very nature of any one sensible thing here and now is true of all sensible things taken together here and now (the universe). This is not an example of the fallacy of composition and division because all sensible things share in common their accidental nature and the priority of the cause of their existence. Since the universe as a whole cannot account for its own existence, it must have been caused by an existentially independent being, namely God. If every other possible existing external explanatory cause has been exhausted with respect to the existentially dependent being that is the universe, then it is caused by an existentially independent being, for a series of existential zeros that extend however far back in time would still yield zero in terms of actual beings. Nothingness cannot be the cause of anything. The existentially independent Being is a Being whose essence is to exist and Who is totally transcendent to the world. And here the God of religion is the same as the God of science.

In *The Mind-Maker* Russell Pannier and Thomas Sullivan argue for the existence of God from the existence of irreducibly immaterial features of our experience, with specific reference to the ontology of "universals". While citing materialists who admit that there is no plausible physicalist explanation of consciousness, freewill or language, the authors turn to a phenomenon that is perhaps most puzzling of all for reductionists, our ability to be intentionally aware of obviously immaterial objects of thought. Concepts in general have posed a significant barrier for naturalists and those who posit mindless, purposeless theories of Natural Selection. Here, the authors go beyond the issue of "concepts" and argue that the existence of non-local (i.e., non-spatial) instantiable characteristics (characteristics that can have instances)—and these instantiables are so fundamental that human thought is hardly possible without them—shows that the human mind could not have been generated by Nature. From the existence of the human mind, they deduce the existence of a divine Mind. Along the way the authors argue against anti-realist and mind-dependent theories of instantiables. Some eliminativists, they also point out, now admit that we can actually be conscious of feelings and sensations but balk at admitting that we do have intentions and beliefs!

In *The Awareness and Certainty of the Existence of God*, Illtyd Trethowan offers a novel pathway to the apprehension of God's existence that is ancient in provenance. His basic thesis, one shared by Augustine and many others, is that God is present to the human mind. This is not the traditional argument to God's existence from "religious experience" but an intellective process of becoming aware of God acting upon us, of His becoming evident in His action upon us (as the cause is evident in its effects). This awareness of God is present even in the exercise of our human powers, of our willing and our knowing for instance. Trethowan's own major contribution in this area is his analysis of the absoluteness of our moral experience: in our recognition of value and our awareness of absolute obligation we begin to be aware of the summons of the Absolute Good, the Unconditioned, Who is God. Due to space limitations, Trethowan can only offer a survey of the contemporary response to this approach. The situation is most promising in France, particularly in the work of Maurice Blondel, but not much progress has been made on this front in the Anglophone world.

In the next paper, the volume moves on from a consideration of the basis for belief in God's existence to a study of what we can know about God's nature. Those who believe in God's existence usually assume that God is infinite, that He is free of any limitation. What does it mean to say that God is infinite or perfect and on what basis can we affirm this? These questions are addressed by one of the foremost authorities on infinity in contemporary philosophy, Leo Sweeney. In *God: Subsistent and Infinite Being*, Sweeney first reviews two recent critiques of traditional conceptions of infinity and divine perfection and notes that approaching God from infinity as taken from mathematics and the natural sciences is of little help in a philosophical context. He then develops an argument for God's existence, and His existence as subsistent and infinite being, from the existence of the actual material universe. After re-discovering the great insight that actually existent beings are "signposts" pointing to an Existent Whose very essence is to exist, Sweeney proceeds to show that this Being, God, is subsistent actuality; since He has no limiting potency, His actuality is infinite. This being the case, God is the perfect fullness of reality: He not only possesses all pure and transcendent perfections, but possesses them in an unlimited degree.

The divine infinity, inasmuch as it signifies a freedom from any limitation, entails that God is not limited by either space or time. In *A God Beyond Space and Time*, Brian Leftow considers the basis of the traditional affirmation that God is outside space and time while defending its coherence. He starts from the premise that the absolute nature of theistic worship calls for "perfect being" theology, a theology that recognizes every possible perfection in God while denying any imperfection. He first considers the thesis that God has a body that is either a part or the whole of the universe. After showing the absurdities entailed by such a view (e.g., city dumps would be part of such a body; what effect does the destruction of one or more atoms in the universe have on this body, etc.), he moves on to an analysis of God's basic actions and shows that in His very act of creating the universe, God wills its every state of affairs. And although God is not spatially present in the universe, Leftow speculates that His relation to those who dwell in the space-time web may be likened to the relation of the three-dimensional interior of a sphere to the points on its two-dimensional "skin". (In a later chapter, *God and the World*, Russell Pannier and Thomas Sullivan also adduce various arguments against the idea that God is identical with the world—He is ontologically independent of the world, He is the ontological ground of the world and His existence is necessary—while also trying to show how He can act in the world, through creation, conservation and causal interaction, without being spatially present).

If God is not in space then God cannot be in time at least under the Minkowskian interpretation of Special Relativity. From the standpoint of perfect being theology, Leftow argues that God must exist outside time since to live in time means that different parts of one's life come to an end, a clear imperfection. To say that God's life is timeless is also to say that He sees the whole span of time "at once", lives His entire life "always," does all that He ever does at once and does not change in any way in what He knows or intends. There is no monotony in His timeless existence because the infinity of the truth He sees and the perfection of His grasp of it, the infinity of His knowledge and love of the infinite Good that He is in Himself, necessarily results in a state of the greatest possible joy in His timeless and "unimaginably intense" present.

If God's infinity and timelessness are as mysterious as they are awe-inspiring, His absolute simplicity is even more of a challenge to the human mind. In *Absolute Simplicity*, Eleonore Stump and Norman Kretzmann present a comprehensive exposition and defense of the assertion that there are no real distinctions in God either among His properties or between Him and His properties. God is entirely actual and has no unactualized potentialities. What we describe as God's omnipotence or His omniscience are just different ways for finite minds to describe a single eternal action or different manifestations of the action, this single action being God Himself. The authors show that God's simplicity is not incompatible with His free choice nor His omnipotence with His goodness through an analysis of the divine will: God's acts of will with reference to Himself are necessary but with the necessity associated with a final cause (the perfect will wills what the perfect intellect presents to it as perfectly good). His acts of will include "conditionally and absolutely necessitated" acts of will. One key obstacle in explaining absolute simplicity is its relation to God's choice of creating the universe: since it is not absolutely necessary that God create the universe, would some potentiality of His be unactualized in a possible world in which He does not create a universe? The authors respond with Aquinas that creation of a universe is just an instance of God willing goodness—and that this potentiality of willing goodness is supremely actualized in God willing Himself (whether or not He creates a universe). Absolute simplicity rules out metaphysical differences within God but allows for logical and conceptual differences.

Absolute simplicity has several important applications. Take the traditional question, is an action good because God says it is good or does God declare an action to be good because it is good? If the answer is that actions are declared good by divine fiat, then there seems to be something arbitrary and subjective about the moral law. The second answer seems to undermine divine sovereignty. But a grasp of divine simplicity makes it obvious that God's nature is identical with His perfect goodness: so whatever He wills to be morally good is identical with His nature; and it is His nature which is the standard for morality. Absolute simplicity is also an important adjunct to the cosmological argument for God's existence. For instance, to the question, why does God exist, the response is that He cannot not exist, this necessity being a logical consequence of His absolute simplicity. God is the best explanation for the existence of the universe—in the context of this discussion—both because He is self-explanatory and necessary.

The traditional objection to belief in a God Who is both infinitely good and infinitely powerful is the problem of evil: if He is infinitely good He would not want any evil and if He is infinitely powerful He could prevent evil and so how can a believer reconcile belief in such a being with the existence of evil. The standard freewill response goes a long way in mitigating the force of the critic's argument for if God has indeed created us free and if freedom necessarily involves the possibility of choosing either good or evil, then the exercise of freedom is responsible for the evil in this world (and God permits such evil in order to bring about the greater good of enabling us to freely love Him). In *Doestoevskian Horrors and the Problem of Grading Worlds* and *Homer, God and Evil*, Sandra Menssen and Thomas Sullivan offer two non-traditional responses to the problem of evil.

In the first paper, they argue that the question of why God permits evil does not have to be answered in order to resolve the apparent incompatibility between the existence of a good God and the existence of evil. In order to speak about a problem of evil, we must have criteria specifying what constitutes a "good" world. There are four possible criteria for judging the "goodness" of a world: functional, utilitarian, aesthetic, theistic. It may be said that whether a world is good or bad will depend on whether it fulfills its function. But a world can have a function only if it exists *for* something and such a function would have to be given by a Designer. Utilitarian criteria for the goodness of a world face various criticisms: who is to decide what is beneficial to the utility of the world as a whole? and if the world has an infinite Creator, utility for Him comes before utility for anyone else. Aesthetic criteria cannot suffice to satisfy our general criteria of good and evil. The authors argue that the only viable criterion for judging the goodness of the world presupposes the existence of God—so God's existence is acknowledged before the problem of evil and suffering is even addressed.

In the next chapter they consider the role of claims of divine revelation in addressing the problem of evil. Some philosophers have tried to argue that the quantity of evil in the world will help determine the probability of God's existence but the authors do not believe that this data alone is sufficient to make the existence of a good God probable. They hold, however, that the introduction of the content of the revelatory claims of Christianity will raise the probability of God's existence above .5. In addition, they recommend and apply certain guidelines in exploring the content of the Christian revelation, namely the consistency and development of this revelation and the fittingness of its content. The Christian revelation offers a paradigm of human freedom and responsibility and of the "economy of salvation" that helps one make sense of the mystery of evil and endure suffering.

The next two essays address some common causes of unbelief. The first, *The Philosophies of Religion of Russell and Flew* by Andrew Beards, is an analysis and critique of the metaphysics and epistemology of two of the best-known critics of Christian theism in the English-speaking world in this century. Beards applauds Bertrand Russell and Antony Flew for taking Christianity seriously enough to consider it a claim to truth (a claim which, of course, they go on to reject) while spurning fideism as intellectual hypocrisy. Nevertheless he is severely critical of their philosophical views and contends that the superficial epistemological skepticism they inherited from the Humean tradition led in turn to metaphysical skepticism. Whereas Russell tended towards subjectivism and anti-commonsense realism, Flew accepted a form of naive realism. And where Russell finally adopted a position of reductive materialism, Flew accepted human freewill while still taking a naturalist view of the human person. Beards notes that our familiar experience of performing various conscious operations and our awareness that we are a conscious unity of such acts are both ignored by the Humean enterprise and consequently neither Russell nor Flew could move beyond a skeptical impasse (some of the self-contradictions of Humean skepticism are usefully unpacked). When it comes to the existence of God, Beards sees the basis of belief in God in the metaphysical intelligibility of what exists. Where Flew and Russell are content with terminating the process of inquiry at an ultimate brute fact, namely the universe, Beards holds that brute facts are only for the brutes and God is not a brute fact but a comprehensive explanation of everything. Since contingent beings cannot give a sufficient reason for their existence and since whatever exists is intelligible, there must exist a Being that explains both its own existence and that of everything else.

In *The Psychology of Atheism*, Paul Vitz puts the atheist on the couch. Vitz contends that the major barriers to belief in God are not rational but neurotic psychological barriers of which the unbeliever may be unaware. Intellectuals may become atheists to gain social and academic acceptance and for personal convenience. But there are also psychoanalytic motives: reversing Freud's claim (inherited from Feuerbach) that belief in God is a wish fulfillment driven by a desire for security, Vitz points out that within the Freudian framework, atheism is actually an illusion caused by the Oedipal desire to kill the father and replace him with oneself. The well-known skeptic Voltaire vehemently rejected his father (and even refused to take his father's name). But the Oedipal explanation is not the whole story. In Vitz's view, it is the "defective father" hypothesis that covers a wider range of data: when a child is disappointed in the earthly father it becomes impossible to believe in a heavenly Father. As evidence for this thesis, he cites the case-histories of various well-known unbelievers: Sigmund Freud himself was deeply disappointed in his father, a weak man; Karl Marx did not respect his father; the young Ludwig Feuerbach was deeply hurt by his father. The death of a father is sometimes also seen as a betrayal: Jean Paul Sartre's father died before he was born and both Bertrand Russell and Albert Camus lost their fathers when they were very young. Vitz supports the defective father hypothesis with excerpts from the personal correspondence of some of the atheists.

The exploration of Theos in the first section of the volume is followed by a consideration of Anthropos. The first four entries in this section are concerned with defending the reality of a mind separate from the brain—two of the contributors are professional philosophers of mind (John Foster and Charles Taliaferro) and the other two (John Beloff and Daniel N. Robinson) work in both psychology and philosophy of mind.

In *Minds or Machines*, Beloff analyzes the claims of Functionalism with particular reference to computers and so-called Artificial Intelligence. Although computers perform information-processing, they are not aware of what they are doing unlike human beings who are aware of themselves thinking. And only humans know what they are thinking about or when they reach a conclusion; they have an insight into what is going on unlike the machine. Moreover, there is no simple correlation between brain processes and conscious experience because a lot of thinking (particularly in problem solving) takes place at an unconscious level. The Functionalist fallacy is to look at what an entity is used for rather than what constitutes it ontologically. A computer program is not a program if it has no user but a human mind with its subjective experiences exists in its own right. Some of the greatest contributions of the human mind are in areas that have no computer simulations such as intuitive insights on which we constantly depend and which cannot be reduced to explicit rules.

In *The Case for Dualism*, John Foster refutes various forms of materialism—conceptual materialism, metaphysical materialism and the token-identity and logical dependence theses—while defending dualism against such critiques as the traditional objection that a non-physical entity cannot affect a physical entity, the causal pairing of mind and brain critique, anomalous monism and epiphenomenalism. Generally speaking, Foster's main objection to materialism is the fact that it does not do justice to the nature of conscious experience. He illustrates his points with numerous instances of experiences that can be explained within a dualist frame of reference but not a materialist one. Experiential states and events are radically non-physical and are not the product of anything physical (although there is causal interaction between mind and brain). Moreover, thoughts, judgments and decisions are essentially conscious acts—and hence resistant to materialist and identity descriptions. Beliefs too involve dualism since they rest on judgmental dispositions and are thereby essentially linked to states of consciousness.

The Embodiment of Mind is an entertaining but profoundly enlightening description of the debate between Materialism and Dualism. Robinson outlines the obvious absurdities entailed by any form of materialism. The so-called "Folk Psychology" of the masses is built on the ageless activities of reflective and intelligent beings who have more authority to speak about their own experiences, feelings and aspirations than scientists and philosophers.

In *Philosophy of God and Mind: Theism and the Queerness of Consciousness*, Charles Taliaferro is concerned with recent materialist attempts to portray dualism as "queer" since it is different from anything else in the universe. Eliminativists try to eliminate "consciousness" from any view of the world. Non-eliminativist materialists acknowledge the existence of consciousness but claim that all mental states are explainable within the natural sciences. In this paper, the author considers dualism as part of an overall non-materialistic metaphysic; problems facing eliminativism and other forms of reductionism; and the case for dualism. Within a theistic framework, the emergence of consciousness is natural and not a freak occurrence: consciousness no longer appears "queer". Within the framework of eliminative materialism (as promoted, for instance, by Paul Churchland), neither moral practice nor reason can survive in any coherent or consistent sense. Reductionists fail to recognize the radical difference between processes described in terms of physics and chemistry and our first person feelings and subjective apprisal of our states. Taliaferro finally develops a case for dualism derived from Descartes' famous modal argument: if persons are the same things as their bodies then whatever is true of their bodies must be true of them but this is not the case.

The second half of the section on Anthropos moves from the mental life that is a datum of immediate experience to the moral dimension that is just as experientially immediate to the human person.

In *Dimensions of Cultural Relativity in the Moral Realm*, Jorge Garcia addresses the cultural relativities that impinge on moral issues and its significance for a thesis of moral relativism. He notes that it is notoriously difficult to muster empirical evidence for the theory that different cultures differ fundamentally in morality. Such theories require clear concepts of what constitutes a culture or what functions as a moral judgment/practice in a culture not to speak of the need for a paradigm of moral standards required for making cross-cultural comparisons. Relativists also sometimes assume that there is a single set of moral practices associated with a culture when in fact there tends to be diversity. Again, diversity in moral judgments does not in itself establish a relativity thesis as superior to competing explanations (e.g., parametric universalism). Thoroughgoing moral relativism also requires its proponents to reject a priori any moral reasoning offered by a culture in justifying a particular practice or judgment. The endorsement of such relativism requires the relativist to accept any judgment or practice as permissible simply because it is part of a cultural code: no cross-cultural standards exist and therefore, for instance, no argument against polygamy is applicable in a society that accepts it. The relativist position also undermines any case for inter-cultural tolerance since there are no cross-cultural values and tolerance therefore has no special status as a value.

In *Reason, Relativism and Christian Ethics*, John Finnis addresses various relativist challenges to morality ranging from subjectivism to proportionalism. Certain relativities are, of course, recognized by Christian ethics—for instance, a universally applicable norm has to be applied differently in different situations—but these do not undermine the objectivity, universality and absoluteness of Christian ethics itself. Christian ethics—which Finnis describes as reason's most comprehensive effort to understand right and wrong choices in light of the fullest information on humankind's situation and destiny—proposes norms and principles that are true in all times and places for all human beings and can be critically justified. Reason can recognize goods that are intrinsic to persons and their communion as well options that are destructive of a good. Disagreements do exist in ethics but the fact of disagreement on a particular moral judgment does not undermine the judgment any more than general agreement serves as sufficient ground to justify it. Sound ethics provides the distinctions required to clarify virtue and vice and identify right and wrong choices or dispositions. These distinctions range from the difference between reason (intelligible goods) and feelings (emotionally motivating goals) to first and intermediate principles of practical reasoning on basic human goods. Finnis outlines eleven distinctions of this nature—distinctions which, he says, are never refuted and rarely mentioned by critics—and then scrutinizes the relativism/subjectivism of certain moral theologians who reject traditional Christian ethics on the ground that it does not consider the entire reality of actions (circumstances, intentions, effects). The main fallacy of these moral theologians is their failure to recognize that, while there are relativities in choices between morally upright alternatives, one cannot, under any circumstance, choose evil for the sake of good. If this imperative is not recognized, then feelings and conventions, rather than reason will drive moral judgments. Christian ethics is directed to the fulfillment of persons in the heavenly kingdom by revealing truths about human willing, self-determination and intercommunion that are related to goods intrinsic to human persons and their communion.

In *Abortion: Can It Ever Be Justified?*, John Foster applies moral reasoning to one of the most urgent issues of our time, the deliberate, intentional killing of a pre-natal human organism. In the first part of the discussion, he treats the question of whether abortion is ever permissible in secular terms acceptable to any rational person and in the second he considers the question from a theological standpoint. Foster points out that the pre-natal human organism is a human individual from the time of conception (fertilization)—in the development process, there is no decisive transition from the non-human to the human other than conception. In its genes the conceptus contains a plan of what the developed organism will be like and, by drawing nourishment from the mother, it grows on its own by a process of cell-division. Both pre-natal and post-natal development are phases in the growth of a single biological continuant. Furthermore, this individual is morally innocent prior to birth. An abortion, therefore, is an act of grave injustice that is tantamount to murder. Foster also addresses various arguments adduced by abortion defenders—what about the welfare of the mother, risks to the mother's life, pregnancies brought about by rape, etc.—and notes that such arguments are based on utilitarian theories of morality that go against our ordinary moral intuitions (the end does not justify unjust means). In discussing abortion from a theological standpoint, he notes that the Christian revelation tells us that the human individual comes into existence at conception: the Gospel accounts of Matthew and Luke specify that the Son of God took on human nature and human life at conception. The Incarnation also shows that each human being has a value that is ultimate, objective and infinite and any action by one human being to another should respect this value if it is to be morally right. The deliberate killing of an innocent human individual is not consistent with such respect and is therefore morally wrong.

The final paper of this section, *Do We Have Too Many People?* by Julian Simon, is not, strictly speaking, a work of moral philosophy or theology. Its importance is in furnishing empirical data for moral debates that are centered on such data particularly in the area of population control. The population controller argues that too many people strain the world's resources and will bring about economic and ecological ruin. Therefore every means should be employed in limiting births. Although the premises of this argument are often presented as self-evident truths, Simon argues that they are demonstrably false. As the world's population has risen so has its standard of living. Natural resource scarcities decrease rather than increase in the long run for all raw materials. Food has become cheaper and more available as the population increases—moreover, less and less agricultural land is required as the decades pass because of increases in productivity per unit of land. Pollutants in air and water have been decreasing contrary to public belief (although this is not the case in socialist countries). Population growth and population density favor economic growth and an increase in population brings an increase in the stock of useful knowledge: in the long run, more people imply more available resources and higher income for everyone. In Simon's view, the world's problem is not too many people but a lack of political and economic freedom (compare the development of East and West Germany, North and South Korea and Taiwan and China).

Christos is the shortest section of the volume and comprises two papers, one a phenomenological analysis of the Gospel narratives as they relate to Jesus Christ by Josef Seifert, and the second an attempt by Horst Burkle to convey the uniqueness of the claims of Jesus vis a vis the paradigms of the major world religions.

In his *The Uninventable Glory of God as the Deepest Reason for Our Faith in Jesus Christ*, Seifert uses the Gospel narratives themselves as the datum that draws us to a recognition of the divinity of Christ. While acknowledging that faith is a gift of grace, Seifert also sees it as the supreme act of human reason. Faith requires belief in the trustworthiness of Jesus, of His Apostles, His Church and His Bible; it is belief *in* Jesus, in the sense of loving surrender, and belief *that* what He says is true. But neither the moral goodness nor the miracles of Christ are sufficient grounds for accepting His divinity. The ultimate ground for our unwavering faith in Christ is our awareness that the uninventable eternal glory of God, His necessary sacred holiness, is encountered in an incarnate/visible form in Jesus Christ. The glory of God that we glimpse, if only barely, in philosophy shines most clearly through the incarnate Word of God, in His miracles and the inner holiness and glory of His words, in the divine beauty of His mercy (Prodigal Son, Mary Magdalen) as well as His horror of sin: the irreducible and unique glory of God manifests itself in the newborn Savior announced to the shepherds, the Sermon on the Mount, the forgiveness of the adulteress, the piercing of the Heart of Jesus on the cross for our sins and the gloriously risen Christ. This glory is a spiritual splendor that can only proceed from the inner holiness of God and that presupposes the uninventable inner perfection and truth of the divine nature. The divine glory and uninventable holiness of charity that permeates the words and miracles, the life and death of Christ, not only justify faith but elevate it beyond probable opinion to an inner certainty and absolute, unconditioned Yes. A similitude of this glory is visible in true followers, the saints, as well as in the doctrines of Jesus and His Church (the inner truth and unity and beauty of the doctrines reveal the glory of God). The most reliable approach to Scripture scholarship, in this context, would be to delve into the glory of God in Christ and into the inner spiritual meaning of the scriptural texts in their "divine form".

In *Christ, Christianity and the World Religions*, Burkle emphasizes the importance of remaining true to the original insight that God was in Christ. The doctrine of the divinity and humanity of Jesus Christ was defined by various Church Councils partially in order to preserve Christian truth in its wholeness in the face of heresies that emphasized one truth at the expense of other essential truths. The never-ending hermeneutic task of the Church is to speak the Christian message in the language of our time without losing the original content of the message. In the contemporary context, a central challenge for the Church is the encounter with the world religions—it is in this encounter that theologians are often tempted to sacrifice certain elements of Christian truth. Burkle cites examples of this with reference to Islam and Hinduism.

The identity of religion and politics found in the Koran, he says, is not found in Christianity where the new reality of Christ's presence cannot be identified with any social structure. Burkle sees an Islamic approach to the Christian message in theologies of liberation and revolution that turns the New Being in Christ into a political program. Another example is the inclusive religious pluralism of Hinduism which stands in contrast to the uniqueness and exclusiveness claimed by Christianity with respect to Jesus Christ. In Hindu terms, Jesus is seen by some as guru, by others as avatara. Among "progressive" Christian thinkers—for whom Hegel, Marx, Freud and the like are the new Church Fathers—Jesus simply becomes a guru with an exemplary existence in his role as revolutionary and new proletarian. But Jesus Christ, as the New Testament portrays Him, is the LOGOS in Whom every being in the cosmos has its origin and final destiny: all that God can reveal to humanity has been revealed in Christ. The miracle stories of the New Testament in different ways function as a fulfillment of the unresolved experiences of the world religions (His healing miracles proclaimed His authority in heaven and on earth; His multiplication miracles show that He provides satisfying food for every need). The modern attempt to demythologize the biblical texts simply results in the loss of the divine secret of Christ in its universal dimensions. Many of those who reject the supernatural message of Christianity simply migrate to a different kind of supernatural reality (with doctrines such as astrology) by embracing eastern religions and even Shamanism and animism. The only remedy for the exodus from traditional Christianity is a return to a true exegesis of the identity of Jesus and a rediscovery of His presence in His mysterious body, the Church.

The Christos Who is Theos and Anthropos

We have seen above that a phenomenological analysis of the Jesus of the Gospels can help us recognize His divinity. But the field of biblical studies has not been amenable to such phenomenological analyses and has more often than not been antagonistic to traditional theological affirmations. The history of skepticism in the nineteenth and twentieth centuries finds a mirror image in the history of the search for the Jesus of history. The skeptical challenge to traditional theological affirmations came to a head in the work of Rudolf Bultmann who was to modern New Testament studies what Charles Darwin is to modern biology and Albert Einstein to modern physics. Bultmann's radical skepticism had a significant impact on biblical studies.[6] Nevertheless, not a few major mainstream biblical scholars have looked beyond skepticism to a serious appraisal of age-old affirmations.

The importance of serious appraisal is most evident in the context of the popular impact of books like *The Myth of God Incarnate* and *The Five Gospels* (a product of the Jesus Seminar). The success of such books illustrates the perennial fascination of attempts to relate the Jesus of history to the Christ of faith. Just as the datum of departure for science and philosophy is the existence of the Universe, the datum of departure for Christian biblical studies and theology is the New Testament record in the context of the dramatic developments associated with it.

In the case of the Universe, numerous attempts have been made to explain its existence without reference to a transcendent ground. The unsatisfactory nature of such skepticism is demonstrated by the very fact that it has to be defended with entirely new arguments on a regular basis. The puzzle posed by the existence of the Universe cannot be brushed under the carpet by appeals to the authority of sheer speculation.

Likewise the continuing discussion on the historical Jesus indicates that sensational speculations which thrive on shock-value have a short life span. The "Jesus of history" is often just the figment of a particular historian's imagination. Also, writes one scholar, "A feature of the recent lives of Jesus phenomenon is the degree to which works marked by tentative hypothesis and tortuous scholarly analysis of obscure material have been marketed for a more general public. At the very least, there are serious ambiguities in this phenomenon, and it is difficult to determine whether the scholars or publishers are to be challenged. When flimsy hypotheses masquerade as exciting new hard scientific discoveries it can be difficult for the lay person to tell the difference. One can excuse authors for proffering a new hypothesis with enthusiasm, but such needs to be debated among their peers in the first instance before being marketed in a misleading way. A scholar who decides to go public with a hypothesis owes it to the public to label the product clearly 'hypothesis on hold'. ... Dogmatic claims are not be made about hypothetical constructs. This is to traffic in ignorance and emotionalism."[7] The numerous speculative lives of Jesus have not given us any new hard data on Jesus: "Since Bultmann, progress has been made in the area of the world of Jesus, but not a jot of firm knowledge of the individual historical person of Jesus has been garnered."[8]

If plausibility is any consideration, the "historical Jesus" emerging from the critic's "quest" must satisfactorily serve as an explanatory ultimate in accounting for the origin of the Christian phenomenon (and few critics have even considered this requirement). The Christian Faith is rooted in the historical process. Inevitably then the Christ of faith cannot be at odds with the Jesus of history. But the Jesus of history is not necessarily the Jesus of reductionist historians and fair-minded scholars must remember that the Christ of faith came to be understood in the experience of the Christian community as it reflected on the Jesus of history over centuries. Any serious analysis of the Christological claims must attempt to enter the thought/experience-world of the Christian community if it seeks to do justice to the data.

Theological skepticism of the Bultmannian variety is at least partially the result of certain philosophical presuppositions. In this context it would not be out of place to mention here some developments in current philosophy of religion that may be relevant to modern biblical studies and theology particularly with respect to the question of presuppositions.

A number of influential philosophers of our time have turned their minds to a study of the logical structure of the Christian belief-system in terms of actual historical practice as well as the demands of consistency and cogency. These philosophers include Michael Dummett, Wykeham Professor Emeritus of Logic, Oxford University; Professor Peter Geach, Professor Emeritus of Logic, University of Leeds; Richard Swinburne, Nolloth Professor of Philosophy of the Christian Religion, Oxford University and Peter Van Inwagen, Professor of Philosophy, Syracuse University. In pursuing this analysis the philosophers have paid close attention to the presuppositions and implications of New Testament criticism. Their arguments represent a significant challenge to skepticism in biblical studies and skeptics would do well to consider the case they make.

A philosophical presupposition must be judged on its philosophical merits— whether the presupposition is made by a scientist or a New Testament scholar. It is in this area that professional philosophers have something to offer the New Testament scholar. The citations below from the relevant works of Dummett, Geach, Swinburne and Van Inwagen help us consider the relationship between the Jesus of history and the Christos of faith without losing our way in the thickets of reductionism and the swamps of speculation.

Michael Dummett: Axioms of Exegetical Theology and Fundamental Theological Judgments:

Although it does not strictly speaking constitute a school, I shall, for the sake of a name, call it 'exegetical theology', as shorthand for 'theology inspired by current biblical exegesis.' It is defined by two fundamental principles or axioms. The first is that the Gospels, and the New Testament generally, do not provide a reliable witness to what Jesus said or did. The Evangelists did not hesitate to make up sayings and parables which they put into his mouth but whose message was one they themselves wanted to convey in the light of conditions prevailing at the time when and in the area where they were writing. We can therefore arrive at the actual words of Christ, or something approximating to them, only by laborious critical inquiry, the conclusions of which will be at best uncertain and speculative. ... The second axiom is that Jesus had no powers lacked by the common run of humanity and no source of knowledge unavailable to ordinary men and women. His beliefs cannot therefore have included any which a Jewish religious reformer of his day would not be expected to have, and were accordingly as liable to error as those of any other devout Jew of the time ...

Thus we cannot know with any certainty what Jesus taught and, even if we did, we should have no special reason to believe it, since he may have been in error. We do, however, know with fair assurance that his teaching was not the source of any of the characteristic Christian doctrines. How, then, were these arrived at? The only possible answer is: by subsequent reflection. This answer seems to me preposterous. Nothing could, of itself, be evidence for the astonishing idea that a particular man was God, through whom all things were made. A man might live a very holy life, exhibit extraordinary insight or wisdom, possess a charismatic personality, work astonishing wonders: but none of that would approach being a ground for holding him to *be* God. Similarly, the doctrine of the Trinity, if purely the result of human speculation, would be no more than a bizarre theory, for the truth of which we could not have any cogent ground. ....

The traditional conception may provide a basis for believing in the Trinity, if the Gospels enable us to conclude that Christ said enough to convey the difficult idea that God is not one Person, but three Persons. The divinity of Christ cannot be believed on the same basis, however: some kind of bootstrap operation is needed if there is to be any reason to think that any revelation from God was made at all. It would be senseless to believe to be true whatever Christ said, on the ground that, being God, he must know and would not lie, and, on that basis, to believe that he was God because that was one of the things he said.

It remains that there would be no reason to believe him to be God unless he knew himself to be and gave us, through the Apostles, reason to think that he knew himself to be. It would not be enough to suppose only that he *came to the conclusion* that he was God and subsequently gave his disciples to understand as much; for, if he had no greater source of knowledge of such matters than, say, John the Baptist, that would merely be a conclusion of whose truth there could be no assurance and which could not in fact have been reasonably, or even sanely, arrived at. Why, then, should we not simply think him deluded, a victim, as others have been, of the ultimate megalomania? That is certainly a rational option, as is the view that, contrary to what appears from the Gospels, he did not say it and we have no reason to believe it. The only irrational option is that offered by exegetical theology, that he did not say it, but that we have good reason to believe it. Should we then speak of a leap of faith at this point? I should rather speak of an act of judgment, involving far more than, but comparable in character to, those we perform whenever we assess the credibility of testimony or the mental balance of an individual. It is in no way irrational to judge, on the basis of what (if we reject the skeptical assessments of the biblical critics) we know from the New Testament of Christ and of the actions of his Apostles, that the astonishing doctrine of the Incarnation is more credible than the rival hypotheses ...

Judgment does not dispense with the need for a rational ground: it is the discernment of such a ground. If there are facts which a given supposition satisfactorily explains, and if these facts are sufficiently bizarre that resort to an apparently bizarre explanation is not patently disproportionate, then, if no alternative supposition is truly explanatory, there is rational ground for that supposition. Judgment is required to determine what is proportionate and what is explanatory...

Modern exegetes and theologians frequently assume that, to be 'scientific', biblical criticism must prescind completely from Christian faith. To treat the New Testament writings like any others demands that they be judged on the same basis as anyone would judge them, whatever religious beliefs he had or lacked. That is, however, utterly irrational. Whatever has been conclusively demonstrated must be accepted: fossils were not put into the rocks by the Devil to seduce us into unbelief, or by God to test our faith. But virtually nothing proposed by New Testament scholarship has been conclusively demonstrated: it consists entirely of hypotheses judged to be more probable than others. Estimates of probability depend crucially on background assumptions, since probability is a relation between a proposition and a body of evidence. What is probable if there is no God, or if Christ and his disciples were misguided fanatics, becomes quite improbable if Christianity is true. Without some background beliefs, no judgment of probability can be made; there is nothing scientific about setting aside your background beliefs in order to arrive at such judgments, and then, on the basis of those judgments, either leaching most of the content out of the beliefs you started with, or explicitly rejecting them altogether.[9]

Peter Geach: The Authority of Christ: Logical Presuppositions:

If we know anything at all of his [Christ's] teaching from the Gospels, he taught with absolute authority, and not as the scribes; he taught as one who saw and knew; knew who and what he was, to what end he was here on Earth, how his earthly life must end, and what joy and glory lay before him.

I may well be accused of ignoring assured results of critical scholarship, confusion about literary forms, and so on. But as a logician I am quite competent to judge the sort of argument I find used by Bible critics; and I judge the arguments to be very ofteb bad arguments, because where the truth-value of premises and conclusion is known independently of any theological disputes, arguments parallel to the critics' would lead from true premises to a false conclusion. ...

It is anyhow clear that we know nothing at all about Christ's words except by way of the Gospel record. By that record Christ did claim to teach with absolute certainty and authority. If the records are in this respect unreliable, two things follow.

Firstly: in this case there is a wide gap between the historic figure of Christ and the figure presented in the Gospel: a gap so wide that we could then know only in a theoretical and conjectural way what the actual teaching of Christ was. We should be in the same position as Platonic scholars trying to divine what Socrates actually thought and said. But then for us Christ would be such a figure of theory and conjecture that faith in him would be as much of an absurdity as faith in Socrates; there could be no question of believing his word or following his precepts; for we could have no well-grounded opinion about what he taught or prescribed, if the only clues to this were as untrustworthy as they would be on the present supposition.

Secondly: Let us consider directly what follows if indeed Christ did not claim knowledge and authority in the style reported in the Gospels. We are in that case simply crazy if we stake our lives and souls on our belief in a teaching which he may never have put out at all in the form that has come down to us, and which we are now to suppose was in any case an expression only of what he thought or conjectured, not of what he claimed to know. Obviously our having faith also requires that Christ did really know, not just claim to know; if he were one of the many people who put on airs of authority because they have strong unfounded convictions, then we need pay no special heed to his teaching at all.[10]

Peter Geach: The Authority of the Christian Tradition: Logical Presuppositions:

If a remarkable tradition has been continuously preserved through many centuries, continuously from the time when this body of belief first arose, this of course does not exclude its having been from the first a fantastic delusion. But if a tradition really is continuous—and I maintain history shows that this is true of Christian tradition in some of its most important traits, in spite of the lamentable divisions of Christendom—then we are believing what was believed by the founders of the tradition, and we are right in believing it if they were right. Like the gold and cedar of the Ark, truth does not grow old. The founders of the tradition claimed to have their teaching from the lips of the Son of God and from the Holy Spirit that had been given them.

Do we accept this claim or do we not? If we accept it, there is an end of the matter; we must hang on to that truth, though one claiming the authority of an apostle, or an angel, should teach us otherwise. And if we reject it as unfounded, then by all means let us follow this way of the world and try to determine for ourselves how the world came to be and what man's place in it is; but it is mere impertinence for somebody now to set up a claim that he can teach a revised Christian doctrine, superior in important ways to the old doctrine. He cannot establish the truth of his claim by reason. ... Can he then establish that he has some God-given authority? I do not see how he can. 'Jesus I know, and Paul I know, but who are you?' we may say to him when he sets up as a teacher. Assuredly he cannot say to a sick man 'Get up and walk' (nor is he likely to be able to say 'Silver and gold have I none', either!) and he will be entirely unable to show any sign that he is inspired by the Holy Spirit. His teaching will be a matter of learned conjectures intermixed with such fragments, few or many, of the old tradition as he chooses still to believe. He may choose to believe all this; but he will scarcely persuade a rational outsider, and he can claim no authority that should bind the conscience of a Christian.[11]

Richard Swinburne: Historical Evidence and the Witness of the Church:

The historical evidence (if we ignore the crucial route of argument to which I am about to draw attention) may be a bit shaky as to what Jesus said when, and what the early community said; but it is a great deal less shaky on what he did. And, I suggest, interpreted in the light of reasonable prior beliefs, it indicates that he taught a message, died on the cross for it (and by that death intended to make available for us an atoning sacrifice) and was brought to life again by God. God thereby signified that the message was true. If God through Christ proclaimed an important message, so important that he gave that unique signature of the Resurrection to its truth, he must have made provision for its continued proclamation—and since he founded a church to carry on his work, it must be the authorized proclaimer of that message. Messages can get misremembered or misunderstood or blown away in the wind unless they are entrusted to a body who can in the end be relied on to proclaim them aright. If Christ founded a church, he taught what it said he taught. I say that without judging between the many different views ranging from a conservative Roman Catholicism to a conservative Protestantism about just how and when the Church has given us authorized teaching about Christ's message; but one thing that all Christians for a millenium and a half have agreed is that the Church has taught that the New Testament is a faithful guide to what Christ said ... The first role of the New Testament as historical evidence leads it via the Church to authorize its second role as the content of revelation. We trust it because, by normal historical criteria, a part of it shows that a community is reliable and that community says that the rest of it is reliable (at any rate, when interpreted in the way the Church says it is to be taken).

Biblical critics have wrongly supposed that only exact detailed historical work on the texts would reveal Jesus' message. We do indeed need historical work—for Christianity is a historical religion—but only to legitimize a broad framework. If historical work, in the light of an overall worldview justified by wider considerations, cannot do that, then there is no authority to the scriptural text. But if it can do that, the text gains its own authority without the need for detailed proof with respect to each passage.[12]

Peter Van Inwagen: The Authority of Critical Studies Critically Considered:

There are good reasons for thinking that Critical Studies do not cast any doubt on the historical reliability of the New Testament, and that one does not have to be a highly educated person to understand those reasons.

This is not surprising. In general, it is much harder to find reasonable grounds for deciding whether a certain proposition is true than it is to find reasonable grounds for deciding whether so-and-so's arguments for the truth (or for the falsity) of that proposition are cogent. If the proposition under consideration is one whose subject-matter is the "property" of some special field of study (like 'The continents are in motion' and unlike 'Mario Cuomo is the governor of New York'), and if the "reasonable grounds" are those that can properly be appealed to by specialists in that field of study, then it is almost certain that only those specialists can find reasonable grounds for deciding whether it is true. ... But if the "reasonable grounds" are ones that it is appropriate for the laity to appeal to, then it is almost always possible for the laity to find reasonable grounds for deciding whether the arguments employed by some group of specialists are cogent ...

Some facts about New Testament studies are accessible even to me. One of them is that many specialists in the field think—in fact, hold to have been demonstrated—that the New Testament narratives are, in large part, narratives of events that never happened ... On the other hand, one can easily find respectable workers in the field who take precisely the opposite view ... A philosopher, at any rate, will not be at a loss of a possible answer to this question. A philosopher will suspect that such radical disagreement means that New Testament scholarship is a lot like philosophy: Either there is little *knowledge* available in the field, or, if there is, a significant proportion of the experts in the field perversely resist acquiring it.

Is New Testament scholarship a source of knowledge? Or, more exactly, is what I have been calling Critical Studies a source of knowledge? Well, of course, the *data* of Critical Studies constitute knowledge: we know, thanks to the labors of those engaged in Critical Studies, that about ninety percent of Mark appears in closely parallel form in Matthew, and that the phrase *en tois epouraniois* appears several times in Ephesians but in none of the other letters that purport to be by Paul, and many things of a like nature. But such facts are only as interesting as the conclusions that can be drawn from them. Or if, you don't like the word knowledge, can any of these conclusions be described, in Perrin's words, as a "fact" that Critical Studies "make unmistakably clear"? ... I suppose that if any of the conclusions of Critical Studies is known to be true, or even known to be highly probable, it is this: Mark's Gospel was composed before Luke's or Matthew's, and both Luke and Matthew used Mark as a source. But this thesis, while it is almost universally accepted (at least everyone I have read says it is) has periodically been controverted by competent scholars, most recently by C.S. Mann in his Anchor commentary on Mark. One might well wonder whether this thesis is indeed known to be true. If it is, how can it be that Mann, who is perfectly familiar with all the arguments, denies it? If it is unmistakably clear, why isn't it unmistakably clear to *him*? And if the *priority* of Mark has not been made unmistakably clear, can it really be plausible to suppose that the much more controversial thesis that Mark is "a strange mixture of history, legend, and myth" has been made unmistakably clear?

My suspicion that Critical Studies have made nothing of any great importance unmistakably clear, or even very clear at all, is reinforced when I examine the methods of some of the acknowledged experts in that field. Here I will mention only the methods of Perrin and his fellow redaction critics, for it is they and their predecessor, the form critics, who are the source of the most widely accepted arguments for the conclusion that the New Testament is historically unreliable; if someone supposes that Critical Studies undermine my supposed grounds for believing in the historical reliability of the New Testament, he will most likely refer me to the redaction critics for my refutation. ...

I have few of the skills and little of the knowledge that New Testament criticism requires. ... But I do know something about reasoning, and I have been simply amazed by some of the arguments employed by redaction critics. My first reaction to these arguments, written up a bit, could be put in these words: "I'm missing something here. These *appear* to be glaringly invalid arguments, employing methods transparently engineered to produce negative judgments of authenticity. But no one, however badly he might want to produce a given set of conclusions, would 'cook' his methods to produce the desired results quite so transparently. These arguments must depend on tacit premises, premises that redaction critics regard as so obvious that they don't bother to mention them." But this now seems to me have been the wrong reaction, for when I turn to commentaries on the methods of the redaction critics by New Testament scholars, I often find more or less my own criticism of them—although, naturally enough, unmixed with my naive incredulity.

I could cite more than one such commentary. The one I like best is an article by Morna Hooker, now Lady Margaret Professor of Divinity in Cambridge University. The article is called "On Using the Wrong Tool," and it articulates perfectly the criticisms I would have made of the methods of redaction criticism if I had been as knowledgeable as she and had not been hamstrung by my outsider's fear that there had to be something I was missing. If Professor Hooker, as she is now, is right, I have certainly not missed anything: All of the premises of the redaction critics are right out in the open. If she is wrong—well, how can *I*, an outsider, be expected to pay any attention to redaction criticism? If its methods are so unclear that the future Lady Margaret Professor couldn't find out what they were, what hope is there for me? I might add that Professor Hooker's witness is especially impressive to an outsider like me because she does not criticize the methods of the redaction critics in order to advance the case of a rival method of her own; rather, their methods are the very methods she herself accepts. She differs from a committed and confident redaction critic like Perrin mainly in her belief that these methods can't establish very much—perhaps that certain logia are a bit more likely on historical grounds to be authentic than certain others— and she adheres to these methods only because (in her view) these methods are the only methods there are. ...

I conclude that there is no reason for me to think that Critical Studies have established that the New Testament narratives are unreliable. In fact there is no reason for me to think that they have established *any* important thesis about the New Testament. ...

Let me close by considering a *tu quoque*. Is not philosophy open to many of the charges I have brought against Critical Studies? Is not philosophy argument without end? Is not what philosophers agree about just precisely nothing? Are not the methods and arguments of many philosophers (especially those who reach extreme conclusions) so bad that an outsider encountering them for the first time might well charitably conclude that he must be missing something? Must one not devote years of systematic study of philosophy before one is competent to think philosophically about whether we have free will or whether there is an objective morality or whether knowledge is possible?—and yet, is not one entitled to believe in free will and knowledge and morality even if one has never read a single page of philosophy?

Ego quoque. If you are not a philosopher, you would be crazy to go to the philosophers to find anything out—other than what it is that the philosophers say. If a philosopher tells you that you must, on methodological grounds, since he is the expert, take his word for something—that there is free will, say, or that morality is only convention—you should tell him that philosophy has not earned the right to make such demands. Philosophy is, I think, valuable. It is a good thing for the study of philosophy to be pursued, both by experts and by amateurs. But from the premise that it is a good thing for a field of study to be pursued by experts, the conclusion does not follow that that field of study comprises experts who can tell you things you need to attend to before you can practice a religion or join a political party or become a conscientious objector. ... This is very close to some of the depreciatory statements I have made about the authority of Critical Studies.[13]

A transition from dogmatic skepticism to a rational consideration of the canons of evidence and explanation is under way in several spheres of intellectual inquiry. The works cited above are relevant in the context of this transition as it applies to biblical studies. Moreover the issues and principles of analysis raised by these authors must be addressed and incorporated in any attempt to construct the logical scaffolding of the Christian belief-system on the bedrock of biblical studies.

Faith in the affirmation that Jesus Christ is truly God and truly human, it has often been said, is not a leap in the dark but a leap to the light. The phenomenological analysis and the logical scaffolding outlined above may serve as the launching-pad for a rationally grounded leap of faith to the affirmation of Christos as Theos and Anthropos—for this affirmation, I believe, furnishes us with the most satisfactory explanation of all the data of Christian history and the Gospels. But faith remains a gift: a gift which the Triune God revealed in the Gospels invites us to accept: and yet a gift that can have a recipient only if it is accepted.

NOTES

[1] J.J.C. Smart and J.J. Haldane, *Atheism and Theism* (Oxford: Blackwell, 1996), 118–9.

[2] C.D. Broad, *The Mind and Its Place in Nature* (London: Kegan Paul, 1925), 623.

[3] John R. Searle, *The Rediscovery of the Mind* (Cambridge: MIT Press, 1992)

[4] A.N. Whitehead, *The Function of Reason* (Princeton: Princeton University Press, 1929), 12.

[5] "Standard evolutionary explanations posit replication as spontaneously arising some three or four billion years ago in a form more primitive than DNA. Needless to say there is no direct evidence of this, rather it is an assumption of

naturalistic theory. The behaviour of DNA itself is acknowledged to be so qualitatively advanced that is unimaginable that it could just have sprung into being
uncreated. So the task is to show how DNA could have arisen from more primitive replication, say RNA, and how that could have resulted from non-replicating
systems. Although molecules exhibit dynamic properties they are not normally
self-duplicating, so the question remains: how could replication and hereditary
variation arise? Talk of proto-replicators' is vulnerable to a version of the dilemma with which I challenged the claim that intentionality arose from proto-repre-
sentation. ... *Low level is not no level*, and it is the jump from none to some that
needs to be effected. I conclude, a priori, that this gap is one of kind not quantity. The emergence of reproductive beings is radical and thus by definition not
naturalistically explicable." J.J.C. Smart and J.J. Haldane, *Atheism and Theism*
(Oxford: Blackwell, 1996), 198–9.

[6] One reviewer has given an apt description of the contemporary situation in biblical studies: "An important factor in evaluating the present condition of biblical
studies is its shift in social location away from the church and synagogue to the
academy, and increasingly to an academy shaped by opposition rather than allegiance to traditional faith. That shift removes biblical scholarship from any read-
ership for whom questions and answers about the texts have genuine existential
significance, and leaves thousands of scholars dancing for no apparent reason
around a very small book." Luke Timothy Johnson "The Crisis in Biblical
Scholarship", *Commonweal*, December 3, 1993, p. 18.

[7] Michael Cahill "An Uncertain Jesus: Theological and Scholarly Ambiguities",
Irish Theological Quarterly, Volume 1, 1998, 28.

[8] Ibid., 26

[9] Michael Dummett, "The Impact of Scriptural Studies on the Content of
Catholic Belief" in *Hermes and Athena: Biblical Exegesis and Philosophical
Theology* edited by Eleonore Stump and Thomas P. Flint (Notre Dame, Indiana
46556: University of Notre Dame Press, 1993), 3–22.

[10] Peter Geach, *The Virtues* (Cambridge: Cambridge University Press, 1977), pp.
67–9.

[11] Peter Geach, *Providence and Evil* (Cambridge: Cambridge University Press,
1977), pp. 85–6.

[12] Richard Swinburne, "Interpreting the New Testament: Comments on the Paper
of Harold W. Attridge" in *Hermes and Athena: Biblical Exegesis and
Philosophical Theology*, 225–234. See also Richard Swinburne, *Revelation:
From Metaphor to Analogy* (Oxford: Clarendon Press, 1992).

[13] Peter Van Inwagen, "Critical Studies of the New Testament and the User of the
New Testament" in *Hermes and Athena: Biblical Exegesis and Philosophical
Theology*, 159–190.

Section I: Theos

A. *The Existence of God*

1

From Cosmos to Theos

The Compatibility of Natural Science and Natural Theology

F.F. Centore

The Subjective Turn in Modern Thought

With good reason, Rene Descartes (1596–1650) is called the father of modern philosophy. In order to combat the skepticism of his day he decided to start afresh, casting aside everything that had gone before. Doubting everything, he withdrew within his own mind and emerged a short time later with the unshakable conviction that he existed as a thinking thing. Indeed, he was, as far as he knew with certainty, nothing but a thinking thing, a mind, a consciousness.[1]

His next step was to go out from his own mind, not to the world of sensible things, but to the existence of God, the perfect being, the creator of all, whose primary trait with respect to science was his honesty and trustworthiness. Since the certainty of his own existence as a substance of consciousness was founded on a clear and distinct idea that could not be denied or suppressed, Descartes figured that we could be equally certain of the existence of anything else also founded on a perfectly clear and distinct idea.

And this was exactly what he claimed to have with respect to God, to wit, an idea of God as the perfect being, the cause of everything, a being whose existence could not be doubted. The only place an idea of perfection can come from, he reasoned, is perfection itself. It certainly could not come from an imperfect being such as himself, and neither could it come by way of any accumulation of imperfect things, no matter how vast. Even an infinite number of imperfections would still total up to imperfection.

Descartes's next step was to turn his attention to the world of nature. Here also he developed a clear and distinct idea, one of nature as nothing but matter in motion, the very thing needed in order to make it perfectly suitable for mathematical analysis. His idea of nature was one of pure extension. Space, matter, and extension were all one and the same thing. The world of nature was created by God, who provided it with a certain fixed amount of matter. God also provided a certain fixed amount of motion. Furthermore, God's immutability and trustworthiness guaranteed that neither matter nor motion could be either augmented or diminished. Hence the basis for all of the conservation laws needed to guarantee that every correct formula would always balance. The last thing a scientist wants is a change in the laws of nature.

Thus was the world made safe for science—forever. Unfortunately for Descartes and his disciples such a thing was not to be, at least not for very long. What sort of God was this who created a world with fixed amounts of matter and motion? Was he the God of religion or just a God of science? Was his name He Who Is or just the Author of Nature? It wasn't long before it became obvious that, in the process of saving science, Descartes had managed to lose the God of Abraham, Isaac, and Jacob. Blaise Pascal (1623–1662), for instance, who was at first impressed by Descartes's clarity and precision, later turned against him, saying that he wasn't worth a moment's consideration. Pascal, however, did not zero in on Descartes's fundamental error, which was to try spinning the world out of his own mind. Instead of allowing reality to dictate to him, Descartes wanted to dictate to reality. This was his subjective turn, something that is still very much with us today in many fields of study, especially philosophy.[2]

Although it was not his intention, what Descartes actually accomplished was to separate the God of science from the God of religion. By the end of the seventeenth century it became clear that the Author of Nature was very much limited to being the great mathematician, architect, and engineer in the sky. He was the perfect mind, and, as later thinkers such as Voltaire and Charles Darwin would point out, a perfect mind should have created a world in which all the parts fitted together properly. If the great engineer in the sky really is all that believers say he is he should have made the best world possible. In such a world, perfect adaptation should be the obvious thing, and, since we don't have it, we have to wonder about divine providence and even God's perfection itself. Could God have created the world and left it to run on its own? Was God even capable of creating a perfect world in the first place? Thus arose a practical atheism, one that could admit the theoretical existence of God but that could then proceed for all practical intents and purposes as if God didn't exist.

This view is called deism. Descartes created God and then God created just the mechanistic, mathematical world that Descartes wanted in order to make the world safe for science. In effect, the infinite richness of God was reduced to one function. It's like asking who Jane is and answering that she's a student. Certainly Jane is a student and certainly God is the Author of Nature but that hardly tells us who they really are in their fullness.

The doctrine of deism was popularized by John Toland (1670–1722) within

Descartes's own time. According to deism, the world is perfectly understandable by science, there are no miracles, no divine providence, and the world is like a great clock that God wound up and set in motion to run on its own. We have been abandoned by God; he has left us alone. Nevertheless, still clinging to a residue of the natural moral law, there are still moral rules for us to follow. Toland taught at Glasgow, Edinburgh, Leiden, and Oxford. His main works were *Christianity Not Mysterious* (1696) and *Pantheisticon* (1720). Toland's views became widespread, and can be found underlying the views of Jean-Jacques Rousseau, Voltaire, and in the thinking of some of the most influential leaders of the American and French Revolutions.[3]

By the middle of the 1800's the separation of the God of religion from the God of science had become painfully obvious to many thinkers. Some of them then set out to counteract it. However, the intellectual tools needed for the task were by then largely lost or forgotten. The result was that such thinkers ended up doing one of several things. Some simply repeated the Newtonian-inspired argument of William Paley (1743–1805), who, in chapter I of his famous *Natural Theology; or Evidences of the Existence and Attributes of the Deity* (1802), compared the need for a maker of a small mechanism, for instance, a pocket watch, to the need for a maker of a large mechanism, the cosmos as a whole. This book work went through several editions even before Paley died, and was reprinted over and over again for many years afterward. Darwin himself said that it showed him how to think in such matters.[4]

In order to make his case, Paley assumes Isaac Newton's (1642–1727) mechanistic worldview. Newton had also used the orderliness of the universe to show the need for a divine creator. For Paley, both the large and the small mechanical devices demand an intelligent, purposeful maker. If Paley were alive today he would undoubtedly use a lap top computer as an example of a small mechanism that could not possibly fall together by accident. Both the parts and the construction of the whole would certainly require a creator. In chapter II of his work he amplifies his argument by observing the wonder of reproduction. Imagine that the watch were able to reproduce itself. Amazing! Yet this is what we find in even the simplest organism. The creator of such a thing must be truly amazing as well. Even assuming that there was an immense amount of time to work with, such wonders of nature could not be explained by any sort of haphazard, unguided process. Paley recognized the fact that time is not a causal agent. How did you get from here to London? Saying that it took a long time is no answer. Insofar as a theory of accidental development depends solely upon long periods of time for something to be accomplished, it explains nothing. Even a self-replicating machine cannot be the cause of itself. And regardless of how many links there are in the chain, there has to be a first support for the chain. If this is true of a simple mechanism, how much more does it hold for a very complicated one.

This approach is fine as far as it goes. It even went far enough to convince

John Stuart Mill of the need for some sort of designer of the universe.[5] That, though, is the troublesome point. Does the scientific design argument go far enough to bring about the reunification of the God of science with the God of religion? The standard rebuttal to Paley-type arguments was given by David Hume (1711–1776) even before Paley wrote his famous work. Hume, assuming that the scientific design argument is the only kind which can be derived from our experience of the cosmos, points out that all such arguments must fail to achieve their goal.[6]

This is because they do not arrive at the God of religion. Paley's God is too anthropomorphic, finite, and imperfect to be useful to religion. And could the world have been made by a committee of scientists (polytheism)? To Hume, this is obviously not the best of all possible worlds, and the God of science need be no more perfect than the actual level of perfection of the universe. In addition, maybe the whole world is one great living organism, with God as the world-soul. The rebuttal to Hume is not to be found in Paley, but in Aquinas, who had, a long time before Hume, already understood the main point of Hume's objection to scientific design-type arguments. Aquinas stated: "Hence, from the knowledge of sensible things, the whole power of God cannot be known, and neither can his essence be seen."[7]

Others gave up on reason and science altogether, falling back into a fideistic position, which was in effect an admission of intellectual defeat. You could either be rationalistic and scientific or religious but not both at the same time. This same temptation still exists today, especially among those who are inclined towards Protestant Fundamentalism. Simply assert the Bible and have little if anything to do with using reason or science to support biblical statements. When mentioning science, show its weaknesses and limitations, thereby removing it as a threat to religion. This, however, is a dangerous path to follow. There's no guarantee whatsoever that suppressing reason will elevate religion. It could well be, as in the case of postmodernism and contemporary pragmatism, that skepticism will overwhelm everything, including religion. It's possible to lose both science and religion at the same time.[8]

Still others tried a process philosophy compromise with Scripture and theism, which was also a defeat in its own way insofar as it was forced to admit that the Bible had lost out to science with respect to the nature of God and God's relationship to the world and to human beings. As becomes quite obvious in the case of someone such as Alfred North Whitehead (1861–1947), any relationship between process philosophy or theology and traditional religion is purely coincidental. Whereas traditional religion says that the relationships among God, man, and the world are essentially fixed forever, Whitehead said that whatever suggests a new cosmology also suggests a new religion.[9]

His cosmology-religion turned out to be a form of pantheism, a doctrine that is just the opposite of deism. According to his doctrine, which he considered to be a compromise between atheism on one hand and the out-dated old religion of a supreme being separate from the world on the other hand, religion must be rational, not just emotional, and evil is a necessary aspect of reality and occurs when things are at cross-purposes. Evil is an internal inconsistency, not some imagined violation of some imagined divine law. Overall, the modern attitude is to reject extremes. Both God as the impersonal order of the world, for example the view of someone such as Albert Einstein, and God as a separate personal creator of the world, as was taught in the old religion, must be replaced with a new process paradigm.

In his work *Process and Reality* (1929) we learn that the philosophy of nature is "first philosophy" or metaphysics, religion is the ultimate craving to rationalize emotions, the separation of flux and permanence is vicious, reducing the world to mere appearance is vicious, everything must be unified into one universal system of things, everlastingness and temporality must be together, God is the World and the World is God, all opposites are elements in the very nature of things, and that everything is in the grasp of the creative advance into newness. Although they have no objection to innovation and creativity, it should come as no surprise to also learn that no one interested in worshipping the God of Abraham, Isaac, and Jacob wanted anything to do with such a remodelled scheme of things.

These process-pantheistic themes have now become commonplace in much of modern religious thought. The main point of process theology is that God is not altogether perfect, but is in the process of becoming more and more perfect, just like other things in the world. In order to have God avoid knowing evil, God is gaining knowledge just like other things. In order to avoid having to conquer evil, God is gaining in power just like other things. So, to account for evil, God must be imperfect. Either God is not all-knowing or not all-powerful or both. If God were all-knowing he would know about evil and would do something about it. If God were all-powerful he would be able to get rid of evil. By having imperfect knowledge God avoids knowing evil. By having imperfect power God avoids having to conquer evil. In this way the responsibility for evil is removed from God.

This means that God is a part of the world. God grows and develops along with the world and the things in the world, including human beings. There is real change in God. Thus God progresses along with the world and its people. Evil, therefore, is inherent in the world-process. There is a lack of perfect adaptation, just as Darwin said. But as the world progresses the mismatch of parts will be lessened, and we will move into a better and better world in the future. Every day in every way things get better and better, as the nineteenth century religion of Christian Science used to teach. Everything moves from the less perfect to the more perfect, and will continue to do so for a very long time to come.

It follows from this that process theology has no use for institutional churches which claim to have a lock on truth. All hierarchies must be levelled; all the marginalized must be taken into the mainstream. Everything must be adjusted and modified as we move ahead into the future. We must constantly reinvent the church and religion as we go along. New times demand new doctrines and new theologies. Those who resist change are backward, regressive, authoritarian, popish, and insensitive to the needs of the people and to the needs of science. Talking about something as being "from the beginning" (e.g., Matthew 19:5) makes no sense in process thinking. The Bible, Koran, etc., are, at best, only interesting stories, written by well-meaning people, containing many useful insights into human life. They are not, though, Revelations from a God who must be strictly obeyed. And there are no real miracles in the world. The only way to really know about the world is through the scientific method of experimentation.

A Partial Rebuttal by John Henry Newman.

A good example of the realization of the problem of reunifying the God of religion with the God of science, although not of its solution, can be found in some of John Henry Newman's (18011890) early writings. In 1841, while he was still the Anglican vicar of St. Mary's Church in Oxford (1827–1841), as part of a series of miscellaneous writings (later put together under the title of *Discussions and Arguments*), Newman explicitly discusses the relationship between science and religion. He begins by criticizing the plan of Sir Robert Peel (1788–1850) for the establishment of a series of public libraries and reading rooms as a means of educating the general populace in the latest views of modern science, thereby assuring that the masses would become more religious. Newman, however, cannot see any necessary connection between religiosity and worldly knowledge. Does science create faith, he asks, or does it only confirm it? Peel himself, observes Newman, being a religious man already, reads science with religious thoughts. But, asks Newman, would someone without religious faith feel so inclined?[10]

According to Francis Bacon's view of the Greek atomists, for instance, as found in his *Advancement of Learning* (III, 4), the reason why they were able to be resurrected in modern times (1400–1600), and why they should be used for making penetrating insights into the physical causes of natural events, is due precisely to their atheism. Talking about God's creative power, and using the language of formal and final causality, does not explain things about nature nearly half as well as concentrating upon the more immediate material and agent causes. Thus does Bacon argue for leaving God out of the early stages of science.

As an aside here, it's interesting to observe that at the same time that Newman was reminding people about what Bacon had to say on the subject, Darwin, in his "B" notebook (July 1837–February 1838, page 104), was complaining to himself about the way a creationist theory of speciation fails to explain anything. A completely materialistic approach, employing rigid universal laws, and without the interference of God, would be much more fruitful, he thought, when it came to explaining the biosphere.[11]

"Lord Bacon," continues Newman, "gives us both the fact and the reason for it. Physical philosophers are ever inquiring whence things are, not why; referring them to nature, not to mind; and thus they tend to make a system a substitute for a God."

It is possible, nonetheless, thinks Newman, for a thinker to rise above the limitations of his own peculiar perspective and, if not embrace, then at least admit the existence of, other perspectives. This is in fact what Bacon himself did. But this is often a very difficult thing to do, and Newman is not surprised to find that many cannot do it. In any event, as far as physics qua physics is concerned, it can never make people religious. Nature can be interpreted as merely a series of causes and effects. Are we to refer everything to the future (design), or backwards to a series of material causes? "Does the sun shine to warm the earth," asks Newman, "or is the earth warmed because the sun shines?" This was exactly the same sort of question that Darwin was asking himself about the same time, and answering in a deistic way.

How you read nature is not decided by the data, says Newman, but by faith. In response to Peel's insistence that anyone studying nature assiduously is bound to end up glorifying God for God's great works, Newman asks if it's not more likely that the scientist will end by glorifying himself. Newman finds evidence for this in that Peel himself glorifies his own mental powers before he goes on to praise God. This is even more clear, points out Newman, in the case of the abolitionist Henry Peter Brougham (1778–1868), the founder in 1825 of the Society for the Diffusion of Useful Knowledge, and who, in 1828, was a prime mover in establishing London University, organized along non-denominational lines. Lord Brougham, notices Newman, is forever praising the powers of the human mind. What science teaches Brougham, it seems, is not so much that God is great as that Lord Brougham is great. To this situation Newman exclaims: "So, this is the religion we are to gain from the study of Nature; how miserable! The god we attain is our own mind; our veneration is even professedly the worship of self."

Wonder should not be confused with religion, explains Newman. The system of nature, divorced from religion, is as religious as a watch or a steamcarriage. If wonder alone were sufficient to found a religion we should be worshipping our rail roads. Science teaches us that nature is a piece of machinery, and that the Author of Nature is no more the living God of Abraham, Isaac, and Jacob than a spring is the god of a pocket watch, or steam is the god of a steam engine. What a religious scientist might worship is the animating principle of the world system. Such a principle is subject to laws, and is as natural as the world it animates. "Well does Lord Brougham," ends Newman, "call it 'the great architect of nature;' it is an instinct, or a soul of the world, or a vital power; it is not the

Almighty God."

Newman's main attempt to explain how we can come to an intimate sense of God's existence and presence is contained in his *An Essay in Aid of a Grammar of Assent* (1870, part I, chapter 5, section 1). God does not come to people through dialectic, but through love. And where do we find this aspect of life most poignantly displayed if not in our interpersonal relationships? As human beings we all make moral judgments of some sort or another; if not about the evils of racism, then about child abuse or pollution, and so on. Such judgments cannot be based solely upon the facts of sense-level observations or upon scientific data. All such judgments must transcend the data; they are evaluations of the data. Saying, for instance, that someone is burning a three year-old child with a hot iron is quite different from saying that the action is evil and should not be done. Recognizing the difference between the fact and the evaluation of the fact is a part of ordinary human experience, common to all people and cultures all over the world.

On this foundation Newman wants to talk about God as the Moral Governor. The feeling of conscience, or the moral sense, is both a judgment and a sense of duty. We judge that there is a right and a wrong, and that we must do the right. This, though, it must be emphasized, is not a rule of what is right, but a sanction of right conduct in our actual lives. It should not be confused with taste or good taste. This latter contemplates an object in only a remote and impersonal way. It's quite possible that doing something which is in bad taste is very remote from us emotionally. Not so with conscience. Conscience can never be remote. It is always something of a personal and immediate concern to the active human person.

What Newman is talking about would be a situation, for example, in which someone arrived at a performance at the Royal Opera House in London dressed in some old dungarees and a dirty T-shirt. Now compare this to the situation where someone is witnessing a child being tortured with a hot iron. In the first situation, the person involved might be embarrassed for a while, but then that would be the end of it. In the second situation, however, there would be moral outrage and a strong motivation to actually do something about remedying the situation. The difference between the two is the difference between manners and morals. Similarly, a male wearing an ear-ring would be a matter of manners; for him to beat his child black and blue would be a matter of morals, and so on. Newman is talking about morals.

Newman then goes on to argue that the sense of morality cannot come from the world of mundane facts and manners; it can come only from the supernatural world of God and divine judgment. The fact that all human beings have a moral sense, a sense of sanction, regardless of the particular content of that moral sense from one culture to another, shows that there is a direct and immediate connection between God and the individual human person.

It's possible, though, for this connection to be weakened or broken. Although we are all born with this moral sense, Newman is willing to admit that it can be lost over time. However, stamping out your moral conscience so that you can rob, torture, maim, kill, and destroy takes time and practice. And even then there is usually some residue left behind to nag you. Regardless of how the situation may be later rationalized, on the subconscious level political leaders know that their duty is to serve the common good rather than line their own pockets; fathers understand that they are not to use their daughters for animal pleasures; mothers realize that it's wrong to kill their own children; judges know that they must be impartial; witnesses understand that they cannot lie to the judge if justice is to be done; prostitutes and drug addicts, on the subconscious level at least, realize that they are degrading themselves, and so forth. Hence, in our own day, the attempted self-delusion on the conscious level of the pro-choice phraseology rather than spelling out the dirty deed.

In modern philosophical terms, the lack of charity and justice has been rationalized in various ways, for instance by claiming that the world itself is cruel and that we must imitate the world. There may in fact be no objective difference between good and evil. It may be, as taught by Friedrich Wilhelm Nietzsche (1844–1900), that the dirty and evil things of life are on a par with the good and clean things of life, and so should be accepted and accorded equal respect. In the words of Newman, towards the end of section 1, "Good and evil meet us daily as we pass through life, and there are those who think it philosophical to act towards the manifestations of each with some sort of impartiality, as if evil had as much right to be there as good, or even a better, as having more striking triumphs and a broader jurisdiction."[12]

Newman, however, cannot accept such ambiguity as the normal human condition. He thinks that the normal condition is for people to grow in their openness to God. Conscience is the living and active link between two personal beings, one finite, the other infinite. By God, though, he does not mean a mere world-soul, or some initial principle of creation which has now abandoned the world (deism), or humanity taken collectively, so that religion, after the fashion of Ludwig Feuerbach (1804–1872) and Auguste Comte (1798–1857), is only a disguised way of worshipping ourselves.

By God Newman means a personal being separate from the world. The religious creeds, which formulate religious beliefs more precisely and which guide our conscience, must be taken seriously. Dogmas help us live better; they help cement the connection between God and man. There is no incompatibility between dogma and living faith. For this reason, churches and creeds are extremely important. This is so even if the individual believer is not an expert in theology. As stated by Ian Ker, "As for the many dogmatic propositions to which a Catholic is required to give notional assent, his assent is implicitly given when he gives a real assent to the Church."[13] Adhering to religious dogmas, even if it is only done indirectly, is necessary in order to maintain a coherent and rational approach to God.

When all is said and done, though, and without in any way doubting Newman's intelligence, piety, and sincerity, his approach still partakes of the subjective turn. In order to establish the existence of God he had to retreat into his own mind. There was no appeal to the cosmos as a foundation for approaching God. This must leave an uneasy feeling in the minds of many when they contemplate the fact that, within an integrated human setting, the God of religion and the God of science must be one and the same being. After all, were not the human intellect and the cosmos made by the same God? And if so, why would the Creator place a barrier between the mind and the world on one side and God on the other?

The Dawning of the Age of Destruction.

By the late 1870's the situation had gotten so bad that Pope Leo XIII felt the urgent need to issue an encyclical on the restoration of Christian learning (*Aeterni Patris,* 1879). In this letter he urged a return to the spirit, even if not the letter in all respects, of the intellectual approach of St. Thomas Aquinas. The core of this approach is the view that science, philosophy, and theology can coexist with each other without contradiction. The Thomistic philosophy of being provided a basis for the integration of all of the main areas of intellectual endeavor, such that both the supremacy of love within religion and the role of the intellect within natural learning could both be safeguarded, nurtured, developed, and expanded. He urged further that this approach become the standard one throughout the Church in all of its teaching facilities.[14]

In our own century, this approach has been confirmed by the Second Vatican Council. In the Declaration on Christian Education (#10) we read that the sciences must be arduously pursued so that "the convergence of faith and reason in the one truth may be seen more clearly. This method follows the tradition of the doctors of the Church and especially St. Thomas Aquinas."[15] This represents the first time that Thomism was recommended to the whole Church, both East and West, as an intellectual model.

Yet, with respect to the decline of religion in the Western world, and, as it turned out, with respect to much of the rest of the world as well, worse was yet to come. Beginning in the 1880's with Nietzsche, who simply assumed that science and technology had made God into an unnecessary hypothesis, through to Marx, Engels, Lenin, Stalin, Hitler, James, Dewey, Freud, Skinner, Camus, Sartre, and many others, the trend has continued. The twentieth century has been the age of nihilism, which is another way of saying that moral relativism reigns supreme.

The doctrine of moral relativism teaches that there are no absolutes with respect to what we should and should not do. Following in the footsteps of the old Greek sophist Protagoras, man is the measure of what is and is not, of what is good and evil, of what can and cannot be done. Without God all things are permissible, and morality is mainly a matter of seeing what you can get away with, regardless of who or what is harmed in the process. This attitude is widespread in the popular media and also dominates in most of our educational institutions at all levels.[16]

One of the most obvious examples of what can happen when moral relativism gains ascendancy is the relationship between Nietzsche and Hitler. The connection between what Nietzsche preached in the nineteenth century and what actually happened in the twentieth century should be obvious enough. Although, in his own life, as far as we know, Nietzsche did not actually practice cruelty and torture, and chose to live the life of a lonely, anti-Prussian hermit, there is nothing in his doctrine and preaching requiring others to do likewise. Although one would-be superman need not use his claws if he doesn't want to, there is nothing to forbid others from doing so. Obviously, you cannot very well say that there are no ideals, no eternal, objective standards of morality, and then claim that Nietzsche's own personal lifestyle is the one ideal, eternally true, lifestyle that everyone else must follow. The whole point is to do your own thing, and no one else can tell you what your own thing is.

This was indeed the attitude of someone such as Adolf Hitler (1889–1945), someone who is supposed to be universally hated but who has shown up in more motion pictures than Jesus Christ. (If Hitler were alive today no doubt the popular media people would be using him to advertise mustache wax.) Hitler saw himself as a bold, sincere, lonely, lucid, loving, hard-working, faithful secular servant-figure, in love with beauty and goodness, especially in architecture, answering the call of his natural destiny. Bereft of any objective Judaeo-Christian or natural moral law moral standards, he was free to be his own master, to think with his guts and blood, and work his terrible, triumphant will on other people.

He was even able to enlist the aid of many outstanding minds, certainly a sign of a great leader, overflowing with self-confidence, marching to the beat of his own drummer, drawing, like a magnet, brilliant men and women into his vision of the world. In science, many outstanding intellectuals came to his side, including Philipp Lenard and Johannes Stark, both of whom were Nobel Prize winners in Physics, in 1905 and 1919 respectively.[17]

In philosophy, Martin Heidegger responded with enthusiasm to his call. As David H. Hirsch has reported with respect to Heidegger, Heidegger's complaint to Herbert Marcuse after the Second World War that he (Heidegger) was no prophet and so could not be expected to see the consequences of Nazism, is nothing short of a lie. As pointed out by others, for instance, Martin Buber, Laszlo Versenyi, and Victor Farias, both before and after the war Heidegger's philosophical and personal views were in perfect harmony with the views of Hitler, from the supeiiority of the Germans to the inferiority of individual human beings relative to the race.[18] Indeed, according to David Lehman, the whole emphasis on hermeneutics and deconstructionism after the Second World War can be considered as an effort to hide the Nazi roots of thinkers such as Heidegger and Paul de Man.[19]

The Return to Reason and Religion.

Nevertheless, despite the spread of irrationalism and irreligion in the twentieth century, there are some signs that things may be changing back in favor of reason and religion. The failure of the Logical Positivism movement (1920–1950), which attempted to set up a completely materialistic, "bread alone" doctrine founded upon nothing but mathematics and sense knowledge, has led many thinkers to reconsider the whole question of religion. Statements about the soul and God are indeed meaningful after all. The failure of Logical Positivism might even serve as an inoculation against any future attempt to ever try the same sort of thing again.[20]

Likewise, the collapse of Communism is now causing a new intellectual and emotional crisis in many parts of the world today. In addition, there is the growing realization among many well-versed thinkers that even Darwin's special theory of evolution is not above criticism, and may indeed be basically false from a scientific viewpoint with respect to the notion that one species can gradually grow out of another species.

In his own day, it was only by extrapolating a long way beyond the evidence that Darwin was able to make a case for a mechanistic process whereby one species transmutes into another. According to Darwin, the French naturalist Jean Lamarck (1744–1829) had offered the philosophers and scientists of his day a fairy tale theory of species origination based on an anthropomorphic wish fulfillment on the part of all organisms. Darwin, though, in conformity with what was then regarded as good science, wanted to be strictly mechanistic. Yet today, after many years of investigation and research, there is still no well-documented case of species transformation. Drosophila (fruit flies) are still fruit flies, butterflies, even though they may change their wing color, are still butterflies, finches are still finches, iguanas are still iguanas, and people are still people. A superficial physical change, such as in size, color, weight, and the like, does not place something in a different species. Does having different skin colors mean that Whites and Blacks belong to different species?

In a way, therefore, it doesn't make too much sense to talk about Darwin's special theory of evolution today. The theory has undergone such radical changes in the last few decades that it's doubtful if it can any longer be regarded as viable. Darwin thought in terms of a gradual process of change, proceeding in minute steps, taking an almost infinite amount of time to accomplish. In keeping with his mechanistic, materialistic, atomistic view of the world, all change had to take place along a smooth curve, with no intervening gaps or leaps. Today, though, this can no longer be maintained. The more modern scientific view of punctuated equilibriumism, which shows that there must have been great gaps and leaps in the evolution of new species, destroys the classical Darwinian theory.[21]

In addition, we now know that at various times in the past all life, or nearly all life, on earth has been wiped out by various natural disasters, such as the earth's being struck by some giant meteor. In light of this new evidence it seems clear that there was not sufficient time for the gradual changes postulated by Darwin's theory to take place. Instead of having an almost infinite amount of time to work with, during which an almost infinite number of generations could live and die, we are now down to mere millions of years between catastrophes.[22]

Moreover, as can be seen in recent scientific research, nobody knows where and when the higher primates, which are supposed to include human beings, really came into existence. A recent article in *Science,* dealing with the subject of the origin of the ancestors of the higher primates, states that at some point the higher primates (the anthropoids) diverged from the lower primates (the pro-simians) but that scientists are at a loss to say when or where. In comparison to the lower primates, the higher primates are so distinctive that we cannot imagine how they managed to evolve from the lower primates. All transitional fossil forms are lacking.

More recently, Richard F. Kay has stated that "the problem of anthropoid origins is still among the most hotly contested in the literature of primate evolution; no consensus has yet emerged regarding the relationships of several groups of Paleogene fossil primates to living strepsirrhines [lemur-like creatures] and haplorhines [monkey-like creatures]. This lack of consensus has stemmed principally from an absence of morphologically transitional taxa between anthropoids and any of the better known Paleogene primate groups."[23] In other words, not just a few links here and there, but most of the chain, is missing.

This lack of fossil evidence, together with the very restrictive time frame in which the forces of natural selection had to operate, render the original Darwinian theory of common descent with modification by means of natural selection, which was based upon minute variations, some of which were preserved because of their usefulness for survival at their time and place of occurrence, pretty much inoperative.

There are also the social and political consequences of Darwinism to contend with. The ethical shortcomings of Darwinian evolutionism are immense. Early in the twentieth century this was noticed by G.K. Chesterton. In his 1910 book *What's Wrong With the World* (1, V) there is a chapter entitled "The Empire of the Insect" in which he mentions how he once shocked some Tory friends of his by calling the famous Conservative Prime Minister of England, Edmund Burke (1729–1797), an atheist and by calling M.M.I. Robespierre (1758–1794), the infamous leader of the Great Committee that staged the Reign of Terror, a theist. This was because the Frenchman agreed with the revolutionaries in their appeal to standards of eternal justice beyond all local custom and convenience, while the Englishman, in his defense of non-revolution, appealed to relativism and evolution.[24]

In a nutshell, Robespierre thought that the state should adjust itself to the Rights of Man; Burke thought that man should adjust himself to his circumstances. In this way Burke was the essential atheistic evolutionist. Being born under the House of Lords was an accident. Through good fortune Englishmen are born in England, just as by accident Negroes are born under the tropical sun and are thereby suited to work as slaves on plantations. It's not Burke's fault that this is the way things are; if we must blame someone or something blame Mother Nature. Like an animal in the forest, man must adapt himself to his surroundings; it's not for him to change his environment. His surroundings would include his political condition. Burke claimed to know nothing about the Rights of Man; only something about the rights of Englishmen.

In this case, how can anyone be both a believing evolutionist and a believing environmentalist at the same time? Chesterton notes that there is an instinctive resistance to evolutionary ideas on the part of the average person. This is not due to an anti-scientific attitude but rather to the fact that the average person does not like being pushed around. If people are supposed to adjust to the circumstances rather than having the circumstances adjust to what is right for human beings, then I'm fair game to be remodelled by any force, human or non-human, which cares to use me to serve its own ends. Everyone becomes a victim, with absolutely no possibility of an appeal to a higher court. Chesterton imagines political dictators deliberately engineering things such as ten-foot tall basketball players and three-foot tall mine workers.

A long time before genetic engineering was actually possible, years before the horrors of social engineering described in Aldous Huxley's *Brave New World* (1932), and decades before TV ads and announcements showing us the disfigured, grotesque, and deformed future humans who have adapted to a polluted earth, Chesterton foresaw the social and political implications of denying a fixed human nature. Without the eternal truths of God's Eternal Law and the ensuing stability of human nature, the state and the mad scientist can do whatever they want with us.

If we have a natural contempt for such things then we had better wonder why that is the case. The answer is that moral relativism must be fundamentally wrong. There must be something in our nature that is more fundamental than the civil laws, and whatever whims and fancies may fill the heads of political leaders and judges, at any particular time and place. This, though, must mean that there is some law that is binding on both the ruled and the rulers, some divine standard that cannot be ignored by either the private citizen or by the lawmakers of the land. Morally speaking, as Voltaire once said, if God did not exist it would be necessary to invent him.

This then brings us back to the main point, namely, can we know the existence of God by a study of the cosmos? Are there in fact certain permanent features of the cosmos that can lead the perceptive intellect to a knowledge of an eternally existing personal God? And what is the most striking feature of the world, its orderliness or its existence?

Some Preliminary Points.

In order to be useful in a Judaeo-Christian context, any rational argument for the existence of God must meet certain minimum conditions. These conditions would be the following:

(A) An argument for the existence of God founded on a knowledge of the cosmos must be accessible to anyone with a basic education. It should not be restricted to only a few specialists in science, philosophy, or theology.

(B) It should be accessible to anyone with basic reasoning power. It should not require that someone be a specialist in all of the fine points of humanistic or computer logic.

(C) It must be free of any particular scientific cosmology. The natural sciences keep advancing in their discovery of more and more certainties about nature. When the sciences enter upon the philosophy of nature, however, they are not at all certain in their results. For example, what are the ultimate constituents of nature? Matter and form? Atoms? Looking back over the centuries we find that, at one time, the latest word in scientific cosmology was Plotinus (205–270), with his universe full of many layers of gods, magic, and mysticism, all coming from the great non-being by a fatalistic, necessary process. We have also seen the worldviews of Aristotle, Descartes, Newton, and Darwin come and go. Any argument which is bound to the latest scientific worldview is sure to die as soon as the worldview dies. Today, for instance, we can ask how long will the pantheism of process philosophy and theology last after Darwin's original position is shown to be false by more advanced science? History tells us that we must also be cautious with respect to the most contemporary "final" theoretician, Einstein.

(D) It must show an agreement between reason and Revelation. Such a convergence must not be forced. At each stage it must be possible to check the argument against the standards of ordinary sensible human experience and the rules of logic. In this way, if there is a convergence of the God of reason with the God of religion, it will be free of prejudice.

From Having Existence to He Who Is Existence.

The philosophical proof for the existence of God begins with our ordinary experiences of the world around us, the cosmos in which we live and breathe. Our commonsense understanding of the world is always two-fold. Such ordinary experience informs us that both sense experience and intellectual thinking are used in our everyday life. We are aware of both (A) that something exists and (B) what something is, even if it's only as a vague "something." In ordinary life our knowledge is always directed first and foremost to real things outside of our own mind. Contrary to Descartes's reversal, the cosmos informs the mind.[25]

Our experiences tell us that things can be grouped into sets, classes, species, and so forth, and that one thing within a given species can never be the cause of the specific nature of another thing within that same species. For instance, human parents can bring about this particular human child, but they do not cause the existence of human nature itself. This leads us to realize that the nature, essence, definition, the "what," of something cannot exist simply as a nature. It must exist either as a thing outside the mind or as an idea in the mind. How it exists is not determined by the nature itself. Expressed otherwise, essences are existentially neutral. This also explains why the definitional approach to God of someone such as Anselm can never work. In order to be real an essence requires some cause that removes its indifference to existence.[26]

Such a cause must be outside of the nature that is being actualized and must be a real thing in the real world. A mere idea, a mere possible, or another naked nature (essence), won't do. Children are produced by real parents, not possible parents; tables are made by real carpenters, not possible ones. Since any essence whatsoever is indifferent to how, when, and where it will exist, there must be some already and externally existing thing that can bring the new being into existence. For example, in modern science, the scientist who creates a new virus, genetic structure, chemical compound, and so on, in the laboratory must already exist, along with all of his or her material, equipment, and the like. In this way, in the real world, existence always precedes essence, that is to say, a real being must be responsible for any new being that actually comes into existence. This is another way of saying that in the cosmos insofar as we presently know it every sensible thing is dependent upon some other, already extramentally existing, thing external to itself for its existence.

I. Anything whose essence (nature) does not include its own existence is something dependent upon some other, already extramentally existing, thing external to itself for its existence.

Every sensible thing is something whose essence does not include its own existence.

Ergo, every sensible thing is dependent upon some other, already extramentally existing, thing external to itself for its existence.

The conclusion means that every sensible thing must be efficiently (existentially) caused by some other already existing thing that is both real and external to the thing caused. Note, though, that it does not say that the cause must also be a sensible thing. For metaphysical materialists of one stripe or another to assume beforehand and without argument that the cause must also be a sensible thing would be a rather obvious case of begging the question in their own favor. All that can be said at this point is that, in the case of any being whose existence is accidental (contingent) to its actual, real, extramental existence, there must be something other than the being in question that already really exists and upon which the being in question depends for its existence. But, does this apply to the whole universe?

In modern times this is the crucial point in the argument. Can we say that whatever is true of the very nature of any one sensible thing here and now is true of all sensible things taken together here and now, that existential dependency is true of the very nature of any one sensible thing here and now (the conclusion reached above), and that therefore existential dependency is true of all sensible things taken together here and now?

II. Whatever is true of the very nature of any one sensible thing here and now is true of all sensible things taken together here and now.

Existential dependency is true of the very nature of any one sensible thing here and now. (See I. above)

Ergo, existential dependency is true of all sensible things taken together here and now.

Is this an example of the fallacy of composition and division? The answer here is that this is not fallacious reasoning, and in fact is very much in keeping with everything we know from modern science about the universe. This is not an example of the fallacy of composition and division, that is, the major premise is in fact a true universal affirmative proposition. We know that there is something wrong with the following sorts of reasoning: John is a champion hockey player and so his team will win the Stanley Cup; leader X (president, pope, police chief, labor leader, school trustee, etc.) is a bad person and so his whole organization is evil; each brick in the wall is 10 inches long and so the whole wall is 10 inches long; each thing in the universe is finite and so the whole universe is finite. These illustrate the fallacy of composition, which means taking collectively what should be considered separately.

On the other side of the coin is the fallacy of division, which means taking separately what should be considered only collectively. Examples of this sort of bad thinking would be the following: All these straws put together broke the camel's back and so this one straw can do it too; everyone in the class weighs 2000 pounds and so Sally must weigh 2000 pounds; Canada is a rich nation and so Canadian citizen Jane must be rich; this is a championship hockey team and so player John must be a championship hockey player; you study hard eight hours a day during exam periods and so you should be able to do so all term long.

In contrast to these fallacious ways of reasoning, however, the argument from cosmos to God as inspired by Aquinas is not jumping from the part to the whole or vice versa. He is referring to the very nature of each sensible thing, which means that all sensible beings are homogeneous with respect to both the accidental nature and the priority of the cause of their existence. It follows the valid logical pattern of saying something like: Everyone (taken individually in his or her own nature) in the class is a human being, Jane is in the class, and so Jane is a human being. The predicate applies to each and every case in the subject.[27]

Note also that the argument is concerned only with the here and now, thereby avoiding the old problem of the chicken and the egg and which came first. As everyone knows from his or her own personal experience, we live in an ever-changing world, a universe of constant process and becoming. This incessant and ceaseless becoming is going on right now. This is a fact, a datum of experience. Nonetheless, as far as moving from the cosmos to God is concerned, it has nothing to do with a long series of events going into the past or the future. Contingency for Aquinas does not mean merely being here today and gone tomorrow. Its primary meaning is not about the constant cycle of generation and corruption. For Thomas, contingency primarily means the existential dependency of beings, not a temporal sequence.

For the old essentialist Aristotle, reality, being, and unity were all the same thing. He took existence for granted. Not so for Aquinas. As a Judaeo-Christian thinker he had to redefine contingency. Even if the world were eternal it would still require a creator. Contingency is not time-dependent (here today, gone tomorrow). Even if the chicken and the egg business went back forever, they would still require a creator. Time per se doesn't explain anything. Anything that exists requires the constant activity of God to maintain it in existence. Things are liable to death and destruction, not because they exist in time, but because they are composites. Where there is a composite nature, decomposition is possible.

For instance, in human nature, both the matter of the body and the soul are incorruptible; yet we die. Because things have essences (natures) which are fixed and permanent, science is possible. But because all things also have an existential dimension, science is not the last word about the cosmos. Certainly things change, but existential annihilation should not be confused with the corruption (substantial change) of things. According to Gilson, this is one of the most difficult points to grasp in the whole Thomistic philosophy of being. Concerning contingency, says Gilson, here we are invited to conceive creatures as being, at one and the same time, indestructible in themselves, yet wholly contingent in their relationship to God.[28]

The notion that the cosmos as a whole can be eternal in duration and yet still contingent is something that many critics, such as Bertrand Russell, who lack an existential outlook, cannot understand. Substantial corruption, that is, the decomposition of things, the death of organisms, etc., should not be confused with existential dependency. When water, for instance, breaks down into hydrogen and oxygen, this shows the contingency of water, but it does not deny its dependence upon a cause in the first place. To understand Aquinas's existential way we must think vertically (existential dependency here and now) rather than horizontally (a line stretching back into the past).

Interestingly enough, on this score, Aquinas's argument is stronger today than it was in his own day. When the science of Aristotle reigned as the last word in science, it was taken for granted that the universe was eternal. Today, however, the situation has changed quite a bit, and all in favor of religion. With the Big Bang theory, and especially after Einstein's theory of a finite universe that is homogeneous throughout, we now have science coming in to support Aquinas.[29] In addition, as described by Heisenberg, although the geocentric view of the universe, with its concentric spheres, is not returning, Aristotle's doctrine of matter and form (potency and act) is making a comeback.[30] Worse than that for the old-fashioned materialistic atomists, we now have actual pictures of individual atoms and they do not show us anything like little specks of stuff moving around in space.[31] Moreover, the old idea of time as something relative to and dependent upon the existence of a material and changing universe, as held by Aristotle, Augustine, and Aquinas, is now the accepted view among modern scientists.[32]

More recently, Jeremy Campbell, in his often reprinted work *Grammatical Man*, includes a special appendix on Aristotle and the discovery of DNA. He refers to the way Nobel Prize winning biologist Max Delbrueck has proposed a Nobel Prize for Aristotle in honor of Aristotle's discovery of the principles underlying the functioning of DNA, even though Aristotle of course knew nothing about the actual existence of DNA. Aristotle's philosophy, from the notion of the unmoved mover, the highest of the gods, to the notion of a form acting through the matter towards a predetermined goal, describes very well just how DNA functions. The unchanging DNA provides the pattern for the developing organism as it changes from a nondescript entity to a fully grown being of a definite type.

Aristotle's philosophy, very much concerned with teleology as discerned in all aspects of nature, found a use for teleological thinking in all areas of biological life as well. This approach to the world goes well beyond mere description and the mere accumulation of large quantities of data to an interpretation of the data. It moves, as science should, from the facts to an explanation of the facts. This is the true work of science, and, in modern times, the interpretive role of teleology can no longer be ignored as science advances.[33]

This does not mean that the argument for the existence of God is dependent upon the latest scientific theories. It does mean, though, that those who would pit science against religion are now having a very hard time doing so.

We are now ready for the last stage of the proof. So far we have seen that, insofar as the structure of the cosmos is concerned, all sensible things taken collectively here and now can be regarded as one existentially dependent being. We can then go on to ask what the situation must be if the one existentially dependent being, that is, the cosmos considered as a whole, cannot account for its own existence—and yet most certainly is. There is only one possible conclusion, to wit, that the universe as a whole is caused by an existentially independent being. And this being we call God.

III. Any existentially dependent being which has completely exhausted every possible other already really existing external explanatory cause is caused by an existentially independent being.

The universe as a whole is such. (See the conclusion of II.)

Ergo, the universe as a whole is caused by an existentially independent being.

As Aquinas saw very well, in a world composed exclusively of dependent beings there would be no real beings at all. This, though, is obviously contrary to fact. The cosmos does indeed exist. What could possibly explain it? A series of existential zeros, however long, however far back in time we might wish to go, would still add up to a great big nothing in terms of actual beings. Neither can we appeal to nothingness. From nothing we get nothing. Nothing can't be the cause of anything; it can't even be thought in any direct way. Appealing to nothingness would be the height of irrationality.

What, then, is the nature of this existentially independent being? Is it the HE WHO IS of the Bible?[34] Recall that the cause of a sensible being, although it must be, does not necessarily have to be a sensible thing. It's logically possible to maintain that the cause of the world is totally transcendent with respect to the world. And this, in fact, turns out to be the case. The whole point of the argument is that the existentially independent being (whom we may call God) is a being whose essence is to exist. As such, he is absolutely unique, transcendent, and holy. This is the very same being who gave his proper name to Moses as I AM WHO AM.[35] Thus the God of religion is the same as the God of science.

A clear statement of the existential way goes a long way in clarifying the difference between it and other arguments often confused with it. Aristotle's scientific (for his day) design argument for a prime mover, who is needed to maintain the eternal and uniform rotary motions of the heavenly spheres, and Paley's scientific design argument, based upon Newtonian physics, are not existential arguments at all. Paley, for instance, reasons by analogy as follows: The small mechanical devise (is to) its manufacturer (as) the large mechanical devise (is to) its manufacturer (the Author of Nature). In both cases intelligence and will, knowledge and power, although on vastly different scales, are required.

With Thomas Aquinas, however, the situation is quite different. Aristotle was a pagan (i.e., a polytheist) who knew nothing of creation ex nihilo and God's continuous providence over his creation. With respect to Paley, even though everything Paley says of God is true, his notion of God remains inferior to Aquinas's understanding of God. Thomas's argument, expressed in a fashion parallel to

Paley's, would be: A single existentially dependent being (is to) its efficient cause (as) the whole existentially dependent cosmos (is to) its efficient cause. Such a cause can only be the unique ipsum esse, the one and only Supreme Being.

Now and only now does it make sense to talk about creation, that is, a real creation rather than a rearrangement of pre-existing things. God's proper name is not the Author of Nature, for God would still be God even if he had never created the least little thing. When God freely does choose to create, however, he gives what only he can give, namely, existence. God's first gift to the world is not order (although this does indeed come along with essence) but existence. God creates neither essences alone, nor existences without essences, but beings, that is to say, things with both essence and existence. This means that the world has both species (essences, law and order, science) and individuality. This emphasis upon a one unique cause of all being also turns out to be the special and unique feature of *Genesis* in contrast to the many other similar stories circulating at the time in the Middle East.

Once this is clearly understood many other subsidiary points also become understandable. First, any doctrine of either deism or process philosophy (pantheism) must be rejected. God is not the world and neither is he absent from the world. He is in fact continuously present to everything and everyone.[36] Next, the giver of being also gives everything else of a positive nature. Evil, as a negation, deviation, or privation, is not caused by God.

It also explains why there can be several "ways" to God. These are summarized by Aquinas at the beginning of his *Summa Theologiae* (I, 2, 3): (A) In our world of constant becoming, God is the unchanging changer, the unmoved mover. (B) In our world of efficient causes and their effects, God is the uncaused cause,—not the self-caused cause, which makes no sense in an existential context. (C) In our world of contingent things, of things that might or might not be, God is the one necessary being. (D) In a hierarchical world of good, better, and best, God is the highest being in any order of perfection, the exemplary cause of everything that's good and true. (E) In our teleological world, a world of operations moving towards definite goals, God is the final cause, and Omega as well as the Alpha of existence.

At the end of the day, therefore, we see that it is possible to harmonize science, philosophy, and theology. This is certainly nothing to be sneezed at. Nonetheless, it's not the last word on the subject. Aquinas was the last person in the world to impugn in any way the simple faith of the uneducated person. As Aquinas himself knew very well, knowledge does not guarantee sanctity, and he never forgot that it's possible for the most uneducated person, even at a tender age, to be a saint. How many times must the brilliant Italian have read the inspired Saint Paul's first letter to the Christian community living in Corinth, chapter 13, informing him that the three great virtues are faith, hope, and love, and that the greatest of these is love. Still, it's nice to know that you don't have to become irrational in order to be religious. If anything, it's the other way around: it's the opponents of religion who are acting like irrational people.

NOTES AND REFERENCES

[1] All of the pertinent Cartesian texts can be found in *Descartes: Philosophical Writings*, Trans. and ed. by E. Anscombe and P.T. Geach, London: Nelson, 1966.
[2] With respect to Pascal's opinion of his fellow Frenchman see Blaise Pascal, *Pensees. The Provincial Letters*, Trans. by W.F. Trotter and T. M'Crie, NY: Modern Library, 1941, sections 76–79.
[3] On deism see Robert E. Sullivan, *John Toland and the Deist Controversy: A Study in Adaptations*, Cambridge, MA: Harvard UP, 1982. See also Etienne Gilson, *God and Philosophy*, New Haven: Yale UP, 1959, 104–108; *The Unity of Philosophical Experience*, NY: Scribner's, 1947, chapter 8, "The Breakdown of Cartesianism."
[4] On Newton and religion see Isaac Newton, *Theological Manuscripts*, Ed. by H. McLachlan, Liverpool: Liverpool UP, 1950. At one point Newton states: "Atheism is so senseless and odious to mankind that it never had many professors."(p. 48) On Paley see Martin Lowther Clarke, *Paley: Evidences for the Man*, London: SPCK, 1974; D.L. LeMahieu, *The Mind of William Paley: A Philosopher and His Age*, Lincoln: Nebraska UP, 1976.
[5] Although he started out as a complete atheist, as we see from his autobiography, Mill later reconsidered, as we see from his essay on theism. See the *Autobiography of John Stuart Mill*, NY: Columbia UP, 1924. Mill's essay on theism was published posthumously as one of a set of three essays: *Three Essays on Religion*, NY: Henry Holt, 1874. The three essays are on nature, the utility of religion, and theism. The last one is twice as long as either of the other two and is concerned with the existence and nature of God. Mill concludes: "The indication given by such evidence as there is, points to the creation, not indeed of the universe, but of the present order of it by an Intelligent Mind, whose power over the materials was not absolute, whose love for his creatures was not his sole actuating inducement, but who nevertheless desired their good." (pp. 242–243) Mill thought that his idea of God was in keeping with the love of Humanity (Comte) and the ethics of Duty (Kant). In the end, the highest possible human aspiration is to contribute to the final victory of goodness. (See pp. 255–257.) About 1880 Newman used the example of Mill as a basis for claiming that atheism is an unnatural condition for human beings. See Ian Ker, *John Henry Newman: A Biography*, NY: Oxford UP, 1990, p. 730. This is the best biography of Newman to date.
[6] For Hume's critique see his *Dialogues Concerning Natural Religion*, Ed. by N.K. Smith, Indianapolis: Bobbs-Merrill, 1947 and *An Enquiry Concerning the Principles of Morals*, LaSalle, IL: Open Court, 1938.
[7] Thomas Aquinas, *Summa Theologiae*, I, 12, 12. This statement is part of an arti-

cle on whether or not God can be known by natural reason, which is part of the question concerning the names of God. We can, however, be led by our knowledge of the cosmos to know that God exists, even though we cannot grasp from the cosmos (the caused, the effect) the full richness of the cause. This seems to be plain commonsense. Is an artist equivalent to one of his paintings? As Aquinas points out elsewhere, to say that our present world must be the best of all possible worlds is not to praise God but to insult him. It implies that God's infinite power has been exhausted by an imperfect world. See the Summa Theologiae, I, 25, on the power of God. See also my "Lovejoy and Aquinas on God's 'Need' to Create," *Angelicum,* 59, 1982, 23–36.

[8] On fideism see Terence Penelhum, *God and Skepticism: A Study in Skepticism and Fideism*, Dordrecht: Reidel, 1983. Karl Barth, Martin Buber, Rudolf Bultmann, Karl Jaspers, Soren Kierkegaard, and Gabriel Marcel showed a marked tendency towards fideism. On the beginnings, in the Catholic Church, of modern fideism as a reaction against modern science see Walter Marshall Horton, *The Philosophy of the Abbe Bautain*, NY: NYUP, 1926. See also Etienne Gilson, *The Philosopher and Theology*, Trans. by C. Gilson, NY: Random House, 1962; *God and Philosophy,* New Haven: Yale UP, 1959.

[9] See Whitehead's *Religion in the Making*, Cleveland: Meridian, 1969, p. 136. See also his *Science and the Modern World*, NY: Mentor, 1964; *Process and Reality: An Essay in Cosmology*, NY: Harper Torchbooks, 1960; *The Function of Reason,* Boston: Beacon, 1958.

[10] This material is taken from John Henry Newman, *Selections from the Prose Writings of John Henry Cardinal Newman,* Ed. by L.E. Gates, NY: Henry Holt, 1895, 101–105. See also *An Essay on the Development of Christian Doctrine,* Garden City, NY: Image, 1960; *Letters of John Henry Newman*, Ed. by D. Stanford and M. Spark, Westminster, MD: Newman, 1957; *An Essay in Aid of a Grammar of Assent,* Garden City, NY: Image, 1955; *Apologia Pro Vita Sua: Being a History of His Religious Opinions,* NY: Longmans, Green, 1927; *Two Essays on Biblical and on Ecclesiastical Miracles,* 9th ed., London: Longmans, Green, 1890.

[11] The texts related to Darwin's notebooks can be found in H.E. Gruber and P.H. Barrett (eds.), *Darwin on Man,* NY: Dutton, 1974. The best biography of Darwin to date is by Adrian Desmond and James Moore, *Darwin,* NY: Warner, 1992.

[12] Newman, *Grammar,* p. 106.

[13] Ker, *Newman,* p. 641.

[14] The text of the encyclical, with variant readings and notes, can be found in Jacques Maritain, *Saint Thomas Aquinas,* Trans. by J.W. Evans and P. O'Reilly, NY: Meridian Books, 1958, 179–214. A good indication of the low state of philosophy and theology at the time, even in Rome itself, can be found in Newman's letters and diaries. There was no coherent, systematic curriculum at all; nothing but a haphazard collection of bits and pieces, an eclecticism gone wild. See A.J.

Boekraad and H. Tristram, *The Argument from Conscience to the Existence of God According to John Henry Newman,* Louvain: Nauwelaerts, 1961; Ker, Newman, p. 327. Behind the scenes, however, there was a neo-Thomism movement well under way in Europe in the second half of the nineteenth century. See Thomas J.A. Hartley, *Thomistic Revival and the Modernist Era,* Toronto: Griffin House, 1971.

[15] The Council text can be found in *Vatican Council II: Documents,* 2 vols., Ed. by A. Flannery, Northport, NY: Costello, 1975–1984, Vol. I, p. 735.

[16] For an account of what is known about Protagoras of Abdera see Joseph Owens, *A History of Ancient Western Philosophy,* NY: Appleton, Century, Crofts, 1959, 155–160. On relativism see Charles Habib Malik, A *Christian Critique of the University,* 2nd ed., Waterloo, ON: North Waterloo Academic Press, 1987. Also of interest would be Etienne Gilson, *The Breakdown of Morals and Christian Education,* Vancouver: British Columbia UP, 1952; Paul Vitz, Letter to the editor, on the inculcation of secularism in the public schools, *Science,* 235, 27 February 1987, p. 955. See also F.F. Centore,"The 'Creative' Ethics of Nietzsche and Sartre," *Faith and Reason,* 10, 1984, 222–241.

[17] Further to Nietzsche and Hitler see Larry Azar, *Twentieth Century in Crisis: Foundations of Totalitarianism,* Dubuque, IA: Kendall/Hunt, 1990; and also his *Man: Computer, Ape, or Angel?,* Hanover, MA: Christopher, 1989. See also Allan Bloom, *The Closing of the American Mind,* NY: Simon & Schuster, 1987; Daniel Goldhagen, *Hitler's Willing Executioners: Ordinary Germans and the Holocaust,* NY: Knopf, 1996; Paul Hilberg, *Perpetrators, Victims, Bystanders: The Jewish Catastrophe,* 1933–1945, NY: Harper Collins, 1992; Stefan Kuehl, *The Nazi Connection: Eugenics, American Racism, and German National Socialism,* NY: Oxford UP, 1994; Deborah E. Lipstadt, *Beyond Belief: The American Press and the Coming of the Holocaust,* NY: Free Press, 1986; Robert Marshall and Charles Donovan, *Blessed are the Barren: The Social Policy of Planned Parenthood,* San Francisco: Ignatius Press, 1991.

[18] See David H. Hirsch, *The Deconstruction of Literature: Criticism after Auschwitz,* Hanover, NH: Brown UP, 1991.

[19] See David Lehman, *Signs of the Times: Deconstruction and the Fall of Paul de Man,* NY: Poseidon, 1991.

[20] According to Gustav Bergmann, one of the original Logical Positivists, "An unexamined metaphysics, that is, one implicitly held, is for a philosopher the worst metaphysics of all." *The Metaphysics of Logical Positivism,* NY: Longmans Green, 1954, p. 51. The main reason the movement failed was because it could not provide science with what science needed most, namely, a foundation for universal and necessary truths about the cosmos. The reason it could not do so was because it simply assumed, contrary to the evidence of both ordinary experience and science itself, a totally atheistic, materialistic, reduc-

tionistic view of the cosmos. On Logical Positivism and its demise see Alfred Jules Ayer, *Philosophy in the Twentieth Century,* NY: Random House, 1982; *The Central Questions of Philosophy,* NY: Penguin, 1978; *Language, Truth and Logic*, 2nd ed. [1946], NY: Dover, n.d.

[21] With respect to the new doctrine see Niles Eldredge, *Reinventing Darwin: The Great Debate at the High Table of Evolutionary Theory,* NY: Wiley, 1995. See also my "Is Darwin Dead?" *The Thomist,* 47, 1983, 550–571. On various occasions Darwin's American pen-pal had tried telling him that even imperfect adaptation is still adaptation and that it could not be explained by a series of accidents alone. See Asa Gray, *Natural Science and Religion,* NY: Scribner's, 1891.

[22] Further to this see Richard A. Kerr, "Cores Document Ancient Catastrophe," *Science,* 275, 28 February 1997, p. 1265; "New Way to Read the Record Suggests Abrupt Extinction," *Science,* 274, 22 November 1996, 1303–1304; "A Piece of the Dinosaur Killer Found?" *Science,* 271, 29 March 1996, p. 180; "Did Darwin Get It All Right? The most thorough study yet of species formation in the fossil record confirms that new species appear with a most un-Darwinian abruptness after long periods of stability," *Science,* 267, 10 March 1995, 1421–1422; "Huge Impact Tied to Mass Extinction," *Science,* 257, 14 August 1992, 878–890. See also Philippe Claeys and others, "Microtektites and Mass Extinctions: Evidence for a Late Devonian Asteroid Impact," *Science,* 257, 21 August 1992, 1102–1104. And also Paul R. Renne and others, "Synchrony and Causal Relations Between Permian-Triassic Boundary Crises and Siberian Flood Volcanism," *Science,* 269, 8 September 1995, 1413–1416. This last article tells of a huge volcano that killed off life by covering the earth with a thick layer of dust for a very long period of time.

[23] See on this Richard F. Kay and others, "Anthropoid Origins," *Science,* 275, 7 February 1997, 797–804; the quotation is from p. 797; and Elizabeth Culotta, "A New Take on Anthropoid Origins," *Science,* 256, 12 June 1992, 1516–1517. See also Michael Behe, *Darwin's Black Box:* The Biochemical Challenge to Evolution, NY: Free Press, 1996.

[24] See Gilbert Keith Chesterton, *What's Wrong With the World,* 2nd ed., London: Cassell, 1910.

[25] The following is based largely on the work of Joseph Owens. See his *An Elementary Christian Metaphysics,* Bruce, Milwaukee, 1963. See also his *Cognition: An Epistemological Inquiry,* Houston: St. Thomas UP, 1992. And also F.F. Centore, "Logic, Aquinas, and utrum Deus sit," *Angelicum,* 63, 1986, 213–226 The main source of inspiration for this approach to God is Aquinas's relatively brief work *De Ente et Essentia* (On Being and Essence), originally written at the request of his fellow Dominican students at the University of Paris. It has been called by I.T. Eschmann, in his catalogue of Thomas's works, one of Aquinas's most admired and popular works. See Gilson, *The Christian Philosophy of St. Thomas Aquinas,* Trans. by L.K. Shook, NY: Random House,

1956, p. 411.

[26] On this see Aquinas, *Summa Theologiae,* I, 45, 5, ad 1; and 104, 1. On Anselm's "ontological argument" see the first five chapters of his Proslogium.

[27] Further to the fallacy of composition and division, and the gratuitous assertion on the part of some atheists that the world is a brute fact, meaning that it has the divine attributes of necessary and eternal existence, see P.J. McGrath, "Professor Flew and the Stratonician Presumption," *Philosophical Studies,* 18, 1969, 150–159. With respect to Flew's position McGrath states: "It overlooks the fact that what is wrong with naturalism from the theistic point of view is not that it ends by appealing to unexplained facts, but that the facts which it leaves unexplained are the ones which demand an explanation."(p. 159)

[28] See Gilson's *Being and Some Philosophers,* 2nd ed., Toronto: PIMS, 1952, 161–162.

[29] The current consensus is that the cosmos began 15 to 20 billion years ago. According to two physicists, there are a few great ideas that underpin all science. Among them are (with boldface removed): "13) The universe was born at a specific time in the past, and it has been expanding ever since; and 14) Every observer sees the same laws of nature, which is a summation of Einstein's special and general theories of relativity." Robert Pool, "Science Literacy: The Enemy Is Us," Science, 251, 18 January 1991, 266–267. The quotation is from p. 267. See also Albert Einstein, *Essays in Science,* Trans. by A. Harris, NY: Philosophical Library, n.d.; *Ideas and Opinions,* Trans. by S. Bargmann, NY: Crown, 1962.

[30] See Werner Heisenberg, *Physics and Philosophy: The Revolution in Modern Science,* NY: Harper Torchbooks, 1962. See also F.F. Centore, "Potency, Space, and Time: Three Modern Theories," *The New Scholasticism,* 63, 1989, 435–62.

[31] Concerning actual pictures of individual atoms, the following is a sample of the numerous articles on the subject: David A. Jefferson, "The Imaging of Individual Atoms," *Science,* 274, 18 October 1996, 369–370; Steve Nadis, "Two Versions of Holography Vie to Show Atoms in 3D," *Science,* 272, 3 May 1996, p. 650; S. Manne and others, "Atomic-Resolution Electrochemistry with the Atomic Force Microscope: Copper Deposition on Gold," *Science,* 251, 11 January 1991, 183–186; Hans Dehmelt, "Experiments on the Structure of an Individual Elementary Particle," *Science,* 247, 2 February 1990, 539–545.

[32] On the nature of time see G.J. Whitrow, *Time in History: Views of Time from Prehistory to the Present Day*, NY: Oxford UP, 1989; John F. Callahan, *Four Views of Time in Ancient Philosophy,* NY: Greenwood, 1968.

[33] See Jeremy Campbell, *Grammatical Man: Information, Entropy, Language, and Life,* NY: Simon & Schuster, 1982, 266–273. For more on the harmony of religion and science see Henry Margenau and Roy Abraham Varghese (eds.), *Cosmos, Bios, Theos: Scientists Reflect on Science, God, and the Origins of the Universe, Life, and Homo Sapiens,* LaSalle, IL: Open Court, 1992.

[34] See Exodus 3:13–14; John 4:26 and 8:58.

[35] Further to this see Giuseppe Ricciotti, *The History of Israel,* 2nd ed., 2 vols., Trans. by C.D. Penta and R.T.A. Murphy, Milwaukee: Bruce, 1958, Vol. I, 176–180.

[36] See Aquinas, *Summa Theologiae,* I, 8. See also F.F. Centore, "Classical Christian Philosophy and Temporality: Correcting a Misunderstanding," *The Monist,* 75, 1992, 393–405.

2

The Mind-Maker

Russell Pannier and Thomas D. Sullivan

Introduction

Does the existence of human minds argue the existence of a divine Mind? Can we infer *Nous* from *nous*? This is the question we will be dealing with as we develop a particular form of an important but generally neglected line of reasoning for the existence of God.

A "Mind-Maker Argument," as we will call it, has the general form:

(A) Some minds have property P.

(B) No entity that has a mind with property P can be produced by nature acting on its own.

(C) If something whose mind has property P cannot be produced by nature acting on its own, then it must owe its existence in part to a supernatural Creator. So,

(D) Some things owe their existence to a supernatural Creator.

Locke argued this way, and so did Aquinas before him.[1] Though few these days consider connecting mind to Mind, a non-theist, Colin McGinn, nicely articulates one form such an argument might take.

> I do not know if anyone has ever tried to exploit consciousness to prove the existence of God, along the lines of the traditional Argument from Design, but in this post Darwinian era, this is an argument with more force than the usual one, through lack of an alternative theory. It is indeed difficult to see how consciousness could have arisen spontaneously from insentient matter; it seems to need an injection from outside the physical world. Only something of the same kind could bring it about to begin with, it might be thought.[2]

In this case it is consciousness of course that is property P.

A second substitute for P is free will. If nature consists of fundamental physical particles and their relationship to each other, and if everything in principle is explicable in terms of those particles and relationships, then it is exceedingly difficult to understand how we could have libertarian freedom. Recognizing this conflict, John Searle reasons that freedom *must* be an illusion which, for inexplicable reasons, evolution has built into the very structure of intentional human behavior. As far as Searle can see, no discussion will ever convince us that our behavior is unfree.[3] But if we *really* cannot discard the belief that we are free, and if we also hold that freedom is inconsistent with a total physicalist world-picture, it certainly looks as if we have all the materials we need for a Mind-Maker Argument.

Yet a third way to build a Mind-Maker Argument is start with the capacity for language. It is again hard to see how an evolutionary account of this capacity is possible, at least as far as the greatest theorist of language in our time is concerned. Referring with dismay to Noam Chomsky's *Cartesian Linguistics*, one non-theist writes, "Whose side was he on anyway? Not Darwin's in any case. If Darwin dreaders want a champion who is himself deeply and influentially enmeshed within science, they could not do better than Chomsky."[4]

Neither McGinn, Searle, nor Chomsky commits to any of these forms of the Mind-Maker Argument, and neither do we. There is, however, a fourth form of the argument that impresses us as considerably more promising. The argument takes property P to be the *intentional awareness of instantiable characteristics — universals*. As we will explain along the way, the Mind-Maker Argument we will develop takes some inspiration from the writings of Aquinas, Locke, John Eccles, and indirectly non-theist Karl Popper.[5] So far as we know, however, our argument differs in important ways from any found in the literature in as much as it relies on fewer controversial premises. We will not here be concerned much, however, with comparisons and exegesis. Our main aim is just to get the argument on the table and to set out the principal assumptions with sufficient clarity to allow readers to determine whether they think it is worth further consideration.

Like just about any argument for a causal hypothesis, our Mind-Maker Argument is only a probable argument, not a knock-down demonstration. Now what one makes of a causal hypothesis depends partly on the assumptions one brings to the inquiry. No Mind-Maker Argument will strike anyone as plausible who begins with either of two assumptions. The first is that a mountain of scientific evidence leads inexorably to the conclusion that there is no God. The second is that, whether there is a God or not, science is well on its way to explaining all the mysteries of life, including every form of mentation — it is hopeless to argue for a "God of the gaps." Now although we obviously cannot consider here all that might be said in favor these assumptions, we can ask whether there might be a way to reassure ourselves at the outset that we should not be deterred from considering a Mind-Maker Argument. In Part I we will suggest that there is. In Part II we will begin our considerations of our Mind-Maker Argument. In Parts III and IV we will take up some major objections. Part IV is a brief defense of a realistic theory of instantiable characteristics (universals). An Appendix provides a formal derivation of a key premise.

I. Doubts About the Project

1. A Short Cumulative Case For Atheism

In memorably vivid language, Daniel Dennett has given voice to what is probably a fairly common view:

> The kindly God who fashioned each and every one of us (all creatures great and small) and sprinkled the sky with shining stars for our delight—*that* God is, like Santa Claus, a myth of childhood, not anything a sane, undeluded adult could literally believe in. *That* God must be turned into a symbol for something less concrete or abandoned altogether.[6]

Why is it that anyone should come to feel so strongly that belief in a God who has any influence on the cosmos or on our lives is simply irrational? Probably the most common reason for believing that there is no God is that it is extremely difficult to reconcile the existence of an omniscient, omnipotent, and wholly good Being with the existence and distribution of evil. Alvin Plantinga argues brilliantly that the existence of evil is not logically incompatible with the existence of such a Being. Others have argued that the existence of the worst kind of evil, moral wickedness, implies existence of a God, since such wickedness presupposes free-will, which as we have seen, feeds right into a Mind-Maker Argument. Still, it must be acknowledged that philosophical responses with respect to the problem of evil fail to provide much of an answer to the questions, Why evil? Why so much? Why do such awful things happen to animals and to the best among us? Surely it takes something more than philosophy to make sense of all this.[7]

For present purposes, however, the problem of evil can be gently laid to one side, for our question is not whether there is an omniscient, omnipotent and wholly good God, but rather whether there is a God. Period. The issue is theism. A person who accepts the God of the Hebrew scriptures is a theist, even if she thinks that God literally "repented of his choices." Of course if the question *Does God exist* is to have any meaning for us, some attributes must be attached to "God", but we can give meaning to the question without raising problems about omniscience, omnipotence, and total goodness. We can simply ask whether there is a being distinct from the physical universe and causally responsible for at least part of it.[8] Nothing in this description explicitly requires a God be unique, or omniscient, or omnipotent, or good, though it may be the case that any being meeting this description of a God necessarily has these attributes.[9]

Putting the problem of evil to one side, it may be felt, hardly changes anything. Dennett's equating belief in a Creator with belief in Santa Claus has little or nothing to do with the problem of evil; the word does not even appear in the ample index of *Darwin's Dangerous Idea*. Dennett's reasons for rejecting a Creator are chiefly scientific. It is Darwin's dangerous idea that wrecks theism. What best accounts for "the speed of the antelope, the wing of the eagle, the shape of the orchid, the diversity of species, and all other occasions of wonder in the natural world" is a mindless, mechanical algorithm. The lesson we must draw from Darwin is that the biosphere issues from nothing but a cascade of algorithmic processes feeding on chance. Who designed the cascade? "Nobody. It is itself a blind algorithmic process."[10]

Cosmology, many argue, backs the idea that there is no Mind behind the algorithm. Recent theorizing shows quite conclusively that we do not need to postulate a Creator to explain the existence of the universe. Steven Hawking is often quoted to this effect.

> So long as the universe had a beginning, we could suppose it had a creator. But if the universe is completely self-contained, having no boundary or edge, it would have neither beginning nor edge: it would simply be. What place then for a creator?[11]

And drawing on the work of Einstein, Hawking, Penrose, Friedmann and other distinguished physicists, Quentin Smith tells us: "there is sufficient evidence at present to warrant the conclusion that the universe probably began to exist over 10 billion years ago, and that it began to exist without being caused to do so."[12]

Now, again, we cannot here begin to do full justice to such claims, but we can ask whether there might be a way to see, even without going into a great deal of detail, that such confident atheism is unwarranted. We think there is.

2.   *Why Confident Atheism is Unwarranted*

Consider the following propositions:
(1)   The world came to be.[13]
(2)   Necessarily, whatever comes to be has a cause.
From these two propositions it follows that there exists a Creator. Therefore, the existence of a Creator is not extremely improbable unless the conjunction of (1) and (2) is extremely improbable. But it is not.

Start with (1). It may not be true, but does anybody have conclusive evidence that it is false? — not a decent theory favoring its contradictory, not a good bit of evidence against it, but conclusive evidence? Not only does no one seem to have such evidence, no one seems even to claim to have it. In fact, some knowledgeable *opponents* of theism often insist that (1) is in fact true. Recall Quentin Smith: the evidence warrants the conclusion that universe probably began to exist over 10 billion years ago.[14] Smith might be wrong. After all there are now quite a few competing theories about the universe.[15] Still, the least that can be said for (1) is that it is not known to be highly improbable.

What about (2)? Again, it hardly seems like a foolish or absurd idea. In fact, some philosophers have thought it is dead evident. The great Scottish philosopher Thomas Reid put it this way: "That neither existence, nor any mode of existence, can begin without an efficient cause is a principle that appears very early in the mind of man; and it is so universal, and so firmly rooted in human nature, that the most determined skepticism cannot eradicate it."[16]

But hasn't Hume given us excellent reasons for doubting (2)? Well, it is true that Hume has raised very searching difficulties about how we can come to know that one thing causes another, but this is quite different from showing that some things can come to be without a cause. Hume argues: "The separation, therefore, of the idea of a cause from that of a beginning of existence, is plainly possible for the imagination and consequently the actual separation of these objects is so far possible, that it implies no contradiction or absurdity."[17] Hume may be right about the absence of contradiction. The statement *Something might arise without a cause* is not self-contradictory; it is unlike the statement *It is possible to carry home a universal solvent in a leak-proof container.* As for absurdity, that is another question. A proposition might be absurd without being self-contradictory. *Somebody lives in a straw hut on the face of the sun* is not self-contradictory, but it is absurd. The same may be true of the principle of causality. In certain moods, even Hume seems to have thought so. "But allow me to tell you," he writes John Stewart, that I never asserted so absurd a Proposition as that *anything might arise without a cause.* I only maintain'd that, our Certainty of the Falsehood of that Proposition proceeded neither from Intuition nor Demonstrations; but from another Source."[18] For our present argument we do not need to go this far. Maybe the denial of (2) is neither self-contradictory nor absurd. But surely neither is (2). In fact, it seems quite plausible.[19] And for present purposes, that is all we need.

But hasn't quantum mechanics shown us that (2) is false? Quentin Smith argues it has. "It is sufficient to understand causality in terms of a law enabling single predictions to be deduced, precise predictions of individual events or states. That there are uncaused events in this sense follows from Heisenberg's uncertainty principle...."[20] Indeed it does follow from Heisenberg's uncertainty principle that there are uncaused events, if causality is defined in terms of the possibility of making precise predictions about individual events. But there is little reason to define causality this way. Suppose someone claims that it feels different when your hair is combed one way rather than another partly because pushing the hair in one direction depolarizes the hair cell, increasing the amount of transmitter released into the interneuron, while pushing it the opposite direction hyperpolarizes the hair cell. This claim could scarcely be overturned by noting that it is impossible to predict *exactly* how it will feel pushed this way rather than that. The claim that polarization plays a causal role is independent of any claim about exact predictability. The underlying problem with the objection to (2) is that it presumes x causes y can be equated with x *necessitates* y. But this is a highly dubious analysis of the causality. For there is no good reason to deny that x contributes causally to the coming to be of y if x is a necessary, though not a necessitating (sufficient) condition.

Moreover, even if we suppose for the sake of argument that causality is properly identified with necessitating condition, and that therefore (2) is demonstrably false, it turns out that the argument against confident atheism is little affected. This is because all we need do is replace (2) with:

(2*) Necessarily, whatever comes to be has necessary antecedent conditions.

Now while quantum mechanics dispenses with necessitating (sufficient) conditions, at least in some circumstances, it does not do away with necessary conditions.[21] The final location of an electron scattered by an atom is not precisely predictable, but that does not mean scattering is not a necessary condition (in the circumstances) for the electron's following a particular path.

It is sometimes suggested that (2*) is false because there are no necessary conditions for the spontaneous emergence of virtual particles in quantum mechanical vacuums and because real particles pop into existence in strong electromagnetic or gravitational fields, but this is at least dubious. Quentin Smith himself explains why. The emerging particles have to borrow energy from fields. Because of quantum indeterminacy, the precise strength of the field is not fixed; therefore a field with a precisely fixed strength is not a necessary condition for the emergence of particles. However, a field with a strength that falls within certain ranges of values is a necessary condition of emergence.[22] It is important to bear this in mind when encountering remarks such as Paul Davies's that "the spontaneous appearance of the universe is not such a surprise, because physical objects are spontaneously appearing all the time—without well defined causes—in the quantum microworld."[23] The qualification "well defined" makes all the difference. Davies's contention is entirely consistent with the claim that necessary conditions are always required.

Smith has argued that while events *within* the physical universe need a cause, the physical universe itself could arise from absolutely nothing because of its unique condition at its origin. Since one of us has replied to Smith's argument elsewhere at some length,[24] we will not consider this objection here. We would note, however, that even if a case could be made for the *possibility* of the universe's being exempted from the general rule that what comes to be has a cause, it can hardly be maintained that we know or have excellent reason to believe it actually occurred.

We have been arguing that confident atheism is misplaced if for no other reason than that there is a good chance that the universe came to be. This possibility alone should give us pause before accepting the claim that belief in a Creator in on a par with belief in Santa Claus, fairies, or unicorns. But that is not the end of the matter, for even if the world did not come to be, it is by no means obvious that there is no Creator.

But what about Hawking? Doesn't his theory do away with a Creator? Well, it is only a theory, one that Hawking keeps evolving. Moreover, Hawking himself does not see it as having such dire implications for theism. In response to a complaint that he was afraid to admit the existence of a Supreme Being, Hawking has written, "I thought I had left the question of a Supreme Being completely open.... It would be perfectly consistent with all we know to say there is a Being who was responsible for the laws of physics."[25] Distinguished physicist Paul Davies goes even further. Noting that according to James Hartle and Seven Hawking there is no origin of our universe, not because it is infinitely old, but because its temporality has no boundary, Davies points out that it still does not follow that the universe is a necessary being. Moreover, reflecting on the fact that the laws of physics take us only so far and that the natural world "is not just any old concoction of entities and forces, but a marvelously ingenious mathematical scheme," Davies has no trouble opting for a necessary being over a necessary world. "In my own mind I have no doubts at all that the arguments for a necessary world are far shakier than the arguments for a necessary being."[26] In other words, in addition to (2*)

(2**) Every contingent entity or system needs a cause (or necessary condition) for its existence

also appears quite plausible. If, as Aquinas long ago saw, an everlasting being may nonetheless be contingent, and if, as Davies now stresses, the physical laws of the universe may themselves be contingent, it is in not highly improbable that there is a Creator.[27]

It might be good to pause for a moment to separate the strands of the argument. So far we have noted that there are two possibilities regarding the origin of the universe. The first is that it had a beginning; the second that it did not. There is a good chance that the first alternative is true. Since this is so, given the plausible principle that (2) *Necessarily, whatever comes to be has a cause*, or even the weaker principle (2*) *Whatever comes to be has a necessary condition for its emergence*, the existence of a Creator is not highly implausible. Even were we to go no further, it should be clear that cocksure atheism is out of place. But we can go further. For even if the universe always existed, it does not follow that there is no Creator. For an everlasting world can still be a contingent being, and (2**) *Every contingent entity or system needs a cause (or necessary condition) for its* *existence* is not implausible. Furthermore, a case can be made for the contingency of the physical laws of the universe. This is why Hawking leaves open the question of God's existence.

Nor is this the end of the matter, for even if the universe existed forever, and even if the Darwinian algorithm is everywhere at work, it may well be that there is a Mind behind the algorithm, despite Dennett's insistence to the contrary. For the universe gives every appearance of having been structured with created minds in view. Many distinguished scientists cannot resist the impression. Nobel-laureate neurophysiologist John Eccles writes:

> My position is this. I believe that my personal uniqueness, that is, my own experience of self consciousness is not accounted for by this emergent explanation of the coming to be of my own self. It is the experienced uniqueness that is not so explained. Genetic uniqueness will not do....
> So I am constrained to believe that there is what we might call a supernatural origin of my unique self-conscious mind or my unique selfhood or soul.... By this idea of supernatural creation I escape from the incredible improbability that the uniqueness of my own self is genetically determined.

And again, Paul Davies:

> "What does it mean? What is man that we might be party to such a privilege? I cannot believe that our existence in this universe is a mere quirk of fate, an accident of history, an incidental blip in the great cosmic drama."[28]

Dennett dismisses Eccles's belief as a scandal[29] and Davies's as "an ill examined prejudice,"[30] but many distinguished men and women of science share similar views. Davies observes that following publication of *God and the New Physics* he was astonished to discover how many of his scientific colleagues practiced a conventional religion.[31] Admittedly, it cannot be claimed on the basis of such a cursory examination of the issues up to this point that theism has the better side of a cumulative case argument. But we have not tried to establish that theism is more probable than not; we have only sought to assure ourselves that it is not so improbable as to render further investigation pointless.

3.   The God of the Gaps?

This brings us to a second assumption that stands in the way of a serious consideration of a Mind-Maker Argument, of an attempt to infer *Nous* from *nous*. How can anyone seriously propose that a Creator must be invoked to explain minds? Once biologists believed it was necessary to invoke a "vital force" or "entelechy" to explain mysteries of life that we now well understand wholly in terms of physical forces acting on matter. Through the whole of the 20th century physical science has been explaining one "inexplicable mystery of life" after another. How can anyone seriously propose that a Creator must be invoked to explain consciousness or anything else about mentation? Like every other "God of the gaps" argument, this one is certain to fail as gap after gap in our understanding of the workings of the mind gets plugged.

So goes an argument that has persuaded even many theists. But is it really all that strong? After all, successful scientific explanations of living operations invariably fall on one side of a bright line dividing what gets explained—matter in motion, not the various manifestations of consciousness.[32] The inductive argument is at least as strong one way as the other.

Preposterous, one might object. Are not library and bookstore shelves sagging with works on consciousness? At least one new journal, *Consciousness Studies*, devotes every issue to the topic. Surely somewhere in all this is at least the beginning of an explanation of how the phenomenon arises. Can it really be the case that Dennett's *Consciousness Explained* provides no understanding whatever of how consciousness emerges?

Indeed it can. For it obviously is impossible to explain the emergence of X if you deny X emerges. *Consciousness Explained* is filled with wonderful accounts of a wide range of data, but in the end Dennett himself makes it quite clear that consciousness is not so much explained as explained away. "In the previous chapter I seemed to be denying that there are *any* such properties ["raw feels," "sensa," "phenomenal qualities," "intrinsic properties of conscious experiences," "the qualitative content of mental states," and "qualia"] and for once what seems so, is so. I am denying there are any such properties."[33] As for the rest of what is out there, consider Ned Block's assessment: "We have no conception of our physical or functional nature that allows us to understand how it could explain our subjective experience." And again, "But in the case of consciousness we have nothing—zilch—worthy of being called a research program, nor are there any substantive proposals about how to go about starting one."[34] Then there is Jerry Fodor: "The *really* most important thing we know about minds is that their states are often conscious. About this, here as elsewhere, I maintain a gloomy silence. Whereof there is nothing to be said...."[35] Colin McGinn chimes in: "While there has been much optimism about the prospects of success in accounting for intentionality, pessimism about explaining consciousness has deepened progressively. Indeed standard approaches to content tend simply to ignore the problem of consciousness, defeatedly postponing it until the next century."[36] Why not, when physiologists write like Jacqueline Ludel? After 366 pages of detailed explanation of sensory processes, Ludel states with remarkable candor:

> Finally, we need to add the fact that, in us, all this modification, comparison, and abstraction is somehow interpreted, resulting in the personal experience of

awareness. I wish I could tell you how the interpretation is performed. However, with all we do know about the workings of the brain, no one is able to explain how the movements of ions across the membranes of neurons finally produce the overwhelmingly important, undeniable experience that 'yes, I exist'—'yes, I perceive'—'yes, I feel and think and know.'[37]

But just because we cannot *now* explain consciousness, how does it follow that we never will? It doesn't. Not all by itself. But two points should be observed about the fact that at the moment we have no explanation of the emergence of consciousness. First, as already noted, the inductive argument cuts both ways. There is much evidence that science is on its way to explaining a great deal about everything this side of the bright line; but the inductive evidence also points in the direction of certain phenomena forever remaining closed to explanation.

Second, it is not too difficult to see why. There is more to explanation than correlation, even perfect correlation. We need insight into the causal flow. Consider, for example, our present situation with respect to the investigation of AIDS. There is mounting evidence that HIV is both necessary and sufficient for the presence of AIDS. Even so, it cannot be said that we now have a satisfactory causal explanation of AIDS. The reason is we have little understanding of the causal mechanisms. As scientists lament in a recent authoritative account, The Molecular Biology of HIV/AIDS, edited by A.M.L. Lever:

> Despite knowing so much about the molecular biology of HIV we still have lit-
> tle understanding of how HIV causes AIDS, and why progression to the disease
> can take a long and variable time. It still remains to be established precisely
> how viral replication and viral gene expression are regulated and how they influ-
> ence progression to clinically significant immunodeficiency.[38]

The mere fact that AIDS correlates with HIV does not definitively establish even a causal link: HIV could be a confounding variable. But even if we can now claim to know that HIV causes AIDS, we cannot claim to possess an explanation until we grasp how HIV impairs the immune system. So even when we have suc-ceeded in establishing necessary and sufficient conditions we sometimes do not have a satisfactory explanation of the phenomenon. When we do not grasp the causal flow, we are left wondering how to complete the answer to the original question "Why does the phenomenon occur?" As long as it makes good sense to ask this question, we do not completely understand the causal mechanism. No matter what physical explanation we give of consciousness, we will always be left with the question, "But why does the phenomenon occur?" For a reason that is quite simple. All physical explanations must be given in purely physical terms. And no matter how elaborately the theory is worked out in such terms, we will always be left wondering why the phenomenon occurs.

But doesn't this argument depend on a narrow, 20th century conception of physical science? Surely science of, say, the 30th century will certainly be vastly different from science today. By then all kinds of new physical concepts will have been introduced. How can we be sure that these new concepts will fail to reveal completely the causal flow? Because if the claim that *physical* science will offer satisfying explanations is to have any meaning, some sense must be attached to "physical explanation" that connects it with our current understanding. It will not do at all to allow that a future physical explanation might invoke something like Leibnizean points of consciousness, for if it does that, the claim that physical science explains consciousness will be nugatory.[39] One might as well allow that the physics of the future will explain gravity in terms of the love bodies have for one another. If the claim that consciousness is a physical state or process is to make sense, it must be possible to specify the primitive terms of the explanation without reference to psychological states as constituents of the terms. Explanations with primitives so specified always will leave us with the question, But *why is this thing conscious*?

II. The Mind-Maker Argument

1. The Need for Another Kind of Argument

The trouble with a Mind-Maker Argument based on consciousness as such is, as McGinn points out, that while we may not be capable of understanding just how it arises from physical causes, consciousness still might be nothing but a physical state or process. As beavers cannot understand particle theory, we may not be able to understand what nature does to bring about this mysterious state. So while McGinn thinks that consciousness probably will forever elude physicalistic explanation, he also thinks that rather than infer that an injection of causality from the outside is necessary, all we need do is "face up to the depth of our ignorance."[40] With respect to any argument based on consciousness as such, McGinn may be right.

It does not follow from this, however, that the same should be said about *every form* of consciousness. Conscious awareness of instantiable characteristics may be a very different matter.

2. The Immediate Premises of the Mind-Maker Argument

Let's see if it is. Plugging the relevant terms into the general framework we set out in the beginning, we get these immediate premises for our Mind-Maker Argument (hereafter MMA*).

(A)* Humans consciously intend non-local, instantiable characteristics.

(B)* If so, nature acting on its own cannot produce human minds.

(C)* If nature acting on its own cannot produce human minds, then human minds (and thus human beings) must owe their existence in part to a Creator.

Consider first Premise (C)*. It is quite unproblematic, unless it takes nothing at all to gets certain kinds of minds into existence.

Premise (A)* involves a number of terms that need some explaining, though none is used in a way deviating from common practice. By "instantiable characteristic" we mean a characteristic that can have instances, can be exemplified. Hot, blue, spinning, having angular momentum, and carrying an action potential are all instantiable characteristics. Instantiable characteristics are often called "universals" and "types", but we will avoid these terms because of the historical baggage they bring with them. By "x consciously intends y" we mean first that x is about y, bears on y; second, x does so occurrently, not just dispositionally. It is possible to be conscious without intending, and to intend without being conscious. If you have a painful throbbing in your leg, you are in a conscious state, but the conscious state of pain is not about anything. If you know your way around New York, then your thoughts are about New York and therefore are intentional, but this can easily be the case when you are not consciously thinking of New York. Nearly every waking minute of the day, however, we are in states at once conscious and intentional, as when looking at a map and trying to figure out how to get from Watertown to Poughkeepsie. Finally, by "x is non-local" we mean that x is not the space-time web, not a segment of the web, and does not occupy a spatial position within it.

These explanations can be further refined, and some of that refining will take place as we move through the argument, but we have enough in front of us to see why (A)* seems at once obvious and highly problematic. (A)* seems obvious because it is embedded in the understanding we have of what it takes to think. If Wanda now consciously thinks *This argument is valid*, then she must somehow grasp instantiable characteristics *argument* and *valid*. Such instantiable characteristics are not part of the space-time web. There is no answer to the question "Where is valid?" or "Where is validity?" But of course as soon as we make (A)* explicit to ourselves, we begin to wonder how, if universals are non-local, they can exist at all. Furthermore, it may strike some that acknowledging (A)* puts us well on the way to a dualistic theory of any entity deemed to have powers of thought. For some, this alone is enough to prompt a search for a way to make sense of thinking without admitting what seems to be the intentional data.[41] Proposition (A)* therefore needs to be defended. This we will do in Parts III and IV.

So let us then turn to (B)*. Our argument for it rests on two premises. The first is:

(B)*-1 Nature cannot produce entities with cognitional powers that achieve their objects without having a physical relationship to the object.

This proposition is taken for granted by physicalists such as McGinn who, while admitting consciousness is inexplicable, hold that we are just ignorant of the connection between cognitive act and object.[42] For if there is no physical link between act or state and object, then there is no physical cause of the power's attaining its object, and no physical explanation even in principle.

In illustration of (2*)–1 consider how the male silkworm moth locates females by using specialized hairs on its antennae to detect the sexual attractant, bombykol.[43] Early investigators thought the process worked quite differently; they thought the male antennae picked up infrared radiation emanating from the female's thorax. All investigations, however, presupposed that the male was detecting something given off by the female. Baffled researchers who realized that it was not radiation certainly did not seriously entertain the possibility that the antennae hairs are the male's instrument of detection, but there is no physical contact at all with anything emitted by the female or with signals in the environment. No one would say that the male's antennae just put the male in a position to know where the female is, that it does not matter how the antennae are pointed or whether the moths are inches or thousand of miles apart, that the male just knows and that is all there is to it. On such a proposal, the male silkworm moth would be in a state that was partly physical, but only partly. His antennae would be located in space and time, and they would respond to the physical environment, the hairs gently swaying in response to the movement of the surrounding air, but there would be *no physical link* between organ and object of detection. Nature acting alone presumably cannot create such a creature. Were it possible for the male to detect the female without the act or state of detection being physically related to either the female herself or an attractant, the bug might well have a nice evolutionary advantage over rivals who had to depend on the picking of signals that only last so long. But no evolutionary mechanism for the production of such a wonderful cognitive system even seems imaginable. Talk all we want about information chains of DNA and RNA, about structural chains of proteins, about algorithms of selection, or any surrogates for them, we are still left with no explanation of how the capacity works.

The second premise of the argument is:

(B)*–2 If a human being consciously intends a non-local instantiable characteristic, then there is no physical link between its cognitive state and the object of the cognitive state.

Here's the nub of the argument for that claim:

Suppose Wanda considers a particular non-local instantiable I*. Breaking the supposition into two propositions we have:

1.   I* is a non-local instantiable.

2.   Wanda consciously intends I*.

Now by definition:

> 3.   For any x, if x is a non-local instantiable, then x does not have a position
> in space.

It furthermore seems quite obvious, even by the lights of physicalists, that:

> 4.   For any non-local instantiable, I, If Wanda consciously intends I, then there
> is a state, s, such that Wanda consciously intends I in virtue of being in state s.

While it is difficult to give a satisfactory definition of "physical" there is widespread agreement[44] on a necessary condition of x being physically related to y, namely:

> 5.   For any x and for any y, if x does not have a spatial relationship to y, then
> x does not have a physical relationship to y.

But it is quite evident that:

> 6.   For any x and for any y, if y does not have a position in space, then x does
> not have a spatial relation to y. (You cannot be to the north of Wanda if Wanda
> is nowhere.)

From a chain of steps according with the standard principles of derivation (see the Appendix), it follows that:[45]

> 18.   Wanda consciously intends I* in virtue of being in state s*, and I* does not
> have a physical relationship to s*.

Proposition (18) is just a way of putting (B)*–2.

III. *Some Objections and Replies*

This, then, is the Mind-Maker Argument.[46] The main premises of the argument, let us recall are:

> (A)* Humans consciously intend non-local, instantiable characteristics.
> (B)* If so, nature acting on its own cannot produce human minds.
> (C)* If nature acting on its own cannot produce human minds, then human
> minds (and thus human beings) must owe their existence in part to a Creator.

What might be said against it? Plenty, of course. Let's consider a few that are often brought up.

Objection 1. It might be argued that we know or have excellent reason to believe that there are no private, subjective mental states. Talk about conscious states is just folk psychology doomed to give way to a more scientific account of the nervous system and behavior that nowhere invokes any everyday terms such as sensation, pain, feeling, or thought.

We cannot here consider at any length the putative advantages of eliminitivism, but perhaps we can reassure ourselves that this objection should not stop us in our tracks until we can find a knock-down refutation. After all, when doing theoretical work we are entitled to assume what we assume in our ordinary activities unless confronted with an imposing difficulty.[47] But what is the imposing difficulty here? What compelling argument has anyone ever given us that we never had a single conscious experience, never had an itch, a memory, a longing, or a doubt? A compelling argument would have to be based on premises at least as seemingly obvious as such statements as *I have at some time felt a pain.* But how could any argument embedding a theory about a theory possibly satisfy that requirement? A measure of the difficulty of holding firm on eliminitivism is Paul Churchland's apparent reversal on qualia.[48]

Objection 2. Some will protest that while we of course have to admit experience of qualia, we do not have to accept conscious awareness of universals. We may properly refuse to allow that it is possible to intend instantiables for just the reason Churchland gives. We have no business positing a form of consciousness unless we can explain it. Qualia are acceptable because we now can explain qualia very nicely. "This is an example of how something need not be eliminated, but can be explained and therefore kept." But "maybe there is no way to explain them [belief and desire], in which case—at least in the long run, in science and in the laboratories—we will stop using that vocabulary."[49]

Maybe so. Perhaps some day we will keep talking about beliefs and desires only in the marketplace and over the dinner table, but if this is what happens, will it come to pass for a good reason? Which proposition, after all, is more obvious to us, (a) *We are entitled to accept an apparent datum of experience only if we can explain the apparent datum in terms of physical science,* or *(b) Somebody once had a thought about her mother*? According to its own terms, eliminativism with respect to belief means that the theory itself can be mouthed but not believed. It hardly seems necessary to refrain from accepting the introspective data on the basis of a theory that can be true only if no one, including its propounders, has ever believed it.

Objection 3. It is possible to explain thinking without introducing non-local instantiables as mental accusatives. As Hobbes pointed out, we can regard thinking as just the manipulation of symbols. The Hobbesian idea has been effectively expressed in a variety of linguistic theories that take semantics as fixed by the relationship of terms *to each other* rather than to the world. As Fodor remarks about this distinguished Hobbesian tradition, "It is pretty close to a literal truth that the tradition of theorizing about the mind offers only two options: either thinking is talking to yourself, or there is no such thing as thinking."[50] And again, "the most important fact that we know about minds," the reason "God bothered to give us any," is that "if you start out with a true thought, and you proceed to do some thinking, it is very often the case that the thought that the thinking leads you to will also be true." And so, as Turing pointed out, "if you have a device whose operations are transformation of symbols ... it is possible to arrange things so that, in a pretty striking variety of cases, the device reliably transforms true input symbols into output symbols that are also true." And if that is the case, then we have every reason to believe that Turing was right that the mind is some sort of computer. "This emphasis on the syntactical character of thought suggests a view of cognitive processes in general—including for example—perception, memory, and learning—as occurring in a language like medium, a sort of 'language of thought'." [51]

It is indeed amazing how far the Hobbesian idea has taken us, how fruitful it has been in computer science. But is it really the case that there never is anything more to thinking than "just going through the motions *in crania* without applying them to any real objects at all?", as some physicalists suggest?[52] Or is it at least sometimes the case that we do apply a term to something, and in so doing, recognize a conventional tie, between sign and the abstract characteristic signified? Is it the case that we can do all manner of things with words, but the one thing we cannot do with them is use them to call abstractions to mind? It is all very well to say with Fodor that the most important fact that we know about minds is that starting with one true thought you can by thinking get to another, provided we add, as Fodor does in qualifying footnote, "The *really* most important thing we know about minds is that their states are often conscious," and go on from there to recognize that unless we can bring consciously to mind instantiable characteristics, unless we can conceive of properties and relations apart from their conditions of space and time, there is no genuine language at all to manipulate *in crania* or out loud.[53]

Objection 4. It cannot be the case that we can intentionally relate ourselves to abstract, non-spatial instantiables unless such instantiables exist. But there are no such non-local instantiables. Since this is perhaps the most pressing objection, we will now consider it at some length. Part IV amounts to a short defense of a realist theory of universals.

IV. Realism About Instantiable Characteristics:

To reply to this last objection, let us begin by returning to the concept of an instantiable. An *instantiable* is an entity which can have instances. A grammatical criterion for identifying instantiables is asking, with respect to an entity, F, whether it makes sense to ask whether there is an F. If so, at least a prima facie case exists for classifying F as an instantiable.

Asserting that instantiables exist in some sense is not saying much; philosophers have used "exists," and related terms such as "thing," "object," "entity" and "being," in many ways. Claiming that an entity exists might mean at least one or more of the following: (1) The entity can be thought about in the minimal sense that someone could truthfully answer the question, "What are you thinking about?" by mentioning it. (2) It can be linguistically invoked in the minimal sense that words semantically tied to it can be used to make assertions. (3) Linguistic invocations of the entity cannot be translated into equivalent statements which do not linguistically invoke the entity, either directly or indirectly. (With respect to those entities for which such reductive translations are possible there is a philosophical tendency to say that in some sense there is really no "it" there at all.) (4) The entity exists independently of any human mental or physical act or state. (5) It has a spatial location. (6) It has causal powers. For example, the average plumber exists in senses (1) and (2) but not (3). A memory image exists in senses (1), (2) and (3) but not (4). God exists in senses (1), (2), (3), (4) and (6), but not (5).

We shall argue that instantiables exist in senses (1), (2), (3) and (4). It seems obvious that they exist in sense (1). We can think about such things as the instantiable, being an apple, or, being an apple falling from a tree. Indeed, a stronger claim can be made. Not only *can* we think about instantiables; we *must* think about them. The formulation of any thought whatever requires the mental invocation of at least one instantiable. Every act of thought directly refers to at least one intended object and predicates something of it. If the thought directly refers to one or more instantiable(s) then the thought directly invokes an instantiable. On the other hand, if the thought directly refers to a non-instantiable then the thought's predicative part necessarily invokes, albeit "indirectly," an instantiable, either in the form of a one-place characteristic or an n-place relation.

One might question this line of reasoning by supposing that cases of the first kind ("direct" references to instantiables) are always avoidable and that cases of the second kind ("predicative" invocations of instantiables) are ontologically harmless in that they involve only "indirect" cognitive invocations. But the objection fails. Any indirect cognitive invocation of an instantiable provides an epistemological foundation for additional thoughts "directly" invoking the instantiable. Imagine thinking about any non-instantiable you please, say, Dobbin, the horse. In thinking about Dobbin you must apprehend him as an F, for some characteristic, F. You might, for example, think of him as "a horse," or as "an animal owned by Ms. Jones." But in any case, you must apprehend him as a token of some type, as an instance of some instantiable. Now with some such thought in mind, you cannot then avoid the possibility of having additional thoughts focussing directly upon that instantiable itself. Having entertained the thought, say, that Dobbin is a horse, you cannot avoid the possibility of entertaining additional thoughts such as that the instantiable, being a horse, is instanced by Dobbin, or that the instantiable, being a horse, is a one-place instantiable, and the

like. Such thoughts exceed the cognitive confines of the first thought and directly refer to instantiables. One might think that such additional thoughts are equivalent to thoughts not directly invoking instantiables. But this is a vain hope.
Given any thought expressible in the form, "F(x)," where "F" is either a single-
place predicate or a relation-term, and where "x" could be either a single term or
an ordered n-tuple, for any finite n, it is always possible to turn one's cognitive
focus upon F itself. In short, every thought asserts that some entity is a token of
some type. But every such predicated type is itself a potential object of direct
thought. There is no possible way of thinking which could avoid the possibility
of providing a basis for such thought sequences.

From the assumption that instantiables exist in sense (1) we can immediately infer that they exist in sense (2). Given the fact that thinking necessarily
involves the direct and indirect invocation of instantiables, any adequate linguistic expression of those thoughts must semantically invoke them as well.
Instantiables which are the objects of a thought's direct focus are semantically
invoked by referring expressions (e.g., "the characteristic, being a book written
by Quine"). Instantiables indirectly invoked by thoughts are semantically
invoked by predicative expressions (e.g., "___is a book written by Quine").

Instantiables exist in sense (3) if at least some apparent linguistic invocations
of them cannot be fully translated into statements which neither directly nor indirectly linguistically invoke them. That they do exist in this sense follows from
what we have said. If every thought is linguistically expressible in the form
"F(x)" then any adequate linguistic formulation of a thought necessarily directly
or indirectly (or both) invokes instantiables. But then language could not be
cleansed of all semantical invocations of instantiables, at least if the cleansing is
to be accomplished in the form of linguistically expressible thoughts.

Do instantiables exist in sense (4), that is, exist independently of any human
mental or physical act or state? We shall refer to entities which exist in this sense
as mind-independent entities; the others are *mind-dependent*. For example, a
memory image of a six-pound brown trout being caught on a Muddler Minnow
is a mind-dependent entity; the trout itself is mind-independent. We shall refer to
theories asserting that instantiables exist in sense (4) as realist theories of instantiables and to theories denying it as *anti-realist* theories.

We believe that some version of realism is correct. This can be argued for in
at least two ways. First, a large variety of instantiables seem obviously mind-
independent. Consider instantiables such as being a horse, being a horse eating
grass, or being the universe containing a brown trout. The existence of such
instantiables does not depend upon any human mental or physical act or state.
Suppose, for example, that Dobbin is presently drinking water and that it is possible for him to eat grass five minutes from now. Then the instantiable, being
Dobbin eating grass five minutes from now, exists. But its existence does not
depend upon anyone's thinking about it or upon any other mental or physical act

or state. Thus, at least some (in fact, a great many) instantiables are mind-independent.

But can this be plausibly asserted of all instantiables? What about instantiables such as having a memory-image of a six-pound brown trout? Aren't they mind-dependent? We shall counter this objection by turning our attention directly to the effort of anti-realist theories to identify instantiables with mind-dependent entities. We shall use the term "concepts" to designate whatever entities any such anti-realist attempt purports to identify with instantiables. The basic strategy of anti-realism here is arguing that instantiables can be identified with concepts and that the latter are mind-dependent. We shall argue for two points. First, the general project of identifying instantiables with concepts must fail. Second, even conceding for the sake of argument that an identification can be made, the most that could be shown is that instantiables are identical with concept-types, not concept-tokens, and that because types themselves are not mind-dependent, anti-realists cannot in the last analysis consistently avoid positing mind-independent instantiables.

What theories of concepts might be enlisted by anti-realists in this identification project? We mention only a few possibilities, hoping to broadly invoke at least some of the major alternatives. A concept is necessarily a concept of something, say, F-ness. Thus, a useful way of sorting theories of concepts is distinguishing different ways in which one might consider articulating what it is to have a concept of F-ness, for an arbitrarily selected F.

(1) *Concepts as mental objects*—One might think that concepts can be identified with mental objects or representations (understood as thing-like entities of some kind)—perhaps images. Thus, one might hold that having a concept of F-ness is having in one's consciousness a mental image of an F. Having a concept of the instantiable, being a horse, just is calling to mind an image of a horse.

(2) *Concepts as sets of beliefs* (understood as the "contents" of acts of belief) —One might suppose that concepts can be identified with sets of beliefs. Thus, a concept of F-ness might be a set of beliefs concerning F-ness. Possibilities in this regard include at least the following: beliefs about the characteristics whose possession is necessary for something's being an F; beliefs about the characteristics whose possession is sufficient for something's being an F; beliefs about the characteristics which Fs typically, but not necessarily, have; beliefs about the characteristics which Fs may, but need not, have; beliefs about methods for identifying Fs; beliefs about the relationships between F-ness and other instantiables, and so on.

(3) *Concepts as mental acts*—Perhaps concepts can be identified with mental acts. In particular, perhaps they can be identified with ways of thinking about things. On such a view one might suppose that having a concept of F-ness is the act of thinking about the characteristic F in some particular way. Thus, if A believes that every brown trout eats insects at all times of its life while B dis-

agrees, then A's concept of the instantiable, being a brown trout, differs from B's.

(4) *Concepts as sets of human capacities*—Concepts might be identified with sets of human capacities. Thus, having a concept of F-ness might be identified with having one or more cognitive capacities regarding F-ness. Possible candidates for the role of capacities are the capacity to identify instances of F-ness; the capacity to call up mental images of Fs; the capacity to describe Fs; the capacity to define what it is to be an F; the capacity to trace inferential relationships between F-ness and other characteristics, and so on.

(5) *Concepts as words*-It might be thought that concepts can be identified with words. Perhaps having a concept of F-ness just is having a word or words in one's vocabulary. For example, perhaps the concept of being a brown trout is identical to the word "brown trout."

(6) *Concepts as brain states*-Physicalists might prefer theories which identify concepts with brain states or processes. On such a view one would be entertaining the concept of, say, being a brown trout, just in case one's brain was in a certain state.

These alternative views of concepts are not mutually exclusive. The concept of having a concept is itself probably a very complicated concept whose complete analysis requires a combination of several of these alternatives (and perhaps more besides). But we are not concerned here to evaluate them on the merits as theories of concepts. Rather, we focus upon them only insofar as they might be used in the anti-realist's project of identifying instantiables with some class of mind-dependent entities.

It seems that any such attempted identification must inevitably fail, at least with respect to instantiables whose instances are not themselves concept-tokens in any of the above senses of "concept." At least three points can be made in this regard. First, thinking about such instantiables does not by itself involve thinking about any of the above candidates. Consider, for example, the mental-object theory of concepts. Suppose, contrary to fact, that whenever one thinks about the instantiable, being a brown trout, one has an image of a brown trout. But even if this were so, it would not follow that in thinking about that instantiable one is thinking about a mental image. At best, the image is usable as an aid in thinking about the instantiable; the image cannot plausibly be identified with it. Similar points can be made for the other theories of concepts. Thus, in thinking about the instantiable, being a brown trout, one is not thinking about any cognitive capacities.

Second, whatever predicating an instantiable might ultimately involve, it surely does not involve predicating any of the listed entities. Thus, whatever one means to say by asserting that Dobbin is a horse, one does not intend to say that Dobbin is a mental image, a belief, a mental act, a human capacity, a word or a brain state.

Third, it seems that all of these theories of concepts ultimately require some account of mind-independent instantiables. For example, identifying a mental image of a brown trout as an image of a brown trout ultimately requires a reference to the instantiable, being a brown trout. Identifying an intellectual capacity to identify brown trout ultimately requires a reference to the instantiable, and so on. In brief, individuating concepts as defined in any of the above ways seems to ultimately require an appeal to some realm of mind-independent instantiables of which concepts in that particular sense *are* concepts.

But suppose we grant these issues for the sake of discussion. Suppose that the instantiable, being a brown trout, is identical to some concept understood in one of the above-mentioned ways. Nevertheless, even in this case one would be compelled to invoke types, that is, instantiables, which cannot themselves be plausibly characterized as a mind-dependent. For example, consider again the mental-object theory. Suppose for the sake of argument that some mental image of a brown trout is somehow identical to the instantiable, being a brown trout. Call this image B*. Imagine yourself thinking about B*. Isn't it obvious that in thinking about B* you would be thinking about the *type* of which one's own mental images of B* are merely *tokens*? But types are instantiables and, as such, cannot themselves be plausibly characterized as mind-dependent entities, although, of course, particular tokens of types are mind-dependent entities. Further support for the thesis that thinking about instantiables necessarily involves reflection about types, rather than tokens, is afforded by the observation that when two persons are thinking about the same instantiable, say B*, they must be thinking about the image-type rather than any of their respective image-tokens. Otherwise, they could not be described as thinking about the same instantiable.

Similar points can be made for the other theories. For example, even if the instantiable, being a brown trout, can be identified with the capacity to identify brown trout, it seems that in thinking about the instantiable one must be thinking about the *type* whose instances are particular capacities to identify brown trout. In general, thinking about a concept in any of the above six senses must involve thinking about types, not tokens, and while tokens of such types are mind-dependent entities, their types are not.

So much for our sketch of considerations supporting realism. We turn now to the question whether instantiables, understood as mind-independent, are non-local, that is, do not have spatial locations. We shall argue that they do not. Realism about instantiables comes in two major varieties. *Transcendent* realism denies that instantiables have spatial locations; *Immanent* realism asserts that they do. We shall argue that instantiables are non-spatial by arguing against immanence theories.

Transcendence theories typically make three claims. First, instantiables are not literally in their instances. Thus, the instantiable, being a brown trout, is not literally embodied in any particular brown trout. Second, instantiables are abstract in the sense that they are not constituents of the spatial order. Thus, although any particular brown trout has a spatial location, the instantiable, being a brown trout, has no spatial location at all. The correct answer to the question, "But where is the instantiable itself located?" is, "Nowhere." Third, instantiables may exist even if they have no instances. Thus, the extinction of the species of brown trout would not somehow destroy the instantiable, being a brown trout, and the instantiable, being a brown trout eating a kernel of corn, exists even if in the entire history of the universe no brown trout ever eats a kernel of corn.

Immanence theories typically make three claims, as well. First, instantiables are literally embodied in their instances. Thus, the instantiable, being a brown trout is incarnated in every particular brown trout and the instantiable, being a brown trout taking a #6 Wooly Bugger, is embodied in every concrete event of some brown trout taking a #6 Wooly Bugger. Second, an instantiable is embodied wholly and completely in each of its instances, whether those instances exist simultaneously or successively. If there are presently 100-million brown trout in the universe, the instantiable, being a brown trout, is presently wholly and completely incarnated in every one of them. Third, a necessary condition for the existence of an instantiable is its possessing at least one instance. Thus, the instantiable, being a brown trout taking a #6 Wooly Bugger, exists only if a brown trout is now taking one. More relaxed versions of immanent realism allow the existence of at least one instantiating event, past, present, or future, to suffice for the existence of the instantiable. Thus, on these versions, the instantiable exists only if at some time in the past, present, or future (understood as already existing in some tenseless sense) a brown trout takes (tenselessly) a #6 Wooly Bugger.

There are at least three reasons for rejecting immanence theories. First, such views commit a category-mistake in literally identifying instantiables with their instances. We assume here the plausibility of identifying at least some instantiables with possibilities. Consider the possibility (i.e., the instantiable), being a person catching a five-pound brown trout on July 13, 1998. Suppose that you catch such a trout on that date. It would be metaphysically inappropriate for someone watching you catch the fish to point at you and say, "*There* is the possibility, being a person catching a five-pound brown trout on July 13, 1998." What one would have here is an actualization of the possibility, not the possibility itself. A possibility necessarily leaves the stage upon the appearance of any of its actualizations.

Second, the immanence claim that instantiables exist only if they have at least one instance is mistaken. Imagine yourself a genetic engineer who has been asked to create an organism answering to specifications, F. Suppose that the specifications are internally consistent, that creating an organism of that kind is technologically possible and that you work on the project for four years, but, for a variety of reasons, abandon the project before actually creating any Fs. Suppose further that no Fs ever have been created by anyone else and never are created in the future. It would be odd, to say the least, for anyone to describe this situation by saying that the instantiable, being an F, did not exist. If it did not exist then what were you thinking about during that four-year period? Nothing? It seems that a correct account would have to say something like, "The instantiable, being an F, has always existed; it's just a contingent fact that it was never actualized."

Third, there appear to be instantiables whose instances are non-spatial. But if that is so, then those instantiables themselves could not possibly be spatially embodied. Consider, for example, instantiables such as being a recursive function or being a two-term relation. Any particular recursive function or two-term relation is a non-spatial entity. But then the instantiables themselves could not be spatial entities since there are no spatial instances in which they could incarnate themselves.

We have gone into the ontology of universals to reassure ourselves that there is good reason to hold that humans consciously intend non-local instantiable characteristics. Given this fact, we have been arguing, that there is good reason to believe that nature alone cannot produce the human mind. From the existence of *nous* we can infer the existence of *Nous*.

Appendix I

Derivation of (B)*–2
Suppose:
1. I* is a non-local instantiable.   [Premise]
2. Wanda consciously intends I*.   [Premise]
Now it seems quite obvious that:
3. For any x, if x is a non-local instantiable, then x does not have a position in space.   [Premise]
4. For any non-local instantiable, I, If Wanda consciously intends I, then there is a state, s, such that Wanda consciously intends I in virtue of being in state s.
    [Premise]
5. For any x and for any y, if x does not have a spatial relationship to y, then x does not have a physical relationship to y.
    [Premise]
6. For any x and for any y, if y does not have a position in space, then x does not have a spatial relation to y.
    [Premise]
7. If Wanda consciously intends I*, then there is a state, s, such that Wanda consciously intends I* in virtue of being in state s.
    [From 4 by Universal Instantiation, using I* as the instantial constant]
8. There is a state, s, such that Wanda consciously intends I* in virtue of being in state s.
    [From 2 and 7 by Modus Ponens]
9. Wanda consciously intends I* in virtue of being in state s*.

[From 8 by Existential Instantiation]

10. If I* is a non-local instantiable, then I* does not have a position in space.

[From 3 by Universal Instantiation]

11. I* does not have a position in space.

[From 1 and 10 by Modus Ponens]

12. For any y, If I* does not have a position in space, then I* does not have a spatial relation to y.

[From 6 by Universal Instantiation, using the instantial constant I*]

13. If I* does not have a position in space, then I* does not have a spatial relation to s*.

[From 12 by Universal Instantiation, using s* as the instantial constant]

14. I* does not have a spatial relation to s*.

[From 11 and 13 by Modus Ponens]

15. For any y, if I* does not have a spatial relationship to y, then I* does not have a physical relationship to y.

[From 5 by Universal Instantiation]

16. If I* does not have a spatial relationship to s*, then I* does not have a physical relationship to s*.

[From 15 by Universal Instantiation]

17. I* does not have a physical relationship to s*.

[From 14 and 16 by Modus Ponens]

18. Wanda consciously intends I* in virtue of being in state s*, and I* does not have a physical relationship to s*.

[From 9 and 17 by Conjunction]

NOTES

[1] John Locke, *Essay Concerning Human Understanding* Bk. IV, x, 10; Thomas Aquinas, *Summa Theologiae* I, Q. 90, a.3.

[2] Colin McGinn, *The Problem of Consciousness* (Oxford: Blackwell, 1991), p. 45.

[3] John Searle, Minds, *Brains, and Science* (Cambridge, Mass.: Harvard University Press, 1984), Chapter 6, pp. 86–101.

[4] Daniel Dennett, *Darwin's Dangerous Idea* (New York: Simon and Schuster, 1995), p. 386.

[5] Karl R. Popper and John C. Eccles, *The Self And Its Brain* (London and New York: Routledge & Kegan Paul, 1977).

[6] *Darwin's Dangerous Idea*, p. 18.

[7] This point is pursued in Menssen and Sullivan elsewhere in this volume.

[8] By "part of the physical universe" we mean not just the things that have physical properties, but those things, if there are any, that are not themselves physical, but are tied to physical things, as perhaps minds are. On the relationship of non-physical things and the concept of pantheism, see Russell Pannier and T.D.

Sullivan.

9 In order to underscore the limitation of the question, we will generally use "Creator" instead of "God."

10 *Darwin's Dangerous Idea*, pp. 18 and 59.

11 Steven S. Hawking, *A Brief History of Time* (Toronto: Bantam Books, 1988), pp. 140–141.

12 William Lane Craig and Quentin Smith, *Theism, Atheism, and Big Bang Cosmology* (Oxford: Oxford University Press, 1993), pp. 108–109.

13 The expression "the universe came to be" can be understood in a number of ways. We mean that it is not the case that the universe is infinitely old. For a discussion of the complexities surrounding the definition of the expression see Quentin Smith, *Theism*, pp. 115–119.

14 Paul Davies, a theist, writes: "Nearly all cosmologists now accept that we live in a universe that had a definite beginning in a big bang...." *The Mind of God* (New York: Simon and Schuster, 1992), p. 57.

15 Smith himself points this out later in *Theism*, pp. 196–197.

16 Thomas Reid, *Essays on the Active Powers of the Human Mind*, ed. Baruch Brody (Cambridge, Massachusetts and London, England: MIT Press, 1969), Essay IV, Chapter II, p. 267.

17 *Treatise of Human Nature*, ed. P.H. Nidditch (Oxford: Oxford University Press, 1978), Bk. I, Part I, Section III, pp. 79–80.

18 *The Letters of David Hume*, ed. J.Y.T. Greig (Oxford: The Clarendon Press, 1932), Vol. I, 187. Quoted by Brian Davies in An *Introduction to the Philosophy of Religion* (Oxford: Oxford University Press, 1982), p. 44.

19 Theism, p. 121.

20 For a defense of this claim see T. D. Sullivan, "Coming To Be Without a Cause," *Philosophy* 65 (1990), pp. 266–268.

21 See Richard W. Miller, *Fact and Method* (Princeton, New Jersey: Princeton University Press, 1987), especially pp. 60–64.

22 "Can Everything Come to Be Without a Cause?", *Dialogue* XXXIII (1994), p. 320.

23 *The Mind of God*, p. 62.

24 Thomas D. Sullivan, "On the Alleged Causeless Beginning of the Universe: A Reply to Quentin Smith", *Dialogue* XXXIII (1994), pp. 325–335.

25 S.W. Hawking,"Letters to the Editor: Time and the Universe", *American Scientist* 73 (1985), p. 12. Quoted by William Lane Craig in *Theism, Atheism, and Big Bang Cosmology* pp. 281–282.

26 *The Mind of God*, especially pp. 62–67, 189, 191 and 213. Davies does not argue for a traditional God, but this only underscores the point made earlier about the need to separate questions. We are concerned with the existence of a Creator, not its various attributes.

27 Contrary to what some commentators have said, Aquinas's Five Ways in the

Summa Theologica do not presuppose that the world had a beginning in time. Like Kant, Aquinas held that the temporal beginning of the universe is indemonstrable.

[28] Paul Davies, *Mind of God*, p. 232.

[29] Dennett, *Darwin's Dangerous Idea*, p. 446.

[30] Dennett, DDI, p. 66.

[31] *The Mind of God*, p. 15. For additional statements by Nobel-laureates and other distinguished scientists see Henry Margenau and Roy Abraham Varghese, ed., *Cosmos, Bios, Theos* (La Salle, Illinois: Open Court Press, 1992).

[32] Cf. David Chalmers, *The Conscious Mind* (New York and Oxford: Oxford University Press, 1996, pp. 168–169.

[33] Dennett immediately continues, "But (here comes that theme again) that there seem to be qualia." *Seem*? Imagine someone saying there are no real pains, it just seems that there are. See also Dennett, *Kinds of Minds*, pp. 54–55, where intrinsic intentionality is also explained away.

[34] Ned Block, "Consciousness," in Samuel Guttenplan, ed., *Companion to the Philosophy of Mind* (Cambridge, Mass.: Blackwell, 1994), pp. 210–211.

[35] *The Elm and the Expert* (Cambridge, Mass: MIT Press, 1994), Note 1 to Lecture 1, p. 121.)

[36] *The Problem of Consciousness*, p. 24.

[37] Jacqueline Ludel, *Introduction to Sensory Processes* (W.H. Freeman and Company), 1978, p. 366.

[38] Quoted by Richard Horton, "Truth and Heresy About Aids," *New York Review of Books* XLIII (May 3, 1996), p. 16.

[39] Compare: we can explain all of reality using only mathematics if we broaden our concept of math to include elements of space, time, and force. Or again, we can reduce mathematics to logic if we allow ourselves the concept of set membership.

[40] *The Problem of Consciousness*, p. 45.

[41] See, for example, Hartry Field, "Mental Representation," in Steven Stitch and Ted A. Warfield, ed., *Mental Representation* (Cambridge, Mass.: Blackwell, 1994), pp. 34–77.

[42] It is not easy to tell just how (B)* is generally regarded among physicalists since it rather oddly is seldom directly discussed. Recent analytic philosophy has quite emphatically rejected reductionism, and that *might* mean, in some cases, that (B)* is rejected by implication. But it is not only far from clear that this is so, but it is also unclear whether it is coherent to hold that all that exists in space-time is physical while maintaining a property dualism about psychological and physical properties. On the difficulties of middle of the road positions such as Donald Davidson's and Jerry Fodor's, see Jaegwon Kim, "The Myth of Nonreductive Materialism," in Richard Warner and Tadeusz Szubka, ed., *The Mind Body Problem* (Oxford: Blackwell, 1994), pp. 241–260.

[43] See William C. Agosta, *Chemical Communication: The Language of Pheromones* (New York: Scientific American Library, 1992), pp. 1–3.

[44] Cf. Jaegwon Kim, "Non-Reductivism and Mental Causation" in John Heil and Alfred Mele, *Mental Causation* (Oxford: Clarendon Press, 1995), p. 193.

[45] For a derivation, see the Appendix.

[46] MMA*, it should be noted, is not just an argument from intentionality of the human mind, for intentional acts could be directed to particular entities which are in space and time. And if it is a particular spatio-temporal entity that is the object of the act, it may be the case that the link between state and object is physical, though beyond our ken. But the situation is entirely different when the conscious, intentional object is a non-local instantiable characteristic.

[47] For a defense of this methodological principle, see Roderick Chisholm, *Person and Object*, (La Salle, Ill.: Open Court Press, 1976).

[48] "In the case of qualia, I am disinclined to be an eliminativist." Paul M. Churchland, "Neural Networks and Common Sense," in Peter Baumgartner and Sabine Payr, ed., *Speaking Minds* (Princeton N.J.: Princeton University Press, 1995), p. 42. It is not easy to tell exactly what eliminativists like Paul and Patricia Churchland hold about the data. Patricia Churchland maintains that though they are widely understood to be denying existence of the common sense data, this is just a mistake. "Do We Propose to Eliminate Consciousness?" in Robert N. McCauley, ed., *The Churchlands and Their Critics* (Cambridge Mass.: Blackwell, 1996), p. 298.

[49] Paul Churchland, "Neural Networks," p. 42.

[50] *A Companion to the Philosophy of Mind*, ed. Samuel Guttenplan (Cambridge: Blackwell, 1994), p. 295.

[51] *The Elm and the Expert*, p. 9

[52] See Ilya B. Farber and Patricia S. Churchland, "Consciousness and the Neurosciences," in Michael S. Gazzaniga, ed., *The Cognitive Neurosciences* (Cambridge, Mass.: Bradford Book, The MIT Press, 1995), p. 1298.

[53] Commenting on John Searle's Chinese room argument, Jerry Fodor distinguishes two questions: The first is, *What is it for a physical state to have semantic properties?* The second, *Given that a physical system does have semantic properties, how could state transitions preserve those properties?* Fodor holds that Turing's idea answers the first question, but agrees with Searle that it does nothing for the first. If one chooses to use "intelligent" for linguistic behavior that respects the content of mental states, then we can say that computers *in this sense* are intelligent, but we then need to reserve a term like "intentional" to designate the mental relationship that connects the subject to the object of cognition. "The Folly of Simulation," in *Speaking Minds*, p. 89.

3

The Awareness and Certainty of the Existence of God

Dom Illtyd Trethowan

The belief that God is present to the human mind (or soul) and can be found there is part of the Christian tradition. Many Christian philosophers seem to regard this as the concern only of specially devout persons and of no interest for philosophical purposes. The evidence for it, they think, is too slender to be taken seriously by academic philosophers without particular interest in religion, who tend to regard anything in the nature of religious experience as suspect. So philosophical discussions about religion are usually concerned with rational arguments for and against theism, usually of a technical kind.

In this article, I want to suggest that there is another attitude of mind which has become more widely shared as the century has advanced, especially in France. The last section of the article, summing up the situation in England, has been added by way of appendix. I have concentrated on developments in Roman Catholicism because I think them to have special significance.

1. The Augustinian Claim

This claim, which I accept, will be set out, in the first instance, by the quotations from a work by Henri (now Cardinal) de Lubac:

> Every human act, whether it is an act of knowledge or an act of the will, rests secretly upon God, by attributing meaning and solidity to the real upon which it is exercised. For God is the Absolute; and nothing can be thought without positing the Absolute in relating it to that Absolute; nothing can be willed without tending toward the Absolute, nor valued unless weighed in terms of the Absolute.[1]

There is no proof of these assertions in the sense of a logical argument enforcing acceptance of them on pain of logical contradiction. All that can be done, in the face of objections and incomprehensions, is to talk, like Plato, around the topic, in the hope that light may break through. Augustine finds what has been called a "quasi-immediate" [2] knowledge of God in the recognition of him as the truth by which the mind is illuminated. He finds that there is something above and beyond his own mind to which he has to submit, which is there waiting for him.

I shall try to put this insight into a form suited to our present situation. We heard a good deal not long ago about a problem of identity experienced in particular by the young (older people had either pushed it under the carpet or come to terms with it somehow). Sometimes this resulted in a sense of unreality: we had been thrown, as Sartre put it, into a meaningless world, and what was called our "existence" seemed to be vanishing away. How can life be given a meaning unless there is some sort of plan for it? To say that something is *true*, then, would be to say not just that we have discovered it, but that it belongs to a world which has a purpose. The world has been put there by God, the source of reality; that proves to be what makes it "real," and that is what makes us "real."

It this is right, then it's not enough to claim that there is such a thing as a "foundational belief" in God. Such a belief cannot stand up to the objection that we might be at the mercy of a system of illusions organized by some presumably omni-competent evil power. It might not seem reasonable to take that particular objection very seriously, but the impression can remain that we are unable to cope intellectually with the situation in which we find ourselves placed; is it the whole enterprise of trying to make sense of things the one great mistake? Only an awareness of God is both self-guaranteeing (only for the subject of it, but his claim must be thought about by others) and at the same time the guarantee of such certainty about anything else as we may prove to possess.

In human knowledge there is a unity of subject and object such that the possibility of error in affirming it is wholly excluded. The particular deliverances of our senses may "deceive" us; that is, to speak properly, we may at any time interpret what they present to us in a way which is perfectly reasonable (based as it is, on the lessons of experience up-to-date) but happens by some extraordinary combination of circumstances to be inappropriate. Even so, what is affirmed, as intuitively known, is the presence to our bodies, themselves intuitively known through our sensations, of a foreign body. For instance, if one falls down the stairs, the impact on one's body of other bodies cannot be in doubt because they are directly apprehended *as other*. But how do I know that I have not gone mad and become incapable of valid judgements? The answer, as before, is that the making of a valid judgement is guaranteed as such by the reality which I encounter, guaranteed itself as a reality by the source of reality, not necessarily recognized as such. It is not, as critics of such a view suppose, that there is a claim to a mere *feeling* of certainty, something purely subjective; it is the object with which there is that *union* of knowledge that provides certainty.

It is the recognition of the other as other that is basic for our knowledge. In the case of external objects it is only their activity upon us that we know; that is, we know them *in* their activity and only so; we find the cause *in* its effects. In the case of God, there is a union of a very different import; it arises as the first step towards a personal relationship to which everything else is heading. Far from its being the case that we can never be certain of God, without that certainty we can never be certain of anything. But, as Pascal said, God is always known and seldom recognized.

The following passage from de Lubac may now be useful:

> The idea of the one God springs up spontaneously at the heart of consciousness, whether as a result of the exigencies of reason or of some supernatural illumination, and imposes itself upon the mind, of itself, of its own necessity. In fact, the clearest instance shows God revealing himself, and in doing so dissipating the idols or compelling the man to whom he reveals himself to tear from his heart: 'You have beaten upon the weakness of my sight, shining upon me with power, and I shook with love and dread'.[3]

Reasoning processes, de Lubac is saying, may prepare the way for an awareness of God, but they cannot produce it of themselves. The illumination of faith, he goes on to say, builds on the original awareness and gives it still greater force. And at this point the agnostic interlocutor may play what he considers to be his trump card: if there were a God, the world would not be the terrible place which, to so sad an extent, in fact it is. Something needs to be proposed about that in passing. It is that the "free will defense" of God in regard to the world's woes is perfectly sound: if love is God's meaning, it is unthinkable that his plan for us should be without a hazard; we must choose or reject him personally, willingly, freely; it is sin that is responsible for the world's woes, human or (in the case of physical evil) angelic. Obviously this raises a great number of further questions, but this much might be enough to avoid a breaking off of the conservation. To touch on this topic seems particularly necessary because theologians not otherwise fixed in Thomist positions continue to treat God's dealings with us as presenting at least apparent contradictions which we cannot hope to resolve. Even Karl Rahner, to whom I owe so much, insists on the complete "incomprehensibility" of God and refers to the "free will defense" as a "popular" and unsound enterprise.

At this point de Lubac's words are highly relevant:

> The world is the real work of a beneficent God and has a real value. It is not just a stage on which man has to act and choose, nor is it simply an instrument for him to use; it is, so to speak, the stuff of the world to come, the matter of eter-

ւıity. Man's task, therefore, is not so much to liberate himself from time as to liberate himself through time. His task is not to escape from the world, but to raise it up. Only, in order to understand time and the world, it is necessary to look beyond it; for it is its relation to eternity which gives the world its consistency and makes time a real becoming. And it is the hope of radical and final transformation which saves our terrestrial efforts from futility....⁴

Finally, there is this as a sort of summing up:

If, when night comes, I think back to certain privileged moments when the truth of my affirmation was revealed to me in an experience, I am not living on a deceptive memory, on the recollection of a pleasing experience, but recollecting a value perceived; it is not the recollection of the fulfillment of a value which I love in principle within me, but the recollection of a newly discovered existence which integrates, orders and judges all human values.⁵

2. Dermot Lane's The Experience of God

The index of this little book⁶ written by an Irish theologian, does not contain the name of any British one; the reason for this is that books by British theologians, relevant to Lane's purpose, are not easy to find. The introduction shows that the approach is the same as Cardinal de Lubac's: "The mystery of God is not some theorem to be proved; it is rather an experience to be lived... The proofs for the existence of God are really an elucidation and elaboration of the experience of God".⁷ So far as I know, this is the first book in English to sum up for the general reader in bringing back experience, understood as an affair of the intellect, not just of feeling, to its proper place in traditional theology. There is much, then, of great value in the book; but I use it partly in order to disagree with it on certain issues. It could have been pointed out with advantage that experience in this sense is taken so much for granted by early Christian writers, starting with the New Testament, that it is seldom formally expressed. When Irenaeus, to take one example, speaks of our having an original knowledge of our Creator, a *sensibilitas Dei* (which one might translate "a taste of God"), he is not saying anything in the least extraordinary. Lane's introduction concludes admirably: "Theology is faith seeking understanding that is critically grounded in the experience of the revelation of God".

In this first chapter, Lane tells us that experience in general involves "some form of encounter between the subject and the reality" and that "there is always a reciprocal flow...which creates a new relationship, participation, awareness and understanding in the life of the individual".⁸ The basic element here is awareness; without it, there can be no conscious relationship, nothing to react to or understand. "Participation" means a sharing, and that must be understood in terms of union when we are talking about God; in the ordinary way it refers to having something *in common,* and that, I must urge, is untrue of our relationship with God. The Absolute cannot be reduced to our level. Lane goes on to quote—from Professor J. E. Smith's account of religious experience, in his important and valuable book *Experience and God,* as being "at one and the same time an experience of something else,"[9] adding, that this "serves as the medium disclosing that dimension in life which is called religious".[10] and speaks of the need to find an object of supreme worth; this constitutes "the religious dimension". "For an answer," he goes on, "it is necessary to surmise the possibility of revelation understood as disclosure from the transcendent side and encounter from the side of man".[11] I wish Lane had quoted that too.

Experience of God together with experience of the finite has been called a "mediated" knowledge of him by a number of writers, including myself, but I have come to the conclusion that this language can be misleading. It is suitable when the experience of, for instance, moral value, when its absoluteness comes to be recognized as God's and this seems to be discerned *through* it; thus it can be called a direct but mediate knowledge. But the experience of something incidental which leads indirectly to an experience of God seems properly described as an "occasion" for it. In any case, all experience or encounter, *in itself,* is immediate in the sense that there is an actual contact. To this I shall return.

Lane, however, now rejects the suggestion that some kind of direct or immediate contact with the sacred is possible in religious experience.[12] The first reason given for this is that "the notion of experience, especially at the level of depth-experience, is a little more intricate than one of mere direct vision", because in it the subject moves "beyond the visible frontiers of the empirical world into a new invisible world, mediated by meaning and depth". Here Lane seems to be thinking about religious language and ordinary psychology. But from my point of view the heart of the matter is a non conceptual experience of God which can be evoked on occasion by language and can itself evoke language (it can suggest analogies) but is beyond the power of language to express. In other words, there must be, on this view, a "touch" of God which is the mainspring, as it were, of the whole business.

Lane's second reason is, he says "more serious". It is that from the side of the human person it is extremely unlikely that the individual could sustain direct contact with God in this life: "We must first of all receive the grace of 'light in glory' in order to enter into the beatific vision of God...all human experiences of God are indirect, being mediated through our experience of creation and the revelation of God in Jesus".[13] I accept that they are mediated, in the sense I mentioned above, but that does not seem to me a good reason for calling them "indirect". Indirect knowledge, I would say, is the result of inference; we know that something is there, but we do not at all know it. Lane's objection might seem to be based on the supposition that any direct knowledge of God would be unrestricted and unlimited apart from the beatific vision, whereas even in that vision there is always a further depth to plumb. There can be no doubt that our knowledge of God while we are in our present bodies is limited in comparison with the "face-to-face" knowledge of the blessed, but this does not mean that there is no sort of real vision of God available for us on this earth.[14]

Happily, however, Lane goes some way into reverse a little later: " We need to go beyond the alternatives of 'mediate' and 'immediate' experiences of God. Instead, we would want to suggest that God is co-present and co-known through the different experiences and knowledge of the human person. God is co-present to us from the outset in all our experiences."[15] He goes on to speak of "the God of Augustine who is more intimate to the soul than the soul is to itself". This is the God of many others besides Augustine, but the theme is not enlarged upon in Lane's book. He does, however, add here most usefully: "If we did not know God implicitly in all our experience, we would not even begin to raise the question of God....One of the primary tasks of theology today is to unpack our human experience of this omnipresent God".[16] In this connection he refers to the famous statement of St. Thomas Aquinas that "God is known implicitly in everything that is known".[17] It is surprising because it does not fit in with Aquinas's general principle that man has no direct knowledge of God. De Lubac quotes it in favor of his case. It is perhaps one of those uncharacteristic remarks in which Aquinas the "essentialist" gives way to Aquinas the "existentialist". Father Copleston asks bewilderedly: "Does it mean simply that though one does not know one is capable of knowing?"[18]

Something more may be added, usefully, perhaps, at this juncture on the notion of awareness as "union". It is not a novelty—Thomism speaks of an "intentional union", but seems not to see its importance. It found the action of knowing as a "becoming" in Aristotle, but does not find this pattern of identity without confusion central to epistemology. When we listen with enjoyment to music, it means something to say "we are the music." We are taken out of ourselves and "become" what we were not before. We give ourselves up completely to something and thereby increase our own stature. This can be an intellectual activity of great intensity in which we apprehend the notes in their relationship to one another and to grasp them as forming an intelligible pattern; it is a matter of sustained attention. This is a figure of the transaction which has to take place, in the end, between ourselves and God. It is indeed a beginning of that transaction even if it is accepted only as a mysterious gift of great value. If the mind is in a healthy state, its awareness of God grows as its activity intensifies. Philosophers in the Anglophone world commonly find this sort of talk meaningless and exasperating, because for them experience is bound up so closely with our bodily functions that to speak of a mind which has a life of its own to live seems meaningless. Christian philosophers may be expected to believe that man (philosophically and theologically speaking) appeared on earth at a particular time with fresh powers of supreme importance.

3. Awareness and Christian Faith

It belongs to the philosophy of religion to consider the possibility of a divine revelation and, in particular, whether Christian faith has any relationship with a putative awareness of God. Here again it will be useful to take Father Lane's *The Experience of God* as a basis for discussion. The following passage gets us off to a good start:

> If doctrine is not related to human experience it will inevitably become marginal in the lives of believers. Further, doctrine must be able to evoke religious experience in a way that opens up the individual to the ever present gracious mystery of God. A sign of sound doctrine is its ability to communicate some aspect of the inexhaustible reality of God. A close interplay should obtain between theological doctrine and religious experience.[19]

Lane describes what he calls "the most popular theory" about revelation as follows: "A kind of divine verbal communication took place between God and the world in the history of the chosen people and the life of Jesus. The agents of this divine communication were the prophets and the apostles who were regarded as the messengers of God."[20] It may well seem amazing that such a view should have been so widely held for so long. Lane here rejects "the suggestion that the revelation of God could be reduced to a series of propositions" and the implication that "God has stopped revealing himself to mankind...leaving the human race bereft". This is not to deny that there are propositions the basic truth of which (but not their culturally dependent forms of language) must be accepted by the faithful. The point is that this is not the whole truth of the matter: "God cannot be confined to or captured by a simple set of propositions...Such a view of revelation seems to contradict the important doctrine of the gracious omnipresence of God to the world and the indwelling of his Spirit among his people." The suggestion would seem to be that there is a non-conceptual element involved in revelation. But it is not directly stated.

Lane now turns to the theory of "revelation in history" and pertinently remarks that "a neutral or detached historian would not find the events of Israel's history more revelatory of God than the events of any other nation's history," adding that faith is not just a matter of discovering and arguing from historical facts but one of "grace and offer". A third theory, which "may be loosely designated as the subjectivist or existentialist" one, is summed up as follows: "The Word of God in Scripture call us to a faith-decision. Revelation is not digging up doctrinal information about God from the past. Instead it is about a personal existential decision here and now".[21] Lane adds cautiously in a note: "Traces of this kind of thinking can be found in the works of R. Bultmann". He objects, soundly, that Bultmann's theory "creates something of a divorce between present faith and past history" and that it "neglects the role of tradition as the bearer and the

Christian community as the interpreter of God's revelation to mankind". He concludes: "Each theory contains an important aspect of God's revelation. A balanced and complete account will include all of them".[22] This he will now attempt to provide.

The essential elements of his account are as follows:

> There can be no divine revelation without the response of faith which receives it, and there can be no faith without the grace of God's revelation which draws forth faith in us...revelation, if it is to be genuine, involves a process of conversion for the recipient. Contact with God changes the individual...Revelation is only available in terms of the faith understanding of biblical and ecclesial witness.[23]

The last of these unexceptionable sentences should not be taken to exclude the sort of (not uncommon) conversion which has as its factual basis only the most slender acquaintance with the Bible and the teaching of the Church. The discovery of God in Christ and in his Church can be made in many different ways. Lane continues:

> The revelation of God to us is always addressed to human self-consciousness and as such draws human self-consciousness out of its lonely estrangement into a new liberating communion with God...It is only in and through the revelation of God that we become truly conscious of ourselves, our origin and our destiny.[24]

It seems that here Lane is speaking of revelation in general, not of the Christian revelation in particular which makes possible a union with the Father in the Holy Spirit through the victory over death of Jesus Christ. Are we to say that general revelation happened as soon as human beings appeared on this earth? It seems so, although we may reasonably suppose that there was at the beginning only a vague realization that so momentous a summons was being issued. We may also suppose that primitive man, in his state of innocence, was capable of very rapid development. Lane has not spoken of an "awareness" here, but his reference to "a new liberating communion with God" must imply it. He speaks of an "invitation from God which is mediated to us through our experience of the other who is the image of God in the world."[25] But there is nothing here about the image of God which each of us is and in which each of us can discover him. Lane follows Aquinas in playing down the directness of our self-knowledge. And it is by way of this, I want to suggest, that full conviction is gained. People who attribute it to the effectiveness of rational arguments, which they subsequently find ineffective, will sometimes discover that their conviction is still there underneath.

In regard to Christian faith, Aquinas does appeal to "inner" evidence, but it is of an unsatisfactory kind. Lane quotes him with approval: "There exists in the heart (*in affection*) an inner instinct which impels and moves us to believe...It enables the individual to recognize and respond to the exterior grace of God's revelation in Christ."[26] Notoriously, Aquinas also gives the will a part to play in the production of the act of faith which seems to suggest wishful thinking. And he tells us that we must accept God's authority for His revelation although we have been given no convincing reason for believing in Him and cannot get intellectually "in touch" with Him. The result was that the certainty of faith became for traditional theologians the most difficult of all problems, the crux theologium. Theology had become rationalistic and detached from spirituality to the great impoverishment of both.

Apart from this residual Thomism, Lane is on what I would call the right side, for instance:

> If the reality of the living relationship between God and his people is seen as something that can be summed up in a body of truths, then the emphasis of the Church will be simply one of safeguarding the deposit of faith. This will lead inevitably to an excessive concern with the defense of a verbal orthodoxy at the expense of a living active faith among the people of God....If on the other hand the loving relationship between God and mankind in revelation is seen as something that goes beyond a body of truths...., then the concern of the Church will be to express that relationship in a language and practice that is in touch with people's present, personal, historical experience of God.[27]

4. A Breakthrough: Dominique Dubarle

What I have referred to as Father Lane's "residual Thomism" is a matter of the greatest importance in itself, although it appears only incidentally in *The Experience of God*. For it cannot satisfactorily account for that total commitment which faith, according to the Christian tradition, requires. It was not until 1963 that I was able to find a plain statement of what was needed in an authoritative work by a leading Catholic theologian. Henri Bouillard in his *Logique de la Foi* wrote as follows: "God reveals himself to each of us at the heart of the act of faith which he specifies. Our awareness of this revelation has the character of a direct and personal grasp, an inner experience, supernatural perception analogous to mystical contemplation."[28] It is, in fact, the traditional view that mysticism is simply the development of faith; one would expect, then, to find an intuitive element in faith itself. Such statements as Bouillard's are still hard to find, at least in the Anglophone world (Father O'Collins' *Fundamental Theology*, excellent in so many ways, misses out this crucial point). And it was not until a few years ago that I found in the work of Dominique Dubarle what seemed to me a decisive breakthrough from Thomism to Aristotelianism on the whole philosophical-theological front on this fundamental issue of an awareness of God.

Dubarle is a much revered Dominican at the Paris *Institute Catholique. Le Modernisme,*[29] a collection of essays presented by him, ends with his ninety-page study, *Modernisme et Experience Religieuse*, in which he discusses the failure of the Roman authorities to understand what was going on in people's minds in the early years of the century. First I shall quote a few passages from the short final section of the article[30] in which he sums up his position. After referring to the statement in the Prologue of the Fourth Gospel that the divine Word was life and that the life which was in him was the light of men, he continues: "With Saint Augustine I think—not indeed without my Christian faith's contributing to the thought's emergence—that it is this which gives us the basic truth about man's knowing powers." This, he says (I now paraphrase), is the ultimate truth about the light of the mind in all its dimensions and functions, natural and supernatural. But this truth is not always grasped in the same way at all levels. On the highest level of God-given wisdom it is grasped directly without need of interpretation; in everyday knowledge, science, discursive reasoning and so on, it is grasped through what man has taken from the world and organized, making it part of his mental life. The use of concepts and categories is indeed important and valuable, but this comes second in importance to the Light itself, without which these functions of the mind would not exist. Here I may add that Professor Ronald Nash in his book *The Light of the Mind* has shown conclusively, in my opinion, that this light is, for Augustine, God himself, not just something that he effects (which is the Thomist view of it).

Dubarle goes on to say that he finds the same teaching about human intelligence in what St. Paul said to the Athenians on the Acropolis about God's presence to them. It is a presence of the spiritual or noetic order, "immensely indefinite and confused," yet "it is in the life of the Word that the psycho mental life of the human being is immersed". It is "a sovereign generality" which becomes "specialized and naturalized" as the light of the active intellect turns toward the sensible world in the form of reason and understanding, while still retaining its special active quality for use when opportunity arises. And then, "by a differentiating awareness, by a discrimination, this free and ever-active original register can achieve self-identification (the Word was the light that enlightens every man): ordinary experience takes on the cast of the ungraspable, the sacred....". Dubarle sees in St. Paul's words to the Athenians about man's seeking God "gropingly" the fact that in primitive religion there must be "*contact* with divine truth," although God is still ungraspable and anonymous. Without this contact, "no searching for God would be found among men, nor any other specifically intelligent activity."

Catholic theologians are then asked to consider "whether, in this matter of man's religious life, there would not be an advantage in starting out simply from these Johannine and Pauline texts, taken in all seriousness, instead of beginning with more complicated and technical theories of knowledge such as Aristotelian or some modern one....". The Thomist-Aristotelian theory has in fact been largely abandoned in theological schools with the result that these fundamental questions are often discussed, if at all, in terms of post-Christian philosophies. The following passage from an earlier part of the article will now be clear:

> Why, then, whether it is a question of a 'natural' knowledge of God, or of faith, or of prophecy, or of that knowledge of the 'perfect' spoken of by St. Thomas, or, in fine, of the glorious vision of the blessed, why should there not be....with whatever differences and special characteristics, a simple cognitive contact with the very reality of God, making God known, really known himself, but always in a particular way and more or less profoundly.[31]

This passage seems to me to remove at a blow many unnecessary difficulties which have haunted theology for so long. It will be remembered that Father Lane objected to any talk about direct contact with God except in the beatific vision. Another passage is reminiscent of Lane, but the point of view is different:

> ...if the language of faith is to be more than simply talk, covering an ignorance pure and simple of the first Truth—the truth which faith, reflecting upon its own thinking, declares to be its object—then it is necessary, since the first Truth is simple, that faith's declaration proceed from a previous contact, itself simple, with this Truth. And this is the vital point: without this intrinsic source, the cognitive experience of that which faith principally expresses, the verbal determination of faith would rest on nothing, and faith itself would be reduced to a verbose ignorance.[32]

Lane was saying that the formulas of faith must keep in touch with the actual experience of the faithful. Dubarle is saying that, if Christians are not yet in touch with the inexpressible God, they are in fact only on the way to becoming Christians. The importance of this for Christian education will be obvious. Until "the sense of God" has been evoked, there can be no *religious* interest in what is being taught. One can always hope to evoke it. But the first duty is on the parents. If what has been said here is right, it follows that they should make clear, when opportunity arises, that religion is a matter of discovering God for oneself, something to look forward to when you are a little older, something that begins to appear in loving and being loved, in wanting to know the truth about things, in looking carefully at them, *appreciating* them.

5. Blondelianism

Philosophers in the Anglophone world take remarkable little notice of what their counterparts in France are thinking. There are historical reasons for this, such as the special relationships formed during the nineteenth century with German universities, but there is also a deep-seated difference of attitude to philosophy, at least as regards a concern with the life of the spirit and the pursuit of values, which persists to a considerable extent in France, not always from a Christian point of view but with one profoundly influenced by Christianity, whereas "the Anglo-American empirical tradition" is characteristically post-Christian. Philosophical Augustinianism continues to flourish in France and has come to be called, more precisely, Blondelianism. Books and articles continue to pour out about it.

Maurice Blondel was de Lubac's philosophical prophet; he has at least as much right as anyone else to be called the philosopher of the Second Vatican Council, which did so much to bring back a spiritual empiricism into Catholic thinking. His most famous book *L'Action* (1893) has appeared at last in English.[33] Here I can give only the merest indication of its contents. It is an account of man's various attempts to fulfill himself, and at this point I hope I may repeat a passage written some years ago:

> These attempts follow one another with the inevitability which the 'logic of action' discloses to us, but there is always some fresh obstacle appearing, and there is always a gap between the will which wills particular finite objects (*la volonté voulue*), and the 'underlying' will (as we may call *la volenté volulante*) which always remains dissatisfied.... The need for the absolute which emerges from all of this, combined with the impossibility of attaining to it by any products of human willing, leads to desperate efforts to force the issue...So the result of this 'dialectic' of human action is a requirement that is both necessary and impracticable...

'It is this conflict', wrote Blondel, 'that explains why there must be present in a man's consciousness a new affirmation, and indeed it is the reality of this necessary presence that makes us conscious of the conflict.' That is to say, it is through this world's values but through their irremediable insufficiency that God is made known to us in practice.[34]

Blondel, therefore, is not a voluntarist or an activist. Man's great action, his self-surrender to God is based on his awareness of him. This theme has been taken up by innumerable French writers of whom Gabriel Marcel is probably the best known. Marcel was one of those who had been willing to be called Existentialists (Heidegger was another) until the word came to stand, in the popular view, for the philosophy of Sartre and for irrationalism in general. Marcel does not often mention Blondel and was once asked whether he had been much influenced by him; he replied: "That goes without saying." Blondel recognized himself as standing in a tradition of thought which goes back by way of Pascal, Bonaventure, and the pre-scholastics not only to Augustine but also to the Greek Fathers.

Writers in this tradition remind us of the New Testament theme that the eye of the mind must be kept clear if we are to fix it on God. And that, contemporary philosophers are likely to say, is fair enough in the pulpit but quite unsuitable in philosophical discourse. This separation of philosophy from spirituality is just as arbitrary as its separation from theology; They are all bound up together for Blondel, and in France he has largely succeeded in discrediting their separation, at least among Catholics. Yet he was at the same time most insistent that philosophy is an autonomous science. It is autonomous up to the point at which the summons of God is heard. When the summons has been accepted the philosopher becomes a theologian, and he now knows the answers to questions by which the philosopher is baffled. When he steps back into the philosophical arena, he keeps the rules of the game, but he may know more about the truth of the matter than the philosopher. Such a claim is naturally infuriating to unbelievers, and the theologian will not put it into words on such occasions. But sometimes it has to be pointed out that the discovery or recognition of God cannot happen if one's attention is divided and that, if one is at the mercy of uncontrolled passions, one's attention is very likely to be divided. If desire for the true, the good and the beautiful is not fostered, but neglected, the result will be a growing inability to see what is there to be seen.

Even this is not the end of the matter. The acceptance of God is only the beginning of a journey, the spiritual writers insist, in which, if we do not go onwards, we go backwards. Fresh demands will be made upon us as we move from stage to stage. Fresh powers are an offer, but our existing powers will be lessened if we deliberately refuse to be taken onwards. Theology has turned into prayer, and there can be no advance in prayer unless we live in obedience not only to the first commandment but also to the second.

6. Philosophy of Religion in Britain

With the names of the late Austin Farrer, H. D. Lewis, E. L. Mascall, and H. P. Owen mine is sometimes associated, and it is true that we all reject syllogistic inference as providing a valid way of proving God. Also, I am greatly indebted in different ways to all four of them. But it will soon become clear that I cannot claim the agreement of them all with the emphasis which I place on the "inner," and particularly the moral, evidence. Farrer has written somewhere of the "self" as the quarry from which all our metaphysical notions are hewn, and Owen has written: "The moral argument... is superior to the other arguments in one important way. The datum on which it is based (moral obligation) is in itself—in its very essence or nature—a mode of the Creator's action on his creatures... Its aim is not to show that we cannot explain the existence of God, but to show that we already encounter God within ourselves."[35] Lewis writes that God is "closer to all things than distinct finite things are to one another, and also remote beyond all conception," adding: "This we see, not as inference, but in one insight or leap of thought."[36] On the other hand, he also writes that 'ethics like everything else is dependent on God, but this is a dependence whose exact nature we cannot understand and it is not peculiar to ethics...”[37] He thinks that to allege an anonymous presence of God in the experience of moral obligation could result in reducing religion to ethics, and we have agreed to differ about this. Mascall, too, is unhappy about it, and here it will be convenient to quote from what I have already written about his Gifford Lectures, published as *The Openness of Being-Natural Theology Today:*

> ... Mascall regards all appeals to the moral evidence for God as exposed to hazards which he wishes to avoid and therefore confines himself to insisting upon the discovery of 'radical contingency' uncontaminated by other factors which intrude themselves when I reflect upon my own self (p. 15)....there is a certain difference between the accounts which we give of the fundamental human experience. That, for me, is the knowledge of self and knowledge of the world outside indissolubly united from the start. Mascall holds that knowledge of the world outside, normally at least, comes first[38] ....He writes: 'Now I do not wish to quarrel with the stress which, for their own purposes, both Farrer and Owen place upon the human self as the datum for theistic argumentation....' adding, however, at once: 'I prefer to start from beings that we know more objectively and at the same time less intimately than we know ourselves' on the ground that there is then 'no danger of confusion with those psychological states of insecurity and anxiety to which existentialists attribute direct ontological status' (pp. 108–110).[39]

It will be clear, I hope, that my account of the matter has nothing to do with “psychological states of insecurity and anxiety.” Awareness of moral obligation has its emotional tone like any other awareness, except perhaps that there is, when it is acted upon, the special satisfaction of realizing the truth about one's own condition. It is this awareness, I think, that saves many people from giving up hope of making sense of things. When Mascall insists that the world has to be explained, laying so much stress on rational processes that his thesis about an apprehension of God might seem to have faded from the picture, such people might feel that explaining the world is something that they are not at all called upon to do. Things act on one another in the world, things happen, they might say, but we can no longer think of the world itself as happening. For such people, talk about a creator of the world is useless until they can discover him acting upon themselves.

Father Brian Davies, O. P., also regards the contingency of the world, the argument that it must have a creator, as solid ground for belief in God. In *An Introduction to the Philosophy of Religion,*[40] which is expected to hold the field for some time as a book for students, he writes as follows: “If it is true that the mere existence of things requires a cause, but if that cause requires a cause, and that cause another and so on ad infinitum, then nothing will exist at all.”[41] It may be unreasonable not to accept this, but we have to bear in mind that there are many people who can be led to adopt a more sensible attitude only by being persuaded that there is direct, "inner," evidence of God. Even if this argument for a creator is accepted, there is the difficulty that the cause of all existents cannot be himself an existent. Davies sees this, not as a difficulty, but as the way to show God's transcendence. But it is a difficulty for the sort of person who cannot, so he will say, attach any meaning to talk about someone who does not exist but is the source of existence. And the only way of helping him to see it is to stop arguing and try to widen his horizon on Blondelian lines. Then we may come to see that it is no contradiction to say that God can be known but not named. Causal arguments may prove something but not the God of religion.

In his chapter "Experiences and God" Davies considers claims to an awareness of God, and discusses certain objections to them which, he says, "are not decisive when taken individually." He goes on: "But this is not to say that it is never reasonable to believe in God on the basis of experience of God."[42] His argument then proceeds as follows:

> If there is a God, one might say, it is likely that he would communicate himself to people directly. But the claims that it is reasonable to believe in God on the basis of experience is heavily dependent on the notion of coming across something in the world....the trouble with this suggestion is that God is usually said to be very different from any particular thing which we might come across in our day-to-day lives....According to some of those who appeal to it, our experience of other people can be compared to experience of God because it involves an awareness of what is non empirical; they have a non empirical or non material side to them....In fact, however, the analogy is very weak indeed. One reason is that any human being is a particular thing.... We do not just learn of a person's mental life or non empirical nature independently of their bodily presence and behavior. In the same way....we cannot learn of God's existence independently of his bodily behavior. The trouble is, though, that God is not supposed to have a body.[43]

I have tried to include here everything essential to Davies's case. At this stage in the present article, I need only ask the reader to find my answers when needed, in earlier parts of it.

Davies, in his chapter "Morality and Religion," says some kind things about writings of mine on this topic. I must emphasize that I find his discussions of other topics in this book very rewarding. Speaking of my references to the absoluteness of moral obligations, he says: "This is not a watertight argument, but it does raise a problem for someone who believes in an objective and imperious moral law. If, furthermore, one already has reason for believing in God independently of moral considerations, one might well argue that there is some additional reason for thinking of the moral law with reference to God....If one has reason to believe in God, one would thereby have available some model providing a context for talk about a non-human law-giver."[44] I have only to remark that

I do not base an "argument" on the absoluteness of moral obligation, by which I refer to that phenomenon, still (I hope) generally recognized in our society, known as "having a conscience"; most people think it definitely wrong "to go against one's conscience." Those who do not, it seems to me, need to be introduced to the idea of life as a project which demands thinking about and to that of the presence to their minds of a beneficent power at one and the same time, with emphasis more on one side of the coin than on the other as the particular circumstances suggest. The strategy consists in trying to show that the two considerations are really only one.

The proposal that moral experience might be regarded as a religious matter in view of an already existing belief in God is one which fits in with what is probably the most influential opinion in Britain about experience of God—that it has no evidential value simply in itself, but can be recognized by religious persons as what people with their beliefs might be expected to have: it comes naturally to them to think that God communicates with us in that way. Dr. Peter Donovan in his *Interpreting Religious Experience,*[45] after much emphasis on the unreliability of claims to have experience of God, subscribes to Professor Basil Mitchell's statement: "The correctness of any particular interpretation cannot be guaranteed by the experience itself, but relies on a conceptual framework which draws support also from other, independent, evidence"[46] Mitchell's account of the way in which belief in God can arise is brilliantly done, but it does not leave room for the unrestricted commitment which Christian faith, according to traditional theology, must carry with it. Reasoning processes which, as strong probability (and are in any case beyond the powers of most people), combined with experiences which have no independent evidential value, cannot justify a firm adhesion to Christianity. Acceptance of Kant's view that there we can have no valid intellectual experience makes it hard to see how religion came into existence originally or how belief-systems survive at all. There are, however, signs that a change in the attitude of British academics may be in the way; Professor John Booker, for instance, in *The Religious Imagination and the Sense of God*[47] argues that the massive witness to direct apprehension of God cannot be dismissed on *a priori* grounds.

Father F. C. Copleston's *Religion and Philosophy* appeared in 1974. He is concerned to show in it that one "can see in metaphysics a movement of the spirit toward God."[48] He mentions in a footnote "a recognition of an absolute (moral) claim" and comments: "It is arguable that a recognition of this kind is a response to a self-disclosure of the divine reality under the aspect of the Good....I do not think it absurd to envisage the case of someone calling himself an atheist, who, for human purposes, would have to be classified as such and yet could not count as an atheist in God's eyes."[49] This is most encouraging. In this final paragraph he sums up his position as follows: "The immanent movement of reason towards the absolute manifests the finality of the spirit." For man is "the being who transcends the world as involved in it, and in this sense metaphysics proves to rest on a profound impulse. But in itself metaphysics is precisely a way to the Absolute through the activity of rational reflection, the objectivity of which is not destroyed by the impulse which gives rise to the reflection." It seems to me that, if one becomes conscious of an "impulse," the rational course is to look for its cause, and I see no reason why anyone should doubt its "objectivity" (it is obviously not a bodily but a mental condition). More importantly, what Copleston means by "rational reflection" is not only concentrating on the matter in hand, rejecting this or that putative explanation until only one reveals itself (which is all that he should be meaning by it here) but something which would count as a philosophical argument. I think it a prejudice to suppose that philosophy is nothing but a matter of arguments. Copleston proposes for his purpose a rational process which (he insists) is not an inference.

The argument, which he presents only tentatively, runs as follows in baldest outline. "Reason unifies the world" is the first stage. There is no logical contradiction when X is one finite thing and Y is another in affirming X and denying Y, so that "we may think it metaphysically possible for X to exist in a state of complete isolation." This is the second stage. The third is "the discovery that, in fact, the completely isolated finite thing is unintelligible." Copleston explains: "That is to say, reason cannot remain in the idea of such an individual; it has to relate it to something else as ground of its existence. To understand the finite existent involves this relating...." Thus there has to be a "movement of transcendence" consisting in the recognition of a Creator.[50] This process of thought may indeed *help* somebody to realize that one cannot dispense with a Creator. But there will be, I think, other people who would very much like to achieve this "movement of transcendence" but find it impossible. Actual contact with the Creator will *assure them* that he is there. And only proper attention to their own specifically human characteristics will provide them with this contact.

Philosophical work in Britain is as much concerned as ever with Wittgenstein. Opinions differ sharply about how he is to be interpreted, and I shall not venture to adjudicate between them. From my point of view, the effects of Wittgenstein, which, for all that I can tell, he might have deplored, have been often disastrous. In a recent book by Don Cupitt, Dean of Emmanuel College, Cambridge, there is the following passage:

> ....there is nothing left for faith to be except a free, voluntary and creative decision simply to choose a certain shape and direction for one's life....There is no longer anything out there for faith to correspond to, so the only test of faith is how it works out in life...The objects of faith, such as God, are seen as guiding spiritual ideals that we live by, and not as beings....The world is made not of beings but of meanings, and religious meanings are purely practical....It is only since Wittgenstein that we have dared to say explicitly that the whole of the objective, quasi-factual side of religious belief must now be rejected as superstition.[51]

Cupitt goes on to say, in effect, still appealing to Wittgenstein that we are locked up in the structure of language or other sign-systems which we have invented and that the idea of there being anything beyond them is simply unthinkable. The most influential Christian philosophers in this country are Wittgensteinians who reject, for philosophical purposes, any talk about a spiritual principle in man. I am not the only person to disagree with them, but those who share my point of view have not, as yet, written books about it.

It may seem surprising that I have not discussed at all the positions of Karl Rahner and Bernard Lonergan who, with the exception of Hans Kung, were, I suppose, the best known philosophers-theologians of our time; the reason is that, although they have done so much to shift opinions into more promising directions, neither has made a straightforward appeal to the "inner" evidence. For Rahner, as Father Donceel has put it, we apprehend God only "out of the corner of the eye."[52] Lonergan in his *Second Collection* moves to a position described as "existentialist" in which he says, excellently, much about loving God, but little (and that not very clear) about awareness of him.

NOTES

[1] *Sur les chemins de Dieu* (Paris: Aubier, 1955), p. 45; in the English translation, which I have used, *The Discovery of God*, trans. Alexander Dru (London: Darton, Longman and Todd, 1960), p. 40.

[2] The appropriateness of such a description will be discussed in sections 2 and 4.

[3] De Lubac, *Discovery,* pp. 35–36; p. 40 in the original, quoting Augustine *Confessions* VII.X.16. The vigor of the Latin cannot be reproduced in translation

[4] Ibid., p. 182; in the original, p. 223.

[5] Ibid., p. 151; in the original, p. 180.

[6] Dublin: Veritas Publications, 1981.

[7] Ibid., p. 2.

[8] Ibid., pp. 8–9.

[9] Ibid., p. 13.

[10] (New York: Oxford University Press, 1968), p. 52.

[11] Ibid., pp. 63, 66.

[12] Lane, *Experience,* p. 14.

[13] Ibid., pp. 14–15.

[14] Anyone who doubts the propriety of this statement might read the final chapter of Louis Bouyer's's *Introduction to Spirituality.* The awareness of God being a unique case, the Fathers sometimes call it a "seeing" and sometimes repudiate the description. To call it a "seeing" is only to "point" to it and in the only intelligible way.

[15] Lane, *Experience,* p. 15.

[16] Ibid., p. 17.

[17] *De Veritate* 22.2, ad 1.

[18] *Aquinas* (Harmondsworth, England: Penguin,1955), p. 256.

[19] Lane, *Experience,* p. 21.

[20] Ibid., p. 30.

[21] Ibid., p. 31.

[22] Ibid., p. 32.

[23] Ibid., p. 33.

[24] Ibid., p. 34.

[25] Ibid., p. 39.

[26] Ibid., p. 64, quoting Aquinas *In Johannem*, c. 6, lect. 5.

[27] Ibid., p. 49.

[28] "Specifies" translates *déterminé* it means that the revelation occupies the mind (like music).

[29] Paris: F. Beauchesne, 1980.

[30] Ibid., pp. 263–270.

[31] Ibid., p. 252.

[32] Ibid., p. 248.

[33] Notre Dame, Ind.:University of Notre Dame Press. It will be found, I fear, very difficult to read. Bouillard's book, *Blondel and Christianity* in the English version, is the best introduction to his work. A necessarily bold account of it is to be found in F. C. Copleston's great *History of Philosophy,* Vol. 9: *Maine de Biran to Sartre* (New York: Newman Bek, 1974), pp. 223–237.

[34] *The Absolute and the Atonement* (London: Allen & Unwin, 1971), pp. 78–79, quoting *L'Action,* pp. 334–5.

[35] *The Downside Review* (July 1977), p. 196. On the previous page he points out that the Bible bases this knowledge wholly on a direct, though mediated, apprehension of God's personal presence.

[36] *Philosophy of Religion* (London: English Universities Press, 1965), p. 146.

[37] Ibid., p. 262. Karl Rahner's acceptance of the moral evidence for God has helped to make it something of a commonplace in Catholic fundamental theology.

[38] *Mysticism and Theology* (London: G. Chapman, 1975), p. 121. Many themes in the present article will be found in fuller form in this book.

[39] Ibid., p. 123.

[40] New York: Oxford University Press, 1982.

[41] Ibid., p. 46.

[42] Ibid., p. 70.

[43] Ibid., pp. 71–72.

[44] Ibid., pp. 97–98.

[45] In the series *Issues in Religious Studies* (London: Sheldon Press, 1979).

[46] Ibid., p. 89, quoting Mitchell, p. 112. Donovan refers to Lewis, Owen, and myself as writers whose views he is controverting.

[47] Oxford: Clarendon, 1978.

[48] (Dublin: Gill & Macmillan, 1974), p. 45.

[49] Ibid., pp. 179–180.

[50] Ibid., pp. 158–159.

[51] *Only Human* (London: 1985), p. 202.

[52] The implication seems to be that we are never "in touch" with Him in the sense which I have been trying to indicate.

B. The Nature of God

4

God: Subsistent and Infinite Being

Leo Sweeney, S.J.

Two recent articles can help introduce this chapter. In a "Brief History of Infinity", *Scientific American* (April 1995), pp. 112–16, A. W. Moore presented a history of infinity consisting of two main periods. The first begins in the 5th century B.C. with the paradoxes of Zeno of Elea (p. 112), proceeds through the Pythagoreans (pp. 112–14) to 4th century Aristotle, whose solution to the dilemma of acknowledging yet repudiating the infinite in time, numbers, space and matter was "masterful" by distinguishing infinity into actual and potential (p. 114). This distinction "stood as orthodoxy" for 2000 years until "eventually [Georg] Cantor [1845–1918] challenged the Aristotelian view" by applying infinity "to sets: a set is infinite if it is no bigger than one of its parts. More precisely, a set is infinite if it has as many members as does one of its proper subsets" (p. 115). But "what remains an open question... is whether all infinite sets are equinumerous. Much of the impact of Cantor's work came in his demonstration that they are not. There are different infinite sizes.... No set, and in particular no infinite set, has as many members as it has subsets. In other words, no set is as big as the set of its subsets" (ibid.).

Cantor later "devised infinite cardinals-numbers that can be used to measure the size of infinite sets". But "what happens when one infinite cardinal is added to another, when it is multiplied by another, when it is raised to a power, and so forth? His work showed mathematical craftsmanship of the highest caliber. But even in his own terms, difficulties remained" (ibid.). And Moore ends his article on a pessimistic tone: "I would urge mathematicians and other scientists to use more caution than usual when assessing how Cantor's results bear on traditional conceptions of infinity. The truly infinite, it seems, remains well beyond our grasp" (p. 116).

For purposes of my current chapter, though, it is important to note that Moore's concluding pessimistic words are addressed to mathematicians and scientists and not to philosophers.[1] Are metaphysicians and other philosophers incapable of elaborating positions on infinity? My answer will be "no".

In the second article, Philip Clayton, "The Theistic Argument from Infinity in Early Modern Philosophy", *International Philosophical Quarterly*, 36 (March 1996), 5–17, begins by warning that the conclusions he will arrive at "will be primarily negative" because "perfection is no longer available to philosophy or to a scientifically informed theology as an area of intellectual kinship" and thus infinity will "have to play a rather crucial role in philosophical theology" (p. 5). Why so? Because in the early modern period under consideration "the infinite was in the air.... It began to dominate geometry and natural philosophy as well. With the introduction of the telescope and microscope and with the advent of the infinitesimal calculus by Leibniz and Newton, the sheer size of the universe and its apparently infinite detail had begun to strike home in a new way. Theologians realized that, if a theistic metaphysic was to preserve a coherent place for God in the world, it would have to be based on a convincing and adequately comprehensive theory of the infinite." But "at the same time that the infinite was attracting more scientific attention, the concept of perfection was losing more and more of its credibility" (ibid.).

The reasons for this shift from perfection to infinity in order to ground a valid philosophical theology are presented in the subsequent sections of Clayton's article, in the first two of which he describes the distinction Descartes made between "infinite" and "indefinite" (pp. 5–7) and between the quantitative and qualitative ways of conceiving God (pp. 7–9). Next, he portrays Leibniz's notion of infinity as basically theological and as drawn from God's nature so that "the true infinite is the Absolute... and is the first principle and the source of all else" (p. 9) and "God is infinite in the highest sense as *ens perfectissimum*," possessing "actually infinite qualities" (p. 10), and is tied to the notion of perfection so that "the absolutely perfect being must actualize the fullest (most infinite) and most perfect possible world" (p. 11).

But "Leibniz's theory of perfection had little or no connection with the ontology of (even his) natural science" and, in fact, involved "a number of inconsistencies"—if "this is the best of all possible worlds,... precisely the amount of evil we find in the world has to exist"; moreover, creation of the world by God must be free and yet "the mechanisms of world-production are described as in themselves sufficient to produce a world, leaving little place for divine choice" (pp. 12–13). Hence, "although the concept of the infinite is closely implied by post-Newtonian scientific and mathematical thought (including Leibnitz's own), the *concept of perfection is foreign to it*" (p. 13; italics in original here and later).

Yet if "one removes perfection as a given of philosophy," one "gets something like Spinoza's *deus sive natura*: the absolutely infinite substance with infinite attributes," with the result "that little or nothing can properly be known about it. Spinoza's infinite substance can never be part of the explanation of any finite event or object.... It cannot cause any finite object. The infinite cannot act in the world or know the world since only finite things, limited by other finite things, can do so. In another sense, of course, for Spinoza every thing in nature is God (nature qua *natura naturans*); but this is merely to decide to view the whole of nature as God. To be everything, and for that very reason to be nothing in particular—such is the fate of the infinite in modern thought" (pp. 13–14).

Yet in the modern set theory of Georg Cantor one finds "an additional resource for understanding the significance of the infinite in modern metaphysics". He "transforms Descartes' simple dichotomy [indefinite/infinite] into at least a trichotomy" of finites, transfinites and the absolute infinite, the last of which is "the class of all sets" and is symbolized by capital Omega (p. 14).[2] Because transfinite quantities form the ideal limit of the finite, "the Absolute [is allowed] to be thought... exclusively *as that which is the maximum thinkable in every respect, that which cannot be increased in any conceivable way*.... This is a positive characterization of the absolute," which Cantor arrived at not from metaphysical but mathematical reasons, which however lead "to conclusions that are significantly similar to our own conclusions from the history of modern metaphysics" (p. 15). But "what bearing does the mathematical discussion [such as Cantor's] have on the theological/metaphysical question concerning the nature of an infinite being? Such a being would be, strictly speaking, inconceivable. Still... by way of negation on analogy with the mathematical case, Cantor's absolute infinity is not the set of all sets; it cannot be expressed within set theory; but it would amount to, roughly, the class of all sets. Likewise we cannot think the infinity of divine being, nor can we think it as a being alongside other beings. It would be something like the lack of all limits that we encounter in certain phenomena of natural philosophy, only now *taken in a positive rather than a negative sense*" (p. 16).

Thus we might say "the nature of the transcendent God is to be perfectly infinite, or to have infinite perfections. But given the difficulties with perfection, it is not yet clear what framework the philosopher can employ to give sufficient content to this notion" (p. 16). Perhaps "the infinite emerging from mathematics and the study of nature while clearly pointing beyond it, is indeed a sign of God's transcendence." But beyond a few "general points, a 'natural theology' of the infinite can provide us with little or no information of a positive sort about the nature of God" (p. 17).

Clayton thus ends his interesting and intricate survey of infinity on a negative note: approaching God from infinity as taken from mathematics and natural sciences is of little or no help.[3]

My approach in this chapter is different. Awareness of God as subsistent and infinite being is based on the actual material universe itself, i.e., on evidences from actual material existents in concrete cases therein, which are the content-determining-causes of our knowledge of what those existents are in themselves and as creatures. Such existents thus lead us to affirm God as subsistent and infinite Being and, for that reason, as Goodness, Beauty, knowledge, love and, thus, as Creator.

My chapter thus falls into four main parts because of four convictions: to know is to be the known; second, material existents are each a single composite entity of existence as actuation (and thereby as conferring perfection) and of essence as potency (and thereby as limiting that perfection); third, God exists and is subsistent existence; and, finally, God as subsistent existence is infinite Being.

To Know Is To Be The Known

The realization that to know is to be the known is based in everyday life on our experience of sympathy upon learning of misfortunes affecting loved ones, of joy upon learning of their successes, of fear when hearing of threats to their safety. Such experience indicates that we feel sympathy, joy and fear for others because their situation has become ours through knowledge. We have cognitively become them and cognition is that state of our being one with them.

The realization can also be gained vicariously from what is expressed in drama and other literature. Take as an instance how for Miranda (the heroine of John Fowles' novel *The Collector*), thinking of the world outside the cellar in which she was physically imprisoned made her mentally free because she had intentionally become the boyfriend of whom she was thinking; by her cognitive acts she was with him, and knowledge is thus shown to be becoming and being what is known.

> It's odd (and I feel a little guilty) but I have been feeling happier today than at any time since I came here.... . I feel happy because *I've not been here for most of the day. I've been* mainly thinking about G.P. [her painter friend]. *In his world, not this one here.* I remembered so much. I would have liked to write it all down. I gorged myself on memories. This world makes that [outside] world seem so real, so living, so beautiful. Even the sordid parts of it [italics added].[5]

That dimension of cognition as intentionally becoming the known has been well explicated by the playwright Ossie Davis in commenting on the nature of good drama.

> What are we looking forward to in the theater? What will be the source of the pleasure we [dramatists] will provide? Insight. The immediate, personal apprehension of truth–of the "feel" of truth–about a thing, or a person, or a situation.

For where there is no insight the people perish. And pleasure in art is based upon *the discovery of identity.* I propose as the legitimate business of the theater the eliciting of the simple joy of seeing for the first time, not only what man is, but also what man can be. *By seeing, I mean to experience. For only by experience can we know. And in theater at its best we experience, through our imagination, the feel of what is true. And having felt it, we know it; and having known it, we possess it–and are possessed by it–forever.*
Once I feel the truth, the internal is-ness of, say, a Negro, a Jew, a Gentile, a Catholic, a Communist, a homosexual or a Nazi, I can no longer pretend that he is a stranger, or a foreigner, or an outcast. *What is more, I will be so pleasured in my new knowledge that I would not want to so pretend. I will myself have become, at one and the same time, all of these things* [italics added].[6]

Do not those paragraphs make clear that Davis conception of knowledge is that by which the knower nonphysically and intentionally becomes the known? If so, his next step would be to explain how that nonphysical becoming occurs. His explanation could not consist in any sort of cognitive factor, which would simply initiate an infinite regress. No, it would have to be a noncognitive factor which would entitatively unite the known with the knower prior to the operation of knowledge itself. But this operation would issue from that entitative union of known/knower when the knower through efficient causality comes to be aware of what he/she already had entitatively become.

Such is, in fact, Aristotle's and my explanation. Knowledge requires two actuations, the first of which is the initial, precognitive, entitative, formal actuation (hereafter: actuation "a") of the faculty; the second is the cognition itself (hereafter: actuation "b"). In *On the Soul*, III, 2, 425b26 and 426a10, he speaks clearly of that first actuation with reference to our sense knowledge.

The actuation of what is sensed and of the sense is one and the same (although the being of each is not the same)... but that actuation of what is sensed and of the sense is in the sense [and not in what is sensed].

Η δε του ασθητου ενεργεια και τηζ αισθησεωζ η αυτη μεν εστι και μια το δ ειναι ου το αυτο ανταιζ . . . και η τον αισθητον ενεωγεια και η τον αισθητικον εν τω αισθητικω.

If we transfer that insight from sense perception to any spontaneous or philosophical knowledge (see ibid., III,4,429a13 sqq.), we obtain this: the actuation of what is known and of the faculty knowing is one and the same but it is present in the faculty and not in the known. It is an actuation of the known and is caused by the known, while simultaneously it also is an actuation of the knower too and, in fact, is solely in the knower. This is truly remarkable. The very same actuation which precognitively conditions, determines, forms the faculty by being present in it is also the actuation of that which is known (precisely as known, though, and not as it is outside the cognitive process, where its actuations are its substantial

and accidental forms) and which is causing it in the knower. Through this actuation, which is in and of the knower and of and by the known, the object known
is the content-determining-cause of my knowledge.[7]

Perhaps the following diagram will help by showing the two actuations of
each cognitive faculty.[8]

In that diagram special attention should be directed to the phantasm, which
is crucially important and which is represented as actuation "b_2". The phantasm

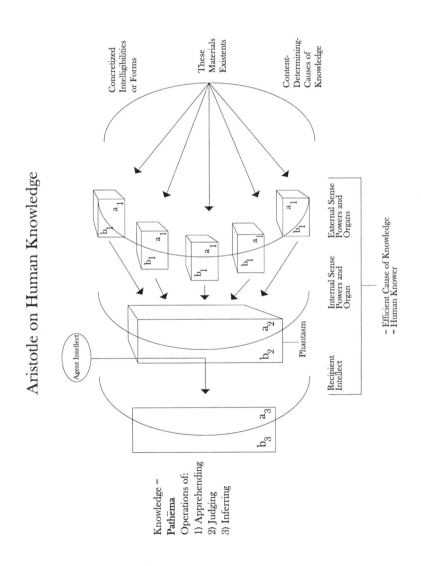

has these six characteristics.

(a) It is my sentient awareness of an individual sensible object such as this brown, wet, barking dog, which is its content-determining-cause.

(b) It is an awareness efficiently produced by the internal senses and based on data from the external senses, as well as from the imagination and memory of previous such data.

(c) It is an awareness whose content is "this-brown-barking-wet-[dog]."

(d) It is the awareness through which I am one cognitively with that dog as "this-brown-barking-wet-[dog]" because also I am one noncognitively through actuation "a_2" with that dog as "this-brown-barking-wet-[dog]."

(e) The result is that my knowledge terminates directly not at the phantasm (which is a medium quo) but at the dog itself.

(f) The phantasm is that which the agent intellect uses as an instrumental formal cause to produce the spiritual actuation "a_3" in my recipient intellect, which then as an efficient cause produces "b_3" and which is now intellectually aware of "dog" itself as a direct universal.

What is the end result? The human knower knows, and thus is cognitively one with, this brown-barking-wet-dog both as "dog" (through the intellect) and as "this-brown-barking-wet" (through our external and internal senses) so that human knowledge directly terminates not with the content of the phantasm and of the direct universal but with the dog itself.

Can anything more be said of the bracketed word in the phrase "this-brown-barking-wet-[dog]"? The bracketed word indicates what is genuinely but only implicitly contained in the initial, entitative and noncognitive actuation and in the sensation, waiting to be explicated in and by the process of intellection. Or one might say that the bracketed noun points to what is virtually present in the initial entitative actuation and in the sense experience itself and which will become formally present through intellection. But no matter whether the couplet used is implicit/explicit or virtual/formal, two important points must be remembered, the first of which is that the content of both sensation and intellection is radically the same (e.g., "this-brown-barking-wet-[dog]), although the former centers on "this-brown-barking-wet", the latter on "dog". Second, if the intelligibility expressed by "dog" is taken to be identical with form itself (that by which this animal is dog), it is actually and not merely potentially present in the dog itself and is universal only through extrinsic denomination inasmuch as it causes us intellectually to know "dog" as what several such animals have in common. But if form is taken precisely as concretized in and individuated by matter, form is an intelligibility only potentially because that concretization and individuation so permeates it that it can be intellectually known only if abstracted from those material conditions, as a result of which abstraction form is actually intelligible in actuation #a3 (see diagram). But even when thus identical with actual intelligibility, form is not in itself intrinsically universal (which is a direct characteristic solely of the content of intellection, of form-as-known) but (as we said earlier) only through extrinsic denomination as that which causes that content, which alone is a direct or reflex universal.[9]

One last comment on the phantasm, this time on its cooperation with the agent intellect in effecting actuation "a_3". The agent intellect is itself without content. The phantasm has content, which however is explicitly particular, concrete and sensible. The actuation "a_3", as well as the consequent concept, is in content explicitly abstract and actually intelligible. Consequently, the determinate content of actuation "a_3" and ensuing intellection must come solely from the phantasm but only when utilized by the agent intellect as its instrument and, thereby, when elevated to a level of activity and to an effect which surpass it if left to itself. This elevation the agent intellect can accomplish because it is a faculty of the human soul, whose nature is to be both the substantial form of matter and spiritual.[10]

Material Existents: Composites Of Existence/Essences

So far we have talked about material existents in relation to knowledge, but what of such existents in themselves? Such is the topic of this section, which will deal with metaphysics, although even the previous epistemological section had its metaphysical moments, as when "form" was described as "that by which this animal is dog" and "that which is concretized and individuated by matter[11]" and when the human soul was described as by nature both spiritual and the substantial form of matter.[12]

Those descriptions issue, in fact, from Aristotle's (and my) metaphysics based on concrete cases in which individual material things (e.g., angry dogs, fragrant rose bushes, generous human persons) change but remain stable. Take this instance: Dr. Larry Ebert, an Arlngton Heights, Illinois 48-year-old dentist who died Friday, June 28, 1996, in an automobile accident in Ghana, Africa. As a lay minister active through African Partners in soliciting used medical equipment for people in Africa, he had been in Ghana for a week and at the time of his death was delivering donated supplies. He had gone to Africa four times in the last six years to take medical equipment and help teach doctors and other medical personnel how to use it.

The changes which such a concrete case reveals are twofold. Over a period of time Dr. Ebert became intellectually aware of the need of medical equipment in Africa, he was religiously motivated to help, he collected supplies, he traveled to Africa with them, he trained personnel to use them. Yet during all such changes Larry remained human. He combined what can be called "accidental" changes with "substantial" stability or continuity. But on the occasion of the automobile accident a second and much more radical change occurred: he who was alive now is dead, that which was human is now a mass of chemical compounds.

Those two combinations of change/stability are sufficient evidences to allow one inductively to infer, first, that Dr. Ebert was a composite of accidental perfections (e.g., that by which he was generous, was prayerful, was hard working) and substance (that by which he remains human and yet receives numerous accidental perfections or forms). The second inductive inference allows one to realize that his substance itself was composed of two components: substantial form (that by which he was human and, hence, with distinctively human characteristics and powers) and prime matter (that by which he received his substantial form or soul in such a manner as to be open to the substantial change of death, when prime matter then becomes actuated by the substantial forms of various chemical compounds.)[13]

That expression "becomes actuated" illustrates another dimension of the components just described: they are related to one another as potencies to actuations. That is, some are the fulfillment or enrichment (and, hence, are "actuations") of the others, which by and in themselves are without those actuations but which they can receive (and, hence, they are potencies). Thus, substance is in potency to the actuations of accidental forms; prime matter is in potency to the actuations of substantial forms.[14]

One additional relevant point. Actuation and potency have reference to one and the same perfection: an actuation confers the same perfection which a potency limits. For instance, being-human was the perfection bestowed on Dr. Ebert by his substantial form and limited and substantially individuated by prime matter. The relevance of this will be clear later when being itself is the perfection conferred by act and limited by potency: if there turns out to be an existent who is subsistent being free of potency, that existent is *infinite* being (see below).

But first we must consider the actuation of existence. Let us reflect again on the case of Dr. Ebert. For Aristotle contemplation is the perfection which actuates that Doctor most fully; it is that which makes him be truly human–in fact, it is that which allows Aristotle to affirm that God is the subsistent act of contemplation.[15] But to Thomas Aquinas (and me) actual existence is the actuation *par excellence*. It is that by which Larry Ebert or any human person is perfect, significant and, in that sense, real.[16] It also is (mediately through his/her essence) that by which he is human and is this or that human person. As autodetermining, existence in a person thus not only confers but also limits essential perfections.[17]

But how does one become aware that the fact something exists also is its prime actuation? That is, how does that fact become evidence for existence as a component? The answer again comes from concrete cases: observe actual existents in their day-by-day situations where who they are and what they do depend upon their be-ing, their existing. If they exist, they can be human, courageous, loving and so on. If they do not exist, all such essential traits are absent.

Or reflect upon the fact presented by Rollo May, *Existence: A New Dimension in Psychiatry and Psychology* (New York: Touchstone Books, 1978), pp. 47–48,–namely, the fact

> that non-being is an inseparable part of being. To grasp what it means to exist, one needs to grasp the fact that he might not exist, that he treads at every moment on the sharp edge of possible annihilation and can never escape the fact that death will arrive at some unknown moment in the future. Existence, never automatic, not only can be sloughed off and forfeited but is indeed at every instant threatened by non-being. Without this awareness of non-being-that is, awareness of the threats to one's being in death, anxiety, and the less dramatic but persistent threats of loss of potentialities in conformism–existence is vapid, unreal, and characterized by lack of concrete self-awareness. But with the confronting of non-being, existence takes on vitality and immediacy, and the individual experiences a heightened consciousness of himself, his world, and others around him.[18]

The following paragraphs are less technical than May's presentation but they are equally or, perhaps, even more helpful in our appreciating existence as a unique value and perfection. They are accounts given me by two former students of their intuitive experience of being and existence. From Michael:

> This experience has always stood out distinctly in my mind. It occurred the summer after junior year of high school. We had gone to visit some friends at a lake cottage. It was a beautiful, sunny day and I happened to be sitting alone on a hill overlooking the lake and chewing on a piece of grass. I happened to notice, as I recall, how intricately that piece of grass was constructed, that it was a work of marvelous, detailed complexity, and much more than "just a piece of grass." Then it came home to me that that piece of grass was real, and that I too really existed. As a result everything took on a kind of terrible significance: whatever act I would perform in this real world had its own, irreversible value; I was, and I couldn't avoid having everything I did mean something, and mean something eternally for me since I would always exist. This last gave this realization a religious import; the world really was, and I was in it, and because we were both real what I did had a value for eternity. I felt a great weight of responsibility that I was and had to do something so significant as manage that existence somehow for an eternal reward or punishment I almost felt trapped by having all this significance thrust upon me with no way of getting rid of it.

From another student:

> A vivid realization of existence came a first time when I was walking across our lawn at home one evening in the spring after supper. I was about ten years old at the time. As I walked across our lawn, I happened to notice our neighbor's dog trotting across the grass beneath some old cedar trees. My mind was at rest at the time; I was simply enjoying a beautiful spring evening. As I watched, the dog headed for the woods about a block from our home. It struck me that I was not that dog. I then glanced at one of the small cedars, and again it struck me

that I was not that tree; rather I was myself, a ten-year-old boy out enjoying a beautiful spring evening. Then it struck me even more radically that I was, I existed. I was not nothing. But why? This was a great mystery to me, and I often reflected on this mystery afterwards as I hunted in silent winter woods or slowly waded through the streams checking my trap lines in the autumn.[19]

What relevant points do Rollo May's and the two students' paragraphs make? Human persons continue to be composites of changes and stability. In May's account a human person engages in cognitive activities (e.g., he grasps what to exist and not to exist mean) and thus in accidental changes. But he also is aware of death as a threat and thus is aware of himself as liable to substantial change. Hence, for Aristotle such a human person shows himself to be a composite of accidental forms, substantial form and prime matter. But in May's presentation the threat from death, anxiety and conformism gives "existence... vitality and immediacy" and causes the individual to experience "a heightened consciousness of himself, his world and others around him" as existing, with the result that for Aquinas (and me) the fact of existence is evidence that existence is also the primal actuation in a person.

The same result issues from the two students' accounts. Michael, the first student, underwent accidental change: he was sitting, chewing on a piece of grass, noticing its complexity. But then he suddenly *realized* (literally) that the grass, the world and he existed, as did all the activities he would ever perform. He and they had eternal significance. Likewise, Marvin (the second student) was involved in the accidental changes of walking across the lawn, noticing the neighbor's dog, enjoying the beauty of the spring evening—all these while remaining human. But suddenly he was struck by his not-being the dog or cedar but by being himself. Then came an even more radical, striking and mysterious realization: he *was*, he *existed*, he was not no-thing.

Obviously, Mike and Marvin were each not only an aristotelian composite of accidental perfections, substantial form and matter but each was actuated by existence and they became the two students who now marveled at the enriching and fulfilling role existence as actuation played in their lives. To put the situation in the technical language of components: essence is that by which each student is who he is both generically, specifically and individually, and hence essence stands for prime matter, substantial form and all accidental perfections and is potency; existence is that by which each student *actually is* and thus it is the actuation fulfilling and enriching that essential potency. Together they *are* Mike and Marvin.[20]

In my previous paragraphs I have been claiming existence as the primal component in individual material things to be Thomas Aquinas' position. Nowhere does he speak of his encountering it in an intuition, as do Mike and Marvin. What he explicitly does present is the awareness that existence is that primal actuation. When (he asks) is the perfection of being a man or that of being fire actually achieved? When it exists in dry wood [to restrict ourselves to the latter example], or in the hands of the man holding a piece of flint, or in his mind as he thinks about starting a fire? No, fire is *fire* only when it actually exists. This fact shows that the act of existence is the actuality of all actuations and the perfection of all perfections.[21] Again: everything is perfect because of and according to its existence. For example, wisdom would be no perfection for a man unless because of it he *actually* is wise. And the same holds true for all other perfections. Accordingly, the manner in which a thing exists also determines the degree of its perfections.[22] Again, you actually do not have goodness or humans unless they actually exist. Hence, existence is the actuality of every form and nature.[23] Again, absolutely nothing has actuality except inasmuch as it exists. Hence, the act of existing is the actuality of all things, even of forms. Accordingly, existence for a horse, a man, or anything whatsoever is its actuation and perfection.[24]

When he came to write the *Summa Contra Gentiles* and other late treatises, then, Aquinas was not only aware that the act of existence is really distinct from essence (this awareness he seems to have had from the first moment he took up his pen),[25] but he also realized that the way in which to establish their real distinction is to turn to the actual universe. Contemplate the myriad existents it contains: the actually existing horses and fires, the women and men who actually are wise and good and virtuous. There one discovers both what actual existence is and that the fact things actually exist is an evidence different from what they are. The consequence is that the real otherness of the act of existing from essence, as well as its primacy in the existent, opens up before him.[26]

We may add that this interpretation of the genesis of Thomas' position on the real distinction does not deny that Thomas may first have elaborated his notion of the act of existing while engaged in theological meditation upon *Exodus* 3, 14, and other Scriptural texts,[27] but it suggests that he simultaneously had his finger on the pulse of the actual world. This it was which had initially conveyed (and was still conveying) to him the everyday notions of existence, actuality, and the like, now being examined under the light of the Scriptural text. Under that illumination they would be transformed, sublimated and deepened both with regard to God and to creatures. Nonetheless, it was they which would be transformed. They had first to be in his mind in order to undergo that change. Without them there was nothing to work upon.

This interpretation also implies that although a theologian originated the notion of esse as the actualizing component within creatures, still that doctrine does not belong of its very nature to theology. It is not a strict mystery, transcending the grasp of human reason. That is to say, the illumination which Thomas experienced while reflecting upon Exodus 3, 14[28] did not superimpose any intelligible content upon the data already gained from material existents through direct experience. Rather, its function was to enable him to *see what actually was already contained within that data* but heretofore overlooked. And

Thomas' role with reference to subsequent thinkers can be conceived somewhat on a parallel–having discovered the nature and primacy of esse, he now can point out to us what to look for within the data delivered by the actual world.

God: Subsistent Being

As an entrance to establishing that God exists and is, in fact, subsistent existence, let us recapitulate how the actuation of existence has primacy in individual material existents.

In what, then, does that primacy consist? In the fact that the act of existing in any existent is such in nature and in function as to outrank the essence it actuates. It realifies and perfects; the essence is realified and perfected. It is pure act, whereas an essence is solely potency in the order of being and even in its own order is always a combination of potency/act. Existence is absolutely necessary for any essence whatsoever, since no essence can be what it is unless it actually exists. But no one essence is absolutely necessary in order to have an act of existing; otherwise, existence would be confined to this one existent. It is a factor common to all existents; the quiddity is unique in each.

In short: existence precedes essence. In opposition to Jean-Paul Sartre,[29] we argue that material existents have genuine essences (concretized, intimate combinations of change and stability, of accidents and substance), but that they are subordinated to the acts of existing which actualize them and which relatively are more important.

Can the reason why esse is of great importance and enjoys such precedence be stated more precisely and developed more thoroughly? First of all, the act of existing takes precedence because it is the source of all other perfections.

1. It is the perfection *par excellence* because it is what any and every existent must have if they are to exist. It is a transcendent perfection since of itself it contains no limitation and imperfection–it is limited only by the essence it actualizes, it is entirely independent of matter as such. Moreover, it is the only component which even *as a component* is a transcendent perfection and pure act.

2. It is the source of all other perfections because of the fact that it is the ultimate reason why an individual thing has those other perfections, as this consideration shows.

A perfection is a possession due to (say) an individual man;

But he has nothing unless he exists;

But that by which he exists is his act of existing;

Therefore, his act of existing is fundamentally that by which he has whatever he does have;

Therefore, his act of existing is the ultimate source of all other possessions or perfections.

The second reason for the primacy of the act of being is that it is autodetermining: it limits itself through the essence it actualizes. Why so? An essence limits the act of existing by specifying-individuating-individualizing it; but no essence can specify-individuate-individualize *unless it actually exists*; therefore the act of existing limits itself through the essence it actualizes by enabling it to be this or that essence and to carry out its causal function of specification-individuation-individualization. Even in its uniqueness and particularity the essence of this man absolutely depends upon the act of existing, which, however, is relatively independent: in order to have an act of existing, there must be some essence or other, but it need not be this essence. Consequently, in any existent the essence is subordinate to the act of existing which is actualizing it, which thereby limits itself through the essence actualized and which is thus shown to have primacy in the existent.

A final reason why the act of existing has primacy is its unique independence of matter even in a material existent: it has no direct connection with matter whatsoever, it is simply *amaterial*. Every component without exception is immaterial of and in itself in the sense that it itself has no extended parts outside of parts. But actual existence is extraordinary in that essential components are present in a material existent because the existent is *material*, whereas existence is present only because the existent is an *existent*. To express this diversity among components, let us say that

1. with the exception of the human soul (together with its intellect and will and their operations and operative habits), essential components are "barely immaterial" because *they are within a material essence and yet are immaterial in such a way as to be intrinsically dependent on matter*;

2. the human soul (as well as its intellect and will and their operations and operative habits) is "spiritual" because *it is a component within a material essence and yet which is immaterial to such a degree that it is intrinsically independent of matter*;

3. but esse is "amaterial" because *it is a component which is within a material existent but is other than the material essence, and hence is immaterial in such way as to be both extrinsically and intrinsically independent of matter*. Accordingly, the act of existing has no direct connection with matter at all, and thus is a component with a unique status of immateriality and with a consequent primacy over all essential components.

This primacy makes the act of existing an excellent basis for easily proving the existence of God, because it reveals material existents to be signposts pointing to an Existent Who is totally greater and significantly other than themselves. Why so? Because actual existence, which is perfection *par excellence* and which is autodetermining and amaterial, is other than the essence of a material existent; hence it does not belong to the nature of any such existent: none exists of its very nature. Nevertheless, they do exist, they do have that supreme and unique perfection. Therefore, there must be an Existent Whose very essence is to exist, Who of His very nature is actuality and thus needs no cause, and yet Who can and does cause all else to exist.

The situation here is like that which occurs when one sees a young, indigent, and (let us suppose) entirely honest child playing with a diamond necklace. We know that the youngster does not have those precious jewels of and from himself, and yet he now does actually possess them; therefore, someone must have given them to him. In a word, wherever there is a gift, there must be a giver. The gift with regard to the very existential status of material things is their actual existence, and the donor is an Existent Who is actuality.

Rather obviously, this line of reflection not only establishes that God actually exists but also enables us to know to some extent the sort of existent He is.[31] In order to be the cause of existents in whom actual existence is really other than what they are, He must Himself not be that sort of existent. He is necessarily a noncreature. As we have already stated, He is actual existence. His very nature is to exist, and in Him existence is identical with what He is. The consequences of this identity are multiple and important. Actuality is being, its lack is nonbeing. Because God is actuality, He is Being, the subsistent and perfect fullness of reality. Moreover, since unity, truth, goodness, and beauty are all inevitable consequences of being (by the very fact and to the extent that something actually *is*, it is also one, true, good, and beautiful),[32] He also is subsistent unity, truth, goodness and beauty. Furthermore, He is endowed with intellection, volition, love and freedom, because these perfections[33] are ultimately rooted in and flow from actual existence. In order to know, choose, or love we must first actually be, but there are actual existents without knowledge, freedom or love. Again, intellection is intellection only because there actually *are* beings which know; love is love and freedom is freedom only inasmuch as there actually are existents who love and freely choose. In brief, then, actual existence is more common, more universally present than any other perfection, and it is the ultimate source for them all. Consequently, He Who is actuality is thereby also intelligent, loving and free.

Admittedly, this sketch of God needs much development in order to be satisfactory,[34] but enough has been said, we hope, to indicate that the act of existing in its primacy and real otherness from essence allows us to answer affirmatively to the question, "Is there a God?" Yes, God does exist, because how else could these material existents possess actual existence, that pearl of great price? It is other than what they are; it neither has been nor ever will be part of their essential natures. And yet they do exist. Hence, there must be an Existent Who by nature is actual existence and Who is giving them that gift.[35] This existent we call God, Who by the very fact that He is *actuality* is also all-perfect (He possesses all pure and transcendent perfections) and by the fact that He is *subsistent* actuality is infinitely perfect (He possesses each perfection in an unlimited degree as well as seen later).

J.J.C. Smart, an Australian analytical philosopher, openly admitted the awe he experiences from reflecting upon actual existence.

> The only rational thing to say if someone asks "Why does this table exist?" is
> some such thing as that such-and-such a carpenter made it. We can go back and
> back in such a series, but we must not entertain the absurd idea of getting back
> to something logically necessary. However, now let us ask, "Why should any-
> thing exist at all?" Logic seems to tell us that the only answer which is not
> absurd is to say, "Why shouldn't it?" Nevertheless, though I know how any
> answer on the lines of the cosmological argument can be pulled to pieces by a
> correct logic, I feel I want to go on asking the question. Indeed, though logic has
> taught me to look at such a question with the gravest suspicion, my mind often
> seems to reel under the immense significance it seems to have for me. That any-
> thing should exist at all does seem to me a matter for the deepest awe.[36]

The awe Smart feels before existence is, as he has rightly concluded, no
request for a logically necessary being. Yet it is the initial and valid step toward
an Existent Who is necessarily known to exist and to exist of His very nature,
because material things do exist and yet in such a way that existence is always
other than what they are. This Existent we call God as subsistent Being.

God: Infinite Being

God is, then, subsistent Being, but is He *infinite* Being? The answer is "yes",
relying on factors we have to a large extent encountered already. It is advanta-
geous to speak first of finite/infinite as determinant/indeterminate-but-deter-
minable. Next, "determine" has two meanings: it can signify to confer a perfection (as an act does on potency) and, second, to limit a perfection (as potency
does to an actuation). Consequently, if a potency would be without an act, it is
without the perfection which act would otherwise bestow upon it and, thus, such
a potency would be in a state of imperfection and thus be indeterminate or infinite and imperfect. But if an act is without potency, it is without that which would
otherwise detract from its perfection, and thus without determination in that
sense it is infinite in whatever the perfection in question is. If that perfection is
existence itself, the actuation and perfection *par excellence*, existence is infinitely perfect—it is the subsistent and infinite Being which is God.

That process of concluding that God is not only subsistent but also *infinite*
Being is so straightforward that one might think that infinity is easily known. Not
so: a human knower can know infinity only with difficulty because human
knowledge arises by the object known *determining* the knower as to what he
knows, due to the fact that the object is the content-*determining*-cause of knowledge through the determination (= actuation "a") it produces in the knower.[37]
Thus the obstacle which this approach to human cognition puts in our way of
knowing the infinite or indeterminate seems obvious.

Human knowledge arises when the object known determines the knower as to
what is known;
But determination is intimately connected with the finite;   in   fact,   the
finite is the determinate;
Therefore, human knowledge is marked by finitude: we know only what is
finite;
But the finite and infinite are opposites;
Therefore, the human knower cannot know the infinite.

That obstacle can conceivably be removed in several ways. One might challenge the first proposition of that syllogism: the object known does not determine
the knower, who rather determines himself as to what is known. Such would be
the answer of any sort of neo-Kantian.

But if one prefers to retain that first proposition in order to preserve cognition of noumena, one modifies the third proposition: human knowledge is directly and first of all marked by finitude—we immediately and primally know only
what is finite—but we mediately and negatively know what is infinite. This modification then changes the final proposition: the human knower cannot know the
infinite except indirectly (through the finite) and negatively (through denial of
the determination which would come from the finite were it a factor within that
which is infinite). This negation signifies a state of imperfection if the infinite
should have what is denied (e.g., matter re form or act) but a state of perfection
if the infinite ought not have what is denied (e.g., subsistent forms or acts re matter or potency). Manifestly, the divine entity is infinite in this second sense since
infinity in Him is both the absence of all imperfection arising from any potentiality and the presence of total perfection issuing from His subsistent actuality.

Before moving on to a final point, let us note how complex the situation is
in which human knowledge of infinity takes place. This complexity flows from
the fact that determination is twofold (as seen previously): conferring a perfection and limiting a perfection. Each object known entails both sorts and thus
determines the content of human knowledge in a twofold manner. Take, for
instance, this red rose bush, which is the content-determining-cause of my
knowledge. That this red rose bush is *red rose bush* is determined by its essence
and, therein, by its forms. That it is *this* red rose bush is determined by the matter which is limiting and individualizing its forms. Both those determinations are
operative in my perceptual/intellectual knowledge of "this red rose bush" (and
both will be denied in my knowing infinity).

Hence, this first positive stage of cognition is followed by my denying the
double determination, a denial which issues into an awareness of two sorts of
indetermination or infinity. The first is the lack of perfection in matter or potency, when these are considered without form or act. The second is the presence of
perfection when form or act is considered without matter or potency, which when
present limits it. Into this latter sort fits the infinity of the subsistent and divine

act of existence with no potency or matter whatsoever.

One last point. A corroboration that the human knower can know infinity comes at the very beginning of philosophy in the West when Anaximander said that primal reality is the Infinite. His statement witnesses to what matter and the human knower each is. In its extent, variety, duration, continuity and cyclic process, the material universe points to a basis and cause which differs from and is greater than any of its parts or even their sum-total. *To apeiron* is such a basis and cause and, accordingly, reveals what matter really is. It has aspects which infinitude alone can express. On the other hand, human knowledge is neither a mere inventory of individual material things nor a surface-appraisal of them. Rather, the human knower can transcend their classifications and penetrate their interiors so as to question what they really involve. *To apeiron* is the answer.[38]

Thus the human mind is revealed as an openness to infinity, a capacity for it through its ability to deny that the determinateness of individual existents, which distinguishes them one from another and constitutes their uniqueness, exhausts their reality. No, they involve more: the underlying infinite nature which their determinations and individualities manifest.

But shortly afterward Pythagoras added to Anaximander's *to apeiron* a co-principle: *peras* or limit. If the infinite may legitimately be likened to the breath, air or void which initiates, encircles and nourishes the world, the limit is like an organism which inhales and draws it in, thereby limiting and determining it, structuring and transforming it into the numbers which constitute the various individual natures of material things. Pythagoras and his followers thereby disclose themselves to have a more adequate understanding of material reality and human cognition.

> The material universe is not accounted for entirely by what explains and grounds its immense extent, endless variety and duration, continuous and radical mutations-in a word, by to *apeiron*. Material things also involve determinate structures, definite natures and tendencies, forms—in a word, *perata*. Human knowledge, too, does not consist solely in liberation from the here and now, in transcendence of this and that. It is not merely a penetration into what things have in common and undergirds them. Knowledge should be definite also— awareness of various sorts of existents, of determinate structures and proper natures, all of which are on the side of *peras*. Consequently, the human mind is not only open to infinity: it is also anchored in determinateness.[39]

Determinateness and indeterminateness, finitude and infinitude—each is a necessary dimension of reality. And in Aristotle's and Aquinas' epistemology, our awareness of determinateness or finitude comes first. Our awareness of indeterminateness or infinity comes in a second moment and movement of negating the first. Yet the human intellect does have that ability, the highest philosophical use of which is, after our affirming that God is subsistent actuality, to deny that He has any limiting potency and, thus, to affirm that His actuality is infinite.

Let me bring this chapter which is fast becoming endless to an end with these words of G.K. Chesterton emphasizing the importance of actual existence.

> There is at the back of all our lives an abyss of light, more blinding and unfathomable than any abyss of darkness; and it is the abyss of actuality, of existence, of the fact that things truly are, and that we ourselves are incredibly and sometimes almost incredulously real. It is the fundamental fact of being, as against not being; it is unthinkable, yet we cannot unthink it, though we may sometimes be unthinking about it; unthinking and especially unthanking. For he who has realized this reality knows that it does outweigh, literally to infinity, all lesser regrets or arguments for negation, and that under all our grumblings there is a subconscious substance of gratitude.[40]

With and to these words I say Amen!

NOTES

[1] Also see A. W. Moore, *The Infinite. Problems of Philosophy: Their Past and Present* (London: Routledge, 1990),—a book which emphasizes mathematical over metaphysical infinity and, in fact, characterizes "the metaphysically infinite as a kind of incoherent compromise between the metaphysical and the mathematical, whereby endlessness was supposed to be wholly and completely present all at once" (p.44). Such a characterization is a serious misconception, as I pointed out in my review of the book in *Review of Metaphysics*, 47 (1994), 834–35.

[2] On Omega as symbolizing Absolute Infinity, Clayton refers (p.15, n.17) to Rudy Rucker, *Infinity and the Mind: The Science and Philosophy of the Infinite* (Boston: Birkhauser, 1982), who characterizes the Omega as "an object of our immediate pre-rational experience... . We have a primitive concept of infinity. This concept is inspired, I suspect, by the same deep substrate of mind that conditions religious thought. Set theory could even be viewed as a form of exact theology. By means of the set-theoretic analysis of Absolute Infinity, we attain knowledge of many lower infinities—the transfinite ordinals and cardinals." In Chapter I Rucker gives "A Short History of Infinity" (pp. 1–9).

[3] Also see P. Clayton, *Das Gottesproblem: Gott und Unendlichkeiten in der modernen Philosophie*, vol.I: *Descartes zu Schelling* (Paderborn: F. Schöning Verlag, 1996). An English version is under preparation.

[4] This and the next paragraphs are excerpted from my *Christian Philosophy: Greek, Medieval, Contemporary Reflections* [hereafter: *Christian Philosophy*] (New York/Bern: Peter Lang Publishing, Inc. 1997), ch.11.

[5] John Fowles, *The Collector* (New York: Dell Publishing Co., 1936), p.136. Another example can be gathered from Jimmy Hoffa's interview while in prison. When asked why imprisonment had not beaten him down, he answered: "My body was in the prison, sure. But I never let my mind believe it. That cell is 7 1/2

feet by 9 feet, and if you want to know what that's like you go home and spend the rest of the day in your biggest closet.

"But my mind was always somewhere else. I read books, and my mind wasn't in the cell. It was away somewhere in the books... And I had people send material for me to study" (Al Stark, "Hoffa on Prisons," *The Washington Post* for April 2, 1972).

[6] Ossie Davis, "Plays of Insight Are Needed to Make Stage Vital in Our Lives", *The New York Times* for August 23, 1964. Also see Oscar Wilde, as quoted by Owen Dudley Edwards, *The Fireworks of Oscar Wilde* (Trafalgar Square: Barrie and Jenkins, 1992): "We become lovers when we see Romeo and Juliet, and Hamlet makes us students. The blood of Duncan is upon our hands, with Timon we rage against the world, and when Lear wanders out upon the heath the terror of madness touches us. Ours is the white sinlessness of Desdemona, and ours, also, the sin of Iago".

[7] Here *energeia* does not mean activity or operation but the nonoperational and formal actuation which is prior to and content-determining-cause of the operation of knowledge.

[8] For the diagram I am grateful to Carson R.Yeager, Cherie Rascop and Carol Szablewski. The diagram aims at showing the two causes of nonconstructural knowledge (both spontaneous and philosophical)—material existents as its content-determining-cause, the human knower through its cognitive faculties (external and internal senses, recipient and agent intellects) as its efficient cause. Both the five external senses (seeing, hearing, smelling, touching, tasting) and the internal senses (imagination, memory, cogitative and unitive senses) are represented by solid geometrical figures so as to show them to be operative powers within physical organs (the latter are obvious in the case of the external senses; the brain is the physical organ of the internal sense powers). The recipient and agent intellects are each represented by a plane geometrical figure because they have no physical organs. In all cognitive powers actuation "a" is noncognitive, entitative and formal; actuation "b" is the cognition efficiently produced by the formally actuated and determined power, which thereby becomes aware of what it had entitatively become by actuation "a". The three intellectual operations of apprehension, judgment and inference, represented as actuation "b_3" on the diagram, are each multiple-for example, apprehension can be simple or complex, judgments can be perceptual or intellectual, inference can be inductive or deductive. See my *Authentic Metaphysics in an Age of Unreality* [hereafter *Authentic Metaphysics*] (3rd ed., New York/Bern: Peter Lang Publishing, Inc., 1996), pp.326–33. On the diagram "knowledge" is termed *pathéma* (see Plato, *Phaedo*, 79D; *Republic*, VI, 511D6–E2) because as nonconstructural and re its content knowledge is "what is done to us" by material existents as its content-determining-cause.

On the contrast between nonconstructural and constructural knowledge, see ibid., p.146, n.10: "What is constructural knowledge? From reflection upon various sorts of constructs found in logic, mathematics, physics, and other empiriological sciences, as well as in our spontaneous knowledge of physical and moral evils, constructural knowledge seems to consist in these two factors: (a) The mental activity involved helps constitute (and thus affects) the very content of the intelligibilities in question, within which it shows up as an integral part. (b) Consequently, the basis of those intelligibilities is not directly any actually existing item, but rather that mental activity.

"By contrast, in nonconstructural knowledge (a) the mental activity involved is merely the means the knower uses to receive the intelligible message which actual existents themselves deliver; (b) accordingly, the basis of the content of such knowledge is directly those actual existents."

[9] On predication through extrinsic denomination see my *Divine Infinity in Greek and Medieval Thought* [hereafter: *Divine Infinity*] (New York/Bern: Peter Lang Publishing, Inc.), p. xiv, n.2: "'Extrinsic denomination' is the application of a predicate to a subject not because what the predicate signifies is itself found in the subject but because the subject is related to something in which that signification is intrinsically verified. For example. 'The wind is cold' means not that coldness as such is found in the wind but that the wind causes someone to be cold. Hence, the sentence is equivalent to "'The wind is the cause of coldness in me'". Thus, an actual dog is universal through extrinsic denomination insofar as it causes us to know "dog" as a direct and reflexive universal. Again, form as that by which this dog is dog is universal similarly through extrinsic denomination as causing our knowledge of "dog" as universal. Also see my *Authentic Metaphysics*, p.88, n.35.

[10] On the human soul as by nature (and not merely in function) both spiritual and the substantial form of matter, see my *Authentic Metaphysics*, pp.131–32 and 135, from which paragraphs in my section "God: Subsistent Being" below are excerpted.

[11] See penultimate paragraph of my immediately previous section.

[12] See ibid., last prgr.

[13] On substance/accidents and substantial form/prime matter see *Authentic Metaphysics*, pp.50–64. On prime matter as the ultimate cause of substantial individuation see ibid., pp.188–93. Prime matter as substantially "individating" a material existent is in contrast to its accidental perfections as "individualizing" it-see ibid., p.115, n.18.

[14] On those components as actuations and potencies, see ibid., pp. 66 and 102–106.

[15] On Aristotle's view that contemplation is the highest actuation of a human person, see his *Nicomachean Ethics*, ch.7; Joseph Owens, "The Reality of Aristotelian Separate Movers," *Review of Metaphysics*, 3 (1950), 326–30; idem, *Doctrine of Being in the Aristotelian Metaphysics* (Toronto: Pontifical Institute

of Mediaeval Studies, 1978), pp.460–70.

For Aristotle the actuation which is common to all material (terrestrial and celestial) things is local motion, from which we prove that God exists. We know what God is from our realization that contemplation is the highest human actuation. [16] Actual existence performs that function, of course, not only in human persons but in every existent, whether subhuman or superhuman, including God. See *Authentic Metaphysics*, p.133, n.44.

[17] On autodetermination see ibid., pp.119–29 and 134 (this last is used as an excerpt in the section below, "God: Subsistent Being").

[18] May begins the next paragraph with the sentence, "Death is of course the most obvious form of the threat of non-being" and then discusses what Freud meant by "death instinct" (see pp.48–49). May ends his discussion by turning again to *conformism*: "We need not "go as far as the extreme example of death to see the problem of non-being. Perhaps the most ubiquitous and ever-present form of the failure to confront non-being in our day is in *conformism*, the tendency of the individual to let himself be absorbed in the sea of collective responses and attitudes, to become swallowed up in *das Man*, with the corresponding loss of his own awareness, potentialities, and whatever characterizes him as a unique and original being. The individual temporarily escapes the anxiety of non-being by this means, but at the price of forfeiting his own powers and sense of existence" (p.49).

[19] Marvin continues his narrative: "The second time existence struck me was six or seven years later. I was sitting in our kitchen at home chatting with mom as she was preparing the evening meal. After a lull in the conversation, I happened to glance at the handle on our refrigerator. It was a solid metal object worn smooth with use. Then it struck me: it existed! My amazement centered around the fact that this dull metal actually was there before me. This common door handle was and I couldn't explain it. Again, I was struck deeply by a mystery that I first made acquaintance with as a ten-year-old youngster."

[20] See *Authentic Metaphysics*, pp.93–102. My subsequent paragraphs corresponding to notes 21–28 are taken from ibid. pp.79–81.

[21] *De Polentia*, q.7. a.2 ad 9 (Marietti Ed., p.192). The Latin reads: "Quaelibet autem forma signata non intelligitur in actu nisi per hoc quod esse ponitur. Nam humanitas vel igneitas potest considerari ut in potentia materiae existens, vel ut in virtute agentis, aut etiam ut in intellectu: sed hoc quod habet esse, efficitur existens. Unde patet quod hoc quod dico esse est actualitas omnium actuum, et propter hoc est perfectio omnium perfectionum."

[22] *Summa Contra Gentiles*, I, c.28 (Leonine Manual Ed., p.29d). The Latin: "Omnis enim nobilitas cuiuscumque rei est sibi secundum suum esse: nulla enim nobilitas esset homini ex sua sapientia nisi per eam sapiens esset, et sic de aliis. Sic ergo secundum modum quo res habet esse est suus modus in nobilitate."

[23] *Summa Theologiae*, 1, 3, 4 resp. (Leonine Manual Ed., p.17b). The Latin: "Esse

est actualitas omnis formae vel naturae: non enim bonitas vel humanitas signifi-
catur in actu nisi prout
significamus eam esse."
[24] Ibid., 1, 4, 1 ad 3 (p.21d). The Latin: "Ipsum esse est perfectissimum omnium:
comparatur enim ad omnia ut actus. Nihil enim habet actualitatem nisi inquan-
tum est; unde ipsum esse est actualitas omnium rerum et etiam ipsarum for-
marum. Unde non comparatur ad alia sicut recipiens ad receptum; sed magis
sicut receptum ad recipiens. Cum enim dico esse hominis vel equi vel cuiuscumque alterius, ipsum esse consideratur ut formale et receptum."
[25] In treatises written ca. 1254–1260 and hence earlier than those cited in notes
21–24 above, Thomas affirms that the act of existence is really distinct from
essence approximately thirty-five times. For a list of texts, see my *Christian
Philosophy*, ch.19: "Existence/Essence in Thomas Aquinas' Early Writings,"
pp.448–51. These texts are especially significant: *In de Hebdomadibus*, Lect.2,
#32 (Marietti Ed., II, 398), *De Veritate*, 27, 1 and 8 (Marietti Ed., p.513b); *In I
Sent.*, 19, 2, 2 sol.(Mandonnet Ed., pp.470–71); *Quodl.*,IX, 4, 1 resp. (Marietti
Ed., p.185b); *In II Sent.*, 16, 1, 2 ad 5 (Mandonnet Ed., p.419). For a study of
those texts see my *Christian Philosophy*, pp. 483 sqq.
[26] Thomas' concern to ground his metaphysics of esse upon direct contact with
actual existents is matched by a similar concern in psychology, where important
doctrines are established through observation of human existents in actual cognitive and appetitive situations. For instance, S.T., I,76, 1 resp. (p.358c): man's
intellective soul is the form of his body because "intellection is an operation of
this man: everyone *experiences* that he it is who intellectually knows (*experitur
enim unusquisque seipsum esse qui intelligit*).... One and the same man perceives
that he knows both through intellection and through sensation (*ipse idem homo
est qui percipit se et intelligere et sentire*)." Among numberless other instances
which could be given, see ibid., I,84,7 resp. (p.414c):"Videmus... experiri
potest"; *Expositio in Librum de Causis*, Prop.10 (Saffrey Ed., p.70,
1.19sq.):"...etiam experimento in nobis percipimus: videmus...."
[27] This is Etienne Gilson's position. For example, see his *Elements of Christian
Philosophy* (Garden City, N.Y.: Doubleday and Co., Inc., 1960), pp.124–33.
[28] Aquinas expresses that illumination in texts such as In I Sent., d.8, q.1, q.1 sol
(Mandonnet Ed., p.195): "In every thing which is, there is a quiddity to consider
(that by which the thing subsists in a determinate nature) and also an act of existing (that by which it is said to actually be). Now the term 'thing' arises from the
quiddity, as Avicenna teaches in his *Metaphysics*, whereas the expression 'He
Who is' or 'being' arises from the act of existing. Since *in every creature essence
is other than existence*, a creature is properly named from its quiddity (for example, 'man' from humanity) and not from the act of existing. But God's very existence is His quiddity and, consequently, the expression which properly describes
Him and is His own unique name is that taken from existence [namely, 'He Who

Is']. The Latin :"Cum in omni quod est sit considerare quidditatem suam, per quam subsistit in natura determinata, et esse suum, per quod dicitur de eo quod est in actu, hoc nomen 'res' imponitur rei a quidditate sua, secundum Avicennam, Metaph., cap.1, hoc nomen 'qui est' vel 'ens' imponitur ab ipso actu essendi. Cum autem ita sit quod in qualibet re creata essentia sua differat a suo esse, res illa proprie denominatur a quidditate sua et non ab actu essendi, sicut homo ab humanitate. In Deo autem ipsum esse suum est sua quidditas; et ideo nomen quod sumitur ab esse proprie nominat ipsum et est proprium nomen ejus, sicut proprium nomen hominis [est] quod sumitur a quidditate sua."

[29] For Sartre the statement, "Existence precedes essence", has at least two meanings, which are quite different but closely related. First of all, existence precedes essence by abolishing and destroying it. This destruction arises from the fact that every existent is nothing more than a mere stream or series of appearances. This identification of existence and reality with total fluency automatically entails that no existent can have any stable nature or essence. Nor does he have one even in the mind of God, and this for an obvious reason: "There is no human nature, since there is no God to conceive it." (*Existentialism* [N.Y., Philosophical Library, 1947], p.18.)

In its second signification the statement is entirely restricted to humans. "If God does not exist, there is at least one being in whom existence precedes essence, a being who exists before he can be defined by any concept, and... this being is man, or, as Heidegger says, human reality. What is meant here by saying that existence precedes essence? It means that, first of all, man exists, turns up, appears on the scene, and, only afterwards, defines himself. If man, as the existentialist conceives him, is indefinable, it is because at first he is nothing. Only afterward will he be something, and he himself will have made what he will be. Thus, there is no human nature, since there is no God to conceive it. Not only is man what he conceives himself to be, but he is also only what he wills himself to be after this thrust toward existence" (ibid.).

For an explanation of Sartre's position, see my *Authentic Metaphysics*, pp. 24–28 and 111–12.

[30] But why must the cause be an existent in whom actual existence and essence are identical? Why could no other material existents suffice? Because also in such existents existence is really other than essence and, hence, instead of a solution we merely have another question: Who causes *them* to exist? We have only managed to transfer the problem back one step. No solution is possible as long as the cause posited is merely a *creature*: an existent (whether material or immaterial) whose existence is really distinct from his essence. No creature can properly cause the existence of another because one properly causes only what he efficiently causes in acting according to his nature, and it is
not the nature of any creature to exist.

But might not an infinite series of such existents be an adequate cause? No, because even if creatures are endlessly added to other creatures, they still remain creatures, just as the endless addition of zeros to other zeros never amounts to anything other than zero, and creatures are zeros when it comes to properly causing existence. In a word, an infinite series is no more powerful than any of its members, each of which is a creature and, accordingly, incapable of properly causing another creature to exist, as we have just seen.

On the impossibility of an infinite series, see Henry J.Renard, S.J., *The Philosophy of God* (Milwaukee: Bruce Publishing Co., 1951), pp.22–25; Maurice R. Holloway, *Introduction to Natural Theology*, pp. 83–8; Arnold Benedetto. S.J., *Fundamentals in the Philosophy of God* (New York: The Macmillan Company, 1963), pp. 44–49; G. Smith, *Philosophy of Being* (New York: The Macmillan Company, 1961), pp. 369–71.

For a nontechnical version of this line of reflection based upon the existentiality of things, see Jacques Maritain, *Approaches to God* (New York: Harper & Row, Publishers, 1954), pp. 1–15. It is what he calls, "The Primordial Way of Approach: Natural or Prephilosophic Knowledge of God." See my *Christian Philosophy*, ch.24: "The Christian Existentialism of Jacques Maritain," pp. 589–99; also "God Does Exist," *Ensign*, 1 (1967), 5–10.

[31] This knowledge will be largely negative and indirect because derived through creatures. On the difficulties encountered in knowing God, see my *Christian Philosophy*, ch.10: "Divine Attributes in [Augustine's] *De Doctrina Christiana*," pp. 241–61; ibid., ch. 18: "Metaphysics and God: Plotinus and Aquinas," pp. 429–39; ibid. ch.25: "Whitehead's Cosmology: A Monism of Creativity?" pp. 637–42.

[32] Unity, truth, goodness, beauty, etc. are what I call "transcendent" perfections because they are not confined to any class of existents but rather transcend them—see my *Authentic Metaphysics*, pp. 161–75.

[33] Such are "pure" perfections: unlike "mixed" perfections (which are due to a material existent precisely as material and intrinsically depend upon that material status), they are present in material existents but only extrinsically depend on matter and hence are spiritual perfections and thus I call them "pure" perfections. See ibid., pp. 116–17.

On "perfection" itself as "that which an existent ought to possess in view of what it is; it is a possession due to an existent," see ibid., pp. 115–16. That definition of perfection issues from concrete cases in which material existents such as (say) these human persons show themselves to be capable of mathematical thinking, rollerblading and playing basketball in contrast to others who are incapable of those activities. The former sort have what they ought to have to be the sort of people they are; the latter do not, even though they may have talents such as writing poetry, ballet dancing, tennis playing and, thus, be "perfect" too in their own way. The definition of "perfection" as "that which an existent ought to have in view of what it is" is based on data from such concrete cases and entails the Aristotelian epistemology described above in the section "To Know Is To Be the Known." Aquinas as theologian subscribes to that epistemology (see my *Christian Philosophy*, ch. 21, pp. 519–28 and 534–38) and thus escapes the dilemmas in which Clayton puts the Dominican theologian (see Clayton, pp. 12 and 17).

[34] For that development see the treatises on natural theology cited in n.31 above. Also see Roy A. Varghese (ed.), *Great Thinkers on Great Questions* (Oxford, UK: OneWorld Publishing Co., 1998).

35 Interestingly and significantly, James Collins has reviewed the positions taken by modern and contemporary philosophers on God and then concluded that one can legitimately attain a philosophical knowledge of God only by moving from the structure of material existents precisely as existents. See *God in Modern Philosophy* (Chicago: Henry Regnery Co., 1959), pp. 394 and 399: "[The proposition that God exists] rests upon an inference, the force of which comes from the given, actual existents of our experience. The proposition which gives meaning and validity to our philosophical conception of God ultimately gets its casual foundation and inferential warrant from our analysis of composite, sensible beings. There is no more radically determinate and relevant a basis for assent than this one, since the inference is made and the assent given to God as a consequence of inspecting some given sensible things in their composing principles of being.... A humanly developed philosophy of God must examine the structure of the existing sensible thing of our experience, discover its intrinsic composition and casual dependence in being for its concrete act of existing, and in this way infer the truth of the proposition that there exists a first, purely actual cause of this being." See ibid., p. 387.

[36] J.J.C. Smart, "The Existence of God," in *New Essays in Philosophical Theology*, ed. A. Flew and A. MacIntyre (London: SCM Press, 1955), p. 46. Robert Nozick, more recently, has penned similar comments in his *Philosophical Explanations* (Cambridge, Mass.: Harvard University Press, 1981). See especially Chapter 2, "Why Is There Something Rather Than Nothing?"

Richard Swinburne also experiences that awe before existence, which however leads him (unlike Smart and Nozick) to affirm that God exists: "It is extraordinary that there should exist anything. Surely the most natural state of affairs is simply nothing: no universe, no God, nothing. But there is something. And so many things. Maybe chance could have thrown up the odd electron. But so many particles!" (*Is There a God?* [Oxford University Press, 1996], pp. 48–49). He rejects chance as explanation and writes his book on God as that explanation— see especially, chs. 4–7.

[37] See Section "To Know Is To Be the Known" above, where Aristotle's epistemology is called "remarkable." Subsequent paragraphs in this current Section are from *Divine Infinity*, pp. 561–64.

[38] L. Sweeney, *Infinity in the Presocratics: A Bibliographical and Philosophical Study* (The Hague: Martinus Nijhoff, 1972), p. 176.

[39] Ibid., pp. 176–77

[40] G.K. Chesterton, *Chaucer* (N.Y.: Pellegrini and Cudahy, n.d.), p. 33.

5

A God Beyond Space and Time

Brian Leftow

I am a philosopher and a Christian. I spend much of my working time as a philosopher thinking about what God is like. As a Christian, I am told that where there is knowledge, it will pass away.

> For we know in part... but when perfection comes, the imperfect disappears... Now we see as in a mirror, dimly. Then we shall see face to face. Now I know in part. Then I shall know fully, even as I am fully known.[1]

So I work with a guarantee that the best I can do is not good enough and will be obsolete.[2] Why then try to describe God? Some of us just can't wait to open our Christmas present. If my beliefs are true and I explain them well, we may all get a glimpse of it. If my beliefs are false and I explain them well, I still help make the truth better known, as I push others to show where I err. In this essay, I am a lawyer defending a set of ideas. Even those who defend the guilty help the truth prove itself, if they argue fairly. Gregory the Great spent long years writing a tome on angels. There is a story that when he got to heaven, he found that he was dead wrong. His reaction? He laughed. I hope someday to react that well.

Having made my disclaimer, I now try to say what God is like. I first explain my method, then argue that (leaving aside the Incarnation), God has no body. If He does not, I argue, He is not in space at all. This leads me to the parallel claim that God is not in time.

How to think about God

The concept of God has its home in religion, not philosophy. To be thinking about God, one must be thinking about the being whom religions seek to address.

So philosophers should take some religion's lived belief as a starting-point for describing God, and be guided to some degree by how the religious think about God, and find Him to be.

Theistic religions all *worship* the being they call God. To worship is to praise, to proclaim that someone is worthy or great. The very gestures one uses to worship display this: bowing the head, bending the knee, hands joined in supplication (as commoner to prince) or lowering one's face to the ground all say "I am less than You. You are greater than I." Worship is not just praise, but an absolute praise. The Psalms make this vivid:

> Your righteousness reaches to the skies, O God,
> you who have done great things.
> Who, O God, is like you?[3]
> Praise be to the Lord God, the God of Israel,
> who alone does marvelous deeds.
> Praise be to His glorious name forever;
> May the whole earth be filled with His glory.[4]

By the skies, the Psalmist means "as high as one can go," or "as elevated as can be." Incomparably greater than anyone else is as great as anyone can be. "Forever" is as long as praise can go on. To the Psalmist, "the whole earth" is the greatest extent to which we can give glory. A sincere worshipper believes that God *deserves* such praise. Again, theistic religions make demands on one's whole life, not just the occasional Sunday hour. Implicit in this is the idea that God is more worthy than anything else, that nothing deserves to rival Him in our lives.

These facts of religious life lead to a method for thinking about God, *perfect being theology.*[5] Believers see God as a being who deserves worship. Worship is the greatest possible praise. So many thinkers take it as an axiom that God is a being who deserves the greatest possible praise—that is, a perfect being. This axiom dictates a rule. Suppose that one is trying to learn whether God has a certain property P. The rule is: "ask whether God would be greater if He had P or if He did not, other things being equal. If God would be greater with P than without it, infer that God *has* P unless good arguments require one to deny this. If God would be greater without P—i.e. if P is an imperfection—infer that God lacks P unless good arguments require that God have P."

There is no guarantee that what *we* think greater really is so. So when we use this rule, we may err. But this does not show that the rule is wrong. It is just one more proof of the adage that even if a machine works, put garbage in and you get garbage out. In fact, philosophy has no better way to think about God. I use this rule throughout this essay.

A personal God

Religions which worship God must hold that God is personal, i.e. knows and wills. For those who worship must suppose that worshipping God makes sense. If God has no awareness, or (lacking will) cannot attend to one thing more than another, worshipping Him makes no more sense than worshipping a rock. Now the sheer *size* of a rock can provoke awe: mountains do this. The universe dwarfs us and mountains, and so can deserve awe. So an impersonal God—either the universe, or something beyond it—could also deserve awe. Carefully cultivated, such awe might induce something like a religious perspective on life. But worshipping is more than feeling awe. It is a form of *address*. It makes no sense to address something which can never know that one is speaking to it, even if there are (say) moral or aesthetic benefits in rituals which do so. Perhaps awe of an impersonal deity can support something like a life of religious emotion. Even so, it cannot support a religion of worship.[6]

The rest of this essay concerns what God is like. Each person we know has a body. So if God is personlike, one wonders whether God does, too. Some strands of Eastern religion think so.[7] Many ancient Western philosophers also held this. The Stoics, for instance, thought that only material things can affect material things.[8] They inferred that God must have a body, since a God who could not affect the world could do nothing to deserve praise, and would be most weak rather than most powerful. The Stoics then reasoned that since God is perfect, God's body must be the greatest, most perfect material thing, the cosmos. Today "process" thinkers, feminists, and such writers as Swinburne, Jantzen and Sarot argue that God has a body.[9]

I now ask whether He does. I first look briefly at what it is to have a body. I then argue that God could not have a body which is just part of the universe, and that the whole universe cannot be God's body. If neither part nor all of the universe can be God's body, then God has no body.

Embodiment

There are (I think) just a few basic accounts of what it is to have a body, or be embodied. They differ over what relation we have to our bodies.

This relation might be *identity*. That is, we might just *be* our bodies, purely physical things.

Again, this relation might be *composition*. I might be a physical object distinct from but composed by the matter of my body, as (some say) Michaelangelo's *David* is distinct from but composed by a particular block of marble. If so, my body wholly composes me.

Aquinas thought that I consist of chunks of matter (the parts of my body) and an immaterial part, my soul. If so, my body partly composes me, and my soul is a part of me which is not part of my body.

Again, the relations which make some chunks of matter our bodies may be *causal*. To Plato, we have bodies, but we are not even partly made of matter. For Plato, we are *souls*, not humans. A human is composed of body and soul. A soul is not. Its body is not part of it, but a tool it uses: souls "have" bodies as humans "have" cars. Now most who believe in souls think that they have no location in space at all. So if we are souls, we may not literally be "in" our bodies. This raises a question. If I am no more "in" this body than that, why is just this one mine, and not that one instead? Causal theories of embodiment reply: well, why do we say that this one is my body? If you stick this one with a pin, I feel pain. Stick any other body and I feel none. I feel this body's insides, not that one's. I see through these eyes and from their perspective. I think with *this* brain. I move *this* body's parts in basic acts.[10] (A basic act is an action I do, but not *by* doing *other* actions. I open a window by raising my arm. So opening the window is not a basic action. I do not raise my arm by doing something else. I just raise it. If I raise it, arm-muscles contract. But contracting muscles is not a separate thing I do: not another action. If so, raising my arm is one of my basic acts.) It is common sense that all these things are so. Causal theories say: these things are what *make* this chunk of matter my body. The way I use this body and the way it affects me are causal relations that link it to me as my body.

Each embodying relation, taken by itself, yields a simple view of what it is for something to be one's body. More complex theories (I suggest) will be at root hybrids of these. I soon argue that God cannot be identical with, even partly composed of, or causally embodied in the universe. If I rule out the simple views, I rule out their possible hybrids too.[11]

A partial divine body?

I now argue that God's body cannot be just part of the universe. The Stoics were right to this extent: leaving aside the Christian doctrine of the Incarnation, the only material thing which *could* qualify to be God's body would be the universe as a whole.

Suppose first that God is identical with or at least partly composed of His body. If God is the greatest being, He is greater than any relevant rival in any relevant respect.[12] If God is or is partly composed of His body, sheer size is a relevant respect of greatness. It is one way mountains and universes provoke awe. So if God is the greatest being and has a physical extent, God should be the largest being, unless this is somehow not compatible with some more important divine property. But if only part of the universe were God's body, something would be greater than God in size, namely the entire universe. Further, if the size difference were great enough, in this respect, God would have to stand in awe of something greater in some respect than He.

Again, if just part of the universe is God's body, the universe includes God and not *vice-versa*: God has an environment into which He must fit. This is incongruous. It is part of the concept of God that God be the ultimate reality, the final context of all else.

Again, if only part of the universe embodies God, this raises questions. Where does God stop and the rest of the universe begin? *Why* does God stop just here? These do not sound like questions that have good answers. Like "how do I get out of this?," if you find yourself asking them, you know you've gone wrong somewhere.

If God is identical with or *wholly* composed of part of the universe, another problem arises. For whatever value some part of the universe has, the whole has that, plus the value of the rest of the universe. So if God is part but not all of the universe, and is nothing beyond the universe, there is something more valuable than God.[13]

A purely causal account of embodiment, on which God is something like a Platonic soul of some part of the universe, could sidestep these problems. If God is "really" a "soul," size is not a relevant respect of greatness in His case, God is not really part of the universe at all, and presumably God's choice (which one can hope to explain) is why His body goes only so far and no further. But on a causal account of embodiment, it is hard to keep God's body from being the whole universe.

Suppose e.g. that God is embodied in any part of the universe He can move as a basic action, or whose insides He feels, or which He makes. God makes everything. If God is omniscient, He knows as much as He can possibly know, and so likely feels the insides of everything if He is able to feel the insides of anything. If God is omnipotent and can move at least some part of the universe as a basic act, it is hard to see why He would not be able to move all parts of the universe as basic acts. If these things are so, a causal theory can say that not all but only some of the universe is God's body only by qualifying God's omniscience, omnipotence or creatorhood. These costs will seem too high to most.

The Christian doctrine of the Incarnation does say that God the Son, the second person of the Trinity, has a body which is just part of the universe—namely, the body of Jesus of Nazareth. All the same, it escapes these problems. For Christians, God is incarnate not *qua* God but qua Son.[14] As God *qua* God is not incarnate, God *qua* God *has* no size, and so size is not a relevant respect of comparison with the universe.[15] Christians hold that God also exists *outside* Jesus' body even while He is incarnate. If He does, the universe is not God's environment.[16]

Christianity tells a detailed story about why God the Son is embodied only in Jesus' body. This limited embodiment is purely causal and by choice. It does not rest on God's feeling Jesus' insides but nothing else's, or being able to move Jesus' body and nothing else's by basic action, or making only Jesus' body.[17] So it does not imperil God's creatorhood, omniscience or omnipotence.

I submit, then, that if we leave the Incarnation aside, God cannot have a body which is just part of the universe. So let us turn to the claim that the whole universe is God's body. I now argue that this claim is false.

Identity or Composition arguments

Identity and Composition theories of embodiment share the claim that each part of a person's body is part of the person.[18] This claim makes it hard to hold that the universe is God's body.

1. If the universe is God's body, each part of it is part of God. Could any being partly composed of the Newark City Dump really deserve worship? There are many disgusting things in the universe. None are good enough to be part of God. So to speak, their being parts of God seems beneath God's dignity.[19]

2. Push part of a thing around, and you push that thing around. We can push parts of the universe around. So if each part of the universe is part of God, we can literally push God around.[20] Is this plausible?

3. We can damage material things. To damage a thing's parts is to damage the thing.[21] So if all material things are parts of God, we can damage God. Being liable to damage is an imperfection.

4. If each part of the universe is part of God, and we can destroy parts of the universe, we can destroy parts of God. Consisting of destructible parts is an imperfection.

5. If part of my body is diseased, I am ill. So if part of God's body is diseased, God is to that extent ill. So if I am part of God's body, then when I am ill, God is ill. Being able to be ill is an imperfection.

6. Nonhuman animals also fall ill. They too are parts of God. If each human illness is a divine illness, and God also has illnesses which are not human illnesses, there is more illness in God than in the whole human race. This seems an imperfection. Further, if we destroy parts of God's body, and particularly if we do so against His will, we become (in effect) parasites of God. So on this view, God has parasites. He is not just ill if anything else is, but even if nothing else is. This seems an imperfection.

7. Again, if God is aware of what goes on in His body, presumably He is perfectly aware of it. So arguably He in some way feels our pains and those of all live things. Further, live things usually feel pain when their parts are damaged or destroyed. So arguably God feels all natural disasters as pains in His body. So on this view, it seems that God feels more pain than the whole human race, or even the sum total of sentient creatures. This seems an imperfection.

8. If we are parts of God, our freedom is a lack of divine self-control—one radical enough to let parts of His body sin, i.e. act against the basic goodness of His nature. So if the universe is God's body, God is imperfectly self-controlled.

This is an imperfection.

Arguments (2)–(8) court a reply: perhaps all this paradoxically redounds to God's perfection. It is good to be loving. Perhaps God makes live creatures because He loves them, or from the same desire to love that leads parents to have children. If so, perhaps (2)–(8) point out things to which God subjects Himself for love's sake. If so, these flaws of God's being display a virtue of God's character. If it is greater to be sacrificially loving than to be (say) pain-free or perfectly self-controlled, then perfect being theology might use (2)–(8) to rule for, not against, God's having a body.

This reply fails. For one thing, God/the universe would still be pushable, open to damage, destructible, and able to feel pain, be ill or lose control whether or not anyone were here to push, damage, etc. These very abilities are liabilities, or flaws. They are there whether or not God makes live creatures. So making live creatures cannot be the whole reason a material God is flawed. At most, a material God lets creatures exploit flaws which would be there anyway.

Further, the reply invites us to pay a high price for claims we can have for free. For instance, the reply to (8) is that God is so loving that to give us freedom, He gives up a measure of His self-control. But on *any* view, God can have the power to control us without exercising it, and can leave us free because He loves us. Only if we are parts of God's body does not controlling us imply a loss of divine self-control. Again, on any version of Christianity, God can be self-sacrificially loving: the Crucifixion gives this ample scope. If one can have a God without flaws but just as loving, why accept the theological cost of divine flaws?

9. Even if one denies that (2)–(8) pick out flaws in the universe, one must grant that the universe is flawed. For there are floods, hurricanes, and mutations of micro-organisms which bring pain, disease and death. Either the floods etc. are natural evils, or at least the pain and death they bring are. Any natural evils are flaws in the universe. If the universe is God's body, flaws in the universe are flaws in God's body. If my body is flawed, *I* am flawed; we say that *I* have a bad back, not merely that my body has one. So flaws in the universe are flaws in God. Having a flawed body is an imperfection.

10. In fact, many natural events bring natural evils. If the universe is God's body, then each natural event is either

    a. an autonomous process in His body which God cannot fully control,

    b. a body-process which God can control but does not, or

    c. an act of God, a case of His deliberately changing His body.

On (a), God is not fully in control of His body—a flaw which makes Him seem all too human. As to (b), what we let our bodies do when we are able to stop them, *we* do. If we are on a bus and the bus passes over a speed-bump, you may or may not blame me for jostling you. If we were too close together for me to have a chance to brake my body, you will excuse me ("it wasn't his fault, it was the bus"). If I was standing far enough away to catch myself before I struck you, you will be annoyed, and blame me for not controlling my fall when I could have. You will treat my striking you as something I *did*, even though I did not initiate it. On (b), avalanches which crush people are similar preventable divine accidents.

On (c), infecting our bodies with disease and breaking our bones *via* laws of gravity are things God actively does, rather than just permitting (as He would do if they occur in a universe which is not His body). The difference between doing and permitting is morally significant. If Cain kills Abel, and Adam merely looks on and does not stop him, Adam is not a murderer. If Adam kills Abel, Adam murders. Thus the claim that the universe is God's body either worsens the problem of natural evil or radically detracts from God's perfection by embodying Him in a way which we judge imperfect in our own case.

11. If the universe is God's body, then either God can exist only if a universe does, or God can exist without a universe. Suppose the first, i.e. that

a. necessarily, if God exists, then a universe also exists.

Philosophers are near unanimous that

b. necessarily, if there is a God, He cannot fail not to exist.

(A) and (b) jointly imply that

c. there cannot fail to be a universe.

Philosophers are near unanimous that (c) is false.[22] If (c) *is* false, (a) or (b) must be and (a) seems far less certain than (b).

Suppose on the other hand that God can exist without a universe. Then perhaps

d. God at some time had no body, but then made the universe and embodied Himself in it.

If this is not so, then either

e. God has always had a body, and that He can exist without a universe means that He could have failed to have one, or

f. God has always had a body, and that He can exist without a universe means that He can continue to exist without it.

I now argue that none of (d)–(f) is acceptable.

If He at some time had no body, then given what we have said so far, a rational God reasonably able to foresee consequences would not choose to embody Himself in the universe. So (d) is false.

If (e) is true, then either it was up to God whether He ever had a body or it was not.

It cannot have been up to Him. For a God whose body is the universe is in time, and so it is up to Him whether to have a body only if this is up to Him at some time. But at any time, He either already does or does not already have a body. If He has always had one, then at any time, He already does. But then whatever time it is, it is too late for having a body to be up to Him.

So if (e) is true, it was not up to Him whether to have one. But then a basic aspect of God's being is both contingent and yet not within His power. God is just like us, a being whose body is a given He must simply accept and try to improve. This is *too* like us. It is an imperfection. So (e) is false.

If (f) were true, a rational God would disembody Himself and keep the universe in being by other means, without wearing it. (If God cannot do the latter, this is a serious limit on His power.) So on (f), God does not now have a body.

12. Theists usually suppose that God can destroy the universe. If the universe is God's body, either this implies that God can commit suicide, or it implies that God can bring Himself to exist unembodied. The first is false, if only because a perfectly good God would not destroy anything as good as He Himself is, or by killing Himself cut off all possibility of future good forever. On the second, we are back to argument (11).

13. If the universe is God's body, God has a size. The question of how big He is or could be raises difficulties. The matter which composes *me* would still compose me with one atom less. So it seems that if the universe is God, it would still be God if there were one less atom. If so, then surely it would still be God without yet another atom. It does not seem that the bare removal of a single atom could make the difference between God's existing and not existing (save for the special case of a *last* atom), or the universe's being divine and being non-divine. But if one atom after another disappears, eventually the universe consists of just one atom. If the universe at no point in this process of atoms disappearing ceases to be God, then at this point, it is still God, and God consists of one atom.

I do not think that something consisting of just one atom could deserve worship. If there were just one atom, I could not be there to worship it, but the next best thing is imagining that there exists just one atom, plus myself in an environment-suit, hanging about to do worship: and I cannot imagine worshipping the whole composed of me, my suit, and one more atom. So it seems to me that by the time the universe got down to one atom, it would no longer be God. But is this true?

We face three propositions which are jointly inconsistent,

i. the universe with its present number of atoms is God.
ii. no removal of a single atom (save the last) would make God not exist, or make the universe cease being God.
iii. a universe consisting of just one atom would not be God.

At least one of (i)–(iii) must be false. We must figure out which is.[23]

(II) appears true. For if (ii) is false, there is a cutoff point for God's size, a minimum number of atoms or mass which the universe must have to be God: as long as the universe is above this cutoff, it is God, but the loss of one more atom places it below the cutoff, and then it is no longer God. But what could determine such a thing? *Why* would that be cutoff for Godhood? And since the universe could have had any size, what would have happened had it always been below that cutoff? Would there have been no God? In that case God exists contingently, a claim which (again) most theists reject, and there could have been a universe without a God, a claim all theists reject. Or would God have then been unembodied? If so, we are back to argument (11).

(III) seems true. For a single atom is certainly destructible. So if God is possibly a single atom, God is possibly destructible. In a suitably strong modal logic, it follows that God is destructible now. But if God is destructible, either He can destroy Himself, or something else can destroy Him, or He can pass from existence without a cause. The first, divine suicide, we have already rejected. The second no theist could accept. As to the third, if this would happen by divine permission, it would be suicide, and if it would happen without divine permission, God would suffer the radical imperfection of being unable to guarantee His own future existence.

If (ii) and (iii) are both true, (i) is false. I infer that (i) is false.

I submit, then, that on Identity or Composition accounts of embodiment, the universe cannot be God's body. We must now consider Causal accounts, on which God is as it were the world's soul.

Causal embodiment

On a Causal account, what embodies me in some matter is that I (or an immaterial thing, a soul) have certain causal relations with it. Identity and composition are all-or-nothing relations. There is no such thing as being a little bit identical with anything or a little bit made of something.[24] So on Identity or Composition accounts, embodiment too is all-or-nothing. Nothing can be my body to just some degree. But causal ties do admit of degrees. So causally-based embodiment might come in degrees. An item might e.g. be the more my body (or part of my body) the stronger my causal ties to it. Again, Swinburne states five different embodying causal relations. On his view, if my relation to A involves all of them, A is my body. If it involves none, A is not. If it involves only some, A embodies me "to some degree."[25]

What causal relations between a soul or person and some matter make that matter embody the soul or person (to some degree)? The best account of this I can give builds on Swinburne's.

> Swinburne writes that one thing which I am saying when I say that this body is my body... is that disturbances in it cause me pains... whereas disturbances in the table or the body over there are unfelt by me.[26]

Swinburne likely means that *if* the right sort of disturbance in A would bring me pain, A is at least temporarily to some degree my body. But earthquakes are disturbances in the earth. I feel them. They give me pain if they make me fall down. So why is the earth not part of my body? Perhaps because the sensations earthquakes cause do not feel as if they are located in the earth, or because the earth can only hurt me if I am in the wrong place at the wrong time. By contrast, my pains feel located in my body, my body can hurt me no matter where or when I am, and whatever else gives me (at least physical) pain does so by disturbing part of my body in some way.[27] Perhaps, then, Swinburne means something like if at t whatever gave me pain-sensations would do so by disturbing A and causing sensations which feel located in A, at t, A is to some degree my body. But this cannot be right. Whatever disturbs and feels located in part of the universe disturbs and feels located in the universe. So by this principle, "the universe" is a value of A, and so is to some degree my body. Best, then, to say that

> 1. if at t something could give B pain-sensations by all parts of A or cause sensations which feel located in all parts of A, at t, A is to some degree part of B's body.

Swinburne continues that

> the second and related thing is that I feel the inside of this body. I feel the emptiness of this stomach and the position of these limbs.[28]

A physician, examining me, could feel both things by hand. So Swinburne's point must be not *what* I feel, but *how* I feel it: I feel these things "from the inside." As there is something it is like to be a bat, there is for me something it is like for Leftow's body to have this emptiness or limb-position. But though the doctor can see the position or palpate the stomach, there is not for the doctor something it is like for Leftow's body to have this emptiness or limb-position. So perhaps Swinburne's claim is that

2. if at t there can be for B something it is like for all parts of A to be in some physical states, at t, A is to some degree B's body.

Swinburne continues that

the third thing is that I can move directly many parts of his body ... moving the limbs of this body is ... a basic action of mine.[29]

Wanting again to keep the universe from being my body, I read this as

3. if B can move A in a basic act, A is to some degree part of B's body.

As we soon see, this suffices for Swinburne's purposes.[30]

I doubt (1) and (2). Perhaps telepathy is possible. If it is, it is possible that I feel pain in a body which is not mine, or feel it from the inside, i.e. that there be something it is like for *me* for this body to be in a certain inner state. Some might reply that if I were telepathically aware in this way of goings-on in your body, this would really mean that for a while, I was partly embodied in your body. But this would imply that for a time, either one human had two bodies at once or one human's body included two spatially separated full-body-shaped parts. Neither seems possible to me. More basically, (1) and (2) are supposed to be conceptual truths. They are supposed to set out part of what it means for A to be my body. If (1) and (2) *were* conceptual truths, telepathy would be inconceivable save as temporary embodiment. We can conceive of telepathy and yet deny that it is temporary embodiment. There seems no contradiction in doing so. This is some reason to think that (1) and (2) are not conceptual truths. But we have only conceptual grounds for thinking them true at all—i.e. we have reason to think them true only if we have reason to think them conceptually true. So we have reason to doubt that (1) and (2) are true.

> Swinburne's argument for partial divine causal embodiment is that
> God is... able to move any part of the universe directly... as a basic action (and) knows without inference about any state of the world (whether he 'sees' it or 'feels' it we do not know); he does not need some parts of the universe to convey information to other parts... in order to know. The traditional theistic view that God has no body has always been supposed to be compatible with the above limited embodiment.[31]

It proceeds, then, by (3), and not (2) but

2*. if at t I know about states of A without physical intermediary processes, A is part of my body.

But Swinburne himself cannot accept (2*). He believes in an immaterial soul, of some of whose states we are immediately aware. If there are such souls, they are not parts of our bodies. Nor does the claim that God knows the inside of everything (which follows from His omniscience) entail that God knows everything from the inside, or that there is for God something it is like for Leftow to have an empty stomach. So (2) is no help, even if it is true. For Swinburne, then, the issue comes down to God's basic actions.

God's basic actions

If body-movements are basic actions, they may not be the only ones. I am responsible for some of what I think. So at least some of my thinkings are actions. If so, they can only be basic acts. Yet they may not be movements of any parts of my body. More to the point, we need not know that they are movements to know that they are basic acts. If this is so, it is not a conceptual requirement of being a basic act to be a body-movement.

If a thinking is a basic act, any matter-movement it causes is a non-basic act or a pure effect which is not also an action. Now God does not need a universe in order to think or act.[32] He can think even if no universe exists. Any such thinking which does not create something is a divine basic act if it is an action at all. Again, if God creates an entire universe *ex nihilo*, this act does not require a universe's existence, nor then His having any body: I need an arm to raise an arm, but God does not need a universe to create a universe.[33] So the thinking or willing which creates is also a divine basic act. Thus at least some of God's thinkings are, by themselves, basic actions. If some are, it may be that all are. If all are, God never moves the universe in a basic action at all.

Still, perhaps only thinkings which do not move matter are divine basic acts. Perhaps no thinking by which God moves matter is a basic act. But even if this is true, it does not follow that God always moves matter by basic acts. God might move some objects by moving others, e.g. my car by spinning its wheels. True, if God does so, God intends both the spin and the car's motion. But God might intend the car to move *because its wheels spin*. God may want the wheels to be causes which carry out His act of moving the car. In such cases, God spins the wheels, and by doing so, God moves the car. So God's moving the car is a non-basic act.

If God moves the car by a *non*-basic act, this does not make the car part of God's body. Non-basic acts often include events in items outside our bodies. By moving my arm, I knock over a vase. Knocking over a vase is something I do. But I do it only if the vase falls over. The vase's falling is part of my non-basic act, but the vase is not part of my body. Non-basic actions may include events which are not actions.

So if there are ultimate sub-atomic particles, perhaps God's basic acts move only *these*, and God moves all other material things by moving them. If so, God moves things these particles compose only in non-basic acts. Or perhaps God moves (say) cars and stones directly, and moves their ultimate particles *by* moving them. Further, perhaps matter is infinitely divisible. If it is, matter is infinitely complex downward: for every level n of parts, there are parts of level n+1 downward which compose the parts of level n. If this is so, then perhaps for every level n, God moves particles of level n *by* moving particles of level n+1 downward. If so, God moves everything, yet no moving of matter is a divine basic action.[34] On this alternative, either the thinkings by which God moves matter are divine basic acts, or when God moves matter, He does *no* basic act. Either way, God never moves matter by a basic act.

Now given human powers, it is not contingent whether a kind of human act is basic. If we do not have the power of telekinesis, we *cannot* open a window without moving some body-part, and so window-opening cannot be basic. Telekinetically opening a window might perhaps by its nature be a basic act. If it is likewise not contingent whether a certain kind of divine act is basic, then if it is a live option that God never moves matter by a basic act, it is a live option that God *cannot* move matter by basic act, i.e. that any matter-moving He does is non-basic. I now argue that God in fact cannot move matter by a basic act.

I begin from a claim of Aquinas, that creation *ex nihilo* is the "proper action" of God.[35] One thing this means is that nothing other than God can create *ex nihilo*. Another is that due to His very nature, this is the primary, basic way God acts—that necessarily, whatever else God does, He does by creating. Let us focus on this last point.

It is false that God creates the world and it then exists on its own, with no further need of Him. Rather, God creates the world, and it remains in existence only because He supports it, as a book remains aloft only if I continue to hold it up. To destroy the world, God would not have to *do* anything. He would just have to stop doing what He is always doing to keep it in existence.[36] At the world's first moment, if it had one, we say that God creates the world, meaning that He causes it to exist, and it had not existed earlier.[37] At later times, we say that He conserves or sustains the world, meaning that He causes it to exist, and it had existed earlier. The difference between creating and sustaining is in the world, not in God's contribution to these two actions. Whatever else God is doing, God is always creating the world, i.e. always making the difference between its existing and its not existing. At each moment, God is making the same difference for the world that He made at its first moment of existence.

So if God is now (say) moving the Earth through space, He is really bringing *two* things about, that the Earth exists and that it moves. Is God bringing these about in one act, or in two? If the Earth moves from here at time t to there at time t2, perhaps God conserves its existence from t to t2 and by a separate action moves it. But God could move the world by conserving it. For He could cause the Earth to exist at t by causing it to exist here at t, and cause it to exist at t2 by causing it to exist there at t2.

Let us say that if God actively causes the world to move, He actively moves it, and that if God merely permits the world to move, but something else or nothing at all actively moves it, God inactively moves the world. It seems to me that if an omniscient and ideally rational Creator actively moves something, He does so *by* causing it to exist.

For suppose that God actively moves the Earth. Before making it, God already knows that He wants it to be here at t.[38] He also knows that He wants to bring this about actively. Since He knows these things, why would He not will both at once? Not because He does not know that He wants to will both or by not attending to both (as omniscient, God always actively considers all He ever knows). He fails to will both only if He *wants* to will them separately. Now the very act by which God makes the Earth exist can also make it be here at t. If it does not, God does with more acts what He could do with fewer. There is nothing to gain by doing more acts. An ideally rational God would not multiply acts without reason. So such a God would kill these two birds with one stone. There is just no reason for Him to split up the state of affairs He wants actively to bring about into two components, the Earth's existing and the Earth's being here at t, and bring those about separately.[39] As omniscient and ideally rational, God fully specifies His every act of willing—i.e. wills each state of affairs He actively wills under its fullest, maximally specific description. So God causes the Earth to exist at t by causing it to be here at t, and God moves by conserving. This follows because God is omniscient, perfectly rational and the conserver of all matter. But

He has these properties necessarily. So necessarily, whatever God actively moves, He moves by conserving.[40]

God also *inactively* moves whatever moving thing He does not actively move. If God is omniscient, He knows in intending the Earth to exist at t where it will be at t if it exists. If He does not actively move it there, He permits it to be there by conserving rather than annihilating the physical forces which bring it there. Permitting is a way of inactively moving; I can move furniture by giving the movers permission to cart it away. If this is true, God inactively moves by permitting and permits by conserving. So necessarily, by conserving things, God *inactively* moves whatever moving thing He does not actively move. Necessarily, whatever God moves, He actively or passively moves. So necessarily, God moves whatever He moves by conserving it.

If this is right, it tells us that conserving or creating necessarily is God's sole basic act involving other things. If this is true, then God cannot move matter by a basic act, though He can of course move matter. If so, then even if Swinburne's (3) is true, nothing in the universe is part of God's body.

But it may in fact be that if there is a God, (3) is false, and God's is the case that falsifies it. Even if we say that God does move some matter by basic acts, there seem to be important differences between God's moving matter and my (say) raising my arm.

I can raise my arm only by contracting muscles, and do many tasks only by raising my arms. What embodies me *limits* how I can act. No material thing limits the way God can act. Even if God moves a whole by moving its parts, He need not. He could move the whole directly.

I *use* my body to do basic actions: I raise my arm by contracting my muscles. My arm is not just what I move, but that by which I move it. My muscles' contractions are an instrument of my raising it.[41] God can move a wheel by moving its parts, or move the parts by moving the wheel, or move the wheel by moving the wheel, i.e. move it directly, as a whole. In none of these cases does God use an instrument to move the wheel.

If God moves a wheel by moving its parts, God *intends* to move the parts and does an act of part-moving. I raise my arm by contracting my muscles. But if asked what I am up to, I say "raising my arm," not "contracting my muscles and raising my arm" or "raising my arm by contracting my muscles." I do not intend the muscles to contract. I only intend to raise my arm. So I do no *act* of contracting, though my intent makes the contractions happen. I do only an act of raising. The contractions are an instrument because I do not directly intend them. God directly intends the part-motions. So they are not God's instruments, contractions (as it were) of God's muscles. Our bodies do things we do not intend to implement our intentions. Nothing plays this role if God moves a wheel by moving its parts. Asked what He is up to, God would reply, "moving a wheel by moving its parts."

If God moves the parts by moving the whole wheel, then here too there is a difference. My raising my arm consists of my contracting my muscles and not vice-versa, roughly as a statue consists of a chunk of marble but not vice-versa. (Thus Aquinas writes that "just as a whole is composed of matter and form, so in human acts, the act of a lower power is as matter in regard to the act of a higher."[42]) If God moves the parts by moving the wheel, His moving the wheel does not consist of His moving the parts, even though the wheel's moving consists of the parts' moving. There is no more basic expenditure of divine effort which counts as a part-moving due to God's intent, as there is a muscle-contracting which counts as an arm-raising due to my intent.

Finally, if God just moves the wheel as a whole, directly, the wheel's motion is not an *instrument* to His moving it, as my muscles' contractions are an instrument of my raising it. Rather, God just moves the wheel, by just willing it to move. The parts also move, but this is as it were a side-effect. My muscles' contracting is not a side-effect of my arm-raising.

An embodied being *uses* its body to move whatever it moves, even its own body.[43] Its body is always an instrument of its movings. If we are necessarily embodied, we can only move things by using our bodies. This is why (3) is true for embodied beings. If something moves what it moves *by* moving its body, its basic acts of moving can *only* be movings of its own body, and so what it can move basically must be part of its body. But God need not move what He moves *by* moving anything. He can just move things directly. If He does move some things by moving others, those others are not instruments of His acts as our bodies are for ours. So there is no reason to expect (3) to apply to God. (3) is true of *me* because

3a. if I can move A in a basic act, A is an instrument of my basic actions, and

3b. if A is an instrument of my basic actions, A is to some degree part of my body.

But no analogue of (3a) and (3b) is true of God, for nothing is an instrument of God's basic actions.

In sum, God does not in fact move matter by basic acts, and if He did, that would not embody Him in matter He is able to move. Swinburne's is the best argument I know for divine causal embodiment. So there seem to me to be no good reasons to hold that the universe is God's body. There are many good reasons to deny this, and deny too that (apart from the Incarnation) any part of the universe is His body. I conclude that God has no body. God is immaterial.

God and space

The Western religions hold that God is omnipresent, i.e. in some sense everywhere.[44] If God has no body, this cannot mean that He fills space by having part of His body in every place. But God might literally be in space in some other way. Some items are in space even though no matter composes them.

Two steel beams may have the same length. Their length is a property they have in common. This property is in some way where they are, for we can in some way see their length when we see them. Yet the beams' matter does not compose their lengths. It composes the beams, which *have* lengths. If lengths are literally present in space, they are not there as material things are. Material things occupy places because their boundaries coincide with the boundaries of those places. A length does not have a boundary.

I think God cannot be in space even in the attenuated way lengths are. If one passes through a space, one passes through whatever is in that space. If I walk through a room suffused with red light, then if the redness is in some way in the room (a controversial claim), it seems reasonable to say that in some sense, I walk through the redness as well as the room. If this is true, then if God is in space as redness (a color, a property) is, one walks through Him all the time, and slams the door on Him whenever one leaves a room. This is too odd to tolerate. So I infer that God is not in space. No place is a place God occupies. Nothing shares its place with God.

If God is not in space, how then is He related to space? Let us turn to the Western concept of God's Scriptural sources. *Jeremiah* depicts God as asking

> Am I only a God nearby... and not a God far away? Can anyone hide in secret places so that I cannot see him?... Do I not fill heaven and earth?[45]

This passage seems to link God's knowledge to His spatial presence. It suggests that nothing can escape God's gaze because God is everywhere, and sees everything at all places He "fills." But the passage may not say that God is literally in space. God does not literally see. Talk of God "seeing" is metaphor for His knowing. The passage links this sight metaphor with its talk of God "filling" space. So its talk of "filling," too, may be a metaphor for something. Perhaps the idea is that the bare fact that God knows what happens everywhere constitutes a way He is present everywhere. Denizens of Orwell's *1984* might well say "Big Brother is everywhere" if Big Brother finds out what they do, no matter where they are.

Consider now Psalm 139, the most important Old Testament passage on God's omnipresence:

> O Lord, you have searched me and you know me. You know when I sit and when I rise. You perceive my thoughts from afar... Before a word is on my tongue, you know it completely, O Lord... Such knowledge is too wonderful for me...
> Where can I go from your spirit? Where can I flee from your presence? If I go up to the heavens, you are there. If I make my bed in the depths, you are there. If I rise on the wings of the dawn, if I settle on the far side of the sea, even there

your hand will guide me, your right hand will hold me fast.[46]

This text suggests the extent of God's knowledge, then links this to the thought that God is everywhere, and then links God's being everywhere to His power's being effective everywhere. But though the text links God's knowledge, power and presence, it does not explain the relation between them.

The text may say that because God's knowledge and power are everywhere, God is everywhere. That is, perhaps talk of God as present everywhere just sums up the claims that God knows and guides everything everywhere. We might along similar lines say that in the "world" of the Sherlock Holmes stories, Arthur Conan Doyle is everywhere. This would not mean that he actually is a character in the stories or has a location in their "space," but rather that his influence and knowledge are all-pervasive, making everything there what it is: to exist in those stories is to be thought of in the right way by Doyle.

But the text has another reading. On this second reading, because God is everywhere, God knows all and is effective everywhere. That is, perhaps the text uses God's presence to explain His knowing and doing what He does, not *vice-versa*. Certainly this would be a familiar order of explanation. I know and can affect what goes on in my house because I live there. It is not the case that I live there because I know and can affect what goes on there.

The Old Testament, then, speaks of God as in some way spatially present with His creatures. This may be just a suggestive shorthand for claims about God's pervasive power and all-encompassing knowledge. But it may have some literal spatial or spacelike core, even if God is not located in space. For perhaps even if God is not *at* or *in* any place, He is *near* every place. A waiter may be near my table, and so present to it, without sharing its place. Let me suggest an analogy.

Consider the surface and interior of a sphere. For the sphere to have a certain surface is for its interior, its full three-dimensional spread, to end in a particular place. The sphere is a 3-dimensional object. But its surface or "skin" is a two-dimensional object. It has no thickness at all. Now suppose that we are two-dimensional beings living in the sphere's skin. We are not aware of the skin's third dimension. It plays no role in our lives. As the skin is a 2D object, we can individuate each point in it given just its co-ordinates in the skin's two dimensions. So we treat the skin and those who dwell therein not just as two-dimensional but as located in only two dimensions. Now suppose that God is the sphere's interior. (The surface and all that is in it exists due to the interior, after all.) As God is that of the sphere which is not its skin, God is not anywhere in the skin. But He is just next to any point in the skin. The very "next to" relation which links points in the skin also links points in the skin and the interior. But skin-dwellers cannot define the direction in which God/the interior lies. For them, it is as if God lies in no direction at all, and at no place in space. For they have no grasp of the third dimension and its directions, and the only places they recognize as in space are places in the skin. So as skin-dwellers see it, God is literally near any place on the skin, and yet there is no way to say what direction He lies in, or where He is.

It may be so with God. God is not in our space, as the sphere's interior is not in its skin. God does not lie in a spatial direction from any point, as the sphere's interior does not lie in a two-dimensional direction from any point on its skin. But perhaps God is literally near each point in space. Because the world is related to God, perhaps we exist in a higher dimension than we know, and the very relation we have to objects close by in the dimensions we recognize, namely nearness, links us to God in this higher dimension.[47] Or at least perhaps God's relation to space is *as if* He were just next to each place, in a higher dimension than ordinary space involves.

God beyond time

Many people treat time as a fourth dimension of our world. Many think that even if God is not in space, He is literally at our location in time—that He exists in time, and while we exist. But there are good reasons to think that God is not in time. I now give two, an argument from physics and a "perfect being" argument. I then try to say what a timeless God is like.

If God is not in space and the orthodox (Minkowskian) reading of Special Relativity is correct, then God is not in time, either. The orthodox reading of Special Relativity includes the claim that time is a fourth dimension of things. That is, it treats time and space as a single four-dimensional (4D) co-ordinate system, over which all matter is spread. If this is how things are, then every item with a co-ordinate in any one of these dimensions has a co-ordinate in all of them. I cannot give an item's place in a 4D co-ordinate system by giving only co-ordinates in three dimensions. This would be like trying to tell you where an earthly object is in relation to New York by telling you only how far north or south it is and how far east or west it is. To give its precise place, I must also tell you how far above or below New York it is. (We might after all be talking about an airplane or submarine.) So if space and time make up a 4D co-ordinate system, to give a thing's precise place, one must give not just a location in the three dimensions of space but one in the fourth dimension, time. Similarly, to say "when" a thing is, one must give not just a co-ordinate in time, but a place in space too. In short, on the orthodox reading of Special Relativity, whatever is in time is also in space. But God is not in space. So on orthodox Special Relativity, God is not in time, either.

I now take up a "perfect being" argument.[48] If God truly is perfect, He lives His life in a perfect way: His life is free of the imperfections of ours. Now our lives have parts we are glad to see end. (I hope that reading this article is not one of them for you.) But we sometimes regret that parts of our lives are over. A widower grieving for his wife grieves that he no longer lives with her—that that part of his life is over. He wishes that it would continue, or that he could have (much of) it again. He grieves not that he no longer can *experience* his wife, but that he can no longer *live* any part of his life with her. Living and experiencing parts of one's life are independent matters. In some memories, one may experience a part of one's life one no longer lives. While one sleeps dreamlessly, one lives a part of one's life one does not experience. Perhaps a widower with continuous perfect memory of his wife would in some way continue to experience her. But she would still be gone. He could not live with her any more. That part of his life would still be over, and perfect memory would be no consolation or substitute. Sometimes a vivid memory makes things worse, not better.

What the widower grieves over is a basic facet of temporal lives: for a life to be temporal is for it to have parts which eventually are over. Lives in time consist of parts. Parts which have not yet begun (like the part after you have finished this paragraph) are in our futures. Parts which have begun and not yet ended are present, going on now (the present minute, day, year). Parts which have begun and also ended are in the past: for a part to be over is for it to be past. So what the widower grieves over is that a good part of his life is now past. Necessarily, every proper part of a temporal life is eventually past. This is why what the widower grieves over is a basic, ineluctable fact about temporal lives.

We may be right to regret that good parts of our lives are over. If we are, then having its good parts end is an imperfection in our lives. This leads directly to my "perfect being" argument. If God is perfect, His life is so good that on balance, God is better off if no parts of it ever are over than He would be if each proper part of it were eventually over.[49] Thus God would be better off if no part of His life ended. So if God is perfect and it is an imperfection to have good parts of one's life become past, God's life never has past parts—no part of God's life is ever over. But every life in time eventually has some past part. So if God is perfect, God's life is not in time: God exists outside time.

This argument does not depend on the idea that what is past is "gone," i.e. no longer exists. Even if the past is fully real though no longer present, the argument holds. For even if the past still exists, past episodes in our lives are over. The "existing past" theory just offers a particular reading of what this means. On this view, events' ending is not their disappearing from reality. Instead events end in time as things do in space, by existing but not including further parts in themselves. On such a view, an event's being over is its being over *there*, its ending where I (at this point in time) am not. So if I grieve, I regret not that the past is gone (since it is not), but that it is not *here*, at the site of this remembering. This just means that I cannot *now* live it. That the past is still there does not affect this, for at this point in time, I am here, not there. So to speak, even if I could experience my past, I could not *get* to it. Even if the past still exists, we are separated from it as from a spatially distant region we cannot reach. It can be quite rational to regret that pleasant items are out of reach. So my argument's point, if the past in some way exists, is that every part of a timeless life includes every part of a timeless life, so that at no point in a timeless life is any part of it past. This makes sense: it is true if a timeless life has no parts.

If a timeless life has no past, it has no future either. For part of one's life is in one's future only if the present part of one's life will eventually be past. So a timeless life is a life without a past or a future. No event in God's life has past or future parts. Nor is any event outside God's life past or future to any event in God's life. For if any event E were *before* some event E2 in God's life, then when E occurred, every part of E2 would then be future. So an event in God's life would have future parts—and only events in time do. Like reasoning applies if any event is *after* some event in God's life.

I now consider two objections to this argument. One is that the argument underestimates the value of God's memory. Our memories are pale, sketchy and fragmentary. So for us, to only remember an experience is to lose most of it. But if God has a memory, it is *perfect*. So He can remember earlier parts of His life as vividly as if they were still happening. If He can, what is the loss in their being over? I reply that even if God's memory is this good, there is a difference between merely remembering events and actually living them. Maybe God can later perfectly recall the part of His life spent with a friend. But would He not care whether it is over, so long as He recalls it? *We* do not feel this way. What is worth living is worth missing.

Another objection is that God could never be in the widower's position, for all those He loves continue to live with Him in some sort of afterlife. One problem for this claim is that arguably, even on Christian doctrine, when we die, we entirely cease to exist, and God later re-creates us: i.e. we are not immortal, merely resurrected. Paul seems to think this.[50] One finds it asserted as early as the second-century Apologists[51] and in authors as orthodox as Aquinas.[52] Christians may well *prefer* to say this, for if we do not cease to exist when our bodies die, then either we then exist disembodied, or we shift instantaneously to some quite different sort of body. Either claim is problematic. But if we do for a while not exist, God really does have to miss us for a while.

A more basic problem for the objection is that whether we continue to live with God later has no bearing on whether it is better for the parts of God's life He spends with our earlier selves to be over. Even if we never cease to exist, a temporal God still loses those parts of His life in which He co-exists with our earlier selves. Some people have a second child because as their first grows, they miss having a *baby*, even though they do not miss their first child. My parents like me as I am, and are still with me, but sometimes miss the child I was. If God is temporal, so may He. If God is timeless, He cannot miss any stage of any person. His life with each is never over.

The life of God

A timeless God's life is hard to describe, for it is little like ours.[53] A timeless God does not remember anything. For one can remember only what is past, and a timeless God has no past. A perfect God would never forget. But a timeless God cannot forget, for one can forget only what is past. God neither remembers nor forgets. He just sees the past, for it is not past to Him: if it were, He would have a past. Nor does a timeless God literally foreknow the future. My death is future for me. But if it were future for Him too, God would have a future. God has no future. So even what is future to us is not future to Him. All that is future to us is given and before God's gaze. What we call His knowing the future is for Him just seeing part of what is there to see.[54] If God is timeless, He sees the whole span of time at once. Nor can "at once" mean "at the same time" here. Instead, it means "in the same part of His life."

A perfect God would never have anything to regret, save perhaps our sins and sadnesses, for He would never err or sin. But a timeless God *cannot* feel regret, for one can regret only what is past.[55] Nor can a timeless God wait, anticipate or hope. For a timeless God has no future, and one can anticipate etc. only what is in one's future. There is no time at all between God's making any plan and executing it, or His executing it and His seeing all the results, responding to these, etc. God lives His whole interaction with humanity at once, i.e. in the same part of His life. I pray to God in an earlier part of my life, and His answer comes in a later. But I pray, He hears and He acts in the same part of His life. In fact, He hears and does all that He hears and does in the same part of His life.

A timeless God always lives His entire life. "Always" here has two meanings. One is that for us in time, at each time, it is true to say that God is living His entire life, meaning not that some part of His continuing life is now going on, but that all of it is timelessly going on. The second is that in each part of His life, God lives every part of His life. Again, this makes sense if God's life has no parts: because a geometric point has no parts, every part of it (namely all of it) is present wherever any part of it (namely all of it) is.

Because God always lives His entire life, He does at once all that He ever does. That is, His creating the world, parting the Red Sea and giving Final Judgment are in exactly the *same* part of His life. If we lived through all three, they would have to be in different parts of our lives, and so happen at different times. But God timelessly makes His contribution to them all at once.

This is not as odd as it sounds. If Mom packs you a week's worth of lunches, then does nothing else about lunch, she makes in one period all her contributions to your week's lunchtimes. But there is a difference. Mom takes some short stretch of time to make the lunches, and then ceases to make lunches. A timeless God takes no time to do anything at all, and never ceases to do whatever He does. For one ceases to do something only if one's doing it becomes past, and a timeless God has no past. Nor does a timeless God begin to do anything, if one can begin to do only what one then continues to do, at later times. Rather, God just *does* what He does. God is always creating, judging—or hanging on a Cross.

If He is timeless, God does not change. For if I change, I first have, then lack some property: if my going bald was a change, this is because I first had then lacked hair. Now nobody can both have some hair and lack that hair at the same time. So whatever goes bald must exist at at least two times—and so, generalizing, whatever changes in any way must exist in time. Thus a timeless God never learns (i.e. has His knowledge change). Instead, He always knows all that He ever knows. Nor does a timeless God change His attitudes or plans. Instead, He always intends all that He ever intends. His plans thus are infinitely complex. He does not first say "I'll create Adam," then wait to see whether Adam sins, then figure out how to deal with that. He instead has at once a huge, branching, conditional plan: "if Adam doesn't sin, I'll do X, and if He responds to X with Y, I'll do Z, and if instead He responds to X with W, I'll do... and if Adam *does* sin, I'll do X2, and if He responds to X2 with Y2, I'll do Z2, and..."

This does not mean that God's life is an unending monotony. I think this is a fairer picture: from His own perspective, God at once knows everything, loves everything, does all that He ever does, achieves incredible triumphs and brings all things to their consummation. God's life is the flash of "I've got it" in seeing the truth, multiplied by the infinity of truth God sees and the perfection of His grasp of it. It is also at once the joy of realizing "I love you" and (in some cases) "YOU love ME!," and the exaltation of "I've done it!" and "I've done it for YOU!," similarly multiplied. Beyond all this, God knows and loves Himself: and this not as narcissism, but because God is so good that even God cannot resist Him, and God of all knowers can most fully appreciate this. The Beatific Vision—our best grasp of God—is supposed to be the crowning joy of our lives. This may be in part because we lacked it before, and strove long to attain it. But it is mostly because of what God is, not what we are or have done. God cannot have whatever part of this joy stems from our lacking and striving. But we cannot have as much of this joy as He can. God's goodness is so far beyond us that it overloads our capacity for joy. Only God can appreciate all there is to appreciate in God. So I suggest that God's joy in Himself exceeds our joy in the Beatific Vision.

For God, all this is not momentary, as our peak experiences are. Neither does it continue, in the sense of having earlier parts recede into a past. If God is timeless, all this lasts forever, in two senses: it is so in each part of God's life, and at every time, it is true to say this. But God's life is neither long nor short. For both being long and being short are a matter of how much time a life takes, and God's life is just outside time. In one way, God's life is like both an instant and an infinitely extended timeline. Like an instant, it has no parts. Like the timeline, it would be co-extensive with even the whole of an infinite time. In another way, point and line are alike bad models: for the point is the shortest interval, the infinitely extended line the longest. But God's life is neither. There is no "how much" or "how long" to it. It is just present, and unimaginably intense.

NOTES
[1] *I Corinthians* 13: 8–10, 12.
[2] Some truths we now know about God are negative—they are about what He is not or is not like, e.g. that He has no body (apart from the Incarnation) and is not in space. These are "not good enough" because they give us no positive information at all. They will be obsolete when we "know fully," I suggest, in the sense that though still true, they will seem hardly worth thinking about. Some truths we now know about God are positive—i.e. about what He is or is like. These are "not good enough" in that they give us very limited information. We may know that God has knowledge, but we do not know in any detailed, concrete way what omniscient, eternal, omnipresent knowledge is like. When we "know fully," these truths will be obsolete (I suggest) in the sense of being the least interesting or important part of a much fuller, more concrete knowledge.
[3] Ps. 71:19.
[4] Ps. 72:19.
[5] For a fuller treatment of this, see my "Concepts of God," in *The Encyclopedia of Philosophy* (Routledge, forthcoming).
[6] Much of this essay consists of "perfect being" theological arguments. While I take as live options only concepts of God which let Him have some sort of knowledge and will, at least some of what I say will apply to an impersonal God too if it is correct to use perfect being theology to think out the concept of an impersonal God. I am not sure that this is correct, though. For it seems plausible to me that anything personal is in some way more valuable than anything impersonal. It seems to me, for instance, that it is wrong to kill an innocent person, but would not be wrong to destroy an entire universe, if that universe were devoid of life or the prospects of life. It also seems to me that the relative value of the items involved must ultimately figure in the explanation of this, if it is correct. If the personal is more valuable than the impersonal, anyone opting for an impersonal God rules out the use of perfect being theology to develop a concept of that God—unless that person can make a good case that there is some property incompatible with being personal which renders God even greater than He could be if personal. (Thus Plotinus, who held that the ultimate source of all is the impersonal One, also held that the One is not a being or a perfect being, but "beyond being." Plotinus' perfect being is Nous, the divine mind.)
[7] E.g. Ramanuja.
[8] Cicero, *Academica* I, 39 The early Christian thinker Tertullian agreed (*Against Praxeas*, 7).
[9] For a "process" view, see e.g. Charles Hartshorne, *Man's Vision of God*

(Hamden CT: Archon Books, 1964) or *The Logic of Perfection* (LaSalle, Ill.: Open Court, 1963). For a sample feminist see Sallie McFague, *Models of God* (Philadelphia: Fortress Press, 1987). See also Grace Jantzen, *God's World, God's Body* (Philadelphia: Fortress, 1984); Richard Swinburne, *The Coherence of Theism*, 2d ed. (N.Y.: Oxford University Press, 1993); Marcel Sarot, *God, Passibility and Corporeality* (Kampen: Kok Pharos, 1992). Sarot provides an extensive bibliography.

[10] Swinburne, *Coherence*, 104–5; Charles Taliaferro, *Consciousness and the Mind of God* (N.Y.: Cambridge University Press, 1994), 116–8.

[11] At least one account of embodiment is possible in God's but not in our case: one could hold that God has a non-material body by holding that there is an absolute Space, independent of matter, and it is God's body. As I cannot imagine a reason to believe this, I do not pursue it.

[12] Unless problems of coherence require otherwise. If being greater than all else in respect A and being greater than all else in respect B are not compatible, the perfect-being thinker must try to see which respect matters more to the overall greatness of God, and say that He is greatest in that respect.

[13] Unless the non-divine part of the universe is wholly valueless. But saying this would raise its own questions. For either God made this part or He did not. If He did, then apparently God acted irrationally in making it, for if something has absolutely no value in any respect, there can be no reason to produce it. If He did not, God is not the source of all things which are not God, violating a primary tenet of theism.

[14] Were God incarnate qua God, then since all three Persons are God, all three Persons would be incarnate.

[15] The universe is of course larger than Christ—but than Christ *qua* human, not *qua* God.

[16] It is Christ's, but qua human, not qua God.

[17] What it *does* rest on is a long story I cannot broach here.

[18] So too Wainwright, "God's Body," 79. On a Platonist view, each part of the body is part of the human, but not part of the person, since the person = the soul.

[19] The doctrine of the Incarnation does not entail that Jesus' body was part of God. So it escapes this point, and all others in this section which trade on the claim that parts of the universe are parts of God.

[20] So Wainwright, "God's Body," 75–6.

[21] So Lactantius, *Divine Institutes*, quoted at Taliaferro, *Consciousness*, 334.

[22] Taliaferro, *Consciousness*, 252–3, and Wainwright, "God's Body," 76, also give this horn of this argument.

[23] This is what philosophers call a *sorites* argument. For a survey and analysis, see Timothy Williamson, *Vagueness* (N.Y.: Routledge, 1994).

[24] Some argue that there are vague cases of identity and composition (e.g. Peter Van Inwagen, *Material Beings* (Ithaca, N.Y.: Cornell University Press, 1992)).

But if there are any, they are vague cases of non-degreed relations, and I would argue that the best way to explicate them is not by taking vagueness as a matter of degrees of identity. David Lewis construes the part-relation as a form of partial identity (see *Parts of Classes* (Basil Blackwell)). But again, he does so without allowing degrees of partial identity, i.e. of parthood.

[25] Swinburne, *Coherence*, 105.

[26] Swinburne, *Coherence*, 104.

[27] Swinburne believes in an immaterial soul, and holds that states of this soul have real effects in other states of the soul (Richard Swinburne, *The Evolution of the Soul* (N.Y.: Oxford University Press, 1986), 82–4). If so, he would likely grant that one thought could be a total cause of another thought, in having which I feel psychological or emotional pain.

[28] Swinburne, *Coherence*, 104.

[29] Ibid.

[30] Swinburne mentions two other embodying relations. But as his case for God's embodiment does not appeal to them, I pass them by.

[31] Swinburne, *Coherence*, 105.

[32] Unless the universe is functionally a divine brain—a claim which to my knowledge nobody has dared to make.

[33] In fact, if God is already embodied in a universe, then if I was right earlier in arguing that an embodied God could not make a second, discrete universe, the most an embodied God could create would be not a universe, but a further part of the universe which already embodies Him.

[34] I have said that God may move wholes by moving parts, or parts by moving wholes, or both wholes and parts directly (as He would in willing directly that my car move and willing directly that its wheels spin—in which case God overdetermines the whole's motion) or (as in my last scenario) both wholes and parts indirectly. These distinctions may seem specious. After all, one thinks, the whole just is the sum of its parts, and so moving the whole by moving the parts must (it seems) be no different from moving the parts by moving the whole. In either case, the same matter moves. But where the parts are sub-atomic particles and the whole is (say) a human being, the whole in one sense is not the sum of its parts. Even if there is no more matter in a human than in the particles composing the human, the whole may well have properties qua human which go beyond its properties qua mass of particles. Again, if Professor Moriarty steals the English crown, he may mean to steal the crown, or only to steal the gold of which it is made. He walks off with the same matter either way, but which intent he has makes a difference later on—he either melts the crown into an ingot, or keeps it intact and struts about his lair wearing it. So either Moriarty intended to steal the crown, and as part of this stole the gold of which it is made, or Moriarty intended to steal the gold, and in order to do so stole the crown. In the one case stealing the crown and in the other stealing the gold are incidental to what

Moriarty means to do—and so it is not specious to say (depending on his intent) either that Moriarty stole the gold by stealing the crown or that he stole the crown by stealing the gold.

[35] *Summa Theologiae* (ST) Ia 45, 5; *Summa Contra Gentiles* II, 21; *De Potentia* 3, 4.

[36] See *ST* Ia 104, 1.

[37] Some physicists speculate that though time does not extend backward infinitely, the world had no first moment (see e.g. Stephen Hawking, *A Brief History of Time* (N.Y.: Bantam Books, 1988), 136–41. They think, then, that there has been just a finite amount of time, but before each time there were other times: as if time asymptotically approached an origin outside time, without ever reaching it. If this is true, then in the narrow sense, God does not create the world, but at each time, He conserves it: for at each time, He causes it to exist, and it had existed earlier. In the broader sense of "creates," if Hawking is right, God creates by conserving.

[38] If God is in time, this "before" may be temporal. If He is not, it is not, but is instead a way of logically representing relations among things God timelessly knows and does.

[39] The bare fact that the states of affairs *the Earth's existing* and *the Earth's being here at t* are distinct does not entail that the acts which effect them are distinct. By one and the same arm-motion I bring it about that the ball moves and that the ball moves toward the infield. The states of affairs are distinct, since the ball can move in other directions too. But I make just one arm-motion and one throw.

[40] Or by creating, if He so acts as to cause some things to be in motion at the world's first instant (if there is one).

[41] In Aquinas' sense: see *ST* I–IIa 17, 4.

[42] *ST* I–IIa 17, 4.

[43] This is false only if there can be telekinesis, and it can fail to involve any use of one's brain.

[44] For one source of this, see *Psalm* 139.

[45] *Jeremiah* 23:23–24.

[46] *Psalm* 139:1–10.

[47] In the Hermetic corpus, one reads that "God is a circle whose center is everywhere and whose circumference is nowhere." Perhaps the Hermetic writer had something like this in mind.

[48] With obvious debts to Boethius.

[49] Here "ever" has the force "at some time." If God is timeless, the parts of His life never end in this sense: at no time is it true of any of them that it has ended.

[50] See *I Corinthians* 15: 18–9.

[51] Tertullian (in his orthodox phase), Athenagoras and Justin.

[52] While Thomas holds that our *souls* never perish, he is clear that we are not our souls, and while our souls exist unembodied, *we* do not exist (see his commen-

tary on *I Corinthians* 15).

[53] Here I can only sketch some aspects of this, and cannot answer the questions the sketch raises. For a much fuller treatment, see my *Time and Eternity* (Ithaca, N.Y.: Cornell University Press, 1991).

[54] There is a strong case that this does not in any way remove our freedom. For its classic version, see Boethius, *The Consolation of Philosophy* V, 6; for an update, see my *Time and Eternity*, 246–66.

[55] Can't I regret a sin while I commit it? What I regret as I (say) finish telling the lie is that it is now too late not to have lied—i.e. that the point at which I could have avoided the lie has passed.

6

Absolute Simplicity

Eleonore Stump and Norman Kretzmann

Abstract

The doctrine of God's absolute simplicity denies the possibility of real distinctions in God. It is. e.g., impossible that God have any kind of parts or any intrinsic accidental properties or that there be real distinctions among God's essential properties or between any of them and God himself. After showing that some of the counter-intuitive implications of the doctrine can readily be made sense of, the authors identify the apparent incompatibility of God's simplicity and God's free choice as a special difficulty and associate it with two others: the apparent incompatibilities between essential omnipotence and essential goodness, and between perfect goodness and moral goodness. Since all three of these difficulties are associated with a certain understanding of the nature of God's will, the authors base their resolution of them on an account of will in general and of God's will in particular, drawing on Aquinas's theory of will.

Taking creation as their paradigm or divine free choice, the authors develop a solution of the principal incompatibility based on three claims: (i) God's acts of choice are both free and conditionally necessitated; (ii) the difference between absolutely and conditionally necessitated acts of will is not a real distinction in God; and (iii) the conditional necessity of God's acts of will is compatible with contingency in the objects of those acts. The heart of their solution consists in their attempt to make sense of and support those claims. The authors extend their solution to cover the two associated apparent incompatibilities as well.

The article concludes with observations on the importance or the doctrine of God's absolute simplicity for resolving problems in religious morality and in the cosmological argument.

1. The doctrine of divine simplicity and some of its difficulties

The doctrine that God is absolutely simple derives from the metaphysical considerations that have led philosophers and theologians to maintain that God is a being whose existence is self-explanatory, an absolutely perfect being or pure actuality.[1] We are not concerned here with the foundations of the doctrine, however; for our present purposes we take the doctrine as a datum,[2] referring the reader to its classical derivation in Augustine, Anselm, and Aquinas, for instance.

Because the doctrine is notoriously difficult, and because our treatment of it will emphasize its difficulties, it is worth noting at the outset that simplicity also offers advantages for constructive rational theology. For instance, it provides a way out of a dilemma for religious morality and a way of strengthening the cosmological argument; as we will try to show in the last section of our paper.

Despite its metaphysical credentials, its long-established position at the center of orthodox Christianity's doctrine of God, and its advantages for rational theology, the doctrine of simplicity is not used much in contemporary philosophy of religion, primarily because it seems outrageously counter-intuitive, or even incoherent. In attributing a radical unity to God, and to God alone, it rules out the possibility of there being in God any of the real distinctions on the basis of which we make sense of our cognition of other real things. The doctrine's general denial of distinctions can be sorted out into several specific claims, three of which will be enough for our purposes.

The first two are claims of a sort that might also be made about numbers, for instance; only the third is peculiar to divine simplicity. (1) It is impossible that God have any spatial or temporal parts that could be distinguished from one another as here rather than there or as now rather than then, and so God cannot be a physical entity. Next, the standard distinction between an entity's essential and accidental intrinsic properties cannot apply to God: (2) It is impossible that God have any intrinsic accidental properties.

Before going on to the third claim, it may be useful to say a little about the familiar distinction between intrinsic and extrinsic properties, between real properties and Cambridge properties, on which we rely in claim (2). We do not know of a satisfactory criterion for precisely distinguishing intrinsic or real properties from extrinsic or Cambridge properties, but the distinction is widely recognized and sometimes easy to draw. For present purposes it is perhaps enough to say that a change in x's extrinsic properties can occur without a change in x, while a change in x's intrinsic properties is as such a change in x., Ronald Reagan's belief that he is of Irish descent is one of his intrinsic accidental properties; his being mentioned in this article is an extrinsic accidental property of his. The intrinsic properties of numbers are all essential; numbers, like God, cannot have intrinsic accidental properties. But no entity, not even a mathematical or a divine entity, can be exempted from having extrinsic accidental properties.

The third of our claims illustrating the denial of distinctions in the doctrine of simplicity stems from the fact that the doctrine rules out the possibility of components of any kind in the divine nature. So even when it has been recognized that all God's intrinsic properties must be essential, it must be acknowledged as well that (3) It is impossible that there be any real distinction between one essential property and another in God; whatever can be intrinsically attributed to God must in reality be identical with the unity that is his essence. Furthermore, for all things other than God, there is a difference between what they are and that they are, between their essence and their existence; but on the doctrine of simplicity the essence which is God is not different from his existence. Unlike all other entities, God is his own being.

In these claims the counter-intuitive character of absolute simplicity emerges more flagrantly, as we can show by examining particular problems stemming from one or another of those denials of distinctions. The problems that are going to concern us are raised primarily by claims (2) and (3). From those claims it seems to follow, for instance, that God's knowledge is identical with God's power and also with anything that can be considered an intrinsic property of his such as one of God's actions, his talking to Cain, for instance. Moreover, God's talking to Cain must, it seems, be identical with talking to Abraham and, for that matter, with any other divine action, such as God's plaguing Pharaoh's Egypt with a hailstorm. And it is not only the drawing of distinctions among God's attributes or actions that is apparently misleading. God's talking to Cain is evidently not really an action of God's, as your talking is an action of yours, but rather part of God's essence. Even that formulation is apparently too broad:

> God's talking to Cain is not part of his essence; it is his essence, and God himself is identical with it.

These unreasonable apparent implications of the doctrine of simplicity lead to further embarrassments for the doctrine. If God's talking to Cain is essential to God, it is necessary and thus not something God could refrain from doing. Moreover, since God's talking to Cain begins at some instant, t1, it is apparently God's-talking-to-Cain-beginning-at-t1 that is essential and therefore necessary, so that it is not open to God even to initiate the conversation a split second earlier or later. So if in accordance with the doctrine of simplicity each action of God's is in all its detail identical with the divine essence, the doctrine entails that God could not do anything other or otherwise than he actually does. Indeed, given the doctrine of simplicity, it is not clear that God can talk to Cain at all, even under the severe restrictions just considered. Every temporal action, unless it is coextensive with all of time, begins and/or ends. If it is true that God talks to Cain, then at t1 God is talking to Cain and sometime after t1 God is not talking to Cain. But in that case it seems that God has an intrinsic property at one time which he lacks at another time, and no such distinction is possible under the doctrine of simplicity.

2. Resolving some of the difficulties

Many, but not all, of these counter-intuitive appearances can he dispelled by clarifying the view of God's nature that gives rise to the doctrine of simplicity and by developing the distinction between intrinsic and extrinsic properties. In virtue of being absolutely perfect God has no unactualized potentialities but is entirely actual, or in act. No temporal entity could satisfy that description,[6] and so no temporal entity could be a perfect being. Nevertheless, the atemporal pure actuality that is God can have various manifestations and effects in time.[7] It is in that way that there is a mistake in thinking of God's talking to Cain as one of the things God does in the strict sense in which a temporal agent's action is an intrinsic property of the agent. Rather, the one thing that is God and is atemporally actual has a variety of effects in time: a conversation with Cain at t1, a conversation with Abraham at t2, and the production of a hailstorm in Egypt at t3. Of course God's talking to Cain is not the same as God's talking to Abraham, hut that undoubted distinction does not compromise God's absolute simplicity because those events are to be understood as various temporal effects of the single eternal act identical with God, God's action in the strict sense. Everyone recognizes analogous characterizations of ordinary human actions: the man who flips the switch on the wall may be correctly described as doing just that one thing or he may, equally correctly, be said to do many things in doing that one thing (turning on the light, waking the dog, frightening the prowler, etc.)—a case of one action with many correct descriptions or many consequences, of one action in the strict sense and many actions in a broader sense. But in this ordinary case there are many really distinct facts about that one action—that it results in the turning on of the light, that it results in the waking of the dog, etc. If the conversation with Cain and the hailstorm in Egypt are analogous to these, won't there be many really distinct facts about God's one action and thus, in that special case, about God himself? Yes, but not in a way that compromises simplicity. As a standard characterization of the single divine action we can use Aquinas's formulation.. "God wills himself and other things in one act of will" (SCG I 76). As Aquinas understands it, God's willing himself and other things consists in God's willing at once, in one action, both goodness and the manifestation of goodness,[8] and there is no special difficulty in understanding goodness to be manifested differently to different persons on different occasions (even in the form of different speeches or meteorological displays appropriate to different circumstances) in ways that must be counted among the extrinsic accidental properties of the goodness manifested.

The absence of real distinctions among divine attributes such as omnipotence and omniscience is to be explained along similar lines. According to the doctrine of simplicity, what human beings call God's omnipotence or God's omniscience is the single eternal action considered under descriptions they find variously illuminating, or recognized by them under different kinds of effects or manifestations of it. What the doctrine requires one to understand about all the designations for the divine attributes is that they are all identical in reference but different in sense, referring in various ways to the one actual entity which is God himself or designating various manifestations of it. 'Perfect power' and 'perfect knowledge' are precise analogues for 'the morning star' and 'the evening star': non-synonymous expressions designating quite distinct manifestations of one and the same thing. There are as much truth and as much potential misinformation in 'Perfect power is identical with perfect knowledge' as there are in the morning star is identical with the evening star'—and 'Perfect power is identical with perfect knowledge' does not entail that power is identical with knowledge any more than the fact that the summit of a mountain's east slope is identical with the summit of its west slope entails the identity of the slopes.[9]

Most of the problems we have so far raised about absolute simplicity are resolved or at least alleviated on the basis of these considerations. The respect in which God is utterly devoid of real distinctions does not, after all, preclude our conceptually distinguishing God's actions in the world from one another or from God himself. And insofar as an eternal being can eternally produce various temporal effects, variously timed, nothing in the doctrine of simplicity rules out God's intervention in time.[10] But these difficulties for absolute simplicity strike us as the easy ones; the hardest one to resolve is the apparent incompatibility of God's simplicity and God's free choice. For all we have said so far, the doctrine of simplicity still seems to entail that the only things God can do are the things he does in fact.[11]

3. The apparent incompatibility of simplicity and free choice

Since no one whose will is bound to just one set of acts of will makes real choices, it looks as if accepting God's absolute simplicity as a datum leads to the conclusion that God lacks freedom of choice. If we begin from the other direction, by taking it for granted that God does make choices—another central tenet of Christian theology—it seems God cannot be absolutely simple. For the doctrine of divine free choice can be construed as the claim that some of God's properties are properties he chooses to have—such as his being the person who talks to Cain at t1. But it makes no sense to suppose that God freely chooses all his properties, so that it is up to him, for example, whether or not the principle of non-contradiction applies to him, or whether he is omnipotent, good, eternal, or simple. Considerations of this sort evidently require us to draw a distinction between two groups of God's properties: those that are freely chosen and those regarding which he has no choice. And this distinction, it seems, must be intrinsic to God. It cannot be explained as only a reflection of diversity in the temporal effects brought about by the single eternal activity which is God, or as no more than different manifestations of a single active goodness. Instead, this distinction appears to express a radical diversity within divine agency itself, in that some truths about God—such as that he exists—are not subject to his control, while others—presumably such as that he talks to Cain at t1—are consequences of his free choice.[12] Nor can this distinction be explained away as an instance of referring to one and the same thing under different descriptions in ways suited to human minds, which can acquire only fragmentary conceptions of the absolute unity that is God. As we have already indicated, we think there is no inconsistency in the claim that an absolutely simple entity is correctly described as omnipotent regarded in one way and as omniscient regarded in another way. But recourse to the human point of view appears to be unavailable as a basis for explaining the apparent distinction between necessary and non-necessary divine properties. Moves in that direction would either present the necessary properties as really indeterminate or deny free choice to God, by suggesting that the appearance of free choice in God is really only a consequence of certain extrinsic accidental properties of his or by presenting the apparently freely chosen properties as not really objects of God's choice.[13] So our earlier defense of absolute simplicity against imputations of inconsistency cannot reconcile divine simplicity with divine freedom of choice.

4. Two related apparent incompatibilities

The apparent incompatibility of freedom of choice and simplicity in God strikes us as closely connected with two others. Because our proposed resolution of the first incompatibility has some bearing on the other two, we will present them briefly before developing our resolution.

In the first place. there seems to be an inconsistency in the concept of a being that is supposed to be both essentially omnipotent and essentially perfectly good.[14]

An acceptable definition of omnipotence is notoriously hard to formulate,[15] but any serious candidate has at its core the idea that an omnipotent person can do anything logically possible. An essentially perfectly good person, however. cannot perform any evil action, or is essentially impeccable. Since evil actions are among the logical possibilities. there are many things an essentially perfectly good person cannot do which, on the face of it, an omnipotent person must be able to do. And so it seems that no person can be essentially both omnipotent and perfectly good (as God is said to be).

The second of these two associated apparent incompatibilities lies within the notion of essential perfect goodness itself. Some important accounts of perfect goodness have emphasized desirability, which surely is to be acknowledged as the passive, esthetic aspect of goodness; but any acceptable notion of perfect goodness must also include its active, moral aspect. The notion of a morally good (or evil) person seems to entail that person's capacity to do both good and evil, however, and on that classic understanding of moral agency the idea of a person who is essentially morally good is inconsistent. The classic understanding might be sketched in this way: A person P in a world w1 is morally good in deciding to perform action x at time t only if there is some possible world w2 like w1 in all respects up to t, but at t, in w2 P does not decide to perform action x but decides instead to do something evil. But a person who is essentially perfectly good is by definition a person who does only good in every possible world inhabited by that person. So it seems that one requirement for moral goodness (and hence for perfect goodness) is incompatible with one requirement for perfect goodness; and so no person can be essentially perfectly good (as God is said to be).

In our view these two problems are associated with our main problem regarding simplicity and choice because in all three of them the appearance of incompatibility between characteristics of a perfect being depends on a certain understanding of the nature of God's will. If God's will regarding his actions in time is thought to be free to choose evil, it seems God can be neither absolutely simple nor essentially good. On the other hand, if in an attempt to preserve simplicity and essential perfect goodness God is conceived of as incapable of choosing evil, it seems he can be neither omnipotent nor morally good.

Our three apparent incompatibilities are generated by adding to perfect-being theology the familiar assumption that a free will is essentially an independent, neutral capacity for choosing among alternatives. Our attempt to dispel these appearances of incompatibility depends on replacing the assumption with a theory we take to be both helpful and plausible: Aquinas's account of the will as a natural inclination toward goodness associated with the agent's understanding of goodness.[17]

5. Will

Although Aquinas is convinced that freedom of choice is a characteristic of human wills as well as of God's will, his general account of the nature of will presents it as fundamentally neither independent nor neutral:

> In their own way, all things are inclined by an *appetitus*[18] toward what is good, but variously.... Some things.. are inclined toward what is good along with an awareness of the nature of the good—a condition that is a distinguishing characteristic of an intellect—and these are the things most fully inclined toward what is good. Indeed, they are, so to speak, directed to the good not merely by something else (as are things that lack cognition), or directed only to some good in particular (as are things that have only sense cognition); instead, they are as

if inclined toward goodness itself considered universally. And that inclination is
called *will*.[19]

General and specific links between will and goodness are built into this definition. Will is understood by Aquinas not as an equipoised capacity, but rather
as falling under the genus of natural inclinations toward what is good. And what
distinguishes will from other species of that genus (such as the instincts to seek
food and shelter) is will's essential association with intellect rather than merely
with sensation (*appetitus rationalis vs appetitus sensitivus*). In associating will
with intellect (as the appetitive and cognitive faculties of the rational soul)
Aquinas means to claim, among other things, that will, naturally inclined toward
goodness itself considered universally, inclines the agent toward subsidiary ends
which the intellect presents to the will as good. Will understood as naturally
inclined toward goodness and as relying to a considerable extent on intellect is
obviously neither neutral nor independent, and such an account of its nature is
bound to raise questions about its freedom and its capacity for genuine choice.
But, as can be seen in the quoted passage, Aquinas also understands will to be
self-directed and to be presented with more than one particular good: moreover,
he expressly argues elsewhere that human beings do have free choice (*liberum
arbitrium*).[20] His conviction that all these features can be consistently and plausibly ascribed to will is founded on an analysis of necessity that is incorporated
into his theory of will.

In general, on Aquinas's view what is necessary is what cannot not be; the
species of necessity are sorted out on the basis of the four Aristotelian causal
principles. Two of those principles—matter and form—are intrinsic to what is
necessitated, and necessity of the sort associated with them is exemplified.
Thomas says,

> with respect to an intrinsic *material* principle when we say that it is necessary
> that everything with contrary components be perishable, or with respect to an
> intrinsic *formal* principle when we say that it is necessary that a triangle have
> three angles equal to two right angles. (ST Ia q. 82, a. 1)

Necessity of both these sorts Aquinas calls "absolute" (or "natural"). The two
extrinsic causal principles, on the other hand, are associated with two distinct
sorts of necessity. The "necessity of the *end*, sometimes called utility" is exemplified when something is recognized as necessary in that someone cannot attain,
or cannot readily attain, some end without it—as food is necessary for life, and
a horse for a journey. (ibid.)

Finally, the necessity associated with *efficient* causation, "the necessity of
coercion,"

> occurs whenever someone is compelled by some agent so that he cannot do the
> contrary [of what he is compelled to do]. (ibid.)

On this basis the obvious questions raised by the directedness and dependency of the will as understood by Aquinas can be answered. Isn't a will that is naturally directed toward goodness naturally necessitated and hence unfree? The will's being directed toward goodness, the ultimate end for all things, is naturally necessitated; but that natural necessity, far from threatening freedom, is a precondition of the will's making choices. Aquinas, following Aristotle, takes the will's activity of choice to depend on its inclination toward the ultimate end as the intellect's activity of reasoning depends on its grasp of the first principles.[21] Choice, as distinct from whim or chance, is motivated, and some motives are subsidiary to others, happiness being the supreme motive or highest good for human beings. So the ultimate end, recognized as a precondition of choice, lies outside the scope of choice, the objects of which are means or subsidiary ends leading more or less directly to that necessitated end or, more broadly, things willed for the end.

Still, doesn't the end necessitate the means? Necessity of the end in its weak, horse-for-journey variety obviously poses no threat to freedom of choice: you can walk rather than ride. Thomas takes it to be no more threatening in its strong, food-for-life variety, presumably because even when an end such as the continuation of one's life cannot be attained without a specific means such as food, one can choose to reject the end—a presumption that is even more plausible in his other example of this variety: "from the volition to cross the sea comes the necessity in the will of wanting a ship" (ST Ia q. 82. a. 1). In the strongest and most clearly relevant variety of necessity of the end, the ultimate end, happiness, is itself absolutely necessary and hence impossible to reject; but the necessity of the end appropriate to human happiness is the weak variety, allowing for choices among more or less (or equally) efficacious means to the unrejectable end.

Even if this summary account of will's involvement with necessity of the sorts associated with matter, form, and end is given the benefit of the doubts it is likely to raise, it answers only questions raised by the natural directedness of will. But what about will's dependence on intellect? Can't that be construed as involving necessity of the sort associated with efficient causation, the one sort of necessitation Thomas admits is incompatible with freedom of will?

The plainest, most familiar evidence that the intellect, in presenting to the will what it conceives of as good, does not cause the will to will anything is that the intellect sometimes presents what it takes to be equally good alternatives, offering no supplementary considerations on which the will might base its choice among the alternatives. A more theory-laden but no less effective sort of evidence is available in a closer look at Aquinas's conception of the relationship between intellect and will. When the intellect presents what it takes to be good, without alternatives, the intellect does indeed move the will, but only as an end moves an agent, "because what is conceived of as good is an object of the will and moves it as an end" (ST Ia q. 82, a. 4). The only necessity emanating from the intellect, then, is the necessity of the end, and we have already seen that such necessity does not preclude choice: the will can refrain from acting, rejecting a subsidiary end presented to it by the intellect. Even more important is the fact that the will also moves the intellect, and that this moving is carried out "in the way an agent moves something" (ibid.), the will compelling the intellect to attend to some things and to ignore others. So if there is efficient causation anywhere in the relationship between intellect and will, it occurs only in the will's occasional coercion of the intellect—a consideration that enhances rather than threatens the will's freedom. What the intellect comes to consider good is thus to some extent under the influence of the will, an influence that is especially powerful because almost everything that is an option for the will can be considered under different descriptions and can consequently be presented as good or as bad depending on which features of it are being attended to and which, are being ignored.

So the self-directedness or freedom of the will considered as its partial independence from the intellect is manifested in three capacities: (1) to choose among alternatives presented as equally good, (2) to refrain from pursuing a subsidiary end presented as good, and (3) to direct the intellect's attention.

Against the background of this much of Aquinas's theory of will we can sketch an account of moral goodness and evil sufficient for our purposes here. The will, a self-directed rational wanting of the good, can turn to evil in either of two ways. First, for various reasons ranging from ignorance to the complex interaction of will and intellect we have just summarized, the intellect can mistakenly present a bad thing as good or a good thing as better than it is. In the second place, the will of any temporal, imperfect entity is capable of leaving some of its potentialities unactualized, and so it is possible for a human will to do nothing even when presented with a genuine good. It follows that nothing in this theory of will or its accompanying explanation of morality requires will to have a capacity to choose evil over good. Evil does get chosen, of course, but only because it has been presented as good in some respect. And so the possibility of moral evil in the will stems from a defect in the agent whose will it is: it must be either that the agent's intellect is mistaken in its evaluation of the options or that the agent's will remains in a condition of potentiality when it should be actualized. It is for that reason that there is no possibility of moral evil in the will of an absolutely perfect being, whose intellect is incapable of error and whose will is eternally actual.

6. God's will

The divine will would not count as will at all if it were not like the human will in being essentially an inclination toward goodness as presented by intellect, but it differs from the human will in being characterized by only the first of the three capacities we picked out as manifesting the self-directedness of will—the capacity to choose among alternatives presented as equally good—in ways we will be considering. As for the second of those capacities, however, since an absolutely perfect being cannot have unactualized potentialities, God's will is entirely actual, or in act, and so has no capacity to refrain from willing anything presented by God's intellect as good without alternatives, And as for the third of those capacities, since God's intellect is likewise entirely actualized, it could not attend to one thing rather than another even if God's will could be imagined, *per impossibile*, as willing that his intellect be directed in such a way.

That difference between the ways in which the divine will and the human will manifest self-directedness reflects the perfection of the former and the imperfection of the latter, For instance, the necessary impeccability of God's will, considered in Section 4 above, is to be understood in terms of these considerations. God's will cannot manifest self-directedness by refraining from choosing between alternatives or from willing what is presented to it as good without alternatives, because it is entirely in act; and so it cannot bring about moral evil by failing to will when it should. And since God's intellect cannot be ignorant of anything, because it is eternally omniscient, it cannot present a mistaken assessment of goodness. It is for those two reasons that neither of the ways in which a will comes to be responsible for evil can characterize the will of God.

But it is not only in lacking two of the modes in which imperfect wills manifest self-directedness that the divine will differs from the human. God's will is also correctly described as self-directed in a way that cannot characterize human wills. Every human will is so constituted as to have happiness as its specific natural end, regardless of its intellect's level of understanding of that goal. God's will, on the other hand, has its natural end, the universal ultimate end, simply in virtue of his perfect understanding of the nature of goodness. Since God is omniscient, he knows himself perfectly; and, in accord with the doctrine of simplicity, he is identical with his goodness, which is perfect goodness itself. Therefore, what God's intellect infallibly discerns as perfect goodness is God himself. And so God's will, which necessarily wills what God's intellect understands to be absolutely good and presents as such to the will, necessarily wills the divine nature: "God necessarily wills his own goodness, and he cannot will the contrary" (SCG I 80).

Although God's willing perfect goodness is necessary, as is a human being's willing happiness, the differences between the divine and human wills in this respect are more significant than that similarity. The essential inclination of the human will toward happiness is part of the constitution of human beings, which they are caused to have, regarding which they are as unfree as they are regarding being animal. Consequently, it can be misleading to describe human beings even as willing their natural end, which is simply what they find their wills essentially directed toward. But since God's willing of the ultimate end is self-directed in the way we have described, it is free in the sense of having no external cause, in having its sole source in God himself. And so for Aquinas it counts as genuine willing even though it cannot involve choice: "in respect of its principal object, which is its own goodness, the divine will does have necessity—not, of course, the necessity of coercion, but the necessity of natural order, which is not incompatible with freedom" (DV q. 23, a. 4). This necessity of natural order is the necessity of a perfect will's willing what a perfect intellect presents to it as perfectly good. It is a necessity compatible with freedom because the necessity of the willing stems only from the impossibility of any obstacle to the will's performing its self-directed function or of any defect in the will's functioning.

So the impression of incompatibility between God's free choice and absolute simplicity is lessened, if not entirely removed, by Aquinas's conception of God's will. When God's acts of will have himself as their object, they are necessary and hence not incompatible with simplicity; and yet their necessity is the necessity associated with a final cause when that final cause is clearly and fully understood as such, and necessity of that sort is not incompatible with the will's freedom.

Furthermore, Aquinas's theory of the nature of will in general and of God's will in particular is enough both to resolve the apparent incompatibility of omnipotence and impeccability and to allay worries about the compatibility of the freedom of the divine will and such conditionally necessitated divine acts as keeping the promise to Abraham. God's keeping his promise to Abraham is conditionally necessitated because once the promise has been made (the condition without which there is no necessitation), he cannot fail to keep it since promise-breaking is wrong (except in circumstances inapplicable to an omniscient, omnipotent being), and it is impossible for an essentially good person to do anything wrong. This sort of conditional necessitation is compatible with the freedom of the divine will in just the same way and for just the same reason as the absolute necessity of God's willing himself does not infringe God's freedom of choice. The necessity in each case is the necessity of the end. Since will is by its nature a self-directed wanting of the good, which is its final cause, when the goodness of some object (such as God's nature, or the keeping of a promise) is not overridden by other considerations, and when the intellect clearly and completely recognizes it as such (as an omniscient intellect cannot fail to do), then the will associated with that intellect necessarily wants that object, not because the will is compelled by anything outside itself to will the object, but because there is no defect or obstacle impeding the will from exercising its self-directed function. In this way God's keeping his promise to Abraham is both freely willed and necessitated by its goodness, which is the final, not the efficient, cause of that divine act. And analogous considerations will apply to any act which is said to be impossible for God to will because it would be evil for him to do so. Consequently, the paradox of essential goodness is resolved on the basis of Aquinas's theory of will: there is no absurdity in postulating a perfectly good moral agent for whom doing evil is impossible. Furthermore, so far from being incompatible with impeccability, omnipotence in fact entails impeccability on Thomas's theory of will: if the will and its intellect are not defective—that is, if a being is perfect in power with respect to its will and intellect—it follows that that being is impeccable, since only a being defective in intellect or will ever wills evil.

An important part of the apparent incompatibility between divine free choice and absolute simplicity is still left unresolved, however, because it is only God's nature (perfect goodness identical with himself) and conditionally necessitated acts of will (such as keeping his promise) that God is said to will in such a way that he cannot will the contrary, either absolutely or conditionally. His willing of other things is said to be characterized not merely by the absence of any coercion but also by freedom of choice, According to Aquinas, the reason for this difference is that "the ultimate end is God himself, since he is the highest good" (SCG I 74), and "since God wills himself as the end but other things as things that are for the end, it follows that in respect of himself he has only volition, but in respect of other things he has selection (*electio*). Selection, however, is always accomplished by means of free choice" (SCG I 88). Of course these passages must not be read as claiming that God wills his own goodness as the end and everything else he wills as *means* to that end, with the implication that perfect goodness (or God himself) is in the process of becoming fully actualized or is in need of things other than itself for its perfection. Thomas's point is that God's goodness is the final cause for the sake of which he wills other things. So, for example, God wills that a certain sort of animal be rational in order to make a human being, he wills to make a human being in order to complete his making of the universe, and he wills to make the universe because it is good—that is, for the sake of goodness, with which he is identical and which is the end, the final cause, of all his actions (SCG I 86). But that end can be served in various ways, and therein lie the alternatives without which free choice could not be ascribed to God, God might have chosen to create a different universe, provided it was good and created because it was good—e.g., a universe with different physical laws, different elements, different forms of life. And there is reason to suppose that a more fundamental sort of alternative is also open to him. Since goodness, the end served by his actions, is present and perfect even if nothing else exists, because he himself is identical with perfect goodness, it seems open to him not to create at all.

In willing things other than his own nature, then, God's will is not absolutely necessitated to will what it wills. But it does not follow that all the acts of God's will within the created universe, for example, can be instances of free choice. If God does freely choose to make the promise to Abraham, then some divine actions—such as willing that the promise be communicated to Abraham—will be necessitated by logical considerations, while others will be necessitated by moral considerations—such as willing that the promise be fulfilled, For reasons already stated, neither of those forms of necessitation constitutes a restriction on God's will, but they do preclude ascribing freedom of choice to every divine action having to do with creatures.

So far, then, it may look as if the acts of God's will can be classified into three sorts: first, the one absolutely necessary act of willing himself; second, acts contingent in themselves but conditionally necessitated either logically or morally; and, third, acts that are not only contingent but freely chosen. But an analysis of God's acts of will that entails contingency in God does seem to leave God's willing incompatible with God's simplicity. Any hope of showing the incompatibility to be only apparent must rest on a different analysis of God's acts of will.

Before introducing such an analysis, we want to replace our hitherto serviceable paradigms of God's free choice. There are two reasons why talking to Cain or to Abraham and subjecting Egypt to a hailstorm are not the sort of actions best suited to provide paradigms of free choice or most threatening to simplicity. In the first place, the clearest instances of free choice are cases of choosing between equally good contrary alternatives, and it is far from clear that *not* counseling Cain, *not* promising Abraham a glorious progeny, or *not* punishing a recalcitrant Pharaoh are alternatives as good as those God chooses. In the second place, as we have seen, all such actions in the world are at least *prima facie* explicable as extrinsic accidental characteristics of the unique divine action, various manifestations of the eternal diffusion of divine goodness. But there is an act of the divine will that seems (a) distinguishable from God's willing of himself, (b) representable as a choice between equally good alternatives, and (c) not even *prima facie* explicable as no more than an extrinsic accidental characteristic of God's willing of himself—and that is God's choosing to create. So for the remainder of this discussion we will take creation as the paradigm of God's free choice, although much of what we have to say about this crucial case will apply as well to any other genuine case of divine choice.

7. *A solution to the problem of God's simplicity and God's free choice*

Aquinas's solution to the problem represented in the three-part classification of God's acts of will consists fundamentally in claiming that the third group, those acts that are freely chosen, are like those of the second group in being conditionally necessitated.[22] Because of the implications of absolute simplicity,Thomas believes that the logical distinction between conditionally and absolutely necessitated acts of divine will does not constitute a real distinction within the divine nature.[23] Consequently, he holds both that God has free choice and that there is no contingency in God himself. Instead, God's nature is altogether necessary, either absolutely or conditionally. And yet Aquinas also maintains that this view of God's nature, this interpretation of absolute simplicity, is entirely compatible with the claim that there is contingency in the created world;

the necessity of the Creator and his act of creating does not preclude contingency in what is created.[24]

And so Aquinas's solution to the apparent incompatibility between God's simplicity and God's free choice rests on three highly counter-intuitive claims:

(i) God's acts of choice are both free and conditionally necessitated;
(ii) the difference between absolutely and conditionally necessitated acts of will is not a real, metaphysical distinction in God's nature; and
(iii) the conditional necessity of God's acts of will is compatible with contingency in the object of those acts of will.

It seems to us that if those three claims can be made sense of and adequately supported, God's free choice and absolute simplicity will have been shown to be compatible after all. In that event, what strikes us as the hardest of the problems for the doctrine of simplicity will have been resolved, and the doctrine will have been resuscitated as a respectable, useful part of philosophical theology. We will consider each of the three claims in order.

7(i). Freedom and conditional necessity

On Aquinas's view, any divine act that is an instance of free choice, such as creation, is necessitated conditionally, but not absolutely. It is not absolutely necessitated because, to put it roughly and briefly, the proposition 'God does not create' does not by itself entail a contradiction.[25] That God's willing to create (or any other act of divine free choice) is conditionally necessitated is a consequence of God's eternality. Because God is timeless, no change in him is possible. If he does will to create, then, it is not possible for him to change and will not to create. Nor can it be supposed that it is open to God either to create or not to create and that he exercises his option to create, because of course this supposition also entails a change in God: that he is first in the state of neither willing to create nor willing not to create and then is in the state of willing to create. So because he is eternal, since he does will to create, the state of not willing to create cannot be attributed to him. Willing to create, then, is necessary to God, but only conditionally necessary, where the condition is the fact that he does will to create.

And so, (A) it is not logically possible for a timeless and otherwise simple being that creates not to create. That observation about God may seem trivial, for it may seem precisely analogous to this observation about a human being: (B) it is not logically possible for the entity that is Socrates and running not to be running. And observation (B) is trivial because, of course, (C) it is logically possible for Socrates not to be running. Although it is necessary that if Socrates is running he is running, it is not necessary that Socrates is running.

Both claims (B) and (C) may be made about Socrates because Socrates can be dissociated from his running in two ways. In the first place, running is just an (intrinsic) accident of Socrates's; Socrates would be Socrates even if he never ran. In the second place, the sort of necessity with which running is connected to Socrates is just the necessity of the present. On the supposition that Socrates is in fact running now, that present state of affairs cannot now be otherwise. And yet, we are entitled to assume, before now it was open to Socrates either to run now or not to run now—i.e., before now Socrates could have exercised (and presumably did exercise) free choice regarding his running now.

But neither of those ways of dissociating Socrates from his running in order to show the triviality of (B) can be used to dissociate God from his creating (or choosing to create[26]), to show that (A) is trivial in the way (B) is. We cannot dissociate God from his creating by claiming that his creating is an intrinsic accident of his, because on the doctrine of simplicity God has no intrinsic accidents. Nor can we dissociate God from his creating merely by pointing out that the necessity with which creating is connected to him does not preclude his freely choosing not to create, because it is not clear that that is true in God's case. The reason why the necessity of Socrates's running while he is running does not preclude his freely choosing not to run is that before the time of his running Socrates could have brought it about that he not be running at that later time. But nothing of that sort can be said of God with regard to his creating. His act of creating is a timeless action in the eternal present, and so it is logically impossible for there to be anything before his act of creating and consequently logically impossible that before the eternal present God do something to bring it about that he does not create in the eternal present.

And yet God's creating is not itself logically necessary or necessitated absolutely; it is not entailed by the laws of logic or by the nature of deity or by the combination of them. Because God is eternal and consequently immutable, we cannot accurately say that God could have willed not to create. But because God's willing to create is not absolutely necessary, we can correctly say that it might have been the case that God willed not to create. If we suppose that the actual world is a world in which God wills to create, then on the doctrine of simplicity (which entails God's eternality), although there are possible worlds in which God wills not to create, none of those worlds lies along any branches of the time-line of the actual world. Considered in the abstract, God's not creating is logically possible; it is for that reason that God's creating is not absolutely necessary. But given that God is timeless and does will to create, there cannot be a branch of the world's time-line on which not willing to create is correctly ascribed to him. And so God's willing to create is necessary, but only conditionally, given the fact that he does create. And nothing in this sort of necessity impugns the freedom of his will, because which logical possibility is actualized and which logical possibility is left unactualized depends on nothing other than God's will. And yet his willing is necessitated since *as things are* it is not possible that not willing to create ever be correctly ascribed to him.

According to this account, one we think is faithful to the spirit of Aquinas's position on these issues, God is not the same in all possible worlds. That result seems to raise difficulties for other features of Aquinas's conception of God's nature—e.g., for the interpretation of absolute simplicity as entailing the absence of contingency and of accidental properties in God. But the notion of contingent or accidental properties that is operative in Aquinas's understanding of simplicity (the one on which we are building) is confined to one or another set of worlds. The counter-intuitive character of the claims we are now investigating is naturally a function of twentieth-century philosophical intuitions, and it is clear that Aquinas's conceptions of contingency and essentiality differ from those taken for granted by most of us now. The fact that he maintains views entailing both that there is no contingency in God and that God's status as creator is not a feature of God in every possible world strongly suggests that he does not conceive of contingency in terms of differences across possible worlds generally but, rather, in terms of branching time-lines emanating from a single possible initial world-state. And so we propose taking Thomas's 'essential', 'necessary', 'accidental'. and 'contingent' to refer to modalities that can be determined by inspecting some subset of possible worlds consisting of the branching time-lines emanating from a single possible initial world-state—an initial-state set, we will call it.

In a sense, then, we are weakening the claims basic to the doctrine of simplicity. When Thomas maintains that there is only necessity in God, and that whatever is true of him is essentially true of him, we take him to mean the following: Within any initial-state set of possible worlds God's nature is fully and immutably determinate, and it is so as a consequence of the single, timeless act of will in which God wills goodness (himself) and whatever else (if anything) he wills for the sake of goodness in that initial-state set.

Finally, it may seem that Aquinas's position is nevertheless inconsistent; for consider an initial-state set in which God chooses not to create. Isn't it clear that in such a set of possible worlds God must have an unactualized potentiality, his potentiality to create?

Aquinas addresses questions of this sort in SCG I 82. There he argues—persuasively, it seems to us—that a will can have open to it an option which it does not take either (a) because it is not actualizing some potentiality it has, or (b) because there is more than one way, equally good, of actualizing the same potentiality. Albert Schweitzer, for example, had open to him the options of becoming either a medical missionary or a concert pianist, and it seems unreasonable to deny that in not opting for the latter career he left unactualized a potentiality he had—an instance of type (a). On the other hand, when the family doctor cures a child's strep throat with Keflex rather than with Ampicillin, it does not seem sensible to say that he leaves some potentiality of his unactualized. Instead, this seems to be an instance of type (b): there is an alternative that is not adopted because the state of the doctor's medical art is such that there is more than one, equally good way for the doctor to actualize his potentiality for practicing medicine.

On Thomas's view, such acts of divine will as creating are instances of type (b). God's end or aim is goodness; he wills what he wills for the sake of goodness. Since according to the doctrine of simplicity he himself is goodness, he is in this respect in the same position as the family doctor: there is more than one, equally good way in which he can achieve his aim, and one of those ways consists in willing just himself and not creating anything.[27] From this point of view it is misleading to say that God has a potentiality for creating—even an unactualized potentiality (in the case of the God-only world)—just as it would be inaccurate to say that the family doctor has an unactualized potentiality for prescribing Ampicillin rather than Keflex. Rather, if it makes sense to ascribe a potentiality to God at all, then God has a potentiality, invariably and ineluctably actualized, for willing goodness, and *this* potentiality is actualized in God's willing himself, whether or not he wills anything other than himself. Therefore, on Thomas's view, even the supposition that God does not will to create—probably the most troublesome supposition for his view that God is entirely actual—would not entail that God has any unactualized potentialities.

It is clear that this account rests on a particular understanding of potentiality, one that distinguishes sharply between potentiality and real possibility. We cannot now provide an exposition of Thomas's theory of potentiality, but we are in any event inclined to think that such an exposition is more than is needed for our present purposes. Thomas's solution to the problem of freedom and conditional necessity, which rests on his notion of potentiality, is a solution to a problem raised by his claim that God is essentially without unactualized potentialities. Consideration of whether his use of '*potentia*' matches the prevailing use of the word 'potentiality' is, then, in an important respect irrelevant to an evaluation of his position; the problem and his solution to it could always be reformulated in different terminology. So in this context it seems to us that the only important consideration regarding Thomas's conception of potentiality is whether or not it is consistent, and we see no reason to think that it is not.

7(ii). Two sorts of necessity without a real distinction

Aquinas's position so far comes to this: the necessitation, absolute or conditional, of everything God wills in no way impugns the freedom of his will; and the conditional rather than absolute necessitation of some of what he wills is compatible with his nature's being completely actual, essential, and non-contingent, in Thomas's understanding of those terms. In order for his position as developed so far to avoid inconsistency, however, it must also include the claim that the difference between absolutely and conditionally necessitated acts of will does not constitute a metaphysical difference in God's nature. God's absolute simplicity entails the absence of any real distinctions within God's nature, and yet Thomas's solution to our problem involves distinguishing conditionally from absolutely necessitated acts of will in God.

Our discussion of this difficulty will be helped by further clarifying the claims of the doctrine of simplicity. As we have seen, maintaining that there are necessarily no metaphysical distinctions in God is not the same as claiming that (a) God is the same in all possible worlds. Rather, it amounts only to claiming that (b) within any given initial-state set of possible worlds there can be no real distinction within God's nature. But God's having some acts of will that are only conditionally necessitated is incompatible only with claim (a), not with claim (b). The conditional necessitation of God's willing to create, for example, presupposes the logical possibility of his not willing to create and so is incompatible with claim (a), but it is entirely compatible with claim (b).

Someone might object that the difference between being conditionally necessitated and being absolutely necessitated does indeed mark a real distinction in God's nature, between the metaphysical "softness" of willing to create (for example) and the metaphysical "hardness" of willing goodness.[28] Willing to create, the objector might say, characterizes God's nature in only some possible worlds, while willing goodness characterizes it in all possible worlds; therefore, there are at least two different sorts of characteristics in the divine nature, distinguished from one another by having or lacking the characteristic of obtaining in all possible worlds.

This objection strikes us as confusing a logical distinction to which we have every right with a metaphysical distinction for which there is no basis. On Thomas's account of God's will, God wills himself and everything else he wills in a single immutable act of will. Because some but not all of the objects of that single act of will might have been other than they are, we are warranted in drawing a logical distinction between the conditionally and the absolutely necessitated objects of that single act of will; but nothing in that warrant licenses the claim that the act of will is not one and the same, that there are two really distinct acts of will, or one act of will in two really distinct parts. Even if we should go so far as to say that with regard to some but not all of its objects God's will itself might have been different from what it is, this counterfactual claim shows us again only a logical distinction and not a metaphysical difference within the divine will itself; for even with regard to the objects of the will which might have been other than they are, there is no mutability in the will, as we showed in Section 7(i) above in our discussion of Thomas's claim regarding conditional necessity and divine freedom. So the logical distinction between conditionally and absolutely necessitated aspects of the divine will does not reflect a metaphysical difference in which one part of the divine will is more mutable or less ineluctable than another. What the logical distinction does pick out is solely a difference in the ways in which the single immutable act of divine will is related to the divine nature and to other things. But the mere fact that one thing is related in different ways to different things does not entail that it has distinct *intrinsic* properties, only distinct Cambridge properties, The difference between the relationship of the divine will to the divine nature and the relationship of the divine will to creatures stems not from a metaphysical difference in the divine will itself but from metaphysical differences among the diverse objects of that will.

An analogy may help clarify this part of Thomas's position, even though it is fully suitable in only a few respects. If some woman, Monica, looks directly into a normal unobstructed mirror, then in a single glance she sees herself and other things. On any such occasion Monica invariably sees herself, so that in the context of the example her seeing of herself is physically necessitated. But what she sees besides herself will vary from context to context and so is not physically necessitated. We might therefore draw a warrantable logical distinction between the necessitated seeing of herself and the non-necessitated seeing of other things. Still, that logical distinction provides no basis for inferring that there is a real distinction within Monica's *act* of seeing. Her *act* of seeing remains a single undivided glance in spite of its being properly subjected to our logical distinction. The basis for the logical distinction is not some division within Monica's glance but is rather the difference among the objects of her glance and the different ways in which those objects are related to Monica's one undifferentiated act of seeing.

Something like the line of thought in this unsurprising account of familiar circumstances is all Thomas wants or needs with regard to God's single act of will and its differing objects. The fact that we can distinguish conditionally from absolutely necessitated aspects of God's will shows us an appropriate logical distinction but provides no basis on which to infer a metaphysical distinction within the divine will itself.

There is a necessary relationship between God's willing and God's nature considered as an object of his willing because his will is by definition a wanting of the good and he is identical with goodness. But any other things God wills for the sake of goodness are such that goodness is realizable without them, and so the connection between God's will and these objects of his will is *not* necessary. So the distinction we point out between those aspects of the divine will which could have been otherwise and those which could not reflects a difference in the ways in which the divine will is related to itself and to other things. And these different relationships give rise to different counterfactual truths—e.g. 'God might have willed not to create' 'Even if God had not willed to create, he would still have willed himself'. But although the differing relationships and differing counterfactuals imply that God is not the same in all possible worlds, they do not show that in any given initial-state set of worlds God's act of will is not one single metaphysically indivisible act. They provide the basis for drawing a conceptual distinction among Cambridge properties of God's will, but because the distinction arises just from considering the different ways in which the divine will can be related to its objects, they do not constitute a metaphysical distinction among God's intrinsic properties any more than Monica's single glance is intrinsically divisible because of the different sorts of objects to which it is related. But absolute simplicity rules out only metaphysical differences within God's nature; it does not and could not provide any basis for objecting to logical or conceptual differences. And so the conceptual distinction between those aspects of the divine nature which could have been otherwise and those which could not is entirely compatible with the doctrine of simplicity.

7(iii). Necessity in the will and contingency in its objects

It seems to us, then, that our development of Thomas's position so far justifies the conjunction of the apparently incompatible claims that God's will is free, necessitated either conditionally or absolutely. and devoid of real distinctions. But what about the modal status of created things and temporal events involving them? If all God's willing is necessitated one way or another, how can there be contingency in the creation God wills?

To some extent we have already offered our answer to this question in our discussion of the conditional character of the necessitation of God's will regarding creatures. The nature of that conditional necessitation is not such as to preclude the contingency of the creation or contingency in the created universe. It is, for example, compatible with all of our development of Thomas's position so far to claim that there is a possible world in which God does not will to create, and Thomas himself takes that line when he addresses this problem in SCG I 85:

> Conditional necessity in a cause cannot result in absolute necessity in the effect. But God wills something with regard to creatures not with absolute necessity but only with the necessity that comes from a condition, as was shown above. Therefore, absolute necessity in created things cannot result from the divine will; but it is only absolute necessity that rules out contingency.[29]

But in the same place Thomas provides another way of supporting the same conclusion, one that is worth adding here:

> God wills everything that is required for a thing that he wills, as was said. But some things have a nature in accordance with which they have to be contingent, not necessary, and for that reason God wills some things to be contingent. The efficient causality of the divine will requires not only that what God wills to exist exists, but also that it exists in the mode God wills it to exist in... And so the efficient causality of the divine will does not preclude contingency.[30]

As Thomas sees it, then, one of the reasons why God's absolute simplicity does not entail the absence of contingency in the world created by him is just that part of what God wills with conditional necessity is that there be contingency in what he creates. There is more than one way of explaining how God might do so. We might, for example, suppose that the contents of God's will include references to possible worlds. On that supposition an accurate description of the contents of his will would include not the volition that Rebecca bear twins in Israel at time t, but that Rebecca bear twins in Israel at time t in worlds w1 and w2 (say) but not w3. This approach strikes us as interesting but problematic. Thomas's own suggestion seems to be that God wills to create things with components that guarantee their contingency (SCG I 85). His example involves the, nature of matter, but a better example might be the free will of human beings, where free will is understood in an incompatibilist sense. By willing to create an entity with such free will, God would bring it about that there is contingency in creation.[31] In any event, then, by one means or another it seems open to an omnipotent being to specify not just the things whose existence he brings about but also the manner in which they exist, including the mode of their existence. And for that reason there is no incompatibility between holding all God's acts of will to be necessitated, whether absolutely or conditionally, and maintaining that at least some features of the world are contingent.

So the three counter-intuitive claims on which Thomas's account of divine simplicity rests can be given a rational interpretation. Consequently, it seems to us that the doctrine of divine simplicity has been shown not to be incoherent in any of the respects in which we have investigated it.[32]

8. Implications of the doctrine of divine simplicity

Having worked to defend the coherence of the doctrine of divine simplicity, we want to conclude by saying something about its usefulness. From our discussion earlier in this paper, it is clear that the development of the doctrine and the resolution of its difficulties provide grounds on which to resolve the apparent incompatibility of omnipotence and impeccability and the seeming paradox of essential goodness (with its tension between impeccability and divine free choice). These are important subsidiary results, by-products of the effort to make sense of simplicity. But what we want to bring out now is the more direct importance of the doctrine for the consideration, first, of God's relationship to morality and, second, of the cosmological argument.

The question, 'What has God to do with morality?' has typically been given either of two answers by those who take it seriously.[33] God's will is sometimes taken to create morality in the sense that whatever God wills is good just because he wills it: consequently, (TS) right actions are right just because God approves of them and wrong actions are wrong just because God disapproves of them.[34] Alternatively, morality is taken to be grounded on principles transmitted by God but independent of him, so that a perfectly good God frames his will in accordance with those independent standards of goodness: consequently, (TO) God approves of right actions just because they are right and disapproves of wrong actions just because they are wrong. The trouble with (TS) is that it constitutes a theological subjectivism in which, apparently, anything at all could be established as morally good by divine fiat. So although (TS) makes a consideration of God essential to an evaluation of actions, it does so at the cost of depriving the evaluation of its moral character. Because it cannot rule out anything as absolutely immoral, (TS) seems to be a theory of religious morality that has dropped *morality* as commonly understood out of the theory. (TO), on the other band, obviously provides the basis for an objective morality, but it seems equally clearly not to be a theory of *religious* morality since it suggests no essential connection between God and the standards for evaluating actions. Furthermore, on (TO), the status of the standards to which God looks for morality seems to impugn God's sovereignty.

So the familiar candidates for theories of religious morality seem either, like (TS), to be repugnant to common moral intuitions or, like (TO) to presuppose moral standards apart from God, which God may promulgate but does not produce. For different reasons, then, both these attempts at a theory of religious morality seem inadequate; neither one provides both an objective standard of morality and an essential connection between religion and morality.

The doctrine of divine simplicity entails a third alternative which provides what neither (TS) nor (TO) is capable of. Because God is simple, he is identical with his goodness; that is, the divine nature itself is perfect goodness. Thus there is an essential relationship between God and the standard by which he judges; the goodness for the sake of which and in accordance with which he acts, in accordance with which he wills only certain things to be morally good, is identical with his nature. On the other hand, because it is God's whole nature, not just his arbitrary decision, which is said to constitute the standard for morality, only things consonant with God's nature could be morally good. According to the doctrine of simplicity, then, God's essential connection with morality provides an objective rather than a subjective moral standard.

These sketchy remarks of course suggest no more than the outline of an objective theological metaethics, and it is a long way from even a fully worked out metaethics to a set of specific moral prescriptions. To progress from the metaethical foundations inherent in absolute simplicity to a full-fledged moral system seems to us to require expounding, defending, and developing the theory which originated in pagan antiquity and was transmitted by Augustine and Boethius—that 'goodness' and 'being' are different in sense but the same in reference;[35] and such an undertaking is obviously not possible here.[36] But despite the prodigious effort it calls for, a religious morality of the sort that might be based on the doctrine of divine simplicity is, we think, much more promising than its competitors and worth the effort.

The other set of issues in connection with which the doctrine strikes us as making a major difference has to do with the cosmological argument. Some philosophers—Leibniz, for instance—have held that unless we admit the existence of a being that exists necessarily we are reduced to pointing to a brute fact by way of answering the question why there is something rather than nothing, and the principle of sufficient reason leads such philosophers to claim that there cannot be brute facts.[37] Other philosophers, most recently Richard Swinburne,[38] have held the more modest thesis that theism provides a simpler explanation for the universe than atheism does. Swinburne thinks that God is a simpler and thus a more rational stopping-point for explanation than is the universe itself, because "there is a complexity, particularity, and finitude about the universe which cries out for explanation, which God does not have. ...the supposition that there is a God is an extremely simple supposition."[39]

The trouble with Swinburne's thesis is that he rejects the notion of God as an entity whose existence is logically necessary, and so it is not clear why we should share his intuition that theism constitutes a more rational stopping-point for explanation than atheism does. Philosophers such as Leibniz and Clarke, who rest their versions of the cosmological argument on the principle of sufficient reason, do tend to hold that God is a necessary being. But the trouble with their position is that they seem unable to account for the necessity of God's existence even though they appear to be obliged to do so by the very nature of the principle of sufficient reason that warrants their cosmological arguments. They apparently both cannot find and must have an explanation for the necessity of God's existence. Finally, the principle of sufficient reason, which cosmological arguments depend on, has itself been called into question. William Rowe, for instance, has recently argued that the principle is not a metaphysically necessary truth but rather a logically impossible falsehood.[40]

We think the doctrine of simplicity significantly alters the discussion of all these related issues. In arguing against the principle of sufficient reason, Rowe attempts to show that it is impossible for every contingent fact to have an explanation. A crucial premiss in his argument is the assumption that (R) "For any contingent fact C the fact which explains it cannot be a necessary fact, otherwise C would not be contingent." And he goes on to show that every other possible explanation of any contingent fact C is such that it entails at least one unexplained contingent fact. The effect of the doctrine of simplicity on this intriguing argument is to call (R) into question. As we have explained it here, the doctrine of simplicity entails that God is a logically necessary being all of whose acts of will are at least conditionally necessitated, and that among those acts of will is the volition that certain things be contingent. No matter what the modal status of God's conditionally necessitated acts of will may be, if it is possible for a logically necessary, omnipotent being to will that certain entities or events be contingent, as we have given some reason for thinking it is, then (R) is false. Consequently, a crucial premiss in Rowe's argument against the principle of sufficient reason is false.

Furthermore, the doctrine of simplicity can supply what Clarke's version of the cosmological argument lacks, the explanation of the necessity of God's existence. The answer to the question 'Why does God exist?' is that he cannot not exist, and the reason he cannot not exist is that because he is absolutely simple he is identical with his nature. If his nature is internally consistent, it exists in all possible worlds, and so God, identical with his nature, exists in all possible worlds. The necessity of God's existence is not one more characteristic of God which needs an explanation of its own but is instead a logical consequence of God's absolute simplicity. The short answer to the further question 'Why is God simple?' is 'Because God is an absolutely perfect being, and absolute perfection entails absolute simplicity', and the fuller version of that answer is to be found in Christian rational theology as developed by Augustine, Anselm, and Aquinas, for instance.[41]

Given the doctrine of simplicity, then, it is reasonable to claim that God is an entity whose existence—whose necessary existence—is self-explanatory in the sense that the explanation of the existence of the entity that is absolutely simple is provided entirely by the nature of the entity. And that conclusion supplies the justification, lacking in Swinburne's account, for claiming that God is a simpler stopping-point for universal explanation than the universe itself is. If we assume that God does not exist, the answer to the question 'Why is there something rather than nothing?', or the search for an explanation of all contingent facts, leaves at least one brute fact, at least one inexplicable contingent fact.[42] But given our explanation of the way in which a necessary cause could bring about contingent effects, if God exists and is absolutely simple, the causal chain of contingent facts has its ultimate explanation in a cause that is both necessary and self-explanatory.

The concept of God's absolute simplicity, then, brings with it not only metaphysical intricacy but also considerable explanatory power. Of course our remarks in this concluding section of our paper are not nearly enough to settle the issues raised in it, but we think we have done enough to indicate that if the doctrine of God's absolute simplicity is coherent, as we have worked to show it is, it provides a very promising point of departure of work on some of the most fundamental issues in the philosophy of religion.

NOTES

[1] The derivation or divine simplicity from such considerations is apparent in Aquinas's *Quaestiones disputatae de potentia* (DP) q. 7, a. 1, as Mark D. Jordan has recently pointed out in his article "The Names of God and the Being of Names" in Alfred J. Freddoso, ed., The Existence and Nature of God (Notre Dame, Ind.: University of Notre Dame Press, 1983), pp.161–190; see esp. pp. 176–179.

⁵ In this paper. as in our previously published article on God's eternality (see n. 7 below), we proceed on the hypothesis that God is an absolutely perfect (hence absolutely simple) being whose actions and personal characteristics are accurately portrayed and expounded in the Old and New Testaments. We do so because we are interested in presenting and resolving a problem in Christian doctrine, and no conception of God that omits either perfect-being theology or biblical accounts of God as a person can count as fully Christian on a historical understanding of orthodox Christianity. The problem we are concerned with is not exclusively Christian, but we believe that its components as well as some elements of its solution have been most fully developed by Christian theologians and philosophers. In any case, it is that tradition, especially as represented in the work of Thomas Aquinas, on which we draw in our discussion. On the combination of biblical data and rational theology in Christianity see Thomas V. Morris, "The God of Abraham, Isaac, and Anselm", *Faith and Philosophy* 1 (1984), 177–187.

³ See. e.g., Augustine, *De trinitate* VI, 7–8; Anselm, *Monologion* XVII; Aquinas (besides the source cited in n. 1 above), *Summa contra gentiles* (SCG) I 18, 21–23, 31; *Summa theologiae* (ST) Ia q. 3. For the development, criticism, and defense of the doctrine in recent philosophical literature, see, e.g., Mark D. Jordan's article cited in n. I above; Daniel Bennett, "The Divine Simplicity", *Journal of Philosophy* 66 (1969), 628–637; Richard LaCroix, "Augustine on the Simplicity of God," *New Scholasticism* 51 (1977), 453–469; James F. Ross, *Philosophical Theology*. Indianapolis and New York: Bobbs-Merrill, 1969 (esp. pp. 51–63); Alvin Plantinga, *Does God Have a Nature?*, Milwaukee.. Marquette University Press, 1980 (esp. pp. 26–61); and in particular the inter-related articles by William E. Mann, including "The Divine Attributes", *American Philosophical Quarterly* 12 (1975), 151–159; "Divine Simplicity", *Religious Studies* 18 (1982), 451–471; and "Simplicity and Immutability in God", *International Philosophical Quarterly* 23(1983), 267–276. For an assessment of some of this work of Mann's, see Thomas V. Morris. "On God and Mann" (forthcoming).

⁴ In Chapter 4 of his *De trinitate* Boethius draws a distinction between what might be called intrinsic and extrinsic predicates, attempting to found it on a distinction between the first three and the remaining seven Aristotelian categories. Although his attempt has certain obvious shortcomings, we think it has merit and deserves further attention and perhaps further development. See Eleonore Stump, "*Hamartia* in Christian Belief: Boethius on the Trinity" in D.V. Stump et al., ed.s, *Hamartia: The Concept of Error in the Western Tradition*, New York & Toronto: The Edwin Mellen Press, 1983; pp. 131–148.

⁵ The most familiar problems of this sort are associated with the claim that there can be no real distinction between what God is and its being the case that he is; for God, as for no non-simple entity, essence and existence must be identical.

Robert M. Adams has worked at rebutting the familiar philosophical objections to the essence-existence connection and to the concept of necessary existence, and we are in agreement with much of what he says in his articles "Has It Been Proved that All Real Existence is Contingent?" (*American Philosophical Quarterly* 8 (1971), 284–291) and "Divine Necessity" (*Journal of Philosophy* 80 (1983), 741–752).

[6] Entities existing only at an instant could satisfy that description, and they are sometimes discussed, notably by Duns Scotus. But strictly instantaneous temporal existence strikes us as theoretically impossible.

[7] See our article "Eternity", *Journal of Philosophy* 78(1981), 429–458.

[8] For a discussion of the essential connection between divine goodness and the manifestation of it in things other than God, see Norman Kretzmann, "Goodness, Knowledge, and Indeterminacy in the Philosophy of Thomas Aquinas", *Journal of Philosophy* 80 (1983), 631–649.

[9] Bowman Clarke. in commenting on our paper, forcibly and succinctly raised a criticism that had occurred to other auditors and readers as well. He claimed that it is "plainly false" that perfect power is identical with perfect knowledge "unless perfect power bears no resemblance to power, and perfect knowledge to knowledge." While there is indeed an essential resemblance between creaturely attributes such as power and their perfect counterparts among the conceptually distinguishable divine attributes, the resemblance must be confined to the formal, abstract aspect of the attribute. God in his perfect power can raise 100 pounds a foot off the floor, and a man can raise 100 pounds a foot off the floor; but it is inconceivable that the means by which a temporal. material creature achieves that result with some effort be like omnipotent God's doing it in any respect other than, perhaps, the fact that an act of will initiates it. Without now providing details or support, we are willing to say that the same sort of claim can and should be made regarding every divine perfect $\phi/$ attribute and its corresponding creaturely $\phi/$. In this same vein, Professor Clarke also objected to our summit-slope analogy, pointing out that a summit is not a perfect slope. At least part of the trouble here is with the apparent contrast between 'perfection' in the sense of 'ideal '—less important for our purposes and sometimes misleading—and 'perfection' in the etymologically fundamental sense of 'culmination', 'completion'. In that latter, more directly relevant sense, the single summit is indeed the perfection of all the slopes. The slope-summit analogy was intended to suggest that the idea that perfect $\phi/$, and perfect $\psi/$, might be identical despite the plain difference between $\phi/$ and $\psi/$ cannot simply be dismissed as incoherent. Here is one more analogy offered with that same intention. Consider two sets of geometrical elements: A (three two-inch line segments lying parallel to one another) and B (three 60-degree angles with one-inch legs lying with their vertices toward a single point). In this analogy the analogue for the perfection/completion of A and of B is the construction of closed figures involving all three elements of each; and,

of course, the resultant figures are identical two-inch equilateral triangles, despite the essential differences between A and B. (We are grateful to Sydney Shoemaker for help with this analogy).

[10] See our article "Eternity" (n. 7 above).

[11] The question whether God could do what he does not do, or refrain from doing what he does, is a well-recognized problem in the tradition of rational theology. Aquinas, for instance, discusses it several times, e.g., *Scriptum super libros Sententiarum* (SENT) I d. 43, q. un., aa. 1 & 2; SCG II 23, 26–27; DP q. 1, a. 5; ST Ia, q. 25, a. 5. But none of the discussions of this problem we have seen associate it specifically with the doctrine of simplicity.

[12] This apparent diversity is clearly expressed by Aquinas in such passages as these: "God necessarily wills his own being and his own goodness, and he cannot will the contrary" (SCG I 80); "in respect of himself God has only volition, but in respect of other things he has selection (*electio*). Selection, however, is always accomplished by means of free choice. Therefore, free choice is suited to God" (SCG I 88): "free choice is spoken of in respect of things one wills *not* necessarily but of one's own accord" (ibid.). Notice that even though God's existence and attributes are conceived of here as being *willed* by God, they are expressly excluded from among the objects of God's free choice. (We discuss these passages further below.)

[13] For developments of this last sort. see. e.g.. Nelson Pike, "Omnipotence and God's Ability to Sin", *American Philosophical Quarterly* 6 (1969), 208–216; Thomas V. Morris, "The Necessity of God's Goodness" (forthcoming).

[14] Besides the article cited in n. 13 above, see, e.g., Peter Geach, *Providence and Evil*, Cambridge: Cambridge University Press, 1977 (esp. Chs. I and II); Joshua Hoffman, "Can God Do Evil?" *Southern Journal of Philosophy* 17(1979), 213–220; Jerome Gellman, "Omnipotence and Impeccability", *The New Scholasticism* 51(1977), 21–37.

[15] For good recent surveys of the difficulties and significant contributions to the discussion see Thomas P. Flint and Alfred J. Freddoso, "Maximal Power", in *The Existence and Nature of God* (n. 1 above), pp. 81–113; Edward Wierenga, "Omnipotence Defined", *Philosophy and Phenomenological Research* 43 (1983), 363–376 (including a very useful bibliography of recent literature on the subject).

[16] The conception of God's goodness as exercising final causation. a conception at the heart of Aquinas's account of creation and its relationship to God, seems particularly likely to emphasize the esthetic aspect of perfect goodness at the expense of the moral. See Kretzmann 1983 (n. 8 above), esp. p.637and n. 16.

[17] Some recent interesting discussion of the will shows signs of moving in the direction of such a conception without any explicit trace ofan association with (or even awareness of) Aquinas's account. See, e.g.. Harry Frankfurt. "Freedom of the Will and the Concept of a Person", *Journal of Philosophy* 68 (1971), 5–20;

Gary Watson, "Free Agency", *Journal of Philosophy* 72(1975), 205–220; Susan Wolf, "Asyrnmetric Freedom", *Journal of Philosophy* 77(1980), 151–166.

[18] It is not easy to provide a satisfactory translation of *'appetitus'*, especially in a single word: 'desire', 'tendency', 'inclination', 'attraction' are all more or less unsatisfactory possibilities. The basic sense of the verb *'appeto'* involves the notion of striving after, which also seems to play a part in Aquinas's account of the will. Perhaps the least unsatisfactory one-word counterpart of *'appetitus'* is 'wanting', as long as 'wanting' is not understood as implying the absence of the object of appetitus. On this basis we could say that for Aquinas the will is a self-directed intellectual wanting of the good, or a self-directed wanting of what is good, essentially connected with some understanding of goodness in general.

[19] ST Ia q. 59, a. 1; cf. SCG II 47 and *Quaestiones disputatiae de veritatae* (DV) q. 23, a. I.

[20] See, e.g., STIaq. 83, a. l; IaIIae q. 13, a. 16; DV q. 22, a. 6; *Quaestiones disputatiae de malo* q.6.

[21] See, e.g., ST Ia q. 82, a. 1: "in practical matters the end plays the role played by the principle in speculative matters, as is said in Physics II [9]".

[22] See, e.g., SCG II 83; ST Ia. q. 19, a. 3; DP q. 1, a. 5.

[23] Thomas's commitment to this position is entailed by his holding both that some of the things God wills are willed with conditional necessity and that God's nature is absolutely simple. See, e.g., ST [a. q. 19, a. 3 (esp. ad 4) and SCG 182; cf. DP q.l, a. 5, adS & ad 6; q. 3, a. 15, ad 6 & ad 11; q. 7, a. I; a. 6; a. S, ad 6; a. 10.

[24] See, e.g., SCG I 85 and ST Ia q. 19, a. 8.

[25] Cf. ST Ia q. 19, a. 3.

[26] In the case of an omnipotent being, choosing to do something is tantamount to doing it, and so we will treat God's choosing to create and God's creating as interchangeable characterizations of the eternal action that is at issue here.

[27] There are elements of Aquinas's theology not directly relevant to those under consideration here that suggest he is not entitled to this claim; see Kretzmann 1983 (n. 8 above), esp. pp.632–635.

[28] Christopher Hughes offered us an important objection of this sort, one that forced us to try to clarify our position.

[29] "Necessitas ex suppositione in causa non potest concludere necessitatem absolutam in effectu. Deus autem vult aliquid in creaturs non necessitate absoluta, sed solum necessitate quae est exsuppositione, ut supra (capp. 81 solq.) ostensum est. Ex voluntate igitur divina non potest concludi in rebus creatis necessitas absoluta. Haec autem sola excludit contingentiami:..."

[30] "Vult enim Deus omnia quae requiruntur ad rem quam vult, ut dictum est (cap. 83). Sad aliquibus rebus secundum modum suac naturac compelit quod sint contingentes, non necessariae. Igitur vult aliquas res esse contingentes. Efficacia autem divinae voluntatis exigit ut non solum sit quod Deus vult esse, sed etiam

ut hoc modo sit sicut Deus vult illud esse:.... Igitur efficacia divinae uoluntalis contingentiam non tollit."

[31] For an account of Boethius's explanation of all contingency in terms of free will, see Norman Kretzmann, "*Nos Epsi Principia Sumus*: Boethius and the Basis of Contingency" in Tamar Rudavsky, ed.. *Divine Omnisicience and Omnipotence in Medieval Philosophy*, Dordrecht & Boston: D. Reidel, 1984, pp. 23–50.

[32] There are, of course, problems for the doctrine of divine simplicity other than those we have dealt with, especially the specifically Christian problems of Trinity and Incarnation. But we hope to have removed enough of the more fundamental obstacles in the way of taking the doctrine seriously to encourage others to look more closely at such further difficulties.

[33] Most of this treatment of the issue of religious morality is adapted from Norman Kretzmann, "Abraham, Isaac, and Euthyphro: God and the Basis of Morality" in *Hamartia* (n. 4 above), pp. 27–50.

[34] For an interesting, sophisticated treatment of divine-command theories of morality, see, e.g., Philip Quinn, *Divine Commands and Moral Requirements*, Oxford: Clarendon Press, 1978.

[35] Scott MacDonald's Cornell Ph.D dissertation (1985) provides a great deal of illumination of the historical development and philosophical implications of this theory.

[36] We hope to make some contribution to such an undertaking soon.

[37] See, e.g., "On the Radical Origination of Things," tr. Letoy E. Loemker in *Gottfried Wilhelm Leibniz: Philosophical Papers and Letters* (2nd edn.), Dordrecht: D. Reidel, 1969; pp. 486–491.

[38] In his book *The Existence of God* (Oxford: Claendon Press, 1979), p.132.

[39] Op. cit.. p. 130.

[40] William Rowe, "Rationalistic Theology and Some Principles of Explanation", *Faith and Philosophy* 1(1984), pp.357–369.

[41] See n. 3 above.

[42] As both Swinburne and Rowe argue, in their writings cited in nn. 38 and 40 above.

[43] This paper has been presented to various audiences in various drafts and has also been read and commented on by individuals. We have benefited enormously from all the criticisms and suggestions we received in those ways, and we are grateful for all of them. Among those who helped us are William Alston, Bowman Clarke, Leon Galis, Joshua Hoffman, Christopher Hughes, William Mann, Deborah Mayo, Alan McMichael, Philip Quinn, Gary Rosenkrantz, James Ross, Joseph Runzo, Christopher Shields, Fred Feldman, Richard Sorabji. Robert Stalnaker, and John Wippel.

7

God and the World

Russell Pannier and Thomas Sullivan

A. Pantheism-A Question of Meaning

What is orthodox theism's account of the relationship between God and the world? Of course, that's a very large question. Here we take on just part of it—the negative side. One way of understanding the affirmations of a metaphysical theory is understanding its denials. We hope to gain some understanding of orthodox theism's affirmative account of God's relationship to the world by first understanding at least some of the accounts it rejects.

Orthodox theism is conventionally characterized as rejecting pantheistic accounts of God's relationship to the world. That much is clear. But what exactly is a "pantheistic" account? What exactly is this heresy to which orthodox theists are presumed opposed? Unfortunately, that isn't so clear.

Indeed, the word "pantheism" apparently has no single precise usage in philosophy. At least this is what a random sample of respectable sources suggests. Consider, for example, the entry under "pantheism" in *The Oxford Dictionary of Philosophy*: "The view that God is in everything or that God and the universe are one." Whether or not the author of the entry regards the two disjuncts as meaning the same, it is not obvious that they do. It seems easy to imagine ways in which God might be thought to be "in" the universe without being "one" with it. For example, orthodox theists presumably believe that there is a sense in which God is present at every spatial location without being "one" with the universe in any literal sense.

It might be thought that ambiguities could be eliminated by discarding the first disjunct of the definition in favor of the second—the claim that the universe and God are "one." But this would not suffice; there are different ways of under-

standing "one," and related words such as "unity," "unified," "unit," etc.
Consider in this regard *The Oxford Companion to Philosophy*: "... the term 'pantheist' designates one who holds both that everything there is constitutes a unity
and that this unity is divine." The difficulty is that "unity" has no single sense.
On the one hand, it might be interpreted as positing a strict numerical identity
between God and the universe. On the other hand, it might be construed as positing only a relationship of some kind.

Even opting for strict numerical identity would not yield complete precision.
Consider, for example, the entry under "pantheism" in *The Cambridge
Dictionary of Philosophy*: "... the view that God is identical with everything." Is
this the view that God is numerically identical with the universe as a whole, or
that He is numerically identical with each proper part, just to mention two of the
possibilities? Presumably, these are different claims.

Such examples could be multiplied indefinitely, but perhaps the few we have
offered will suffice to make our first point: characterizing a theory as "pantheistic" is not, by itself, philosophically useful. The term has no precise usage.

A better approach to the matter would proceed in two stages. First, one
would look for ways of systematically distinguishing significantly different ways
of understanding the relationship between God and the world. It might or might
not turn out that one or more of these distinct conceptions deserves the label
"pantheistic" in some suitably refined sense. But the important thing would be to
get clear about the substantive differences between the alternative views, as
opposed to engaging in wheel-spinning debates about terminology. ("You're a
pantheist." "No I'm not; you are." Etc.) Second, with a firm grasp of the alternatives, one would then turn to the task of evaluating them. We do not undertake
here either of these tasks in anything close to the detail they ideally merit.

We shall primarily focus upon the first project. In that regard we shall try to
set out in a clear fashion at least some of the alternative ways of understanding
God's relationship to the world. In doing so, we shall limit ourselves to a discussion of *possible* accounts of that relationship; we deliberately refrain here
from engaging in historical exposition or analysis. We approach the matter in this
way because we think that in philosophy it is usually best to begin the study of
an issue by getting as clear as one can about its general nature and the surrounding logical landscape before plunging into historical exposition and analysis.
Thus, we won't be discussing any of the historical positions sometimes classified
as "pantheistic" in one or another sense—e.g., the theories of Plotinus, Spinoza,
Hegel, Schelling, Fichte, Hartshorne, Whitehead, and so on. In making this
choice of approach, we do not intend to suggest that historical investigations are
inappropriate or useless. Of course, they are not. But our purpose here is setting
out in a *general* way at least some of the distinctions that should be drawn and at
least some of the available alternative accounts of God's relationship to the
world. Our hope is that such a discussion will help facilitate mutual understand-

ing between orthodox theists and those with doubts about orthodox theism. One of the traditions expressing such doubts is often referred to as "panentheism." One of the tasks we shall undertake here is sorting out at least some of the issues raised by panentheistic theories and distinguishing some of the ways in which such ideas might be expressed.

As for the second project, we shall limit ourselves to discussing just some of the difficulties confronting the views we distinguish. We shall make no attempt to offer exhaustive evaluations. Again, our primary purpose is to contribute to the clarification and specification of the issues.

B. Alternative Ways of Characterizing God's Relationship to the World

So, our question is: What are at least some of the alternative accounts of God's relationship to the world? Before attempting an answer, we find it useful to address three preliminary matters.

1. "God" and "the world" as successfully referring terms

First, because the question of pantheism, whatever its ultimate meaning, concerns the relationship between God and the world, it can appropriately arise only for those who believe that the terms "God" and "the world" can be used to successfully refer. Only one who thinks that these terms have referents can legitimately go on to ask about the relationship between those referents.

2. Meaning of "the world"

The second preliminary point concerns the meaning of "the world." How should it be understood in this context? One possibility can be rejected out of hand. Sometimes the term is used in a way intended to draw a contrast between God and the world—for example, "the world is the aggregate of entities which are distinct from God." Whatever the merits of such an analysis in other philosophical contexts, it is not useful here. Its use would beg the very question at hand—whether there is a sense in which God and the world are distinct.

The moral to be drawn is that a condition of adequacy for any interpretation of "the world" is that it beg no questions about the relationship between God and the world. One possibility immediately suggests itself. Why not say that the world, for purposes of the pantheism issue anyway, is the aggregate of material entities? Surely, the term is often used in that way. But there is a difficulty with the suggestion. Imagine a philosopher who believes that human minds are not material entities and that God is numerically identical with one or more of those minds, (e.g., Buddha). It seems that one would be naturally inclined to characterize such a theory as asserting *some* kind of substantial identification of God and at least part of the world, and, indeed, that would seem to be a philosophically illuminating way of expressing the claim. But if the world has already been characterized as excluding non-material entities, the claim could not be consistently put in that way.

So, the proposal fails. A characterization of the world as the aggregate of material entities is too narrow. But our imagined objection to the proposal suggests what is perhaps a better approach. Why not say that the world is the aggregate of all entities which in *some* sense are "part of" or "in" the spatio-temporal universe? Thus, "the world" would be construed simply as referring to the spatio-temporal universe. Such a characterization would, of course, include all material entities. But it seems that it would also include anything else which people commonly regard as included in some sense in the spatio-temporal universe. Even those who believe that human minds are immaterial entities, or at least have immaterial powers, would presumably be willing to say that minds are "among" (in *some* sense) the things existing in the spatio-temporal universe. Thus, according to this proposed usage, human beings would be properly deemed members of the spatio-temporal universe, even if it should ultimately turn out that they are not purely material entities. Perhaps the essence of this usage-proposal can be grasped by imagining a person standing on a mountain top, waving and pointing his arms in all directions, and saying, "By 'the world' I mean *all* of *this*—*whatever* 'this' turns out to be." Of course, after adopting this usage, a philosopher might conclude that God is identical in some sense with all or part of "the world" so understood. But that outcome would not retroactively show that the philosopher had begged the question of pantheism in adopting the recommended usage. On the contrary, he would have succeeded in giving semantic content to the term "the world" by means of an ostensive method which does not, by its own terms, beg any questions about pantheism. That is the most that could reasonably be expected of any semantical clarification in this context.

A simple example might help illuminate the point. Imagine that the main issue in a criminal trial is whether the defendant is the person who robbed the bank. It would obviously be inappropriate for the prosecutor to refer to the defendant either as "the person who robbed the bank" or as "the person who did not rob the bank." Either usage would beg the very issue at hand. In contrast, referring to the defendant in some neutral manner—e.g., by name—would not beg any legally relevant questions concerning identity, even if the trial should eventually demonstrate that the defendant did indeed rob the bank. The crucial referential requirement is that there be some neutral method of identifying the referent, where a neutral method is one which does not beg the ultimate question of identity. It does not matter so much which of possibly several neutral methods is chosen, so long as one of them is used. Similarly, with respect to the matter at hand, the crucial requirement is that there be at least one way of identifying the world which does not by its own terms beg the ultimate question of identity between God and the world. It seems that we have succeeded in describing one such method.

3. About identity

Any reasonable discussion of pantheism is bound to touch upon the idea that God and the world are identical in some sense. Thus, something should be said about the meaning of "identical" in such contexts. We offer a few comments on this score, hoping to say just enough to illuminate the particular use we make here of the concept of identity, without purporting to offer anything close to a systematic or full treatment.

By "identity" we shall understand "strict identity," a concept which can be explained as follows. Any assertion of identity requires the use of at least two referring expressions, say, "x" and "y." Then an assertion of identity expressed in the form, "x is identical to y," is true only if "x" and "y" are used to designate the same entity. If such an assertion is true, we shall say that x is *strictly identical to* y. Thus, to assert that God is strictly identical to the world is to assert at least that "God" and "the world" designate the same entity.

Of course, there is more to an identity assertion than the mere claim that the syntactic entity-type "God" designates the same thing as the syntactic entity-type "the world." There is also at least an implied claim about "meaning." Anyone asserting an identity claim presumably wants to be understood as saying something like this, "Given what I take "God" and "the world" to mean (in terms of semantic content), they refer to the very same entity."

There are different ways of making this intuitive idea more precise. We offer just one. Let "x" and "y" be referring expressions. Suppose that the speaker believes that "x" is semantically tied to the characteristics, x^*-1, ..., x^*-m, in the sense that she believes that any entity correctly designated by "x" exemplifies x^*-1, ..., x^*-m, and that "y" is semantically tied to the characteristics, y^*-1, ..., y^*-n, in the same sense. Then to assert that x is identical to y is to assert (at the very least) that "x" and "y" designate the same entity, E, and that E exemplifies the characteristics, x^*-1, ..., x^*-m, and y^*-1, ..., y^*-n. Thus, with respect to the issue at hand, anyone asserting that God and the world are strictly identical should be understood as asserting at least this: "The referring expression "God" is semantically tied to the characteristics, G^*-1, ..., G^*-m, and the referring expression "the world" is semantically tied to the characteristics, W^*-1, ..., W^*-n. The expressions "God" and "the world" designate the same entity, and that entity exemplifies the characteristics, G^*-1, ..., G^*-m, and W^*-1, ..., W^*-n."

Given this, what would it mean to assert that God is strictly identical to just a part of the world? Suppose, as seems plausible, that we at least roughly understand the notion of something's being a *part* of the universe. For example, the solar system, the earth, the Atlantic Ocean and Dobbin the horse are parts of the universe in our intended sense. Then to assert that an entity E-1 is *strictly identical to a part of the universe* is to assert at least that there is at least one part of the universe, E-2, which is strictly identical to E-1. Given this usage, to assert that God is strictly identical to a part of the universe is to assert at least that there is at least one part of the universe which is strictly identical to God.

What about the meaning of the assertion that the world is strictly identical to a part of God? Assume for the moment that we understand what it would mean to say that God has parts and that God has parts in that sense, whatever it is. Then, presumably, to assert that the universe is *strictly identical to a part of God* is to assert at least that there is at least one part of God which is strictly identical to the universe as a whole. But this for-the-sake-of-discussion assumption is obviously debatable. We shall return to it later.

4.   Strict-identity accounts of God's relationship to the world

With these preliminary matters at least temporarily resolved, we turn to the task of sketching at least some of the alternative ways of characterizing God's relationship to the world. Thus, our question is: Assuming (1) that "God" and "the world" have referents, (2) that "the world" is understood as designating the spatio-temporal universe, and (3) that "is identical to" means "is strictly identical to," what are at least some of the interestingly distinct ways of describing the relationship between God and the world?

One way of approaching the question is to draw a line tied to the relation of strict identity. What are at least some of the ways in which one might assert a strict identity between God, or a part of God, and the universe, or a part of the universe? It seems that one might assert (i) that God and the universe as a whole are strictly identical, or (ii) that God and at least one part of the world are strictly identical, or (iii) that the world and a part of God are strictly identical. It should be noted that these alternatives are generic and not necessarily mutually exclusive. For example, in a moment we shall distinguish two versions of (i), one of which combines (i) with (ii).

We shall place any theory asserting at least one of (i), (ii) or (iii) on one side of the line, referring to them as *strict-identity* theories. On the other side of the line we shall place any theory denying (i), (ii) and (iii), referring to them as *dualist* theories.

We begin by focusing upon strict-identity accounts. What are at least some of the possible varieties of such theories? One way of sorting the alternatives is to ask the question: What exactly is supposed to be strictly identical to what? We shall mention a few of the apparently possible responses, making no attempt at a complete inventory.

(1) God is strictly identical to the world as a whole and to every part of the world. According to conceptions of this sort God would be conceived of as

numerically identical to the spatio-temporal universe and to every constituent of the universe. Thus, God would be understood as strictly identical to every electron, every tree, every human being, and so on, as well as to the total aggregate of all such entities.

(2) God is strictly identical to at least one part of the world, but not to every part of the world nor to the world as a whole. Thus, some might be inclined to strictly identify God with, say, a statue, or a mountain, or a particular human being, while denying that God is strictly identical to the world as a whole or to every part of the world.

(3) God is strictly identical to the world as a whole, but not to any of the world's parts. According to this conception God and the spatio-temporal universe are numerically identical—literally the same entity. But God is not strictly identical to any part of the universe; hence, any part of the universe is in some sense a part of God. It seems that there are several ways of understanding this proposal. One possibility is attributing to God some kind of personal or conscious unity in His own right and correspondingly understanding the material universe as God's "body" in some sense. Variations of this kind naturally tend in the direction of mystically-oriented views some of whose proponents are perhaps likely to describe the material realm as "God-suffused." Matter is not "just" matter; it is the transparent garment of God Himself, so to speak.

Another quite different possibility is a view which refuses to attribute to God any sort of conscious unity in His own right. God is identified with the world, where the world is understood as a simple aggregate of distinct entities. The aggregate has no intrinsic unity *qua* aggregate; whatever intrinsic unities there may be exist only at the level of the distinct parts of the aggregate. Variations of this sort naturally tend to become regarded as sugar-coated, tender-minded versions of atheism. "God" is understood as just one of the terms which can be used in referring to the spatio-temporal universe as a whole, and the latter is not understood in any special religious or spiritual light. The material realm is not portrayed as the transparent garment of God Himself. Indeed, if anything, God is portrayed as just one of several linguistic garments with which some speakers choose to semantically clothe the universe.

(4) The world as a whole is strictly identical to a part of God. Here the idea is that God incorporates the world as a part of Himself. The world is one of God's constituents, but not the only one.

There are probably other possible varieties of strict-identity responses to the question. For example, someone might think that God is strictly identical to every part of the world, but not strictly identical to the world as a whole. Whether this would be a coherent position might be doubted, but we shall attempt no resolution here. Neither do we stop to consider other possible variations on the strict-identity theme. Our purpose is simply to offer enough examples to illustrate the general nature of such theories.

What should be said about such conceptions of God's relationship to the world? One of the issues any serious strict-identity account must eventually address is the large question of how the Principle of Substitutivity of Identity bears on the matter: Entities which are strictly identical share all of the same characteristics. More precisely, $(x)(y)(F)[(x=y) \longrightarrow$
$(Fx \longleftrightarrow Fy)]$. One general question then for at least several of the strict-identity accounts is: What should be done about certain seemingly awkward entailments generated by applying the Principle of Substitutivity?

5.   *The first strict-identity variation*

For example, consider the first of the strict-identity variations just mentioned—the claim that God is strictly identical to the world as a whole and to every part of the world. If that is true, then God is identical both to, say, Dobbin the horse and to that particular brown trout which is just now hitting a Number-6 Mickey Finn streamer. Dobbin is presumably not a brown trout. If God is strictly identical to Dobbin then, by Substitutivity, God is not a brown trout either. But we have assumed that God is strictly identical to a particular brown trout. This has the look of a contradiction.

It seems that our hypothetical strict-identity proponent would have at least three options at this point. He could reject the Principle of Substitutivity. He could accept that principle, but contend that all philosophical accounts of God's relationship to the world are inherently self-contradictory. Or, he could deny the proposition that horses are not brown trout. None of these alternatives seems especially attractive. The Principle of Substitutivity seems certain, if anything is. Contending that philosophical theology is inherently self-contradictory seems, at best, a prelude to madness. Denying that horses are distinct from brown trout seems to require a substantial alteration of our ordinary beliefs about the world. It is perhaps of interest in regard to this last point to note the tendency of some strict-identity views to maintain that nothing is "really" distinct from anything else.

The first strict-identity variation encounters similar difficulties with respect to its identification of God with the world as a whole. Again, according to this variation God is strictly identical to the spatio-temporal universe as a whole and to every part of the universe, e.g., to Dobbin the horse. Dobbin exemplifies the characteristic, being a horse. God is strictly identical to Dobbin. Hence, according to the Substitutivity of Identity, God is a horse. But God is also strictly identical to the universe. Hence, according to Substitutivity, the universe is a horse. Now, of course, the universe is a wonderful and mysterious thing, and one should presumably hesitate to summarily dismiss even apparently unlikely accounts of its nature. But at the very least it seems fair to place the burden of persuasion upon anyone who would maintain that the universe is a horse.

A particularly striking application of the Substitutivity Principle generates an argument trading on one of Aristotle's. If God is strictly identical to every part of the universe then He is strictly identical, say, to the two particular human beings, A and B. Suppose that A believes that God exists and that B believes that God does not exist. But then by Substitutivity God both believes that God exists and that God does not exist. But there could be no such entity. For, as Aristotle argues in *Metaphysics* IV, c.3, (1) nothing whatever can be in two contrary states at the same time and (2) believing a proposition P, on the one hand, and believing not-P, on the other hand, are contrary states. The reason (1) is true should be obvious, provided that "can be" is understood occurrently, as opposed to dispositionally. Someone could at t-1 be *capable* of going south on I-35 at t-2 and also *capable* of going north on I-35 at t-2, but nobody at t-1 can go in opposite directions at once. Aristotle astutely notes with respect to (2) that, although P is the contradictory of not-P, the belief that P is the contrary of the belief that not-P. That is, P is the contradictory of not-P, but believing that P is the contrary of believing that not-P. A conscious being might well be in neither state.

Of course, someone might *say* that he believes that God exists and also believes that God does not exist. But there is no reason in general to think that introspection is infallible with respect to what we believe, and this argument shows that with respect to *this* kind of claim, that person must be in error. Thus, our first version of the strict-identity account appears to confront formidable difficulties. Of course, it would presumably always be open to proponents of the view to dilute their claims by saying that they didn't, after all, mean to say that God is *literally* identical to the world as a whole and to every part of the world. Of course, that would present a different question. Any new formulation would have to be examined on its own merits. But the very fact of any such attempted reformulation would tend to show that the original formulation was misleading, at best.

6.   The second strict-identity variation

What about the second strict-identity variation—the claim that God is strictly identical to at least one part of the world, but not to the world as a whole nor to every part of the world? Theories asserting a strict identity between God and two or more parts of the universe would confront difficulties of the sort we have just discussed. Thus, for example, a theory which identifies God both with, say, a golden statue of a calf and a river would have to somehow deal with the apparent entailment that God is both a river and not a river.

But turning aside from these already-canvassed problems, consider versions of the second strict-identity variation which maintain that only one part of the universe is strictly identical to God. One of the apparent difficulties for such a view is that God is presumably confined by the Substitutivity of Identity

Principle to whatever characteristics happen to be exemplified by whatever particular entity is singled out for identification with God. Thus, if the claim is that God is strictly identical to, say, a golden statue of a calf, then God presumably has all, but only all, of the characteristics exemplified by that particular statue. If the statue is made of gold then God is made of gold. If the statue weighs fifteen pounds then God weighs fifteen pounds, and so on. So, "What's the problem?" one might ask. The problem is that of attributing to God properties which seem to conflict with those properties one would naturally tend to expect from any entity alleged to have God-like status.

What might such properties be? Without trying to give an exhaustive list, it seems obvious that at the very least one would want to say that if God exists at all, He must have two characteristics. (1) He must be *ontologically independent* in the sense that His existence does not depend upon any factor distinct from Him. (2) He must be an *ontological basis* for everything else in the sense that any entity distinct from God, if any, depends for its existence upon God's existence. Fulfillment of the first condition is obviously a necessary condition for fulfillment of the second. Now, the point is that a golden statue of a calf is apparently not an ontologically independent entity, and therefore could not be an ontological basis either. So, one is seemingly forced to the conclusion that, while God might not exist at all, if He *does* exist, He could not be strictly identical to a golden statue of a calf.

Similar reasoning would apply to *any* choice of a proper part of the universe. Whatever such entity is selected, it would not be ontologically independent, and thus could not be plausibly identified with God.

In the face of such criticisms there might surface a tendency on the part of strict-identity proponents to either retract the claim that God is strictly identical to the statue, settling for some looser sense of "identity," or maintaining that the statue is really not a statue at all, but something with more "ontological power." The first move would constitute giving up altogether on the strict-identity project. The second move would change the essential nature of the account and raise other questions. If it's not really a statue, then what exactly is it, and what's the point of calling it a statue in the first place?

7.   *The third strict-identity variation*

What can be said about the third strict-identity theory—the theory that God is strictly identical to the world as a whole, but not to any of its parts? The Substitutivity Principle causes difficulties here too. If God is strictly identical to the universe then God necessarily exemplifies any characteristics which the universe exemplifies, and fails to exemplify any characteristics which the universe fails to exemplify. But there is reason to believe that the universe lacks at least some of those characteristics which God presumably must exemplify, if God exists at all. Consider again the characteristic of ontological independence. It is surely not obvious that the universe has this property; it seems possible to imagine, without self-contradiction, that the universe does not exist. These reflections suggest the following line of reasoning:

1] No entity whose non-existence can be self-consistently imagined is an ontologically independent entity.

2] The universe is an entity whose non-existence can be self-consistently imagined.

3] Hence, the universe is not an ontologically independent entity.

4] No entity which is not an ontologically independent entity is strictly identical to God (if God exists).

5] Hence, the universe is not strictly identical to God (if God exists).

We shall not undertake here to offer a full-scale defence of the argument. Suffice it to say that it is deductively valid and its premises are not obviously false. Indeed, the premises seem quite plausible. Consider (1), for example. Isn't it at least prima facie reasonable to suppose that the possibility of imagining the non-existence of an entity is sufficient to show that it is not ontologically independent? Premise (2) also seems plausible. It is apparently possible to describe without self-contradiction a state of affairs in which the universe does not exist.

An additional difficulty for the third strict-identity variation concerns the proposition that every part of the universe is a part of God. The case for attributing this view to the third variation is easily stated. God is strictly identical to the universe. By the Substitutivity of Identity, every characteristic of the universe is a characteristic of God. One of the universe's apparent characteristics is having parts. Hence, God has parts. Consider any arbitrarily selected entity, E-1, which is a part of the universe. Then one of the universe's characteristics is having E-1 as a part. By another application of Substitutivity, God has E-1 as a part. But E-1 was arbitrarily selected. Hence, generalizing, every part of the universe is a part of God. Now, if every part of the universe is a part of God, then every human consciousness is a part of God (assuming, of course, that human consciousnesses are parts of the universe). But this conclusion raises questions, one of which is, How exactly should we understand the claim?

It might be understood in more than one way, depending upon what one takes the third variation to maintain about God's consciousness. There appear to be at least two possibilities: (1) God does not have a single unitary consciousness in His own right. (2) God has a single unitary consciousness in His own right.

Consider the first alternative: God has no unified consciousness in His own right. He is simply the brute aggregate (*not* the set-theoretic class) of all entities which happen to be parts of the universe. Insofar as the universe contains individual consciousnesses as parts, each of them is a part of God, but they do not somehow combine to form a higher-level divine consciousness with its own unity. They no more combine to form a higher-level unified consciousness than do individual apples in a basket combine to form a higher-level apple. On this view of things, God has a consciousness only in a very tenuous sense—He happens to be the brute aggregate of a large number of entities, some of which happen to be (or have) individual consciousnesses themselves. For example, suppose that the universe contains just three individual consciousnesses (along with some purely material entities): St. Thomas Aquinas, Lucretius and Dobbin the horse. Then "God's consciousness" in this somewhat strained and artificial sense would simply be the aggregate of those particular consciousnesses. There could be no such event as God Himself having a thought or experience—no event of the form, "I am God and I think that P." The only possible events of consciousness would be events whose immediate subjects were Aquinas, Lucretius or Dobbin. God *Himself* could not be the immediate subject of an event of consciousness.

We shall mention just two apparent difficulties with this view, one of which might be thought of as at least partly theological in nature. Such an entity does not seem to be what at least many religious persons would expect of an entity alleged to be God. God understood as merely the aggregate of all the particular entities in the universe would not seem to have the requisite natural unity to be reasonably expected of an ontological ground. How could God be just a *collection* of things? Why use the term "God" at all for an entity which is just a collection?

A second difficulty concerns the position the view must take on the relationship between God and the individual consciousnesses within the universe. If God does not have a unified consciousness in His own right, then it seems that the fact of consciousness in the universe (in the form of individual consciousnesses distinct from God) must be somehow explained without recourse to any ontological ground with a center of consciousness itself. But if our argument in "The Mind-Maker Argument" is sound, any such attempted explanation must fail. For, as we have argued, the existence of consciousness in the world provides a good reason for believing in the existence of an ontological ground which is itself conscious.

The second alternative is that of attributing to God a unified consciousness in His own right. There are at least two ways of understanding such an attribution.

One way is to understand it as the claim that, while God has a single unified consciousness in His own right, the events occurring in that consciousness are in a sense nothing over and above the events occurring in the individual consciousnesses which are parts of the divine consciousness. An example may help. Suppose that there are only four consciousnesses in the universe: Aquinas's, Lucretius', Dobbin's and the universe's—that is, God's. Whenever, say, Aquinas has a conscious experience, God has that very experience Himself, and similarly for the experiences of Lucretius and Dobbin. God never has any conscious experiences of "His own," so to speak. All of the events in His consciousness originate from the other three, but God does not realize it.

This view is susceptible to the Aristotelian challenge sketched earlier. There could be no such divine consciousness. For, suppose that at a given moment, Aquinas judges that God exists and Lucretius judges that God does not exist. According to the view under review, God would simultaneously believe and disbelieve in His own existence. But that is impossible. Hence, there could be no such consciousness.

The second way of understanding an attribution to God of a unified consciousness is construing it as the claim that, although the individual consciousnesses "in" God's mind are *parts* of God's consciousness, the divine consciousness has a higher-order unity which somehow enables God to distinguish between the "inputs" of the "lesser" consciousnesses and those conscious events which are truly "His own." Thus, the events occurring in, say, Aquinas's consciousness would occur in God's consciousness, but God would immediately recognize those events *as* originating in Aquinas's mind and would presumably have the power to "accept" or "reject" any information content they happened to contain. Suppose again that, at a given moment, Aquinas judges that God exists and Lucretius judges that God does not exist. According to this second account of God's unified consciousness, both judgments would occur in God's consciousness, but God would have to have the power to "distance" Himself from those judgments. That is, He would be able to identify them as originating from sources of consciousness outside Himself and thereby realize that He has the power to accept or reject them.

A major difficulty with this view is that it is not obvious that the events in, say, Aquinas's consciousness could be "parts" of God's consciousness in any serious sense. On the contrary, it seems that the very description of the view under discussion presupposes that God's consciousness is really *distinct* from Aquinas's. Think about the form of the events supposedly occurring in God's consciousness in such cases: "I, God, am now immediately apprehending the content of Aquinas's conscious experience and I am apprehending it *as* originating from Aquinas." It seems that the very formulation inevitably distinguishes between God, as the ultimate conscious subject, and Aquinas, as the "transmitter" of the event of consciousness. It seems that any event of consciousness that was truly a "part" of God's own consciousness could not be experienced by God as anything but His own conscious event. On the other hand, if God experiences an event of consciousness as originating in another mind, then it seems that it could not possibly be *His own*.

The upshot seems to be this. On the one hand, if the conscious events originating from other minds are not experienced by God *as* events originating from elsewhere then there is indeed a serious sense in which those other minds would be "parts" of God. But the Aristotelian argument shows that such a divine consciousness is logically impossible. On the other hand, if the conscious events

originating from other minds *are* experienced by God as events originating from
elsewhere, then those other minds could not be "parts" of God's consciousness
in any interesting sense. Thus, the theory confronts an apparent dilemma. If it
uses the term "part" literally, then its God is logically impossible. On the other
hand, if it does not use "part" seriously, then it is not proposing a strict-identity
view at all, but rather a form of dualism.

Strict-identity proponents might counter by denying that consciousnesses
other than God's being "parts" of God's consciousness is logically impossible.
They might urge that the part-whole relationship between the individual consciousnesses which are "in" God's consciousness and God's consciousness itself
is strictly analogous to the part-whole relationship between the parts of any complex physical entity and that entity itself, and that relations of the latter kind are
not only possible, but actual. For example, they might point to the relationship
between a living organic body and its individual cells and argue that it is precisely analogous to the relationship between God's consciousness and other consciousnesses.

But the analogy is doubtful. While there is a sense in which individual cells
can be parts of complex organic bodies, it does not seem that two distinct centers
of consciousness could come together to make up a single consciousness in *any*
sense. Consider, for example, what we would feel obliged to say if studies of
individuals whose corpus callosum has been surgically severed to control epilep-
tic seizures not only showed, amazingly enough, that separated cortices experience and in some sense can learn separately, but that they can form simultaneously opposed judgments, in the full sense of the term, about the truth of propositions. It is very hard to see how it could be reasonably maintained that there was
but one person. There seems to be no *pertinent* difference between siamese twins
connected from the chest down, on the one hand, and cortices joined in the head,
on the other hand, if both cortices, like both twins, can have truly divergent
thoughts. It seems rather that a sufficient condition for a center of consciousness,
C-1, being distinct from a center of consciousness, C-2, is the possibility of C-
1's judgments contradicting those of C-2. And if the contents of C-1 and C-2's
judgments are somehow transmitted to a consciousness (e.g., God's) which in
turn somehow records those contents and uses them for its own cognitive purposes, there would necessarily be three distinct consciousnesses, rather than just
two.

Of course, a strict-identity defender might respond by simply denying that
human consciousnesses are distinct from one another. We have already discussed
similar moves in other strict-identity contexts. Once again, we would be faced
with a strict-identity attempt to avoid the force of obvious objections by denying
presumptively true, common sense, beliefs—in this case, the belief that human
consciousnesses are distinct from one another.

8.   *The fourth strict-identity variation*

We turn to the fourth strict-identity variation—the claim that the universe is a part of God. One of the versions of this variation is the so-called "panentheist" account, according to which, while God contains the universe in some sense, God is a more inclusive entity than the universe.

Obviously, the claim presupposes that God has parts. Now, we have already addressed one aspect of the question of God having parts in our discussion of the third strict-identity variation. There we focused upon the suggestion that individual consciousnesses are parts of God. Obviously, in that regard the fourth variation encounters the same difficulties as the third. If the universe is a part of God, then presumably every part of the universe is a part of God, including any individual consciousnesses there may be. We have tried to sketch at least some of the difficulties inherent in this idea.

We would like to move on to a difficulty for the fourth variation not already addressed in our earlier discussion. In order to formulate that difficulty it is useful to think about the idea of God having parts in a more comprehensive way than we did in the previous section. The claim that God has parts raises at least the following questions: (1) What could it mean in general to say that God has parts? (2) Given each of these possible senses, if there are any, does God have parts in that sense?

We begin with a sense of "part" which seems most immediately accessible— the sense in which one spatial entity can be part of another spatial entity. Does God have parts in that sense? Perhaps He does, but, in any case, saying so would not be open to a proponent of the fourth variation. For, the assumption of the fourth variation is that all spatial entities are included in the universe, which, in turn, is a part of God. If God were a spatial entity Himself, then He would have to be part of the universe, contrary to the assumption.

Thus, if God does not have parts in the way in which some spatio-temporal entities have parts then exactly how does He have parts? Assuming that there is some legitimate sense in which the universe is itself a spatial entity, the question is: In what sense could a non-spatial entity (here God) have a spatial entity (here the universe) as a part? What could "being a part" mean here?

It seems plausible to say that an entity, E-1, is a *part* of an entity, E-2, only if (1) E-1 is not identical to E-2, and (2) any complete description of E-2 would have to mention E-1. Then one might distinguish between two kinds of parts— essential and accidental. An entity, E-1, is an *essential part* of an entity, E-2, only if (1) E-1 is a part of E-2, and (2) E-2 could not exist without E-1. An entity, E-1, is an *accidental part* of an entity, E-2, only if (1) E-1 is a part of E-2, and (2) E-1 is not an essential part of E-2. Presumably, the fourth strict-identity variation must choose between the assertion that the universe is an essential part of God, on the one hand, and the claim that the universe is an accidental part of God, on the other hand.

Suppose that it chooses the first alternative—the universe is an essential part of God. Would that choice result in a conflict with either of the two necessary conditions for an entity's qualifying as God we mentioned earlier—being ontologically independent and being an ontological basis? There seems to be no immediate problem with the first condition. True, the view in question claims that God is ontologically dependent upon the universe, but it maintains that the universe is a *part* of God. Thus, it would not necessarily be logically committed to the thesis that God's existence depends upon at least one factor distinct from Himself. Similarly, there is no apparent problem with the second condition. The fact that God has an essential part—the universe—does not necessarily entail that God, so understood, could not serve as the ontological basis for everything else. Of course, if there was not anything "else," then God would be an ontological basis by default. And if there was something else, then the fact that the universe is an essential part of God would not, by itself, prevent God from providing the ontological basis for those other entities.

However, there is a third often-assumed necessary condition for an entity's qualifying for God-like status, one we have not yet mentioned—a condition which does raise a difficulty for the view under consideration. That condition is *necessary existence*: Whatever other characteristics God might have, He must exist necessarily, if He exists at all. Now, the version of the fourth variation we are now discussing asserts that the universe is an essential part of God. But it seems possible for the universe not to exist at all. Hence, it is possible for God not to exist. But then God could not have necessary existence. Thus, one of the difficulties with this particular version of the fourth variation is its apparent conflict with the view shared by many that existing necessarily is a necessary condition for an entity's being God.

What about the other alternative—that the universe is an accidental part of God? Here a distinction can be drawn between two ways in which this proposal might be understood. On the one hand, it might be understood as the proposition that, although no particular universe is necessary to God's existence, God needs at all times some universe or other. God does not need any particular universe, but He could not exist without a universe. On the other hand, it could be understood as the claim that not only is no particular universe necessary to God's existence, but God doesn't need any universe at all.

Consider the first alternative. It seems that this conception of God conflicts with our third condition of Deity—necessary existence. If God at all times needs some universe or other, then since it is possible for no universe to exist at all, it is likewise possible for God not to exist. But if that is possible, God does not necessarily exist.

What about the second alternative—God could exist without any universe at all? It seems that this position would, in effect, constitute giving up altogether on the claim that the universe is a "part" of God. If God could go right on existing even after the extinction of the universe, it seems that a "complete" description of God would not require a mention of the universe at all.

Of course, there are other potential difficulties with the fourth strict-identity variation. For example, its claim that God has parts apparently conflicts with the belief of many traditional theists, such as Aquinas, that God is a simple (i.e., non-complex) entity. But such issues raise deep and complicated questions we cannot explore here.

9.   *Dualist accounts of God's relationship to the world*

What about the orthodox theistic claim that, while God is distinct from the universe in the sense that He is neither strictly identical to either the universe as a whole or to any part of the universe, He is nevertheless somehow "in" the universe? It might be doubted whether the claim is even coherent. The following line of reasoning might stimulate the doubt.

One might think that the relation, x is in y, is satisfiable in only two possible kinds of situations. In the first, the entity which includes the other (the "inclusive" entity) is not itself identical to the spatio-temporal universe as a whole. Here one might say that the relation, x is in y, is satisfied only if (i) x and y are spatial entities in the sense that each has a location in space, and (ii) the location of x is a part of the location of y. Examples of something's being something else in this sense are an apple's being in a box or Dobbin's brain being in Dobbin. We shall call this the "Sense 1" sense of "in."

In the second kind of situation the inclusive entity is the universe itself. Here one might say that the relation, x is in y, is satisfied only if (i) y is the spatio-temporal universe, and (ii) x is a spatial entity in the sense that x has a location in space. For example, Dobbin is in the universe in this sense. We shall call this the "Sense 2" sense of "in."

Given these analyses, one might reason in the following way. To assert that God is in the universe could only be to assert that God is in the universe in either Sense 1 or Sense 2. But God could not be in the universe in Sense 1, because the universe does not itself have a location in space. Hence, if God is in the universe at all, He must be in it in Sense 2. If so, God must Himself be a spatial entity with a location in space. Then God would Himself would have to be a part of the universe, that is, God would have to be strictly identical to a part of the universe. If God is strictly identical to a part of the universe, God is not distinct from the universe. Hence, orthodox theism contradicts itself in maintaining that God is both distinct from the world and yet in the world.

Indeed, the challenge can be made even more general by eliminating the step denying that God is in the universe in Sense 1. One could simply argue that if God is in the universe at all, He must be in it in either Sense 1 or Sense 2. But in either case God would have to be a spatial entity. Hence, theism contradicts itself, whichever is the case.

The challenge seems invincible, at least on its own turf. So, any theist hoping to meet the challenge must try to put that turf itself in question. That is, a necessary condition for a minimally adequate theism is the articulation of a way in which an entity, x, can be in another entity, y, without x being a spatial entity itself.

It seems that the theist should respond by contending that a non-spatial entity possessing the power to causally interact with the universe in a direct and immediate fashion would properly be deemed "in" the universe in some serious sense. Presumably, such an entity would have the power to causally interact with the universe as a whole; it would have the power to create the universe in the first place, the power to continuously maintain it in existence and the power to extinguish it whenever it chose. It would also have the power to causally interact with any part of the universe in an immediate way; that is, it would not need to use any causal intermediary. It could, for example, directly cause a bush to burn without being consumed, or directly transform the heart of a persecutor of Christianity on the road to Damascus. If these things are possible and if there were an entity which acted in such ways, it would surely seem legitimate to say that it is "in" the world in a significant sense.

Is it possible? How might one go about showing that it is? Perhaps the easiest way of showing something possible is pointing to an actualization of the possibility. Orthodox Christians can point to a great many things: burning bushes, loaves of bread feeding thousands, people raised from the dead, hearts inexplicably transformed and martyrs walking calmly to their deaths singing the praises of God. Christians believe that these, and many other, events furnish grounds for believing in both the possibility and the fact of God's immediate and direct causal intervention in the world. We think that they are right.

C. The Problem of Evil

8

Dostoevskian Horrors and the Problem of Grading Worlds

Sandra Menssen and Thomas Sullivan

Why would a good God make a world with suffering and sorrow and sin? Countless thinkers have taken the question to pose an insurmountable obstacle to religious belief. Countless theists have worked to answer the question. Here we suggest that the traditional "problem of evil" may be resolved *without* answering this question, without speculating about reasons a good God might have for permitting affliction and sin. To this end we argue that:

1. If there is a problem of evil then there is a criterion of goodness for worlds.
2. If there is a criterion of goodness for worlds then the criterion must pre suppose God's existence.
3. So either there is no problem of evil or God exists.

We take up each premise in a separate section.

(1)

What is a criterion of goodness for worlds? It's simply a standard of judgment or evaluation. We commonly evaluate various sorts of things in the world, things that have associated with them general criteria of goodness: knives, for instance (a good knife cuts well), and planes (a good plane flies well), and zoos (a good zoo satisfies visitors and promotes the well-being of its animal inhabitants). There are also things in the world that don't seem to have associated criteria of goodness: clouds, for instances, and minutes, and numbers. It is worth our while to consider whether there is a criterion of goodness for worlds, a standard that makes it meaningful to say a world is good, or that determines which worlds are good and perhaps how the good worlds rank against one another. It is worth our while to take this question up in the course of discussing the problem of evil in part because only if there is a criterion of goodness for *worlds* does it make sense to say that God must (or need not) create a good world. Furthermore, we suggest, investigation of the question leads to a startling result: one ends up concluding that either there is no problem of evil or God exists.

In this first section we argue that if there is a problem of evil then there is a criterion of goodness for worlds: if there is a problem of evil then there are criteria of goodness that apply to *some* states of affairs or phenomena, and if there are criteria of goodness that apply to some states of affairs or phenomena then there are criteria of goodness that apply to the world as a whole. We assume (and expect it to be widely agreed) that if there is no criterion of goodness for worlds, then either there are no criteria of goodness that apply to any states of affairs or phenomena, whether these states of affairs be proper parts of the whole world or not; or while there may be criteria of goodness that apply to states of affairs or phenomena within the world, there are no criteria that apply to the world as a whole.

How does the problem of evil present itself? A person encounters particular evils—he witnesses the suffering of others, he discovers the depths of his own depravity. And on the basis of such experiences he asks: How could a good God make a world like this? That's to say: why would a good God do it? Or perhaps he thinks: I wouldn't expect to understand the reasons an infinite, divine being might have for making a world of some sort, but I do expect to understand *that there could be such reasons*, and this I do not understand. Or perhaps he thinks: OK, I'll grant that there might possibly be such reasons, but it seems to me immensely unlikely that the reasons do exist, so I don't take the possibility seriously.

Each of these lines of thought generates a problem of evil. The precise formulation of the problem will depend on the antecedent beliefs of the person doing the formulating, and the particular aspects of the world that strike him as troublesome, and ways in which they strike him as troublesome. As our Questioner develops his formulation—somewhere along the way—he needs to refer to the goodness or badness of the world as a whole, we suggest. Let's consider why.

In the first place, anyone formulating a problem of evil will need to recognize that there are general criteria or factors that underlie the problem. In the face of the most extreme cases of affliction and wickedness it may seem tempting to think that we just *look* at the evils and see that they couldn't have been made by a good, all-powerful, all-knowing being, or that it's highly improbable they were, or that it's improbable enough to prompt the question "why?". If the evil viewed is very close to home (the torture and murder of one's own child), or, though distant, of great magnitude (the genocides of the twentieth century, the conscription of young children into armies and their subsequent brutalization), then one need not go to great lengths to elaborate what it is about the situations that's appalling. But though it may seem in some way crude and repellent to try to articulate what it is about such evils that we find appalling, it's all too easy to begin the task. One can always cite some general factors to take into account. Extreme physical suffering, psychological pain so profound that there is a disintegration of self, moral decay — all of these factors can be mentioned and described in detail for anyone obtuse enough to request it, the Questioner will say.

How general must the general factors be? A person might say: here's the factor: God can't make a world where I or mine suffer. But even if this is the first, almost instinctual response, no one publicly articulates the position, and for good reason. Actually, for a variety of good reasons. It can't be my suffering *qua my suffering* that's the problem partly because we all can imagine deserving pain. The point is strikingly illustrated by Solzhenitsyn's account of the Gulag. At one point in his discussion he offers the sobering reflection that those imprisoned with him, though convinced they were wrongly imprisoned, were also convinced that they had done something at some point in their lives that merited the suffering they were experiencing.

And if the Questioner still insists that it's *his* suffering *qua his* that's relevant, he can be asked to imagine a possible world like our own where he has a counterpart, a person very like him but not him. It would be absurd for a person to insist that his own suffering poses a problem for theism but the suffering of his counterpart, which is similarly intense and similarly extensive, does not.

So the Questioner generalizes: suffering and sorrow and sin *of a particular sort* generates the problem of evil (or various problems of evil). And of course in explaining what sort of evil is problematical one dismisses small inconveniences, little pains and little trials. The fact I have a hangnail and no scissors at hand to remove it immediately may safely be ignored; the fact my counterpart in some other world has a hangnail is likewise insignificant.

Furthermore, as a Questioner reflects on the matter it becomes clear that there are some large inconveniences, some big pains and some major trials that we may also set aside in demarcating the evils that generate a problem for theism. Imagine, for instance, that a little girl in second grade is having some trouble adjusting to the new school she's been attending since her father's recent job relocation. There's a little boy that pulls her ponytail during class, sometimes really hard; there's another child who won't share crayons unless the teacher is looking; the lunches that are served contain vegetables she doesn't like, and the teacher is demanding, to the girl's dismay, that as the students read out loud they try to sound out the words they don't know. From the little girl's point of view these aren't insignificant matters at all. She is genuinely quite unhappy, and desperately tells her mother that she doesn't want to go back to school. It occurs to no one to say: a mother who doesn't take her daughter out of the school can't be good. We commonly think that there's a whole set of fairly significant inconveniences, pains, and trials that can be permitted because they are intrinsic to greater goods.

Let's assume that there's a range of minor evils that are not objectionable, perhaps because they're too insignificant to matter whether or not they conduce to greater goods, or perhaps because they have some small significance, but it's outweighed by the fact that they conduce to, and are necessary for obtaining, goods of one sort of another. Let's also assume, however, that as one gradually intensifies or extends the pain and suffering, physical and psychological and spiritual, one approaches the threshold of the permissible. Let's call the suffering on the other side of the threshold "Affliction". It's profound human suffering and sorrow and sin that matter; it's human Affliction that matters. Now it is our contention that one can't generalize in this way, one can't refer to "human Affliction" without having criteria that apply to whole worlds. Protesting the existence of afflicted humans is protesting the design or structure of the world.

Imagine that someone responds to our contention as follows: "Look, the evils in the world that strike me as inconsistent with a good God, or at least as providing strong evidence against a good God, are really a small part of the whole world. Of course the troublesome evils go further than my own back yard; I'm not claiming that I alone suffer in such a way as to generate the problem of evil. Of course they don't include hangnails or even rather strong childhood anxieties about the school cafeteria serving green beans instead of corn. But I can give a fairly precise characterization of the troublesome evils without passing any judgment on the world as a whole, without invoking the claim that the world as a whole is bad or deficient in some way. I have no idea what it means to say that the world as a whole is good or bad. But I'm quite certain that a particular set of phenomena in the world, and, of course, other similar phenomena, pose a very special problem. My claim is that there is a class of grotesque evils, evils typified by the horrors Dostoevski describes in *The Brothers Karamazov*, that a good God wouldn't permit. More specifically, I contend that if there is something a moral agent can do or refrain from doing that would prevent Affliction from striking the child tortured by her parents, the agent ought to do it."

This "Dostoevskian objection", as we will call it, is similar to a position taken by Marilyn Adams. In recent years she has called our attention to the importance of the "existential" problem of evil, the problem of understanding God's goodness to individual human beings. She recommends that Christian philosophers interested in the problem of evil turn from the global or holistic approach that has dominated discussions of God's goodness, an approach illustrated by Pike's and Plantinga's explorations of ways in which the *world's* goodness can defeat evils, and instead focus on God's justice and goodness to *individuals*. Only by focusing on God's agent-centered goodness, she suggests, will we be able to respond to the existential problem of evil embodied in the claims of an Ivan Karamazov, of one who tells us that higher harmony and *global* goods are no vindication of God's goodness to individuals.

So let us consider the claim that if there is something a moral agent can do or refrain from doing that would prevent Affliction from striking an innocent child, the agent ought to do it. The obvious response to this claim is that the agent's action (the doing or omitting) may have other consequences equally objectionable, may result in the Affliction of a different innocent child. So the objector needs to qualify the principle, needs to change it to something like this: If there is an action a moral agent can perform or refrain from performing that would keep all human beings out of a state of Affliction, then the agent ought to do it. (Although there is a superficial distinction between acting and refraining from acting, it is only superficial.)

But is this principle correct? The principle suggests there are certain conditions that can't be tolerated no matter what the consequences of not tolerating them. Consider a situation where an agent has the option of acting (or refraining from acting) in such a way that one person will be pushed over the "threshold" we have imagined, pushed into a state of Affliction; but at the same time a million persons will be spared a state which is just this side of Affliction. A million persons will be spared intense physical and psychological torment which stops just short of the forbidden threshold. Is it really wrong for the agent to refrain from some action, realizing that as a consequence of inaction a million will suffer almost indescribably, and one will be spared the state of Affliction?

It seems one can put *oneself* in the way of the worst kind of harm in order to obtain some great good for others. And if that is the case, then the principle in question is false. It is heroic to subject oneself to the most intense horrors, heroic to take on the most profound suffering and Affliction for the sake of others. The soldier who throws himself on a grenade to save his comrades, some of whom are at a distance such that their death or disfigurement would not be inevitable, is rightly honored. The mother who enters a burning house to save her children, voluntarily undergoing the severest pain, dying without knowing that her actions have in fact saved her children from death (perhaps painless death by smoke inhalation), is rightly praised. In such actions reside courage and nobility.

Only if the Dostoevskian builds into a description of Affliction a component of sin, sin on the part of the person Afflicted, is it wrong for a person to "accept" Affliction for the sake of others. But the horrors Dostoevski describes certainly do not build sin on the part of the Afflicted into an account of Affliction. On the contrary, the horrors are striking partly because those they mark are *innocent* sufferers: children, mostly; babies bayoneted by soldiers, a little boy forced to play the role of a hunted fox and ultimately torn to pieces by dogs, a little girl tortured by her own parents.

This line of thinking drives us in the direction of saying it's *better* if the soldier who sees the grenade fall nearby throws himself upon it and dies a heroic death, better for his comrades, better for unnamed persons, better for his country. And note that when we say these things we don't imagine that the sacrificial action is better for the hero's country and worse for *all other* countries. Perhaps we take it for granted—perhaps naively—that it will be good for nations at large for our own country to win the war we're imagining. But if it's not, that's relevant to our ultimate assessment of the value of the sacrificial action (though perhaps not of the moral character of the soldier who makes the sacrifice). Plato's account of justice in the city is interesting and insightful in certain ways, but it suffers from its parochialism. A full account of justice will require consideration of the relations between the Republic and other city-states. Similarly, Rawls's account of justice in a nation requires—and in fact lends itself to—supplementation by a theory of international justice. If one accepts the idea that rules of justice for a particular nation can be chosen in an "original position" in which persons do not know their position in the society whose rules they are trying to construct, there seems no reason not to accept the idea that rules of international justice can be constructed by imagining a choice situation in which persons don't know their own country. We find ourselves pushing out the context of who or what counts. Ultimately, it's better, simpliciter, that the soldier or the mother dies the hero. And what is it to be better, simpliciter? It's to be better for the *world*. One cannot stop this process of pushing out the context of what counts short of the world. One can't stop at the level of humankind, for if only humans matter, if other things in the world don't, then one is committed to some criterion according to which only humans matter. And that over-arching criterion gives us a criterion of what it is for things to be better simpliciter. Whether or not only humans matter, one is into a criterion of goodness for worlds.

Another way of making this point (that the soldier's heroic action is better simpliciter) is to note that the kind of morality the atheist is tacitly propounding must be something close to Aquinas's morality, where there is a focus on the common good, on a structured whole that includes the individual. The atheist who puts forth the problem of evil can't be using a Kantian morality; the statement of the problem is too tightly tied to sufferings. It's not an egoist morality; the case isn't made with reference to "me qua me." And it's not a utilitarian morality.

It's worth noting that neither is our own position utilitarian. In claiming that Dostoevskian horrors can in principle be justified, can contribute to greater goods, we're *not* saying that any evil whatsoever can be included in a whole that's sufficiently good. A situation in which God deceived us, or intended our sin, would, we think, be absolutely unacceptable; its inclusion in a world would mark that world as absolutely unacceptable. No matter how great the other goods in the world, a good God could not bring about such a world.

It is of course the case that God *permits* our deception, and *permits* our sin.

But although "it's not the case that there is evil" is the contradictory of "there is evil," the contradictory of "God wills that there is no evil" is *not* "God wills that there is evil," but rather "it is not the case that God wills that there is no evil". There is an intermediate state between "God wills that there is no evil" and "God wills that there is evil." The intermediate state is the state in which God permits evil, but does not will it.

John 3:16 tells us that God so loved the *world* that he gave his only son to die for it. Christ dies a hero's death for the world. Nobody ever says God shouldn't have put Christ through the degradations he suffered if Christ goes on to assume a heavenly throne as savior of the world. Heroism trumps all.

(2)

If there is a criterion of goodness for worlds then, we contend, the criterion must presuppose God's existence. We support this claim by examining various criteria of goodness for worlds that have actually been proposed (functional, utilitarian, and aesthetic criteria), and arguing that only those that presuppose God's existence operate as we reasonably expect a criterion of goodness for worlds to operate. How do we reasonably expect a criterion of goodness for worlds to operate? We want a criterion that matches up in a very general way with our "intuitions" about the goodness of worlds, and (a related point) that allows us plausibly to say a good God has reason for creating a good world, and ought not to create a bad world.

Very often a thing's function determines its criterion of goodness. What might it mean to say that the world has a function? If the world has a designer or maker, then it might seem natural to think its function is set by its designer's or maker's intentions: a good world, on this line, would be a world that did what its maker or designer intended it to do. But while this suggestion at first glance may seem attractive, its attraction is undermined by reflection on the hypothesis that the world's maker or designer is a super-powerful, super-knowledgeable demon, an evil genius. For in such a case a world that did what its evil maker designed it to do would not be a world that matches up with any general intuitions we might have about the goodness of worlds. Since a person who claims the world is good presumably intends to say more than that its maker is smart enough and strong enough to bring his plans to fruition, the criterion under consideration here would not give us a sufficient condition for identifying good worlds. And it doesn't give us a necessary condition, either, if we acknowledge the possibility that a good designer may have intentions which in some sense go unrealized because free creatures the designer has chosen to include in the world do not themselves make the right or the best choices.

It might well be possible to say a good world is one that fulfills its designer's or maker's intentions if we stipulate that the designer or maker, the creator, is a good creator. But with this stipulation the criterion under consideration becomes a theistic criterion.

Perhaps instead of trying to identify the function of the world by attending to a designer's purposes, we could turn to the purposes or needs or desires of the organisms or inhabitants of the world. But since this turn is a turn into utilitarianism, we defer consideration of it for the moment.

Might it be possible to identify a world's function not with its designer's purposes, and not with its inhabitants' purposes or needs, but instead with the world's capacity to sustain itself, to promote its own benefit, to flourish as some sort of organism? Plato's Timaeus portrays the world in such a way, as do contemporary discussions of the "Gaia hypothesis," a hypothesis which takes the world to be itself an organism, a living entity. But here again there doesn't seem to be a close match between our intuitions about good and bad worlds and the kind of sorting this criterion would provide. Our intuitions about good and bad worlds (if we have such intuitions) are likely to be tied to the environment we as humans find desirable. And presumably the criterion at issue would direct us to count as "bad" worlds that weren't sufficiently long-lived, or perhaps worlds that did not contain within themselves mechanisms for regeneration, for reproduction *of the worlds themselves*. Maybe we could have worlds counted as "good" which included terrible suffering and predation among individual species, so long as we had species properly balancing one another in eco-systems that were self-sustaining. So we don't get the requisite match between intuitions and criterion.

Ultimately, all these approaches to generating a criterion of goodness for worlds out of functions worlds may have seem doomed because *absent a theistic context* worlds don't seem to have natural functions. A world qua world doesn't do anything essentially. It's not *for* anything, essentially. Some structure outside the world is necessary in order for a world to have a function. Within a theistic context it is possible to hold that a world is good insofar as it images or represents God; it is possible to see it as having the function of imaging or representing God. Aquinas (among others) has taken this view. He holds that the world's goodness depends on the goodness of its parts (or species) and on the order of the parts; the order of the parts depends on how they are related to one another and on the end to which they are directed—God.

Aquinas's understanding here follows Aristotle in holding that the good is that which all things desire. Although Aristotle spoke of "desire" very broadly, in such a way as to allow that even inanimate things have certain appetites or desires, we may perhaps still see the claim that the good is what is rationally preferable as Aristotelian. Then it seems possible to argue that the world (as a whole) is good if and only if it is good for a conscious being who is either identical with the world or independent of the world. Since the world is not itself a conscious being, if the world is good then it is good for some conscious being independent of the world. And one may well have an understanding of function which permits one to say that the world fulfills its function if and only if it is good for God.

Notice that if we imagine a "demonistic" context for the creation of worlds it is far less plausible to think we can "naturally" identify a function for worlds. If a demon or evil genius makes a world that demon may decree that his creation has some particular function or purpose, but the decree itself isn't enough to guarantee that the function obtains. Inhabitants of the world may rebel against the evil creator's designs, may make their own decisions about what is of ultimate value or import in the world or about what their own flourishing will involve. The intentions of an evil demon would not trump such decisions. It is only in the context of a good creator with good intentions and purposes that it makes sense to say the function simpliciter of the world is to image or represent the creator.

Let us turn to the possibility of finding a non-theistic criterion of goodness for worlds through utilitarianism. Initially this may seem an attractive possibility, since the "intuitions" typically expressed by those who think this is a bad world are intuitions about the balance between pain and suffering, on the one hand, and pleasure and happiness, on the other. And historically the utilitarian option has in fact seemed to some an acceptable way of setting out a criterion of goodness for worlds. Leibniz, for instance, appears to include (as part of a multifaceted criterion of goodness for worlds) the claim that God is an act-utilitarian.

But there are serious difficulties with this proposal. In the first place, we think, various more or less standard objections to utilitarianism will surface. The utilitarian focused on defending a criterion guiding human action needs to offer some way of summing the total amount of happiness or pleasure and unhappiness or pain; similarly, one who suggests that worlds are good insofar as they maximize happiness or pleasure or utility is committed to the idea that it's in principle possible to sum the utility in the world as a whole. We are ourselves highly sceptical that this is possible. The utilitarian offering a theory of morality for humans needs to confront the objection that rights of individuals may end up being wrongly sacrificed for the sake of the greater good. Similarly, one who offers a utilitarian criterion of goodness for worlds faces the criticism that the rights of individuals are ignored. Again, we are sympathetic to this oft-cited problem for utilitarianism. And in fact, the intuition that there are some things individuals shouldn't be asked to sacrifice for the greater good seems to underlie the Dostoevskian principle we considered in section (1) of this paper.

But even if these more or less standard objections to utilitarianism are set aside, even if we just assume for the sake of the argument that the problems can be solved, one who seeks to defend a utilitarian criterion of goodness for *worlds* still faces a serious difficulty. The utilitarian standard presumably rests on an intuition that it is important to make sentient and rational creatures happy, or more specifically perhaps, to satisfy their preferences. But if this intuition is trustworthy, then surely the desires or preferences of beings *outside* the world will also be important. There's no good reason to exclude such preferences from consideration. And if we imagine the possibility of a powerful and highly knowledgeable maker or designer then we imagine the possibility of a being with very heavily weighted preferences or desires: the utilitarian reasonably counts human happiness as at least sometimes out-weighing the happiness of non-human creatures in importance, and likewise, the utilitarian will have to count divine happiness or satisfaction of preferences as out-ranking or out-weighing human happiness. If the creator is infinite, perhaps the weight assigned to satisfaction of its preferences will also be infinite.

So it looks like according to the criterion at issue a creator might be able to make any world it pleased, and the world would be judged good. But if any world a creator makes could be judged good, we certainly do not have a criterion that matches starting intuitions about which worlds count as good and which count as bad.

Might it be possible to articulate an acceptable aesthetic criterion of goodness for worlds? People who judge that the actual world is a good world are often struck by nature's splendor and majesty. And here again, the criterion has had historical appeal: Leibniz did think that God was an act utilitarian, but he also thought God would make the most beautiful world (since we derive pleasure from contemplation of what is beautiful, the two standards are supposed to coincide).

How is an aesthetic criterion of goodness to be specified, if not in terms of the pleasure certain states of affairs produce in sentient or rational beings? Perhaps the criterion could be specified in terms of the degree of organic unity or harmony in a world. And what is organic unity? For a start, we may say that an organically unified whole has diverse parts that fit together in some way judged complementary, some way that makes the whole unified. One whole will have a higher degree of organic unity than a second if the first unifies a larger number of things, or more kinds of things than the second, or if the degree of complementarity or tightness in the whole is higher.

A full account of organic unity would need to be much more detailed than this, but for our purposes here a full account is not necessary. For it is easy enough to see that the criterion of organic unity does not fulfill the expectations we have of a criterion of goodness for worlds. Is it even possible for there to exist disharmonious possible worlds, worlds with some negative score on the scale of organic unity? If not, how do we determine where the mark of "sufficiently beautiful for a good God to create" gets placed? For any such mark we try to set, the question can be raised: why is a world below this mark a world a good God shouldn't create? Imagine a very simple world, with few constituents (no sentient beings, let's say), little diversity, and hence little complexity. Why would a person stipulate that a good God would not create such a world? If, as orthodox theism teaches, there was no necessity attached to God's creation, if God could have chosen not to create, it is hard to understand why it would be impermissible for God to create the simple sort of world we're imagining.

Furthermore, there may be worlds that *do* have a high degree of harmony or organic unity which we'd think a good God shouldn't create. Many atheists probably think the actual world is of exactly this sort. One who is bothered by horrendous suffering and affliction is unlikely to find it comforting to be told that, after all, the whole is quite beautiful when one stands back and looks at it.

In sum: Functional criteria of goodness for worlds require that we identify a function of the world; absent a theistic frame of reference there's no good way to do this, and no way to do it that matches up with our starting intuitions about the goodness of worlds. Within a theistic framework a functional criterion for worlds is attractive. Utilitarian criteria of goodness for worlds, at least those broadened to include preferences and desires outside as well as inside the world, seriously conflict with our most general intuitions about which worlds count as good and bad. Aesthetic criteria do not correspond in any obvious way to our general intuitions about which worlds count as good and bad. So it seems reasonable to think that if there is a criterion of goodness for worlds then the criterion must presuppose God's existence.

9

Homer, God, and Evil

Sandra Menssen and Thomas Sullivan

The Problem

What is the most promising search strategy for a philosophically inclined nonbeliever wanting to investigate the claim that there is a good God, a Creator of the vast oceans and the undiscovered stars whose eye is on the sparrow, and the child in Sudan, and the baby in the next room?

At the beginning of the *Summa Theologica*, after a few preliminary remarks about the nature of theology, Aquinas turns to the question of God's existence. He argues against the position he takes to be St. Anselm's that God's existence is not self-evident in the way that permits us to dispense with argumentation. Our Inquirer, the philosophically inclined nonbeliever, will no doubt side with Aquinas here. Aquinas then asks whether the existence of God is demonstrable. He draws a distinction. No, if we are thinking of the kind of top-notch argument that Aristotle depicts in the *Posterior Analytics*, the kind of argument Aquinas calls a *propter quid* demonstration. A top-notch demonstration not only shows that something is the case but explains why; it is at once a proof and an explanation. But the final explanation of why things behave the way they do, have the properties and relations that they have, involves causal structures dependent on the essence of the entities in question. For a *propter quid* demonstration one must grasp the essence of the thing. And nobody in this world grasps the essence of the Being that is the cause of the world. So there can be no demonstration in this sense.

However, Aquinas says, there can be a demonstration in the *quia* sense, if there is a God. For a *quia*-demonstration is just a proof, not a proof-explanation. You don't need to know the essence of the Being under consideration. Reverse explanation is all this required; move backwards from effect to cause. But (let us assume) our Inquirer encounters notorious difficulties with Aquinasís proofs, and, unhappily, judges that the proofs fall short of what we would expect even of a *quia*-demonstration.

Where does that leave our Inquirer? Well, some answer, there are always non-deductive or probabilistic arguments — for belief in God to be rational it is enough if the argument for God's existence is better than the argument against. And so it is. But it is not at all clear that if one tries to reason from motion, efficient causality, contingency, teleology, and the like, one will end up with a case that is more probable than not on the natural evidence. Richard Swinburne, who explicitly sees his work as carrying on the tradition of Aquinas, as using the science of the day to produce the strongest possible argument for God, is probably the best-known contemporary advocate and technician of probabilistic natural theology. But at least two very serious difficulties militate against his conclusion. First, he assigns exceedingly strong weight to considerations of simplicity as he develops his estimates of the probability that there is an omnipotent, omniscient, wholly good God.

And second, Swinburne's treatment of the problem of evil falls far short of what is necessary to establish that the probability of God's existence is >.5. Swinburne decides (after his discussion of reasons a good God might have for allowing evil) not to allow evil to count at all against God's existence; and Swinburne proceeds on this basis to further develop his Bayesian argument for God.[1] The Inquirer we are imagining need not read tomes of criticism to judge whether Swinburne's decision here is reasonable. The Inquirer can make his own judgment about Swinburne's decision on the basis of the justification offered in the text:

> Everything turns on a quantitative moral judgment (i.e. a judgment about the *quantity* of evil which it is justifiable to bring about or to allow to occur, or the *quantity* of good which it is obligatory to create). Quantitative judgments are the hardest moral judgments on which to reach a sure conclusion.[2]

But lots of people believe (and have argued) that everything does not turn on a judgment about the amount of evil in the world: the *distribution* of evil is at least equally disturbing for many — famously, for Dostoyevsky; less famously, for many of us, who are especially moved by the affliction of the innocent and the vulnerable.

Countless thinkers inquiring into the rationality of religious belief have foundered on the existence of evil. Camus seemed to regard it as conclusive evidence for atheism. Hume, famous for his general scepticism as well as his attack on the "argument from design" for God's existence, may have taken evil to be the only serious obstacle to belief in God. In fact, his *Dialogues Concerning Natural Religion* can be read as suggesting the argument from design would be persuasive were it not for the evil in the world. Darwin, James Rachels, and Iris Murdoch, critics of the design argument, also appear to find evil an insurmountable problem for the theist. Quentin Smith sees the problem of evil as blocking acceptance of the cosmological argument. Scores of other contemporary philosophers could be added here to the list of those who reject the existence of God because of the world's evils. And it is not merely agnostics and atheists who are troubled by the problem of evil. Augustine's great, almost overwhelming intellectual attraction to Manicheism, with its hypothesis of a supreme Evil constantly warring with a supreme Good, can be ascribed to the forcefulness with which the problem of evil impressed itself upon him. Leibniz, increasingly recognized as one of the very greatest of all philosophers, published but one book in his lifetime: *Theodicy*. Virtually every systematic theistic philosopher has offered reflections on the problem of evil (if not full-blown theodicy).

Given the obstacle the problem of evil may pose for an Inquirer following Swinburne's line of argument, it is reasonable to consider other search strategies that may be offered our Inquirer. Throughout the tradition individuals from time to time have pointed to religious experience or miracles as capable of grounding arguments for God, or at least of grounding belief in God. But although it seems conceptually possible that religious experience can impress itself with such force that one no more needs to reason whether light is radiating from God than to reason whether it is radiating from the sun, the Inquirer we are imagining does not claim such experience (neither do many believers). And a contemporary Inquirer will be all too conscious of the notorious unreliability of witnesses to putative miracles.

Accepting these limitations in classical proof strategies, some contemporary religiously-minded philosophers have argued that belief in God is basic for them, is a part of their epistemic foundations. Well, maybe so—for them. But religious belief presumably is not lodged indefeasibly in the epistemic foundations of our Inquirer.

Some philosophically sophisticated believers have suggested that science and religion by their natures cannot conflict, and that the religious language-game has a logic of its own, immunizing it against the traditional problem of evil. A Wittgensteinian fideist might suggest, for instance, that even if there turns out not to be an afterlife at the world's end, Christianity is not thereby falsified, since the meaning and value of a religious life does not lie in the hope or expectation of immortality. In some sense, surely, the meaning would not be drained out of a saint's life should it turn out that the beatific vision Christianity promises in an afterlife does not exist. The love the saint has shown to his or her fellow human beings, the virtues developed, the truths discovered, will still remain. But even though the holy person has not loved, and struggled for virtue, and searched for truth *in order* to gain an eternal vision of God, if there is no such vision his life will have been monumentally misguided, perhaps even foolish. A faith without risk, a faith nothing can show to be false, is a faith without content. And few Inquirers are drawn to such a faith.

What options remain to the Inquirer who has rejected the claim that God's existence is self-evident, who has rejected the possibility of either a *propter quid* or a *quia* demonstration, who has found probabilistic arguments (of the sort Swinburne develops) defective, who hasn't had self-authenticating religious experiences, who is sceptical of reports of miracles, who doesn't have religious beliefs that are properly basic, and who regards Wittgensteinian fideism as vacuous and uninviting? Is there *any* other option, aside from agnosticism?

Yes.

The Existence of Homer: The Significance of the Content of a Text

We want to suggest that if the content of revelatory claims is included in the evidential base used in assessing the probability of God's existence, the probability can be raised above .5.

Our proposal to include the content of revelatory claims in the evidential base may seem paradoxical. After all, the proposition *A good God has revealed thus and thus* embeds the proposition that *There exists a good God.* If the embedded proposition is improbable, so is the more complex proposition. For as the probability of p & q cannot exceed the probability of either conjunct, so the probability of a more complex proposition cannot exceed the probability of a simpler embedded proposition. *Emily ran swiftly* cannot be more probable than Emily ran.

But this is too quick. While it is true[3] that the probability of a more complex proposition cannot exceed that of an embedded component, given the same evidential base e-1, the more complex proposition can be more probable on a fuller evidential base e-2 than the embedded proposition on the slenderer base e-1. And so even if on just the cosmological evidence, or the cosmological plus the teleological evidence, it is improbable that *There exists a good God*, it certainly does not follow that on the total evidence one might have, evidence that includes but goes beyond the cosmological and teleological evidence, it is improbable that *There exists a good God that has revealed thus and thus.*

How can an Inquirer amplify the evidential base to include more than the cosmological and teleological evidence standardly adduced in arguments for God's existence? What we suggest is taking into account the *content* of a putative revelatory claim that is up for evaluation.

It will be helpful to consider a parallel case. The ancient Greeks appear to have believed that both the *Iliad* and the *Odyssey* were written by a single author, Homer. But they seem to have known almost no facts about his life—they didn't even know when he lived. In modern times questions were raised as to whether the two epics had a single author; indeed, some thought it doubtful that either one of the texts had a single author. The argument was put forward that the *Iliad* and the *Odyssey* are too long to have been composed by a single author, given that writing was not known at the time.

If one is convinced by the point that it's impossible for a poem the length of the *Iliad* or the *Odyssey* to have been retained in the memory of one human being (and certainly impossible for both poems to have been retained in one mind), then it's not going to matter much what the contents of the poems are, what the internal or intrinsic evidence for a single author is.

It has turned out, however, that our knowledge of what memory can do when writing is not familiar has dispelled the argument that it would have been impossible for a single individual to have had the two poems in mind. Now the question can arise, given that it is not impossible, was there in fact one author? And in answering this question the content of the poems must be considered. The cohesiveness of each poem as a whole, and the fit between the two poems, can be examined. The consistency of the characters in the poems, the richness of the language, the vocabulary itself (including particular abstract nouns, Aeolic forms, and, patronymics), the type and number of similes, the structure of the action in the two works, the type of transitions used between major scenes—all these elements, and others as well, have been discussed by scholars and used as a basis for making a judgment about whether the *Iliad* and the *Odyssey* have a single author, i.e., whether Homer actually existed. The current consensus of opinion among the classicists seems to be that it is more likely than not that the two poems did have one author, that Homer did actually exist.

So an inquirer begins by wondering whether Homer existed. The chief obstacle to accepting the view that he did exist is that it seems impossible for one person to actually carry off the feat of composing the *Iliad* and the *Odyssey*. But once the inquirer is satisfied that it is not exceedingly unlikely that a person author poems the length of the *Iliad* and *Odyssey* without the aid of writing, the inquirer can then look to the poems themselves to see whether it is probable that one person, a Homer, did produce both works. The content of the poems can bring the probability of the existence of Homer up over .5. Similarly, we suggest, if it can be established that the probability of there being a creator is not exceedingly low on the body of natural evidence, then our sincere, philosophically inclined nonbelieving Inquirer can turn to the contents of documents purported to be revealed (and to other evidence ordinarily left out of the picture), and perhaps bring the probability of God's existence up past .5.

To illustrate the power of bringing the contents of a putative revelatory claim into consideration let us take a specific example. Consider a case in which we find a young man, destitute and starving, who tells us he comes from a wealthy family. We try to assess the a priori probability that his father loves him. We resolve at the outset to set aside questions of the motivation a loving father might have for leaving a son in destitution until we've arrived at an initial a priori calculation — and in so doing we preclude ourselves from understanding this prodigal son and his father.

Probabilistic arguments that follow Swinburne's strategy in assessing the revelatory claim of Christianity — probabilistic arguments that *preclude* the content of putative revelatory claims in making an assessment about whether there is a good God — seem similar to this futile strategy of trying to get at the truth about whether the prodigal son has a loving father. For there are serious insolubilia — the problem of evil is the most noteworthy example — that may well arise in the very beginning stages of an investigation into theism, insolubilia that for some will not be adequately handled without seeing details of the Christian story, without understanding the economy of salvation, for instance, and reflecting on the mystery of human and divine suffering.

What would Swinburne make of this? He does consider the possibility of appealing to Christian doctrine in order to deal with the problem of evil. He writes, for instance, that:

> If any one wishes to add this hypothesis [of an afterlife] to theism to save it from the force of an argument from evil, he must however bear in mind that theism then becomes a more complicated hypothesis, and hence has less prior probability and so needs more in the way of confirming evidence to raise its over-all probability on evidence, to (e.g.) more than 1/2.[4]

And Swinburne comes to the same conclusion about other hypotheses that could be added from Christian doctrine. But the conclusion only makes sense if one can push the probability that God exists given all the natural evidence (but excluding "theistic hypotheses") up over .5. We think that more than a few people aren't going to be able to do this, because they're not going to be able to go along with Swinburne's view that evil does not count at all against the existence of God.

Swinburne says that once his entire line of argument has been accepted a person will be in a position to go back over the argument and strengthen certain premises, including the premise that claims God's existence is probable on the natural evidence. In describing the tetalogy to which *Responsibility and Atonement* and *Revelation* belong, he indicates that having worked through the Christian doctrine treated by the tetralogy a person comes to a fuller understanding of divine goodness, and then naturally

> comes to investigate whether all these doctrines provide more resources than does natural theology on its own for understanding God's purpose in creating a universe, and allowing evil to occur in it.[5]

But again, we suggest, lots of people (including lots of people appreciative of philosophical argument, and in particular including our imagined Inquirer) aren't going to get this far, because the pool of evidence on which Swinburne bases the probability of God's existence is unnecessarily restricted.

In order for an Inquirer of the sort we are imagining to have the requisite motivation to examine the content of a particular revelatory claim (such as the Christian revelatory claim), the Inquirer must think God's existence is not impossible. A classical scholar who believes Homer couldn't have existed will not read the poems with an eye particularly attentive to relevant internal evidence. Natural theology can play an essential role for many a sincere Inquirer simply by arguing that God's existence is possible, or even better, by arguing that God's existence has some degree of plausibility (maybe at least .25).

In our view the most convincing argument natural theology can develop here begins with the following propositions:

(1) The world came to be.

(2) Necessarily, nothing comes to be without a cause.

Who is in a position to be very confident that one or both of these propositions is false? Consider proposition (1). Quentin Smith, a very knowledgeable critic of theism, keeps insisting that there is now enough evidence "to justify the belief that the universe began to exist" (Smith also thinks it began without a cause, but postpone this point for a moment).[6] Given the way theories in science keep getting overturned, perhaps we should not be too surprised if the grounds for Smith's position that the universe began to exist, that it came to be, shift next week. Still, judging from what we are told by many working in the field, it looks as if the worst that can be said is that there is no more reason to reject (1) than to accept it. It looks like we can assign proposition (1) a probability of .5, and this without even adding in the weight of various philosophical arguments adduced through the centuries for (1).

What about premise (2)? Many philosophers have thought (2) is just dead evident. The great Scottish philosopher Thomas Reid put it this way: "That neither existence, nor any mode of existence, can begin without an efficient cause is a principle that appears very early in the mind of man; and it is so universal, and so firmly rooted in human nature, that the most determined skepticism cannot eradicate it."[7] It is not even clear that for all the skeptical questions he raised about causality, Hume actually rejected it. In a letter to John Stewart in February 1754, Hume writes: "But allow me to tell you that I never asserted so absurd a Proposition as that *anything might arise without a cause.* I only maintain'd that, our Certainty of the Falsehood of that Proposition proceeded neither from Intuition nor Demonstrations; but from another Source."[8] It is not necessary for our purposes to insist that the denial of (2) is absurd. For present purposes it is enough to realize that (2) is a quite plausible principle. Assign it a probability of .5; then given that premise (1) has a probability of (at least) .5, it will be (at least) .25 probable that the world was caused to exist.

Of course, nothing in the argument just given entails that the cause of the world is a good God. But that doesn't render the argument useless. Aquinas's procedure in developing the Five Ways and the subsequent arguments in the *Summa* concerning the attributes of the first cause provide one illustration of how a starting argument for a god or a creator can be snowballed into something much bigger. We think there's much to be said for the general approach Aquinas takes here. Begin not by asking whether the hypothesis Swinburne focuses on, the hypothesis that there is an omnipotent, omniscient, perfectly good God is demonstrable or probable; rather, ask the much more manageable question of whether there is some plausibility to the hypothesis that the world had a creator. That is enough, we think, to give an Inquirer the requisite assurance that the existence of God has some degree of plausibility.

Thus the way is open, we think, for applying the lesson of Homer in a discussion of God's existence that expands the traditional evidential base.

Applying the Lesson from Homer: Possible Avenues of Exploration

We cannot give an exhaustive account here of how exploration of the content of Christian revelation might push the probability of God's existence above .5. But we do want to provide first some general comments about the *sorts* of philosophical exploration of content that might be undertaken, and then (in the next section) an extended *illustration* of the exploratory work we recommend, an illustration developed with particular attention to the problem of evil.

Philosophical exploration of the content of revelatory claims is particularly appropriate with respect to the *consistency* of revelation, the *development* of revelation, and the *fittingness* of the content of revelation. In this section of the paper we make a few remarks about what is involved in undertaking these three sorts of investigation. When we turn in the next section to explore a particular aspect of the content of the Christian revelatory claim we hope it will be apparent how the example invokes considerations of consistency, development, and fittingness of content.

The claim that Christianity has a doctrine which has been consistently elaborated over the centuries will be troublesome for many. Given the scandal of Christian schism, how can anybody argue that Christian doctrine is (perfectly) consistent?

To mount the argument that Christian doctrine is consistent one first must identify what Christian doctrine *is*. Swinburne approaches this task by asking which church carries on the original Christian revelation—by asking which church is, as he puts it (using Robert Nozick's terminology) the "closest continuer" of the original. Now in the first place, it is not clear to us that the distinction Swinburne draws between original revelation and interpretation is conceptually coherent or of practical value. If revelation involves God's manifestation of himself at a certain period of time, plus the Holy Spirit guiding people to form various judgments about what was unknown so that what was secreted is made manifest, then we've lost the original expressions of Jesus and the Apostles; what we have are various re-expressions offered by various churches.

Further, Swinburne's method here attributes a relatively high degree of probability to the truth of the "original revelation"—to the assertions of the early Christians, let us say. If evidence to support the claim that the probability of God's existence is > .5 is limited to the assertions of the early Christians, the claim will not, we think, have adequate support. If, on the other hand, one puts a fuller case on the table, and takes the entire testimony of a witnessing church, consistently developed over the centuries in unexpected but fruitful ways, then the plausibility of assertions made by the early Christians goes up dramatically. If the evidential base is limited to an initial deposit of revelation among the apostles, then to get a substantiating miracle the historical evidence needs to support a probability of maybe .4 or .5 or .6 that the resurrection occurred. But given an enhanced base that includes a long tradition of developing doctrine, one needs perhaps only something like a .1 probability on the historical evidence that there was a resurrection. It is reasonable to believe that Christ was resurrected *because* one believes that a particular church has received the fullness of divine revelation, and this church proclaims the resurrection.

Anyway, as Swinburne notes, the task of finding the "closest continuer" of the original revelation is very vaguely defined; it depends on the historians and the biblicists, and it's not clear how it all works out.

But there is an alternative, and that is to present a *particular* body of doctrine that strikes one as having as good a chance as any to be right, to take a particular message proclaimed by a particular church or body, and then consider whether the doctrine is consistent, beautiful, elevated, and fitting. As Catholics we favor the candidacy of Catholic doctrine. But Catholic teaching is not the only possible doctrine that can be investigated.

Once a particular body of doctrine is identified it may be necessary to rebut various arguments that the teaching has been inconsistent on the propositions to which it irrevocably commits itself. Often, of course, one will need to turn to the historian and the theologian for help with refutations. But philosophers who work on theories of meaning and reference have an important contribution to make here. And even philosophers who do not specialize in these areas are trained in such a way that they can help with the assessment of various particular accusations.[9]

In reflecting on the consistency of the Church's teaching it may be helpful to reflect on all the mistakes it has *avoided*. It might have succumbed to the spirit of the age in which it was born and pronounced, for example, that women are not worthy of eternal life. It never did, though the apocryphal *Gospel According to Thomas*[10] makes exactly this pronouncement, adding that Jesus turned Mary into a male so that she could become a living spirit. During the conflict with

Galileo it could have formally declared his doctrine heretical; but it never did.[11] Later, it could have solemnly declared against Darwin, whose teaching was at least as disturbing as Galileo's, that the human species did not evolve from lower forms of life. It could have, but it did not. Reflection on the consistency of the Catholic revelatory claim will (we think) eventually force a key question: does the best explanation of this constant avoidance of error require reference to divine assistance?

Christian doctrine has not merely been consistently proclaimed by the (Catholic) church; it has been elaborated and developed over the centuries. Newman provides a starting point for anyone who seeks to understand that development.[12] He suggests that there is so great a degree of unity in *developed* Christian doctrine that one may actually infer from that unity a providential design:

> Thus developments in Christianity are proved to have been in the contemplation of its Divine Author, by an argument parallel to that by which we infer intelligence in the system of the physical world. In whatever sense the need and its supply are a proof of design in the visible creation, in the same do the gaps, if the word may be used, which occur in the structure of the original creed of the Church, make it probable that those developments, which grow out of the truths which lie around it, were intended to fill them up.[13]

But even if one rejects the particular version of the teleological argument for God's existence Newman seems to have in mind here,[14] one may accept the claim that the development of Christian doctrine points to Providence. Newman articulates in detail "seven Notes of varying cogency, independence and applicability"[15] which allow us to discriminate between true development of an idea and corruption and decay: the preservation of its type, the continuity of its principles, its power of assimilation, its logical sequence, its anticipation of its future, its conservative action upon its past, and its chronic vigor. The general analysis of these "notes" of development, together with their application to the case of Christianity (or any other religion), is a task for the philosopher.

Questions concerning the *fittingness* of the content of revelation must also be addressed. Philosophers have a contribution to make in analyzing the concept of fittingness, and in considering whether some particular revelatory claim (or some aspect of the claim) is in fact fitting for the human situation.

There are at least two general ways in which the content of a revelatory claim may fit human needs. First, it may provide necessary moral guidance; second, it may provide nourishment and medicine for the soul. (These aren't mutually exclusive categories; moral guidance might be medicinal for the soul.)

Can't philosophy by itself provide any necessary moral guidance? Probably not. Consider Aristotle's understanding of certainty. Aristotle is the great demonstrator, the foundationalist of foundationalists, but even he is conscious of philosophy's limitations. For one thing, he doesn't think there are any indubitable principles except the principle of non-contradiction.[16] Further, on Aristotle's own account of things, though we may know that an axiom is true, it's not clear that we can ever know that an axiom is an axiom. Aristotle does provide a criterion axioms must satisfy: the predicate must have an immediate connection with the subject. But according to his account, and according to our own experience, the immediacy of the connection is not demonstrable.[17] Or consider the certainty that attaches to moral principles on Socrates's understanding of philosophy and of certainty. "Never return a wrong or do evil to a single human being no matter what we may have suffered at his hands," Socrates tells Crito as they argue about whether Socrates should escape from prison. And how does Socrates know that this principle is binding? He offers no conclusive proof in the dialogues historians take to represent his views; further, he is arguably committed to a method of investigation that makes it impossible to conclusively demonstrate the principle.

If we are unable to get a completely firm hold on truths of geometry, if we cannot establish with certainty simple ethical precepts such as "do no harm," we will lack certainty about higher or more complex matters. And indeed, many pressing moral questions are notoriously difficult to resolve by philosophy alone. But Christian doctrine resolves these pressing moral questions.[18] It is fitting for us in this respect. And philosophy helps us understand the fittingness.

Admittedly, Christian revelation has not given us the highest possible degree of natural certainty. Why not? Why didn't God use the stars in the sky to spell out a message for us: "Know that the Lord Your God Speaks Infallibly Through the Roman Catholic Church"? Presumably, God had a reason for not just putting us in heaven to begin with. But why didn't he make the evidence of his existence as compelling for us in this lifetime as it is at this moment for the demons? Here again, philosophy has a job to do.

Notice first that the demand for evidence this compelling is a demand for an experience beyond having a message about God's existence and wishes spelled out every night in the stars. For such an experience would not make the consequences of disobedience clear. Perhaps God could put two pictures or displays up in the sky each night, one showing something of the rewards of heaven, the other portraying the pains of hell. But these displays would do justice to neither the glory of heaven nor the misery of hell. We need actually to feel the torments of hell for short bursts of time—maybe for long stretches of time—to understand what it would be like. So we run up here against the problem of evil, which one who demands compelling proof of God's existence presumably wants to avoid. And the displays of heaven which would alternate with the bursts of pain would be misleading because they would not be of the divine essence. So our minds would be directed towards the wrong object: we would have glimpses of a surrogate, which might well be taken for hallucinations. The bottom line here seems to be: God can't give us absolutely compelling evidence of his existence and wishes without putting us in heaven; and once one gets appreciably beneath the point of "compelling evidence" there seems no logical place to break things off.[19]

It doesn't follow from all this that though we have an obligation to believe, God has no obligation to provide *any* evidence of our obligation. We have good reason to expect a divine revelation given that there is a good God who has created human beings. We do not have good reason to expect absolute (natural) certainty that a putative revelatory claim is correct.

For many, the desire or need for moral guidance will take a back seat to the need for spiritual healing and sustenance. Told that God has taken human form, has walked among us and died for us and continues to this day to love us more perfectly than mother or father, husband or wife or friend can possibly love us, we crave contact with the divine. People everywhere seek medicine for the soul the world cannot provide. And we seek bread more nourishing than the loaves fashioned by human hands. Conscious of the malice that streaks our own hearts, we seek a means for the purgation of sin and the making of amends. Shocked by our own weakness of will, we seek help in strengthening resolve. Witness to grotesque afflictions of the innocent, we wonder whether we dare hope they will find peace and justice in an afterlife; we think we will not be whole until they are whole, until they are healed.

Philosophical reflection can display Christian doctrine as fitting for humankind because philosophical analysis can unveil ways in which the doctrine provides medicine and nourishment for the soul. With the understanding thus attained, with the expanded evidential base such understanding provides, we are positioned to handle the problem of evil; without this understanding, we suggest, our Inquirer's attempts to assess the truth of theism will be limited to a meager and insufficient evidential base.

We turn now to develop an extended example of the way in which philosophical reflection can display *developed* Christian doctrine as *fitting* for humankind.

Applying the Lesson from Homer: Evil, Free Will, and the Mystical Body of Christ

Evil and Free Will

Although we referred to "the problem of evil" in the first section of this paper we did not offer a particular formulation of it. It will be instructive here to consider how the problem should be stated. Philosophical orthodoxy bids us begin with Hume's famous paraphrase of Epicurus:

> Is he [God] willing to prevent evil, but not able? then is he impotent. Is he able, but not willing? then is he malevolent. Is he both able and willing? Whence then is evil?

This traditional formulation of the problem suggests a concern with *all* evils, with evil in general. But there is a range of "evils" in the world, and some of them strike virtually no one as prima facie inconsistent with God's existence.

"Evil" can be used simply to mean "harmful" or "thing that harms." One may, for example, say that a long drought which withers plants is an evil for them (it may be a good to some other vegetation or creatures). Such evils of harm do not on the face of it seem inconsistent with the existence of God. The point may be missed because there is a tendency to describe some harmful thing as an evil when one also wants to blame someone for its existence. (Has prostitution been called "the social evil" both because it has been thought to harm certain social structures, and because it is thought to be inherently wrong?) Shakespeare provides a perspicuous example of this double meaning "evil" can carry:

> Hastings: The king is sickly, weak and melancholy, / And his physicians fear him mightily. ...
> Duke of Gloucester: O, he hath kept an evil diet long, / And overmuch consumed his royal person....
> (*King Richard III*, I.1.136–139)

But calling some phenomenon an evil does not imply that someone ought to have prevented it, or that it ought not to have occurred.

Perhaps there are other sorts of evil which aren't prima facie inconsistent with God's existence. One could, 400 years ago, speak of a knife that didn't cut well as an evil knife: "If a man cut with an evill knife, he is the cause of cutting, but not of evill cutting"[20] unless, perhaps, it was his duty to keep the knife sharp. And a piper who didn't pipe well might have been called an evil piper: "He is an euell piper but a good fiddler."[21] And we do even now sometimes use "evil" at least in part as an attributive adjective: we do so when we call a human being evil, if we mean by this that a person lacks some quality a human being should have, or doesn't fulfill the function of a human being.

So various evils do not intuitively strike us as inconsistent with a perfectly good being. In fact, there are some evils theists identify that actually entail the existence of God. Blasphemy is an example. The atheist can only get the problem of evil off the ground by narrowing the set of evils than need some kind of explanation. The "evil" of blasphemy will no doubt be seen by our Inquirer as marginally relevant to the inquiry at hand; the theist who proposes them for consideration will be thought to beg the question at issue. We suggest, however, that there is a very large class of evil *widely recognized as the sort of evil that generates the problem of evil for theists* which is explicitly identified and addressed by Christian revelation, but typically ignored or minimized by contemporary anti-Christian materialistic accounts of the world. This is the class of moral evil, evil that consists in wrong-doing, transgression of moral duties, viciousness, or (as the theist might say) sin.

Philosophical accounts of the problem of evil may begin with homage to Hume's Epicurean formulation of the problem, but authors quickly move on to description of particular evils seen as particularly troublesome. Dostoyevsky's graphic description of cruelty towards children is sometimes offered to the reader. Every one of the examples of *suffering* Ivan provides in explaining why he cannot endorse Christianity is an example rooted in *moral evil*. The babies bayoneted by the Turkish soldiers suffer physical pain (briefly); the mothers who watch in disbelief surely are seized by a lasting and visceral horror. The horror must grow not only from the loss of their children, but also, deeply, from the inhumanity of the soldiers, from the senselessness of the violence, from the depravity and the wickedness of men who, shockingly, are as much members of the human race as any one of us. The young girl Ivan describes as abused by her parents suffers physically, but it is the malice and cruelty of the parents and the psychological effects this has on the girl that sicken us.

Frequently the Holocaust is cited as an example of the sort of thing a good God would obviously prevent. Why does this example come so easily to mind? Not because the physical suffering of the victims was so severe. The Romans' executions by crucifixion, the Inquisitors' executions by fire, the Aztecs' killings of their sacrificial victims all would have been deaths far more physically painful then the gassings Hitler ordered. The Holocaust rightly appears to us as evil of the worst sort: but that is because the sort of evil it embodied was moral evil of the worst sort, genocide which systematically branded men, women, and children who were part of the human family as inhuman and worthless, as refuse. In recent years philosophical articles on the problem of evil have also taken as a paradigmatic example of evil the case of a five-year old girl who was tortured and raped and finally killed by her mother's boyfriend. We do not wish to underestimate the child's physical suffering. But countless children in times past must have suffered equally. It is the moral evil in the situation that is the locus of our outrage.

Sometimes critics of theism focus on the problem of animal suffering. Interestingly, the language they use in setting out the problem is often anthropomorphic. Quentin Smith, for instance, opens his discussion of "An Atheological Argument from Evil Natural Laws"[22] with an account of how he was awakened one night while sleeping in the woods by cries of terror and agony as one animal "savagely" killed and devoured another. He speaks of animal prey as being "tortured" by the predator. Smith's anthropomorphic language reveals a hidden sensitivity to *moral evil*. Smith claims (with breath-taking naiveté) that there is a possible world, W, just like the actual world except that all animals and animal-like creatures are vegetarians. He holds that in W there are wonderful creatures—Florence Nightingales and Beethovens—but they're all vegetarians. Smith maintains that since there is a possible world W, the law of predation in our own world is ultimately evil. But it is not implausible that any counterpart world even remotely similar to our own would include long painful deaths (maybe instead of dying quickly in the jaws of a lion, a zebra dies a slow agonizing death because one of the extra trees that exists due to the vegetarians' need for vegetation falls on top of it). That Smith's concern is focused on predation, on torturous or savage killing rather than on pain, evidences a concern with moral evil.

So: the problem of evil is not the problem of reconciling *all* evil, or "evil in general" with the existence of a good God. The deepest aspect of the evil we decry is moral. The problem of evil is first and foremost the problem of explaining how moral evil and its consequences can exist in a world made by a good God.

Now we must ask: where do we find a world-view able to acknowledge that real evil involves choices? Christian revelation *begins* with an insistence on personal responsibility, responsibility rooted in libertarian freedom. The Hebrew scriptures, foundation blocks for Christian revelation, from the outset portray the human person as free and accountable. Eve and Adam make their tragic choice between good and evil, shaping their destiny and affecting our own. The Lord "created man in the beginning, and he left him in the power of his own inclination.... to act faithfully is a matter of your own choice," Sirach reminds us.[23] The New Testament underscores and develops the concept of the responsibility individuals have to opt for their own good and for the good of the community, a community now broadened through Christ's salvific death to include the gentiles, to include all of humanity. If we abuse our freedom we sell ourselves into the slavery of sin.[24] But if we exercise our freedom responsibly, if we work for "the glorious liberty of the children of God"[25] by directing our wills towards truth and goodness and God, standing fast against adversity, we make it possible for ourselves and for others to attain the deepest human happiness, which is inextricably connected with our moral agency. "For freedom Christ has set us free," the author of Galatians tells us.[26]

The outsider with only the barest understanding of the content of Christian revelation will recognize its foundational commitment to human freedom and responsibility. Christian revelation thus appears as wiser than worldly wisdom. For the paradigm of worldly wisdom, the physicalistic or materialistic world view, is incompatible with libertarian freedom. The most honest of the physicalists recognize this fact with some dismay. John Searle, for instance, after arguing in *Minds, Brains, and Science* that mental states are brain states and that everything explicable is explicable in terms of fundamental physical particles and their relationships, acknowledges that the physicalism he has endorsed entails determinism. Human beings do not have libertarian freedom; the "choices" we make do not involve the freedom to do things differently. Freedom is illusory. Searle accepts the fact that human beings will never actually be convinced that their behavior is determined. He is himself persuaded — *practically* speaking — of the falsity of the determinism implied by the theory to which he has committed himself. We humans are destined to live with the demonstrably false belief that our actions are free, destined by an evolutionary process which has indelibly imprinted the conviction that we are free, and responsible, and accountable for the choices we make.

The common-sense view of the matter, of course, the pre-philosophical or pre-theoretical view of the matter, is that the subjective experience we have of the free will points to a reality: we feel like we deliberate about our choices because we do deliberate; we feel like we're free because we are. This has been the over-whelming verdict of human-kind, and the considered opinion of most philoso-phers and scientists as well. It is a verdict not to be discarded without the most convincing of proofs of the physicalist hypothesis.

And as even the philosophical novice will be able to recognize, convincing proof of physicalism is not forthcoming. Consider, for a brief example, John Searle's attempt to explain the intentionality of thirst, or (to put the point more sympathetically) his attempt to explain what the physicalist would need to do to account for the intentionality of thirst. Searle's discussion of the intentionality of thirst anchors his account of the attractions of physicalism. Searle thinks that what we need to explain thirst, to explain how thirst is directed to an object, is to provide a lot of scientific detail. And he sketches in some details — all going in the wrong direction, starting with the firing of neurons and ending up with the kidneys, when what we need is an explanation of how the firing of neurons is connected with the experience of thirst. Given that the neurons fire in such and such a way, why, we want to know, is this person thirsty rather than itchy? But Searle has nothing to tell us about that.

Consider Searle's account of thirst in light of an example. Imagine a man sees a woman standing on the east side of a raging river, watching the sunset; the man glances away for a fraction of a second and then looks back; amazed, he sees the woman on the west side of the river. How did she get to the west side? An explanation is offered: well, she drove her car to within 100 yards of the east bank of the river and then took the forked footpath to the edge of the bank. The man wants more detail. Well, she decided to drive to the river today because it was her mother's favorite river and it's been exactly one year since her mother died ... and so on and so on. The added details all go in the wrong direction; none of them explains how she got from the east side to the west.

Physicalists will typically acknowledge that science hasn't yet shown we're nothing but material beings with the illusion of freedom; science hasn't yet explained why certain brain states correlate with the perception of pain, others with seeing red, and others with feeling thirst. They will suggest that the science of the future will provide the missing explanations. But an Inquirer, whether philosophical novice or sophisticate, will rightly be sceptical. There is good rea-son to think science cannot, in principle, provide the missing explanations. Consider the following scenario. You have a pull toy for your son, a toy which has a little figure in a box whose head pops in and out of the box as the toy is pulled along. You ask the question: why does the head pop in and out as the toy is pulled along? You examine the toy, and see that the wheels are connected to an axle which is shaped like this:

    _|--|_

and as the wheels turn the middle bar rises and falls. The little figure is sitting on the middle bar, so its head rises and falls with each revolution of the wheels. Now your teen-aged daughter comes in and asks you: why does the head pop in and out as the toy is pulled along? So you explain. But she says: I understand all that, but why does the head pop in and out? You go over everything again. She persists in claiming not to understand what's going on. You decide—on very good grounds—that either she wasn't listening or she's being obstinate. For if she has really understood all that you have said, there's nothing more to add about why the head pops in and out. We may state a general principle here: If a putative explanation, E, of phenomenon P is a genuine explanation, then if you grasp E in relation to P, it makes no sense to ask: "But why does P occur?"

It may take a person a few minutes to puzzle out how the toy with the pop-up rider works. But the phenomena being examined are homogenous and the mystery can be removed. When one starts talking about heterogeneous phenomena, on the other hand, matters are not so simple. Why do we feel an itch and not some other sensation when the neurons are in such-and-such an arrangement? Why do we see red, and not yellow, or feel pleasure rather than pain? These things are mysteries, not just in the sense that they are awe-inspiring, but in the sense that no matter how much detail we are provided about the chemistry of the brain it is always reasonable to go back to the philosophical question, to ask, for instance, why do I feel thirsty rather than itchy?

Perhaps at this point a critic will assert that in fact it *doesn't* make sense to ask why we feel thirsty or why we see red. If the objection here means that it never makes sense to ask the question, of course, then it can hardly be claimed that science will some day explain the phenomenon completely, or that our current knowledge of physiology tells us anything at all about why people have sensations. Presumably the objection here isn't that it never makes sense to ask why we see red, but rather that it doesn't make any sense to keep asking the question beyond a certain point—beyond the point where science can provide answers.

Such an objection presupposes an unduly cramped, limited conception of explanation, one that does not sit comfortably with common scientific practice. For how is it known in a particular case whether or not "science can provide answers"? Frequently scientists find some one-to-one correlation, say a correlation between a gas being heated and its expanding, and they ask: why does the correlation exist? The fact that they don't yet know the answer, that they don't yet have the next step in an explanation, suggests to no one—certainly not to them—that they have a complete explanation. They do not yet have an explanation that provides insight into the correlation at issue, and so they keep looking.

That we do not already have insight into why we see red when we look at a cherry is shown by the fact that it is meaningful to ask whether we might be having our sensations in an inverted fashion, that is, in a fashion where one person sees black and another sees white, and so on. The hypothesis that there might be an inverted spectrum seems meaningful because we can ask whether animals see in color, and we can test for it; furthermore, we can ask whether there might be an inverted spectrum for human beings that isn't reflected in our language. But if it is sensible to ask "do people have different spectra, given the same physical structures?" then it's not obvious straight off why a certain material configuration would give rise to a particular way of seeing the world. It can't be maintained that we already have insight into why we see red.

We have just argued that science has not yet explained sense perception, has not given us reason to think physicalism is true and free will an illusion. And we have argued here and elsewhere that it never will.[27] The determined critic is likely to hang in. Some *super*-science of the future, at present unimaginable, will do the trick, we may be told, will explain what seems inexplicable, will circumvent the principled reason for thinking the scientific explanation is impossible.

David Chalmers has suggested[28] that "the explanatory gap" between talk of neural firings and talk of consciousness may be filled by a future scientific theory, "a true theory of everything," which includes both physical laws that tell us about the behavior of physical systems and "psycho-physical laws, telling us how some of those systems are associated with conscious experience." But wait, you say; what are the entities governed by "psycho-physical laws"? Has conscious experience been introduced as some sort of scientific entity? Are we supposed to imagine something like little Leibnizian monads of consciousness? Well, yes, it turns out: Chalmers proposes that "conscious experience be considered a fundamental feature, irreducible to anything more basic." But any future explanation that is scientific must be tied to basic physics; it won't appeal to "psychic bits" or "pieces of soul", but rather to entities located in space and time that interact in ways that can be quantified. Though the nature of forces may seem different in the future, though science may certainly change its understanding of those forces, the forces that science deals with are and will be physical forces.

We are, almost all of us, unshakably convinced that we are free to choose between good and evil, and ennobled by that freedom. The conviction underlies any respectable formulation of the problem of evil. (It underlies as well our codes of law and punishment, our concepts of honor and responsibility, our dramas and dreams and loves.) The physicalist's account of the world has no place for freedom; if the problem of evil is taken in its most severe form, the physicalistic hypothesis must quit the field. And if the physicalist is right, we must try to extinguish our misguided conviction of our own responsibility — or live in bad faith.

In fact, we suggest, it is the physicalist who condemns himself to living in bad faith. Sartre provides us with the icon here. Recall his description in *Being and Nothingness* of the woman who talks with her dinner companion, aware of his desire for her, but indecisive about her own intentions. The man takes her hand. The action calls for her decision. If she chooses to allow her hand to be held, she has consented to flirtation — at the least. If she rejects the hand, she has broken the charm of the hour and the possibility of involvement. What does she do? She leaves her hand where it is, but *does not notice* that she is leaving it there. That is to say, Sartre suggests, she divorces body and soul: she is a model of bad faith. So also the physicalist, who commits to a theory that precludes free will but neglects to notice the commitment when he goes about the business of living, is in bad faith.

Evil and the Mystical Body of Christ

We have just seen that Christian revelation, with its recognition of the reality of moral evil and good, fits our understanding of ourselves as free and responsible agents. The account we gave of the Scriptural understanding of human freedom only gestured towards the richness and beauty of the Christian picture of the "economy of salvation" in which human freedom is situated, and it now behooves us to explore another part of that picture. For the more one sees of the picture, the more one can understand of Christian revelation concerning the mystery of evil. The part of the picture we now turn to is the portrait of the mystical body of Christ. We begin by considering the origins of the New Testament image, and then go on to discuss a 20th-century Encyclical written during one of our darkest hours, an Encyclical which *develops* (in Newman's very full sense of the word) the New Testament image of the Church as the body of Christ.

In writing to the fractious, unruly members of the church at Corinth Paul suggests a striking image:

> For just as the body is one and has many members, and all the members of the body, though many, are one body, so it is with Christ.... Now you are the body of Christ and individually members of it.[29]

A variety of traditional pictures probably fed into Paul's suggestive identification. In the 1st and 2nd centuries AD Jewish literature presented the image of a gigantic body of Adam which filled the universe and contained the souls of all men; Paul, who was raised a Jew, may have been influenced by the picture. Since he was raised in the Greek city of Tarsus he would also have been exposed to Hellenistic images presented (for instance) by Plato, who in *The Republic* elaborated the metaphor of the city or state as a body, and in *The Timaeus* suggested that the cosmos itself is a living creature with a body, made by the Demiurge.[30] And he may have had some familiarity with Stoic philosophy: Seneca, who lived shortly before Paul, held that the universe which encompasses us is God and that we arc associates of God; we are "parts of one great body." Whatever the sources, the image even in these nascent formulations was extraordinarily powerful, and would grow more so as the Christian church developed interpretations ranging well beyond the boundaries of the Jewish, Hellenistic, or Stoic conceptions.

When Paul addressed the Corinthians with the bodily image he told them that *they* were the members of the body of Christ, and that the local church at Corinth was Christ's body. He thus set up a framework for dealing with the particular problems the church at Corinth was facing. Paul addresses those guilty of fornication by arguing[31] that one who is truly a member of Christ's body cannot associate with prostitutes. He rebukes those who get drunk at communal meals while others go hungry, suggesting that "one who eats and drinks without discerning the body eats and drinks judgment upon himself."[32] And he argues that various functions must be performed in the church for the edification of the whole and that church members who have received the more dramatic gifts of the Spirit should not be prideful.

If we turn to the Colossians we see the church as the entire community of believers (not just a local community) identified with Christ's body. This epistle, written to the church at Colossae either by Paul or one of his disciples, draws (Col. 1:15–24) on an early Christian hymn[33] as it proclaims that Christ is the image of the invisible God, that through Christ and for Christ all things were created, and in him all things hold together: "He is the head of the body, the church; he is the beginning." The church is bearing fruit and growing:

> Let no one disqualify you ... taking his stand on visions, puffed up without reason by his sensuous mind, and not holding fast to the Head, from whom the whole body, nourished and knit together through its joints and ligaments, grows with a growth that is from God.[34]

In the epistle to the Ephesians Paul (or one of his disciples) presents us with a similar picture of the relationship between Christ and his church. Ephesians identifies the church with the body of Christ,[35] constantly growing. It undergoes qualitative growth as individuals who are already in the church attain "to mature manhood, to the measure of the stature of the fullness of Christ." And the church is growing as well in number (partly because of the qualitative growth):

> Speaking the truth in love, we are to grow up in every way into him who is the head, into Christ, from whom the whole body, joined and knit together by every joint with which it is supplied, when each part is working properly, makes bodily growth and upbuilds itself in love.[36]

The author of Ephesians goes even further, with the striking suggestion (reminiscent of aspects of the Jewish, Platonic, and Stoic imagery cited above) that Christ's church, Christ's body, will eventually grow to fill the *entire cosmos*:

And he has put all things under his feet and has made him the head over all things for the church, which is his body, the fullness of him who fills all in all.[37]

God's "plan for the fullness of time"[38] is "to unite all things in Christ, things in heaven and things on earth". The letter to the Ephesians portrays creation as awaiting reconciliation with God in Christ's body; in Romans there is a similar eschatological expectation:

> The creation itself will be set free from its bondage to decay and obtain the glorious liberty of the children of God. We know that the whole creation has been groaning in travail together until now.[39]

The growth of the church is effected through the suffering of its members, who witness their faith to the world. The author of Colossians tells his audience:

> I rejoice in my sufferings for your sake, and in my flesh I complete what is lacking in Christ's afflictions for the sake of his body, that is, the church.

And the author of Ephesians, who refers to himself as "a prisoner for the Lord" tells those at Ephesus not to lose heart over what he is suffering, since what he is suffering is for their glory.

The suffering bears fruit. Newman's criticism of Gibbon's account of the rise of Christianity poses the question: why were early converts won to Christianity? It was, Newman answers, the "*Image*" or "the Thought of Christ, which inspired that zeal which the historian so poorly comprehends...." It was an Image, he suggests, that entered into myriads of men, women, and children, with the

> power to wean them from their indulgences and sins, and to nerve them against the most cruel tortures, and to last in vigour as a sustaining influence for seven or eight generations, till it founded an extended polity, broke the obstinacy of the strongest and wisest government which the world has ever seen, and forced its way from its first caves and catacombs to the fullness of imperial power.[40]

We have in the New Testament epistles the key elements of an image that is developed through subsequent centuries and applied to the particular problems faced by the Church and its members. Pope Pius XII's encyclical on the "Mystical Body of Christ," written in 1943, provides a splendid example. The encyclical was written , as the Pope notes, in turbulent times, times when the skies were "heavy with storm clouds, and exceeding great dangers" threatened all of human society, and fields were "strewn with massive ruins and defiled with the blood of brothers."[41] Around the world people suffered, and questioned the value of suffering, and doubted the existence of a good and loving God.

In these times Pius saw fit to remind people that the members of the Church "glory in a thorn-crowned Head."[42] The Church, the body of Christ, is built on the suffering of Christ and "purchased with his own blood."[43] Christ made the purchase freely, for love of his bride the Church[44] (as the Father had freely given his Son for this purpose). The Church is grounded in love and in affliction endured for the sake of love.

The union which is the Church is seen through tradition from different perspectives. It is not merely the body, but also the image of Christ (and each individual within it images Christ as well). As the body of Christ the Church undergoes bodily affliction; as the image of Christ it undergoes spiritual suffering. As the image of Christ the Church forms with Christ "but one mystical person," "the whole Christ," a union which Christ himself likened "to that wonderful unity by which the Son is in the Father, and the Father in the Son."[45] And so the Church, and its members, are to image the love which Father and Son have shared for all eternity. The perspective grows even broader: "It is the Spirit of Christ that has made us adopted sons of God"; and "as Christ is the Head of the Church, so is the Holy Spirit her soul."[46] Thus the Church imitates not merely the love between Father and Son, but the full Trinitarian exchange of love given and received. And again we may step back for an even wider view: Christ's mother Mary is exemplar for us all; she was "the mother of our Head," and "through the added title of pain and glory became, according to the Spirit, the mother of all His members."[47] She, "bearing with courage and confidence the tremendous burden of her sorrows and desolation, she, truly the Queen of Martyrs, more than all the faithful 'filled up those things that are wanting of the sufferings of Christ' ... for His Body, which is the Church."[48]

New Testament themes and images are developed, elaborated, applied to the situation at hand. Let us consider a further stage of the application. What is the *point* of the suffering which the Church and her members bear in times of war and trouble? What does it mean to "fill up those things that are wanting of the sufferings of Christ"? Pius tells us that through our suffering we become so like Christ that we cooperate with Christ in the "work of salvation, 'from one and through one saved and saviors.'"[49] The Church shares the task of imparting the graces of redemption to humankind, and "the salvation of many depends on the prayers and voluntary penances which the members of the Mystical Body of Jesus Christ offer."[50] If we are bound in ardent love to God, to our divine Head, to one another, if, "on fire with this heavenly flame," we rejoice "to suffer insults for Him, and to face and overcome the hardest trials,"[51] including death, we contribute to the growth of the Church and the salvation of souls. Affliction so borne is integrated into our relationship with other human beings and with God. It is not merely "balanced off" by greater goods; it is transformed and subsumed within the good of knowing and loving God and the people of God.[52]

Our love must extend to all of humankind: "so vast is the love of the divine Spouse that it embraces in His Bride the whole human race without exception."[53] This includes those "not yet joined" to us in the Body of Christ; it includes "not only those who are of a different nation or race, but even our enemies."[54] For the length and breadth and height and depth of the love of Christ knows no bounds. That all of humankind is included in Christ's love does not mean that outsiders are to be forced into the visible Church, for faith "is an entirely free 'submission of intellect and will.'"[55] It does mean, however, that the members of the mystical body of Christ will show a special care of those "who are the object of our Savior's special love": the weak, the wounded, the sick, the poor, the deformed, the insane; all who are vulnerable, all who are preyed upon by the powerful and unscrupulous.[56] The Church in protecting the vulnerable will here look to Christ, who, "with absolute impartiality and incorruptible judgment, rising above the conflicting gales of human passions, takes upon himself with all his strength the defense of truth, justice and charity."[57] Indeed, it appears that the love must (in mysterious ways that we do not now fully comprehend) extend beyond all of humankind. We saw that the New Testament writings urged us to recognize that the body of Christ one day will expand to fill the entire cosmos. We are called upon to recognize and love the intrinsic goodness of non-human realms of creation.

Thus "the inexhaustible fruitfulness of the Mystical Body of Jesus Christ may shine resplendently throughout the whole world,"[58] and as the letter to the Ephesians predicted, and Pius repeats, the Church will grow "to fill not only the whole world but the realms of heaven as well."[59] Exercising the gift of free will bestowed on us by a loving creator we will accept responsibility for establishing true community with the whole of the human race and with creation itself; through loving endurance of tribulation, together with the whole creation groaning in travail, we will achieve the glorious liberty of the children of God and find redemption in Christ.

NOTES

[1] Richard Swinburne, *The Existence of God* (Oxford: The Clarendon Press, 1979) p. 220.

[2] Ibid., p. 220.

[3] Actually, the situation is rather complex. The claim holds only if we leave out (a) the mode of presentation of the evidential base and (b) the subjective estimate of the proposition at issue in relationship to that base.

[4] Richard Swinburne, *The Existence of God*, p. 222.

[5] Richard Swinburne, *Revelation* (Oxford: The Clarendon Press, 1992), p. 5.

[6] Quentin Smith, "The Uncaused Beginning of the Universe," *Philosophy of Science* 55 (1988), p. 39.

[7] Thomas Reid, *Essays on the Active Powers of the Human Mind*, Baruch Brody (ed.) (Cambridge, Mass. & London: MIT Press, 1969), Essay IV, Ch. II, p. 267.

[8] *The Letters of David Hume*, ed. J.Y.T. Greig (Oxford: The Clarendon Press, 1932), Vol. I, p. 187. Quoted by Brian Davies.

[9] And often the training philosophers receive in "dividing and defining" and in identifying fallacies will allow them to offer refutations. Consider, for instance, Jaroslav Pelikan's description of "the various data of church history that seemed to refute the doctrine of the infallibility of the church or the pope":

> "millennialism 'even in the earliest ages, and within thirty or forty years after the apostles'; Origen's preface to *On First Principles*, one of the earliest and most systematic patristic discussions of authority in the church, which was silent about the infallibility of the church; the history of canon law, including the forged decretals, as well as the familiar provision that the pope could be deposed if he fell into heresy; the contradiction (despite their being linked as authorities) between the Second Council of Nicea in 787, which had approved the use of icons, and the Synod of Frankfurt in 794, which had not; the error of Pope John XXII on the doctrine of the vision of God, which required exculpation; and the textbook case of Pope Honorius I, which, despite efforts to dismiss it on the grounds either that in condemning him the Council of Constantinople in 681 was not a legitimate ecumenical council or that the text of its Acts was corrupt, continued to stand, as it would at the First Vatican Council in 1870, as evidence that Honorius 'had been and had remained a heretic and the pope at one and the same time'." (Pelikan, *The Christian Tradition*, Vol. 5 (University of Chicago, 1989), pp. 19–20.)

(1) Why would a belief in millennialism imply that the Church or pope lacked infallibility? Neither the Church nor any Pope has ever infallibly defined the truth of millennialism. (2) Why would the fact that Origen's discussion of church authority doesn't speak of infallibility mean that the church is fallible? (3) The forged decretals (or "the decretals of the Pseudo-Isidore") are an embarrassment to the Church, but no Pope or Council ever infallibly pronounced that the forged decretals were authentic. Pope Gregory VII adopted and proclaimed various of the juridical precepts in the forged decretals, wrongly believing them to have been taught by early Popes, but that is a far cry from infallibly proclaiming their authenticity. (4) Why does either the provision that the pope can be deposed if he falls into heresy, or the application of the provision in the condemnation of Pope Honorius I for his argument (in several personal letters) that the Word has only one will, tell against infallibility? Honorius never infallibly proclaimed the teaching judged heretical. (5) The Synod of Frankfurt was not an ecumenical council. (6) Pope John XXII gave four sermons in 1331–2 which taught, contrary to traditional doctrine, that saints did not have a full vision of God until after the final judgment. He never infallibly defined the contrary view he had set forth, and he retracted that view on his deathbed.

[10] *The Gospel According to Thomas*, Coptic text established and translated by A. Guillaumont et al. (Harper, 1959), Log 114.

[11] Various discussions of Galileo's case make this point. See, for instance, Charles Journet, *The Church of the Word Incarnate, Vol. I: The Apostolic Hierarchy* (New

York: Sheed and Ward), 1955, pp. 354–358; or Germain Grisez, *The Way of the Lord Jesus, Vol. I: Christian Moral Principles* (Franciscan Herald Press, 1983).

[12] John Henry Cardinal Newman, *An Essay on the Development of Christian Doctrine* (Westminster, Md.: Christian Classics Inc., 1968).

[13] Ibid., p. 63.

[14] Many theists who think certain versions of the teleological argument are sound would reject the particular version Newman seems to have in mind here; it seems possible to provide a Darwinian explanation of the needs and supplies to which Newman apparently refers.

[15] Ibid., p. 170.

[16] *Metaphysics* III–IV.

[17] In Bk. II of the *Posterior Analytics* Aristotle says that the immediacy of the connection between a subject and a predicate is not demonstrable. The indemonstrability of the axiomatic character of axioms is, we think, essentially a problem rooted in the indemonstrability that the essence of a thing is the essence of a thing. Aristotle held that essences are not demonstrable.

[18] Christians may speak like faith is knowledge—but it's rooted in the will. It's misleading to speak of certainty ....

[19] The argument we develop here parallels an argument for handling "gratuitous evils" in a theodicy.

[20] This is an entry in the *Compact Edition of the Oxford English Dictionary* under "evil" (p. 91, p. 349 in non-compact edition); the citation given there is: (1583) Babington Commandmt I.7.

[21] An entry in the *Compact Edition of the Oxford English Dictionary* under "evil" (p. 91, p. 349 in non-compact edition); the citation given is (1561) T. Norton, Calvin's Inst. IV 85.

[22] Quentin Smith, "An Atheological Argument from Evil Natural Laws," *International Journal for Philosophy of Religion*, June 1991.

[23] *Eccleciasticus* 15:14–15.

[24] Cf. *Rom.* 6:17.

[25] *Rom.* 8:21.

[26] *Gal.* 5:1.

[27] See, for instance, Russell Pannier and Thomas D. Sullivan, "The Mind-Maker," in the current volume.

[28] *Scientific American*, December 1995; see also *The Conscious Mind*, forthcoming from Oxford Press.

[29] 1 Cor. 12:2, 27.

[30] Cite passages from *The Republic* and *Timaeus*.

[31] 1 *Cor.* 6.

[32] 1 *Cor.* 6:11.

[33] ee, e.g., E. Schweizer in "Christ in the Letter to the Colossians," *Review and Expositor*, Vol. 76 (1973). Schweizer suggests the original hymn went something

like this:

He is the image of the invisible God, the first-born of all creation:
Through him and to him all things have been created.
And it is he who is before all things,
And it is in him that all things hold together,
And it is he who is the head of the body.
He is the beginning, the first-born from the dead;
For in him all the fullness was pleased to dwell,
Through him to reconcile all things to him.

[34] *Col.* 2:18–19.

[35] *Eph.* 1:22–23, 3:6, 4:16.

[36] *Eph.* 4:15–16.

[37] *Eph.* 1:22–23.

[38] *Eph.* 1:10.

[39] *Rom.* 8:21–22.

[40] John Henry Newman, *A Grammar of Assent* (University of Notre Dame Press, 1979), pp. 359–360.

[41] Pope Pius XII, *Mystici Corporis Christi*, June 1943, Sections 4, 109. At: http://www.ewtn.com/library/ENCYC/P12MYSTI.TXT

[42] Ibid., Sec. 2.

[43] Ibid., Sec. 2.

[44] Ibid., Cf. Sec. 92.

[45] Ibid., Sec. 67.

[46] Ibid., Sec. 56, 57.

[47] Ibid., Sec. 110.

[48] Ibid., Sec. 110.

[49] Ibid., Sec. 59; Pius refers here to Clem. Alex., Strom., VII, 2; Migne, P.G., IX, 413.

[50] Ibid., Sec. 44.

[51] Ibid., Sec. 73.

[52] See Marilyn Adams, "Horrendous Evils and the Goodness of God," originally published in *Proceedings of the Aristotelian Society*, Supplementary Volume 63, 1989, reprinted in Marilyn McCord Adams and Robert Merrihew Adams, *The Problem of Evil* (Oxford University Press: 1990), pp. 209–221.

[53] Pope Pius XII, *Mystici Corporis Christi*, Sec. 96.

[54] Ibid., Sec. 96.

[55] Ibid., Sec. 104; Pius is quoting Vat. Council, *Const. de fide Cath.*, Cap. 3.

[56] Ibid., Sec. 93, 94.

[57] Ibid., Sec. 6.

[58] Ibid., Sec. 97.

[59] Ibid., Sec. 21.

D. Atheism

10

The Philosophies of Religion of Bertrand Russell and Anthony Flew

Andrew Beards

For quite a number of philosophers, in both the Anglo-American and the 'continental' traditions, a consideration of the contributions of Bertrand Russell and Anthony Flew to the philosophy of religion would be viewed as a reflection upon philosophical attitudes now to be regarded as passe'. That is, on this view, the positions of these thinkers exemplify the kind of mid-century, Anglo-saxon foundationalism which we are now moving beyond or should move beyond. Consequently, the kind of fideism in theology and the philosophy of religion which both thinkers witnessed the rise of (in its twentieth-century incarnations at least), and which both have spurned and repudiated as a form of moral and intellectual hypocrisy, now appears to be in a triumphalist phase: its exponents now taunt its detractors with the failure to recognise what, surely, anyone in the cultural vanguard must recognise, that philosophy rests as much on 'faith' as does any other human enterprise.

I remain as unimpressed as Russell and Flew by such Protagorean theological strategies, and I believe that the respect they express for Christianity by taking the metaphysical claims implicit in its doctrines seriously is greatly to their credit. Neither has been impressed by attempts to broaden the meaning of those doctrines so as to be maximally, and therefore vacuously, inclusive. If Christian faith does not involve claims about the nature and destiny of the Universe and human persons, about historical events, some of which are miraculous, and if the cogency of such claims could not be argued for in anything like the way in which

Augustine and Aquinas, Descartes and Leibnitz, Butler and Newman argued for them, then, as both philosophers insist, it is not clear why there would be any point in accepting such claims as true and valuable.[1] A judicious application of Ockham's razor would dispose of the pretended dressing up of atheists such as Russell and Flew as "good Christians after all", irrespective of their beliefs. For if such beliefs mean nothing more than being what you are, why use such labels, particularly when for someone like Russell, Christian symbols are caught up with, what he takes to be, the many deplorable features of Christian history and past attitudes? One might put it that for someone like Russell the adoption of Christian symbolism would only be made tolerable by Christianity being true. So in his response to an essay on his Philosophy of Religion by the American philosopher Edgar S Brightman, Russell resists attempts to baptise him as an "anonymous Christian".[2] Of course it is open to the Christian to believe that people who try to be good and upright according to what they, in all sincerity, have come to hold true, will be saved and will be saved by Christ. But that is part of a theological belief Christians may hold, not a neutral philosophical position which anyone, upon a little reflection should subscribe to.

But while I am impressed by the sceptical attitude Russell and Flew demonstrate regarding fideism, I cannot say that this admiration extends to the epistemological and metaphysical positions they adumbrate, nor to the critiques of Christian doctrines essayed on the basis of those prior philosophical commitments. What I shall argue below is that, if the kind of philosophical views which Russell and Flew held on such fundamental issues as the possibility of objective knowledge about ourselves and the world are to be defended in the context of current realist/antirealist debate, then the empiricist and naive realist components of those positions must be transcended. And, ironically, those limitations can be surpassed, I believe, by arguing for a philosophical position which reverses epistemological scepticism in a manner which at once also reverses the metaphysical scepticism inherent in the Humean tradition to which, in quite different ways as we shall note below, Russell and Flew are both heirs. To defeat the philosophical fideism inimical to the epistemological stance of Russell and Flew, (but, it must be said, more so to the latter than the former), one requires a strategy that will also dismantle the kind of objections to the preambles of Christian faith (the existence of God, the reasonableness of belief in life after death and miracles) which occur in their work.

The way a philosophy of religion is manifest in the work of the two thinkers is, it must be said, quite different. As Brightman, in the essay mentioned above, points out, Russell provides no systematic treatment of the preambles of Christian faith we have mentioned. There is some discussion of Leibnitz's arguments for God's existence and nature in an early work on that philosopher, and this is probably the reason why Frederick Copleston chose to engage Russell on the issue of God's existence with reference to Leibnitz in their BBC radio debate of 1948, while one would suspect that it was in fact Aquinas behind Copleston's philosophical position.

Theological issues of a philosophical kind certainly appear in Russell's more popular essays on the question of religion, such as those collected in the book *Why I am not a Christian*. But there is little close analysis offered, rather such essays enhanced Russell's reputation as the champion of those in early and mid-twentieth century Britain and America who saw themselves as free-thinking, reason loving enemies of religious superstition, as with rhetorical flourishes of mordant wit and cool, logically honed, sarcasm he excoriated the evils wrought in society by the legacy of Christianity. To many Russell appeared as a 20th century Voltaire, (although some of the differences between the two over metaphysics and the importance of religion are far from negligible). Beyond this it is clear from Russell's general philosophical position, which underwent considerable development, that any attempt to ground a rational theology or a metaphysics supportive of the preambles of Christian faith is doomed to failure. In this sense he continues the Humean tradition into the 20th century. It would be outside the scope of the present essay to examine how well founded Russell's criticisms of the historical track-record of Christianity are. Suffice it to say that it is easy to acknowledge the rhetorical style of Russell's writing here and that the grounding or the confounding of such historical criticisms requires the analyses of the historian. One does have to recognise that Russell tends to rehash a number of the standard 'black legends' concerning Christianity and, in particular, medieval Catholicism which were a stock in trade of post-enlightenment anti-religious apologists. An example is the way Russell, in his *History of Western Philosophy*, encourages the myth that medieval philosophy is unworthy of study given the religious prejudices of those who produced it. Thirty years ago Anthony Kenny offered a witty riposte to this Russellian thesis when he observed that the man who had spent three hundred and sixty pages in the *Principia Mathematica* trying to prove that two and two are four, a truth which Russell believed, was hardly in a position to take medieval philosophers to task in this way.[3]

I think what can be discerned as the theme underlying much of this Russellian anti Christian rhetoric is a Neitzschean one: there is operative a hermeneutic of suspicion as regards Christianity. In the essay "Useful Contributions to Civilisation?", Russell writes:

> It would seem, therefore, that the three human impulses embodied in religion are fear, conceit and hatred. The purpose of religion, one may say, is to give an air of respectability to these passions, provided they run in certain channels. It is because these passions make on the whole for human misery that religion is a force for evil, since it permits men to indulge these passions without restraint, where but for its sanction they 'might, at least to a certain degree, control them.[4]

The parallels with Neitzschean analyses, as with those of other "masters of suspicion" such as Marx and Freud, are evident: that which ostensibly controls and defeats such emotions as "fear, conceit and hatred", Christianity, actually fosters these undesirable phenomena. Clearly, the immediate response of the Christian here will be that, although inauthentic manifestations of Christianity may provide instances of such inconsistency, authentic Christianity does not. For one's own experience of Christianity, and that of others one has known or read about, has been that it was only through the strength which one's faith gives one that one has been able to resist temptations towards acts of precisely these types. But the further point is that if one ventures upon the Neitzschean path one must realise that such analysis is a double-edged sword. For it was Neitzsche himself who turned the mirror back on philosophy and philosophy of the apparently dis-passionate sort which is represented in a thinker such as Russell. On Neitzsche's view such philosophical professionalism was itself a concealing mask for "fear, conceit and hatred", for a Will to power. It is not my intention to defend Neitzschean analysis, (in fact I think that for all Neitzsche's subtle strategies of subterfuge he cannot avoid revealing the self-referential incoherence of his endeavours), but Alasdair MacIntyre's recent use of Neitzsche and Foucault to reflect on, and reveal some of the presumptions of late 19th century rationalism,[5] suggests to me that Russell's "suspicions" of Christianity and its moral profile invite reciprocal reflections of a fairly personal kind on the moral profile of Russell and the tradition in which he wrote. And it is, in part, to biographical studies that one would have to turn to pursue such a reflection. Finally, it is important to complete the picture of Russell's attitude to religion by taking into account certain personal factors which Russell himself drew attention to: the way philosophy was for him at first seen as a path towards, perhaps, the confirmation of religious belief, and then the way in which the "loss of certainty" gradually spread from religious belief to mathematics and to philosophy itself, and the retention by Russell of a vague notion of the value of a religious "sense".[6] Regarding the latter point, it is important to bear in mind that Russell was, "emo-tionally", as he would put it, an unhappy and reluctant humanist whose writings also manifest, in an idiom expressive of his British philosophical and cultural background, that tragic sense of the loss of faith evident in the writings of so many of the cultural elite of the West in the 19th and 20th centuries; a sense of loss, so powerfully expressed in Matthew Arnold's poem *On Dover Beach*, or, in the 20th century, in the literary and philosophical writings of the Spaniard, Miguel Unamuno. In Russell's words

> "...those who attempt to make a religion of humanism, which recognizes noth-ing greater than man, do not satisfy my emotions."[7]

Anthony Flew, unlike Russell, is a philosopher who is not only more sym-pathetic to the traditions of Christian thought, and has, for example, a high regard for Aquinas as a philosopher, but has also produced systematic treatments of philosophical issues connected with Christian doctrine.[8] Given the more explicit philosophical treatment of theological matters in Flew's anti-theistic writing, discussion below will tend to show a bias in favour of examining his work in more detail than Russell's; for often what is implicit in Russell's rhetorical criticisms of Christianity is given an explicit form in Flew's argument. But there are also significant differences between the two philosophers in the area of epistemology and metaphysics and these need to be highlighted. No doubt there are some for whom post-war philosophers such as Flew and Kai Neilsen assumed the "mantle of Isaiah" from an older generation of atheistic thinkers, Russell being the most notable among them. From the perspective of philosophy this would in many ways be a false lumping together of diverse viewpoints; although the element of truth here, as I have already hinted above, is that Russell's and Flew's anti-theisms have family resemblances based on the fact that the family tree is basically empiricist and Humean. It should perhaps at this point be noted that neither philosopher is, technically speaking, an "atheist" since Russell denied that there were arguments to prove God's non-existence and Flew, in his essay "The Presumption of Atheism", states that what his "presumption" amounts to is that God's existence has to be argued for if one is to accept it other than by faith—a position he argues was also held by Aquinas.[9]

Epistemological and Metaphysical Positions

There is little doubt that Bertrand Russell's position in the history of philosophy is well established on the basis of his contributions to 20th century philosophical logic. This is not to say that the major collaborative effort with Whitehead, *Principia Mathematica*, and the minor classic of Russell's 1905 *Mind* article 'On Denoting' put an end to the questions they set out to answer. It is, of course, the massive contribution these writings made to ongoing debates on mathematical and philosophical logic, as much as anything by the incoherencies and antinomies they threw up, for which they are remembered. However, it would have to be said that Russell's output after World War I, when he turned increasingly to epistemological and metaphysical issues, has not remained a conspicuous element in current discussions of these areas. C.D. Broad's quip that Russell changed his philosophical position every two weeks is rather unfair, but it does perhaps convey the sense his contemporaries had that his researches into philosophical issues were of a tentative and incomplete kind.

A case in point would be Russell's move towards metaphysical monism. That is, he gradually became persuaded that there was only one kind of "stuff" in the universe and that was to be described in terms of the laws of physics.[10] This is, of course, that kind of reductionist materialism which became popular in some philosophical circles in the 19th and 20th centuries. The only really real is what is on the "basement level", other "levels", those explained by sciences such as chemistry, biology, and the social sciences are merely apparent, or fictive epiphenomena. This would include, naturally, the level of human conscious operations. But unlike some recent philosophers of mind who are prepared simply to deny that we have conscious states or say, as does Daniel Dennett, that they are "useful fictions", Russell worried away at the evident difficulties involved in reinterpreting conscious phenomena as something which they are evidently not. In the 1940 work, *An Inquiry into Meaning and Truth*, he made some suggestions in this direction but also made it clear that he could not to his own satisfaction solve the problems involved.[11] And in the later work *My Philosophical Development* it is evident that he draws attention to the importance of such mental acts as "noticing" not on the basis of arguments from physics but in terms of a "reductive" analysis of what is given in consciousness.[12] I will have more to say on this below, but the general methodological point is worth highlighting: Russell's metaphysical procedure is the application of Ockham's razor: entities are not to be multiplied without requirement. In some popular presentations of this precept it is thought that what must follow is the denial of such unobservables as God and spiritual beings. But as anyone who knows a little of the history of philosophy is aware, it appears that the precept can just as well land one in the situation of also denying the reality of personal identities, causal relations in the world (with Hume), other minds, and, as we shall see Russell himself admitted, the world purportedly described by common sense and science. Must all this follow? I shall argue that following this perfectly reasonable precept should not lead into such a morass. The point is that if one has failed to notice a good deal of what is "given" in consciousness to begin with one's subsequent affirmations and denials of what there is sufficient evidence to affirm and to deny will be similarly impoverished.

The adoption of a reductive analysis, as understood by Russell, very rapidly leads to such a philosophical position being impaled on the horns of a dilemma; and it was a dilemma Russell himself boldly described, even if his attempts to shy away from accepting its implications were sometimes in effect a loss of "philosophical nerve". To state the dilemma, in one form at least: reductive analysis might favour a metaphysics of reductionism, i.e. that things are really only a matter of the operation of laws of physics, but it is precisely reductive analysis itself that indicates that all we have are the data of consciousness—the entities postulated by physics, or indeed the external world are mere inferences and are not given. We are back with Hume who denied we had any knowledge of causal relations in reality. So Russell can write, to the chagrin of the "Johnsonian stone-kicking", scientistically minded materialists, and indeed to that of the other philosopher we are here concerned with,

> ...indeed there is little but prejudice and habit to be said for the view that there is a world at all.[13]

Russell was candid in his profession of the reasonableness of solipsism; of the phenomenalist view that all we really, definitely have to go on are our sense impressions. There is an interesting historical irony in the way Russell gradually came to repudiate the assurances of common sense, dogmatic, or naive realism so central to G.E. Moore's turn of the century programme for dispelling the obfuscations of Idealism, a programme with which Russell had thrown in his lot so enthusiastically. Others who did not wish to follow down the path Hume had identified as running from the sunny uplands of empiricism to the lugubrious and intractable forests of idealism, a path Russell now seemed to be retracing, resisted with tenacity. So one can witness the lively exchange between Russell and Ernest Nagel in the Schilpp edited *Festschrift* of the 1940's. Nagel is clearly shocked by Russell's refusal to accept the truth of the direct deliverances of common sense experience.[14] In reply Russell traces out arguments in a 20th century form which have been put forward in one way or another over the last four centuries: modern science reveals that so much of what we take to be the case in common sense judgements is erroneous. To take Sir Arthur Eddington's example, according to common sense the table before me is brown, continuous, solid; according to modern physics it is mostly empty space with 'things' in the domain that I now describe as particles, now as waves. Which is the correct account? Russell writes,

> Since events in my body determine my percepts, this limits the extent to which my percepts can give me information as to what happens outside.. and makes such information dependent upon the laws of physics. I am here assuming physics true; if this assumption is not made, obviously a more sceptical conclusion follows.[15]

The final sentence of this passage, then, acknowledges the dilemma outlined above. Not only do the deliverances of science throw the judgements of common sense into doubt, but, in terms of reason, these deliverances in turn only rest upon assumptions. In a way very akin to Hume's endorsement of the adoption of the, non-reasonably justifiable, "natural attitude", Russell proceeds to see a way beyond his impasse by adopting a "natural attitude" that has two aspects to it. In practice no one lives as a solipsist, for no one takes it that he or she has only come into existence five minutes ago. What we can do here, Russell avers, is to have some sense of what counts as an inference by examining heuristic notions that are at work in current science, and then reflecting on ways these inferences may have arisen in the course of biological evolution as necessary ways creatures like ourselves adapted to the environment for survival.[16]

I said above that much of Russell's philosophical output from the period after the first world war on has not continued to engage the interest of philosophers today in the way his earlier work has. But in many ways the theses I have described above have been developed in new, and indeed more detailed fashion, and have been the issues which have been argued to and fro in much Anglo-American philosophy of science and epistemology over the last thirty years or so. And certainly I would have to say, as will be argued further, that Russell's insights into the paradoxes and dilemmas of epistemology in the context of modern philosophy of science are far more acute than are those evidenced by the dogmatic realism of Anthony Flew.

On the other hand, Russell's move off into the realm of the "natural attitude" in order to bypass the crisis in empiricism he had so eloquently delineated, proves to be no reasonable answer to the reasonable questions he had asked, as subsequent developments in philosophy have made very clear. So Russell's attempt to map out five general notions operative in scientific inference runs into innumerable problems once we see it as very much a pre-Popperian effort in the philosophy of science. By this I mean that with Popper and with the research and debate his work initiated on the reasonableness of scientific change (acknowledging that there were important precursors like Duhem, and Adjukiewicz), Russell's list of scientific notions appear no more than a piece of cultural anthropology that is unconcerned with the problem of paradigm change; the attempt to bolster the list with considerations of the adaptive capacity of human animals can, from this perspective, only appear as an even more lame attempt to elevate the culturally particular to a universal status. One could well imagine the humourous spectacle of a neo-Kantian in the last century trying to carry through just such a task by arguing that Euclidean geometry must be the unique geometry of the real world, or we must take it to be so, because of its relation to the structure of tough, evolutionary specimens such as homo sapiens! Of course such "naturalised epistemology" found a new lease of life with its adoption as a slogan for a research programme by W.V. Quine. But the criticisms this notion has come in for are also by now part of the history of Anglo-American philosophy of the last thirty years, and no doubt the not inconsiderable number of philosophers who follow Rorty, Bernstein, Feyerabend, Laudan, Putnam and the like might suggest that it marked the last brave stand against the swelling tide of anti-foundationalism in Anglo-American philosophy of epistemology and philosophy of science. Philosophers including Sellars, Stroud and Davidson pointed out that the difference between input into mind and output from mind had to be a matter of reasonable inference, not simply of brain states, and that naturalism which failed to reckon with this ends in the usual incoherent fallacies that Frege identified in the case of psychologism: one uses inference and reason to establish naturalism, Darwinian theory and the like![17] One should bear these points in mind not only with regard to Russell's endeavours but as also relevant to an assessment of the "naturalistic" tendencies in Flew's work.

Flew, as was noted above, is as disturbed by Russell's leanings toward subjectivism and anti-common sense realism as was Ernest Nagel. For Flew this demonstrates that Russell was yet another philosopher to fall under the spell of

Descartes and the latter's doctrine of the "Veil of Appearance."[18] As opposed to Russell and as opposed to many of the luminaries of Anglo-American philosophy who have adopted some form of anti-realism over the last twenty-five years, Flew holds fast to a Morean common sense realism. On this view knowledge by immediate acquaintance removes the issues which make hazy and difficult judgements based on inference. So Flew asserts,

> ...we may expect everyday and practically oriented perceptual judgements to be correct.[19]

Descartes, having had such a baneful influence on philosophy over the last four-hundred years, is Flew's prime target. Flew's criticisms take the form of by now fairly familiar moves against Cartesian scepticism, moves far from novel in either Eastern or Western philosophy.[20] With regard to the terms employed in the formulation of the sceptical moves in the Cartesian *Meditations* Flew writes,

> These Cartesian 'doubts' cannot be formulated or understood without assuming some knowledge of kinds which Descartes is setting himself to repudiate. For how could we allow that anyone was master of the concepts of material things and of hallucination, of valid and invalid argument, of dreaming and of waking, if they were unable confidently and correctly to identify any specimen exemplars, however paradigmatic? Descartes is taking for granted his own mastery of colloquial French; and in the somewhat later *Meditations* of Latin also. Yet this is knowledge of a kind and amount which we could not concede to be possessed by anyone pretending to such near total Cartesian uncertainty.[21]

There are elements in this rebuttal of Cartesian scepticism which have something going for them and which, I believe, do provide a hint of what needs to be done to give a more satisfactory account of human knowing than that provided by Descartes. But placed as they are in the context of Flew's argument these elements themselves do not save it from debilitating confusion. Flew has not got the measure of Descartes' "escalating" scepticism, nor the measure of the way that scepticism has been played out in Idealism, or in more recent subjectivism in epistemology and the philosophy of science. An initial question to help one see the sleight of hand here is, "does one always need to know that a paradigmatic instance is actually the case in order to have a paradigmatic concept?" That is, surely I can ask if there are mermaids without ever having had to derive that concept from an encounter with one. But the problem becomes aggravated, as Descartes himself knew, and as those who tease their brains with problems of "brains in a vat" in more recent philosophy know. Descartes' version of that latter day conundrum was the introduction of the "evil genius". Where do I get my experiences from? It could possibly be from the "evil genius" or, in the case of Putnam's brain in the vat, from the stimulating apparatus; the contrasts I make between experiences, between the experiences of words in "different languages" and so forth could be a result of such trickery. As Barry Stroud has argued against similar attempts to refute the sceptic, because the sceptic uses a conceptual scheme that includes contrast terms such as "reality" and "illusion" this does not necessarily imply that he has knowledge of those concepts being instantiated.[22] That the use of such contrasts is a "pointer" to realism is, I am sure, the case, but more will be needed, more than Flew can provide here, to establish and defend realism. And so, for the present, we are back with Russell's subjectivism.

What has been the purpose of the argument of this section so far? I am not going to defend anti-realism and subjectivism for as will be seen below I shall argue for a critical realism and, as I have suggested above, it is on the basis of that position that one can argue for a metaphysics that is at variance with the anti-theistic views of Russell and Flew. But if I am not an anti-realist nor am I a realist of empiricist persuasion and I do not think defending the reasonableness of common sense involves defending such a view. For rather than praising dumb staring at data, common sense also prizes intelligence and reasonableness in coming to know the real. And I do not think, as Flew appears to, that a naive realism which insists that we know reality because, obviously, we get out of the way of oncoming buses and trains is adequate to resolving the complex epistemological issues which vex contemporary philosophy of science, not to mention the epistemology of the last four centuries.[23] For bats and rats also execute such manoeuvres and while we no doubt have something in common with them, such comparisons do not resolve issues about whether or not we are capable of objective knowledge in science or history, and how one is to resolve issues concerning the relation between common sense knowledge and science (is the former a kind of illusion which the latter replaces as some of Russell's arguments seem to imply?). Indeed, such comparisons of similarities, especially when taken to the level of sophistication we find in biology or evolutionary theory, had better not saw off the branch upon which they sit through some kind of simplistic naturalism or psychologism.

In formulating an answer to the sceptic one may usefully begin with a piece of introspective analysis Russell presents, which was mentioned above.[24] Russell writes,

> My abandonment of the relational character of sensation led me to substitute 'noticing' for 'acquaintance'. Most of the occurrences in our sensational life are not noticed; and when they are not noticed they are not data for empirical knowledge. If we use words about them, that is clear proof that we have noticed them ...[25]

Here Russell draws attention, then, to an activity of consciousness that is to be differentiated from simple sensing—it is, rather, a matter of noticing or adverting to some sensation. It is worthwhile in this context to refer to the way

Flew also senses that the data of consciousness as described by, for example, Hume are rather exiguous and wishes to claim that there is more to it than just Hume's "bundle of fleeting perceptions". Flew writes,

> ... Hume refers in his every statement to 'we', or to 'the mind'.. as allegedly reviewing, those successive 'perceptions of the mind.' [26]

A use of Ockham's razor, a "reductive" analysis, in epistemology or metaphysics wishes to cling, parsimoniously to the "given" of consciousness, but that "given" is not so easily characterised as at first it might seem. So we see Russell, in the passage above, revising his own account of what goes on in our conscious experiences. But how would one agree or disagree with Russell here? Clearly, by raising the same question he has answered and by trying to settle it with regard to the data which are one's own conscious experiences: are there or are there not acts of noticing, adverting to sensation over and above sensation itself? The question can only be settled by checking in one's own conscious experience whether the conditions specified by the notion of "noticing" Russell has specified are given, fulfilled. The experiment will not be settled by reading books on the physics of radioactivity or on the archaeology of ancient Rome. But if one performs the necessary experiment of attending to one's conscious experience, one can by a parallel process also not only notice "noticing" of sensation, as distinct from mere sensing, but the activities of questioning and judging as to what is the case which one performed in order to attempt to verify or disconfirm Russell's initial contention. I would suggest that this process of differentiating one's conscious activities involved in attempting to come to know could be continued at some length, and would reveal such conscious and interrelated activities as: raising questions as to 'What?' ("What does Russell mean by 'noticing'?"); having insights, perhaps trying to formulate those insights in some way; raising the further question 'Is that so?', 'probably so?', having understood Russell's notion of "noticing" is it the case that I do that?); and, perhaps, coming to a judgement, tentative or firm on the basis of the evidence—in this case the evidence being the data of my own conscious activities, initially regarding the Russellian notion of 'noticing', but subsequently being the data of all the conscious operations just outlined. And since one would have to engage in those very operations to estimate the truth of the proposed differentiation of one's conscious experience of trying to come to know, it should not be too difficult to verify those operations as, in fact, what occur.

But the rub here is the contention that these operations, which I have only, necessarily, briefly sketched out, are found to be confirmed just as much in the attempt to deny them as to confirm them. That is, in making out the case that I do not have conscious experience, that I do not question, understand anything or make judgements, in short, that I do not carry out processes which are minimally required for the business of arguing, or attempting to establish what is so or probably so, I will be involved in a self-referential incoherence. It may be thought that we are simply back with Descartes here, affirming, at the end of his sceptical peregrinations, his own existence. And there are, indeed, affinities between the approach I am suggesting here and Descartes' refutation of scepticism insofar as his argument stands within the tradition of such refutations running from Socrates through Aristotle, Augustine, and Aquinas to the present.[27] But the differences are perhaps even more significant and would, if one were able to go into more detail here, be found, in large measure, to reflect the way such arguments occur within the context of a philosophical position with more in common with that of Aquinas. The most significant difference is that among such conscious operations of which one is aware and which one can come to affirm as occurring in one's consciousness (and the doubting of which only serves to draw attention to) is the process of verifying those conscious operations themselves. Whatever the precise status Descartes' idea of the 'I think' has in his thought, whether it be some intuited innate idea or no, he does present what appears to be an "intuitionist" version of human knowing which is applied to human conscious activities themselves. Thus it is not true, as Descartes' own practice witnesses, that I cannot doubt my own existence; I can certainly raise the question without being prevented from doing so by some blinding intuition of the truth of the proposition. Just like raising and answering the question "Are there any lettuces in the garden?", the question "Do I exist?" is, similarly raised and is answered, in a similar fashion, by adverting to the data, evidence available. In the case of the lettuces the familiar green items in the garden, in that of my conscious operations, including those of coming to make a judgement, the conscious data on cognitional process. Descartes' oversight of this vital element in human knowing, the process of judgement and its exigencies, leads him to offer as a criterion of estimating the truth of other putative truth assertions beyond the 'Cogito', the "clarity and distinctness" characteristic of the truth perceived. If, on the other hand, one adverts to the facts of consciousness which reveal that any proposed judgement of fact is to be assessed in terms of whether or not its conditions are fulfilled in the data then, clearly, one has a more fertile criterion to hand than Descartes had for moving beyond consciousness.

To begin with, on this view coming to know reality, what is the case, is a matter of: intelligent grasp, the enjoyment of some insight; perhaps the adumbration of some hypothesis or theory in order to explain the data; and reasonable affirmation of whether that insight, surmise, or theory is true, false, probably so, or not so. Therefore the posing of the problem of the "bridge" from an in here consciousness to an out there world is an oversight of the nature of the process of verification. For if I affirm, as part of setting up the problem of the "bridge" to start with, that there is consciousness, and that it is really the case that it is cut off from a world which is really out there, then I have already made a number of judgements about reality to begin with; I have crossed the bridge without adverting to that fact. Despite their ingenuity and subtle and profound insight, then, in the end one has to be brutal about the self-destructive incoherence of Kantian and Hegelian idealisms and their many progeny up to and including the Derridean critique of Husserl: if one brilliantly and impressively argues for the limitations of human knowing such that one ends by affirming "it is really the case that I cannot know what is the case", one has ended in incoherence. But an important point to note here is that the recognition of this incoherence is a further instance of adverting to evidence, evidence provided by the data of consciousness. For the refutation of such positions occurs precisely because I notice that the conscious act of affirming them as true occurs. These are not simply cases of blackboard exercises in logical fallacy, rather those exercises can be written up only because I have first adverted to an instance of a conscious act which I may have denied there are instances of; so I notice that I am judging that "I do not judge".

This means that the judgements of common sense are also reasonable and intelligent, although they may not be as definite as those which have to do with my own conscious process. When I deny that I am making a denial I am clearly aware of all the evidence being in on the type of act I am performing such that my denial denies what is truly the case. But if I deny that this fried egg before me is so, I may be right. Perhaps it is April Fool's Day and although it is an extremely good imitation, still what appears as an egg is not so. But evidently this shows the reasonableness of common sense. For if I have no reason to doubt that the egg is what it appears from sight and smell and even touch to be, then it is reasonable for me to take it as such. If I hear children giggling behind me as I am about to bite and remember it is April the first, I may begin to suspect what appears before me on the plate. While ordinary language uses "know" and "certain" rather loosely, so that by these terms one tends to mean that which given the normal situation (which I have no reason to doubt is normal), I take it that this is an x, still there is a recognition that there is not certainty in the strict sense in these cases; for people do not suffer nervous breakdowns when, in the case of practical jokes, they find out that what they felt was the case was a piece of trickery. One may further note that with regard to the discussion above of "Eddington's two tables", the position outlined here would suggest that any view of common sense as reaching only "appearance" whereas science reaches reality is erroneous. Science begins with the descriptions of common sense and we may say that science attempts to relate things among themselves (as Einstein's "independence from all observers" postulate indicates), whereas common sense judgements, in large measure relate things to us and our concerns. But this does not make the judgements of common sense unreal. The data have to be given for the verification of the "coloured, continuous object" which common sense recognises as a table, just as they have to be given for the verification of the physicist's object.

The point is, therefore, that just as I can intelligently understand the notion of my being a conscious unity differentiated by acts including seeing, smelling, hearing, questioning, imagining, excogitating, asking for evidence, and judging, so I can make judgements on the basis of the evidence, albeit defeasible judgements, that there are chairs, tables, mountains, dogs and other persons. What of the deceptions of the evil genius? On this account the evil genius is just one more hypothesis, and as with any hypothesis in science or the humanities we can say that it may be possible, but that does not mean there is any evidence to suggest that an hypothesis is so or even probably so.

Not only can I verify, under pain of incoherence if I try to deny it, that I perform the conscious operations itemised above in the process of coming to know, but I can also affirm that I am a conscious unity of such acts. For, clearly I must be aware of what I have understood when I try to judge whether it is so or not, and in judging I must not only be aware of the meaning of terms, of the operations of asking are these concepts instantiated, and weighing the evidence for this, but also of the data which provide the fulfilling of conditions, allowing me to affirm rationally that this is so, not so, or probable; and those data may be of sensation, in the case of the table or the clock alarm, or of consciousness, in the case of my own operations. I am, then, aware of a unity, of these acts occurring as linked within the one consciousness as the condition of possibility for the process of my thought. As was noted above, Flew observes that Hume's account of human (and indeed Humean) consciousness is less adequate than it could be, and that inconsistencies show at the margins of Hume's own text (Derrida would, one hopes, be proud of Flew here). And on the view expounded here such inconsistencies run throughout the warp and weft of the Humean enterprise. For example, Hume holds that the distinction between fictional ideas and belief is simply a matter of the force of custom and habit; the effect of repetition is to establish a "strong feeling" within us which is what "belief" amounts to.[28] So the rat turns the treadwheel and is "certain" that, as usual, the cheese will fall. But this is hardly an adequate characterisation of how human beliefs can be changed and how Hume himself attempts to change our past beliefs and establish new ones on the scope and limits of human knowing. It is not a matter of simply reading and rereading the *Inquiry* over and over again to change our beliefs, rather Hume's presumption is that it is by agreeing with his reasoning. Among other things that reasoning entails questioning other views as to their cogency and as to whether they are supported by the evidence, the data of our own conscious activities; and asking us to judge the truth of his own view on the basis of that same data. So do we not find, for instance, that we have an intuitive grasp of mathematical connections but no such intuition as regards the necessary, causal connection of things in the world? In short Hume's reflections are undermined by his own intelligent and reasonable practice in attempting to establish them: he has a bad self-image.

The argument of this section has, then, been to show the inability of either Russell or Flew to move beyond the sceptical impasse created by the weaknesses of empiricist realism; weaknesses which Russell ably identified. In order to meet the sceptical challenges of idealism, social relativism, Kantianism and the like I have briefly sketched out, what may be termed a critical realist position; a position the bold claim of which is that the attempt to deny at least its general and most basic features involves one in incoherence. In the next section I will attempt to tease out the metaphysical implications of that position in order to confront the objections raised by Russell and Flew to a reasoned argument for God's existence.

The Question of God's Existence

Clearly the centrepiece of any anti-theistic philosophy of religion will be the denial of any reasonable grounds on which God's existence may be affirmed. Such is the option taken by both Russell and Flew. Since I take a view similar to that of Aquinas on the ontological argument, I should not want to attempt to defend that approach. However, I do believe, that arguments traditionally known as "Cosmological", and in a sense, "from Design," have force and I wish to mount a defence of these against the criticisms of Russell, Flew and what may be termed the Humean tradition. The fundamental issue in establishing the cogency of such arguments is, I believe, the metaphysical argument as to the intelligibility of what there is; an argument which must show how principles of "causality" or "sufficient reason" are to be known as applying to reality in general (by "sufficient reason" here I intend a principle that is to be understood in Aquinas' terms rather than in Leibnitz's).

In the debate with Fr Copleston on the existence of God, of which mention has already been made, Russell responded to Copleston's argument for God's existence as the ultimate cause or explanation of what is by denying the general validity of the principle of causality. His answer was

> ..a physicist looks for causes; that does not necessarily imply that there are causes everywhere. A man may look for gold without assuming that there is gold everywhere; if he finds gold well and good, if he doesn't he's had bad luck. The same is true when physicists look for causes.[29]

When Russell in his youth encountered James Mill's dismissal of arguments to an ultimate cause by pointing out that they begged the question "Who made God?", this had the same effect of disabusing him of belief in rational argument for God's existence as it had had on the youthful James Stuart Mill.[30] An objection of this kind also plays a role in Flew's critique of the causal argument to God. He writes,

At every stage explanation is in terms of something else which, at that stage, has to be accepted as a brute fact... It would therefore seem to be a consequence of the essential nature of explanation that, however much ultimately be explained in successive stages of enquiry, there must always be some facts which have simply to be accepted... The ultimate facts about God would have to be, for precisely the same reasons, equally inexplicable.[31]

To begin with the last first, one may question Flew's assertion that we take explanations as "brute", or "ultimate" until we decide to move on to further explanations. This leaves unclear how and when we take a series of questions as being satisfied in some factual explanation and when we know not all the answers are satisfactorily met: why is it in some cases we carry on asking further questions and in others we do not? On Flew's account it would seem that we had no way of distinguishing between the two. But if his account does not provide this perhaps his own practice will remedy the deficiency. So we may ask what would be Flew's response if someone were simply to assert to him, as matter of "brute fact", that all he had ever written on the history of philosophy was mistaken. If his interlocutor refused to attempt to establish such "facts" by way of reasoned argument one would expect Flew simply to dismiss him as unreasonable. The point is that "brute facts" are only for the brutes, but for human beings "facts" are known in reasoned judgements; as the attempt to deny this fact and perhaps establish alternatives will itself only serve to testify. We know we have established such facts when we grasp that the evidence is in on some matter, that the conditions are fulfilled, that there is sufficient reason to affirm x is the case. It is the awareness that there are further relevant questions to be asked, that not all conditions are fulfilled that drives us on to ask for further evidence, further explanation. On this view God is not some brute fact but a comprehensive explanation of everything; that is God explains why God as well as why everything else. That we do not enjoy a direct insight into God is evident; for we do not already understand everything otherwise we would not be questioning. But just as in algebra, or physics there are heuristic concepts which involve knowing something but not everything about some explanatory x, so we can unfold some heuristic notions of what such an ultimate explanation which God is would be without having God's knowledge of God. To ask "Who made God?" is a recognition of not experiencing that ultimate insight which (to use language which Aquinas' position suggests) is God; but neither does it get one off the hook, for implicit in the question is the recognition of the demand for ultimate explanation.

Turning to Russell's piece of empiricist mythology about physicists finding, or failing to find causes, as gold-diggers succeed or fail, one realises that, in the context of Russell's position on epistemology and metaphysics as a whole, of which something was said above, this could but be a temporising, *ad hominem*, response to the issues raised by Copleston. For on Russell's own showing the notion of physicists really finding anything is problematic. There is no preventing Russell's weak phenomenology of "some rules contemporary scientists happen to follow", which was the best he could do for scientific rationality, from being hijacked by some version of scientific instrumentalism or conventionalism. In that case there is a self-denying ordinance in Russell's position as far as pronouncements on the ontological or metaphysical structure of reality are concerned.

Flew is fond of alluding to Hume's warnings against anthropomorphic projections of our nature and intentions onto God.[32] But recognising the profound irony of such warnings issuing from a philosopher like Hume brings us to the nub of the issue: for we have to keep before us that on Hume's showing all our anticipations of causal relations, of the unified, substantial persistence of entities and the like as obtaining in reality are likewise mere anthropomorphic projections on our part. But, as I have argued above, the attempt to make affirmations about the scope and limits of human knowing is itself a claim to know what is really and truly the case. When the nature of the reversal of such sceptical positions is understood one may also go on to understand the epistemological and metaphysical implications of that reversal. For such reversals come about when I grasp that the conditions are fulfilled for affirming that I do, in fact, perform intelligent and reasonable operations; the attempt to deny which only provides evidence for the truth of the proposition being denied. As far as metaphysics is concerned one may see how a metaphysics emerges from one of three epistemological alternatives. On the empiricist-naive realist view I know reality simply by allowing my sensory faculties to be flooded by the information which just "flows in from the outside"; given the long history of sceptical objections to this view, some of which we noted above, this is hardly viable. So one arrives at the sceptical, Idealist, social relativist, "locked in the conceptual schema", deconstructionist view. But, to repeat, such views are grasped as incoherent once one adverts to the fact that their affirmation involves variations on the incoherence of claiming to know that one cannot know; and in grasping that incoherence one is grasping in the data of consciousness a mental operation which one affirms to be an operation of 'judging what is truly the case". Just as one can grasp that such a judgement occurs so one can likewise judge as being the case, as being real, the other conscious activities of coming to know some of which were mentioned above. But on this showing reality is precisely that which one knows through the operations of intelligence and reason. And again the attempt to deny or question this heuristic notion of the real as intelligible will be self referentially incoherent; for one will be attempting to show that it is not so, not really the case, through the very operations of intelligence and reason.

If, then, reality is the intelligible it is the case that we can rule out and rule in certain items as possible or impossible. So it was argued above that we know that something is the case if its conditions are fulfilled and any philosophical debate on the nature of human knowledge presupposes just such a notion. For we verify on the basis of the data of our consciousness whether or not the conditions specified in, say, Hume's or Russell's accounts of human knowing are fulfilled. In the case of position on human knowing outlined above, as involving several, interrelated conscious activities, the reader was invited to verify the position in terms of whether or not its conditions were fulfilled in his or her consciousness. A further point must be brought out here: such views on human knowing are not known to be true or false simply by considering their meaning; that must be done prior to raising the question "is it so?", but of itself the process of understanding the meaning and implications of the position does not settle the facts. In other words we are aware that such hypotheses concern contingent notions. Simply by considering them we do not know that they are, we only know that they are if we find their specified conditions fulfilled in consciousness. But, then, if those conditions are fulfilled further reasonable questions occur as to why this particular being, item, system, is, given that it does not have to be. Such questions relate to the conditions, or causes, external to the being or system under question. But the crucial point here is, if reality is the intelligible, and it has been argued that the attempt to deny this only proves the case, then all the conditions necessary, internal and external, for a being to exist must be fulfilled if it is to exist.

Hume thought that he had disposed of the causal argument for God by pointing out that one can imagine a thing coming into existence without a cause. However, imagining is not understanding nor is it knowing. So I can imagine that something exists, but this does not mean that it does exist. To know that something exists I must know that all its conditions, its conditions of intelligible dependence, are fulfilled. Hume also denied our ability to know of any instance of real causal dependence, and he quite rightly pointed out, in the *Inquiry* that I do not directly perceive that my willing causes a picture to appear in my imagination.[33] It might be that God or some other cause always makes the image appear when I wish it to. But it is a different matter, (and one which Hume with his limited account of conscious operations failed to see), with my own attention to the picture or an idea. I am aware of attending to this or that image *because* I want to, *because* I grasp it as a value to do so, and *because* I will to act in accord with that value. Similarly when I make a judgement of fact I am aware of the causal movement of my own activity: I judge because, and am aware of doing so because, I grasp that the conditions are fulfilled in the data, whether this be on the cheese being off or on an account of human knowing itself. Within our own conscious operations then we can identify paradigm instances in which we recognise the intelligible dependence of x on y for the existence of x. We can identify efficient causes in cases as the one above, where judgement occurs (and we are aware of it occurring) because the evidence, data, are given. We can identify examples of the intelligible dependence known as final causality when we are aware of doing x, attending to this argument for example, in order to do y, to get at the truth. We can identify instances of exemplary causality when we attempt to execute or do x in a way which is in conscious dependence on a prior insight into the way of doing x.

One can, then, further differentiate the notion of intelligibility and of intelligible dependence of one thing on another. One can understand in the instances identified in consciousness that the causal relation in question is not simply bound up with this particular case. Rather, as with the principle of non-contradiction, the particular case is assessed, judged, with regard to what is understood as a general requirement for intelligibility. One grasps, then, that if there is not sufficient reason for x then x does not exist. For just as one grasps that the theory of one's own knowing cannot be the case if its conditions are known not to be given, so reflection on the instances of efficient, final and exemplary causality given in one's conscious operations, makes evident the requirement that these further conditions must be fulfilled if some x is to exist. Given that contingent beings, such as we have seen our own identity as a knowing creatures to be, do not provide sufficient reason for their own existence, and given that whatever is is intelligible (to be known through intelligent and reasonable operations) then there must exist a Being which explains both that Being's existence and the existence of everything. Further, given that this Being must fulfill the requirements of efficient, final and exemplary causality this Being must be something that has, in some fashion, intelligence and will. (Although there are other arguments one could advance on the issue, on the basis of Ockham's razor alone, one could only have grounds for concluding to the existence of one such Being). And such a Being, as Aquinas puts it, is what people call God.

If there are reasons for affirming the existence of God what of reasons for affirming the Self-revelation of God to human beings? Flew poses some objections in this regard to arguments put forward for the reasonableness of belief in such a Revelation on the basis of miracles.[34] In his discussion of these questions in *God and Philosophy* it is not always clear that Flew distinguishes between, a) miracles offered as proof for the existence of God, and b) miracles offered as proof, or evidence of God's Self-revelation. Be that as it may, it is clear that in most people's minds there is, justifiably, some connection between the two points. For if one can make a reasoned argument for God in the way offered above, occurrences which appear miraculous are, at the very least, consistent with the position that such a God exists.

There are two aspects of Flew's treatment that I wish to address. The first is Flew's development of Hume's view that the historian must assume continuity with present regularities if he is to begin to understand the past and therefore must discount as actual events stories of miracles from the past.[36] Flew acknowledges that this position requires development, for it is evident that there may be revisions in what is considered possible or probable as the sciences develop, such that what an historian at one period ruled out has having been a fabrication a later historian may be open to accept. But Flew's admission of this possibility is limited to what the "sciences" may discover as possible. As such it is a very modest gesture in the direction of debates which rage over the possibility of objectivity in historical knowing with little less ferocity than they do in the arena of philosophy of science. As a fair number of the participants in those debates, both historians and philosophers, have come to acknowledge the horizon within which the historian operates is a perspective on the possible and probable in history influenced by tacit or overt philosophical commitments. Usually the humanistic bent of historians prevents them from being out and out reductionists or determinists, but the question still arises, and can arise, as to how the question of objectivity is to be settled in the case of a school of historians who, let us say, deny that free human choices were in fact causal factors in past processes. The point is that cultural assumptions bound up with philosophical viewpoints influence the way both commentators on the contemporary scene and historians assimilate the data. This is not to say that all history is irredeemably subjective but it is to make the point that one cannot entirely exclude philosophical considerations in estimating the judgements of an historian. And on this showing an historian who was convinced of the reasonableness of affirming God's existence could also reasonably estimate the probability of event z being a miracle in a way he could not do were he not so rationally persuaded. What is fundamentally at stake here are Flew's own physicalist and scientistic metaphysical views on the basis of which he would propose to rule out and rule in what can and cannot happen and, therefore, what could and could not have happened. As we shall see below, when discussing his views of evidence for life after death, it is the question of the rational warrant with which he upholds this proposition that is the underlying issue.[37]

My second set of observations have to do with Flew's admonition that,

> ...it will not do at all to argue that a wise and good God must wish to reveal himself to his creatures. Still less are we entitled to deduce that this revelation could reasonably be expected to take this particular form, or to be recognisable by these appropriate signs. The theist is only too eager, when hard pressed by criticism, to suggest that the ways of God must necessarily be beyond our unaided understanding and conjecture.. Precisely in so far as, and for the same reasons that, the magnificent attributes specified ensure that nothing which occurs constitutes a falsification of the contention that there is such a Being: to that extent and by the same token it must become impossible to deduce any testable consequences of His existence.[38]

There are a number of points which need to be disentangled in this passage. Firstly, as mentioned above, it is not clear whether evidence for God's existence or for His Self-revelation is the issue. This confusion is enhanced by Flew's drawing parallels, in the paragraph preceding the one quoted, between testing in the case of miracles and testing via the sensible effects which may be expected to confirm a scientific hypothesis. Secondly, one would expect Flew to be aware, with his knowledge of the Christian tradition, that recourse to the "mysterious ways of God" does not function in Christian thinkers such as Aquinas as it does in others of a more fideistic persuasion, or those who think God is utter paradox, or those who take Euthyphro's voluntaristic approach to the question of God and morality. For Aquinas, and in fact for the view enshrined in the dogmatic tradition of the Catholic teaching on God, the "magnificent attributes" of God's goodness and wisdom, although analogically predicated of God are still true of God such that it is in terms of precisely those attributes that we might have some heuristic anticipation of how and what God might wish to reveal to us were He to do so. Note here that since this is a free act of God who is similar enough to us to be called a "person", one would not say on this view that God must reveal Himself but that, as with a free human person, He can do so.

Given that on the view argued for God is complete explanation He is also completely good; for evil is precisely an absence of reasonableness. There follow, naturally, the problems of pain and of reprobation; but whatever the answers to these offered by the tradition represented by Aquinas that tradition has never affirmed that mystery to do with God is a matter of sheer paradox and absurdity. It would seem reasonable, then, that one could expect that if God created and willed creatures like ourselves who have a teleological nature which strives for fulfillment then He might assist us reach the goal or goals He created for us. That we ought to come to know the truth and act accordingly are aspects of that telos to which even those who attempt to deny them as such are clearly, implicitly, committed. Further, we have argued above that God is the ultimate explanation and is therefore the ultimate answer to our questions; our very questioning therefore is orientated to some kind of sharing in the ultimate answer which God is. If this is so one may have reason to anticipate that a revelation of God could be identified as such by being concerned with these very issues. Further, that such and such events were God revealing Himself could be reasonably held were these events: a) to be reasonably held as having no explanation due to secondary causes other than God; b) as fitting into some "dialogical" pattern appropriate to the self-revelation of an intentional entity, a person; c) as concerned with the truths of human fulfillment, including the evident problem of the massive failure of human beings to live up to the demands of seeking truth and acting in accord with it. With regard to a) Flew asserts that what was held as physically impossible at one time may turn out not to be so at another; therefore a "miracle" is no longer seen to be so.[39] That the judgement of "miracle" is defeasible is something I would grant, but then it is no more defeasible than most of our other judgements concerning the existence of other minds, how well established a scientific hypothesis is, and so forth. But persons rising from the dead, and quantities of food being multiplied (as described in New Testament accounts and, also, as far as one can see well attested cases in the lives of recent Saints such as the 19th century St. John Vianney and St. John Bosco), are events which remain inexplicable in terms of the laws of the modern sciences. What Flew returns to, however, is the insistence that such events *will* and *must* be explained eventually by science.[40] I will say something more on this metaphysical commitment of Flew below. But for now, suffice it to say that what is operative here is not some methodological precept of contemporary physics, on the basis of which that science *must* demonstrate that explanations of architectural differences in terms of "renaissance" and "baroque", or explanations of data in terms of chemistry or biology or psychology or the social sciences are merely fictive collocations of data *really* to be explained by physics.

One final item in the above quotation from Flew which it might be worth commenting on is the criterion of "falsification" applied to assessing the hypothesis of God's existence and activity in the world. Since his 1950 essay on "Theology and Falsification" Flew has of course been noted for his employment of this criterion in philosophical theology. However, it is by now a notorious fact, one revealed in debates of the last three or four decades over Popperian versions of falsification in science, that such criteria of rational evaluation are not themselves self-validating. In other words, as far as the old positivist pejorative use of the term goes they are "metaphysical". Popper's insistence that one cannot reach definite truth on any matter, including whether or not the principle of falsifiability does truly operate to increase our knowledge of reality, has of course only enhanced the case of those like Feyerabend and Laudan who argue that scientific problem solving does not increase our knowledge of reality.[41] The only way, I believe, to substantiate the claim that procedures such as falsification and the like (here I do not want to suggest that even if substantiated falsificationism has the whole picture on rational progress) is along the lines of defending the epistemological position outlined above. That is, even in denying that I make judgements or can get to know the truth I can verify that conscious acts of judgement and truth-assertion have occurred. Not only can I verify such conscious acts as really occurring but the process of verification, as a pattern of such interrelated conscious activities, can also be known as such on the basis of the data of consciousness. This is claiming to know what is the case in a way Popper does not advert to, but it is in such terms that one may then validate criteria of verification, falsification and so forth as criteria yielding judgements as to what is so, or probably so with regard to reality. However, the problem here for Flew is evident. For it was argued above that just such an epistemological view yields a metaphysics of reality as the intelligible, and reality can only be intelligible if God exists. Flew can have his verification of the validity of falsification, I believe, only at the price of verifying an epistemological and metaphysical position on the basis of which the existence of God is also to be verified.

Persons, Freedom and Immortality

There are certain views of the human person as characterised by Christian anthropology which are denied and contested by both Flew and Russell. But, again, the differences between the two philosophers are as evident as their agreements on the issues involved. So Russell takes the determinist position and denies freedom while Flew argues that freedom is a fact of our experience.[42] Flew's objection to Christian dogma on the issue of freedom has, rather, to do with the possibility of God's power and human freedom cooperating. He sees two problems here: a) a free act would seem to be one without sufficient reason and, therefore, would be unthinkable in a theistic universe; b) as Descartes puts it, we know of God's irresistible power but we also assert human freedom; these two positions appear irreconcilable.[43] Flew seems to have missed the point of Aquinas' treatment of these issues even though he does allude to St Thomas' discussion of them. To begin with Flew conflates "being caused" with "being necessarily caused"; that is, while every aspect of the universe is intelligible and the requisite causes are there for whatever is, this does not negate the difference between contingency and necessity. If I drive my car today then the requisite causes for that event occur but this does not entail that the event is necessary. Free acts are, then, a species of contingent event. As St Thomas often repeats: Socrates' running is not necessary, but if Socrates runs then, necessarily, he runs.[44] The corollary of this with regard to b) is that if God wills by His irresistible power that a contingent being is, then it will be; but since His power is irresistible it will be precisely that: a contingent being not a necessary one.

Russell, on the other hand, holds for a determinism such that one should not blame persons for apparent wrong doing, and "...we should treat the criminal as we treat a man suffering from plague."[45] This goes hand in hand with Russell's intuitionist-emotive view on ethics which denies an objective possibility of ethics because of the facts of cultural relativity. The position is not, therefore, a particularly original one and it is subject to the usual charges of inconsistency. It is not difficult to discern inconsistency in Russell's own writing. For, if the acts persons perform are not acts for which they can be blamed or praised, any more than a lion can be blamed for killing its prey, then it is senseless to descant on the moral deformities of the human race in the way Russell does: "Of men in the concrete, most of us think the vast majority very bad".[46] But such inconsistencies are more than textual. They are, so to speak, also self-referential. If one's view of morality is totally determined by one's past, one's genetic make up or whatever, there is no point in arguing, as Russell does, that one *ought not* to take a moral absolutist view but that one *should* acknowledge the facts of moral relativity and act accordingly. That is, in so arguing Russell is committed to the position, and is urging that his interlocutor be committed to the position, that the moral requirement for any reasonable and responsible being (such as could participate in the debate) is to *find out the moral truth and act accordingly.*

Another difference between the two philosophers appears in the way they approach the issue of personal identity. Flew is concerned with this issue in as much as it enters the discussion of the possibility of immortality, the possibility of incorporeal persons. Flew is, I think, quite right in drawing attention to the way this question has a bearing, not only on the question of life after death, but of the intelligibility of the Christian doctrine of God as incorporeal.[47] The fundamental problem, as Flew sees it, is that whereas we can identify and reidentify persons as corporeal things of "flesh and blood" we cannot so do in the case of putative incorporeal persons.[48]

What then the difference with Russell? Not the denial of life after death, for Russell, as we saw above holds the determinist-materialist-reductionist creed. The difference lies in the way Russell takes seriously the ontological issues arising from the modern scientific world view for the very identification, and therefore reidentification of individuals.[49] That is, Russell recognises that the problem of "Eddington's two tables" recurs in the case of human beings. From the viewpoint of science, is the table to be identified as one or many? Similarly is this "human being" to be identified as a unity or a multiplicity? A question which has vexed philosophers from Whitehead, and Cassirer, to Quine (in works such as *Ontological Relativity*) and van Frassen is simply ignored by Flew, for whom the "folk ontology" of a certain brand of common sense of a particular period seems all we need to settle ontological issues of identification and reidentification of persons as "flesh and blood" parcels.

But there are indeed some intriguing surprises which emerge for ontology from the rise of modern science. The Eddington picture itself of course needs to be handled with caution. We remember we are told that within the "mostly empty space" of the scientist's table there are things which appear now *like* a wave, now *like* a particle. In fact the upshot of verification in modern science is to bring home the epistemological point, recognised by some in the tradition not by others, that understanding is not simply imagining. That is, only the imaginable percept can be verified as such, and since the entities postulated by science are not perceivable they are verifiable neither as percepts nor imaginative constructs. The point was emphasised by Quine in discussion with Bryan Magee, that what we can visualise may give us no more than an analogy for the entities postulated by science. As a result Quine admitted that his materialism was now a matter of faith.[50] In fact, therefore, the reductionist's picture thinking myth is what is not verified by scientific practice. That myth takes it that the "big things" we see are really epiphenomena made up of tiny little things which we cannot see but imagine. The truth is quite the reverse, as Bernard Lonergan puts it,

> But if subatomic elements cannot be imagined, then atoms cannot be imagined, for one cannot imagine a whole as made up of non-imaginable parts. It follows

that no thing itself, no thing as explained, can be imagined. If atoms cannot be imagined, then by parity of reasoning, molecules cannot be imagined. Neither can cells. Neither can plants. I can imagine the plant as seen, as related to my senses, as described. But if I apply the full principle of equivalence and prescind from all observers, then I also prescind from all observables.[51]

The point is that, as was argued above, what is known is known through intelligent grasp and reasonable affirmation on the basis of the data of sense or of consciousness. Verification, identification, of unities, acts, and so forth is a matter of these intelligent operations being applied, and as Philip McShane writes, "...on any adequate view of verification the laws of behaviour of the elephant are as least as well verified as the probability-laws of electrons".[52] As regards identifying unities it was argued above that one has a privileged case with regard to coming to know oneself as one whose knowing is characterised by acts of sensing, questioning, understanding, judging, for just as one can affirm these acts as occurring so one has evidence of the unity between them: I must be conscious both empirically and rationally when I judge on the basis of data. But science, and indeed common sense also present us with evidence of other unities operative in the world around us.

However, Flew himself begins to muddy the waters of his straight-forward empiricist account of identification of persons by adding to the criterion of "flesh and blood" those of consciousness, rationality and free agency, refusing to follow Dennett into epistemological instrumentalism.[53] For the question arises of how one comes to know these facts. It is not by contemplating flesh and blood as sensed, but by attending to the data of one's own conscious operations. And, further, while it is perfectly reasonable and morally important to conclude to similar operations in others it is the case, as the problem of other minds (and science fiction films of the '50's on loved ones being taken over by aliens) testify, that such judgements are not totally indefeasible.[54]

Flew includes in his discussion of the impossibility or possibility of incorporeal existence a treatment of the apparent evidence in favour of such possibility found in paranormal phenomena. Flew takes this evidence seriously, and although he points to cases in which fraudulent practices have been uncovered, he remains open to the possibility of genuine data accumulated by parapsychological researchers and researchers, such as Raymond Moody and J.C. Hampe, into near-death experiences.[55] Concerning the latter, Flew admits that it is difficult to accommodate within the known scientific laws accounts in which during near-death experiences persons acquire information of events and conversations occurring far away. But Flew is confident that science will explain such phenomena in due course. As he writes,

Certainly their occurrence could present the physicists with a very baffling and even perhaps wholly intractable problem. But the reasons why such changes [to the consciousnesses of human persons] would be the business of physics precisely is that these recipients are creatures of flesh and blood.[56]

Besides this frank profession of materialist metaphysics, Flew's other major response to these phenomena is to follow E.R. Dodds' in applying Ockham's razor to accounts of hauntings, poltergeist phenomena and the like, in order to explain the activity observed not in terms of incorporeal entities, but as that produced by the psi-capacities of the witnesses to these events. [57]

However, a number of problems arise with regard to this approach. Firstly, if such activity is to be explained in terms of the psi-capacities of witnesses, the postulation of such capacities is itself the postulation of that which is beyond explanation in terms of current physics and physiology. Secondly, when one thinks of such occurrences as are related in works by reliable investigators such as Herbert Thurston, (see, for example, his *Ghost and Poltergeists*, London: Burns and Oates, 1952), one realises that there is a fair amount to explain away. That is, the entities apparently involved act in ways typical of a conscious, intentional person; often languages foreign to the witnesses are a means of communication; activity may occur when witnesses are absent, and the activity may be hostile to witnesses; the witnesses involved have no conscious awareness of performing the activity and show no aptitude for such capacities before or after the events. Further, in the case of hauntings, witnesses witnessing similar patterns of events at different times may have no connection with one another and no prior expectation of these events; and the events may be 'particularised' in a way which seems to manifest a slightly different response to different witnesses. It is difficult to explain all this data in terms of the psi-powers of witnesses. Such attempts may postulate some "unconscious" power exercised by a witness. But given all the capacities of this "power", its ability to manifest intelligent intentional activity and powers beyond those the witness is aware of having, the attempt to argue that this entity is 'the same person' as the witness looks like ending up as question-begging. Thirdly, one can ask in the light of these considerations, whether Ockham's razor has not been given an empiricist edge here? If the suggestion is that all activity is to be explained as emanating only from entities which are observed one once again runs into all the problems which the methodology of modern science, and questions concerning knowledge of other minds, throw up for empiricism.

Flew's profession of materialist metaphysics, in the quotation given above, raises further issues. Given that Flew does not argue for this metaphysical position on the basis of an epistemological approach, as I have argued for a metaphysics above, how is he entitled to hold this view? Would it not be more consistent to admit, with Quine, that such materialism is a matter of 'faith'? But for a falsificationist like Flew these difficulties are compounded by the approach that position takes on estimating the intellectual viability of metaphysical research programmes. For from his discussion both of miracles and of paranormal phenomena it looks as if any evidence which appears to offer a challenge to Flew's materialist metaphysics will be met with the expression of hope that, one day, physical science will explain it. But then for the falsificationist such a move means that one has denied any way of knowing what would falsify or corroborate such a metaphysics; in terms of falsificationism itself one holds such a belief without rational warrant.

On the other hand, there are some points we can make in favour of a non-materialist metaphysics. To begin with, it is not the case that the notion of existence is intrinsically linked to those of empirical space-time. As Bernard Lonergan writes,

> 'To be' cannot mean 'to be in space' or 'to be in time'. If that were so, and space or time is, then space would be in space and time would be in time. The further space and time, if real, would also be and still would demand a still further space and time. The argument could be repeated indefinitely to yield an infinity of spaces and times. 'To be' then is just 'to be'.[58]

Flew quite rightly, I believe, has a high regard for Descartes' distinction between imagining and conceiving: Descartes points out that we can conceive of a thousand-sided object, but we cannot imagine it.[59] But, although Flew also recognises the differences between Descartes and Aquinas on the soul, he does not give the attention he might to the way the act of understanding, as distinct from imagining, features in the Thomistic traditions' understanding of the non-material aspect of the human person.

Since, as modern science has witnessed so eloquently, insight, or the act of understanding, is not mere picturing one has to understand that this act involves, rather, the grasp of what is an intelligible 'form' or 'pattern' in the data. The Euclidean understanding of a circle as 'as series of coplanar points equidistant from the centre' may be taken as an example. An essential element to grasp in understanding understanding itself is that the insight, while it grasps the necessary and sufficient conditions of, in this case, circularity in the images or data of imaginative constructs, abstracts or prescinds from the particularities of that data in coming to grasp something which is relevant to any instance of circularity. There cannot be an instance of circularity that is not intrinsically conditioned by the empirical space-time domain; circles have dimensions. But the grasp of the intelligible 'form' of circularity abstracts from the particularity of that domain and so is not intrinsically conditioned by it. If someone were to 'look into my head' when I was thinking of Euclid's postulates perhaps they would see imaginative constructs of circles; but that would not be 'seeing' the insight. For the insight abstract from any particular image. For it regards circularity in general irrespective of, for instance, dimension. The 'form' as it occurs in insight is precisely characterised as what has no specific empirical space-time characteristics;

the form of circularity as actually instantiated cannot but have such empirical spatio-temporal characteristics and dimensions. It is on the basis of such insights into the nature of insight that the Thomist account of the material and the non-material is developed.

Conclusion

I have taken issue with Russell and Flew on some of the key objections they raise regarding the cogency and reasonableness of the Christian world-view. In offering criticisms of their positions I have attempted, by way of contrast, briefly to outline and defend an epistemology and metaphysics which leads to a positive evaluation of that world-view. But I should like to reiterate a positive comment on their work with which I began this essay. That is, their criticisms and objections appear, for the most part, to be honest and to be the kind of objections, given philosophical form, which those in Western culture who still reflect on religion raise against it. And it is just in case Russell's and Flew's objections to Christian dogmas fail because those dogmas are true that there is any point in any person who is concerned with truth and value accepting them.

NOTES

[1] See, Bertrand Russell, (1957), *Why I am Not A Christian?* (London: Allen and Unwin), p.38; Anthony Flew,(1987), *The Logic of Mortality*, (Oxford: Blackwell), p.166.

[2] Schilpp, Paul, Arthur, edited,(1944), *The Philosophy of Bertrand Russell*, Vol II, (New York and London: Harper and Row), p.726.

[3] Kenny, Anthony, (1969), *Aquinas: A Collection of Critical Essays*, (London: Macmillan), p.2

[4] Russell, (1957), p.42.

[5] MacIntyre, Alasdir, (1988), *Three Rival Versions of Moral Enquiry*, (Notre Dame: University of Notre Dame Press).

[6] Russell, (1959), *My Philosophical Development*, (London: Allen and Unwin), Chapters 3 &4; Schilpp, p.726.

[7] Schilpp, p.19.

[8] See, Flew, Anthony, (1966), *God and Philosophy*, (London: Hutchinson); (1976), *The Presumption of Atheism*, (London: Elk/Pemberton); and Flew, (1987).

[9] Schilpp, p.727; Flew, (1976), p.

[10] Russell, (1959), p.135.

[11] Russell, (1940), *An Inquiry Concerning Meaning and Truth*, (London: Allen & Unwin), p. 49ff.

[12] Russell, (1959), p.185.

[13] Russell, (1931), *The Scientific Outlook*, (New York: W.W. Norton), p.98.

[14] Schilpp, pp.703–6.

[15] Schilpp, pp.713–14.

[16] Such are the arguments of the book, (1948), *Human Knowledge: Its Scope and Limits*, (London: Allen & Unwin).

[17] See, Sellars, Wilfred F, (1963), *Science, Perception and Reality* (London: Routledge and Keegan Paul), Chapter 5; Stroud, Barry, (1984), *The Significance of Philosophical Scepticism*, (Oxford: Clarendon Press); Davidson, Donald, "A Coherence Theory of Truth and Knowledge", in, *Kant oder Hegel?*, (1983), (KlettCotta), 429–431.

[18] Flew, (1987), p.94.

[19] Flew, (1987), p.92.

[20] So, as one can see from a recent article by Chakravarthi Ram-Prasad, (*American Philosophical Quarterly* 32, No. 3, July, 1995: 225–239), this debate between Descartes and Flew is a replay of that in Indian philosophy between the fourth-century Vasubandhu and the eighth to ninth-century Sankara, with somewhat similarly inconclusive results.

[21] Flew, (1987), pp.90–91.

[22] Stroud, (1984).

[23] Flew, (1987), p.90.

[24] For the positions on epistemology and metaphysics for which I will argue I am heavily indebted to Bernard Lonergan, especially to his, (1957), *Insight. A Study of Human Understanding*, (London: Darton, Longman and Todd).

[25] Russell, (1959), p. ~85.

[26] Flew, (1987), p.150.

[27] For a brief introduction to some of the important differences between Aquinas and Descartes in their uses of this type of argument, see, Jaakko Hintikka, (1974), *Knowledge and the Known*, (Dordrecht and Boston: D.Reidel), Chapter 5.

[28] Hume, David, (1748), *An Enquiry concerning Human Understanding*, edited by L.A. Selby-Bigge, (Oxford: Clarendon Press, 1902), pp.49–50.

[29] Russell, "A Debate on the Existence of God", in, Russell, (1957), p.146.

[30] Russell, (1957), p.6.

[31] Flew, (1966), p.83.

[32] Flew, (1966), pp.152, 154.

[33] Hume, (1748), pp.60–72.

[34] Flew, (1966), Chapter 7.

[35] Flew, (1966), Chapter 7, see especially sections: 7.20, 7.21, 7.25.

[36] Flew, (1966), p.146.

[37] On this see Part 2 of my, (1997), *Objectivity and Historical Understanding*, (Brookfield, Vermont: Avebury).

[38] Flew, (1966), p.152.

[39] Flew, (1966), p.149.

[40] Flew, (1966), p.150.
[41] On this see, Hugo Meynell, "Infallible fallibilism", (1982), New Blackfriars, Vol. 63, 333–343.
[42] Russell, "Do we survive Death?", in ,(1957); Flew, (1987), pp.59–76.
[43] Flew, (1976), pp.88–89.
[44] St Thomas Aquinas, *Commentary on the Sentences*, d. 38, q.1, a. 5, ad 4m.
[45] Russell, (1957), p.61.
[46] Russell, (1957), p.71.
[47] Flew, (1987), pp.104–5.
[48] Flew, (1987), pp.100, 109.
[49] Russell, (1957), p.73.
[50] Magee, Bryan, (1978), *Men of Ideas*, (London: BBC Publications), pp.175–6.
[51] Lonergan, (1957), p.250.
[52] McShane, Philip, (1971), *Randomness, Statistics and Emergence*, (London & Dublin: Gill and Macmillan), p.127.
[53] Flew, (1987), pp. 142–4.
[54] The denial of certainty in such cases can appear "cold" and "unfeeling", and it is not my intention to deny the very evident and important facts of intersubjective, connatural knowledge of loved ones. But on the positive side, to deny access to the conscious states of one's spouse is also to say something about the dignity of the other person as free. Birthday surprises would not be such were spouses to have direct access to each others' consciousness.
[55] Flew, (1987), Chapter 10.
[56] Flew, (1987), pp.177–8.
[57] Flew, (1987), p.173.
[58] Lonergan, (1957), p.513.
[59] Flew, (1987), pp.108–9.

11

The Psychology of Atheism

Paul C. Vitz

The title of this paper, "The Psychology of Atheism" may seem strange. Certainly, my psychological colleagues have found it odd and even, I might add, a little disturbing. After all, psychology, since its founding roughly a century ago, has often focused on the opposite topic—namely the psychology of religious belief. Indeed, in many respects the origins of modern psychology are intimately bound up with the psychologists who explicitly proposed interpretations of belief in God.

William James and Sigmund Freud, for example, were both personally and professionally deeply involved in the topic. Recall *The Will to Believe* by James, as well as his still famous *Varieties of Religious Experience*. These two works are devoted to an attempt at understanding belief as the result of psychological, that is natural, causes. James might have been sympathetic to religion, but his own position was one of doubt and skepticism and his writings were part of psychology's general undermining of religious faith. As for Sigmund Freud, his critiques of religion, in particular Christianity, are well known and will be discussed in some detail later. For now, it is enough to remember how deeply involved Freud and his thought have been with the question of God and religion.

Given the close involvement between the founding of much of psychology and a critical interpretation of religion, it should not be surprising that most psychologists view with some alarm any attempt to propose a psychology of atheism. At the very least such a project puts many psychologists on the defensive and gives them some taste of their own medicine. Psychologists are always observing and interpreting others and it is high time that some of them learn from their own personal experience what it is like to be put under the microscope of psychological theory and experiment. Regardless, I hope to show that the psychological concepts used quite effectively to interpret religion are two-edged swords that can also be used to interpret atheism. Sauce for the believer is equally sauce for the unbeliever.

Before beginning, however, I wish to make two points bearing on the underlying assumption of my remarks. First, I assume that the major barriers to belief in God are not rational but—in a general sense—can be called psychological. I do not wish to offend the many distinguished philosophers—both believers and nonbelievers—but I am quite convinced that for every person strongly swayed by rational argument there are many, many more affected by nonrational psychological factors.

The human heart—no one can truly fathom it or know all its deceits, but at least it is the proper task of the psychologist to try. Thus, to begin, I propose that neurotic psychological barriers to belief in God are of great importance. What some of these might be I will mention shortly. For believers, therefore, it is important to keep in mind that psychological motives and pressures that one is often unaware of, often lie behind unbelief.

One of the earliest theorists of the unconscious, St Paul, wrote, "I can will what is right, but I cannot do it ... I see in my members another law at war with the law of my mind .. .,' (Rom. 7:18, 23). Thus. it seems to me sound theology as well as sound psychology that psychological factors can be impediments to belief as well as behavior, and that these may often be unconscious factors as well. Further, as a corollary it is reasonable to propose that people vary greatly in the extent to which these factors are present in their lives. Some of us have been blessed with an upbringing, a temperament, social environment, and other gifts that have made belief in God a much easier thing than many who have suffered more or have been raised in a spiritually impoverished environment or had other difficulties with which to cope. Scripture makes it clear that many children—even into the third or fourth generation—suffer from the sins of their fathers, including the sins of fathers who may have been believers. In short, my first point is that some people have much more serious psychological barriers to belief than others, a point consistent with the scriptures' clear statement that we are not to judge others, however much we are called to correct evil.

My second point as qualification is that in spite of serious difficulties to belief, all of us still have a free choice to accept God or reject Him. This qualification is not in contradiction to the first. Perhaps a little elaboration will make this clearer. One person, as a consequence of his particular past, present environment. etc., may find it much harder than most people to believe in God. But presumably, at any moment, certainly at many times, he can choose to move toward God or to move away. One man may start with so many barriers that even after years of slowly choosing to move toward God he may still not be there. Some may die before they reach belief. We assume they will be judged like all of us—on how far they traveled toward God and how well they loved others—on how well they did with what they had. Likewise, another man without psychological difficulties at all is still free to reject God, and no doubt many do. Thus, although the ultimate issue is one of the will and our sinful nature, it is still possible to investigate those psychological factors that predispose one to unbelief, that make the road to belief in God especially long and hard.

The Psychology of Atheism: Social and Personal Motives

There seems to be a widespread assumption throughout much of the Western intellectual community that belief in God is based on all kinds of irrational immature needs and wishes, but atheism or skepticism is derived from a rational, no-nonsense appraisal of the way things really are. To begin a critique of this assumption, I start with my own case history.

After a rather weak, wishy-washy Christian upbringing, I became an atheist in college in the 1950s and remained so throughout graduate school and my first years as a young experimental psychologist on the faculty at New York University. That is, I am an adult convert or, more technically, a reconvert to Christianity who came back to the faith, much to his surprise, in my late thirties in the very secular environment of academic psychology in New York City.

I am not going into this to bore you with parts of my life story, but to note that through reflection on my own experience it is now clear to me that my reasons for becoming and for remaining an atheist-skeptic from about age 18 to 38 were superficial, irrational, and largely without intellectual or moral integrity. Furthermore, I am convinced that my motives were, and still are, commonplace today among intellectuals, especially social scientists.

The major factors involved in my becoming an atheist—although I wasn't really aware of them at the time—were as follows.

General socialization. An important influence on me in my youth was a significant social unease. I was somewhat embarrassed to be from the Midwest, for it seemed terribly dull, narrow, arid, provincial. There was certainly nothing romantic or impressive about being from Cincinnati, Ohio and from a vague mixed background. Terribly middle class. Further, besides escape from a dull, and according to me unworthy, socially embarrassing past, I wanted to take part in, in fact to be comfortable in, the new, exciting, even glamorous, secular world into which I was moving. I am sure that similar motives have strongly influenced the lives of countless upwardly mobile young people in the last two centuries. Consider Voltaire, who moved into the glittery, aristocratic, sophisticated world of Paris, and who always felt embarrassed about his provincial and nonaristocratic origin; or the Jewish ghettos that so many assimilating Jews have fled, or the latest young arrival in New York, embarrassed about his fundamentalist parents. This kind of socialization pressure has pushed many away from belief in God and all that this belief is associated with for them.

I remember a small seminar in graduate school where almost every member there at some time expressed this kind of embarrassment and response to the pressures of Socialization into "modern life." One student was trying to escape his Southern Baptist background, another a small town Mormon environment, a third was trying to get out of a very Jewish Brooklyn ghetto, and the fourth was me.

Specific socialization.

Another major reason for my wanting to become an atheist was that I desired to be accepted by the powerful and influential scientists in the field of psychology. In particular, I wanted to be accepted by my professors in graduate school. As a graduate student I was thoroughly socialized by the specific "culture" of academic research psychology. My professors at Stanford, however much they might disagree on psychological theory, were, as far as I could tell, united in only two things—their intense personal career ambition and their rejection of religion. As the psalmist says. "... The man greedy for gain curses and renounces the lord. In the pride of his countenance the wicked does not seek him; all his thoughts are, 'There is no God'" (Psalm 10:3–4).

In this environment, just as I had learned how to dress like a college student by putting on the right clothes, I also learned to "think" like a proper psychologist by putting on the right—that is, atheistic—ideas and attitudes.

Personal convenience.

Finally, in this list of superficial, but nevertheless, strong irrational pressures to become an atheist, I must list simple personal convenience. The fact is that it's quite inconvenient to be a serious believer in today's powerful secular and neo-pagan world. I would have had to give up many pleasures and a good deal of time.

Without going into details it is not hard to imagine the sexual pleasures that would have to be rejected if I became a serious believer. And then I also knew it would cost me time and some money. There would be church services, church groups, time for prayer and scripture reading, time spent helping others. I was already too busy. Obviously, becoming religious would be a real inconvenience.

Now perhaps you think that such reasons are restricted to especially callow young men—like me in my twenties. However, such reasoning is not so restricted. Here I will take up the case of Mortimer Adler, a well known American philosopher, writer, and intellectual who has spent much of his life thinking about God and religious topics. One of his most recent books is titled *How to Think About God: A Guide for the 20th Century Pagan* (1980). In this work,

Adler presses the argument for the existence of God very strongly and by the latter chapters he is very close to accepting the living God. Yet he pulls back and remains among "the vast company of the religiously uncommitted" (Graddy, 1982). But Adler leaves the impression that this decision is more one of will than of intellect. As one of his reviewers notes (Graddy. 1982), Adler confirms this impression in his autobiography, *Philosopher at Large* (1976). There, while investigating his reasons for twice stopping short of a full religious commitment, he writes that the answer "lies in the state of one's will, not in the state of one's mind." Adler goes on to comment that to become seriously religious "would require a radical change in my way of life ...." and "The simple truth of the matter is that I did not wish to live up to being a genuinely religious person." (Graddy, p.24).

There you have it! A remarkably honest and conscious admission that being "a genuinely religious person" would be too much trouble, too inconvenient. I can't but assume that such are the shallow reasons behind many an unbeliever's position.

In summary, because of my social needs to assimilate, because of my professional needs to be accepted as part of academic psychology, and because of my personal needs for a convenient life-style for all these needs atheism was simply the best policy. Looking back on these motives, I can honestly say that a return to atheism has all the appeal of a return to adolescence.[1]

The Psychology of Atheism: Psychoanalytic Motives

As is generally known, the central Freudian criticism of belief in God is that such a belief is untrustworthy because of its psychological origin. That is; God is a projection of our own intense, unconscious desires; He is a wish fulfillment derived from childish needs for protection and security. Since these wishes are largely unconscious, any denial of such an interpretation is to be given little credence. It should be noted that in developing this kind of critique, Freud has raised the *ad hominem* argument to one of wide influence. It is in *The Future of an Illusion* (1927, 1961) that Freud makes his position clearest:

> [R]eligious ideas have arisen from the same needs as have all the other achievements of civilization: from the necessity of defending oneself against the crushing superior force of nature. (p.21)

Therefore, religious beliefs are:

> illusions, fulfillments of the oldest, strongest and most urgent wishes of mankind . As we already know, the terrifying impression of helplessness in childhood aroused the need for protection—for protection through love—which was provided by the father... Thus the benevolent rule of a divine Providence

allays our fear of the danger of life. (p.30).

Let us look at this argument carefully, for in spite of the enthusiastic acceptance of it by so many uncritical atheists and skeptics, it is really a very weak position.

In the first paragraph Freud fails to note that his arguments against religious belief are, in his own words, equally valid against all the achievements of civilization, including Psychoanalysis itself. That is, if the psychic origin of an intellectual achievement invalidates its truth value, then physics, biology, much less psychoanalysis itself, are vulnerable to the same charge.

In the second paragraph Freud makes another strange claim, namely that the oldest and most urgent wishes of mankind are for the loving protecting guidance of a powerful loving Father, for divine Providence. However, if these wishes were as strong and ancient as he claims, one would expect pre-Christian religion to have strongly emphasized God as a benevolent father. In general, this was far from the case for the pagan religions of the Mediterranean world—and, for example, is still not the case for such popular religions as Buddhism and for much of Hinduism. Indeed, Judaism and most especially Christianity are in many respects distinctive in the emphasis on God as a loving Father.

However, let us put these two intellectual gaffes aside and turn to another understanding of his projection theory. It can be shown that this theory is not really an integral part of Psychoanalysis—and, thus cannot claim fundamental support from psychoanalytic theory. It is essentially an autonomous argument. Actually, Freud's critical attitude toward and rejection of religion is rooted in his personal predilections and is a kind of meta psychoanalysis—or background framework which is not well connected to his more specifically clinical concepts. (This separation or autonomy with respect to most psychoanalytic theory very likely accounts for its influence outside of psychoanalysis.) There are two pieces of evidence for this interpretation of the projection theory.

The first is that this theory had been clearly articulated many years earlier by Ludwig Feuerbach in his book *The Essence of Christianity* (1841, 1957). Feuerbach's interpretation was well known in European intellectual circles, and Freud, as a youth, read Feuerbach avidly (see Gedo & Pollock. 1976, 47, 350). Here are some representative quotes from Feuerbach which make this clear:

> What man misses whether this be an articulate and therefore conscious, or an unconscious, need that is his God. (1841, 1957, p.83)

> Man projects his nature into the world outside himself before he finds it in himself. (p.11)

> To live in projected dream-images is the essence of religion. Religion sacrifices reality to the projected dream. (p.49)

Many other quotes could be provided in which Feuerbach describes religion in "Freudian" terms such as wish-fulfillment, etc. What Freud did with this argument was to revive it in a more eloquent form, and publish it at a later time when the audience desiring to hear such a theory was much larger. And, of course, somehow the findings and theory of psychoanalysis were implied as giving the theory strong support. The Feuerbachian character of Freud's *Illusion* position is also demonstrated by such notions as "the crushing superior force of nature" and the "terrifying impression of helplessness in childhood" which are not psychoanalytic in terminology or in meaning.

The other piece of evidence for the nonpsychoanalytic basis of the projection theory comes directly from Freud. who explicitly says so himself. In a letter of 1927 to his friend Oskar Pfister (an early psychoanalyst, and believing Protestant pastor), Freud wrote:

> let us be quite clear on the point that the views expressed in my book (*The Future of an Illusion*) form no part of analytic theory. They are my personal views (Freud/Pfister, 1963a, P.117).

There is one other somewhat different interpretation of belief in God which Freud also developed, but although this has a very modest psychoanalytic character, it is really an adaptation of Feuerbachian projection theory. This is Freud's relatively neglected interpretation of the ego deal. The super-ego, including the ego ideal, is the "heir of the Oedipus complex," representing a projection of an idealized father—and presumably of God the Father (see Freud, 1923, 1962, pps. 26–28; p.38)

The difficulty here is that the ego ideal did not really receive great attention or development with in Freud's writings. Furthermore, it is easily interpreted as an adoption of Feurerbach's projection theory. Thus, we can conclude that psychoanalysis does not in actuality provide significant theoretical concepts for characterizing belief in God as neurotic Freud either used Feuerbach's much older projection or illusion theory or incorporated Feuerbach in his notion of the ego ideal. Presumably, this is the reason Freud acknowledged to Pfister that his *Illusion* book was not a true part of psychoanalysis.

Atheism as Oedipal Wish Fulfillment

Nevertheless, Freud is quite right to worry that a belief can be an illusion because it derives from powerful wishes—from unconscious childish needs. The irony is that he clearly did provide a very powerful, new way to understand the neurotic basis of atheism. (For a detailed development of this position see Vitz and Gartner, 1984a, b; Vitz. 1986).

The Oedipus Complex

The central concept in Freud's work, aside from the unconscious, is the now well-known Oedipus Complex. In the case of male personality development, the essential features of this complex are the following: Roughly in the age period of three to six the boy develops a strong sexual desire for the mother. At the same time the boy develops an intense hatred and fear of the father, and a desire to supplant him, a "craving for power." This hatred is based on the boy's knowledge that the father, with his greater size and strength, stands in the way of his desire. The child's fear of the father may explicitly be a fear of castration by the father, but more typically, it has a less specific character. The son does not really kill the father, of course, but patricide is assumed to be a common preoccupation of his fantasies and dreams. The "resolution" of the complex is supposed to occur through the boy's recognition that he cannot replace the father, and through fear of castration, which eventually leads the boy to identify with the father, to identify with the aggressor, and to repress the original frightening components of the complex.

It is important to keep in mind that, according to Freud, the Oedipus complex is never truly resolved, and is capable of activation at later periods — almost always, for example, at puberty. Thus the powerful ingredients of murderous hate and of incestuous sexual desire within a family context are never in fact removed. Instead, they are covered over and repressed. Freud expresses the neurotic potential of this situation:

> The Oedipus-complex is the actual nucleus of neuroses... What remains of the complex in the unconscious represents the disposition to the later development of neuroses in the adult (Freud, 1919, Standard Edition, 17, p.193; also 1905, S.E. 7, p. 226ff.; 1909, S.E., 11, p.47).

In short, all human neuroses derive from this complex. Obviously, in most cases, this potential is not expressed in any seriously neurotic manner. Instead it shows up in attitudes toward authority, in dreams, slips of the tongue, transient irrationalities, etc.

Now, in postulating a universal Oedipus complex as the origin of all our neuroses, Freud inadvertently developed a straightforward rationale for understanding the wish-fulfilling origin of rejecting God. After all, the Oedipus complex is unconscious, it is established in childhood and, above all, its dominant motive is hatred of the father and the desire for him not to exist, especially as represented by the desire to overthrow or kill the father. Freud regularly described God as a psychological equivalent to the father, and so a natural expression of Oedipal motivation would be powerful, unconscious desires for the nonexistence of God. Therefore, in the Freudian framework, atheism is an illusion caused by the Oedipal desire to kill the father and replace him with oneself. To act as if God does not exist is an obvious, not so subtle disguise for a wish to kill Him, much the same way as in a dream, the image of a parent going away or disappearing can represent such a wish: "God is dead" is simply an undisguised Oedipal wish-fulfillment.

It is certainly not hard to understand the Oedipal character of so much contemporary atheism and skepticism. Hugh Heffner, even James Bond, with their rejection of God plus their countless girls, are so obviously living out Freud's Oedipal and primal rebellion (e.g., *Totem and Taboo*). So are countless other skeptics who live out variations of the same scenario of exploitative sexual permissiveness combined with narcissistic self-worship.

And, of course, the Oedipal dream is not only to kill the father and possess the mother or other women in the group but also to displace him. Modern atheism has attempted to accomplish this. Now man, not God, is the consciously specified ultimate source of goodness and power in the universe. Humanistic philosophies glorify him and his "potential" much the same way religion glorifies the Creator. We have devolved from one God to many gods to everyone a god. In essence, man—through his narcissism and Oedipal wishes—has tried to succeed where Satan failed, by seating himself on the throne of God. Thanks to Freud it is now easier to understand the deeply neurotic, thoroughly untrustworthy psychology of this unbelief.

One interesting example of the Oedipal motivation proposed here is that of Voltaire, a leading skeptic about all things religious who denied the Christian and Jewish notion of a personal God—of God as a Father. Voltaire was a theist or deist who believed in a cosmic, depersonalized God of unknown character.

The psychologically important thing about Voltaire is that he strongly rejected his father—so much that he rejected his father's name and took the name "Voltaire." It is not exactly certain where the new name came from but one widely held interpretation is that it was constructed from the letters of his mother's last name. When Voltaire was in his early twenties (in 1718), he published a play entitled *Oedipus* (Edipe), the first one of his plays to be publicly performed. The play itself recounts the classic legend with heavy allusions to religious and political rebellion. Throughout his life, Voltaire (like Freud) toyed with the idea that he was not his father's son. He apparently felt the desire to be from a higher, more aristocratic family than his actual middle class background. (A major expression of this concern with having a more worthy father is the play *Candide*.) In short, Voltaire's hostility to his own father, his religious rejection of God the Father, and his political rejection of the king—an acknowledged father figure—are all reflections of the same basic needs. Psychologically speaking, Voltaire's rebellion against his father and against God are easily interpretable as Oedipal wish fulfillment, as comforting illusions, and therefore, following Freud, as beliefs and attitudes unworthy of a mature mind.

Diderot, the great Encyclopaedist and an avowed atheist—indeed he is one of the founding brothers of modern atheism—also had both Oedipal preoccupation and insight. Freud approvingly quotes Diderot's anticipatory observation:

> If the little savage were left to himself, preserving all his foolishness and adding to the small sense of a child in the cradle the violent passions of a man of thirty, he would strangle his father and lie with his mother (from *Le neveau de Rameau* quoted by Freud in Lecture XXI of his *Introductory Lectures* (1916–1917), S.E., 16, pp.331–338).

The Psychology of Atheism: The Theory of Defective Father

I am well aware of the fact that there is good reason to give only limited acceptance to Freud's Oedipal theory. In any case, it is my view that although the Oedipus complex is valid for some, the theory is far from being a universal representation of unconscious motivation. Since there is need for deeper understanding of atheism and since I don't know of any theoretical framework—except the Oedipal one—I am forced to sketch out a model of my own, or really to develop an undeveloped thesis of Freud. In his essay on Leonardo da Vinci, Freud made the following remark:

> Psychoanalysis, which has taught us the intimate connection between the father complex and belief in God, has shown us that the personal God is logically nothing but an exalted father, and daily demonstrates to us how youthful persons lose their religious belief as soon as the authority of the father breaks down (*Leonardo da Vinci*, 1910, 1947 p.98).

This statement makes no assumptions about unconscious sexual desires for the mother, or even about presumed universal competitive hatred focused on the father. Instead he makes the simple easily understandable claim that once a child or youth is disappointed in and loses his or her respect for their earthly father, then belief in their heavenly Father becomes impossible. There are, of course, many ways that a father can lose his authority and seriously disappoint a child. Some of these ways—for which clinical evidence is given below—are:
1.   He can be present but obviously weak, cowardly, and unworthy of respect—even if otherwise pleasant or "nice."
2.   He can be present but physically, sexually, or psychologically abusive.
3.   He can be absent through death or by abandoning or leaving the family.

Taken all together these proposed determinants of atheism will be called the "defective father" hypothesis. To support the validity of this approach, I will conclude by providing case history material from the lives of prominent atheists, for it was in reading the biographies of atheists that this hypothesis first struck me.

We begin with Sigmund Freud's relationship to his father. That Freud's father, Jacob, was a deep disappointment—or worse—is generally agreed to by his biographers. (For the supporting biographical material on Freud see, for example, Krull, 1979, and Vitz, 1985, 1986.) Specifically, his father was a weak man unable to financially provide for his family. Instead money for support seems to have been provided by his wife's family and others. Furthermore, Freud's father was passive in response to anti-Semitism. Freud recounts an episode told to him by his father in which Jacob allowed an anti-Semite to call him a dirty Jew and to knock his hat off. Young Sigmund, on hearing the story, was mortified at his father's failure to respond, at his weakness. Sigmund Freud was a complex and in many respects ambiguous man, but all agree that he was a courageous fighter and that he greatly admired courage in others. Sigmund, as a young man, several times stood up physically against anti-Semitism—and, of course, he was one of the greatest of intellectual fighters.

Jacob's actions as a defective father, however, probably go still deeper. Specifically, in two of his letters as an adult, Freud writes that his father was a sexual pervert and that Jacob's own children suffered from this. There are also other possible moral disasters that I have not bothered to note.

The connection of Jacob to God and religion was also present for his son. Jacob was involved in a kind of reform Judaism when Freud was a child, the two of them spent hours reading the Bible together, and later Jacob became increasingly involved in reading the Talmud and in discussing Jewish scripture. In short, this weak, rather passive "nice guy," this schlemiel, was clearly connected to Judaism and God, and also to a serious lack of courage and quite possibly to sexual perversion and other weaknesses very painful to young Sigmund.

Very briefly, other famous atheists seem to have had a similar relationship to their fathers. Karl Marx made it clear that he didn't respect his father. An important part in this was that his father converted to Christianity—not out of any religious conviction—but out of a desire to make life easier. He assimilated for convenience. In doing this Marx's father broke an old family tradition. He was the first in his family who did not become a rabbi; indeed, Karl Marx came from a long line of rabbis on both sides of his family.

Ludwig Feuerbach's father did something that very easily could have deeply hurt his son. When Feuerbach was about 13, his father left his family and openly took up living with another woman in a different town. This was in Germany in the early 1800s and such a public rejection would have been a scandal and deeply rejecting to young Ludwig and, of course, to his mother and the other children.

Let us jump 100 years or so and look at the life of one of America's best known atheists—Madalyn Murray O'Hair. Here I will quote from her son's recent book on what life was like in his family when he was a child. (Murray, 1982) The book opens when he is 8-years-old: "We rarely did anything together as a family. Hatred between my grandfather and mother barred such wholesome scenes." (p.7) He writes that he really didn't know why his mother hated her father so much—but hate him she did, for the opening chapter records a very ugly fight in which she attempts to kill her father with a 10-inch butcher knife. Madalyn failed but screamed, "I'll see you dead. I'll get you yet. I'll walk on your grave!" (p.8)

Whatever the cause of O'Hair's intense hatred of her father, it is clear from this book that it was deep and that it went back into her childhood—and at least psychological (e.g. p. 11)and possibly physical abuse is a plausible cause.

Besides abuse, rejection, or cowardice, one way in which a father can be seriously defective is simply by not being there. Many children, of course, interpret death of their father as a kind of betrayal or an act of desertion. In this respect it is remarkable that the pattern of a dead father is so common in the lives of many prominent atheists.

Baron d'Holbach (born Paul Henri Thiry), the French rationalist and probably the first public atheist, is apparently an orphan by the age of 13 and living with his uncle. (From whom he took the new name Holbach.) Bertrand Russell's father died when young Bertrand was 4-years-old; Nietzsche was the same age as Russell when he lost his father, Sartre's father died before Sartre was born and Camus was a year old when he lost his father. (The above biographical information was taken from standard reference sources.) Obviously, much more evidence needs to be obtained on the "defective father" hypothesis. But the information already available is substantial; it is unlikely to be an accident.

The psychology of how a dead or nonexistent father could lay an emotional base for atheism might not seem clear at first glance. But, after all, if one's own father is absent or so weak as to die, or so untrustworthy as to desert, then it is not hard to place the same attribute on your heavenly Father.

Finally, there is also the early personal experience of suffering, of death, of evil, sometimes combined with anger at God for allowing it to happen. Any early anger at God for the loss of a father and the subsequent sufferings is still another and different psychology of unbelief, but one closely related to that of the defective father.

Some of this psychology is captured in Russell Baker's recent autobiography (Baker, 1982). Russell Baker is the well-known journalist and humorous writer for the New York Times. His father was taken to the hospital and died there suddenly when young Russell was five. Baker wept and sorrowed and spoke to the family housekeeper, Bessie:

...For the first time I thought seriously about God. Between sobs I told Bessie that if God could do things like this to people, then God was hateful and I had no more use for Him.

Bessie told me about the peace of Heaven and the joy of being among the angels and the happiness of my father who was already there. The argument failed to quiet my rage.

"God loves us all just like His own children," Bessie said.
"If God loves me, why did He make my father die?"

Bessie said that I would understand someday, but she was only partly right. That afternoon, though I couldn't have phrased it this way then, I decided that God was a lot less interested in people than anybody in Morrisonville was willing to admit. That day I decided that God was not entirely to be trusted.

After that I never cried again with any real conviction, nor expected much of anyone's God except indifference, nor loved deeply without fear that it would cost me dearly in pain. At the age of five I had become a skeptic ... (*Growing Up*, p.61).

Let me conclude by noting that however prevalent the superficial motives for being an atheist, there still remain in many instances the deep and disturbing psychological sources as well. However easy it may be to state the hypothesis of the "defective father," we must not forget the difficulty, the pain, and complexity that lie behind each individual case. And for those whose atheism has been conditioned by a father who rejected, who denied, who hated. who manipulated or who physically or sexually abused them, there must be understanding and compassion. Certainly for a child to be forced to hate his own father—or even to despair because of his father's weaknesses—is a great tragedy. After all, the child only wants to love his father. For any unbeliever whose atheism is grounded in such experience, the believer, blessed by God's love, should pray most especially that ultimately they will both meet in heaven. Meet and embrace and experience great joy. If so, perhaps the former atheist will experience even more joy than the believer. For, in addition to the happiness of the believer, the atheist will have that extra increment that comes from his surprise at finding himself surrounded by joy in, of all places, his Father's house.

REFERENCES
Adler, M. (1976). *Philosopher at Large*. Macmillan.
Adler, M. (1980). *How to think about God: A guide to the twentieth century pagan*.
New York: Macmillan.
Baker, R. (1982). *Growing up*. New York: Congdon & Weed.
Feuerbach. L. (1891/1957). *The Essence of Christianity*. Ed. and abridged by E.G. Waring & F.W. Strothman. New York: Ungar.
Freud, S (1910/1947) *Leonardo da Vinci*. New York: Random.
Freud, S. (1927/1961).*The Future of an Illusion*. New York: Norton.
Freud. S. (1923/1962). *The ego and the id*. New York: Norton.
Freud. S. & Pfister, O.(1963). *Psychoanalysis and Faith: The letters of Sigmund Freud and Oskar Pfister.* New York: Basic.

J.E. & Pollock G.R. (Eds.). (1967). *Freud: the fusion of science and humanism.* New York: International University.

Graddy, W.E. (1982, June). *The uncrossed bridge. New Oxford Review*, 23–4.

Krull, M. (1979). *Freud und sein Vater.* Munich: Beck,

Murray, W.J. (1982). *My Life without God.* Nashville, TN: Nelson.

Vitz, P.C. (1988). "Sigmund Freud's attraction to Christianity: Biographical evidence", *Psychoanalysis and Contemporary Thought* 6, 73–183.

Vitz, P.C. (1986). *Sigmund Freud's Christian Unconscious.* New York: Guilford.

Vitz, P.C. & Gartner. J (1984a). "Christianity and Psychoanalysis. part 1: Jesus as the anti-Oedipus", *Journal of Psychology and Theology*, 12, 4–14.

Vitz, P.C. & Gartner. J (1984b). "Christianity and Psychoana!ysis. part 2: Jesus the transformer of the super-ego", *Journal of Psychology and Theology*, 12, 82–89.

NOTES

[1] I understand there is a sequel to the story of Adler. I've been told that Adler became a Christian, an Anglican.

Section II: Anthropos

A. The Existence of the Soul

12

Minds or Machines

John Beloff

Abstract

In this paper we take a look at the "strong claim" of the artificial intelligence movement which here is taken to mean that there is no essential distinction to be drawn between a living mind and some possible mind-like machine, with the corollary that there is no upper limit to the intellectual achievements shown to rest on a particular theory of mind that has come to be known as Functionalism. This theory is discussed but found to be based on a fallacy. The fallacy in question is, primarily, a problem about the ontological status of minds and not, in the first instance, about their functional properties. The conclusion is drawn that the essential distinction between minds and machines remains and cannot be eliminated hence the "strong claim" must be dismissed as must its corollary. How far automation can take us in practice is a matter that can be settled empirically. The paper concludes by suggesting that the main contribution which A. I. can make to our understanding of the mind is the negative one of demonstrating what a mind is not. In other words its value lies in the clearer appreciation it affords of the difference between the mechanical aspects of mental activity as opposed to the intrinsic properties and powers of the mind as such.

The attempt to understand the workings of the mind using mechanical models and analogies is as old as psychology itself. An entirely new chapter began, however, around the middle of this century with the advent of the computer. For the first time we had now to reckon with the fact that machines could perform tasks which had hitherto depended on human ingenuity. From then on the temptation to take the computer as the model for our own cognitive processes became even harder to resist. Yet the time has come to ask ourselves whether this com-

putational metaphor as it has been called might not be more misleading than illuminating. Much will depend on whether we believe that a living mind has properties that distinguish it from any conceivable artefact that might be designed to
simulate its output. What in this paper I shall refer to as the "strong claim" is the
claim put forward by some proponents of artificial intelligence that nothing
essential differentiates the human mind from a possible mind-like machine so
that a perfect simulation of human mental activity using the hardware of a computer would in fact amount to an exemplification of such activity. This strong
claim carries with it the corollary that there is no theoretical limit to what a
machine could be expected to do.

It is clear that the claim we are to consider is a bold one and yet it has already
received widespread endorsement from eminent contemporary philosophers and
psychologists. Nor should this surprise us. Behavioristic and physicalistic theories of mind have been a recurrent feature of twentieth century philosophy and
psychology at any rate in the English-speaking world. Such theories purpose to
cut the ground from under the obvious objection which the claim might otherwise encounter, namely that while minds are conscious machines are not. For, if
mental processes are nothing over and above the workings of the brain conceived
as a self-regulating physical system there seems to be no reason, other than practical limitations in our engineering techniques, why mental processes should not
be exemplified in an artefact. On the traditional dualistic account, of course,
mental events were taken to indicate the interaction between an immaterial mind
and a material brain and, so long as this view prevailed the scope of A. I. was
clearly restricted. Thus, the strong claim is closely bound up with the perennial
mind-body problem and our assessment of it will depend on the position we take
on that issue.

The current theory of mind that is most congenial to the strong claim is that
which goes by the name of Functionalism. It has been expounded and defended
by various philosophers and psychologists among whom one could include
Dennett, Fodor and Boden. Briefly, it is the contention of a Functionalist that a
mental event is to be understood in terms of the function that it performs with reference to a given system or organism. For example, for a Functionalist, a given
sensation is not something that is to be defined ostensively in terms of its peculiar quality but rather by reference to the sort of behavioral discriminations that
it makes possible. Thus a pain should not in the first instance be thought of as
some special kind of private event but as that which brings about avoidance or
escape reactions. Likewise, thinking should not be regarded as a process going
on in some private arena to which the thinker alone has access but as the process
that brings about problem-solving or other such objective achievements and, in
the same vein, a Functionalist analysis can be provided for desiring, intending,
believing, expecting and so on across the board for each instance of what traditionally comes under the heading of the mental. The novelty of the Functionalist

position is that it is neutral with respect to the composition of the system with whose operations one is concerned. That the system in question should be made of neurons rather than wires and transistors, that it should be a living organism rather than an artefact, is, for Functionalism, a matter of indifference since the concept of the mental is to be defined in terms of function not in terms of the nature of the system in which it originates. In this respect it differed from other earlier physicalistic theories of mind. Thus, according to "Central State Materialism" mental events had to be identified with events in the brain or central nervous system. This implied that brain tissues had some special property that could not necessarily be attributed to inanimate systems. It follows that Functionalism is easier to reconcile with our "strong claim" than any version of mind-brain identity theory.

The crucial question we have next to ask is whether Functionalism is, in fact, a tenable position with respect to the mind-body problem? Given its illustrious credentials one hesitates to say no. Nevertheless this is the answer that I propose to make and which I shall endeavor to justify. It transpires that Functionalism falls at the first post inasmuch as it disregards certain facts that are universally acknowledged, at least by everyone who does not happen to be committed to some bizarre philosophical thesis. Consider those objects of introspection which philosophers sometimes refer to as "qualia" or which in ordinary parlance we might call conscious sensations. The fact is that these entities can be recognized and described by those who experience them independently of the function, if any, that they may perform in our behavior or mental life. Indeed, in certain types of passive experience, say in contemplation, it is arguable whether they have any observable consequences but they are none the less real and definite for all that. In short, Functionalism cannot be the whole truth about the nature of mental events. Nevertheless, the Functionalist might well plead that the sacrifice of the "qualia" is a small price to pay for the advantages which his philosophy offers in the wider context of the continuing debate about the compatibility of artificial and natural intelligence. So, rather than digging in our heels over the issue of "qualia", let us move on to something much closer to the heart of this controversy, namely the nature of thinking itself.

Such plausibility as attaches to the strong claim derives from the fact that computers solve complex problems more successfully and always more rapidly than the unaided human intellect. This is a remarkable fact which familiarity tends to make us take too much for granted. There was a time when the very idea that a machine might be able to compete on the intellectual plane with a rational human being would have been regarded as too fantastic or absurd to merit serious consideration. During the early 19th century a certain showman toured Europe and the United States with what was billed as a chess-playing automaton. People would be invited to challenge the "Turk", as the robot figure was nicknamed, and usually they were beaten. Naturally the shrewder onlookers suspected that a human operator was concealed somewhere inside the contraption but the concealment was done with such cunning that the audience would go away thoroughly bemused. The fame of this invention gave rise to a fair amount of controversy that found its way into print over the question of whether, in principle, it was possible to build a machine that was capable of thinking and reasoning. One of those who was fascinated by his encounter with the "Turk" was the American writer Edgar Allan Poe. [1]

Nowadays, of course, we would not be very surprised if we were to read in our newspaper one day that the new world class champion was not Kasparov nor yet Karpov but some chess-playing program with a fancy name conceived in some laboratory of A.I. For the fact is that we have learned to accept the principle that any rule-governed activity that can be precisely formalized can be simulated with a computer program. And even though in chess, thanks to the vast number of combinations, one cannot compute an infallible minimax strategy as one can for simpler board games, the use of appropriate heuristics has made possible increasingly powerful chess-playing programs. If, therefore, what we mean by thinking is finding solutions to problems or answers to questions then we already have all the evidence we need to say that machines can think. But is that all there is to thinking? No one would be tempted to say, for example, of a chess-manual that it thinks or of a textbook that gave answers to the exercises it set. Yet, when all is said and done, a computer program is no more than a glorified book even if the manner in which we interact with the computer is more reminiscent of the way we might interrogate a fellow human. But, if there is more to thinking than just information-processing in the widest sense, what is that something extra?

The answer, I submit, is plain enough when we turn to our own experience of being engaged in thinking. The least that we would require before we were ready to say of something that it was thinking is that it should be aware of what it is doing, that it should know what it was thinking about, that it should recognize when it has reached a conclusion and that, in general, it should have insight into what is going on. So the question is, can a machine have experiences of the sort which this implies? Admittedly one cannot prove that this cannot be the case but, at the same time, there is not the slightest reason for supposing that it does. Since the information-processing that is performed by a machine is wholly explicable in physicalistic terms it would be entirely gratuitous and fanciful to credit it with consciousness as this would imply. One could argue that, if we understood exactly how our own brains were constructed and knew the complete sensory input to which we have been exposed then we could explain our own thinking along physicalistic lines without needing to invoke conscious awareness. That is as may be. The point, however, is that, in the human cases, we do have one instance where it is no longer a question of whether thinking is reflected in consciousness because we know, in a way that leaves no opening for doubt, that this is so, namely when we ourselves are the thinker. For it makes no sense to doubt whether we are conscious since doubting, as Descartes would have said, implies that one is conscious. It is true we cannot prove that other human beings are conscious when they think, logically speaking they might be insentient automata, that is the classic problem of "other minds", the inescapable possibility that the solipsistic nightmare might be true. But neither is there the slightest reason to suppose that we might be unique in this very fundamental way when, in most superficial respects, we are so similar to our fellow beings. In the case of the artefact, on the contrary, there is no reason to think and every reason to doubt that consciousness supervenes when information-processing is going on. Thus the situation as between minds and machines is in this respect by no means symmetrical. Defenders of the strong claim have tried to restore a degree of symmetry by proposing a law of emergence such that, once a given system attains a certain level of complexity and sophistication, it is deemed to be conscious. But it is difficult to see what evidence could be adduced to support such a law when the only known instance where consciousness supervenes is the human one. Moreover a study of brain activity suggests that there can be no simple relationship between brain processes and conscious experience since an important segment of our thinking, including perhaps the critical stages of problem solving, proceeds at an unconscious level.

One of the current cliches about mind and brain is that the brain corresponds to the hardware of a computer while the mind corresponds to its software, that is, to the way in which it is programmed. It is an analogy that is very much in accord with the Functionalist standpoint. A closer examination of the analogy, however, reveals certain confusions. We may compare the description of a computer as an information-processing device with the description of a chair as an item of furniture. The designation in both cases is appropriate and unexceptionable but we must not forget that it specifies the use to which the object is put. Hence, if we were to banish from the scene all potential users there could be neither information-processors nor items of furniture although, of course, computers and chairs would continue to exist as physical objects. Indeed one could imagine a computer, after the ultimate holocaust, continuing to print out information it was programmed to supply for as long as the electricity supply held out. And yet all that would be happening, in this instance, from an objective or ontological standpoint, is that electrical impulses would be passing through its circuitry. The point of this illustration is to bring out the distinction between the functional account of some entity, how it is used, what it is designed to do, etc., and an ontological account, what it consists of, what goes on inside it, etc. The basic deficiency of the Functionalist account of mind which allows for the comparison of mind with a computer program is that a program is a program is a program only for as long as there is a potential user; a mind, on the other hand, exists in its own right, my subjective experiences exist for me whether or not they have any implications for anyone else. We may conclude that Functionalism can at best account for the functional aspect of mental life. It can provide no warrant for the strong claim that there is no essential difference between a machine and a mind.

But where does that leave what we called the corollary of the strong claim to the effect that in terms of achievement, at any rate, nothing was in principle beyond the capacity of an artificial intelligence? Having reconciled ourselves to the advent of an artificial world chess champion have we any reason to doubt the future advent of artificial geniuses of all kinds or of the ultra-intelligent robot such as the science fiction writers have taught us to envisage? Stated thus I do not think there can be a definitive answer to this question. For the question here is no longer whether such machines will resemble minds but rather whether they will be able to do everything and more than the human mind could do. But what a priori principle could we invoke to set an upper limit to the advances of technology in any direction, be it in transport, in manufacture or in information technology? Whether one is optimistic or skeptical about technological progress will depend on which of the various relevant factors one takes into account. An optimist about progress in the field of A. I. will no doubt take heart from the rapid advances that have already been achieved. A skeptic, on the other hand, is likely to dwell on the unevenness of the progress that has so far been made. He may point out that where A. I. has scored its most spectacular successes has been in just such tasks as chess-playing which lend themselves most effectively to formal analysis. Where it has been less successful has been in connection with those skills that are so central in human life, the use of natural language, pattern recognition, the exercise of creative imagination and so on. What lesson can we draw from this comparison?

There is a question which at first sounds odd because we so rarely perceive it as a problem. It is the stark question as to why we should have minds at all. If thinking is an activity of the brain alone why should we not have evolved with brains such as we now possess but without minds? We might even speculate that we would have been even more efficient from the biological point of view if our brain processes were free from any risk of interference from consciousness. However, we know that somehow and at some point in time consciousness emerged and it is a reasonable presumption that it did so because a conscious organism was more effective than one devoid of consciousness. In that case it is meaningful to inquire what specifically consciousness might contribute to thinking which brain activity alone could not have done. It is a question which William James asked himself in opposition to the scientific materialists of his day who took an epiphenomenal view of the nature of consciousness and he speculated about a possible answer.[2] It now seems more plausible than ever that mind is responsible for just those aspects of thinking that are lacking in computer simulations notably the intuitive insights on which we constantly rely but which cannot be reduced to any set of explicit rules or the voluntary aspects of thinking such as attending to the task in hand and striving to attain its fulfillment.

Thus we come back again to the mind-body problem. We already noted that any solution that rests upon a denial of consciousness is a non-starter. This leaves us with two viable contenders. Either consciousness is an entirely superfluous feature of the world which might just as well have run its course as a closed physical system without ever becoming the object of awareness, since there would then have been no conscious observers only anthropoid robots going through the motions of observing, or, alternatively, consciousness could be taken to represent the incidence of mind when it intervenes in the physical world at the juncture that we call the brain. This is the dualist interactionist view of the mind-brain relationship and, if I am right in believing that it is the correct alternative, then it follows that an artificial brain necessarily lacks one vital ingredient of a natural brain, namely its link with the non-physical mind or psyche that activates or animates it. How far this imposes a break on the potential achievements of artificial brains may be a matter for trial and error but it does weaken the assumptions on which the strong claim is based.

There is a further consideration that leads one to doubt the strong claim. There exists a body of evidence that suggests that the mind has certain transcendental powers that cannot be explained in physicalistic terms and are independent of the constraints of time and space. I allude here to what parapsychologists have called "psi phenomena", those transactions between the individual and the external world that do not appear to be mediated by any of the known sensorimotor channels. Of course there is at present no obligation to accept such evidence at face value. The phenomena in question are so unstable and so marginal that, even after a hundred years of psychical research, no conclusive demonstration or unequivocal experiment can be cited to prove that they exist. Nevertheless, my impression, as one who has made a special study of the field, is that it would be unwise and short-sighted to ignore such evidence as of no account. At the very least there remains a real possibility that the evidence may be valid and it is, after all, the only empirical evidence which, if valid, would decisively sway opinion in favor of the dualist position. And, if we do take such evidence into account then it represents another barrier to the pretensions of the A. I. enthusiast as indeed Turing himself recognized when, in his 1950 paper, he introduced the concept of an imitation game.[3]

In my talk I have dwelt on the limitations of A. I. because it was this negative aspect that struck me as being philosophically the most interesting. I hope that, in doing so, I have not given the impression that I do not care about or value the positive achievements of this youthful science. I would like to add, therefore, that psychology is always liable to stagnate unless it can draw sustenance from developments in allied sciences and, in my lifetime, no other developments have made a profounder impact on psychology, more especially cognitive psychology, than those of A. I. What may eventually come of this we can only surmise but it can hardly fail to be of importance. It is my belief that the most important lesson we are likely to learn from A. I. is precisely what mind is not. It should enable us to see more clearly the distinction between the purely mechanical aspects of thinking which are presumably mediated for us by the brain, and what is intrinsically and irreducibly mental. Perhaps we shall even be able to lay down a general principle to the effect that whatever can be fully automated in a machine does not pertain to the mind.

NOTES

[1] This episode is discussed at length by David Fryer in his *Wheels within Wheels* (Unpublished Ph.D. thesis; Edinburgh, 1978) see Chap. 6 "Opinions on Pinions: An Eighteenth Century Turing Game". The inventor of the machine was von Kempelen, a brilliant mechanician who was a court councillor at the court of Empress Maria Theresa of Austria. It was there that the machine was first demonstrated in 1769. It was later taken on tour by the showman Maelzel. Poe published his reflections on it in the *Southern Literary Messenger* for April 1836. Maelzel had a chess-player among his entourage which gave rise to speculations as to who might have been the "ghost" in his machine.

[2] The school of psychology associated with James came to be known as the functionalists on account of their insistence on the efficacy of mind as a force in nature. However, unlike the present day Functionalists who are closer to the behaviorists, the original functionalists were dualist like James.

[3] See A. M. Turing "Computing Machinery and Intelligence", *Mind* 59, 1950. This classic paper has been reprinted many times in various complications, most recently by D. R. Hofstadter and D. C. Dennett (Eds.) in their *The Mind's I: Fantasies and Reflections on Self and Soul* with a commentary by the editors.

13

The Case for Dualism

John Foster

By "dualism" I mean the thesis that the mind and its contents are radically non-physical, that is, that they are neither themselves physical, nor the logical product of anything physical, nor, except causally or nomologically, dependent on anything physical.[1]

I. The Alternatives to Dualism

I.   Conceptual Materialism.

The most radical alternative to dualism is "materialism," the thesis that mental facts (or states of affairs) are nothing over and above physical facts (or states of affairs). This thesis can be interpreted in two ways. I shall start by considering the most straight-forward interpretation: all mental truths (true propositions about the mind) are logically deducible from physical truths (true propositions about the physical world). I shall call this version of the thesis "conceptual materialism." The label "conceptual" is not intended to signify that the materialist thesis is offered as a conceptual (a priori) truth but only to signify the deductive (a priori) character of the logical relation between mental truths and the physical truths from which they allegedly flow.

As defined, conceptual materialism is a very general thesis: it leaves open a wide range of possibilities. But, typically, what the conceptual materialist has in mind is something like this. Take a human organism 0 at a certain time *t*. Suppose, for the sake of argument, we have a complete description of the physical structure of 0 at *t* and know all the physical laws of nature. From this information we can, it is claimed, deduce a complete description (or as close to complete as we care to make it) of how 0 is designed to function in different physical environments.[2] Not all aspects of this total functional organization are relevant to the mental activities of 0. So we next select those that are. For example, we select as one mind-relevant item the functional organization of 0's visual system, noting how, through the reception and processing of different light inputs, this system equips 0 to behave in discriminatory ways with respect to the arrangement of colors in his environment. Likewise, we select as another mind-relevant item the functional organization of 0's hunger system, noting how, by the monitoring of nutrient levels and stomach condition, this system disposes 0 to behave in food-seeking ways (partly under the guidance of the visual system) when appropriate. Once we have selected all the relevant items and, integrating them, have a complete description of the total mind-relevant organization of 0, we then consider the physical state of 0 at *t* and work out its mind-relevant significance with respect to this organization. From this, it is claimed, we can deduce a complete description of 0's state of mind at *t*.

It is, typically, something like this which the conceptual materialist has in mind—the mental description of an organism being deducible from its functional description and its functional description being deducible from its physical description and physical laws. But my objection to conceptual materialism applies quite generally. The objection, which is a very familiar one, is that such materialism fails to do justice to the nature of conscious experience. There are many ways of putting this objection. Here is one way which I find compelling. Consider the situation of someone who is congenitally blind. Could such a person derive from physical information about the sighted a full knowledge of the character of visual experience? Could he deduce from the physiology and functional organization of the sighted human organism (and any other physical truths that might be thought relevant) a full knowledge of what it is like experientially, for such an organism to see? It seems clear that he could not. But why not if conceptual materialism is true?[3]

Does the conceptual materialist have any replies? Well, in the first place, he might say that what prevents the blind man from deducing the experiential conclusion is that being congenitally blind, he is not conceptually equipped to understand it. But this is clearly hopeless. If conceptual materialism were correct, there would be nothing to prevent such a person from acquiring the requisite experiential concepts, assuming he was sufficiently intelligent and was conceptually equipped to understand the relevant physical truths. The presumption that his blindness prevents such acquisition is already a tacit acknowledgment that the physical truths do not implicitly specify, in full, the nature of the sighted organism's experience. In any case, it is not essential to the example that the blind person should lack the requisite concepts. We can suppose that his visual cortex is sufficiently operational to give him, from time to time, visual experiences of a rudimentary kind, though ones which are not, and which he does not take to be, perceptions of his physical environment. These experiences could equip him to understand the experiential conclusion. But it still seems clear that he could not deduce it from the physical premises. For the physical information about the sighted, however comprehensive, would not logically establish that their experience was of the sort to which his experiential concepts, furnished by his own visual experiences, applied.

Alternatively, the conceptual materialist might claim that the blind man is not conceptually equipped to understand all the relevant physical premises. Thus he might argue that one of the physical truths which would be required as a premise is that the sighted organism is equipped by its visual system to behave in ways which are discriminatory with respect to physical color, e.g., in the case of a motorist, to stop when the traffic lights are red and continue when they are green. This is a truth which the blind man cannot fully understand, not having an adequate conception of physical color. But this reply too is quite hopeless. The blind man can acquire an adequate conception of physical color insofar as it is described scientifically, i.e., in terms of wavelengths of light and the reflective properties of pigment. What he lacks is merely a conception of how physical colors look to the sighted. But this deficiency is just one aspect of his not knowing what it is like, experientially, for the sighted organism to see. The only respect in which he fails to grasp what is meant by "the traffic lights are red" is that he does not know what sort of experience the sighted person has when he receives light of the relevant wavelength. But this knowledge is precisely what, if conceptual materialism were true, he should be able to deduce from the physical information available. So the blind man's inability to achieve an adequate conception of color merely reflects the falsity of the materialist's thesis.

The conceptual materialist still has one final line of defense. He might claim that the blind man can, from the physical truths, derive a full knowledge of the character of visual experience, and that what misleads us into supposing otherwise is that the physical truths do not afford that kind of knowledge which is available, through introspection, to the sighted. On this view, there is no more to the character of visual experience than the blind man can deduce; it is simply that, being blind and lacking even the capacity to visualize, he cannot conceptually focus on this character in the way the sighted can. He knows exactly what such experience is psychologically like but cannot achieve, in his imagination, the viewpoint of those who have it. This reply looks more promising than the others. At least the distinction between merely knowing the character of a certain type of experience and knowing it in introspective perspective is sound. To take a different example, there are some pitches which are too high for me to hear or frame a mental image of. Suppose P is the highest pitch I can hear or image. There is a perfectly good sense in which I know what it is like, experientially, to hear the pitch which is an octave higher than P: I can exactly fix the position of such an experience in the auditory spectrum. All I lack is the kind of knowledge available to someone who has the experience or can achieve, in his imagination, the viewpoint of one who has it. However, I do not think that this distinction can be of use to the conceptual materialist. For while it is possible for someone to know the character of a certain type of experience without knowing it in the introspective manner, it is surely only possible in those cases where the person can define that character by reference to other types of experience whose character he does know in that manner. I can grasp the experiential character of hearing the relevant pitch because I can introspectively grasp both the hearing of P and the octave relation. The problem for the blind man is that the physical truths provide no introspective reference points at all. And for this reason, I cannot see how he could derive from them, in any sense, a full knowledge of what it is like, experientially, for the sighted organism to see.

2. Metaphysical Materialism.

The failure of conceptual materialism does not entail the failure of materialism as such. For the thesis that mental facts are nothing over and above physical facts can be interpreted in another way. It can be interpreted as meaning that all mental facts are the necessary consequences of physical facts by some mode of necessity which, while in a broad sense logical (i.e., stronger than mere natural necessity), is not that of deductive entailment. Since this mode of necessity is often called "metaphysical," I shall label this position "metaphysical materialism." It might be objected that this so-called interpretation of the materialist thesis does not do justice to the force of the phrase "nothing over and above." But this is a purely verbal issue. The fact remains that metaphysical materialism as defined is incompatible with dualism.

How could mental facts be the logically (stronger than naturally) necessary consequences of physical facts except by some relation of deductive entailment? Well, the metaphysical materialist invites us to accept a certain analogy. Consider the relationship between the two propositions (A) that this spoon is hot, and (B) that the molecules of this spoon are agitated. Let us assume that our ordinary (i.e., prescientific) concept of physical heat is as that property, whatever it is, which induces heat sensations in us. From this it immediately follows that (A) is not deducible from (B), since it is not an a priori truth that what induces such sensations is molecular agitation. At the same time, it is a truth, and one which science has established. And from this, together with the assumption, it follows that heat is (i.e., is identical with) molecular agitation. But, for reasons which Kripke has made familiar, this obliges us to say that there is no logically possible world in which (B) is true and (A) is false.[4] In this sense, if the spoon is hot, its being so is a logically necessary consequence of the fact that its molecules are agitated. In the same way, it is claimed, mental facts about a person are the logically necessary consequences of physical facts about his body. Thus our ordinary (i.e., prescientific) concept of pain, it is said, is as that state, whatever it is, which reveals itself to the subject under a certain introspective appearance and is expressed overtly through certain forms of behavior. We cannot deduce that a person is in pain from a physical description of his body (not even from one which includes a formulation of physical law), since such a description does not tell us how things appear introspectively: it does not address itself to the character of pain as a subjective experience. But we should, it is claimed, anticipate the scientific discovery that the state which meets our conceptual requirements—the state which, in the actual world, has the required introspective appearance and behavioral influence—is, in its intrinsic nature, physical. And if pain is (i.e., is identical with) a physical state, then it is a necessary truth (true in all logically possible worlds), though not a priori, that a person is in pain if and only if his body is in that state. Admittedly, it may well turn out that pain in one species of organism is a different physical state from pain in another, and it may even turn out that, within a single species, pain in one member is a different physical state from pain in another. But while this would prevent an exact analogy with heat, it does not affect the fundamentals of the account.

However, as Kripke has shown,[5] the suggestion of any analogy at all is totally misconceived. What allows us to identify physical heat with molecular agitation is that we can detach the sensible appearance of physical heat from its essential nature: we can regard the sensible appearance as just the contingent effect of physical heat on human experience. If we are to identify pain with a physical state (whether absolutely or in a way which is species/organism-relative) we must similarly detach the introspective appearance of pain from its essential nature. But how could this be done? Only by separating what pain is in itself from how pain feels to the person who has it. And such a separation is surely impossible. Moreover, even if it were possible, it would be, from the standpoint of the materialist, self-defeating. For, if the experiential character of pain is not part of its essential nature, the identification of pain with a physical state does nothing to make the experiential facts necessary consequences of physical facts and hence contributes nothing to the materialist's program. Nor can I see any other way in which the materialist could attempt to justify his consequentialist thesis without reverting to some form of conceptual materialism (e.g., by analyzing experiential concepts in functional terms), and this we have already refuted. Of course, the materialist could simply assert that experiential facts are metaphysically necessitated by physical facts and challenge us to refute him. But without some explanation of how such necessitation might obtain, we can hardly take this assertion seriously.

3. The Token-Identity Thesis.

The fact that experiential states, as mental types, cannot be identified with physical states does not, as such, entail that experiences (experiential events), as mental particulars, are not identical with physical events. Thus a position which is becoming increasingly fashionable is to hold that mental events are identical with certain neural events, but that the mental properties of these events are not identical with any of their physical properties or indeed with anything, such as their functional properties, whose instantiation could be deduced from purely physical truths. This position is not a form of materialism as defined; it does not claim that mental facts are, either deductively or by metaphysical necessity, nothing over and above physical facts, though in some versions it does claim that mental facts are supervenient on physical facts, i.e., that there cannot be mental differences without physical differences. Rather, the position combines a kind of ontological monism with an attributive dualism. When someone is in pain, the pain event is part of the material world (e.g., the firing of his C fibers at a particular time); but its being a pain (its mental character) is something genuinely additional to, and not logically necessitated by, its physical properties or anything which physical science could describe. This position, or, strictly, the monist part of it, is known as the "token-identity thesis." It is thus contrasted with the stronger "type-identity thesis," which claims that the mental types of which mental events are the tokens are identical with certain physical types, i.e., that mental properties are identical with physical properties.

Once again it is Kripke who has exposed the flaw in this weaker position.[6] Suppose Smith is in pain. Let us call the particular pain event (the particular experiential event in Smith's mind at that time) E. And let us call the particular neural event with which E is supposedly identical (e.g., some particular firing of Smith's C fibers) *B*. Now it is clear that the experiential property "being a pain" is an essential attribute of *E* (the experiential event); that is, there is no logically possible world in which E exists and is not a pain. The only remotely feasible way of denying this claim would be by adopting a functionalist account of experiential properties, as in certain versions of conceptual materialism. For this would allow one to say that *E* qualified as a pain only contingently, in virtue of the causal role which events of *E*'s (presumably physical) intrinsic type played in the whole physical or psychophysical system. But, as we have already seen, the functionalist account is inadequate; the arguments that refute it as an adjunct to conceptual materialism refute it quite generally. But while "being a pain" is an essential attribute of *E*, it is surely not an essential attribute of B (the neural event). For surely there is a possible world (perhaps it has to be one with different psychophysical laws) in which *B* exists and has no experiential character at all. Of course, this would be rejected by someone who identified experiential properties with physical properties, but, as we have seen, this type-identity thesis is unacceptable. But if E is essentially a pain and B is not, then E and B cannot be numerically identical. For if they were, they would have all their properties, including their modal properties, in common.

Granted the rejection of functionalism and the type-identity thesis, the defender of token-identity has, as far as I can see, only one way of trying to resist this argument. He has to maintain that while the experiential character of *B* is not part of the essential nature of the type of physical event of which *B* is an instance, it is, nonetheless, essential to the identity of *B* itself. But even this reply fails, since the identity of *B* is wholly determined by physical factors. Thus, suppose we try to envisage a world W which results from the actual world by (a) removing *B*, (b) filling the gap with an event of exactly the same physical type, composed of exactly the same particle events, with exactly the same causal antecedents, but without *B*'s experiential character, and (c) making whatever further adjustments this requires, e.g., changes in psychophysical law and similar (putative) replacements of other *B*-type events. It is surely obvious that the W event which is the counterpart of *B* is none other than *B* itself. Being of exactly the same physical type, having exactly the same spatiotemporal location, being composed of exactly the same particle events in the same brain, and being caused in exactly the same way, the putative replacement just is numerically the same physical event. It follows that if W is genuinely possible, 'being a pain" is not essential to *B*. And consequently, the only way in which we could hold it to be essential would be by claiming that the experiential character of *B* was logically determined, either deductively or metaphysically, by its physical properties and other physical factors on which its identity depends. This claim would exclude the possibility of W, but it would oblige us to accept a full-blooded materialism of the kind we have already rejected and which the token-identity thesis was designed to avoid.

4. The Logical Dependence Thesis.

The token-identity thesis was one way of trying to get a compromise between full dualism and full materialism. Another way would be to claim that while mental facts are not logically determined by physical facts, they are at least logically dependent on them. There are several positions of this sort. Among the most familiar are the claim that any subject of mental states has to be (or at least to have been) embodied and the claim that the connection between mental states and their behavioral manifestations is not purely contingent. I do not have time to examine such claims in detail, though I find none of them at all convincing. My main objection to all of them is that, in the last analysis, they rest on an indefensible form of the verification principle. They all, in one way or another, appeal to the alleged fact that dualism generates skepticism—for example—(and this is the case most often cited), skepticism about other minds—and that such skepticism can only be avoided by moving, to some extent, in the direction of conceptual materialism—for example, by making certain concessions to behaviorism. But the fact that a philosophical position generates an epistemological problem is not as such a reason for rejecting it. Moreover, in the particular case of other minds, the problem that dualism allegedly generates has been greatly exaggerated. Even from a dualist standpoint, most of our commonsense beliefs about the mental states of others can be justified by an inference to the best explanation. If it is said that such justification falls short of conclusive verification, this is quite true. But it is surely very implausible to maintain that in the case of statements about other minds, conclusive verification is available. The only area, in the topic of other minds, where dualism seems to generate a really acute epistemological problem is that concerned with sense qualia—e.g., how can I tell that your color spectrum is not inverted with respect to mine? But here it seems to me that the problem is a genuine one and that a theory which did not allow it to arise would be defective.

5.   *The Restriction of Dualism to Experience.*

Assuming we reject the logical dependence thesis, we cannot, I think, avoid a dualistic account of experience: experiential states and experiential events are radically non-physical, i.e. are neither physical, nor the logical product of anything physical, nor, except causally or nomologically, dependent on anything physical. But we could still reject dualism with respect to the residual contents of the mind. Thus we could still claim that propositional attitudes, such as belief and desire, are physical states of the brain, or functional states whose instantiation is deducible from a physical description of the brain, or whole organism, together with certain physical laws. And we could still claim that propositional acts, such as thoughts and judgments, are physical events in the brain, or functional events whose occurrence is deducible from a brain/organism-description and physical laws. My arguments against materialism and the token-identity thesis do not directly exclude such claims, since they have exclusively concerned the case of experience.

    Nonetheless, it seems to me that once we have accepted experiential dualism, the extension of dualism to the rest of the mind becomes unavoidable. The first point to stress is that although, as formulated, my arguments against materialism and the token-identity thesis have only concerned the case of experience, they can be generalized to cover all those aspects of our mental life which are essentially conscious—all those aspects which, of their very nature, form part of how it is, subjectively, with the subject. For it was precisely the conscious character of experience that made it resistant to the materialist and identity accounts. This does not oblige us to adopt a dualist account of propositional attitudes, such as belief and desire, since these are not essentially conscious in the relevant sense: a person who is sound asleep can still be said to have beliefs and desires. But it does, I think, oblige us to adopt a dualist account of propositional and quasi-propositional acts, such as thoughts, judgments, and decisions. For these, it seems to me, are essentially conscious. It might be objected, by philosophers of a radically empiricist persuasion, that it is only the phenomenal, not the conceptual, aspects of these acts which are essentially conscious. For example, suppose that in the course of performing some larger arithmetical calculation, I make the judgment that 9 x 7= 63. An empiricist might argue that the only essentially conscious element in this judgment is my mental voicing of the sequence of sounds "nine sevens are sixty-three" and that this phenomenal act only derives its conceptual significance, as a vehicle for my propositional act, from a surrounding mental framework (involving such items as my mastery of English and my knowledge of arithmetic) which is, or could be, subjectively silent. If this were so, then the conceptual aspects of the judgment—in effect, the propositional act itself—could be construed in a nondualistic way. However, I find this empiricist account very implausible. I think we can best see this by beginning with the case of perception. It is quite clear that in most cases of perception, at least after early infancy, there is a large element of conceptual interpretation within the conscious experience itself. Thus in visual perception, the experience consists of more than just the presentation of a color array; it includes seeing the color array as a physical scene of a certain sort. (Seeing "Wittgenstein's ambiguous picture as a duck or as a rabbit is just a dramatic example of this.) Now consider the particular case of hearing the sequence of sounds "nine sevens are sixty-three." There is clearly an experiential difference between hearing it just as a sequence of sounds (this might be the experience of someone who did not understand English) and hearing it as a sentence of English expressing the proposition that 9 x 7 = 63 (this would be the normal experience of a numerate English-speaker). But given that a propositional interpretation of the sounds can be part of the total perceptual experience when the sounds are heard, it can also be part of the total conscious state when they are mentally voiced. And surely this will always be so when the mental voicing is the vehicle for a propositional act.

We are still left with the case of propositional attitudes, which, as I have conceded, are not essentially conscious. Here, the case of dualism rests on the fact that such states, while not in themselves states of consciousness, are essentially linked with states of consciousness. Let us focus on the example of belief. There is no denying that a person can hold a certain belief at times when he is not performing the corresponding act of judgment. But it is surely part of the essential nature of belief that it should dispose the subject to make such judgments when the need arises. Thus it is surely logically impossible for me to believe that 9 x 7 = 63 unless I am thereby disposed to judge that 9 x 7 = 63 when I address myself to the question. If so, then beliefs cannot be identified with physical states, such as neural networks, since such states would at best sustain such dispositions only contingently, i.e., through the contingent obtaining of certain psychophysical laws. Nor, given that judgments themselves are nonphysical, can beliefs be construed as functional states of a kind whose instantiation could be deduced from purely physical truths. It might be objected that in rejecting the identity thesis, I am overlooking the distinction between types and tokens. Thus it may be that as a mental type, a belief state cannot be physical. But why shouldn't the tokens of this type—the particular instances of this belief state in particular minds at particular times—be physical? Why not say that my current token-belief that 9 x 7 = 63 is some current neural network in my brain, while allowing that this network only qualifies as a token-belief in virtue of its contingently disposing me to make the appropriate conscious judgment? But the trouble with this is that while we are free to recognize an ontology of token-beliefs, we cannot do so in a way which leaves their belief character (their character as token-beliefs) only contingent. For our only conception of a token-belief is as something which is, by its essential nature, the particular occurrence of some type of believing, e.g., my believing now that 9 x 7 = 63. And if the token-beliefs are essentially token-beliefs, then their dispositional connection with conscious judgments must be essential too.

Given all this, the only way of avoiding a wholly dualistic account of belief would be to adopt a hybrid form of functionalism, in which belief is construed as a functional state defined partly in terms of its output in nonphysical conscious judgment and partly in terms of its output in physical behavior—in effect, the combination of certain mentalistic and certain behavioral dispositions. All I can say against this is that I find the behavioristic element implausible. It is inconceivable that someone should believe that 9 x 7 = 63 without being disposed to make the corresponding judgment. But it is surely quite conceivable that someone should hold this belief without being equipped with the right kind of neuro-muscular system to express it overtly. Indeed, in the case of stroke victims, this frequently happens. It may be objected that such victims only retain their beliefs because they once possessed the neuromuscular capacity to express them. But we can surely also envisage cases in which someone acquires beliefs without ever having such a capacity.

As I see it, then, we are obliged to give a wholly dualistic account of belief. (Exactly what account we should give I shall not pursue; the fact that belief essentially involves a judgmental disposition may seem to support some kind of dualistic functionalism, but for reasons I shall not go into, I doubt if this is so.) Obviously, if we are dualistic about belief, we must be similarly dualistic about other propositional attitudes. Since we have already established dualism for experience and other essentially conscious states, this means, in effect, that we must accept dualism as such—accept the thesis that the mind and its contents are radically non-physical.

II. Four Objections to Dualism

I have tried to show why the alternatives to dualism are unacceptable. If my arguments have been correct, there is a sense in which I could afford to rest my case there, since if the alternatives are wrong, dualism must be right The reason I continue is that dualism itself is thought to be vulnerable to certain objections, and these objections (or at least some of them) merit answers. Of course, I do not have space to consider all the objections. Some are nothing more than rhetoric (I would put into this category such objections as "'nonphysical entities are queer" and "'postulating nonphysical entities is ontologically extravagant'"); others would require a separate chapter to deal with them effectively (in particular, those objections which concern the problem of other minds and the issue over private languages, though, in the case of other minds, I have given some indication in section I.4 of the line I would take). Apart from these, however, I have tried to cover those objections which I regard as the most important, either because of their intrinsic merits or because of the influence they have exerted.

As it turns out, the four objections I consider all concern, in one way or another, the dualist's account of psychophysical causation—his account of the causal relations between body and mind. Dualism itself, of course, does not entail that there are such relations. There is no contradiction in maintaining that the mind, as well as being nonphysical, is causally isolated from the physical world; and with the help of a suitable theism, it may even be possible to explain why things are empirically organized as if there were psychophysical causation, when there is not. But since I do not want my defense of dualism to force me into such an eccentric position, I shall work on the assumption that parallelism, in this extreme form, is untenable and that mind and body are indeed causally related. This still leaves the dualist with a choice between interactionism, which takes the causal relations to run in both directions, and epiphenomenalism, which takes them to run only from body to mind. Here my sympathies, again in line with common sense, are with the interactionist. And consequently, I would feel at least very uncomfortable if there were something which obliged me to choose between abandoning dualism altogether and adopting its epiphenomenalist version. That I do face such a choice is the substance of the fourth objection.

I. *The Traditional Objection.*

Perhaps the oldest objection to dualism is that if the mind is nonphysical, the very idea of psychophysical causation—of the body causally affecting the mind or the mind causally affecting the body—is deeply puzzling, if not incoherent. How can such different kinds of thing—the physical and the nonphysical—come into casual contact? How can the material body gain purchase on the immaterial mind, or vice versa? However, put like this, I cannot see what the problem is supposed to be. Obviously, dualistic causation does not operate through physical contact, as when one billiard ball displaces another. But why should it not just be in the nature of things that in certain psychophysical conditions, certain types of neural event cause certain types of mental event, or vice versa? According to Thomas Nagel, we cannot understand how such causation would work.[7] Nagel assumes, I think correctly, though contrary to Hume's account, that causation involves some kind of objective necessitation. He then argues, in effect, that so long as we think of mental and physical events as radically different in their intrinsic nature, such necessitation is incomprehensible: "what we cannot understand is *how* . . . the brain process necessitates the sensation."[8] But what I cannot understand is how this "how"-question arises. Since the necessitation is causal, rather than logical, there cannot be any question of construing it as some kind of a priori entailment. Moreover, since the causation is direct (the brain event directly causing the mental event, or vice versa), there is no question of an intervening mechanism. Perhaps it is this very directness which Nagel finds puzzling. For in the physical world causal processes are, in general, spatiotemporally continuous, thus providing an intervening mechanism between a cause and any subsequent effect. But there is surely nothing incoherent or problematic about the notion of direct causation. And where causation is direct, I do not see in what sense there could be a question of how it operates, except as a request to specify the causally relevant properties and covering laws.

II. The Problem of Causal Pairings.

While the traditional objection to dualistic psychophysical causation is totally misconceived, there is a related objection which is more troublesome and for which, ironically, I have to take the credit.[9] It is normally assumed that where two events are causally related, they are so wholly by virtue of the way in which, via their noncausal properties and relations, they fall under some natural law. Thus if, on a particular occasion, my heating of a lump of metal caused it to melt, it is assumed that what makes this true is that the metal was of a certain type and reached a certain temperature and that it is a law of nature (or a consequence of a law of nature) that whenever a lump of metal of that type reaches that temperature, it melts. However, when we apply this model to the case of psychophysical causation, dualistically conceived, we encounter a problem. Suppose that B is the event of Smith's brain being in state ϕ at time t and that E is a mental event of type ψ which occurs in Smith's mind a tenth of a second after t and as the direct causal result of B. What psychophysical law could we postulate to account for this causal episode? We might begin by postulating the law (L1) that whenever a brain is in a state ϕ a mental event of type ψ, occurs a tenth of a second later. But this would be inadequate. For suppose that Jones's brain is also in state ϕ at t, giving us the event B' which is a simultaneous duplicate of B, and that this causes in Jones's mind, a tenth of a second later, an event E' of type ψ, which is a simultaneous duplicate of E. *Ex hypothesi*, B is the cause of E and B' is the cause of E'. But the law L1 does not account for these causal pairings. Because it only specifies the temporal relation between cause and effect, it is neutral between these pairings and the alternative, but false, hypothesis that B is the cause of E' and B' is the cause of E. The obvious remedy is to replace L1 by the stronger law (L2) that whenever a brain x is in state ϕ a mental event of type ψ occurs a tenth of a second later in that mind which x, or the x-containing organism, embodies—in other words, in the mind of that subject whose brain x is. L2 would then yield the unique causal pairings of B with E and of B' with E'. But the problem with this is that, for a dualist, the relation of embodiment itself must be analyzed, wholly or partly, in causal terms: at least part of what makes a particular brain x the brain of a particular subject y is that things are psychophysically arranged in a way which gives x (and x alone) the capacity to have a direct causal influence on y (and y alone) and, for the interactionist, vice versa. It would be circular to account for this arrangement by laws like L2 and, because of the original problem, impossible to account for it by laws like L1. In view of this, it might seem that the right solution is to abandon dualism. For if we identified mental events with neural events, we could envisage laws that guaranteed unique causal pairings by specifying the precise spatiotemporal relation between cause and effect. Indeed, we could hope to account for psychophysical causation wholly in terms of the ordinary laws of physics and chemistry.

When I first wrote about this problem back in 1968, I argued that the right response, for the dualist, was to postulate psychophysical laws restricted to particular pairs of brains and minds (or brains and subjects). Thus in the case of Smith and Jones, we can secure the correct causal pairings by postulating a separate law for each person—the law (relevant to Smith) that whenever brain $x1$ is in state ϕ, a ψ event occurs a tenth of a second later in mind $M1$ (or to subject S) and the law (relevant to Jones) that whenever brain $x2$ is in state ϕ, a ψ event occurs a tenth of a second later in mind $M2$ (or to subject J), where $x1$ and $M1$ are the brain and mind of Smith and $x2$ and $M2$ are the brain and mind of Jones. More recently, I have tried to meet the problem in a quite different way.[10] I have argued that even in the physical realm we can envisage cases in which the fundamental laws do not account for the causal pairings. Thus suppose that, for a certain kind K of metal, it is a law that when any spherical K lump reaches a specified temperature, a flash occurs a tenth of a second later somewhere (unspecified) in the region of points no farther from the center of the sphere than twice its diameter. Suppose further that there is no stronger law which fixes the position of the flash more precisely. Now imagine the case in which two adjacent K spheres simultaneously reach the critical temperature and, a tenth of a second later, two flashes occur, both within the specified region for each sphere. It is coherent and indeed plausible to suppose that each flash is the effect of just one of the sphere-temperatures and that each sphere-temperature is the cause of just one of the flashes. But the causal pairings are not determined by the law and the noncausal conditions, since each flash falls within the specified region for each sphere. From this I concluded that we should abandon the assumption that causal relations can be wholly accounted for in terms of non-causal properties and laws. And once this assumption is abandoned, the problem of psychophysical causal pairings no longer arises; it no longer matters if the pairing of B with E and B' and E' is not determined by the noncausal conditions and the covering law.

Reviewing these alternative responses, I now think that in a sense, both were correct. On the one hand, the hypothetical case of the K spheres does indeed show that causal pairings can be law-transcendent; and, in that respect, the original objection to the dualist's position fails. On the other hand, it does seem quite plausible to envisage laws of the restricted kind as underlying the relation of embodiment. As we have said, at least part of what makes a particular brain x the brain of a particular mental subject y is that things are psychophysically arranged in a way which gives x (and x alone) the capacity to have a direct causal influence on y (and y alone)—and, for the interactionist, vice versa. It is hard to see in what this arrangement could consist except in certain psychophysical laws which specifically link x and y, and such laws would guarantee unique causal pairings. At all events, it is clear that the dualist has sufficient resources to meet the objection.

III. Davidson's Objection.

Even if causal pairings can be law-transcendent, it is still plausible to insist that if an event x causes an event y, there is some covering law which ensures that in relevantly similar conditions, any event of the (relevant) x-type stands in a relevantly similar relation to some event of the (relevant) y-type. According to Donald Davidson, even this relatively weak claim, combined with the acceptance of psychophysical causation, commits us to the token-identity thesis.[11] The reason, argues Davidson, is that the "disparate commitments of the mental and physical schemes" preclude the existence of strict psychophysical laws.[12] "It is a feature of physical reality that physical change can be explained by laws that connect it with other changes and conditions physically described. It is a feature of the mental that the attribution of mental phenomena must be responsible to the background of reasons, beliefs, and intentions of the individual. There cannot be tight connections between the realms if each is to retain allegiance to its proper source of evidence."[13] As he explains the point in a subsequent essay, "my general strategy for trying to show that there are no strict psychophysical laws depends . . on emphasizing the holistic character of the cognitive field. Any effort at increasing the accuracy and power of a theory of behaviour forces us to bring more and more of the whole system of the agent's beliefs and motives directly into account. But in inferring this system from the evidence, we necessarily impose conditions of coherence, rationality and consistency. These conditions have no echo in physical theory, which is why we can look for no more than rough correlations between psychological and physical phenomena."[14] Davidson concludes that where there are causal relations between mental and physical events, the covering law must be physical. This in turn requires identifying mental events with physical events and claiming that it is in respect of their physical, not their mental, properties that mental events have physical causes and physical effects. He calls this position "anomalous monism": "monism, because it holds that psychological events are physical events; anomalous, because it insists that events do not fall under strict laws when described in psychological terms."[15]

When Davidson denies the possibility of strict psychophysical laws, he only intends this, I assume, to apply to those types of mental phenomena, such as beliefs and desires, which have propositional, or in some other way conceptual, content. He is not, I assume, excluding the possibility of a psychophysical law ensuring that a certain type of brain process always produces a certain type of nonconceptual sensation. However, even when we confine our attention to the relevant types of phenomena, Davidson's argument seems very strange. No doubt he is right to stress the holistic character of the mental: we cannot, I suspect, even make sense of the claim that someone has just one propositional attitude, not forming part of some coherent system of attitudes; and certainly, as Davidson sees, it is only by finding evidence of some larger system in a subject that we can be justified in ascribing a particular attitude to him. No doubt too Davidson is right in claiming that the considerations of coherence, rationality, and consistency which form an essential part of the evidence (or of the way the evidence is interpreted) "have no echo in physical theory." My difficulty is in not being able to see why these points should rule out strict psychophysical laws. Davidson seems to be arguing that because the epistemological methods of commonsense psychology and physical science are quite different, psychological and physical facts cannot stand in any tight lawlike connection. But this is just a non sequitur.[16] The only point which even seems to pose a threat to strict psychophysical laws— and it concerns the logical, not the epistemological, holism of the mental—is that the smallest viable unit of propositional mentality is a coherent system. But the most that follows from this is that some of the psychophysical laws would have to be very complicated, e.g., ones which determine how complex neural networks causally sustain complex systems of belief and desire. Maybe such laws would be too complicated for us to discover; maybe even some of them could not be exhaustively specified; but that does not mean that they do not exist. Nor should we conclude that all psychophysical laws are, in respect of their psychological content, of this complexity. If there are laws determining how complex neural networks sustain complex systems of propositional attitudes, then a fortiori there are laws determining how complex networks sustain individual attitudes. Moreover, in the case of causal links from mind to body, there is nothing to prevent there being laws which determine how, given certain brain conditions, certain types of volition (such as the attempt to move one's arm in a certain way) cause certain types of neural response. The fact that such volitions are possible only in the framework of a complex cognitive field makes no difference.

All in all, it seems to me that while we can accept much of what Davidson says about the holistic character of the mind and the difference between the epistemological methods of psychology and physical science, there is nothing here which even looks like an argument against the existence of strict psychophysical laws.

IV. An Objection to Dualistic Interactionism.

Some dualists, while accepting that there are psychophysical causal relations, hold that they only run in one direction—from body to mind. They accept, for example, that if I am stung by a wasp, the subsequent pain is caused by the neural response which the sting induces, but they deny that if I decide to smoke my pipe, the subsequent bodily movements involving pipe and matches are caused by my decision. And, quite generally, they accept that a person's mental states are causally affected by the states of his body but deny that his mental states have any causal influence on the states of his body or on anything else in the physical world. This version of dualism is known as "epiphenomenalism," and the version it contrasts with, which accepts psychophysical causation in both directions, is known as "interactionism." I should add that most epiphenomenalists, as well as denying that the mind has any causal influence on the body, also deny that it has a causal influence on anything at all. In particular, they deny that mental states can cause, or contribute to the causation of, other mental states.

Like most other current philosophers, I regard epiphenomenalism as unnatural and implausible. In the first place, it is in radical conflict with our conception of ourselves as agents. If mental states have no causal influence on behavior, then behavior cannot be thought of as intentional in any decent sense, even if the subject happens to have certain intentions which it fulfills. And if behavior is not intentional, it does not qualify as action in a sense which distinguishes it from mere bodily movement. The epiphenomenalist might reply that the general conformity of our behavior to our intentions is not merely accidental; it is ensured by the very structure of our brains and their muscular extensions in the framework of physical and psychophysical law. But even so, the behavior would not be intentional in the requisite sense, since the intentions and the psychophysical laws that control their occurrence would be irrelevant to its production. Second, human behavior exhibits certain complex regularities that call for explanation and that, at present, we explain (at least partly) in psychological terms. These psychological explanations, though typically of a rational rather than a mechanistic kind, attribute a causal efficacy to the mental; they represent behavior as falling under the control of the subject's beliefs and desires, or under the control of the subject's decisions, which are responsive to (if not determined by) his beliefs and desires. And these explanations gain credence from the fact that, as well as being, in their own terms, successful, they cannot, at present, be replaced by non-psychological explanations that cover the same ground. Third, it is difficult to see how, if epiphenomenalism were true, the mind could form a subject matter for overt discussion. Certainly, if mental states have no causal access to our speech centers, the notion of an introspective report collapses: even if the subject retains an introspective knowledge of his mental states, his utterances would not count as expressing that knowledge if it contributes nothing to their production. But it is not even clear how, on the epiphenomenalistic view, our language, as a medium for our utterances, makes semantic contact with the mind at all. In what sense, for example, could the word pain, as overtly used, be said to signify a certain type of sensation, if neither the occurrence of the sensations nor our introspective conception of their type affects the overt use? Quite generally, it seems that if the mental contributes nothing to the way in which the linguistic practices involving "mental" terms are developed and sustained in the speech community and in no other way affects the production of utterances employing these terms, then, in respect of their overt use, the terms should be analyzed in a purely behaviorist or functionalist fashion—which would deprive the epiphenomenalist of the linguistic resources to enunciate his thesis. It is true, of course, that each language user may mentally interpret each term as signifying a certain kind of (dualistically conceived) mental state. But how could such interpretations have any bearing on the objective meaning of the terms, as employed in speech and writing, if they are causally idle?

None of these points shows that epiphenomenalism is logically untenable, in the sense of being incoherent or self-contradictory. Even the third point, if correct, only shows that when overtly expressed, epiphenomenalism is self-refuting—that the very attempt to provide an audible or visible formulation of the thesis presupposes its falsity. Nonetheless, we have, I think, very strong, and perhaps even conclusive, reasons for rejecting it. And, because of this, I should not want my defense of dualism to involve my acceptance of anything but an interactionist position.

It is at this point that the fourth objection arises. For there is an argument which purports to show that dualism of any but an epiphenomenalistic kind is scientifically unacceptable. The argument runs like this:
1.   The body is a physical system.
2.   As such, the body must be subject to ordinary physical laws.
3.   Our theories as to what physical laws obtain are subject to revision. But our current scientific evidence strongly supports the view that at any level of description relevant to a theory of human behavior, these laws are, for all practical purposes, deterministic.
4.   So we can reasonably conclude that any bodily event, of a sort which might be cited in a description or explanation of behavior, is causally determined by

prioɪ physical events and conditions.

5.   But such a conclusion leaves no room for a nonphysical mind to have any causal influence on behavior.

6.   Hence, on our present scientific evidence, we face a choice between epiphenomenalism and some kind of identity thesis (if only of the token-token variety).

If it is correct, this argument constitutes an objection to dualistic interactionism. It also, on the face of it, constitutes an objection to dualism as such, if epiphenomenalism is, as I would concede, unacceptable. And, nowadays, it is normally as an objection to dualism, and in support of the identity thesis, that the argument is offered[17]. But here we must be careful. It is true that epiphenomenalism is very implausible and, overtly expressed, may even be self-refuting. And this means that, other things being equal, we should reject it. But it does not mean that we should reject it at all costs. If the only alternative were the identity thesis, then, in my view, epiphenomenalism, despite its implausibility, would be the preferable option. For I think that my earlier arguments show that the identity thesis is incoherent. The choice between epiphenomenalism and the identity thesis only counts against dualism on the assumption, which I hold to be false, that epiphenomenalism is not only very implausible but less plausible than its rival. There is also a further point to bear in mind. If the identity thesis is only of a token-token kind, it is not clear how, even if it were coherent, it would avoid the implausibilities of epiphenomenalism. For if mental events have physical effects only by virtue of their physical properties, and if mental properties are not identical with physical properties, or with functional properties of a purely physicalistic kind, then mental properties are causally irrelevant. And if mental properties are causally irrelevant, the identity thesis does not accord the mind the kind of causal efficacy which common sense demands. It does not allow the mental an influence on behavior in any interesting sense. So to provide a genuine alternative to epiphenomenalism, the identity thesis would have to be of a full-blooded materialist form, involving, in addition to token-identity, some physicalistic construal of mental properties. This is something which defenders of token-identity do not always recognize. It is not, for example, recognized by Davidson [19].

However, whether it is an objection to dualism as such or only to interactionism, I have to find some answer to the argument; for I am not willing to concede that epiphenomenalism and the identity thesis are the only empirically acceptable options. In fact, the error in the argument is not hard to identify. We must begin by distinguishing two ways in which science might provide evidence that the functioning of the body is wholly explicable in terms of deterministic physical law. The first way would be by direct research on the body itself—in particular, on the brain, since it is on brain activity, if on anything, that we might expect the mind to exert a direct causal influence. Thus, by monitoring neural activity in various parts of the brain (without disturbing normal functioning), scientists might build up a strong inductive case for the conclusion that the electrochemical state of any neuron at any time is determined by its immediately prior electrochemical state and the states of other neurons directly connected to it. The second way would be by discovering, without reference to the functioning of the human body, that the rest of the physical world seems to be subject to certain physical laws of a sort which, if they applied universally, would make the body a deterministic system. This is the evidence provided by the investigations of physics and chemistry into the properties of matter and energy in general. Now it is predominantly evidence of the second kind to which the argument appeals. The claim is not that a thorough sampling of brain activity reveals a wholly deterministic system, for no such sampling has been conducted. Rather, the claim is that the human body, including the brain, must be physically deterministic if it is to conform to those theories which apply to physical systems in general. But this evidence, just because it bears on the question of the human system only indirectly, is not decisive. It has to be weighed against what we know or have reason to believe, independently, about the relation between body and mind. In particular, it must be weighed against all that makes epiphenomenalism an implausible theory, and this, in turn, must be set against the background of the a priori objections to materialism and token-identity. When everything is taken into account, the most reasonable conclusion to draw is, surely, that through its attachment to a nonphysical mind, the brain is subject to certain influences which do not affect the other physical systems that science investigates and on whose behavior its nomological theories are based. It is conceivable that this conclusion will be called into question by future brain research (if it were, I should have to reconsider my rejection of epiphenomenalism). But as things stand, we are entitled to assume that it will not.

NOTES
[1] I am indebted to Howard Robinson for his helpful comments on an earlier draft of this paper.
[2] On my interactionist view, which I defend in section II, this claim is, in fact, false.
[3] Cf. H. Robinson, *Matter and Sense* (Cambridge: Cambridge University Press, 1982), pp.4–5.
[4] Thus see Kripke, *Naming and Necessity* (Oxford: Blackwell, 1980), pp.131–34
[5] Ibid., pp.148–54.
[6] Ibid., pp.146–47.
[7] T. Nagel, *Mortal Questions* (Cambridge: Cambridge University Press, 1979), pp.185–87.
[8] Ibid., p.187.
[9] See my "Psychophysical Causal Relations," *American Philosophical Quarterly* 5, no. I (1968).
[10] See my "In Self-Defense," in G. F. Macdonald, ed., *Perception and Identity*

(London: Macmillan, 1979), pp.168–70.

[11] D. Davidson, "Mental Events," in L. Foster and J. Swanson, eds., *Experience and Theory* (London: Duckworth, 1970), pp. 79–101.

[12] Ibid., p. 97.

[13] Ibid., pp.97–98.

[14] "Psychology as Philosophy," in Davidson, *Action and Events* (Oxford: Oxford University Press, 1980), p.231.

[15] Ibid., p.231.

[16] This was pointed out by T. Honderich in "Psychophysical Lawlike Connections and Their Problem," *Inquiry* 24:191–93.

[17] This, in effect, is how C. Peacocke argues for token-identity in his *Holistic Explanation* (Oxford: Oxford University Press, 1979), pp.134–43.

[18] For a fuller exposition of this point, see Robinson, *Matter and Sense*, pp. 8–13.

14

The Embodiment of Mind

Daniel N. Robinson

As we prepare for what now must be the fourth decade of "the decade of the brain" it is timely to step back from the anatomical blowpipes, MRIs, PET scans, low-noise amplifiers and kindred *impedimenta*, and attempt to focus more sharply on what the welter of data have added to that venerable *quaestio vexata*, the MIND/BODY problem. Indeed, before one can even begin to apply the "findings" to attempted solutions to the problem, one must have a settled basis on which to regard the problem as amenable to empirical modes of address and inquiry. (If, in the end, the "problem" would abide in the face of any and every imaginable finding, we would have to conclude that science as such is not the arena in which to seek solutions. Where, then?). Then, too, one must remain satisfied that there really is a problem to begin with, and not just one of those irksome verbal controversies arising out of the discursive eccentricities of philosophers.

Early Morning Colloquies

Riders on the Clapham omnibus are said not to recognize the problem, or to have ready but unhelpful "folk" solutions to it. (We all use this conveyance at one time or another, Clapham being the official destination of the metaphysically challenged). Like Descartes, they find themselves thinking, discover that the activity seems to have no moving parts, no weight or azimuth, and conclude that, though it can't occur without a brain, it isn't merely a biological process. Pressed for proof, one rider notes that he can't control his digestion or his brain processes, but he has at least occasional if fitful control over his thoughts, desires and significant goals. Yet another—this one having read *Scientific American*—recalls how even massive lesions in the brain might have no effect whatever on one's consciousness, problem-solving ability, perception and memory. The corporate CEO, whose Daimler is in the shop for repairs and who thinks the ride is entirely too slow, looks up from the pages of the *Wall Street Journal* and asks, with patent contempt, how a "body" can raise questions about a *mind*! But then, what could the untutored classes know about such things?

It is, of course, something of a moral obligation on the part of those occupying the House of Intellect to challenge the complacent by forcing them to see the counterintuitive or logically incoherent consequences of their beliefs. Thus, with apologies to the CEO, the driver is urged to pull over so that idle thoughts might be refined into something of value. To wit:

Query: If "mind" refers to an immaterial, spaceless entity, how can it causally bring about such *physical* events as, e.g., bodily movements?

Reply from Rider-1: "I don't know". (Then, after a pause...) "Maybe the mind changes the brain in some way".

Query: But, to change the brain, *work* must be done. The laws of thermodynamics prohibit such work to be accomplished without a source of energy. Apparently you don't know about the First Law—which we (this "we" being the academic equivalent of the *royal* we) know as the Law of the Conservation of Energy. How do you take *that* into account?

Reply from Rider-2: (This person had been studiously reading a book throughout and only looked up when the word "thermodynamics" was uttered). "Huh? Er, well, actually, no; that's really got nothing to do with it. You see, the First Law just says—well, the equation is $U + L = Q$ and it's really totally neutral as to the sources or the nature of the energies involved. So if there were some kind of *mental* energy that couldn't be physically measured but nonetheless entered on both sides of the equation, the law would be honored and mentalism, if that's what you call it, would still be defensible".

Query: But don't you see that *everything* in the known universe is subject to the laws of physics? How can you believe that something called your "mental" life isn't?

Reply from Rider-3: "Wait a minute. I thought that's just what we've been discussing; we've been discussing whether or not it actually *is* the case that everything in the known universe is subject to the laws of physics. Maybe "mental" things aren't! Needless to say, *if* everything is subject to the laws of physics, and *if* everything thus subjected must also be some sort of material thing, then *necessarily* there are no "mental" things. But you can't begin with the conclusion, can you? Isn't that committing some sort of fallacy?

CEO-Rider: "Look, I've got a company to run. Can we leave the dock and return to earth?"

Rounding Up The Usual Suspects

Aristotle had quite a good head on his shoulders but nevertheless thought it was a kind of refrigerator. Daniel Dennett, who also has a good head on his shoulders, thinks of his as a kind of computer. We are not at a loss for "solutions" to the MIND/BODY problem. There are about a half-dozen generic ones, each yielding an assortment number of variants. The number and nature of these tend to track developments in science and engineering. Some who would defend a given solution draw their support from the neurology clinic and the neuropsychology laboratory; others from what is called "conceptual analysis"; still others from a larger, grander and essentially religious perspective on the nature and purpose of intelligent life. The "data", so to speak, stand as a constant. The traditional solutions to the MIND/BODY problem endure in part because they've been able to absorb such findings, if not without embarrassment then at least without fatal consequences. As for the solutions themselves, most have been on offer since ancient times. For the sake of economy it will be useful to assign all of them to one or another of three very general theoretical categories: *Causal, Reductive, Perspectival.*

Causal Theories of Mind (or of Body!):

A solution to the MIND/BODY problem is achieved by a *causal* theory when any of the ontological contents presumed to comprise one of the classes requires at least one of the ontological contents of the other class as a causally necessary pre-condition. However so modestly or reluctantly, causal theories are dualistic, for there are no "causes" without "effects". Thus, any and every finding emerging from research on the brain and leading to the conclusion that a given mental process or event or state is the efficient consequent of an identifiable physical process, event or state, is further evidence in support of psychophysical dualism.

The nature of the causality here is obscure, but perhaps no more obscure than it is in the purely physical realm. Thomas Reid, in the eighteenth century, pressed the important distinction between the laws that express a causal relationship and the cause itself. The universal law of gravitation does not disclose just what it is that has bodies attracting each other with a force proportional to the product of their masses; it merely sets forth the rule according to which the cause operates. Reid was satisfied that we are of aware of very few if any *causes*, notwithstanding to the contrary the profound discoveries made by Newton and others regarding the *causal laws* or the rules by which causes operated.

Within the context of MIND/BODY phenomena, there are well known and lawful relationships between, e.g., the discharge-frequencies of sensory nerves and the intensity of the sensations experienced by an observer. The neuroelectric coding of sensory magnitude is a well established scientific fact, but just what *causes* a stimulus thereby to become brighter or louder or heavier is something that perhaps must always be elusive. To acknowledge that "qualia" present a difficulty of some sort is to mislead oneself. Experiences are *sui generis*. Hence Du Bois' famous *Ignorabimus!*

Causal theories, it should be noted, work equally well in either direction. In one direction, they legislate against the possibility of an independently subsisting mental realm. For there to be thought, perception, memory, etc., there must be a physical embodiment of all that is causally necessary to bring these about No matter? Never mind! But this gate swings both ways, as is illustrated famously by Berkeley's utterly successful demonstration that all of the possible attributes of the material world subsist dependently on an ideational ontology. Berkeley does not deny the world of matter; only an independently subsisting world of matter. No mind? No matter!

Reductive Theories

The MIND/BODY problem is solved by a *reductive theory* when any of the ontological contents of one of the allegedly real classes is shown to be part of the contents of the other class, the former now regarded as in fact empty. If it seems to have contents these are only apparent or are installed by misleading figures of speech; by Ryle-type "category mistakes", by "Descartes' myth", by ghosts in the machine, and by yet other seductive illusions. Some tall talk has been offered in defense of reductive theories, but behind the rhetoric one finds veils of ignorance and what John Eccles jauntily called a merely "promissory materialism". Try reading La Mettrie's *l'Homme Machine* without chuckling.

The reductive theories that would now be presented as debate stoppers are *eliminative materialism* (new wine from the Churchland vineyards, poured into ancient casks first shaped by the disciples of Leucippus); the *identity* thesis (curiously compatible with nearly superstitious forms of idealism!); and *supervenience* (which tends to be developed with one too few sentences, as I will suggest). The elminativist and identity-theorist offer a solution to the MIND/BODY problem in the form of a solution to the problem of reference: When Smith reports that he sees a blue light, to what is Smith referring? Note that Smith's report can occur in hallucinatory states; under conditions in which 'blueness' is actually the afterimage of intense stimulation by a yellow light; or while dreaming. But under any of these and under all possible conditions, the actual *reference* of the perception-report is an event or a process in the brain. So, if Smith is referring to *anything* when saying, "I see a blue light", then he is referring to a process in his brain. And, by extension, all "mental" events are just brain processes under a traditional but hopelessly pre-scientific set of descriptions. The "mental" and the "physical" here are not causally related, for there is finally only the physical.

The discursively mental is the ontologically physical. Mental events simply *are* brain processes.

Yes, but then by way of the alleged "identity" brain processes simply *are* mental events, and there would seem to be no empirical way of teasing out the bona fide ontology from its mirror-image. The identity-theory would appear to be the specific target of what might be called "Berkeley's revenge"! Then, too, what sort of "identity" is proposed here? It can't be the (trivial) tautologous identity according to which "3" is identical to "one of the prime numbers". It surely can't be a *necessary* identity, for it is surely conceivable that perceptions might occur where there are no "brain processes". (It is conceivable that paramecia have perceptions and we know paramecia have no brains).

On this same point, it has been argued that what we have here is akin to the Phosphorus-Hesperus conundrum. For centuries even the wise believed that there was a 'morning star' and an 'evening star', thus yielding two stars. But then we discovered that the 'morning star' *just is* the 'evening star'. But the 'morning star' *just is* the 'evening star' because something just is itself. What made the 'morning star' seem like a second star was its appearance only at sunrise, the "other one" coming into view much later. There was nothing 'unstarry' about either of "them", however, and thus no property-problem arose. If seeing a blue light *just is* a brain process, it surely is not as a result of being comparable to the Phosphorus-Hesperus dyad. Again, something is itself *necessarily*; but perceptions (if they *just are* brain processes), are not necessarily brain processes.

The next gambit, then, is to argue that mental events are *contingently* identical to brain processes. Are there (and can there be) "contingent" identities? Saul Kripke thinks not and I think he's right. The exemplum of choice for those who think otherwise is some form of "Someone's on the phone/Smith is on the phone", where "someone" is said to be contingently identical to Smith. This doesn't work in the required way, however, for, although it is certainly true that, of all the persons who might be using the telephone, it is just contingently the case that it is Smith, it makes no sense to say that, of all the persons Smith might be, Smith is contingently himself.

This aside, one still wonders what identity-criteria are adopted by the theory? If the more or less standard textbook criteria are invoked, the identity fails. Leibnitz law of identities (the law of universal substitutivity) takes X and Y to be identical just in case everything truly said of X can be truly and relevantly said of Y without there being any alteration in the truth-value of the statements. But whether or not a stimulus can truly be said to *hurt* depends uniquely on whether or not the percipient says it does. However, whether or not a brain process is or is not of a given nature depends on the unique authority of no one. So, as the expression goes, Smith has an epistemic authority in the matter of his sensations that no one has in the matter of brain processes, meaning that at least Leibnitz identity-criteria are not satisfied.

The eliminativist assures interested parties that mentalistic and introspective psychological terms (psychobabble?) will give way to the precise and public observation-terms as the program of the neural sciences proceeds. Competent discussants will speak of activities in, for example, a specific "cortical triune system" of information-processors instead of prating on about "yellow" and "green". The question arises, however, as to why it is that progress in, say, urology or orthopaedics is not expected to have such an outcome. And the answer, unless I'm mistaken, is that there is no known psychological state, no mental event, reliably associated either with urogenital physiology or with the bones of the body. If, however, perceptual *qualia*, obsessional notions, significant aspirations, or evidence of an examined life were all and reliably correlated with the filling and emptying of the bladder, or with stress on the metacarpals, then presumably the eliminativist would give up on the "cortical triune system" and begin to look south, as it were. Here's a thought-experiment: Imagine a species (Churchlandians) whose intellectual history is the reverse of what we take to be our own: It begins in the positivistic scientific phase and moves toward a religio-mystical one. So it begins by speaking of "cortical triune systems". In relation to what? Absent thoughts, ideas, percepts and the like *as such* there could be no basis whatever on which to favor cortical over urinary systems in an attempt to explain behavior, emotion, cognition, problem-solving, and, alas, intellectual history. It's a non-starter.

The ancient Greek physicists, Aristotle especially, had the notion of *supervenience* and employed it effectively. Thus:

LEVEL OF OBSERVATION   -   THE TABLE
COMPOSITION   -   WOOD
CONSTITUENTS   -   EARTH, AIR, FIRE, WATER
ULTIMATE CONSTITUENTS   -   PRIME MATTER

Tables, then, "supervene" on wood, which supervenes on earth, etc., which ultimately supervene on that most basic of ontological entities, *prime matter*. Note that tables don't "look like" prime matter or, for that matter, like earth, air, fire or water. Nonetheless, prime matter is the ontologically necessary substrate of all that occurs at the level of observation.

Might this reductive model embrace the mental as well? Might the mental "supervene" on the physical? Let's see:

LEVEL OF OBSERVATION   -   PERCEPTIONS
COMPOSITION   -   COLORS, SOUNDS, ODORS
CONSTITUENTS   -   BRAIN STATES?
ULTIMATE CONSTITUENTS   -   SUBATOMIC PARTICLES

But what, then, might subatomic particles "supervene" on if not a congeries of attributes at least in principle accessible to human thought and experience. Somewhere down the metaphysical line subatomic particles themselves, to bear an intelligible relation to what is said to supervene on them, must themselves supervene on an ideational ontology. Berkeley's back again.

Du Bois was a great experimental scientist; an associate of Helmholtz's, a fellow laborer in the fertile laboratory of Johannes Müller. *Ignorabimus* was not the ejaculatory utterance of a scientific know-nothing, but the settled position of one who understood the difference between a fact and a proof. The reality of the mental is the necessary precondition even for challenging it—which is all the *Cogito* was intended to make clear—and thus cannot itself be hostage to some other alleged reality somehow either identical to it or having the power of replacing it.

Perspectival Theories

Early in his philosophical development Bertrand Russell advocated a theory he called *neutral monism*, arguing against any sort of eliminativist alternative that would be won at the price of either material or the mental reality. Russell was more comfortable with a neutral position on just what sort of stuff comprises reality, but insisted that whatever it was there was only one kind of it. There's much to be said for a parsimonious ontology and, as the clock shows that it is only 1996, we can safely predict a future big with surprises regarding matter itself. Perhaps what is taken to be the indubitable sign of the mental will come to be recognized at levels of seemingly material organization now beyond reach and comprehension. That is, the matter-mind dichotomy might come to be understood as we now understand the matter-energy dichotomy; a dichotomy that is *perspectival* rather than ontological; a dichotomy arising not from the very nature of things, but from the particular conditions under which a given sort of thing is observed, and the particular state the thing is in when it is observed.

The MIND/BODY problem is solved by a perspectival theory when the allegedly distinct ontological categories containing x and y respectively are understood as being a single category with x and y differing only as a result of the conditions of observations and the states that yield x-type or y-type attributes. The textbook version of a perspectival theory is the so-called "double aspect" theory. It, too, is older than the hills. Aristotle amply discusses the equally valid but utterly different explanations that might be given to account for anger, for example. The natural scientist will explain such a state on the basis of physiological changes in temperature of certain bodily constituents (e.g., blood), whereas the *"dialektikos"* will understand the condition as arising from the sense that one has been treated unjustly. The victim of a murderous assault is dead *because* his heart is no longer beating; the victim of a murderous assault is dead *because* his heir was desperate for the inheritance. Smith is in a sort of reverie induced by reading a passage from Wordsworth's *Intimations*; Smith is in brain state-X brought about by the activation of neurally coded "memories".

What of such *perspectival* theories and their allegedly reductive consequences? At least as the strategy is applied to the MIND/BODY problem, it is not at all clear that anything of ontological consequence has been "reduced", for the very means by which one has a certain *perspective* presupposes the very dispositions one would plausibly take to be *mental* in the first place. That is, there is an important difference between perceptions of reversible figures (e.g., the Necker cube) and reversing one's perspective. The apparent reversal of sides of the cube in the third dimension is not the result of a cognitive or perspectival disposition but the expression of certain laws or principles of visual habituation, inhibition, etc. But to understand that the fate of the victim of a crime can be explained at once in medical, moral and legal terms is not perceptual at all in any relevant sense. Indeed, both of the "double" aspects—both Smith-as-brain-state and Smith-as-in-reverie—are achieved perspectively such that only a mentalistic thesis would seem to account for what the observer is doing, whatever we might offer as an account of what Smith is doing. It would seem, therefore, that double-aspect theories, far from supporting a monistic ontology, are intelligible and even necessary precisely because the actual ontology is dualistic!

Causal and perspectival theories solve the MIND/BODY problem at no cost to dualism, and reductive theories simply don't work, where "don't work" refers variously to a lack of coherence or credibility or consistency. In all, then, there are no compelling reasons not to be a dualist and quite compelling reasons not to be anything else.

The Ride Home

Frustrated by the failure of the garage to deliver the Daimler the CEO is now even more peevish at the end of the day, maybe even somewhat eager to vent his passions at the expense of the first pest he meets. Back in the bus, he spots the morning's chattering don and mutters audibly, "Oh God, not *him* again!"

Query: Say, some of you were on this bus this morning and there were some things we didn't get to. This so-called mind or mental life you claim for yourselves achieves nothing more than what any powerful computational device can do better and faster. Doesn't this convince you that you're no more than such a device?

Reply from CEO: No, it convinces me that *you're* no more than such a device and I'd love to find out where you're plugged in!

Query: Ah, temper, temper. But the question won't go away. There is nothing in principle in our putatively "mental" life that cannot be accomplished by a properly programmed computer, and there's no warrant for assuming that such a device is "mental". Does that not tell decisively against all forms of dualism?

Reply from Rider-6 (a tall distinguished and sandled man with a look of whimsical and perpetual confusion on his face):

"Actually, this is something on which I've penned a line or two myself. This device of yours must be a formal system of some kind with sufficient power to generate an arithmetic. In that case, and by way of Gödel's Incompleteness Theorem, its performance will depend on at least one axiom that cannot be supplied by the system itself. That is, whatever it achieves will depend on axiomatic principles external to the system. So this must be the limit on all such systems, but it clearly is not a limit—or at least was not a limit—imposed on Gödel. So, you see, the "mental" is distinguishable from the *merely* computational. Oh, by the way, driver, I hope to reach Victoria in time for the 6:30 Oxford Tube".

Reply from Rider-2: "Yes, and there's that Chinese Room business I read about in *Scientific American*. All the computer is doing is functioning as some kind of compiler; it just follows assigned steps without any "mental" comprehension at all. It's not enough to show that a computer gets the same answers we do, but gets them *the way* we do".

Query: And what would your position be just in case such a device or some future and far more powerful version of it were to get answers "the way" you do?

Reply from CEO: I'd hire it! Not *buy* it, mind you, but *hire* it. I might even introduce it to my daughter.

Reply from Rider-3: Exactly, for this would not be a "device" at all, but an intelligent and thinking thing. It would have a *mental life* that must be very much like our own.

Query: But how can you claim that any device has a "mental life"? Here's something that has had none of your experiences, none of your education or associations. It's not in any society or culture. How could it possibly be "like" you?

Reply from CEO: I think he's getting the point.

The Point

If there is a disembodied mode of mental life this cannot be known by any sentient being whose own embodied life requires properly functioning and mediating neurosensory and neurocognitive processes. Accordingly, if claims to the effect that there is such mode of mental life are subjected to the only methods of verification available to embodied beings, the claims will fail of proof *necessarily*. If, however, an embodied entity possesses mental attributes that are neither reducible to the properties and processes of matter nor identical to them—even if causally dependent on them—then ontological dualism is confirmed. The point of interest, then, is not *that* the mental has real existence, but *how* this existence is brought about.

Causation, as noted, is elusive everywhere and is not likely to be pinned down in the mental domain. Huxley's graphic defense of epiphenomenalism availed itself of clocks and bells, as if genuinely mental phenomena could be thus analogized. If consciousness answers to the ringing of a neural bell the answer makes no sound. On the question of just how a complex physical system somehow supports an ineliminably mental life, I stand firmly with Du Bois: *Ignorabimus*!

Does this itself constitute some sort of superstition or atavistic slide? I would argue quite the opposite. It has long seemed to me that a firm belief in the materiality of the mental—a firm skepticism toward the very notion of the mental—was itself a form of superstition; a species of religious zeal that will not quail in the face of reason or daily experience; the utter triumph of hope over reality.

The core beliefs of those who are the authors and the subjects of "Folk Psychology" are grounded in the ageless doings of reflective and intelligent beings who, in the very nature of things, have greater epistemic authority on the matter of their own experiences, feelings and aspirations than all scientists and philosophers who will ever have lived. The blazing irony finds the productions of one set of cognitive and perceptual achievements being used against another set to show that neither is anything but a physical process. One is reminded of old Professor Weigandt's comment on Freud's theory: "This is not a fit subject for academic discussion. This is a reason to call the police!"

Is not the point, then, whether or not one is a theist? Again I would resist so facile an interpretation which sooner or later will fuel an *argumentum ad hominem*. Modern distinctions between the natural and the supernatural are largely the gift of seventeenth and eighteenth century trends in the sciences; trends that would surface in the various scientific "positivisms" advocated by the *philosophes* of the Enlightenment, by Comte, J. S. Mill, Ernst Mach, the Vienna Circle, behaviouristic and materialistic psychologies. Aristotle was not a very good Christian, even if Thomas Aquinas did all he could to save his pagan soul. But Aristotle found no justification for excluding from the realm of the "natural" whatever is a regular and consequential part of the overall scheme of reality. Mental life is not "unnatural", nor is the *polis* itself somehow inauthentic or merely contrived. What figures centrally in the flourishing life of a species must be the result of the order of nature itself. That this very order suggests an intelligent principle at work was obvious to Aristotle who, in his *Physics*, noted that, "If the art of shipbuilding were in the wood, we would have ships by nature".

If a lonely and tiny planet within an immense universe has come to host a staggering variety of sentient beings, dazzling in their beauty and complexity and in the overall harmonious patterns of life they've achieved, and if all this has come about through what are finally random collisions of matter, then I, for one, not only believe in the miraculous but would claim to have proof of it!

In matters of this sort the extreme positions are to be eschewed. One extreme is occupied by members of the "nothing-but" school. Apart from the simplistic and hubristic philosophical impertinences emanating from such precincts real harm is either done or countenanced. Descartes, insisting that non-human animals are irrational and essentially mechanical devices, not only diminished his own reputation but put in place a philosophical justification for acts of torture and violence that continue to this day. Those who would absorb humanity into a totally physical ontology, treating morality, justice, aesthetics and political life as but fictions of discourse, would surely not want to be treated in a manner that such a theory would sanction. At the other extreme are found those whose intellectual inlets are closed to all traffic that does not fly the doctrinally "correct" flag. Three centuries of witch-persecutions should have a chastening effect on those claiming such certainty, but such is not the case. The zealot is lost without an enemy. Between these extremes is that massive majority that each faction would seek to convert. If they move chiefly on the Clapham omnnibus rather than on the weightless wings of thought, so also do they move in ways that would foster a better, a richer civic life in which decency counts for more than metaphysical agility. By and large, they are easily gulled, easily tamed by experts in science, philosophy, religion, engineering, computer science, and the like. But when it comes to telling them, one and all, what is in their minds and hearts and hopes, on these matters they become stubborn to the point of rudeness. On these matters, Smith knows more about his toothache than his dentist does or can or ever will. Try as the expert may, Smith reserves the right to say, "No, that's not really what I think at all. And that really isn't why I went there, though my original plan changed in the process. And, no, this is not something you can confirm by consulting anyone else, or anything else, or even my own brain. For if my brain says otherwise, my brain is wrong".

May such refractoriness be deathless!

15

Philosophy of God and Mind: Theism and the Queerness of Consciousness

Charles Taliaferro

J.L. Mackie developed an argument against moral realism he called "the argument from queerness" (Mackie 1977, pp.3842). He contended that the existence of objective values would be queer or, to use less colorful language, objective values would be unique and unlikely given a materialist understanding of the cosmos. "If there were objective values, then they would be entities or qualities or relations of a very strange sort, utterly different from anything else in the universe" (Ibid., p.38). A similar thesis about the existence of consciousness is advanced by many in the philosophy of mind. Some philosophers contend that the existence of consciousness is itself an entity, quality or relation of a very strange sort, utterly different from anything else in the universe. Some of these philosophers are called "eliminativists" because of their project of eliminating "consciousness" and other mental states from a comprehensive view of the world. Others are considered noneliminative materialists (or identity materialists) because while they allow for the existence of consciousness and various mental states (beliefs, hopes, fears and so on), they maintain that all such mental life is describable and explainable within the natural sciences. By their lights, the mental is the physical, and it would be queer to think of the mental as nonphysical.

Various forms of dualism, according to which consciousness or persons themselves are nonphysical but materially embodied, are often given short shrift in the literature. In *Kinds of Minds* Daniel Dennett describes and dismisses dualism in one blow. Dualism is the "view that minds are composed of some non-physical and ultimately mysterious stuff... relegated to the trash heap of history, along with alchemy and astrology" (Dennett 1996, p.24). Dennett elsewhere lampoons nonmaterialist opponents as "cartoon characters" (Dennett 1993, p.135).

There are many reasons for the widespread dismissal for dualism. I believe at least three factors are at play behind the current disdain for dualism. First, I believe there is a failure to appreciate that dualism is compatible with the findings of the physical sciences. Second, dualism is often caricatured in the literature as promoting a disjointed, fragmented, bodyhating view of human nature. In the modern literature, this is the preeminent character of Gilbert Ryle's *The Concept of Mind* (1949). Unfortunately, Ryle's explicit project of deliberately caricaturing dualism is alive and well (Ryle 1949). In my view, there is no reason to think dualism is saddled with this misshapened portrait; dualism can instead underwrite a profoundly integrated view of embodied persons (Taliaferro 1994). And third, I believe that many who reject dualism fail to take seriously the prospects of an alternative, overarching, nonmaterialist metaphysic. That is, some of the arguments for and against dualism are carried out as though the debate is over a relatively localized philosophical terrain and not as a debate that is connected with the deepest of one's philosophical commitments.

This paper touches on each of these topics, beginning with this last one. I contend that the case for dualism can gain considerable support from theism, for theism provides an alternative framework in which one may understand the emergence of consciousness as something natural and not unlikely or unique. One of the goals of this paper is to outline a position similar to George Mavrodes' in his reply to Mackie, "Religion and the Queerness of Morality" (1986). Mavrodes argued that moral realism is not "queer" if seen against a theistic backdrop, whereas it does seem odd if seen in the context of Mackie's or Bertrand Russell's naturalism. Following Mavrodes' example, I contend that what Dennett and other critics of dualism dismiss as a cartoon looks more like an accurate picture of our lives, once the debate over consciousness is placed in a broader context and some of the views wrongly associated with dualism are shaken loose.

There are four sections in what follows. The first considers the metaphysical background to the debate over consciousness, focusing on theism and naturalism. A second section notes some of the problems with eliminative materialism. A third section examines some problems with materialist theories that are less radical than eliminativism, but still identify the mental with the physical. A fourth section develops an argument for dualism and concludes with observations about the prospects of a combined dualisttheistic philosophy.

Clearly this paper covers a great deal of territory, and so at points I develop the arguments in a succinct fashion. I also narrow the scope of the paper by attending to Paul Churchland's materialist account of persons in *The Engine of Reason, the Seat of the Soul*. Dennett's and other materialists' works are referenced and discussed, but greater focus is given to Churchland's arguments for they are upheld by a wide range of contributors to the literature and there is not space to survey an array of figures. Churchland's work also has the advantage of containing arguments for eliminativism as well as for the identity theory. His view seems to be that whichever view is elected in philosophy of mind, be sure that it is not dualism.[1]

(I) Background assumptions in the philosophy of mind

If one assumes a thoroughgoing, exclusively physical beginning to the cosmos, then positing consciousness as an emergent nonphysical reality seems to face a weighty burden of proof. Churchland utilizes a physicalist cosmology to ground his subsequent physicalist treatment of persons and their mental states.

> Most scientists and philosophers would cite the presumed fact that humans have their origins in 4.5 billion years of purely chemical and biological evolution as a weighty consideration in favor of expecting mental phenomena to be nothing but a particularly exquisite articulation of the basic properties of matter and energy (Churchalnd 1995, p.211).

Against such a cosmic scenario, Churchland develops his eliminativist project, according to which all mental events (thoughts, feelings, sensations) must either be categorized as physical or eliminated from our view of the cosmos. Daniel Dennett adopts a similar position. From the vantage point of a fundamentally materialist cosmology, the emergence of consciousness seems strange; it is likened to claiming "then a miracle happens" (Dennett 1993, p.141). Because of background physicalist assumptions about the structure and origin of the cosmos, dualism looks particularly out of character—as does any view of human life that exempts us in whole or in part from the natural sciences.

In light of this philosophy of the origin of humanity and the universe, Dennett privileges explanations of nature that are, at base, nonmental and make no use of mental terms like "consciousness," "intelligence," and "purpose." In his view, a fully satisfactory explanation of human intelligence requires that one not invoke ever increasingly intelligent forces to account for human intelligence and the cosmos tout court, but, rather, one accounts for intelligence in categories that do not involve intelligence at all. Dennett contends that explanatory accounts that leave intelligence unexplained are question begging.

> The account of intelligence required of psychology must not of course be question begging. It must not explain intelligence in terms of intelligence, for instance by assigning responsibility for the existence of intelligence in creatures to the munificence of an intelligent Creator (Dennett 1978, p.83).

Dennett's position feeds into the project of securing the unity of science. By explaining intelligence in categories that do not invoke it, one can aim to unify the kinds of explanations used in science. By comparison, dualists seem left with intelligence *plus all the rest*; the mental appears to dangle. In the 1960s materialists castigated dualists with leaving "nomological danglers," items that simply did not fit in with a unified theory of the laws of nature. Some 30 years later Dennett sets forth the conditions for a unified, materialist theory of human life in succinct terms: "Only a theory that explained conscious events in terms of unconscious events could explain consciousness at all" (Dennett 1991, p.454).

It is common to take what is termed here "the argument from queerness" in the philosophy of mind to establish a burden of proof on those who introduce nonmaterial forces. Of course some burdens of proof may be overcome, and a natural question is whether the burden has indeed been met by appealing to the lived experience of consciousness, thinking, feeling, and the like. Churchland, Dennett, and many others think not. Marvin Minsky represents this latter camp as he counsels caution in employing ordinary psychological terms in scientific theorizing.

> [T]hough prescientific idea terms like 'believe,' 'know' and 'mean' are useful in daily life, they seem too coarse to support powerful theories; we need to supplant rather than to support and explicate them. Real as 'self' or 'understand' may seem to us today, they are not (like milk and sugar) objective things our theories must accept and explain; they are only first steps toward better concepts (Minsky 1980, p.439).

Daniel Dennett likewise seeks to dispel confidence in what appears to some to be the irrefutable experience of beliefs and desires (1978, p.xx and elsewhere). Stich (1983) and others concur.

But let us now drop back and reconsider the metaphysical terrain. Churchland views the person as "a particularly exquisite articulation of the basic properties of matter and energy," but it was not too long ago that a majority of philosophers in the West viewed the human person as a particularly exquisite articulation of God. Churchland seems aware of the linkage between dualism and theism for he refers to "the religious hypothesis of mind-body dualism" (p.18). I believe that in developing a joint case for dualism and theism with its deep intentional explanation behind everything ("the munificence of an intelligent Creator," in Dennett's phrase), one can advance a theory of nature that is both diverse and unified: diverse in terms of the variety of things that exist but unified by the comprehensive intention of God to create and sustain this diversity. The workings of both the physical and mental in creation are thereby viewed as the creation of an encompassing, all good, powerful intelligence. A comprehensive theistic philosophy offers an alternative framework in which the emergence of consciousness is natural and not some freak occurrence. In short, theism can dispel the notion that consciousness is "queer" and in doing so it outlines a fundamentally unified philosophy. The strategy of a *religious* hypothesis of mind-body dualism here is similar to one in the philosophy of religion about miracles. Miracles are unusual, indeed, but the case against them can partly (and perhaps only partly) be met by taking into account theories of nature and God according to which all laws of nature are accountable by God's activity. The Enlightenment, rationalist objection to miracles is largely constructed on prior, naturalistic assumptions. An effective defense of miracles cannot flinch, but must challenge the naturalistic starting point and defend a comprehensive worldview. So, the strategy proposed here is to not leave unchallenged a naturalistic framework which from the very start makes dualism Pickwickian.

I believe that one of the reasons why this standoff between theism and naturalism is unappreciated is partly due to a failure to take seriously the breadth and power of theistic explanations and a related, disparaging view of the power of mental life. A good representative of someone who seems to underestimate both is Brian O'Shaughnessy.

> Well, four centuries of triumphant advance by the rockbottom physical sciences of physics cannot but leave some mark on philosophy. When you can predict the wave length of a spectrum line to eight decimal places it is rather more difficult to believe that the underlying reality of everything is spiritual, e.g. an immaterial Deity. After all, should a Deity be so fastidious? (O'Shaughnessy 1980, vol.1, p.xvii).

I offer a twofold response, first highlighting the resources of theism and then taking note of the power of mental life.

The Resources of Theism:

Contra O'Shaughnessy's comment about God, I note that few, if any, philosophical theists today or in the history of philosophy have thought God was anything other than maximally precise in knowledge and creation. Anselm of Canterbury provides a classic statement of the unparalleled magnitude of divine omniscience (*Proslogium* VI) as did Thomas Aquinas (*Summa Theologiae*, 1a.14.7). Earlier Augustine mocked the supposition that God might lose track of the details of creation, forgetting the number of planets and so on. "For God I think it is no great matter to count all the stars. Or doth He perhaps go over the number, lest he forget it? Is it any great thing for God to number the stars, by whom 'the very hairs of your head are numbered?'...His understanding surpasses all calculators" (Augustine 1989, p. 666, 667).[2] The better critics of theism have always taken this high view of divine omniscience and creativity seriously. Witness, for example, Ludwig Feuerbach's biting comment: "A God who is injured by determinate qualities has not the courage and the strength to exist... An existence in general,

356 *Philosophy of God and Mind*

an existence without qualities, is an insipidity, an absurdity" (1957, pp.1517). Indeed, historically, many scientists have described their task as trying to approximate and measure up to the precision of God's thoughts and intentions (see references in R.A. Varghese 1992).

Some critics of theism appear to work with very weak estimates of the scope of God's intentions. Thus Mackie argues for the improbability of the thesis that God has direct access to all that exists, but this is built on an analogy with human intelligence and not based on an appeal to any conceptual restraints on the magnitude and precision of God's cognition and will. In general, I believe that any philosophical theism worth defending must take the high ground: If theism is true, then God's intentions are maximally precise (Swinburne 1994 and Morris 1991).

The Power of Mental Life:

O'Shaughnessy and others have sometimes assumed that the categories employed to describe our mental life (beliefs, desires and so on) are too coarse to be used to describe the precise determinate details of the physical world. By way of a rejoinder, theists may find a strange ally among nonrealists. According to many versions of nonrealism (quasirealism, internal realism), all our scientific categories with their 8 decimal measurements are themselves the result of our mental powers, our concepts and frameworks. Hilary Putnam, among many others, insists that "'Objects' do not exist independently of conceptual schemes" (Putnam 1981, p.52). Paul Feyerabend, Michael Dummett, Nelson Goodman, may also be used here in stressing how the sciences are themselves human activities. I do not wish to endorse a version of nonrealist theism here. I only note how some nonrealist philosophers have brought to light the richness and power of the mental in general and, insofar as they are successful in highlighting this richness they show that at least one objection to theism can be effectively challenged.

So, I propose that the prospects of theism and dualism be weighed together. Theism has greater resources than some of its critics grant, so linking the two is not like tying an albatross around the dualist's neck. (See Taliaferro 1997 for further reflections on the coherence and plausibility of theism.) Stephen Jay Gould comments "If mind has no real existence beyond the brain, can God be anything more than an illusion invented by an illusion?" (Gould, 1977, p.25). If there is some plausibility in believing that God is not an illusion beyond the brain, can acknowledging the existence of the mind be far behind?

(II) Some challenges facing Eliminative Materialism

In this section I note some of the difficulties facing eliminative materialism. My focus is on the moral and cognitive problems and I offer a modest ethical argument as to why one should not adopt a full scale eliminativism. First, however, I reproduce Paul Churchland's eliminativism as found in his *The Engine of Reason, the Seat of the Soul*. The eliminative project emerges as part of a humanistic effort to live in an ethical "nurturing" fashion, and the project comes to the fore in stages.

Churchland's book is designed to exhibit some of the ways in which contemporary science can shed light on humanistic concerns.

> One's first impulse, perhaps, is to see the vocabulary and framework of a general theory of the brain as something alien and cold. But it will not be alien if it depicts all of us, at last, as we truly are... Whatever the distractions, we must continue to exercise our reason. And whatever the temptations we must continue to nurture our souls. That is why understanding the brain is so supremely important. It is the engine of reason. It is the seat of the soul (p.324).

Talk of nurturing the soul seems a long way from talk of neuronets, but Churchland sees the two languages as fitting and important. Churchland asks: "How does the brain work? How *does* it sustain a thinking, feeling, dreaming self?" (p.xi) This seems to involve a straightforward acknowledgment of the reality of thinking, feeling, and dreaming, and a unitary subject that engages in each. Indeed, some of Churchland's depictions of the findings of the brain sciences seem compatible with a philosophy of mind and body that is either a form of *none*liminative materialism or even dualism.

> [W]e are now in a position to explain how our vivid sensory experience arises in the sensory cortex of our brains: how the smell of baking bread, the sound of an oboe, the taste of a peach, and the color of a sunrise are all embodied in a vast chorus of neural activity (p.3).

Reference to how a psychological phenomena "arises" suggests a distinction between the psychological and physical, and talk of "embodiment" seems as at home in theories by noneliminative materialists as it is with dualist theories that uphold the metaphysical distinction between the mental and physical and yet insist upon their causal interaction. But this open-ended description of the mind and body is soon put aside.

One of the themes of Churchland's book is that our typical theory or working assumption about ourselves needs to be radically revised in light of the natural sciences. Churchland has elsewhere construed dualism as "mankind's official view of itself" and so it is often his foil in the course of his arguments for a thoroughgoing materialism (Churchland 1979, p.64).

> Is our basic conception of human cognition and agency yet another myth, moderately useful in the past perhaps, yet false at edge or core? Will a proper theory of brain function present a significantly different or incompatible portrait of

human nature? ... I am inclined toward positive answers to all of these questions (p.19).

Churchland assumes that the average reader, or newcomer to the field, is not an eliminativist when it comes to sensations, beliefs, perceptions, desires, and preferences. Following a current convention, Churchland refers to the assumption that these items exist as a case of "folk psychology."

> You came to this book assuming that the basic units of human cognition are states such as thoughts, beliefs, perceptions, desires, and preferences. That assumption is natural enough: it is built into the vocabulary of every natural language... These assumptions are central elements in our standard conception of human cognitive activity, a conception often called "folk psychology" to acknowledge it as the common property of folks generally. Their universality notwithstanding, these bedrock assumptions are probably mistaken (p.322).

This is a radical claim; it takes us some distance beyond the customary attack on dualism. Churchland claims that the disposal of such folk "bedrock assumptions" and the building up of an alternative, scientificallyinformed understanding of human nature will lead us to new insights into moral life. New scientific discoveries can "set us free, and allow us to achieve a still higher level of moral insight and mutual care" (pp.17,18). He endorses a form of moral realism and indicates his preference for an Aristotelian as opposed to Kantian ethic. Brain and physiological testing provide Churchland with evidence that moral judgments on specific cases comes prior to our grasping and applying moral rules.

Regrettably, it is not clear how Churchland can succeed both in advancing eliminativism and redeeming the promise that it will assist us in an effort to "nurture our souls" and care for one another. Obviously the brain sciences can assist us insofar as they enable us to treat physiological illness and the organic basis for psychological dysfunction. They can provide the noneliminative philosopher with insights as to the material underpinnings of our mental life. But it is not clear how we can make use of notions like "assist," "care" and so forth, if we must shed bedrock assumptions about thoughts, beliefs, perceptions, desires, and preferences. In most contexts, "care," "compassion," and "love" appear to make sense only within a context of beliefs and desires. At a minimum, love between persons seems to involve beliefs about oneself, beliefs about the other person and some desire for the other's well being. In *The Engine of Reason, the Seat of the Soul* we are not given a clear guide as to how what, in folk language, we refer to as "love," "care," "compassion," and so on, can be given any purchase in an eliminative world.

Churchland does not see a problem here and, perhaps to put on display his settled view on the compatibility of eliminativism and his philosophy of personal relations, he includes several personal allusions in the text. There is, for example, a photograph of his daughter and her "soulmate," which is then analyzed in terms of retinavisual cortex interaction (p.58 and following). And there is figure 7.1, an MRI image of Patricia Churchland's brain (p.155). Paul Churchland comments: "This particular brain is in fact well known to me via more conventional informational pathways. It is the brain of my wife and colleague, Patricia Churchland, and it is very dear to me" (p.155). But if we shed folk psychology, what are we to make philosophically of the claim that anyone is dear to anyone? Consider the plight of Roland, a fictional character in A.S. Byatt's novel *Possession.*

> Roland had learned to see himself, theoretically, as a crossing place for a number of systems, all loosely connected. He had been trained to see his idea of his 'self' as an illusion, to be replaced by a discontinuous machinery and electrical messagenetwork of various desires, ideological beliefs and responses, languageforms and hormones and pheromones. Mostly he liked this. He had no desire for any strenuous Romantic self-assertion (Byatt 1990, p.459).

In the novel, Roland does not know how to fall in love. The failure even to be interested in such a fall seems natural given a view of persons that denies they have thoughts, references, beliefs and so on.

Something like Pascal's wager can be formulated that can, I believe, tip the scales in the direction of folk psychology. What follows is a condensed version of such a wager.

Assume, if only for the sake of argument, that folk psychology is essential for moral practice. That is, for there to be moral truths like killing innocent persons is wrong or compassion is good, there must be beliefs, desires, preferences, and feelings of the kind that elminativists target (see Kim 1985). Assume the further position of someone who is deciding between eliminativism and a combination of folk psychology and moral realism. Imagine the evidence seems equally weighted and our would-be betting person, Jane, thinks that if the folk world is real then moral realism is true, whereas if there is no folk world there is no fact of the matter about the moral rightness or wrongness of any action. Let 'A' stand for the truth of moral realism and folk psychology and 'B' for eliminativism, viz. the falsehood of folk psychology and moral realism. Jane desires to promote good and prevent evil. The wager may now be cast as follows: Imagine Jane opts for A and A is true. Great gains are in the offing in that it is likely good is done, ill avoided. Imagine A is elected and yet it is false. There is no big loss if eliminativism is true, for there is no pain and sorrow. Imagine Jane chooses B and B is true. There is no personal loss or gain because there is no pain, sorrow, pleasure, good or evil. Imagine Jane chooses B and it is false. At best, perhaps by accident, no great harms are done, but certainly there would be no point to promoting good if you think there is no such thing. To the morally conscientious person, there are reasons of a moral kind to elect for 'A' rather than 'B.'

Obviously, this wager can be challenged. Perhaps eliminativists can articulate some "successor-terms" by which to underwrite moral realism. At the present stage, however, it is not clear what these successor-terms amount to. The wager needs to be read as a wager that is restricted to the choice at hand, namely Jane's (I believe, quite reasonable) subjective apprisal of the options. The wager argument can be improved to the extent that one can plausibly argue that the person making the wager can control her/his beliefs, but even if not it can carry some weight as far as prompting persons to at least act on certain folk assumptions.[3]

Notwithstanding the pride of place that Churchland gives to the moral benefits of the position he defends, I think the overall, eliminative project gives rise to considerable worries about whether the brain (or "enbrained body," to use an awkward phrase) as Churchland describes it can indeed function as an engine for reason.

It is difficult to conceive of how reasoning can survive in an eliminativist framework. In a world that eliminates the intentional world of folk psychology, how can one make sense of reasoning? In a standard case of reasoning, one accepts a conclusion in virtue of believing the premises of an argument and acting on one's grasp of the nature of entailment. Jane accepts conclusion B, because she believes that "If A then B" and she believes there is compelling evidence that A. I am skeptical about whether reasoning can be given any intelligible place in our view of what we do when we undertake philosophical reflection (or any other norm-governed reflection in which conclusions are derived on the basis of beliefs) if one does away with beliefs or, if one acknowledges the existence of beliefs and yet gives them no role to play in a causal explanation of why, say, Jane reasons as she does. Thus, even when Churchland permits (if only as by way of marking a starting point for further analysis) attributions of "beliefs" in describing our activities, I contend that these beliefs are not given a sufficient role to describe and explain (what at least appears to be) our reflection—our coming to hold certain beliefs on the basis of others. Here, I think Churchland's privileging of physics and chemistry causes problems. He is careful to limit causal accounts to physics and chemistry.

> I do not mean to suggest that social properties are anything more, ultimately, than just intricate aspects of the purely physical world. Nor do I wish to suggest that they are independent causal properties over and above what is captured by physics and chemistry (p.131).

But unless physics and chemistry include the stuff of reason and beliefs (which, at least in conventional versions of physics and chemistry, they do not), I do not see how Churchland can do justice to our capacities to reason and argue rationally.

Obviously this argument admits of various replies and it is not possible to go over all moves, pro and con.[4] I note only that one reply seems to be ruled out by Churchland and other eliminativists. Some philosophers adopt noncausal theories of agency, and simply hold that reasoning is not the sort of thing that admits of causal analysis (e.g. Fred Stoutland's noncausal theory of agency). If the stronger aim of eliminativism is secured, however, then it appears that there is no such thing as reasoning at all, causal or noncausal.

(III) Some Problems with reductionism

As noted above, Churchland is an eliminativist, but he also advances various arguments that if the mental does exist then it turns out to be physical. What follows in this section is a modest defense of those Churchland attacks who uphold the ineliminability and irreducibility of the mental. I comment on Churchland's dismissal of a dualist thought experiment taken from Leibniz' work, an argument from analogy designed to disperse the appeal of subjectivity, his specific criticism of Thomas Nagel and Frank Jackson, and, finally, I offer a brief defense of modified privileged access to mental states. Obviously, given limited space, the observations that follow are extremely compressed. A common thread in these observations is the conviction that Churchland has not given sufficient weight to the subjective character of the mental.

Dualist Thought Experiment.

Consider first Churchland's description and dismissal of Leibniz' thought experiment taken from *The Monadology* (published in 1713). Leibniz asks us to imagine that we are so reduced in size that we can examine first-hand the brain of a wide awake subject; we can stroll through his brain as one might stroll through a mill. Would we see the subject's thinking and feeling? Arguably not. Dualists make much of the charge that we would not directly observe any such thoughts or feelings (whether seen from the post of a reduced, Leibnizian or from the vantage point of neuroscience) and utilize this in arguing for the distinction between the physical and mental. Churchland replies:

> It remains possible, even granting Leibniz' story, that the taste sensation of a peach is identical with a four-element activation vector in the gustatory pathways. And it remains possible that, should you and I happen to know what vectors constitute what sensations, and should we happen to know where and how to look for those activation vectors, then we might recognize those sensations, from our mite-like perspective, as they go by (p. 193).

This is in line with Churchland's claim about locating sensations elsewhere in the book, when he compares the taste of peaches and apricots.

This is why the tastes of those two fruits are so similar: the subjective taste just is the activation pattern across the four types of tongue receptors, as rerepresented downstream in one's taste cortex, and the peach pattern differs from the apricot pattern by only a few percentage points in each of the four dimensions (p.23).

But in knowing what peaches taste like and knowing the location and character of a four-element activation vector, are we attending to two distinguishable processes (properties or activities), or just one? I believe that a natural (and plausible) view is that we do not know, nor can we observe, the *constitution* of one by the other, but, rather, we can take note of the link, the interaction or "embodiment," if you will, of the one by and in the other. We do not observe the taste in the pattern or the brain pattern in reflecting on the taste, but, so it appears, we may well discover that the two are intimately, causally connected such that the differences in taste are causally explained (in part) by the proximity, configuration and speed of brain activity. As many dualists argue, one can conceive of subjective properties like *being such that one tastes peaches* without conceiving of *being gustatory pathway XYZ* (however this is described in the language of current physics and chemistry) and this is an important ground for concluding that the properties are distinct. I have defended an intentional distinction of properties elsewhere (see Taliaferro 1994, chapters one and two). If this criterion is plausible, then one has grounds for regarding the relevant mental and nonmental, physical properties as distinct. For scientific and other practical purposes, one may well elect to treat the two as a single thing, but it remains a philosophically substantial issue as to whether one should collapse the two metaphysically. This is the point that many dualists have made: correlation is not equivalent to identity (e.g. the older generation of 20th century dualists: H.D. Lewis, A.C. Ewing, C.A. Campbell, C.J. Ducasse et al, and "the next generation," e.g. Richard Swinburne, W.D. Hart *et al*). Correlation is a necessary but not sufficient condition for identity. Even correlation in all possible worlds does not amount to identity (presumably the properties *being the successor of 5* and *being the smallest perfect number* are distinct but necessarily coextensive).[5]

An Argument from analogy:

Churchland objects that dualists who resist identifying the mental and physical are no different from a stubborn vitalist who assumes that life must be different from what one observes in the natural sciences. This objection may be cast as an argument from analogy. I believe Churchland's analogy between dualist and vitalist arguments is shaky. Notice first Churchland's depiction of a vitalist claim.

However closely you might watch these molecular structures folding, unfolding, hooking together, unhooking, and drifting aimlessly around in the soup, it is obvious that you would never observe the impulse of life that urges its growth; you would never observe the telos of life that knows and guides its species-specific development (p.192).

The problem is that if vitalism is understood as asserting that there is such a thing as knowing, felt urges, guidance on the basis of some grasp of (or maybe belief in) purpose and so on, then the difficulty of identifying these with physical processes observed in the natural sciences is very much in place. It is only because the concept of "life" as it is employed by most contemporary biologists seems to be a straightforward non-mental category (defined in terms of cell replication and so on) that there is no philosophical puzzle about the claim to observe life or identify it with physical processes. The question remains, however, whether the dualist position about our own (and some nonhuman animal) mental lives should be jettisoned as quickly as we have given up thinking of "life" itself in quasimental terms. It is one thing to give up the notion that "life" should be understood in mental categories and another to give up the notion that our thinking, believing, feeling, sensing and the like should be understood in *bona fide* mental categories, distinguishable from the physical world disclosed in the natural sciences.

Objections to the Appeal to Subjectivity:

Churchland dismisses antieliminative arguments advanced by Thomas Nagel and Frank Jackson. Some of their arguments are built on the thesis that there are distinct ways of knowing about world; the mental is disclosed in a privileged, immediate fashion, whereas the physical is publicly observable. In brief, they appeal to the apparent fact that there is a felt quality that characterizes sensory awareness and our other mental states. There is a *what-it-feels-like* to experience pain, see colors and so on. If they are right, there is a nonpropositional state of awareness, a felt way things are, involved with mental life. Churchland thinks the arguments introduced by Nagel, Jackson, and others, involves "a conflation between different *ways of knowing* on the one hand, and different *things known* on the other" (p.201). To bring to light his point, Churchland notes how the same physical state, the location of one's limbs for example, can be known in different ways.

> Here, however, the object of knowledge is exactly the same from both perspectives, the subjective and the objective, and it is something paradigmatically physical: the configuration of your body and limbs (p.197).

Other analogies involve access to one's bladder, bowls, stomach, micromuscles in one's skin, lungs, flushed skin, and so on.

Such examples can be tripled, quadrupled, and more, but these eight will serve to make the point. The existence of a proprietary, firstperson epistemological access to some phenomenon does not mean that the accessed phenomenon is nonphysical in nature. It means only that someone possesses an information-carrying causal connection to that phenomenon, a connection that others lack (p.198).

Has Churchland thereby defeated Nagel's appeal to subjectivity? I do not think so.

The different ways of knowing the object(s) Churchland cites by feeling it oneself rather than not feeling it and knowing it in some other way, e.g. observing it scientifically, constitute different things that are knowable. To know the feel of one's flushed cheeks is different as a feeling than knowing what it looks like from a few yards away. The point of arguments like Nagel's is that the perspectives of the mental and physical are different sorts of things (where a "thing" is understood broadly to cover properties, activities, processes, and not limited to concrete individual substances). Insofar as Churchland allows that there truly is a difference between the subjective apprisal of one's body, desires, tastes, and knowing about these in other ways, by external observation, say, then he is paying homage to the kind of subjectivity that philosophers like Nagel seek to bring to light. Churchland's reference to "information carrying processes" to cover both first person observation and the observations that are registered in the language of physics and chemistry tends to override the radical differences in the mental as gleamed, on the one side, in our first person feeling and subjective apprisal of our own states and attitudes, and, on the other, that which is depicted in physics and chemistry. The distinct reality that is manifested in subjectivity is not exhausted by citing its information content; its content is nonpropositional. Even when one is thinking propositionally, I suggest there is a felt awareness of the process (there is *qualia* or what its like to thinking). Apprehending information is a matter of subjective awareness (Strawson 1994).

Churchland's disregard of the subjectivity of the mental emerges in his depiction of what he depicts as a massive confusion. He examines a microwave instruction book and complains about its confused metaphysics. The manual includes this claim:

> The microwaves agitate and vibrate the moisture molecules at such a great rate that friction is created; the friction, in turn, creates heat and the heat causes the food to cook (p.207).

Churchland comments:

> This raises a problem: how to connect heat with the rest of what is going on. Here the authors fall back on their prescientific folk understanding of one of the many things that can cause heat: friction! The result is massively misleading to

the innocent reader, who is left with the impression that rubbing two molecules together causes heat in the same way that rubbing your two hands together causes heat (p.207).

There is a confusion in the manual, but I take issue with Churchland's diagnosis.

The puzzle created by the manual results because it can be read as switching from talk of "heat" as molecules in motion to talk of "heat" as a feeling of warmth, and then the manual appears to revert back to talk about molecules in motion. In outlining how a microwave cooks (though not how microwaved food tastes) there is no more need to invoke feelings of warmth than there is a need to invoke vitalistic talk of "urges" when describing the growth of a tree. Instead of playing into Churchland's hands, I believe his pointing to an awkwardness in the manual brings to the fore an awkwardness of entirely dispensing with folk, subjective notions of warmth. I suggest we do wind up with a truncated and unsatisfactory theory of what it feels like to be warm if we were to construct a manual on rubbing hands together using Churchland's data that only referred to molecular friction. In a sense, then, Churchalnd's use of the example can be turned around. He seems to acknowledge there is a difference between "heat" when this is engendered by rubbing hands and "heat" when this designates molecules in motion when no sentient being is in the vicinity. Advocates of Nagel's et al would pay him the compliment of taking up this distinction more seriously, though they would carry it to a conclusion Churchland would reject.

A modest defense of privileged access:

Finally, in this section, consider Churchland's case against the notion that the mental cannot be indubitable. On this point he claims that the traditional model "cannot possibly be true" (p.319). The tradition seems to hold that we know the mental immediately, with certainty (directness and indubitability). And yet no neural system can have this. Churchland's argument can be represented in the following way, set up to refute the first premise. (Passages cited are from p.319.)

(1) "The mind knows itself directly and indubitably."

(2) "[N]eural networks have automatic and certain knowledge of their own cognitive activities"

(3) "A neural network has no direct or automatic knowledge of anything at all, let alone of its own cognitive activities."

(4) '1' is false.

The indubitability thesis has indeed been attacked by a host of philosophers. But it has also been defended with some nuance specifying types of awareness and the like. A modest claim is that there are certain mental states in which a subject cannot but know of this state while in it; the state is self-presenting (to use

Roderick Chisholm's term for this rock bottom certainty). On this view, one cannot be in excruciating, piercing pain without knowing it. If this is not true of any neural or other physical network, then one may have reason to discount an identity of the two. Churchland notes at some length the problem of a bodily infallibility.

> [F]or a neural network to have knowledge of any particular domain is for it to have acquired an expertise in discriminating some important and recurring set of features within that domain.. This requires in turn the development of a suitable configuration of synaptic connection weights, one that partitions the network's neuronal activation space into a useful set of categories...But there is nothing "automatic" about the network's grasp of the target domain, whatever that domain might happen to be. Success still requires development of an appropriate configuration of synaptic connection weights... Neither will the exercise of that acquired cognitive capacity ever yield "certain" knowledge, as the tradition claims. Nothing ever guarantees that the category or the prototype activated on some occasion must be a correct or an accurate representation of the input reality that led to its activation. Networks are always hostage to the possibility of error (p.320).

This opens the way for the following dualist strategy: Allow for lots of fallibility with respect to knowledge claims about many first person mental states and yet claim that there are at least some mental states that one cannot but know, e.g. I cannot be in excruciating pain without knowing it. If this is plausible, the tradition seems to be in less of a sad condition than Churchland has demonstrated. Churchland leaves open the possibility of revising "1" to:

> *Some* mental states are such that it is impossible for a subject to be in those states without knowing it.

If there are plausible cases that fit this condition, and nothing can fill this bill physically, then some form of dualism would be secured.[6]

(IV) A Humble Argument for Dualism

There are a host of reasons for adopting a dualist philosophy of persons. I shall simply outline one here, a version of Descartes' famous modal argument.

If persons are the very same thing as their bodies then whatever is true of their bodies must be true of them. This follows the law of the indiscernability of identicals; if A is B, then there is nothing true of A that is not true of B. If Tully is Cicero then whatever we say to one we say to "the other." On this schema, if persons are bodies then whatever happens to their body happens to them. But, so the argument goes, certain things *can* happen to them that does not happen to their bodies. What are these? Consider the stories that are widespread through many cultures in which persons survive their bodies or switch bodies (reincarnation, reembodiment in an afterlife). A good annotated bibliography of these is offered in Terry Basford's *NearDeath Experiences* (1990). The argument here does not require that any of these cases actually occur, only that they reflect what appear to be bona fide possibilities. If we may reasonably believe such cases are indeed possible, we may reasonably conclude the person and body are not identical.

The argument is akin to one that we find in Descartes' *Meditations*, but it is muted in strength. The argument is developed in terms of what we may reasonably believe, not in Descartes' terms of what we may clearly and distinctly see to be possible. For those interested in a modest use of the modal argument, an analogy with C.S. Peirce's "socalled humble argument for theism" may be useful. Peirce advanced an imaginative thought experiment that theism is true and then argued for its reasonability. First comes imaginative thought experiments, arguments to the best explanation or, as Peirce would say, abduction, comes later.

I clarify three points about the argument and then reply to three objections.

(1) Prima facie justification.

One fairly wide complaint is that even the finest of thought experiments establish only what might be called negative, conceptual results. That is, the claim to imaginatively picture or conceive of some state of affairs is often taken to be evidence only of the fact that the person making the claim has not (as yet) noticed that it is impossible. Margaret Wilson writes: "Thus, the fact that we can conceive of p does not entail that p is even possible: all that follows (at best) is that we have not yet noticed any contradiction in p (Wilson 1982, p. 191)." This is a far cry from the relatively more optimistic claim of Hume that "... nothing we imagine is absolutely impossible" (Hume 1965, p. 32). One important mark of the modal argument advanced here is that it involves imagining a positive state of affairs obtaining (disembodiment, bodyswitching), not merely the absence of certain conditions. The modal argument is "humble" but it is built on more than the failure to see these states of affairs are impossible.

(2) Dualism and Theism.

The "humble argument for dualism" is vulnerable to the charge that the modal intuitions on which it is based are rogue sentiments that are in conflict with a rigorous systematic naturalism. That is, if naturalism has no competitors, why should one entertain these thought experiments, these "miracles"? It is here that dualists may appeal to theism to provide the comprehensive framework that can bolster and further refine the dualist picture of persons. If an overriding materialist cosmology and philosophy is "the only game in town," one might well dismiss the modal argument as well as the appeal to subjectivity canvassed in the last section.[7]

(3) Dualism and Science.

Do the natural sciences exclude dualism? Arguably not. The appearance of a conflict here may result if one ties dualism down to a particular, scientific hypothesis of mind-body interaction. But dualism is quite compatible with a range of theories about the brain, nervous system *et al.* I have addressed this problem elsewhere, but here I shall focus on Churchland's work.

It is not clear that any of the findings that Churchland cites in his book *establishes* that "the religious hypothesis of mind-body dualism" is false. Churchland seems to hedge some of his arguments against dualism, referring to the difficulty of dualism rather than its impossibility.

> It will be evident from the rest of this book that this familiar hypothesis is difficult to square with the emerging theory of cognitive processes and with the experimental results from several neurosciences. The doctrine of an immaterial soul looks, to put it frankly, like just another myth, false not just at the edges, but to the core (p.17).

But none of the solid scientific findings he cites shows that one *cannot* square dualism with the neurosciences, and it is easy to wonder whether the reason why dualism (or dualism plus theism) looks mythic is because of prior materialist commitments. Given an overall materialist metaphysic, there is not going to be much motivation for recognizing some relatively local exceptions in human and nonhuman consciousness to the general order of nature. But leave the door open to an alternative metaphysic, and I suggest that Churchland's project will not seem an open and shut affair.

By way of underlining the way in which Churchland blends his science and metaphysics, I take note of the ease with which a dualist can accommodate many of his scientific claims. Dualists can readily understand Churchland to have located key physical causes in shaping our consciousness. Addressing some neurological processes, Churchland writes: "This is where past learning shows itself, where character and insight come in, and where intelligence is ultimately grounded" (p.11). This may readily be seen as identifying the bodily backing or foundation of our mental lives, but it is quite a different, and decidedly metaphysical, matter to charge that intelligence and so on is the brain and body. The blending of science and philosophy emerges at various point. I suggest the following claim seems more metaphysics than science: "Without a neural network in place, there can be no self, neither an emotional self, nor a perceiving self, nor a deliberating self, nor any other kind of self" (p.308). Imagine science shows the exact correlation in our own case of selves and neural networks and does not give us evidence of there being any immaterial being (God, say) that is a person or personlike. Why would this be taken to demonstrate a *necessary* connection between selves and neural networks? I think Churchland's claim is *informed* by the sciences, but it reflects considerable speculation beyond what is dictated by the sciences alone.

Consider three brief objections and replies.

The Animalist Objection: It has been objected that dualism faces a burden of proof from the start. Surely, it is a fundamental and well grounded belief that we are animals. Dualists challenge this because they are committed to believing human beings are nonphysical things inside of animal bodies. Paul Snowdon and Quassim Cassam advance this charge.

Reply: The most plausible version of dualism is one that highlights the integrated respects in which human persons are embodied. There is no reason why dualists should deny we are animals. To be a fully functioning human animal is to be a fully embodied person. It should also be noted that most contemporary dualists do not follow Descartes on all matters, for they typically attribute consciousness and feeling to nonhuman animals.

Modal Skeptic Objection: Many things may appear possible but turn out to be false, even necessarily false.

Reply: Granted, we may well be mistaken in many cases but certainly not all. The case for dualism has the advantage that it is based on widespread testimony that its modal assumptions are not just held to be possible but actually believed to be true. If one cannot find reasons to dismiss them as nonsense and, indeed, they appear to be positively conceivable (imaginable, even picturable), then it is *prima facie* warranted to accept them.

Begging the Question: In order to hold that one could survive the death of one's body one must already accept dualism. The argument therefore only brings to light the dualist beliefs already in place.

Reply: Modal thought experiments of disembodiment and bodyswitching would probably not be judged to be genuine possibilities if one were already committed to rejecting dualism. But, if one is open to electing dualism or, say, materialism, the thought experiment can provide some evidence on behalf of the former over the latter. Consider analogies with the use of thought experiments in other areas of philosophy. One may not be sure whether utilitarianism or, say, virtue theory is true. In many moral arguments a thought experiment is described in which utilitarianism (or some other theory) leads one to judge the case at hand is just, while a competing theory like virtue theory leads one to judge the case unjust. Moral disagreement often seems quite rightly to be adjudicated by such a method in through which one may come to see that some theory is unacceptable. This technique is at home not just in ethics, but epistemology, the theory of art, other areas of metaphysics, and so on. If sound, modal thought experiments bring to light our understanding or grasp of our identity and how this identity diverges from the identity of our bodies. For superb defense of thought experiments in philosophy see Sorenson (1992).

Obviously this "humble" argument leaves much to be discussed and the aim of this chapter is not to proclaim it arrogantly as established, but to advance it here for further analysis. A crucial point I have sought to make is that such subsequent discussion should not take place in total isolation from the broader discussion of the reigning metaphysical schemes at work.

There is an analogy in contemporary philosophy of language to what I have sought to do here. Philosophy of language can be carried out without much attention outside it, but this is increasingly difficult to do since the work of J. L. Austin (d. 1960). Austin and others have provided good reasons to believe that to understand language-usage we must tackle philosophy of mind and behavior. My thesis is that in order to rekindle the case for dualism one does well to entertain a philosophy of God. Similarly, I believe the philosophy of God needs to take very seriously the philosophy of mind. If theism can provide a background that makes dualism look natural, whatever plausible arguments that can be mustered for dualism give one some reason for considering theism. They at least provide reasons to explore a philosophy that is not narrowly materialist. Traditional philosophical theists have often taken note of the link between our thinking about human persons and not just their sensations or other qualia in thinking about God. As Austin Farrer put it, "It is from 'creatures,' not *qualia* that the ascent of the mind to God takes its spring" (Farrer 1943, p. 20).[8]

NOTES

[1] Because I make so much use in this paper of Churchland's *The Engine of Reason, the Seat of the Soul* I simply reference it by providing page numbers in the text. Churchland's position appears to be the opposite of John Foster's. Foster defends idealism (*The Case for Idealism*), but also dualism (*The Immaterial Self*). Although he is an idealist, his view appears to be that dualism is preferable to materialism.

[2] In this passage Augustine cites the New Testament, *Matthew* 10:30. This robust affirmation of God's knowledge of the mundane stands in contrast with Plato's hesitancy to think that the forms traffic with terrestrial items we judge of little account: mud, hair, and "vile matter" (see the *Parmenides*).

[3] See Taliaferro (1992) for a parallel wager argument against some forms of scepticism about the external world.

[4] In essence, I think the selfrefutation argument works. A superb development of the refutation is developed in an unpublished paper of William Hasker's "What Can't be Eliminated?" See also Lynne Baker's *Explaining Attitudes: A Practical Approach to the Mind*.

[5] This demarcation of properties here does not amount to demarcating concrete individual substances; one should grant that the ability to conceive of distinct

properties is *prima facie* evidence of their genuine metaphysical distinctness while holding that they are properties of the very same thing (e.g. the property of *being the tallest spy* is distinct from the property of *being the shortest American*, but they could both be borne by Jane Doe. For a further defense of dualism against some of the usual objections see Joshua Hoffman and Gary Rosenkrantz's very fine *Substance Among Other Categories*, chapter five.

[6] I address some the problems involved with attributing privileged access to persons, e.g. the private language argument in CMOG (1994), chapter two.

[7] Theists have not always supported a dualist view of persons. This is brought out in clear terms by C. Williams' interesting paper "Christian Materialism and the Parity Thesis" (1996). I believe that the plausibility of Williams' defense of a limited materialism within Christianity would be mitigated if he expanded the scope of his concerns to include classic beliefs in the afterlife. "Nothing I have said," Williams notes, "shows that dualism and materialism are on a par with respect to life after death." For a superb review of Jewish and Christian commitment to dualism, see Cooper's *Body, Soul, and Life Everlasting* (1989).

[8] My thanks to comments on earlier versions of this paper by members of the Philosophy Departments at Bethel College and St. Cloud State University, and the The Divinity School at the University of Chicago. Thanks especially to Paul Griffiths, Mel Stewart, Paul Reasoner, James White, Charles Matthews, Derek Jeffreys, and Trina Jones.

BIBLIOGRAPHY

Augustine (1989 printing) *Exposition on the Book of Psalms*, ed. by P. Schaff (Edinburgh: T & T Clark).

Baker, L.R. (1995) *Explaining Attitudes: A Practical Approach to the Mind.* (Cambridge: Cambridge University Press)

Basford, T. (1990) *Near-Death Experiences* (New York: Garland Press).

Bryatt, A.S. *Possession.* (1990) London: Chatto and Windus

Churchland, P.M. (1995) *The Engine of Reason, the Seat of the Soul.* Cambridge, MA: MIT Press.

Churchland, P.M. (1979) *Metaphysics and the MindBody Problem* (Oxford: Clarendon Press)

Cooper, J. (1989) *Body, Soul, and Life Everlasting* (Grand Rapids: Eerdmans).

Dennett, D.C. (1993) "Living on the Edge," Inquiry. 1/2, pp.135159.

Dennett, D.C. (1996) *Kinds of Minds* (San Francisco: Basic Books).

Dennett, D. (1991) *Consciousness Explained* (Cambridge: MIT press)

Dennett, D. (1978) *Brainstorms* (Cambridge: MIT Press)

Farrer, A. (1943) *Finite and Infinite* (Westminster: Dacre).

Feuerbach, L. (1957) *The Essence of Christianity* (Harper Torchbooks).

Gould (1977) *After Darwin* (New York: Norton).

Hoffman, J. and Rosenkrantz, G. S. (1994) *Substance Among Other Categories*

(Cambridge: Cambridge University Press).

Hume, D. (1965) *A Treatise of Human Nature*, ed. by L. A. SelbyBigge (Oxford: Oxford University).

Kim, J. (1945) "Psychophysical Laws" in *Actions and Events*, ed. by E. LePore and B. McLaughlin (Oxford: Basil Blackwell).

Mackie, J.L. *Ethics: Inventing Right and Wrong* (1977) (Harmondsorth: Penguin).

Mavrodes, G.I. (1986) "Religion and the Queerness of Morality," in *Rationality, Religious Belief and Moral Commitment* ed. by R. Audi and W.J. Wainwright (Ithaca: Cornell University Press).

Minsky, M. (1980) "Decentralized Mind," *Behavioral and Brain Sciences* vol. 3.

Morris, T. (1991) *Our Idea of God* (Notre Dame: University of Notre Dame Press)

Putnam, H. (1981) *Reason, Truth, and History*. Cambridge: Cambridge University Press.

Ryle, G. (1949) *The Concept of Mind* (London: Hutchinson).

Sorenson, R. (1992) *Thought Experiment* (Oxford: Oxford University Press.

Stich, S. (1983) *From Folk Psychology to Cognitive Science: The Case Against Belief* (Cambridge: MIT Press).

Strawson, G. (1994) *Mental Reality* (Cambridge: MIT).

Taliaferro, C. (1997) *Contemporary Philosophy of Religion* (Oxford: Basil Blackwell)

Taliaferro, C. (1994) *Consciousness and the Mind of God* (Cambridge: Cambridge University Press)

Taliaferro, C. (1992) "Imaginary Evil; A Skeptic's Wager," *Philosophia* 21:3,4, pp.221233

Varghese R. and Margenau, H. (1992) *Cosmos, Bios, Theos*, (LaSalle: Open Court).

Williams, S. (1996) "Christian Materialism and the Parity Thesis," *International Journal for Philosophy of Religion* 39:1, pp. 114.

Wilson, M. (1982) *Descartes* (Boston: Routledge & Kegan Paul).

B. The Moral Order

16

Dimensions of Cultural Relativity in the Moral Realm

Jorge Garcia

I. Dimensions of cultural relativity

The cultural relativist sees the moral realm as a personal (better, an interpersonal) order in which groups of people organize their lives together by expressing, acting from, and inculcating such shared mental responses as disapproval, shame, guilt, and so on.[1] From this vision of the moral realm, it follows both that, insofar as humans comprise different groups, there is not one moral community but many, and that 'perspective', understood as a standpoint from within some group, is a pervasive and inescapable feature not only of moral judgment, but of moral rights, duties, and virtues themselves.

We can say that someone holds the doctrine of cultural relativism within the moral realm if and only if she accepts the following claim, which we may call the *comprehensive relativity* thesis:

(CRT) All moral judgments are relative to the codes, practices, customs, language games, etc. of human cultures.

When she says that they are 'relative' to cultures, she means, roughly, that moral judgments, including the moral standards on whose bases people judge personal attributes and behavior, are created by human cultures, and have meaning and application only within them, and that these standards will vary with relevant cultural changes as our survey moves from one culture to another, either across places or across times.[2]

This sort of view can be found especially among social scientists.

I wish to approach the topic of the way in which morality may be related to culture from a rather unusual angle. Rather than focusing directly on whether the doctrine of cultural moral relativism, strictly speaking, is true, or the question of whether we have adequate warrant to believe it, I wish to consider the degree to which a theory is relativistic, the degree to which it contains an element of relativity, even when it is not relativistic enough to be called a form of relativism *tout court*. After all, even the doctrine of cultural moral relativism, as we have defined it, has forms in which it does not pose a serious challenge to the non-relativist's moral judgments about what is right and wrong, even what is right and wrong everywhere and for all people. The disagreement between *some* non-relativists and some relativists may lie only in their differing accounts of why certain actions are right or wrong, that is, about *what makes them* to have the moral status they have. Imagine, for example, a certain relativist who thinks that all morality is a creature of human cultures, but also thinks that every human culture creates substantially the same moral code. Or, imagine a certain non-relativist who thinks that not all, but most moral judgments are creatures of widely diverse human cultures, so that a certain type of practice changes from morally right to morally wrong and back again several times across human cultural groups. One accepts the doctrine of moral relativism and is thus a relativist, while the other rejects the doctrine of relativism and is thus a non-relativist. However, the relativist we have imagined is closer to what we usually think of as non-relativism than is our non-relativist, and our non-relativist is closer to what we usually think of as relativism than is our relativist.

This suggests that the more interesting question may be not whether a certain position counts as relativism *tout court*, but the degree to which it contains relativistic elements. The form of relativism we imagined is not very deeply relativistic, we might say, while the non-relativism we conjured up is deeply relativistic. Things are, however, more complicated than this suggests. I will suggest that there are at least three different dimensions in which we may assess the degree of cultural relativity that a position or theory contains. We can begin to understand these "dimensions", if we first state three theses.

Insofar as a position is relativistic, it involves:

(RT) a *relativity* thesis, holding that some moral judgments, but not necessarily all, are somehow relative to the codes (or customs, practices, life-styles or whatever) of cultural groups;[3]

(DT) a *diversity* thesis, holding that these groups codes, life-styles, etc. are not entirely identical in what they commend, enjoin, and so on; and

(NT) a *non-hierarchy* thesis, restricting the extent to which different codes, or opposed provisions drawn from different codes, can be ordered as better or worse.[4]

Each of these elements affords a dimension, which I shall label *breadth* (or judgmental scope), *depth*, and *strength*, respectively, in respect to which any two moral views can vary in their relativity.

Regarding the first dimension, consider the view of a person who believes in some measure of moral cultural relativity but thinks it doesn't apply to judgments about justice.[5] She thinks that standards of justice have a different basis, rooted not in culture, but in, say, a hypothetical contract or in the general requirements for civil communal life. Similarly, consider the position of those thinkers who hold that there is irreducible cross-cultural conflict only among judgments in which people in different cultures rank the various virtues or which presuppose a certain claim about the relative stringency of moral principles.[6] This sort of restriction makes the relativity of their position less *broad* than is that of a view which holds *all* moral standards to be creatures of cultures, and thus relativized to them.

Regarding the second dimension, consider the claim that some types of behavior, for example, killing a group-member's children just for fun, are disallowed in every culture. (This kind of claim is attractive to those who hold the functionalist belief that the purpose of a moral code is to harmonize the pursuit of individual interests within the group.[7] More on this belief later.) Such a position displays a relativity that doesn't go as *deep* as that found in the view that there are *no* such cross-culturally universal moral norms.[8]

Regarding the third dimension, consider the position of someone who, while she thinks that morality is just a matter of a group's code and that codes differ in content from group to group, nonetheless maintains that there are some *non-moral* standards that can sometimes legitimately serve as a non-relativized basis for saying that the code of, say, Group Number One is better than is that of Group Number Two.[9] Anyone who holds the functionalist belief mentioned above seems to be thereby *committed* to the existence of such non-relativized bases for evaluating codes, since some group's code may fulfill these functions, for example, insuring the survival of its group's culture, less effectively than does that of another group. Such a relativity is not so strong as that of someone who insists there are no such non-relativized standards by which different codes can properly be evaluated. It is, however, stronger than that of a theorist who holds that while morality is a creature of culture, thinks most cultures can be ranked according to how well they fit the demands of a common human nature.[10]

We may clarify one important implication that what we have said has for the logical relations that hold between two important and closely related terms. As we use the terms here a position or theory counts as a form of *relativism*, that is, relativism *tout court*, just when it endorses the thesis of comprehensive relativity (CRT). A position or theory, however, is *relativistic* (to a greater or a lesser degree) when it endorses *some* relativity thesis (RT). Thus, in our usage, a position or theory may be more or less relativistic even though it is not a form of relativism. To avoid confusion, I will use the noun 'relativity' as the cognate substantive term corresponding to 'relativistic', talking, for example, about the comparative relativity (but never the comparative relativism) of two non-relativist positions. I shall similarly restrict the adjective 'relativist' to use as the cognate adjective corresponding to 'relativism', using 'relativistic' as the term in which we measure a position's relativity. Thus, 'relativism' and 'relativist' are either/or matters: a view is relativist when it endorses the doctrine of relativism. They are non-scalar: it will not make sense, as we use the terms hereafter, to talk of the degree of a position's relativism or to ask how relativist it is. 'Relativity' and 'relativistic', in contrast, are scalar concepts as we will employ them henceforward: it will make sense to talk of the degree of the relativity a position involves and to ask how relativistic it is. I shall call someone a relativist only when she accepts a form of relativism; that her view involves some degree of relativity will not be sufficient to warrant application of the term 'relativist'.

II. Assessing seriously relativistic moral positions

Let us call a position seriously relativistic when its relativity is significantly broad, deep, and strong. There are serious problems confronting any position whose cultural relativity is serious in this sense.

Any claim that much of morality is relative to culture is doubtful for several reasons. In the first instance, it is notoriously difficult either to identify the components of a culture (what does it consist of?) and to individuate cultures and subcultures, distinguishing one culture from another.[11] Second, we should remember that in the older, clearer, and more useful senses of the term 'culture,' not every set of customs that a group acknowledges, uses, or teaches will count as a culture. Culture, on this understanding, is a process of tending and nourishing which results in individual growth and development. (This image endures in our talk of 'agriculture' or of a 'cell culture', as well as in talk, still sometimes heard, contrasting 'popular entertainment' and 'high culture'.) There can be differing cultures, inasmuch as there can be differing social regimens each of which still tends to help the person's humanity flourish. However, there is no good reason to suppose that the customs of every group will tend to human development and flourishing. Not all values, then, can be logically identified merely as the norms of a certain culture. For some standards of what is good and bad for people must be presupposed if we are even to identify a group's customs as a 'culture,' that is, as a social environment that helps people thrive.

In addition, it is doubtful that there is much empirical evidence for the cultural relativity of moral standards. "It is unlikely that we will find genuine empirical evidence of societies that differ fundamentally from us in...morality."[12] Thinkers who endorse seriously relativistic positions sometimes neglect to distinguish evidence that there is some measure of cross-cultural disagreement about what is good and right from evidence that goodness and requirement are creatures of various cultures and inseparable from them. Moreover, it is difficult to see just how the needed empirical evidence could be amassed. There is no reason to call any set of judgments or practices in a society we encounter *moral* judgments or practices unless they are recognizable as such. And, of course, we can recognize them as moral only insofar as they pertinently resemble what we ordinarily call 'moral'. How do we know to translate certain dyslogistic terms in their language as 'unjust' or 'morally vicious', for example? Presumably, we should look to the same factors we would look to in deciding whether to translate certain descriptive terms by the English words 'circular' or 'sickening' or 'oral'—we should need to find out if they applied the term largely to the same things we should call circular, sickening, or oral, and whether they would explain, vindicate, and ground these attributions by appeal to the same sort of considerations we would. In the absence of any such similarities, it is difficult to see what could justify the translation. It is difficult to see how we can, or why we should, proceed otherwise in the case of the moral terms.

MacIntyre has protested against this sort of emphasis on translation, insisting that what is required is that we be able to *understand* the others' judgments not that we able to translate them.[13] Even if that is correct, however, our point still holds. Quine has proposed a "principle of charity" which "entitles" us to be "suspicious" of understandings that ascribe to people "absurd or exotic...beliefs."[14] Similarly, Richard Grandy's "principle of humanity" demands that the "pattern of relations among beliefs, desires and the world" that we impute to others "be as similar to our own as possible."[15] There are difficulties at the margin in applying these principles, but their general force still holds.[16] To understand the other as making moral judgments we must be able to recognize those judgments by their similarity to our own in such respects as their content and their grounds of application.

This suggests that, insofar as we can be sure that the members of a distant cultural group are making *moral* judgments, they must, by and large, claim that the same things are moral rights, duties, and virtues as we claim are; or, if they do not, then they must at least offer largely the same kinds of reasons for the set of things they think are rights, duties, and virtues as we offer for the set of rights, virtues, and duties we believe in. This fact, however, pits some claims made by the proponent of a seriously relativistic position against others to which she is committed, especially as the relativity becomes broader and deeper. This is because someone arguing for a seriously relativistic position needs the judgments and practices in question to be similar enough to our own to be recognizable as moral, but she also needs them to be different enough from our own to support her relativity thesis. Nor will it do for her to say that the other cultural group's judgments differ from ours in content but are similar in the rationale supporting them, for this will tend to mean that her position's relativity evaporates as we approach the deeper moral claims which serve as our judgments' or practices' epistemic or justificatory basis. At that point, her best hope is to insist upon some purely formal criteria for recognizing moral judgments and practices.

Unfortunately for her, however, the familiar forms of formalism are all problematic in the light of philosophical criticism in the last few decades, and, in any case, they merely beg the question against those who hold that nothing should be counted as a moral judgment or practice unless it is substantially similar in subject, content, and rationale to the only paradigms we have of the moral—that is, the judgments we ordinarily make in our cultures, the practices in which we ordinarily participate.[17]

There is an additional problem besetting the formalist's way out of this internal tension within her system. The most common and appealing purely formal criteria of the moral are those that pick out a judgment or practice as moral just when it serves a certain social end, such as the survival of the group-members' lives or unity. Such a view seems to be popular among anthropologists. However, as we noted above, any strongly relativistic position is implausible if we assume functionalist accounts of morality, since, from whatever function they take as definitive of moral codes, we can extract a non-relativized standard for evaluating such codes.[18] Moreover, those who accept seriously relativistic positions want cultural codes and practices to play various explanatory roles, helping us to understand why individuals endorse the moral beliefs and practices they do, for example. As a culturally relativistic position approaches subjectivism, the notion of culture plays a less serious role and begins to lose the explanatory power these thinkers want for it.

The formalist might reject functionalism, however, and instead try to identify a society's moral judgments as those triggering such responses as guilt, shame, praise, blame, and ostracism. (Rather than identifying the moral judgments within a given culture by looking to what fills certain functions (e.g., perpetuating the group's way of life or determining which judgments in that culture have roughly similar extensions and grounds of application as do our moral predicates). This procedure, however, is likely to prove circular. Moral judgments must be tied to moral guilt, moral blame, and so on. However, there is no way to tell if this person's guilt or that person's blame is *moral guilt* or *moral blame*, unless we can already recognize the judgments on which it is based as moral judgments. It follows that we cannot rely on our recognition of moral guilt, etc. to identify moral judgments.[19]

What we have said so far poses a problem for the proponent of a seriously relativistic position in her effort to establish that there is as much diversity among moral judgments as she claims. The seriously relativistic position is also threatened from the other side. There may be more diversity of moral judgment than seriously relativistic positions can allow, diversity that arises at the wrong level. Consider a case. Someone notes, for example, that persons in various Arab cultures hold that a male is morally permitted to take several wives (though cautioned against doing so), while the Western feminist holds that polygamy is immoral because it violates the rights of women and upholds their patriarchal domination. She then concludes that both sides are right in the only way in which they can be right. That is, each correctly applies her own moral code. There is, then, no such thing, as polygamy's simply being right or wrong. There are only polygamy's 'being-permitted-within-the-code-accepted-by-Arabs', and its 'being-forbidden-within-the-code-accepted-by-Western-feminists'. (Or, in a somewhat different kind of relativistic view, there are only the 'being-justified-by-the-set-of-standards-used-by-Arabs' of the judgment that polygamy is permitted, and the 'being-justified-according-to-the standards-used-by-Western-feminists' of the judgment that polygamy is forbidden.) Relativistic positions accommodate in this way the diversity of moral judgments from one cultural group to another.

What does the proponent of a seriously relativistic position have to say, however, about diversity of moral judgments *within* each group? Not much, as it turns out. There may, after all, be some Arabs, even some Arab Muslims, who agree with the feminist that polygamy is immoral, and there may even be some feminists who hold that polygamy does not degrade women but frees each wife from household responsibilities she might have if she were alone. These dissident individuals, however, upset the tidy cultural relativistic picture, which sees moral judgments as differing across cultures and subcultures but as uniform within them. The diversity we are now considering comes at the wrong level for seriously relativistic positions easily to accommodate it. It makes it harder and less plausible to say simply that *the* morality of the Arab group permits polygamy while *the* morality of the feminist group forbids it. We now need to ask, *Which* morality within each group? Of course, a proponent of a relativistic position can always spin more and more subcultural groups, even as the geocentrists postulated more and more epicycles, in order to match a cultural group to each dissident opinion. However, this becomes more and more patently contrived, and, in any case, it begins to replace the thesis of cultural relativity that morality is relative to culture with the subjectivist's claim that morality is relative to the individual. This maneuver, then, is not so much a defense of cultural relativity, as its abandonment.

It remains open to the proponent of a serious relativistic position to avoid denying the diversity that exists within a culture group by treating the dominant view as constituting the group's view. She may admit the existence of dissident voices within a cultural group, but ignore them overtly as a matter of methodological principle, rather than covertly. This, however, betrays the shallowness of the liberalism that seriously relativistic positions can accommodate. (Contrary to the image of liberal tolerance that such positions tend to enjoy.) This is because, in taking this tack, the proponent of a serious relativistic position must abet the marginalization, silencing, and subjugation of minority, dissident voices. This sort of absolute majoritarianism stands in need of justification even as a matter of scientific methodology. More troubling, however, is its politics. The "dominant" view may be precisely the view of those who dominate, and it is disturbing to see the proponent of the seriously relativistic position merely acquiesce in the domination of dissident minorities by agreeing to treat them as beneath notice.

Of course, even if someone overcomes all the difficulties I have sketched, and succeeds in showing that there is as much diversity across cultures as the proponent of moral relativism or of any seriously relativistic (but non-relativist) position needs, but not more diversity within cultures than she can allow, that would establish only the first premise of the kind of argument needed to establish any sort of relativity thesis, whether CRT or some limited relativity thesis (LRT). It would establish that there is the right amount of diversity and at the right level. It would still remain for the proponent of the seriously relativistic position to show that this diversity among moral judgments is better explained by the claim that moral judgments are culture-relative than by any competing explanation available. Why think that it is? One alternative explanation is that of what we can call "parametric universalism".[20] According to this doctrine, there are certain deep and very general universal moral principles, but these principles themselves allow for differing prescriptions in differing circumstances. This sort of view is not a form of relativism *tout court*, because it does not entail the comprehensive relativity thesis, CRT. Parametric universalism does, of course, involve a measure of relativity, since it allows some moral judgments to vary from culture to culture. However, this relativity is of crucially limited breadth, because it exempts some moral judgments from the scope of relativization. The deepest principles are not themselves cultural inventions.

We charged above that, in an important respect, the liberalism that any seriously relativistic position can accommodate is shallow.[21] This shallowness is also manifest in the weakness and inadequacy of any case against intolerance that seriously relativistic positions permit one to make. The proponent of a seriously relativistic position endorses the moral judgments made about cases within each culture, and this latitudinarianism, this indifference has the appearance of liberalism. However, she rejects all the moral reasoning those within the culture might offer in explaining and vindicating these judgments about cases. She rejects the claims that people make about what makes this action right and that one wrong— claims about human nature, say, or about the divine will, or about the group's history. The proponent of a seriously relativistic position is likely to judge all these claims false. More important than this is that she is committed to denying that, even if they were true, these claims *would* or even *could* establish the moral judgments in whose support they are offered. Rather, if her position's relativity is broad in our sense that its relativity thesis applies to a wide range of moral judgments, then she is committed to claiming that, for all the moral judgments within that range, only a cultural group's code or practice can make them true. What is sufficient, and what is necessary, to establish the moral judgment that, say, polygamy is permissible is simply *that* the cultural group accept it.[22] *Why* the group accepts it doesn't matter within a seriously relativistic position.

Indeed, within such a relativistic view, the reasons that those within the group offer for their belief that this or that practice is morally required or forbidden are none of them relevant to the justification of the judgment. Those within the group may think what they are doing is the right thing because it is the will of the divinity, or because it honors the ways of their ancestors, or because it fits their understanding of what human beings need and where they are going. However, the proponent of a seriously relativistic position dismisses all these claims as wrong, without even bothering to assess the truth of the historical or theological claims made. They are wrong because morality is not, as the local group may think, the sort of thing that flows from our nature as humans or from the demands of whomever they recognize as their maker. Such are the limits to any endorsement of local cultural values that a seriously relativistic position can allow. The proponent of such a view endorses the group's practice while systematically denying all that on which the group bases its practice.

Seriously relativistic positions also undercut the tolerance that they are said to support in another way, one that has been often noted: they undermine the cross-cultural moral case for intercultural tolerance. In raising a moral challenge to intolerance, we want to be confident that the bigot is not on just as solid ground in defending her intolerance as we are in attacking it.[23] Seriously relativistic positions tend to deny us this assurance, whatever their pretensions to liberalism.

Faced with these difficulties, the proponent of a seriously relativistic position may want to restrict the breadth of her position's relativity, retreating to a position like that of some recent philosophers who maintain that cultural relativity applies to assessments of personal ideals and social 'ways of life', but who exempt judgments about justice from this relativity's scope.[24] There are reasons for pessimism about such a strategy's prospects. It seems likely, for example, that your right to my assistance in securing health care grows less stringent as the assistance becomes more onerous for me, interfering with my legitimate ideals and way of life. However, this means that the correctness of a judgment about the legitimacy of a way of life (a relativized judgment, on the view in question) will depend on a judgment of justice (a non-relativized judgment), and vice versa. Perhaps this can be worked out, but it seems to me that this sort of interdependence of judgments of justice and judgments about ways of life will make it difficult to keep the two kinds of moral judgment segregated in the way this sort of narrow cultural relativity requires.

It may be objected to my argument that it is Eurocentric, taking the moral judgments and practices of some Western cultures to be normative in that no other culture's judgments or practices are to be counted as moral unless they sufficiently resemble the Western paradigm. There is, of course, some truth to this objection, but I don't see that as very damaging to my argument. First the "Eurocentrism" is not essential but is merely a function of the fact that we are speaking a Western tongue and asking in it a question about what has to be true of a judgment or practice for us to properly apply to it an English term, 'moral', which term picks out certain concepts that, even if they arose in Africa or Asia, have developed in a peculiar way in the West. In an exactly parallel way, a Polynesian examining whether modern Americans have a code of *tabu* must determine whether anything in this society closely enough matches what she is familiar with in Polynesian culture as *tabu* that it warrants her saying that modern American society has such a code as well. Thus, while there is an essential element of the ethnocentric in the methodology, there is nothing essentially *Euro*centric in it.

Second, as I have just pointed out, the ethnocentrism is merely methodological, and even there this ethnocentrism lies mainly in the starting point of the method. This may be disappointing to those who, like certain optimists with Cartesian leanings, think they can begin their scholarly inquiries from some neutral territory unmarked by the folkways of any particular cultural tradition. The point, however, is merely a familiar one: there are no presuppositionless starting points in philosophy or in life; we must begin from where we are. That means that when we look to see to what the term and concept of 'the moral' can be applied, we must begin with the English term and the particular concept, shaped by its historical development in Western tongues and thought, we express when we use it.

III. Conclusion

In this discussion, I have tried to offer a way of understanding of cultural relativity within the moral realm, and to raise certain problems for it. I have argued, first, that tensions among the three theses I mentioned make it difficult for the proponent of a seriously relativistic position to establish the cross-cultural diversity among moral judgments that she needs in order to mount an argument for relativity. This is owing to the difficulty of identifying judgments made in another culture as moral ones when those judgments differ significantly in content and rationale from our own, and the related difficulty of translating terms in another language as moral terms, when their application and their use in the 'language game' of justification is markedly different from familiar paradigms. Second, I have argued that intra-group diversity among moral judgments makes it difficult to establish the intra-group uniformity that her argument for the *cultural* relativity of moral judgments presupposes. Strategies for avoiding this, I claim, tend to collapse cultural relativity into subjectivism, or objectionably threaten to replicate and even to re-enforce the marginalization and silencing of dissident minority voices. Third, I have argued that, even if someone can establish the right amount and level of diversity among moral judgments, it will be difficult to establish any relativity thesis, either a comprehensive one (CRT) or a limited one (LRT), as a superior explanation of this diversity over various plausible competing explanations. Fourth, I have tried to show that and why it is implausible to maintain, as people commonly do, that accepting the claims that morality is broadly, deeply, and strongly relativistic promotes tolerance and reflects liberal values. On the contrary, any seriously relativistic position: (a) threatens to whitewash hegemonic power relationships within groups, (b) undermines the cross-cultural moral case against intolerance, (c) requires us to reject as wholly irrelevant to morality the explanations and justifications people may offer in their intra-group moral discourse and in their efforts to explain and to justify their moral judgments to outsiders, and (d) requires a comparable rejection of the understandings of the world, of morality, and of themselves as a people that these explanations may reflect.

My arguments here, then, serve to indicate that any moral position whose cultural relativity is broad, deep, and strong will suffer from serious difficulties. To these internal tensions plaguing all seriously relativistic positions, we have added others, which afflict efforts to link such positions to a principle of cross-cultural tolerance. The proponent of any such position is in no position to claim for tolerance status as anything more than simply another local value of certain cultural traditions.[25] Moreover, it is not at all clear on what basis she could argue even that Westerners should put greater store in tolerance than they should invest in such other items from their stock of values as individualism (or, for that matter, monotheism). It is difficult to see how, without contradicting her own relativistic view, the proponent of a seriously relativistic position could so much as *endorse* the claim that tolerance has such moral primacy, let alone *argue* for it.

NOTES

Sabbatical support from Georgetown University, and grants from Georgetown's Graduate School, from the National Endowment for the Humanities, and from Harvard's Program in Ethics and the Professions afforded me time to develop these thoughts. I am grateful to audiences at the Harvard Program, at the University of Rhode Island, and at the Harvard Medical School for their responses to earlier versions of some of this material, and to Arthur Kleinman, Barbara Koenig, and Marsha Witten for discussion of issues and bibliographic suggestions.

[1] Cultural relativism as I define it here is to be distinguished from both moral skepticism—the thesis that no genuine knowledge of right and wrong, good and evil, etc. is attainable, and from moral nihilism—the thesis that nothing really is morally right, wrong, good, bad, forbidden, required, virtuous, vicious, etc. Below I distinguish relativism from relativity. This latter distinction will play a prominent role in my discussion.

[2] When I say that the relativist believes that moralities are creations of human culture, this characterization is, I realize, rather rough. She may think that human social groups create morality at the same time as, and together with, the other social practices and doctrines that together constitute their culture. She may also think that a group's morality, in turn, helps to shape the culture that spawns it and which it comes partially to constitute. (I owe these points to conversations with Marsha Witten and Arthur Kleinman.)

[3] The relativity thesis (RT), of course, entails, but is not entailed by, the comprehensive relativity thesis (CRT) which we said above was constitutive of relativism. This is as it should be. Every position that counts as a form of moral relativism is very relativistic in at least one dimension, as I define these terms below. However, not every position that is relativistic to some extent should therein count as a form of moral relativism.

[4] The idea and terminology for the first two theses I borrow from John Ladd's Introduction to his collection *Ethical Relativism* (Belmont: Wadsworth, 1993). The idea, and awkward terminology, for the third is my own. I add this thesis to reserve the term 'cultural relativist' for those who think that ultimately there is no legitimate and objective basis on which to rank and choose among cultures, and to distinguish such thinkers from those who, while strongly linking morality to tradition, insist upon our ability for such rational appraisal and choice. My terminology is probably somewhat idiosyncratic, but not entirely without rationale.

[5] For two recent examples of this sort of view, see Bernard Williams, *Ethics and the Limits of Philosophy* (Cambridge: Harvard University Press, 1985), and Stuart Hampshire, "Morality and Convention," in Hampshire *Morality and Conflict* (Cambridge: Harvard University Press, 1983).

[6] For an example of this sort of position, see Wong, *Moral Relativism* (Berkeley: University of California Press, 1984). T. M. Scanlon also discusses a related view in an unpublished paper.

[7] Many social thinkers seem thus to combine a seriously relativistic position with functionalism. The philosopher Alain Locke seems to espouse some such combination. He writes approvingly of Pareto's "historical and functional relativism of cultural values," and concludes the most important of his philosophical essays, titled "Values and Imperatives," by invoking "a new center for the thought and insight of our present generation,...a philosophy and a psychology, and perhaps too, a sociology, pivoted around functionalistic relativism." Alain Locke, "Values and Imperatives," in *Philosophy Born of Struggle*, ed. Leonard Harris (Dubuque, Iowa: Kendall-Hunt, 1983).

[8] I say that a theory's relativity is deeper the further it extends cross-cultural diversity of moral judgments because, as it thus extends, it will both: (i) approach those moral judgments which are foundationally basic in the order of moral justification, and (ii) reach to those moral judgments of which we are most deeply

convinced. As Mill famously noted, foundational judgments (such as, in his view, the greatest happiness principle) need not be the ones we find it hardest to doubt.
[9] Sometimes philosophers build what I call the dimension of strength into their definitions of relativism itself. Thus, one writer defines relativism within the theory of knowledge in this way: "'Epistemological relativism may be defined as the view that knowledge (and/or truth) is relative—to time, to place, to society, to culture, to historical epoch, to conceptual scheme, framework, or to personal training and conviction—so that what counts as knowledge depends upon the value of one or more of these variables. If knowledge and truth are relative in this way, this will be because different cultures, societies, etc. accept different standards of evaluation for knowledge claims, and there is no neutral way of choosing between these alternative sets of standards." (Harvey Siegel, "Relativism," in *A Companion to Epistemology*," edited by Jonathan Dancy and Ernest Sosa (Oxford: Blackwell, 1992), pp. 428–9.
[10] Some who have been called 'communitarians' may think this. A communitarian might consistently hold that morality derives from one's community, but also hold that 'community' itself is a teleological notion, such that any given form of community is answerable to our needs as social animals.
[11] Roger Scruton says that in recent British discussions of 'multiculturalism' in education, "the following have all been included as parts of 'culture': (1) Language, including dialect, speech melody, and idiom. (2) The 'deep' customs and beliefs of religion. (3) The 'shallow' customs of social intercourse: feasts and ceremonies, manners, and courtesies. (4) Morality, and especially sexual morality. (5) Popular entertainment, sport and leisure. (6) 'High' culture, in which aesthetic values are paramount. (7) 'Political' culture, including a sense of law and justice, and expectations as to the correct way to resolve conflicts." (Scruton, "The Myth of Cultural Relativism," in *Anti-Racism—An Assault on Education and Value* (London: Sherwood, 1986))

The U. S. National Commission on AIDS has been quoted as pronouncing that "A culture is a way of life grounded in a particular past experience and environmental context. In important ways it differs from any other culture in content and form. One challenge...is to comprehend and respond to the distinctiveness of varying cultural experiences, including each community's fundamental assumptions and beliefs, ethical and aesthetic values, ritual and material preferences, and historical burdens." (Quoted in "Viewing Science and Technology through a Multicultural Prism," a draft report of the AAAS Directorate for Science and Policy (March, 1993), p. iv. AAAS cites the AIDS Commission's *The Challenge of HIV/AIDS in Communities of Color*, (Washington: December, 1992), p. 23.) We can presume that, in pontificating on matters so far from their charge and expertise, the members of the AIDS Commission are merely echoing what they have picked up from the intellectual air.

A recent authoritative source says simply, "[T]here is no current, widely accepted, composite resolution of the definition of culture." It adds that "the omnibus tradition form the cultural anthropology tradition has been generally relegated to introductory texts," and quotes a recent review's claim that sociologists still sometimes follow the anthropologists in understanding culture as a "code of conduct embedded in or constitutive of social life." (Samuel Gilmore, "Culture," *Encyclopedia of Sociology*, vol. 1, edited by Edgar Borgatta and Marie Borgatta (New York: Macmillan, 1992), p. 409.)

Separate cultures have been found in the most surprising places. A newspaper headline on alleged employee thefts in the Boston municipal transit system (popularly called 'the T') recently read: "T's culture seen ripe for corruption." (Boston Sunday Globe, March 7, 1993, p. 1)

[12] David-Hillel Ruben, "Relativism," in *The Concise Encyclopedia of Western Philosophy and Philosophers*, edited by J. O. Urmson and Jonathan Ree (London: Unwin Hyman, 1989), p. 275.

[13] Alasdair MacIntyre, "Relativism, Power, and Philosophy," in *Relativism: Interpretation and Confrontation*, edited by Michael Krausz (Notre Dame: University of Notre Dame Press, 1989).

[14] W. V. O. Quine, *Word and Object* (Cambridge: MIT, 1960), p. 69.

[15] Richard Grandy, "Reference, Meaning, and Belief," *Journal of Philosophy* 70 (1973): 443.

[16] See the discussion of Quine's and Grandy's principles in Wong, *Moral Relativity*, ch. 8. Wong and others use the following sort of case in arguing against such principles. Alicia, at a party sees a man, Bao, who is drinking water from a martini glass. Alicia says of him, 'The person drinking a martini is a male.' The critics point out that there is a charitable interpretation of Alicia's statement, the one that makes it true. Unfortunately, that interpretation, that someone else at the party—say, Carlos, who is drinking a martini—is male is also probably an incorrect interpretation.

This is an interesting observing, but it leaves unaffected our point about moral relativity. Alicia's statement can properly be understood as mistaken because we assume that she believes as we do about other things—that someone drinking from a martini glass is probably drinking a martini, for example. This is precisely what is missing in the moral realm as relativity becomes broader and deeper, covering more moral judgments and more basic ones. For as the relativity grows, the needed agreement between the members of another culture and ourselves recedes. Thus, these critics' case against Quine and Grandy's principles, whatever its merits, rests on the existence of general agreement between speaker and evaluator in the more basic judgments used to justify more particular claims. Such agreement at the level of justificatory judgments in the moral realm is one of the casualties of the broad and deep relativity that characterizes seriously relativistic positions. So, while they may have pointed out cases where the principles' presumption is overridden, those cases do not seem to apply in the kind of context where we deploy the principles against the more deeply relativistic moral positions.

[17] The arguments I make here are presented with a little more detail in Garcia, "Relativism and Moral Divergence" *Metaphilosophy* 19 (1988): 264–281. The general anti-relativist strategy resembles that of Donald Davidson's in "On the Very Idea of a Conceptual Scheme," *Relativism: Cognitive and Moral*, ed. Jack Meiland and Michael Krausz (Notre Dame: University of Notre Dame Press, 1982).

For some early and influential criticisms of formal criteria of morality, see Philippa Foot's "Moral Beliefs" and "Moral Arguments" in her *Virtues and Vices* (Berkeley: University of California Press, 1978).

[18] This undermines at least some versions of the position called "cultural equity", which holds that all cultures are of equal value. It is hard to know how to assign a single value to a whole culture and, once such assignments are made, it is incredible to suppose that, for any two cultures, C1 and C2, the value of C1 will be exactly equal to that of C2. Of course, in general, it will be difficult to judge the value of a culture as a whole. However, it is often not at all difficult to judge how well a culture is doing in this or that respect, say, in providing for the health or liberty of the people living in it. And surely a cultural that does a bad enough job in all the pertinent areas can properly be said to be worse on the whole than one that better succeeds in all of them. Perhaps what the proponents of cultural equity mean to say is that all cultures are equally valueless in the sense that there are no true judgments of the comparative value of two cultures. Many philosophers, influenced by logical positivism, used to think that value-judgments lacked truth because they had a special kind of meaning that made them more like imperatives or ejaculations than like statements of fact. However, this claim makes it extremely difficult to explain the logical behavior of value judgments and the thesis of cultural equity is insecure indeed if its fate depends on such discredited theories of language.

Some maintain that African-American culture is not merely equal but superior to its chief domestic rival. Dr. Cheryl Sanders maintains that "the African-American ethos...is characteristically human in ways that the European-American ethos is not." According to unsympathetic press reports, Professor Leonard Jeffries holds Nazism to be the ultimate culmination of the white value system, which supposedly derives from deformation of white genes during the Ice Ages, while blacks hold "the value system of the sun." (Sanders, "Theological View," p. 3. Conservative journalist Dinesh D'Souza summarizes Professor Jeffries' views in "Illiberal Education," *The Atlantic vol.* 267 (March, 1991), p. 54.) Now, of course, people shouldn't say things like the ones cited at all unless they have the best of evidence, and even then they shouldn't say them without some qualification to disavow any suggestions that African-Americans are themselves more human than are European-Americans. Nonetheless, it is possible and even likely that some cultures will, in some of their aspects, surpass others, and it is surely romantic to imagine that all these factors will even out so as to leave every culture on the whole exactly equal to every other one.   Some   people claim to hold versions of this thesis of cultural equity, but I do not know how their views can avoid running afoul of arguments of the sort adduced here.

[19] Tom Beauchamp suggests that the term 'moral' may be a "family resemblance" term. (See Beauchamp, "Response to Jorge Garcia," in *African-American Perspectives on Biomedical Ethics*, edited by Harley Flack and Edmund Pellegrino (Washington: Georgetown University Press, 1992).) This would, I think, somewhat lessen the impediments I have pointed out in arguing for a seriously relativistic position. It would not, however, remove them. The fact remains that the more dissimilar a person's statement S is from some uncontroversial paradigms of moral judgment in its content, justificatory basis, emotional hold, etc., the less plausible becomes the relativist's insistence that S is a radically opposed moral judgment and the more attractive becomes the option of saying that S is not a moral judgment at all.

[20] I borrow this term and the idea it expresses from Scanlon's unpublished paper. Ruben also makes this now-familiar point: "[T]here might be a single ethical principle which entitles or requires persons in different circumstances to perform different actions. . . Relativism should be defined as the assertion that some of these differences are (or at least may be) fundamental rather than derivative." (Ruben, "Relativism," p. 275.)

[21] Relativistic positions *may* encourage the practice of cross-cultural toleration. (They also may not.) More important, they undermine the intellectual foundations for any moral principle of tolerance. This is bad trade-off. For comprehensive opposition to intolerance, it is not enough to be disinclined to practicing intolerance oneself. One should also be committed to discouraging others' intolerance, preventing and discontinuing others' intolerance, and responding to incidents of intolerance. For this, it is best to have a principled disapproval of intolerance, not just the sort of tolerance toward other views that is born of indifference to moral matters and of a deflated conception of the moral. Yet the latter is the best support for tolerance that seriously relativistic positions can muster.

[22] Different seriously relativistic positions may diverge over whether this agreement must come in (non-verbal) conduct or in doctrine or in some particular combination of the two.

[23] Here, again, my thinking is influenced by Scanlon's unpublished work.

[24] Hampshire, "Morality and Convention," and "Morality and Conflict, in *Morality and Conflict*. Williams, *Ethics and the Limits of Philosophy*.

[25] Alain Locke's view that his relativistic "pluralism" somehow supports a principle of tolerance is disturbingly close to the position Bernard Williams rightly castigates as 'vulgar relativism' in his book, *Morality* (New York: Harper & Row, 1972).

17

Reason, Relativism and Christian Ethics

John Finnis

Introduction

The term "relativism" is used rather variously in contemporary philosophical and other scholarly discourse. Some use it to pick out (A) the whole range of opinions which deny that ethical judgments can be true ("objective"), that ethical or moral reasoning can yield genuine ("objective") knowledge. Others (B) distinguish "relativism" from "subjectivism": then, according to *relativism*, ethical judgments are true only relative to the accepted norms of a given society, norms which are themselves not true hut merely the conventions settled upon in that society; according to *subjectivism*, moral judgments do no more than express the attitudes of the subject who makes them. According to a rather different usage, (C) a relativist can accept that some moral norms and judgments are objective and true, and proposes no more (and no less) than: no moral judgment about right and wrong choice is valid for all times and places, for moral judgments are relative to human nature, and human nature changes; so moral judgments have their truth only relative to particular social contexts (eras, etc.)

In this last sense (C) of "relativism", not a few contemporary Catholic theologians propose a relativist moral theory, and some are even willing to be called moral "relativists"[2]—though they perhaps rather prefer labels such as "historical-minded".[3] But the claims made in the theological community about changing human nature, and about "historical-minded" as opposed to "classicist" world-views are, in my opinion, of little plausibility or philosophical interest.[4] Decades after such claims became fashionable, we still await any serious attempt to show

how human nature may have so changed, or might in future so change, as to render untrue the type of moral judgment whose truth those who make such claims seem to wish to put in doubt—e.g. about intentional killing of innocents.[5] So I shall not in this paper have more to say about relativism of this sort, even though I shall say much about other aspects of the work of a theologian who defends it. My focus will instead be upon the more radical (A) or (B) relativism, or subjectivism, into which theological accounts of moral right and wrong fall willy nilly when, like that theologian, they embrace one or other of the ethical theories commonly (and by him) labeled "proportionalist".

Theologians who adopt proportionalism commonly seem to do so from dissatisfaction with Christian ethics in its classic forms (rather than from an articulated philosophical exploration of the groundwork of ethics). And their dissatisfaction involves (along with valid insights) some large misunderstandings of Christian ethics. So I shall begin by identifying (*Part I*) the relativities which that ethics freely acknowledges, and (*Part II*) the absoluteness and universality which, despite those acknowledged relativities, it affirms. In *Part III*, I indicate some of the resources which Christian ethics possesses not only for showing the reasonableness and truth of the moral absolutes it teaches but also for explaining why moral judgments vary as they do from person to person and society to society—the variability which is still today the principal weapon of the moral sceptic, the type (A) or (B) relativist. Finally, in *Part IV*, I suggest that proportionalism came to seem attractive to some theologians through inattention to those conceptual resources of a refreshed and developed classic Christian ethics; and that theological proportionalism, though wishing to regard moral judgments as *recta ratio* and true (or *contra rationem* and false), results in a position which understands judgments of right and wrong in the way they are understood by Part III's secular (A) or (B) relativists—i.e. as judgments directed to their conclusions by feelings and/or personal choices, or by public opinion and/or social conventions.

Relativities Recognized by Christian Ethics

Christian moral reflection willingly acknowledges that right reason, sound moral judgment, is in many ways relative to situations and thus varies with times, places and persons.

In the first place, it is part of the very meaning, force and truth of many moral principles and norms to be applicable *variously*—i.e. in varying ways on varying occasions. Consider, for example, all those principles and norms which Christian ethics describes as valid, binding and applicable *semper sed non ad* (or: *pro*) *semper*—as always true and potentially relevant, but not on every occasion actually definitive of one's moral responsibility. It is always and everywhere true that one must honour one's parents, and this norm must always inform one's dispositions; but what the norm itself requires varies with persons and situations, and in many situations it has no actual part to play in one's reasonable deliberations.

Again, people today often assume that an ethic which, like the ethics of St. Paul and St. Thomas, thinks in terms of right reason must postulate that to every morally significant question of the form "What is to be done?", there is one right answer, an answer which reason requires (however difficult it may in practice be to find that uniquely correct answer, in complex situations). Some think they find this postulate in St. Thomas.[6] But he rejects it. Practical judgment on morally significant matters must never, and need never, be at variance with the principles and norms of reason (natural law). But judgments which fulfil that condition are of two different types. Some can be reached *by reasoning*, as conclusions or deductions from those principles and norms; and in these cases, as in all other cases of valid reasoning, one will have uniquely correct answers—in each case the one answer required by reason. But other judgments (St. Thomas explains), while not at variance with reason's principles and norms, are nonetheless not deducible from any set of true practical principles and norms—not even with the aid of additional true premises about the facts of the situation.

These reasonable judgments are not required by reason, but are specifications (*determinationes*) which give to reason's principles and norms a *chosen* application in much the same way as an architect *choosing* to make the doors in his building six feet five inches rather than six feet six inches high *makes a reasonable decision* which is *oriented* by and *gives effect to* the rational principles and norms of architecture yet is not (in its precise content) required by them; just the same could have been said of a decision (had he so chosen) to make the doors six feet six.[7] In short, one's choices are often: not simply between a right option and a wrong option, between the reasonable and the unreasonable, but: between two (or more) right, reasonable options. So there is another important relativity in Christian ethics: in many situations, various incompatible decisions are consistent with right reason, with *prudentia*, with upright practical wisdom.

So it is important to distinguish the question (i) What is the right course of action in this situation? from the question (ii) If such-and-such were done in this situation would it be right (i.e. *an* upright) course of action or would it be morally wrong? To the second question there is always one, and only one, right answer.[8] To the first, there is sometimes just one right answer, but very often not. Moreover, options can more easily be judged *wrong* options than *right* options. For: *malum ex quocumque defectu, bonum autem ex integra causa.*[9] An option will be wrong if its ulterior purpose(s) be wrong, or its context, or the means chosen to accomplish the purpose(s). To be right, purpose, context and means must each and all be upright. Rightness is much more relative to situation than wrongness is.

I return to the relativity which consists in the co-presence of incompatible right options. St. Thomas's account of this relativity is put forward by him in explanation of yet another type of relativity. Where the affairs of a community are at stake, those who have responsibility for managing those affairs for that community's common good often make decisions which commit the members of the community to a course of conduct which they would otherwise have had no commitment to, and no obligation to pursue. Custom, legislation, and judicial decisions with the force of precedent all can make morally obligatory what was not morally obligatory.[10] Thus what is morally obligatory in one community may be morally permissible, or even morally forbidden, in other communities, including communities whose relevant circumstances (apart from the law-making act itself) are identical. I gloss: Such a "legislative" decision, being between morally upright options, is not simply a matter of following or applying reason's requirements; it will be uprightly made if it is made by (a) a careful and fairminded attention to the human goods and bads involved in the alternative upright options, an attention which results in an "intuition" not of the *intelligibly* better or less bad option but rather of the option more appealing or less repugnant to feelings, or (b) by a fair *conventional procedure*, such as voting.

Significantly related to that type of relativity is yet another, which Aquinas puts like this. God can and does will the good of the whole universe, but human willing concerns particular objects (i.e. practical proposals for choice) which often enough are good in some respects but bad in others—as just punishment is good for the community but bad for the convict's family. So people of good will, St. Thomas continues, can rightly will incompatible objects. The judge rightly wills the suppression of the criminal's life or liberty, while the criminal's wife—though she could not rightly try to sabotage his trial or spring him from jail—rightly *wills his release.*[11] The connection with the previously mentioned type of relativity can be seen if one reflects on a situation common in modern politics: the rich and powerful propose a program to relieve the plight of the very poor, the program to be funded by imposing taxes which bear most heavily on the not-quite-so-poor. In such a situation, the very poor can fairly and rightly support and vote for the program, while the not-quite-so-poor can fairly and rightly oppose and vote against it.[12] And even a program which (unlike this one) involved no unfair scheme of funding could be funded in a number of different (fair) ways, about which fair-minded middle-income voters—while agreeing that *some* such program must be instituted with some such method of funding—could reasonably differ amongst themselves.

II. Absoluteness and Universality Affirmed by Christian Ethics

None of these ethical relativities undermines the objectivity, universality and absoluteness which Christian ethics, notoriously, affirms.

Christian ethics proposes its principles and norms as critically justified and true, as practical knowledge available to open-minded reason.

Moreover, Christian ethics proposes its principles and norms as universal, as true in all times and places for human beings, who all share in the human nature assumed by Jesus Christ, who fully reveals man to man himself and makes clear the supreme calling of every human person[13]—a calling to the Kingdom in which, transformed and purified, will be found all the goods intrinsic to human persons and their communion: "a kingdom of truth and life, of holiness and grace, of justice, love and peace".[14] By reason's grasp of these fundamental forms of human opportunity as intelligible benefits making sense of choice and action, and reason's ability to identify some options as truncations of human opportunity and destructive of a good or goods intrinsic to persons and their communion, moral requirements are known in conscience. As St. Paul puts it: human hearts are inscribed with moral requirements known in conscience—so that Gentiles who do not have God's revealed law can nonetheless know and do "by nature what the Law requires" (Romans 2:14–15). And he goes on to make it clear (Romans 13:8–10) that the law which Christian love fulfills finds a kind of summary in the Commandments, the observance of which Jesus had identified as a condition for eternal life (Matt. 19:16–20; Mk. 10:17–19; Lk. 18:18.21). Christ's own moral teaching was at its most specific in defining true marriage's indissolubility. This definition pivots on the commandment against adultery, and it is precisely here, in proposing a moral absolute and its implications, that Jesus affirmed that his moral teaching is grounded in the order of creation.[15]

Commenting on Paul's statement that love fulfils the commandments, Aquinas asks himself why Paul, in *Romans* 13:9, exemplifies the point by itemizing negative commandments of the Decalogue's second table. Aquinas's answer: Because the negative precepts are "more universal" than affirmative precepts such as "Honor your parents". They are more universal in respect of situations (*tempora*), for they are binding *semper et ad semper*—for there is no situation *[nullo enim tempore] in* which one is to (say) commit adultery—not even, as he states elsewhere, where an act of adultery would save a whole community from tyranny and ruin.[16] Affirmative precepts, on the other hand, bind indeed *semper, sed non ad semper, sed pro loco et tempore*, relative to situations. Moreover, negative precepts can have a greater universality *ad personas*, for no-one has the capacity to serve everyone, but we can all abstain from deliberately harming anyone at all.[17]

So: In the exceptionless applicability of these negative precepts or norms, these girders of the positive love of neighbor as oneself which flows from love of God, we find another absoluteness, a further non-relativity, in Christian ethics.

III. Accounting For Disagreement

Anyone who teaches young people today knows how thoroughly our culture puts into question the objectivity, the universality and the absoluteness of moral principles and norms. Students emerging from high school-freshmen—almost all see ethics as a projection of opinion; as a realm of subjectivity, of "value-judgments" which by definition are not truths; as an expression of attitudes peculiar to this or that culture, if there are ethical truths, they must remain at the level of generalities such as "Be well disposed towards your neighbor" or "Be tolerant and not judgmental"; specific norms about honesty or killing or sexual conduct could never be exceptionlessly true.[18] One might concede the truth of tautologies such as Always act honestly, Never behave unchastely, Never kill unjustly, and so forth; but what counts as honesty, chastity, injustice varies from culture to culture; there is no basis for an objective critique of cultures, validly transcending them all.

Those students who go on to philosophical studies find, of course, that their scepticism about ethics is not easily justifiable. It turns out to be difficult, or indeed impossible, to give an account of human knowledge which, while accounting for knowledge not only in the natural sciences but also of colors, meanings (whether of facial expressions or of statements), and philosophical conclusions, will leave no room for ethical knowing.[19] And it turns out to be fallacious to point to the sheer fact that opinions differ on ethical matters—for just as rational judgments in ethics, as in every other exercise of intelligence, do not appeal to the opinion of the judger or the agreement of other persons as a *ground* for making the judgment, so such judgments are not undermined by an appeal to the fact that the critic or other persons disagree. Indeed, a fine example of a "naturalistic fallacy" is supplied by any argument of the form:
"The fact of variety of opinion, and disagreement, about whether X is good/right/obligatory shows that it is not true that X is good/right/obligatory"—an invalid argument from "is" to "ought".

Contemporary English-speaking philosophers have, indeed, turned the fact of disagreement into an argument *against* this subjectivism and/or relativism. For: the subjectivist who thinks that "X is right" *means* "X is right *for me*" (or *means* "I think—i.e. it is a fact about me that I think—that X is right") fails to account for the facts. For: people often enough disagree with those who make statements such as "X is right", yet have no interest in what is right *for the speaker*, or in denying *the fact that* the speaker thinks what he thinks.[20] Moreover, moral disagreement very often takes the form of *argument*, in which the disputants take for granted that one or other (or perhaps each of them) is mistaken —but not mistaken about himself or about the autobiographical fact of what his views happen to be. And such argument is unintelligible unless the disputants treat at least some moral views as *not* matter for rational disagreement.

Still, the same contemporary philosophers—I think for example of Bernard Williams, the professor-elect of Moral Philosophy at Oxford—will not rarely be found supporting a moral relativism by appealing, with many sophisticated precautions, to the same considerations to which freshmen incautiously appeal:

...science has some chance of being more or less what it seems, a systematized account of how the world really is, while ethical thought has no chance of being everything it seems. The tradition is right, moreover, not only in thinking that there is such a distinction, but also in thinking that we can come to understand what it is through understanding disagreement.[21]... .

...An ethical theory might ... rationalize some cultural differences, showing why one local concept rather than others was ethically appropriate in particular circumstances.... But while it might explain why it was reasonable for people to have these various ethical beliefs, it would not be the sort of theory that could explain why they did or did not have them. It could not do something that explanations of perception can do, which is to generate an adequate theory of error and to account generally for the tendency of people to have what, according to its principles, are wrong beliefs.[22]

...[the idea of] our coming to have propositional knowledge of ethical truths ... must at least imply that a range of investigators could rationally, reasonably, and unconstrained come to converge on a determinate set of ethical conclusions. What are the hopes for such a process? I do not mean of its actually happening, but rather of our forming a coherent picture of how it might happen. If it is construed as convergence on a body of ethical truths which is brought about and explained by the fact that they are truths—this would seem the strict analogy to scientific objectivity—then I see no hope for it. In particular, there is no hope of extending to this level the kind of world-guidedness we [were] considering in the case of the thick ethical concepts [such as *coward, lie, brutality, gratitude*]. ... Nor is there a convincing analogy with mathematics... [for] every non-contradictory piece of mathematics is part of mathematics... [b]ut not every noncontradictory structure of ethical reflection can be part of one such subject, since bodies of ethical thought can conflict with one another in ways that not only lack the kinds of explanation that could form a credible theory of error, but have too many credible explanations of other kinds.[23]

I quote these denials of ethical objectivity at some length because the fact that they can be advanced by Williams as, so to speak, premises rather than conclusions—but they are his conclusions, too!—shows how he, not unreasonably, anticipates a set of more or less subjectivist or relativist presuppositions in his audience. Still, as other secular philosophers have observed, these denials all beg the question against ethical knowledge. They either presuppose that ethics attempts a form of explanation that is in fact quite foreign to it,[24] or simply *assert* precisely what needs *argument*, viz. that neither moral consensus nor moral disagreement (between individuals, or between cultures) can be rendered more intelligible by a true ethical theory or less intelligible by a false ethical theory

In fact, all the distinctions developed by a sound ethics serve two points. Their primary point is to clarify the moral distinctions between right and wrong, virtue and vice, and to identify (with reasons) what types of choice are right (or wrong), what types of disposition are virtuous (or vicious), why the judgments informing cowardly, dishonest, brutal and ungrateful choices truly are (as we have seen even Williams accepting) practical *falsehoods*. The distinctions intrinsic to a critically justified ethics serve also a secondary, incidental but important, function: of making it intelligible that morality is a matter of *reasonableness* while yet there are among rational people many disagreements about its content.

The sorts of distinctions I have in mind include the following (all of which need, and have received, much more explanation). First, there is the distinction (1) between reason and feeling, and the corresponding distinction between intelligible goods (benefits) and the merely-emotionally motivating goals of feelings. Then there is the distinction (2) between intelligible goods which are intrinsic to human persons and their communion (e.g. life, truth, friendship), and intelligible goods which have their intelligible attractiveness mediately, as means to the basic, intrinsic goods (such instrumental goods as money, a job, connections). There is here a third distinction to be made: (3) each of the basic goods is intelligible in itself and provides some *reason* for choosing and acting. But only considering all of the basic goods together, and all their possibilities for realization (in various persons and communities) does one have the total reason for choosing and acting. That total reason can be called "integral human fulfilment", the good of the whole human person and of all human persons and communities— compatibility of one's willing with integral human fulfilment is the demand of morality's first principle.[25]

Then there is the distinction (4) between those first principles of practical reasoning in which the basic human goods are identified as to be pursued, and the further "intermediate" principles in accordance with which the pursuit of basic human goods through chosen acts has that thoroughly reasonable character, that full compatibility with integral human fulfilment, which we call moral rightness principles of which the Golden Rule is one example, and the "Pauline principle" that one may not do evil that good may come is another.[26]

In turn, the coherent sense and force of these principles depends upon the distinction (5) between types of act specified by physical characteristics (*in specie naturae*) or by merely conventional descriptions, criteria, or classifications, and types of act specified precisely by the description which they have (*in specie moris*) in the practical deliberations of the agent, i.e. by what he intends as end and chooses as means in the proposal which he adopts by choice.[27] To illustrate this distinction, by reference to the Golden Rule, consider a sharp blow to one's back' by a colleague—struck jocularly and condescendingly to "congratulate" one on a *faux pas*; or struck, perhaps over-anxiously, but with friendly intent to get one's attention and save one from compounding the *faux pas*. The Golden Rule of fairness cannot be applied to the behavior in *genere naturae*: a sharp blow struck to a man's back by a colleague. But it can and must be applied to the two different acts which I described by describing the choices they respectively carry out.

Along with distinction (5) there comes immediately the further distinction (6) between what is intended and chosen (whether as end or as means) and what is knowingly caused, permitted, accepted, but not intended—sometimes expressed (though at the risk of seeming to refer to physical characteristics as such) as the distinction between what is "directly" and "indirectly" willed.[28] To illustrate this distinction, by reference to the Pauline principle, consider the administration of a certain quantity of analgesic drugs—this may be done for the sole purpose of relieving pain, though in the knowledge that life will be shortened; or it may be done for the purpose of shortening life so that death will bring relief from pain. Here there is not one human act, but two different acts according as the identical behavior carries out two different choices, the latter (but not the former) a choice to do evil—to destroy or damage, or to impede the continuance of, human life—for the sake of good.

Reflection on these structuring principles of ethics readily shows how diversity of moral opinion arises, takes shape in lasting cultures, propagates itself. For at every point, the intelligence which should make these distinctions must do so in a context confused by images, feelings, culturally formed concepts, vested interests (starting with one's own).... If even slightly confused or deflected in fundamentals, practical reason will yield countless deformations in the many particular situations of individual and social choice, deformations which in turn will obscure the fundamentals for whole eras and cultures. There is nothing at all surprising in the diversity of incompatible ethical views. Yet that diversity is by no means as great as is often loosely supposed, and there is never a point at which one must, despair of consensus with Williams' "rational, reasonable, and unconstrained" investigators, if they are to be found.

Moreover, the distinctions which I have outlined above make possible an understanding of the coherence of Christian ethics itself, in its historical development. For example: (7) While the basic goods intrinsic to human persons and their communion, such as the good of marriage, do not undergo essential change, social and cultural entities such as borrowing and lending do change, even essentially. So the development of a capital market linking interest on loans with the return on joint productive enterprises means that outwardly similar behavior, in 1288 and in 1988, can involve essentially different relationships between the wills of those doing it and the relevant human goods: same behavior, perhaps same cultural descriptions ("interest on loans") but different actions *in specie moris*.[29] Or again: (8) Options, particularly options for complex forms of social life, can be transformed by conceptual clarification. So a correct but undifferentiated moral judgment on the position which mingled religious freedom with indifferentism[30] can be transformed into two correct moral judgments on alternatives now adequately differentiated. Or again: (9) Emotional biases which blocked differentiation, for example between penal servitude and chattel *servitu-*

do, can be removed by changed social conditions, allowing the latent moral insight to be clearly articulated, as in the specific moral absolute which excludes slavery. Or (10) new or apparently new forms of behavior, such as taking the Pill, can raise the question whether they are instances of a familiar and, more or less well-understood form of action, such as contraception, and that question can clarify and deepen understanding of that action and of precisely why one does wrong in willing it. Finally, (11) other new behavior may prove, on analysis, to be indeed a new form of action, such as baby-production—a new form of action, but one which turns out to possess one morally decisive feature in common with the (fairly recently clarified) moral evil of slavery.[31]

IV. Relativism in Recent Moral Theology

I have just indicated eleven distinctions of importance to any rational ethics, and therefore to Christian ethics as reason's most thoroughgoing effort to understand what should and should not be chosen in the light of the fullest information about humankind's real situation and real destiny. Some of the distinctions are perhaps instantiations or sub-species of others in the list; other distinctions could be added to the list, such as that between negative and affirmative norms: But none of these distinctions, listed or unlisted, is merely a legalistic, apologetic distinction got up in defence of some pre-established position or some quasi-political *via media* between relativism and "classicist" rigidity. All are distinctions important to an understanding of the dynamics *of* the whole process of choice making. Many of them are distinctions fundamental to the logic of free choice between intelligible options, and some are fundamental to the very idea of creation—of divine creation and providence, as well as of human self-determination.[32] A Christian ethics which overlooked even one of these distinctions would be crippled in its attempt to understand our vocation to co-operation with the creator in building up a kingdom of God's redeemed children, *ad maiorem Dei gloriam*. Equally it would be crippled in any attempt to engage in discourse with secular philosophical proposals and critiques of relativism. Finally, it would be crippled in any attempt to understand the development of *doctrina de moribus*, and of Christian ethics itself.

A characteristic pre-Vatican II treatment such as Joseph Fuchs, *Theologia Moralis Generalis; pars prima* (1960)[33] deployed not one of the eleven distinctions.[34]

This is not the occasion for an analysis of the fragile philosophical structure of so many pre-Vatican II moral manuals. My purpose here is no more than to indicate some features of the route by which some of their authors, caught up as leaders in the post-conciliar revolt against main pillars of Catholic moral teaching, arrived at a relativism opposed to the universality and absoluteness always affirmed by Christian ethics.

According to Fuchs' treatise of 1960, the foundation of all moral knowing is in *synteresis*, an infallible knowledge of the first and most general moral principles—principles which one immediately understands and infallibly makes a moral judgment upon, as soon as one is confronted with the "object(s)" of these principles. The very first of these first principles is that *good is to be done*, the meaning of which is twofold: (i) It is good to subordinate oneself to the Absolute; (ii) Whatever, in accordance with right reason, is appropriate to one's own Being is good and to-be-done (as that Being depends on the Absolute).[35] This latter principle was given another formulation: (iia) The personal goodness of the (whole) man is to be expressed and realized by him through particular good acts.[36] The other first principles mentioned by Fuchs are: (iii) It is not licit to kill *whomever one feels like killing (quemlibet)*; and (iv) One should have some order in one's sexual life.[37]

Moral knowledge, continued Fuchs, is most often a matter of subsuming a *physical* object *(aliquod ohgiectum (physicum))* under a more primary, more general principle—or, equally, applying this principle to that *physical* object *(obiecto (physico))*—so as to arrive at, "thus", a less general, more determinate, and secondary principle.[38] Fuchs failed to show, or even to hint at, a way of deriving a secondary principle such as "No-one may directly kill anyone on his own private authority"[39] from a primary principle such as "one may not kill whenever one feels like it". Instead of attempting such a clarification of the supposed derivation of the more restrictive from the less, he lamely remarked that "subsumption" is not a matter of logic, but of holding in view simultaneously the truth of the moral principle and the "quality of the object"; and that the morality of concrete objects is most usually perceived immediately and intuitively.[40] Thus he not only contradicted his earlier assertion that general moral principles are more easily and securely known and understood than the morality of the concrete situation and concrete solutions in that situation.[41] More important, he treated *principled* moral knowledge as a mere ideological superstructure whose connections with right judgment on particular types of act, and particular options, cannot be made intelligible.

Such expositions of Christian ethics were gravely deficient in rational integrity. Their conception of the first principles of practical reason was confused, obscure, question-begging: their exposition of reason's advance from first principles to further principles, norms and judgments was almost non-existent, and where attempted was both incoherent and inconsequent (a series of *non sequiturs*). The exposition was quite inattentive to the problems raised by modern philosophy. And, perhaps more surprisingly, it thoroughly neglected the distinctions I have summarily listed and have suggested are essential to Christian ethics and to its notable explanatory power.

Since 1960, two roads have been followed. Some have undertaken a philosophical reconstruction which is at once attentive to the conceptions and arguments of the greatest Christian philosophers—concepts and arguments radically mutilated and confused in pre-conciliar treatments such as Fuchs's and at the same time an independent philosophical effort, attentive to reasons whatever their provenance. Following this road has yielded a fresh understanding of the distinct types of first and intermediate moral principles, an understanding very close to that of St Thomas—but clarified and further developed.[42]

Josef Fuchs himself, and not a few others, chose another road. While the old structure of self-evident first principles is nominally retained,[43] only one principle now provides a criterion of right moral behavior. In this sense, there is now only one absolute moral duty—the duty to act in the way which conforms to this one primary first principle of moral rightness in behavior.[44] What is this primary principle and criterion of moral rightness in action? It was not a principle identified in Fuchs's pre-conciliar writings. And while professing entire confidence in its decisive directiveness for moral judgment, in its capacity to distinguish right from wrong in moral judgment, Fuchs states the principle itself with a reticence, vagueness and variability scarcely distinguishable from evasiveness.[45]

At one end of the spectrum of versions he offers are formulations which are manifestly empty of criterial content:

> Right human behavior...can be understood only as what is right and appropriate with regard to the acting person. This includes a true relationship to others in all their dignity, rights and justified expectations, as well as to the nature and specificity of the various areas of human-earthly realities.[46]

Other, less frequent formulations allude to criteria embedded within the primary criterion itself, though Fuchs himself in no way attends to the tension between these inner criteria (dignity v. urgency) themselves:

> The question is then which of the qualities/values that are under consideration in a situation of incompatibility are to be given precedence by reason of their hierarchical order or their concrete urgency.[47]

And at the other end of the spectrum, there are the formulations which do succeed in conveying some notion of the principle's demand:

> To put, it positively: because of the coexistence of premoral goods and premoral evils in every human act, we must determine the moral rightness or wrongness of an act by *considering all goods and evils in an act and evaluating whether the evil or the good for human beings is prevalent* in the act, considering in this evaluation the hierarchy of values involved and the pressing character of certain values in the concrete.[48]

As is well known, this "principle", first formulated in the Enlightenment by, at latest, Jeremy Bentham, has encountered vigorous philosophical and theological critiques. For it proposes a "comparative evaluation"[49] of things multiply incomparable. It proposes that reason compare the human goods and bads involved in alternative options. These options include (1) goods and bads which are often of irreducibly different types (such as life and knowledge). But even when the good(s) involved in the alternative options are of the same category, those options must be comparatively evaluated not as states of affairs but *as options* involving (2) usually incalculable probabilities of realization and non-realization.[50] Moreover, the realization of the options by human choice and action itself involves (3) consequences of irreducibly different types (such as the states of affairs transitively caused by the action and the states of character reflexively or intransitively determined by the willing and intentional doing, or the non-intentional but accepting causing, of it). And the attempt to track divine providence by "considering all the goods and evils in an act", including its "outcomes and consequences", in an "all embracing view and total appraisal",[51] ends (unwittingly) in theological absurdity if one's human responsibility is simply to bring about what divine providence will (as faith teaches) bring about in any event—a realization of the world in which good is prevalent over bad—one could as well fulfil that responsibility by doing whatever takes one's fancy: *quodlibet*.

To objections of these forms, which have been very carefully argued, Fuchs makes the briefest and bluntest of replies:

> ...this problem is not new in moral theology, and therefore there is no special need to explain it here. For traditional moral theology was also aware of it, and said that determination of the proportionate reason is possible (for example, in judging an act with a double effect...)...[52]

> ...the accusation [of impracticability] is more theoretical than real: the practice of such evaluation is well established both in theory (e.g. with reference to action involving the principle of double effect, or to the ordering of the works of fraternal love, etc.) and in the area of practical life.[53]

This appeal to a "traditional moral theology"' (from which Fuchs elsewhere departs freely) is quite vain. For the traditional moral theological account of the fourth condition for applying the "principle of double effect"—that the good effect must be proportionate to the bad—offered no "'theory" of this comparison *other than that the comparison must he guided* by *moral norms*[54]—the very guidance which Fuchs rejects as inapplicable in assessing moral rightness or wrongness by reference to his primary principle.[55]

The variety and vagueness of Fuchs's formulations of his first principle of moral *recta ratio*, and the slenderness of his response to criticisms of that principle's rationality, suggest something that emerges in the following key passage:

> Norms and judgments of morally right behavior require an evaluation and a

comparison of the good/ills or values/nonvalues implied by particular conduct
in the human world; for responsible behavior must strive to augment human
goods and values.... One should interpret this position neither as simple utilitarianism nor as calculating consequentialism; *for* in such an endeavor [as Fuchs
proposes) to explain right behavior it is not the case that either means alone or
consequences alone are considered in isolation; rather the *entire reality of a
moral act* is taken into account—its own meaningfulness as seen within the context of the meaningfulness which the *entire act and its result* represent and signify.... final judgment about [such acts] cannot be made in the abstract, that is
without *simultaneously taking into account the circumstances and intentions* of
such acts, only in this way can the moral judgment about them be objective.[56]

What here (as elsewhere) emerges is that Fuchs's real concern is not: to
articulate a systematic ethical theory of principles of right and wrong, a theory
stated with care, defended dialectically, elaborated in a way which would *show*
what Fuchs wants to show—the moral falsity or inadequacy of the specific moral
absolute norms of Christian tradition's ethics. Rather, his concern is simply to set
aside—but without explicitly confronting it at all—the fundamental distinction
which that ethics formulated in a principle of ethical reflection to which I have
already referred: *bonum ex integra causa, malum autem ex quocumque defectu.*
That principle of reflection (articulated clearly before the end of the patristic age)
is tightly linked with another position recalled above, that there are (negative)
norms which hold not merely *semper* but also *ad semper.* For the latter position
entails that an upright person, noticing in the course of practical deliberation that
an option contravenes one of these norms, will simply dismiss that option from
further consideration: "for there is never a time to be considering whether, when,
with whom...to do an act"[57] contrary to such a norm. Similarly, such a person—
a prudent person, for prudence involves all the virtues—will exclude from further deliberation any option which is morally defective, e.g. in its means or
modus agendi, even if it was introduced into those deliberations with the best of
intentions and with a view to good consequences or to the avoidance of very bad
consequences. But one who follows Fuchs (and many others) will regard no
moral norm as capable of holding *semper et ad semper,* will see all norms as pro-
visional generalizations, and will always be open to considering that perhaps *now
is the time* for giving the norm a new formulation according to which *these are
circumstances* for making what, on the norm's old, inadequate formulation,
would be called an *exception.*

A thorough survey of the dissenting ethics of Catholic theologians shows
that their fundamental complaint about the tradition of Christian ethics is: it does
not "take into account" the whole reality of actions, including their circumstances, their motivating intentions, their anticipated effects. This is the complaint to which dissent keeps returning, as its other arguments falter and fail.[58]

The complaint is unwarranted. In judging that one factor is sufficient to render an option wrong, Christian ethics does not ignore any knowable aspect of that option's whole reality. In saying that evil—notably, the intentional destroying, damaging or impeding of a basic human good—must not be chosen for the sake of good, one does not ignore the goods that might have been achieved by choosing that evil. One may and/or should seek those goods by whatever other means (if any) are available. One is not refusing "to take those goods into account". One does not avert one's eyes from the relativities in differing situations. One is only refusing to undertake the rationally groundless "weighing" or "trading-off" of those goods against the bad (harm to persons) done *intentionally*—embraced into the will - by choosing such bad(s) as a means to such good(s).

The "morally neutral" "weighing" which the dissenting moralists invite us to undertake cannot be guided to any determinate conclusion by reason, and so - in the absence of other applicable moral principles—can be directed to a conclusion only by the feelings and/or by the socially existent conventions which impress the person who undertakes it. The invitation entails relativism; it extends to *the whole field* of morality itself the relativities which are inherent in the enactment of positive laws by choice *between morally upright alternatives*. For the invitation entails not only the relativism which Fuchs freely admits and defends: that there are no specific norms of right and wrong behavior which are applicable always and everywhere (since no formulation of such a norm could adequately take into account the variable totality of relevant factors). The invitation to do evil—intentionally destroy, damage or impede instantiations of basic human goods—for the sake of greater quantities (assessed morally neutrally) of good (or lesser amounts, similarly assessed, of evil) entails also a relativism which Fuchs and other Catholic theologians have been anxious to avoid (though less than zealous to rationally *refute*). The relativism it entails is relativism (subjectivity, lack of objectivity) in every moral judgment, a relativism inevitable when judgment can be reached only under the direction of feelings or conventions—including the feeling or convention that such-and-such a moral norm (moral generalisation) is to-be-applied in *these* circumstances.

An ethics grounded on the primary principle proposed by Fuchs and his followers collapses into unbounded relativism in its judgments on human action because that principle irrationally summons us to measure the immeasurable. Richard McCormick, closely following Fuchs, but facing critics and difficulties unnoticed by Fuchs, concludes:

...when dealing with "good things of very different types"... What do we do?

Somehow or other, in fear and trembling, we commensurate. In a sense we *adopt* a hierarchy.[59]

I would grant that the basic goods are incommensurable. One cannot measure one against the other if they are indeed basic. But perhaps we can adopt a hierarchy of values, either personally or socially.[60]

McCormick speaks of this as the "adoption of personal and community policies".[61] But Christian ethics, in proposing its principles and norms, and the supporting methodological distinctions which its theological critics never refute, scarcely mention, and then misstate, is not simply offering the products of some policy-maker's or law-maker's *decision* to adopt these principles, norms, adages and methods in order to give determinacy to what is rationally indeterminate. Nor is it proposing a set of *leges latae in praesumptione periculi communis* for the avoidance of the bad effects of moral anarchy.[62] It is communicating truths about the complex and various ways in which our willing, and thus our self-determination and our communion with other human persons, is related to the various goods intrinsic to human persons and their communion, and thus—though here Christian ethics draws on revelation—to the fulfilment of very many persons in the heavenly Kingdom. That Kingdom is now, by God's gratuitously promised gift, being built up by human choices.[63] It is built up not only by choices to promote those goods. It is built up also by choices to respect those goods, those aspects of persons and their communion—to respect them in the structure of one's choosings, not just in one's feelings and attitudes, and to do so even when our limited human foresight is dominated by the loss and damage which will ensue unless we violate that respect.[64]

NOTES

[1] Professor of Law and Legal Philosophy, Oxford University, and Fellow of University College; Biolchini Professor of Law, University of Notre Dame, Indiana. This paper was prepared for a conference in Washington, DC, in 1990; I have made a few bibliographical additions referring to later publications of my own, but have let the text stand. Many but not all the issues taken up in this paper are more formally treated in FINNIS, *Moral Absolutes* (Catholic University of America Press, 1991); FINNIS, *Absolutos Morales: Tradicion, Revision y Verdad (EIUNSA, Barcelona, 1992)*; FINNIS, *Gli assoluti morali* (Ed. Ares, Milan 1993).

[2] See, e.g., JOSEF FUCHS, *Personal Responsibility and Christian Morality* (Georgetown UP, Washington DC; Gill and Macmillan, Dublin, 1983) [PRCM] 133.

[3] See Lonergan, "Natural Right and Historical Mindedness", in F.E. Crowe SJ (ed.), *A Third Collection: Papers By Bernard J.F. Lonergan* (Paulist Press, New York; Geoffrey Chapman, London, 1985) 169–83 at 171–2, 176. This essay exemplifies the relativism introduced by distinguishing between what Karl Rahner (especially in an article on *Naturrecht*, which treats the matter in a way directly approved by Lonergan in his "The Transition from a Classicist Worldview to Historical-Mindedness", in his *Second Collection*, (Darton, Longman

and Todd, London, 1974) 1–10 at 6) called "transcendental necessities" and what he called "categorial" or "concrete" human nature: for references and comment, see Finnis, "The Natural Law, Objective Morality, and Vatican II" in WILLIAM E. MAY (ed.), *Principles of Catholic Moral Life* (Franciscan Herald P., Chicago, 1980) 113–49 at 139–42, 148; more thoroughly, Finnis, *"Historical Consciousness" and Theological Foundations*, Etienne Gilson Lecture No.15, Pontifical Institute of Mediaeval Studies, Toronto, 1992. For a critique of "classical moral theology" which is much more penetrating and adequate than Lonergan's broad-brush critique of "the classical world-view", see GERMAIN GRISEZ, *The Way of the Lord Jesus*, vol.1, *Christian Moral Principles[CMP]* (Franciscan Herald P., Chicago, 1983) 12–13, 16–17, 105–6.

[4] See FINNIS, *"Historical Consciousness" and Theological Foundations*, supra note 3 at pp. 1–16.

[5] *Ibid.* at pp. 23–25; GRISEZ, *Christian Moral Principles*, supra note3 at 182–183.

[6] Thus R.A. ARMSTRONG, *Primary and Secondary Precepts in Thomistic Natural Law Teaching* (The Hague, 1966) 159: "... implicit through his [Aquinas'] teaching on natural law is the idea that no matter how complex an issue may he, no matter how many different and oftentimes contradictory solutions may be suggested as being the right course of action, it nonetheless remains true that there is only one correct solution; there is one action, out of all the actions, whether suggested or otherwise which is the right action to do". He cites no text from St. Thomas; nor, I believe, could he. M. RHONHEIMER, *Natur als Grundlage der Moral* (Innsbruck & Vienna, 1986) 394, quotes the passage from Armstrong with apparent approval, though in the context of the somewhat different issue whether (as I do not deny) there is always one right answer to the question whether a particular (type of) action does or does not fall within a class of *intrinsece mala* such as adultery or murder. JOSEF FUCHS, *Christian Ethics in a Secular Arena* (Georgetown U.P., Washington DC; Gill & Macmillan, Dublin 1984) [CESA] p.44 goes further and claims that the prevailing conviction in the Catholic moral theological tradition is that "moral norms determine the concrete moral truth through assumed application to the concrete situation. This means that the aggregate of formulated (or formulable) general moral norms contains in itself all concrete moral truth".

[7] *Summa Theologiae [ST]* I–II q.95 a.2; FINNIS, *Natural Law and Natural Rights* (Oxford U.P., 1980), 281–290, 294–296.

[8] See ST I–II q. 18, a. 9.

[9] Cf. ST I–II q. 18a.4 ad 3; q.19 a.6 ad 1; de Malo q.2a.4 ad 2.

[10] ST I–II q. 95 a.2: the products of such decisions (the customs, laws, etc.) have their force just from their having been made: *ex sola lege humana vigorem habent*.

[11] STI–IIq.19 a.10.

¹² See further Finnis, "The Consistent Ethic—A Philosophical Critique", in FUECHTMANN (ed.), *Consistent Ethic of Life* (Kansas City, 1988) 140–181 at 163–4. There I add that the very rich are in a moral perplexity by reason of the prior injustice of their position: they cannot oppose the program without compounding their injustice to the worst-off, nor support it without compounding their injustice to the not-quite-so-poor. This program, which is really just and really unjust—i.e. whose injustice has yet another type of relativity—would not have been needed if they had not been hanging on to their inequitable advantages.

¹³ Vatican II, *Gaudium et Spes22.*

¹⁴ *Gaudium et Spes39.*

¹⁵ As the Synoptics put it: Moses because of the hardness of hearts allowed divorce, but *from the beginning of creation* it was not so; And I [Jesus] say that whoever puts away his wife and marries another commits adultery; and she, if she marries another, commits adultery, too: cf. Matt. 19:4–9; Mk. 10:4–12; Lk. 16:18. So the earliest Christian philosophers and systematic theologians had solid grounds for calling the Decalogue's precepts (at least its second table) natural moral law. In Irenaeus' phrases: *naturalia legis ..., naturalia praecepta quae ab initio infixa dedit hominibus..., naturalia et liberatia et commnia omnium: Adv. Haer.* IV, 13,1; 15,1; 16,5.. On the whole matter of the importance of the Decalogue in the apostolic and early patristic eras, see *GUY BOURGEAULT, Decalogue et morale chretienne: enquete patristique sur l'utilisation et líinterpre'tation chretienne du decaloque de c. 60 a c.* 220 (Paris, 1971). As Justin Martyr had earlier noted, *Dialogue with Trypho* c. 93,1, revealed norms of the Decalogue are also rational, available to any conscience not blinded by sin. Irenaeus links the Decalogue tightly to his theology of human fulfillment: the glory of God is living man, but the life of man is the vision of God; and God has no need of our love or service; it is we who have need of God's glory, which can in no way be attained save through service of God; and to prepare us for this life of friendship with God and concord with neighbor, the Lord articulated the Decalogue which Jesus reaffirmed, amplified and perfected (*Adv.. Haer. IV*, 20,7; 16,3 & 4; 12,5; 13,1 & 3). In short; the moral norms of the Decalogue guide us towards human fulfillment, by disclosing God's plan for our sharing in his glorious kingdom.

¹⁶ *De Malo q.*15 a. 1 arg. 5 [4] & ad5 [4].

¹⁷ AQUINAS, *Commentarium in Epistolam S. Pauli ad Romanos* c. xiii lect. ii (ad v.9).

¹⁸ The denial is less confident when it comes to some specific norms well supported in our culture: "Rape is always wrong"; "Slavery is always wrong".

¹⁹ See the critique of John Mackie's argument from the queerness of ethical knowing, in FINNIS, *Fundamentals of Ethics* 58–60. See also SUSAN HURLEY, *Natural Reasons: Personality and Polity* (Oxford U.P., New York &

Oxford, 1989)302.

[20] See e.g. BERNARD WILLIAMS, *Morality: An Introduction to Ethics* (Harper, New York & London, 1972)15; BERNARD WILLIAMS *Moral Luck* (Cambridge U.P., Cambridge & New York, 1981)142.

[21] BERNARD WILLIAMS, *Ethics and the Limits of Philosophy* (Cambridge, Mass., & London, 1985) 135.

[22] *Ibid.*, 151.

[23] *Ibid.*, 151–2.

[24] See, e.g. HURLEY, *Natural Reasons* 291: "It's false that ethics has 'no hope of being everything it seems', not because it seems to describe reality in explanatorily primary terms and it really does so after all, but because it doesn't seem to do so to begin with, nor should it. Ethics simply doesn't have the aspirations with respect to the explanation of convergence Williams attributes to it".

[25] For a formulation and explanation of the moral first principle, and an explanation of its relationship to the first principle and primary principles of practical reasoning, see FINNIS, BOYLE AND GRISEZ, *Nuclear Deterrence, Morality and Realism* (Oxford U.P., Oxford & New York, 1987) [NDMR] 281–4; GRISEZ, BOYLE and FINNIS, "Practical Principles, Moral Truth and Ultimate Ends", *American J. Jurisp.* 32 (1987)121–2. The moral first principle is equivalently formulated by VATICAN II in *Gaudium et Spes* 35, see GRISEZ, CMP 183–189.

[26] On the various formulations of the Pauline principle, see FINNIS, *Fundamentals of Ethics* 109–127; for a further defence of the attribution of this principle to (*inter alios*) St. Paul (in Romans 3:8) see FINNIS, *Moral Absolutes* 59–67.

[27] The importance of this distinction for a proper understanding of the ethics of St. Thomas, and of Christianity, has been rightly insisted upon by, e.g. RHONHEIMER, *Natur als Grundlage der Moral 61–2*, 81,91–7, 327–345, 352–3, 367–74, 375–77, 398–400.

[28] For the equivalence, in this context, of "direct" and "as an end or as a means", see Pius XII, Discourse to the St. Luke Medical-Biological Union, 12 November 1944, *Discorsi e Radiomessagi* VI (1944–45) 191–2, cited in PAUL VI, *Humanae Vitae*, note 14, and in the CONGREGATION FOR THE DOCRINE OF THE FAITH, *Declaration on Procured Abortion* (1974), para.7 at note 15 ("Pius XII clearly excluded all direct abortion, that is, abortion which is either an end or a means"); also CONGREGATION FOR THE DOCTRINE OF THE FAITH, *Donum Vitae*, 22 February 1987, at note 20.

[29] So to the old, immoral option of usury is added the new or newly clarified option of charging interest on loans at a rate, established by a capital market, which fairly reflects the lender's entitlement to compensation for his risk and for forgoing participation in the equity, the profit, of other economic enterprises.

[30] Or with the opinion that religious liberty entails that religious vows are neither

morally binding nor even morality proper (e.g. the decision of the French revolutionary Constituent Assembly of 12/13 February 1790); or with the opinion that liberty of forming and publicly expressing opinion must be absolutely untrammeled (e.g. the teachings of Lamennais's liberal Catholic newspaper *L'Avenir* beginning in 1830 and condemned by Pope Gregory XVI's *Mirari Vos* in 1832: see BRIAN HARRISON, *Religious Liberty and Contraception*,(John XXIII Fellowship Co-operative, Melbourne, 1988) 34–42).

[31] See *Donum Vitae* (Congregation for the Doctrine of the Faith, Instruction on Respect for Human Life in its Origin and on the Dignity of Procreation, 22 February 1987) II.B.4–5 (AAS 80 (1988) 70–102 at 90–94); FORD, GRISEZ, BOYLE, FINNIS AND MAY, *The Teaching of Humanae Vjtae: A Defense* (Ignatius Press, San Francisco, 1988) 95–97.

[32] See FINNIS, "On Creation and Ethics" *Anthropotes* 1989/2, 197–206.

[33] This is not to deny that Fuchs's treatise has some rather personal, indeed strange, features: e.g. the emphasis on the "call of God in the situation," (*Deus vocans in situatione concreta*: p.40); the claim that, quite ordinarily, a man's situation itself has a *"sensus et intentio"* which come from God and are to be "realized" by that man here and now (pp.40–41); the claim that in *synderesis* "the whole man is present to himself, in the depth (*'scintilla'*) of his soul" (p.154); and the claim that there is a real and important distinction between my judgments of antecedent conscience about the-act-to-be-done-by-me (which he thinks somehow "theoretical" judgments) and my judgments of antecedent conscience about my-doing-the-act (which he thinks truly "practical" judgments) (pp. 164, 152).

[34] And it seems to treat the distinction between affirmative and negative norms as an "adage" (p.51) which is of dubious or no weight (cf. p.83).

[35] FUCHS, *Theologia Moralis Generalis* 154.

[36] *Ibid.*

[37] *Ibid.*, p. 85 (Fuchs's emphases).

[38] *Ibid.*, p. 155.

[39] *Ibid.*, p. 85.

[40] *Ibid.*, p.155.

[41] *Ibid.*, p. 46.

[42] See the annotated bibliography at the end of GRISEZ, BOYLE and FINNIS, "Practical Principles, Moral Truth, and Ultimate Ends", *American J. Jurisp.* 32(1987) at 149–51.

[43] See FUCHS, PRCM 130. The very first principle, of subordination to the Absolute, has now a rather different ring, however: compare, e.g., FUCHS, *Christian Morality: The Word Becomes Flesh* [CMWF] 44–48 with FUCHS, *Theologia Moralis Generalis* I, pp.36–48. And, in general (see e.g. CESA 31), these moral principles are now merely "'formal" (without "material" content) and seem to be removed to a realm of "moral goodness" which Fuchs insists is

radically distinct from the realm of "moral rightness", an insistence never adequately justified and involving a legalistic exaggeration of the distinction between formal and material sin and the reality of invincible and inculpable ignorance of moral norms—an exaggeration which overlooks the way in which such ignorance involves the agent in real loss and self-mutilation in his participation in goods intrinsic to human persons and their communion.

⁴⁴ See CESA 84 (= Fuchs, "'Intrinsece malum'; Ueberlegungen zu einem umstrittenen Begriffî in WALTER KERBER (ed.), *Sittliche Normen* (Patmos, Dusseldorf, 1982) at p.87).

⁴⁵ It is as if he wished to preserve a lofty neutrality between the positions adopted by his influential disciples or former students—say, between Timothy O'Connell and Peter Knauer. The former adheres to "Schueller's preference principle": "Maximize the good and minimize the evil": see TIMOTHY E. O'CONNELL, *Principles for a Catholic Morality* (Seabury Press, New York, 1978) 153, 223. The latter is aware of some of the problems of incommensurability which make that "principle" senseless, and proposes instead a principle directing one to avoid actions which in the long run "contradict" the value they seek: see Knauer, "The Hermeneutic Function of the Principle of Double Effect" in CURRAN AND MCCORMICK, *Readings in Moral Theology* No 1 (Paulist P., New York, 1979 1–39 at 11–13.) (For the failure of Knauer's effort to avoid the problems, cf. FINNIS, *Fundamentals of Ethics* 99–104.)

⁴⁶ *CESA* 40. See also: "...the better human way toward realization of this world": *CESA* 10; "...way of realizing the earthly data of the world of man [which] is really human... conducive to the well-being of man and his world"; *CESA* 52; "...behavior in this earthly reality [which] best corresponds to this human inner-wordly reality..": *CESA* 143; "...serve to enhance the world of human persons—of the individual, of interpersonal relationships, of human society, of the sub-personal world—and thus to realize the true good of the human person (of humanity)": *CMWP* 14; "...actualization of the individual person and of the formation of a human world": *CMWF* 15; "Rightness can he predicated of acts—i.e. whether they are in accord with the shaping of the horizontal reality of the human world as a human reality, or do not contradict it": *CMWF* 96: "action should correspond to concrete being as a given and a task; it must encompass the whole significance of the totality of the unique human reality, insofar as the—at least attempted—personal realization is the acceptance or refusal of self": *PRCM* 214.

⁴⁷ CMWF 132; *PRCM* 131. And what is the order of precedence between hierarchical order and concrete urgency? And between concrete urgency and long-term dangers? Fuchs fails even to identify the relevant questions.

⁴⁸ *CESA* 82. This formulation ends with the same problematic directive as those cited in the previous footnote, but at least identifies the program of deliberation.

⁴⁹ CESA 83; CMWF16.

⁵⁰ *NDMR* 240–54.

[51] *PRCM* 130,131.

[52] *CESA* 83.

[53] *CMWF* 16.

[54] The requirement of "proportionateness" proposed by Aquinas at the origin of the "doctrine" (*Summa Theol* 'II–II q. 64 a. 7, on lethal measures of self-defense) used no concept of greater good or lesser evil, and involved no scrutiny of overall net consequences; it merely required that the action which causes the foreseen harm must be no more harmful than is necessary for defending oneself then and there: the act must be *proportionatus fini*, proportioned to its own end, (See FINNIS, *Fundamentals of Ethics* 85.) When the Salamanticenses, in the mid-seventeenth century, generalized St. Thomas' discussion, they proposed that causing the unintended but foreseen and harmful side-effect is morally upright only when one is "morally powerless to prevent it", bearing in mind the "the virtues to which the evil permitted is opposed". SALMANTICENSES, *Cursus Theologicus* vol.7 *de Peccatis'* (1647) tr. 13 disp.10 dub.6; see J.T. MANGAN, "An Historical Analysis of the Principle of Double Effect" *Theol. St.* 10 (1949) 40 at 57. Similarly, when Joannes Gury SJ in 1850 stabilized the textbook tradition of what thereafter became known as the "doctrine" of double effect, he gave a similar explanation: there is a "proportionately serious reason for actuating the cause" of the harmful side-effect, when "the author of the action would not be obliged by any virtue, e.g. from justice or charity, to omit the action": GURY, *Compendium Theologiae Moralis* I ([1850] 5th ed. Ratisbon, 1874) "de actibus humanis" c. 2 n. 9; see Mangan at 60–61. Thus moral norms were conceived as controlling, not controlled by, any assessing of consequences. (This is no surprise, since the other requirements specified in the "doctrine" of double effect likewise propose moral limits on the pursuit of good consequences—limits such as lead proportionalists generally to reject the "doctrine".)

[55] "The judgment about the rightness of human conduct... replies in a way *that is neutral from the moral point of view* to only one question: which realization of the reality is to be considered humanly—that is, from the point of view of the existence of human beings, appropriate or inappropriate? ...the judgment about right conduct (on its part a morally neutral judgment)..".: Fuchs, "Historicity and Moral Norm" in R GALLAGHER AND B. MCCONVERY (eds.), *History and Conscience* (Gill & Macmillan, Dublin, 1989)32 (emphasis added).

[56] CMWF 16 (emphases added). Cf, among many other passages, PRCM 133: "the decisive truth... that if behavioral norms are to be operative, *the entire pertinent reality* (including the social factor) *has to be taken into account* and enter into the judgment" (emphasis added).

[57] Cf. ARISTOTLE, *Nicomachean Ethics* II.6: 1107 a 9.17; FINNIS, "Aristotle, Aquinas, and moral absolutes", *Catholica* (English ed.) no. 12(1990) 7–15; FINNIS, *Moral Absolutes* 31–37.

[58] See FINNIS, *Moral Absolutes* 95–96, 98–101.

[59] McCormick, in MCCORMICK AND RAMSEY, *Doing Evil to Achieve Good* (Loyola U.P., Chicago, 1978) 227 (emphasis in original).

[60] *Ibid.* 252 (emphasis in original).

[61] *Ibid.* 229.

[62] Cf. MCCORMICK, *ibid.* 44. "...where we view norms as 'virtually exception-less', we do so or ought to do so because of the prudential validity of what we refer to technically as *lex lata in praesumptione periculi conmunis* (a law established on the presumption of common and universal danger)".

[63] Cf. JOHN PAUL II, Encyclical *Sollicitudo Rei Socialis*, 30 December 1987, para 48: "However imperfect and temporary are all the things that can and ought to be done through the combined efforts of everyone and through divine grace, at a given moment of history, in order to make people's lives 'more human', nothing will be *lost or will have been in vain*. This is the teaching of the Second Vatican Council, in an enlightening passage of the Pastoral Constitution *Gaudium et Spes*: 'After we have obeyed the Lord, and in His Spirit nurtured here on earth the values of human dignity, brotherhood and freedom, i.e. all the good fruits of our nature and enterprise, we will find them again, but freed of stain, illumined and transfigured, when Christ presents to his Father an eternal and universal kingdom...'" See Gaudium et Spes 39.

[64] SeeNDMR ch.14.

18

Abortion: Can It Ever Be Justified?

John Foster

I

Can abortion ever be justified? Well, perhaps I ought to begin, in true Oxford-philosophical style, by clarifying the question. What's meant by 'abortion'? What's meant by 'justified'?

First, then, the term 'abortion'. In medical circles, this is sometimes used as a synonym for 'miscarriage'. When used in this sense, we can speak of an abortion even when the miscarriage is purely accidental—for example, the result of a fall. But outside the medical world, the term is normally reserved for cases in which the miscarriage is deliberately induced—cases in which someone deliberately terminates the pregnancy with the intention of killing the unborn child (or perhaps put less tendentiously, of killing the pre-natal human organism). It's this sort of case—the deliberate destruction of the unborn child/organism—that I mainly want to talk about and it's this that I'm going to use the term "abortion" to signify. It's important to realise that abortion in this sense is to be distinguished, not only from cases of accidental miscarriage, but also from cases in which, when the pregnancy is deliberately terminated, the death of the offspring is foreseen but not intended. People sometimes find it difficult to draw this distinction, or having drawn it, to appreciate its moral relevance. But I'll try to explain what I've got in mind here presently.

So much for the term 'abortion'. What about the term 'justified'? Well, the point I want to stress here is that I'm only concerned with the issue of *moral* justification. I've no doubt that, leaving aside the moral dimension, an expectant mother can sometimes find strong *practical* reasons in favour of having an abortion. And these practical reasons, considered in their own terms, could provide a sort of justification—they could show why, ignoring the claims of morality, it was rational for her to have the pregnancy terminated. But what I'm concerned with are the issues of right and wrong. Are there really any cases in which, as well as serving someone's interests, abortion is morally permissible, something which can be done without breach of the moral law, something which, as a Christian would put it, God would not forbid?

So my question becomes: are there any circumstances in which the *deliberate* (intentional) killing of the unborn child—the pre-natal human organism—is *morally* justified (*morally* permissible)? And my answer to that is, unequivocally: 'No'.

In defense of this answer, I'm going to divide my discussion into two parts. In the first part, and in fact this will form the bulk of my discussion, I want to approach the issue in purely secular terms, without presupposing any religious position. I want to try to show that the immorality of abortion (in the relevant sense) can be established from premises which any rational person, of normal sensitivity, can accept. In the second part, which will be much shorter, I shall try to back up my conclusions by appealing to doctrines which are distinctively theological, and indeed distinctively Christian.

II

My case against abortion can be expressed quite simply. Abortion, in the sense, which here concerns us, is the deliberate destruction of the pre-natal human organism. It's my contention that, from conception (i.e. fertilization), this organism qualifies as a human individual, in exactly the same sense as you and I so qualify; and—in case this is thought relevant—I take it as obvious that, prior to birth, this individual is, in all relevant respects, morally innocent. Consequently, I view abortion as an act of grave injustice, morally tantamount to murder, and I regard its institutionalized practice as having no better claim to moral acceptability than Hitler's extermination programme. It goes without saying that, in viewing it as tantamount to murder, I also advocate its legal prohibition.

That, then, is my position put in its simplest terms. I'll concentrate on defending it against objections. The most obvious objection, and arguably the most important, concerns the status of the pre-natal organism, and it's with this that I'll begin.

I've expressed my belief that the pre-natal organism qualifies as a human individual, and does so from conception. But at conception (fertilization) it doesn't have a recognizably human form or organization; for it's just one cell. How can I seriously maintain that this is a genuine human being? To do so might seem as absurd as thinking that you've built a house when you've laid the first brick.

Opponents of abortion sometimes try to meet this objection by posing a challenge of their own. If human life doesn't begin at conception, when does it begin? At what point in its development does the organism become a genuine human being? Because the development is so gradual, any answer, other than conception, seems wholly arbitrary. Apart from conception, there seems to be no momentary change sufficiently decisive to constitute the definite transition from something which lacks the status of a human being to something which has it. But I find this challenge, as it stands, unconvincing. After all, when a house is being built, we can't, without arbitrariness, identify the moment when the house comes into existence. There's no critical episode of brick-laying which constitutes the definite transition from something which isn't a house to something which is. But we can be quite sure that there's no house in existence when only a single brick, or a few bricks, have been laid. Why not construe the case of human development in a similar way, treating the conceptus as the first brick? Why not deny that the conceptus is a human being, but also deny that there is any definite subsequent moment when the human being comes into existence? Why not say that the emergence of the human being is gradual, like that of the house?

It's clear that, to meet the objection effectively, we need a positive reason for taking conception as the decisive moment when human life begins. Such a reason emerges when we look more closely at the supposed analogy between foetal development and house-building. For, on closer inspection, what stands out are not the similarities between the two cases, but the differences. Three differences, in particular, need to be stressed. First, the initial brick which is laid in the process of house-building doesn't contain a plan of what the completed house will be like. But, in contrast, the conceptus *does* contain, in its genes, a plan of what the fully developed organism will be like. Of course, this genetic plan doesn't determine every aspect of the subsequent development. There are many other factors, both during the foetal stage and more especially after birth, which affect what physical and psychological characteristics the mature organism will have. But these factors affect the details of a process which is, in broad outline, genetically determined. Pursuing the building analogy, we may say that, unlike the brick, the conceptus contains in its genetic material, what corresponds, in the case of the house, to the architect's instructions. Second, after laying the first brick, the builder can't just leave it to grow into a house. The brick won't grow into a house even if the builder inscribes the architect's instructions on its surface and leaves a pile of bricks and cement within easy reach. The brick won't grow, into a house or anything else, because it isn't a living organism. But the conceptus, of course, is a living organism, and it will grow into something which is recognizably human just by drawing nourishment from its mother's body. In this sense, as well as containing the architect's instructions, the conceptus possesses the skills and motivation of the builder. It contains a plan of its subsequent development *and* the capacity and disposition to execute this plan on the raw materials at hand. Third, to construct a house, the builder has to keep adding new bricks to those already laid. Once laid, each brick remains unchanged as the rest of the house takes shape. But, in contrast, the embryo develops by a process of cell-division. The fertilized egg grows and divides, the two new cells grow and divide, and so on through all the phases of development, until the mature human form is reached. What we have here is a single expanding organism rather than, as in the case of the house, the mere aggregation of separate bits and pieces. In short, while bricks are merely inert blocks of matter, which can be assembled into some complex structure in accordance with an external human plan and under the control of an external human agent, the conceptus is intrinsically structured in such a way that, given only a suitable environment, it will develop, by an internal process of cell-growth and cell-division, into the new-born baby whose full humanity is not in question. In the light of this, there can be no doubt that, biologically speaking, the human being comes into existence at conception. All subsequent embryonic and foetal development is just the process by which a human individual which has existed from conception gradually realizes its inherent potential. The pre-natal development and the post-natal development are just different phases in the history of a single biological continuant, which started life as one cell at fertilization. This allows us to meet the objection. To say that the conceptus doesn't count as a genuine human being because it lacks a recognizably human form is as inept as saying that a new-born baby doesn't count as a genuine human being because it lacks the form of an adult or that a sprouting acorn doesn't count as a genuine oak because it lacks the form of the mature tree. The fact is that the conceptus has precisely that form which a human being needs to have at that phase of his existence.

At this point, the defenders of abortion may try a different tack. They may say that even though the pre-natal organism, qualifies as a human individual from conception, it doesn't have *initially* the same moral standing as it will come to acquire in its more mature state. If we then enquire what the morally relevant difference is between human beings at different stages of maturity, we'll be told that it's a difference in their mental capacities. The pre-natal organism, or at least the organism in its earliest phase, doesn't merit the same degree of moral respect as (say) the schoolchild or the adult, because it hasn't reached the same level of psychological maturity. The point is sometimes expressed as the claim that the pre-natal organism isn't yet a person.

This view of the matter is a commonly held one, but a little reflection shows it to be both deeply counterintuitive and devoid of any rationale. In the first place, there's no way of developing it which accommodates the moral status we ordinarily assign to a new-born baby, together with the lesser status we assign to such creatures as adult dogs and chimpanzees. The new-born baby has the potential to develop to a point where its psychological capacities vastly exceed, and indeed transcend in kind, those of such animals. But this is a matter of its greater potential rather than of its current mental condition. So if we were to make moral standing depend on current capacities, we would either have to reduce the standing of the baby to match or fall below that which we ordinarily assign to the animals or increase the standing of the animals to match or exceed that which we ordinarily assign to the baby. But surely we wouldn't, in practice, be willing to alter our moral attitudes in either of these ways. Moreover, however the position is developed, there just isn't any rationale for the suggestion that it's the *current* capacities which are morally crucial.

No doubt the special moral status we assign to human beings derives, in part, from the special richness of human mentality in its mature form. But why should it be thought more acceptable to deprive someone of the opportunity of *acquiring* such mentality than to rob someone of it when it's in his possession? We don't think that it's morally better to prevent someone from inheriting money to which he's entitled than to steal it from him after he's received it. And if someone's in a coma from which, with proper nursing, we expect him to recover, we wouldn't count it as less than murder to kill him in his present comatose state. So on what grounds could we discriminate against the pre-natal organism, given that it qualifies as a human individual and is the very thing which, if left to develop, will come to have the mental capacities of the schoolchild and the adult?

It might be objected that we are setting up the issue in the wrong way. We're assuming that, whatever its psychological endowments and moral status, the pre-natal organism is what eventually becomes the adult person—that the adult person can look back and say of the organism, even at conception: 'That was *me*'. But it might be objected that, strictly speaking, a person is not a biological organism, but something purely spiritual. The real *me*—the thing which thinks and feels and perceives and wills—is not this body, but something which, as it were, inhabits it and which may survive after my body has decayed. If so, then what's really at issue is presumably: at what point, in the history of the organism, does this spiritual entity (the soul) enter the body? Does it enter at conception, or when the brain is formed, or at quickening, or at birth, or still later? If it enters at some point after conception, then abortion prior to that point would not be tantamount to murder: the destruction of the organism would not be the killing of a person, or of a human individual in the morally relevant sense.

This Cartesian conception of the self as a purely spiritual entity is a highly controversial one—and indeed most philosophers now would reject it. But even if we accept it (and I've defended it myself in my book *The Immaterial Self*), I see no grounds for revising our conclusion about the point when the human person (or the human individual in the relevant sense) comes into existence. We might concede that until the organism has a working brain, the soul and the body will not interact in the ordinary sense. The soul will not experience anything as a result of what is taking place in the body, and it will not be able to act on the body in the way in which I can now move my limbs. But this doesn't mean that before it has a working brain, the organism does not possess a soul. Given the biological significance of conception, it seems very likely that the soul comes into existence at the same time and that it is attached to the conceptus in virtue of the fact that its potential to acquire a subsequent psychological life is inextricably bound up with the conceptus's potential to develop a central nervous system. I admit that, as it stands, this conclusion is less than certain, since, in the nature of things the creation of the soul and its attachment to the body are not things that we can scientifically detect. But, crucially, this lack of certainty makes no practical difference. For if there is room for doubt, we are morally obliged to give the conceptus the benefit of it. If there is a signifiicant chance that the conceptus has a soul, and thus embodies a person, we should act on the presumption that it does, just as, if there is a significant chance that an accident victim is still alive, we should act on the presumption that he is. It would be far worse to fail to accord the conceptus the respect to which it is entitled than to accord it a respect to which it is not.

It's clear, then, that, whether or not we think of a person as a purely spiritual entity or as something which has both a spiritual and a corporeal nature, the pre-natal organism must, from conception, be accorded the same moral status as human beings at any later stage of development. The conclusion I draw from this is that abortion (the deliberate killing of the pre-natal organism) is an act of grave injustice of the same kind and of the same degree as the deliberate killing of anyone else who is innocent. To put it bluntly, I regard abortion as murder, though a form of murder which, in certain circumstances, our present unjust system of laws permit.

However, I suspect that a number of people who are prepared to accept my premises would want to challenge this conclusion from another direction. They would concede, that other things being equal, the deliberate killing of an innocent human being is an act of grave injustice; but they would also claim that, in the case of abortion, other things are not always equal. There are, they would say, other morally relevant considerations, such as the welfare of the mother, the welfare of her family, and the predicted quality of life of the child himself. What if the pregnancy was the result of rape? What if the mother is an unmarried teenager? What if the unborn child is mentally or physically handicapped? These and many other considerations might be thought to show that, in the circumstances, an abortion, while regrettable, was the lesser of two evils—that, on balance, one would do more harm by allowing the pregnancy to continue than by terminating it. And in any case, however we might assess the moral pros and cons of an abortion on a particular case, shouldn't the decision be left in the hands of the mother? Even if the pre-natal organism is a human individual, with the same moral status as you and I, what right do we have to insist that, irrespective of her wishes, the mother should put her body at its disposal? After all, we probably wouldn't think it appropriate to *force* someone to give a pint of blood to save another's life. And the giving of blood is a much smaller sacrifice than the continuation of an unwanted pregnancy.

This last point is based on a confusion. The anti-abortion position to which I am committed does not claim that the mother should be forced, or legally required, to do something positive to help the continuation of the pregnancy. For example, if the pregnancy has run into difficulties and ones which can only be overcome by the mother taking a certain drug, I'm not saying that she should be legally required to take it; nor, for that matter, am I ruling that out—the position I'm defending simply doesn't commit me either way. All that this position requires is that the unborn child should enjoy the same kind of legal protection as other human beings—so that the mother and her medical practitioners be under a legal obligation to refrain from doing anything with a view to destroying or harming it. Maybe a person should have the legal right to refuse to give his blood to save another's life. But he shouldn't have the legal right deliberately to kill or harm another—at least this other person is, in all relevant respects, innocent. In seeking for the legal prohibition of abortion, all I'm doing is applying the same principle to the case of the born and unborn alike.

I must now clear up a second confusion. It occasionally happens that the continuation of a pregnancy involves a serious risk to the mother's life. For example, let's suppose that, in the fourth month, the mother is discovered to have cancer of the womb. The cancer, we'll assume, is in its early stages, so that there's some chance that if the pregnancy is allowed to continue, she'll give birth to a healthy baby. At the same time, the doctors may know that, from her standpoint, the only safe treatment would be to remove the cancerous womb immediately. If we prohibit abortion, it seems that we're condemning the woman to death; we're choosing to protect the life of the baby at the expense of the life of the mother. And surely, where the issue is between her own life and the baby's, we should allow the mother to decide the matter for herself. Isn't this what natural justice demands?

Well, yes, in the sort of case we're here envisaging, I think it is. But the point I want to stress is that the position which I'm defending doesn't commit me to denying this. As I made clear at the outset, when I condemn abortion, and advocate its legal prohibition, what I'm condemning and seeking to prohibit is the *deliberate* (intentional) killing of the unborn child—the deliberate termination of the pregnancy with the intention of destroying the pre-natal organism. If the doctors remove the cancerous womb, purely with a view to saving the mother's life and without intending to harm the baby, and if they are, as it were, hypothetically committed to doing what they can to save the baby's life in such circumstances, so that if there were a more advanced form of life-saving equipment available they would make use of it, then such an operation, though foreseeably causing the baby's death, would not count as abortion in the relevant sense. It would not be a case of deliberately killing the unborn child, since the child's death would not be something intended, either as an end in itself or as a means to an end. Of course, in condoning such an operation, I'm not implying that it's always morally permissible for doctors to do something which they foresee will cause the death of an unborn baby so long as they are not *aiming* to kill it. All such cases will have to be looked at on their merits, bearing in mind the prima facie duty to protect human life in so far as that's possible. I'm merely pointing out that my condemnation of *abortion itself*, in the way I've defined it, only applies to cases in which the killing is deliberate.

There remains, of course, a large number of so-called hard cases, like rape, teenage pregnancy, and handicap, where the issue *is* concerned with abortion in this sense—with the deliberate killing of the unborn child. I'd like to be able to examine these cases in detail. But I'll restrict myself to two general points, which I hope will help to put things in the right perspective.

Those who think that abortion is morally justified in any of these hard cases are, whether explicitly or implicitly, relying on a utilitarian theory of morality, according to which the right action in any circumstances is the one which has, or which we can expect to have, the most beneficial consequences. The slogan of such a theory is that the end justifies the means. Killing the unborn child may be regrettable, taken on its own, but it will morally justified, indeed morally oblig-atory, if the consequences of doing so are more beneficial, in terms of the pro-motion of happiness and the avoidance of unhappiness, than the consequences of permitting it to live. Now the first point I want to make is that this utilitarian the-ory, despite some superficial appeal, is at great variance with our ordinary moral intuitions. For although it sets a value on human *happiness*, it accords no value to the human *individual* except as a medium in which happiness may be cultured or as an instrument by which happiness may be produced. And, in consequence, it sanctions any treatment of human beings which promotes the general happi-ness, however unjust and callous that treatment would ordinarily be deemed to be. If there's a predictable net gain in happiness by eliminating the severely hand-icapped, by torturing political prisoners, by rounding up vagrants for medical experiments, by enslaving despised minorities, by fabricating evidence to secure a conviction, then, in each case, utilitarianism says: go ahead. But in all these cases, our intuitions are against the utilitarian. We don't accept that the end jus-tifies the means, if the means involve what we perceive to be a grave infringe-ment of the rights of individuals.

My second point is that, if the pre-natal organism is, as I've argued, a human individual in the morally relevant sense—an individual with the same moral standing as the new-born baby, the schoolchild, and the adult—then whatever view we take of abortion has to be in harmony with our views about homicide in other cases. When a born child is physically handicapped, or mentally retarded, or rejected by its parents, or found abandoned on a doorstep, it doesn't cross our minds to think of its deliberate destruction as a morally permissible option. We rule out such a solution as a matter of principle, irrespective of any utilitarian considerations which could be adduced in its favour. But then how can this principle fail to operate in the cases of the unborn? How can a prohibition which is accepted as absolute in the one case become vulnerable to trade-off and compromise in the other? The question is unanswerable, though its force is often obscured by the bland euphemisms by which abortion is described. So often I have heard people say: "But surely, in the circumstances, it would be better not to bring the child into the world". Make no mistake; the unborn child is in the world already, and abortion is the act of pushing him out. In my book that's murder, and to be condemned as such.

III

Well, that completes the basic defense of my position—the defense which avoids religious considerations and merely appeals to our ordinary rationality and moral sense. I dare say there are a number of points where you'd like clarification or elaboration. For example, you may want to look at some of the hard cases in detail; or you might want to raise objections to my claims about when human life begins. But before I open up the discussion, I'd like, though rather briefly, to try to put what I've said in some kind of Christian perspective. My argument has turned on two fundamental claims: First that the human individual, in the morally relevant sense, comes into existence at conception (fertilization); and second, that it's always wrong, and more specifically an act of grave injustice, deliberately to kill an innocent human individual. These claims seem to me defensible in their own right. But I want to reinforce each of them by a distinctively Christian-theological argument.

Let's start then with the first claim—that the human individual, in the relevant sense, comes into existence at conception. I've tried to establish this claim by appeal to the biological findings. But I shall now urge that it is one which, for independent reasons, Christians—at least Christians of orthodox persuasion—are obliged to accept. For it is entailed by the doctrine of the Incarnation, as traditionally interpreted.

The doctrine of the Incarnation, which forms the foundation of the Christian Faith, asserts that God the Son, the Second Person of the Trinity, became a man. In becoming a man, he did not, of course, cease to be God. He retained his divine nature, with all the attributes that are essential to that nature, but assumed human nature as well living a normal human life, with a normal human body and a normal human mind. Now all this is a very large and complicated theological subject (and it also, surely, involves a great deal that we can't, at least in our present perspective, understand). But I want us to focus on just one question. At what point, in the development of the human organism, did the Incarnation occur?

Exactly when, in this developmental process, did the Son take human nature and begin his human life? The answer is implicit in the Gospel records of Matthew and Luke, whose accounts are distilled in the two credal claims: 'He was conceived by the Holy Spirit' (the Apostles Creed) and 'He was incarnate by the Holy Spirit of the Virgin Mary and was made man' (the Nicene Creed). It is clear that the conception-by-the-Holy-Spirit referred to in the first credal statement is the same as the incarnation-by-the Spirit referred to in the second. So conception is marked out as the moment of incarnation—the moment when the Son took human nature, when Christ began his human life. Now, of course, given that Mary was a virgin, this conception did not involve fertilization in the ordinary biological sense. But it must have occurred at the same point in the biological process as fertilization occurs in the ordinary case, and it must have resulted in a conceptus of the normal human type. This means that, in the ordinary case—the case of you and me—conception (i.e. fertilization) must be the beginning of human life in the fullest sense—the point when the human person, or human individual in the morally relevant sense, comes into existence. For Christ could hardly have taken human nature without becoming a human individual in the relevant sense; and he could hardly have become a human individual at a point prior to that at which, in the ordinary case, the human individual exists. In short, if Christ became a human individual in the relevant sense at conception, then conception must be the time when we, as human individuals, come into existence.

This argument, of course, will cut no ice with non-Christians; nor even with Christians who don't accept the orthodox teaching in this area. But for orthodox Christians, it is, as far as I can see, decisive.

Finally, let's turn to the second of the claims on which my argument rests—the claim that it is always morally wrong, and an act of grave injustice, to set out to destroy innocent human life. Certainly, our ordinary moral intuitions endorse this claim. But suppose these intuitions are called in question. Suppose someone demands to know what it is about human beings that makes them morally special, that gives human life this supposed sanctity. Most of us have no absolute objection to killing non-human animals. What makes human beings so different? Aren't they in fact just animals of a highly developed kind?

To meet this sort of challenge, we need to turn, once more, to theology. For it's man's distinctive relationship with his Maker that gives him his distinctive moral status.

We're, in a very special sense, made in God's image, or likeness. In particular, God has given us, as creaturely reflections of his own attributes; rationality, self-consciousness, freedom of choice, a capacity to love, and a moral sense. It is because we are made in God's image that the incarnation was possible. The Word could not have been made flesh unless, within the framework of created human nature, it was possible to express, without compromise, the attributes of the divine nature. Now because we are made in God's image, God *loves* us. The love in question is (in Greek) *agape*. To love someone in this (agapetic) way is to value that person as if he were oneself; it is to project on to the other one's own value (so that, in a sense, the divine command "love your neighbor as yourself" is *pleonastic*). The measure of God's love for us is our Lord's incarnation and sacrificial death ('God so loved the world that he gave his only-begotten son ...' *John* 3.16).

Now God's love for us guarantees that each of us has a value which is *ultimate*, *objective*, and infinite. Our value is *ultimate*, because God's love represents us as having value *in ourselves*; as ends, not just as means to some further end (thus love always represents the beloved as of value in himself or herself in this way). Our value is *objective*, because it is *God's* love that's here involved. To be loved by God is to be valued from that viewpoint at which, uniquely, all distinctions between appearance and reality are eliminated—the viewpoint which is guaranteed to reveal things as they really are. Just as we can draw no distinction between objective truth and what God believes, so we can draw no distinction between objective worth and what God values. Finally, our value is infinite, because, God's own value is *infinite*, and it is this value (his own value) that he agapetically projects on to those he loves. And one other crucial point about all this; whatever our destiny beyond the grave, an individual's God-given value at least rests on him in relation to his life *here*—it is a value which he possesses in the course of this mundane, earth-bound life. Again, this is something made clear by the incarnation. Nothing could demonstrate the eternal significance of our earthly life more clearly than the fact that our Lord chose to live it and manifest the glory of his divine nature through it.

No action by one human individual towards another, or indeed by an individual towards himself, can be morally right if it does not respect that person's God-given value. But the deliberate killing of an innocent human individual is clearly not consistent with a respect for that individual's value. So, whatever the motives and circumstances, any such killing must be morally wrong.

That, then, as I see it, is the ultimate, theological basis of the sanctity of human life. I should add that the point of the qualification 'innocent' (for it's only the deliberate killing of an innocent human being that's explicitly proscribed) is to leave room for cases in which, allegedly, the killing is morally deserved and hence not at variance with a proper respect for the value of the one whose life is taken.

Many Christians would reject this qualification and accept the sanctity of human life in a stronger, unqualified form—a form which prohibits such things as judicial execution and deliberate killing in war. This is clearly an important issue, but my case against the morality of abortion doesn't depend on how it's resolved.

19

Do We Have Too Many People?

Julian Simon

This is the economic history of humanity in a nutshell. From 2 million or 200,000 or 20,000 or 2,000 years ago until the 18th century there was slow growth in population, almost no increase in health or decrease in mortality, slow growth in the availability of natural resources (but not increased scarcity), increase in wealth for a few, and mixed effects on the environment. Since then there has been rapid growth in population due to spectacular decreases in the death rate, rapid growth in resources, widespread increases in wealth, and an unprecedently clean and beautiful living environment in many parts of the world along with a degraded environment in the poor and socialist parts of the world.

That is, more people and more wealth have correlated with more (rather than less) resources and a cleaner environment—just the opposite of what Malthusian theory leads one to believe. The task before us is to make sense of these mind-boggling happy trends.

The current gloom-and-doom about a 'crisis' of our environment is wrong on the scientific facts. Even the US Environmental Protection Agency acknowledges that US air and water have been getting cleaner rather than dirtier in the past few decades. Every agricultural economist knows that the world's population has been eating ever-better since the Second World War.

Every resource economist knows that all natural resources have been getting more available not more scarce, as shown by their falling prices over the decades and centuries. And every demographer knows that the death rate has been falling all over the world—life expectancy almost tripling in the rich countries in the past two centuries, and almost doubling in the poor countries in only the past four decades.

Population Growth and Economic Development

The picture is now also clear that population growth does not hinder economic development. In the 1980s there was a complete reversal in the consensus of thinking of population economists about the effects of more people. In 1986, the National Research Council and the National Academy of Sciences completely overturned its 'official' view away from the earlier worried view expressed in 1971. It noted the absence of any statistical evidence of a negative connection between population increase and economic growth. And it said that 'The scarcity of exhaustible resources is at most a minor restraint on economic growth'.[1] This U-turn by the scientific consensus of experts on the subject has gone unacknowledged by the press, the anti-natalist environmental organisations, and the agencies that foster population control abroad.

Long Run Trends Positive

Here is my central assertion: Almost every economic and social change or trend points in a positive direction, as long as we view the matter over a reasonably long period of time.

For a proper understanding of the important aspects of an economy we should look at the long-run trends. But the short-run comparisons—between the sexes, age groups, races, political groups, which are usually purely relative—make more news. To repeat, just about every important long-run measure of human welfare shows improvement over the decades and centuries, in the United States as well as in the rest of the world. And there is no persuasive reason to believe that these trends will not continue indefinitely.

Would I bet on it? For sure. I'll bet a week's or month's pay—anything I win goes to pay for more research—that just about any trend pertaining to material human welfare will improve rather than get worse. You pick the comparison and the year.

Let me quickly review a few data on how human life has been doing, beginning with the all-important issue, life itself.

The Conquest of Too-early Death

The most important and amazing demographic fact—the greatest human achievement in history, in my view—is the decrease in the world's death rate. Figure 1 portrays the history of human life expectancy at birth. It took thousands of years to increase life expectancy at birth from just over 20 years to the high twenties in about 1750. Then life expectancy in the richest countries suddenly took off and tripled in about two centuries. In just the past two centuries. the length of life you could expect for your baby or yourself in the advanced coun-

Figure 1: History of Human Life Expectancy at Birth (3000BCE–2000CE)

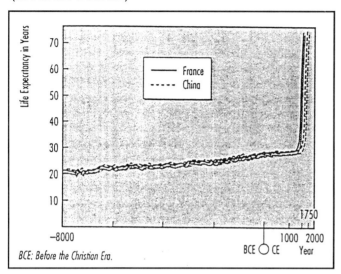

Figure 2: Female Expectation of Life at Birth

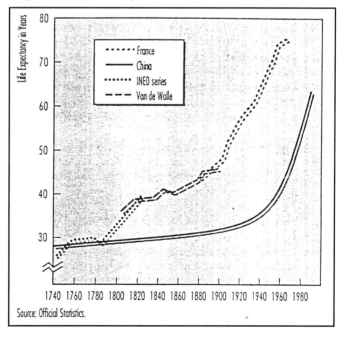

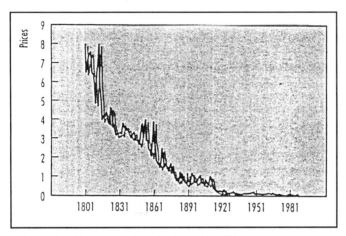

Figure 3: Copper Prices Indexed by Wages

tries jumped from less than 30 years to perhaps 75 years. What greater event has humanity witnessed than this conquest of premature death in the rich countries? It is this decrease in the death rate that is the cause of there being a larger world population nowadays than in former times.

Then starting well after the Second World War, the length of life you could expect in the poor countries has leaped upwards by perhaps 15 or even 20 years since the 1950s, caused by advances in agriculture, sanitation, and medicine (Figure 2).

Let me put it differently. In the 19th century the planet Earth could sustain only 1 billion people. Ten thousand years ago, only 4 million could keep themselves alive. Now 5 billion people are on average living longer and more healthily than ever before. The increase in the world's population represents our victory over death.

Here arises a crucial issue of interpretation: One would expect lovers of humanity to jump with joy at this triumph of human mind and organisation over the raw killing forces of nature. Instead, many lament that there are so many people alive to enjoy the gift of life. And it is this worry that leads them to approve the Indonesian, Chinese and other inhumane programmes of coercion and denial of personal liberty in one of the most precious choices a family can make—the number of children that it wishes to bear and raise.

The Decreasing Scarcity of Natural Resources

Throughout history, the supply of natural resources has worried people. Yet the data clearly show that natural resource scarcity—as measured by the eco-

Figure 4: Copper Prices Divided by CPI

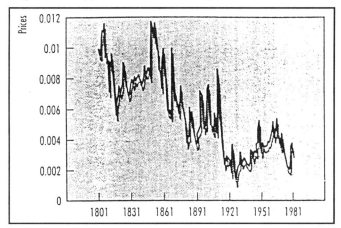

nomically-meaningful indicator of cost or price—has been decreasing rather than increasing in the long run for all raw materials, with only temporary' exceptions from time to time: that is, availability has been increasing. Consider copper, which is representative of all the metals. In Figure 3 we see the price relative to wages since 1801. The cost of a ton is only about a tenth now of what it was two hundred years ago.

This trend of falling prices of copper has been going on for a very long time. In the 18th century BCE in Babylonia under Hammurabi—almost 4,000 years ago—the price of copper was about a thousand times its price in the USA now relative to wages. At the time of the Roman Empire the price was about a hundred times the present price.

In Figure 4 we see the price of copper relative to the consumer price index. Everything we buy—pens, shirts, tyres—has been getting cheaper over the years because we have learned how to make them more cheaply, especially during the past 200 years. Even so, the extraordinary fact is that natural resources have been getting cheaper even faster than consumer goods.

So, by any measure, natural resources have been getting more available rather than more scarce.

In the case of oil, the shocking price rises during the 1970s and 1980s were not caused by growing scarcity in the world supply. And indeed, the price of petroleum in inflation-adjusted dollars has returned to levels about where they were before the politically-induced increases, and the price of gasoline is about at the historic low and still falling. Taking energy in general, there is no reason to believe that the supply of energy is finite, or that the price of energy will not continue its long-run decrease indefinitely. I realise that it sounds weird to say that the supply of energy is not finite or limited; for the full argument, please see my 1981 book (revised edition forthcoming).[2] (Science is only valuable when it arrives at knowledge different from common sense.)

Food—'A Benign Trend'

Food is an especially important resource. The evidence is particularly strong for food that we are on a benign trend despite rising population. The long-run price of food relative to wages is now perhaps only a tenth as much as it was in 1800 in the USA. Even relative to consumer products, the price of grain is down because of increased productivity, as with all other primary products.

Famine deaths due to insufficient food supply have decreased even in absolute terms, let alone relative to population, in the past century, a matter which pertains particularly to the poor countries. Per-person food consumption is up over the last 30 years. And there are no data showing that the bottom of the income scale is faring worse, or even has failed to share in the general improvement, as the average has improved.

Africa's food production per person is down, but by 1994 almost no-one any longer claims that Africa's suffering results from a shortage of land or water or sun. The cause of hunger in Africa is a combination of civil wars and collectivisation of agriculture, which periodic droughts have made more murderous.

Consider agricultural land as an example of all natural resources. Although many people consider land to be a special kind of resource, it is subject to the same processes of human creation as other natural resources. The most important fact about agricultural land is that less and less of it is needed as the decades pass. This idea is utterly counter-intuitive. It seems entirely obvious that a growing world population would need larger amounts of farmland. But the title of a remarkably prescient article by Theodore Schultz in 1931 tells the story: 'The Declining Economic Importance of Land'.[3]

The increase in actual and potential productivity per unit of land has grown much faster than population, and there is sound reason to expect this trend to continue. Therefore, there is less and less reason to worry about the supply of land. Though the stock of usable land seems fixed at any moment, it is constantly being increased—at a rapid rate in many cases—by the clearing of new land or reclamation of wasteland.

Land also is constantly being enhanced by increasing the number of crops grown per year on each unit of land and by increasing the yield per crop with better farming methods and with chemical fertiliser. Last but not least, land is created anew where there was no land.

Figure 5: National Ambient Concentrations of Pollutants:
USA, 1960–1990

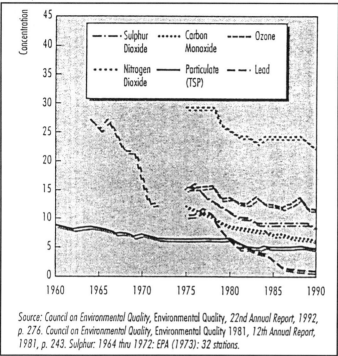

Source: Council on Environmental Quality, Environmental Quality, 22nd Annual Report, 1992,
p. 276. Council on Environmental Quality, Environmental Quality 1981, 12th Annual Report,
1981, p. 243. Sulphur: 1964 thru 1972: EPA (1973): 32 stations.

Figure 6: National Ambient Water Quality in Rivers and Streams,
USA, 1973–1990: Fecal Coliform Bacteria (200+ cells per 100 ml)

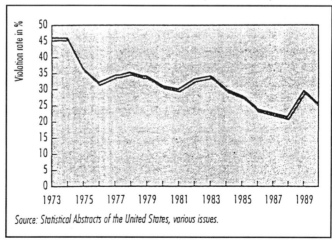

Source: Statistical Abstracts of the United States, various issues.

The One Scarce Factor

There is only one important resource which has shown a trend of increasing scarcity rather than increasing abundance. That resource is the most important of all—human beings. Yes, there are more people on earth now than ever before. But if we measure the scarcity of people the same way that we measure the scarcity of other economic goods—by how much we must pay to obtain their services—we see that wages and salaries have been going up all over the world, in poor countries as well as rich. The amount that you must pay to obtain the services of a barber or cook—or economist—has risen in the United States over the decades. This increase in the price of people's services is a clear indication that people are becoming more scarce even though there are more of us.

Surveys show that the public believes that our air and water have been getting more polluted in recent years. The evidence with respect to air indicates that pollutants have been declining, especially the main pollutant, particulates (see Figure 5). With respect to water, the proportion of monitoring Sites in the USA with water of good drinkability has increased since the data began in 1961 (Figure 6).

Every forecast of the doomsayers has turned out flat wrong. Metals, foods, and other natural resources have become more available rather than more scarce throughout the centuries. The famous Famine 1975 forecast by the Paddock brothers—that we would see millions of famine deaths in the US on television in the 1970s—was followed instead by gluts in agricultural markets. Paul Ehrlich's primal scream about 'What will we do when the [gasoline] pumps run dry?' was followed by gasoline cheaper than since the 1930s. The Great Lakes are not dead; instead they offer better sport fishing than ever. The main pollutants, especially the particulates which have killed people for years, have lessened in our cities. Socialist countries are a different and tragic environmental story, however!

Damage of Wrong Forecasts

The wrong forecasts of shortages of copper and other metals have not been harmless, however. They have helped cause economic disasters for mining companies and for the poor countries which depend upon mining by misleading them with unsound expectations of increased prices; similarly with airplane design, U.S. government-mandated mileage-per-gallon standards (CAFE) have misdirected valuable resources. But nothing has reduced the doomsayers' credibility with the press or their command over the funding resources of the federal government.

Let me dramatise these sets of changes with a single anecdote. The trend toward a better life can be seen in most of our own families if we look. For example, I have mild asthma. Recently, I slept in a home where there was a dog, and in the middle of the night I woke with a bad cough and a shortness of breath. When I realised that it was caused by the dog dander, I took out my 12-dollar pocket inhaler, good for 3,000 puffs, and took one puff. Within 10 minutes my lungs were clear. A small miracle. Forty years ago I would have been sleepless and miserable all night, and I would have had to give up the squash-playing that I love so much because exercise causes my worst asthma in the absence of an inhaler. Or diabetes. If your child had diabetes a hundred years ago, you had to watch helplessly as the child went blind and died early. Now injections, or even pills, can give the child almost as long and healthy a life as other children. Or glasses. Centuries ago you had to give up reading when your eyes grew dim when you reached 40 or 50. Now you can buy magnifying glasses at the drugstore for nine dollars. And you can even wear contact lenses for eye problems and keep your vanity intact. Is there not some condition in your family that in earlier times would have been a lingering misery or a tragedy, that nowadays our increasing knowledge has rendered easily bearable?

With respect to population growth: A dozen competent statistical studies, starting in 1967 with an analysis by Nobel prizewinner Simon Kuznets, agree that there is no negative statistical relationship between economic growth and population growth. There is strong reason to believe that more people have a positive effect in the long run.

Population growth does not lower the standard of living—all the evidence agrees. And the evidence supports the view that population growth raises it in the long run.

Incidentally, it was those statistical studies that converted me in about 1968 from working in favour of population control to the point of view that I hold today. I certainly did not come to my current view for any political or religious or ideological reason.

The basic method is to gather data on each country's rate of population growth and its rate of economic growth, and then to examine whether—looking at all the data in the sample together—countries with high population growth rates have economic growth rates lower than average, and countries with low population growth rates have economic growth rates higher than average. All the studies agree in concluding that this is not so; there is no correlation between economic growth and population growth in the intermediate run.

Of course one can adduce cases of countries that seemingly are exceptions to the pattern. It is the genius of statistical inference, however, to enable us to draw valid generalisations from samples that contain such wide variations in behaviour. The exceptions can be useful in alerting us to possible avenues for further analysis, but as long as they are only exceptions, they do not prove that the generalisation is not meaningful or useful.

Population Density Favours Economic Growth

The research-wise person may wonder whether population density is a more meaningful variable than population growth. And, indeed, such studies have been done. And again, the statistical evidence directly contradicts the common-sense conventional wisdom. If you make a chart with population density on the horizontal axis and either the income level or the rate of change of income on the vertical axis, you will see that higher density is associated with better rather than poorer economic results.

You can check for yourself: if you fly over Hong Kong—just a few decades ago a place seemingly without prospects because of insoluble resource problems—you will marvel at the astounding collection of modern high-rise apartments and office buildings. Take a ride on its excellent smooth-flowing highways for an hour or two, and you will realise that a very dense concentration of human beings does not prevent comfortable existence and exciting economic expansion as long as the economic system gives individuals the freedom to exercise their talents and to take advantage of opportunities. And the experience of Singapore demonstrates that Hong Kong is not unique. Two such examples do not prove the case, of course. But these dramatic illustrations are backed by the evidence from the aggregate sample of countries, and hence do not mislead us.

(Hong Kong is a special thrill for me because I first saw it in 1955 when I went ashore from a US Navy destroyer. At the time I felt great pity for the thousands who slept every night on the sidewalks or on small boats. It then seemed clear to me, as it must have to almost every observer, that it would be impossible for Hong Kong to surmount its problems—huge masses of impoverished people without jobs, total lack of exploitable natural resources, more refugees pouring across the border each day. But upon returning in 1983, I saw bustling crowds of healthy, vital people full of hope and energy—no cause for pity now.)

The most important benefit of population size and growth is the increase it brings to the stock of useful knowledge. Minds matter economically as much as, or more than, hands or mouths. Progress is limited largely by the availability of trained workers. The more people who enter our population by birth or immigration, the faster will be the rate of progress of our material and cultural civilisation.

Here we require a qualification that tends to be overlooked: I do not say that all is well everywhere, and I do not predict that all will be rosy in the future. Children are hungry and sick; people live out lives of physical or intellectual poverty, and lack of opportunity; war or some new pollution may finish us off.

What I am saying is that for most relevant economic matters I have checked, the aggregate trends are improving rather than deteriorating.

Also, I do not say that a better future happens automatically or without effort. It will happen because women and men will struggle with problems with muscle and mind, and will probably overcome, as people have overcome in the past—*if the social and economic system gives them the opportunity to do so.*

The Explanation of These Amazing Trends

Now we need some theory to explain how it can be that economic welfare grows along with population, rather than humanity being reduced to misery and poverty as population grows.

The Mathusian theory of increasing scarcity, based on supposedly fixed resources (the theory that the doomsayers rely upon), runs exactly contrary to the data over the long sweep of history. It makes sense therefore to prefer another theory.

The theory that fits the facts very well is this: More people, and increased income, cause problems in the short run. Short-run scarcity raises prices. This presents opportunity, and prompts the search for solutions. In a free society, solutions are eventually found. And in the long run the new developments leave us better off than if the problems had not arisen.

To put it differently, in the short run more consumers mean less of the fixed available stock of goods to be divided among more people. And more workers labouring with the same fixed current stock of capital means that there will be less output per worker. The latter effect, known as 'the law of diminishing returns', is the essence of Malthus's theory as he first set it out.

But if the resources with which people work are not fixed over the period being analysed, the Malthusian logic of diminishing returns does not apply. And the plain fact is that, given some time to adjust to shortages, the resource base does not remain fixed. People create more resources of all kinds.

When we take a long-run view, the picture is different, and considerably more complex, than the simple short-run view of more people implying lower average income. In the very long run, more people almost surely imply more available resources and a higher income for everyone.

I suggest you test this idea against your own knowledge: Do you think that our standard of living would be as high as it is now if the population had never grown from about 4 million human beings perhaps 10,000 years ago? I do not think we would now have electric light or gas heat or cars or penicillin or travel to the moon or our present life expectancy of over 70 years at birth in rich countries, in comparison to the life expectancy of 20 to 25 years at birth in earlier eras, if population had not grown to its present numbers.

Scarcity and Discovery

Consider this example of the process by which people wind up with increasing rather than decreasing availability of resources. England was full of alarm in the 1600s at an impending shortage of energy due to the deforestation of the country for firewood. People feared a scarcity of fuel for both heating and for the iron industry. This impending scarcity led to the development of coal.

Then in the mid-1800s the English came to worry about an impending coal crisis. The great English economist, Jevons, calculated that a shortage of coal would bring England's industry to a standstill by 1990: he carefully assessed that oil could never make a decisive difference. Triggered by the impending scarcity of coal (and of whale oil, whose story comes next), ingenious profit-minded people developed oil into a more desirable fuel than coal ever was. And in 1990 we find England exporting both coal and oil.

Another element in the story. Because of increased demand due to population growth and increased income, the price of whale oil for lamps jumped in the 1840s, and the US Civil War pushed it even higher, leading to a whale oil 'crisis'. This provided incentive for enterprising people to discover and produce substitutes. First came oil from rapeseed, olives, linseed, and camphene oil from pine trees. Then inventors learned how to get coal oil from coal. Other ingenious persons produced kerosene from the rock oil that seeped to the surface, a product so desirable that its price then rose from $0.75 to $2.00 a gallon. This high price stimulated enterprisers to focus on the supply of oil, and finally Edwin L. Drake brought in his famous well in Titusville, Pennsylvania. Learning how to refine the oil took a while. But in a few years there were hundreds of small refiners in America, and soon the bottom fell out of the whale oil market, the price falling from $2.50 or more at its peak around 1866 to well below one dollar. And in 1994 we see Great Britain exporting both coal and oil.

Here we should note that it was not the British government that developed coal or oil, because governments are not effective developers of new technology. Rather, it was individual entrepreneurs who sensed the need, saw opportunity, used all kinds of available information and ideas, made lots of false starts which were very costly to many of those individuals but not to others, and eventually arrived at coal as a viable fuel—because there were enough independent individuals investigating the matter for at least some of them to arrive at sound ideas and methods. And this happened in the context of a competitive enterprise system that worked to produce what was wanted by the public. And the entire process of impending shortage and new solution left us better off than if the shortage problem had never arisen.

The Role of Economic Freedom

Here we must address another crucial element in the economics of resources and population—the extent to which the political-social-economic system provides personal freedom from government coercion. Skilled people require an appropriate social and economic framework that provides incentives for working hard and taking risks, enabling their talents to flower and come to fruition. The key elements of such a framework are economic liberty, respect for property, and fair and sensible rules of the market that are enforced equally for all.

The world's problem is not too many people, but lack of political and economic freedom. Powerful evidence comes from an extraordinary natural experiment that occurred starting in the 1940s with three pairs of countries that have the same culture and history, and had much the same standard of living when they split apart after the Second World War—East and West Germany, North and South Korea, Taiwan and China. In each case the centrally planned communist country began with less population 'pressure', as measured by density per square kilometre, than did the market-directed economy. And the communist and non-communist countries also started with much the same birth rates.

The market-directed economies have performed much better economically than the centrally-planned economies. The economic-political system clearly was the dominant force in the results of the three comparisons. This powerful explanation of economic development cuts the ground from under population growth as a likely explanation of the speed of nations' economic development.

The Astounding Shift in the Scholarly Consensus

So far I have been discussing the factual evidence. But in 1994 there is an important new element not present 20 years ago. The scientific community of scholars who study population economics now agrees with almost all of what is written above. The statements made above do not represent a single lone voice, but rather the current scientific consensus.

The conclusions offered earlier about agriculture and resources and demographic trends have always represented the consensus of economists in those fields. And the consensus of population economists also is now not far from what is written here.

In 1986, the US National Research Council and the US National Academy of Sciences published a book on population growth and economic development prepared by a prestigious scholarly group. This 'official' report reversed almost completely the frightening conclusions of the 1971 NAS report. 'Population growth at most a minor factor ...' As cited earlier in this paper, it found benefits of additional people as well as costs.[4]

A host of review articles by distinguished economic demographers in the past decade has confirmed that this 'revisionist' view is indeed consistent with the scientific evidence, though not all the writers would go as far as I do in pointing out the positive long-run effects of population growth. The consensus is more towards a 'neutral' judgement. But this is a huge change from the earlier judgement that population growth is economically detrimental.

By 1994. anyone who confidently asserts that population growth damages the economy must turn a blind eye to the scientific evidence.

Summary and Conclusion

In the short run. all resources are limited. An example of such a finite resource is the amount of space allotted to me. The longer run, however, is a different story. The standard of living has risen along with the size of the world's population since the beginning of recorded time. There is no convincing economic reason why these trends towards a better life should not continue indefinitely.

The key theoretical idea is this: The growth of population and of income create actual and expected shortages, and hence lead to price rises. A price increase represents an opportunity that attracts profit-minded entrepreneurs to seek new ways to satisfy the shortages. Some fail, at cost to themselves. A few succeed, and the final result is that we end up better off than if the original shortage problems had never arisen. That is, we need our problems though this does not imply that we should purposely create additional problems for ourselves.

I hope that you will now agree that the long-run outlook is for a more abundant material life rather than for increased scarcity, in the United States and in the world as a whole. Of course, such progress does not come automatically. And my message certainly is not one of complacency. In this I agree with the doom-sayers—that our world needs the best efforts of all humanity to improve our lot. I part company with them in that they expect us to come to a bad end despite the efforts we make, whereas I expect a continuation of humanity's history of successful efforts. And I believe that their message is self-fulfilling, because if you expect your efforts to fail because of inexorable natural limits, then you are likely to feel resigned; and therefore literally to resign. But if you recognise the possibility—in fact the probability—of success, you can tap large reservoirs of energy and enthusiasm.

Adding more people causes problems, but people are also the means to solve these problems. The main fuel to speed the world's progress is our stock of knowledge, and the brakes are (a) our lack of imagination, and (b) unsound social regulation of these activities.

The ultimate resource is people—especially skilled, spirited, and hopeful young people endowed with liberty—who will exert their wills and imaginations for their own benefit, and so inevitably benefit not only themselves but the rest of us as well.

NOTES
[1] National Research council, Committee on Population, and Working Group on Population Growth and Economic Development, *Population Growth and*

Economic Development: Policy Questions, Waahington DC: National Academy Press, 1986.

[2] J.L. Simon, *The Ultimate Resource*, Princeton, N.J.: Princeton University *Press*, 1981.

[3] T.W. Schulz, 'The Declining Economic Importance of Land,' Economic Journal, Vol. LXI, December 1951, pp.725–40.

[4] National Research Council, *op.cit.*

Section II: Christos

20

The Uninventable Glory of God as the Deepest Reason for Our Faith in Jesus Christ

Josef Seifert

And the Word became flesh, and dwelt among us (and we beheld his glory, glory as of the only begotten from the Father), full of grace and truth.[1] (John 1:14)

1. "... for I know him whom I have believed...": The Gift of Faith, Human Reason, and Its Elevation through Grace.

As believers in Jesus Christ we must, in spite of the gift of faith which we received, always continue to speak with the man of the Gospel: "help my unbelief" (Mark 9:24). We acknowledge that our faith in Christ is a gift from God which no man could give to himself. As Christ himself said: "No one can come to Me, unless the Father who sent Me draws him." (John 6:44), and again, "... Jesus answered and said unto him, Blessed art thou, Simon Barjona: for flesh and blood hath not revealed it unto thee, but my Father which is in heaven." (Matt 16:17).

Yet nevertheless, while being a gift of divine grace, our faith is likewise the supreme act of human reason and freedom; and it is, as such, based on the recognition of reasons for the sake of which we believe in Jesus Christ—rather than believing in any other man who claims to be sent by God or to be the Son of God. Otherwise we could not fulfill the admonition of Peter: "... always be(ing) ready to make a defense to everyone who asks you to give an account for the hope that is in you." (*Peter* 3:15).

This aspect of faith which corresponds to our experience is closely related to the great truth that grace and faith presuppose nature and natural understanding. The character of faith as a reasonable surrender to Jesus and assent to the truth-claim of Revelation also shows that God does not treat man as if he were an irrational creature. God does not bestow grace on him entirely outside of, or against, his nature as a being endowed with reason. Rather, it is in accordance with the dignity of man, and with the gift of reason he possesses, that he be convinced also with his reason by the truth of divine revelation and that, while surrendering his reason and free will to God in the act of faith, he does so not without his own reason being convinced that truly God revealed Himself to man in Jesus Christ. There is no better formulation of this truth than the words of Saint Paul (2 *Timothy* 1:12): "... for I know him whom I have believed..."

It would be against the dignity of man to surrender his reason and his free will to God without having gained the profound conviction that it is in fact God to whom he gives, and thus rightfully gives, his faith. Otherwise, it would not be faith but superstition or unjustified belief which may be the largest part of the convictions and beliefs of human persons in the field of religion which is corrupted by idolatry, astrology, false and absurd beliefs of all kinds. Therefore, authentic religious faith involves a conviction of the real trustworthiness of the witnesses of faith and must not be deprived of reason. It rather rests on the *knowledge* of the trustworthiness of Jesus Christ (*scio cui credidi*—I know whom I believed), the Word of God incarnate. Authentic religious faith (as opposed to superstitious faith) also rests on the wellfounded conviction of the trustworthiness of Christ's witnesses, the Apostles and Evangelists, of the Church He founded, and of the Bible. In all of this, human understanding is not bypassed by the grace of faith; rather, it is presupposed, and at the same time elevated and strengthened, by grace so that God draws man to himself through Jesus Christ, appealing to man's reason and to his faith, speaking not only to the innermost recesses of his soul which can be activated solely by grace, but also to his understanding.

Jesus Christ Himself stresses both aspects of faith. He insists not only on grace, telling us that we could never come to Him unless the Father draws us: "No man can come to me, except the Father which hath sent me draw him." (*John* 6:44). He also refers to the role of understanding as the basis of faith, however, when He says: "If I do not the works of my Father, believe me not. But if I do them, though ye believe not me, believe the works: that ye may know and understand that the Father is in me, and I in the Father." (*John* 10:3738). Thus Jesus adduces as reason for faith not solely the hidden operation of divine grace but also His words and His deeds, which we should listen to and understand, so that we may believe in Him.

2. What Is Faith? On the Necessity of Wholly Extraordinary and Stunning Reasons to Believe that a Human Being like us is the "Son of the Living God": Miracles are Not Enough

But what is this act of faith? Is it a mere opinion? Is it only the theoretical conviction that Jesus is God and that what He tells us is true? Is it a "belief that something is true" or an act of trust in a person? Is it a merely "subjective" belief? Some try to reduce religious faith simply to a set of theoretical convictions to which we give a mere "notional assent"[2] Others defend the view that faith has nothing to do with propositional truth and that it is, on the contrary, a mere act of committing oneself blindly, of following the person of Christ. According to them, faith does not involve any specific content of creed or convictions regarding truth-claims made by the Bible.

In reality, however, faith is both, an act of "believing *in* Jesus Christ," an act of loving and believing surrendering of ourselves in the unreserved trust in him, and an act of not only notional but real assent to the truth of what He tells us, an act of *belief that* what he says is true: And this act of believing in Jesus Christ and of committing and surrendering ourselves to Him, in turn, rests on the *belief* that He is the Son of God who is One with the Father and knows God.[3] Faith is thus an act by which we surrender our whole person to Jesus Christ and believe *in* Him, and, because of believing *in* Him, obediently accept the truth of what He reveals to us, i.e., believe *that* His words are true.

Now why should we believe that Jesus Christ truly is God and why should we surrender ourselves and our pride to Him, go beyond all that our reason can comprehend and believe *in Jesus Christ*? And why should we believe that Jesus of Nazareth's stunning claims about His person and our salvation are true? Some might be inclined to think that, when Jesus asks us to believe in Him and to believe His words, He speaks simply of the trust we should normally have in somebody whose truthfulness we have no reason to doubt. One might likewise be inclined to think that the reason for our belief on account of the miracles which Jesus performed lies simply in their extraordinary character, in that these miracles go against the laws of nature or at least are entirely inexplicable by them, and therefore *prove* the truthfulness and divinity of the one who performs them.

Yet this opinion is entirely insufficient to explain what in the words and miracles of Christ actually motivates our faith. For certainly nobody would believe in one of us, if we claimed to be the Son of God. And, more importantly, no one should believe us if we made such a claim, even if we had never given him any sign that we were lying or in any other way untruthful, and even if we had performed miracles. Anyone would be justified in believing that we are mad or liars or demonically possessed, if we claimed to be the Son of God, rather than believing that our claim should be true. In short, the generally proven truthfulness and moral goodness of a man is in no way sufficient to justify the belief in his words when he claims to be God. While the most extraordinary signs and miracles, such as raising the dead Lazarus or the young man of Naim, may well be such that no ordinary man or demon could ever perform them, we might still assume for a moment the impossible and say: Even if a Hitler or Stalin or an ordinary man were capable of performing such signs, this could not as such suffice to justify and to ground our belief that a man who performed such miracles is God. Jesus Christ himself warns us against believing in the truthfulness of a man simply because of signs and miracles, saying: "For false Christs and false prophets will arise and will show great signs and wonders, so as to mislead, if possible, even the elect." (*Matt* 24:24).

To reflect on all of this will reveal a much deeper ground of our faith in Christ and of our assent to the truth of His words than simply the reason that we have no ground to assume the untruthfulness of Jesus. For we recognize that it is such an extraordinary, such a stupendous thing for a man to say that he is the Son of God, that it needs the greatest possible sign of trustworthiness of the person who tells us this in order for us to believe in him. It is by no means enough for us, in order to believe such a claim, that the person who makes it is an honest and kind man, that he loves his family and always showed faithfulness towards his friends, and that he never lied.[4]

No, there must be a much greater, in fact a unique reason which allows us as beings endowed with rationality to believe that a mortal man like us, who lived in time, Jesus Christ, is truly the Son of God. It takes indeed an overwhelmingly weighty reason for not being scandalized by this claim of Christ, as the Jews were scandalized, who grabbed stones when they heard Jesus say, in the same words which God used to Moses in the burning thorn bush: "Truly, truly, I say to you, before Abraham was born, I AM." (*John* 8:58).

As we cannot believe in the truth of the words of Christ simply on account of some purely natural reason, such as the fact that He never gave a sign of being a liar or of being mad, which suffices for believing other people on lesser things, something similar applies even to the belief in Jesus Christ on account of the miracles which He performed. Certainly, these miracles are stunning simply inasmuch as they suspend the laws of nature and inasmuch as it goes against all experience that the dead rise, that the incurably sick are suddenly cured, that the blind receive in an instant the gift of sight. Yet, as we said, we would (it is to be hoped) never believe that an AntiChrist, such as he is prefigured in a Stalin or Hitler, would be the Son of God, even if he performed similar miracles. We would (we hope) never have believed that the magicians of Pharaoh, who operated by some dark force almost the same extraordinary signs which Moses performed through the power of God, were sent by God. Therefore, there must be some other and hidden reason why the miracles of Jesus Christ reveal his Godhead to us, a reason distinct from the mere fact that these signs and miracles are entirely inexplicable through our general experience of the world and through the laws of nature which we come to recognize.

The fact that our faith in Jesus Christ presupposes such another deeper reason becomes particularly apparent when we consider the possibility of a man who would not live an evil life but who would be just like one of us, whose sayings and deeds would be mediocre and purely human as our own, and who would then tell us that he is the Son of the Living God and would undertake to prove this by miracles. Certainly, we could not explain by the laws of nature that such a man would remove mountains or would strike people dead by the mere power of his thought or that he would operate the signs and miracles which the magicians of Pharaoh performed, or even gorgeous miracles such as curing us from cancer. Yet, even the great miracles which he would perhaps perform and which would seduce many, should never suffice to convince the authentic believer that such a man comes from God, given that he says and does mediocre, silly, and at times evil things just like any one of us. In fact, if some ordinary man and sinner had resuscitated many dead and cured many sick but would still have performed some injustices and many mediocre acts, we would have a duty to protest his claim that he is sent by God like a prophet and even more reject his blasphemous claim of being the Son of God.

Thus we come to understand that there must lie in the words, parables, and actions of Christ something else, something which is more significant for our faith than all these elements. What is more, in separation from this central moment which we shall explore, all the other important confirmations of the divinity of Christ and of our faith, miracles especially, would lose their character as aids to our faith. What then is this central moment which, when the grace of God guides us, prompts our faith in the divinity of Jesus Christ?

Don't forget that the claim of a man to be God is something so extraordinary that Kierkegaard often said that we should never take it for granted. This claim is a tremendous scandal and stumbling block for the Jews: "But we preach Christ crucified, unto the Jews a stumbling block, and unto the Greeks foolishness." (1 *Corinthians* 1:23.) The claim of Christ to be the Son of God is indeed at first sight an absolutely incredible and even "scandalizing" claim which should first be experienced in its whole character as a potential "stumbling block".

Therefore, it is incongruous to believe, like many men, that Jesus was just a good or even the best man who ever lived. It is equally illogical to assume that He was a great prophet but not God as Moslems believe. No, He is a stumbling block or the Redeemer. Either he is blasphemer (or a madman)—or *He* is "the Christ, the Son of the Living God."[5] For someone who takes Jesus seriously, there is only this Either/Or. Only when we realize the infinite distance between God and man, between an eternal self-possession of all life and the temporal unfolding of human existence, only when we realize the abyss between finite human beings and the infinite divine being, can we come to realize the immensity of the

claim of a mortal human being to be the Son of God. Only then can we understand why Christ Himself repeatedly said that those are blessed who do not take
scandal in Him. Kierkegaard reflected deeply on this scandal and paradox of the
claim to divinity by Christ and he saw his task in leading people to hesitate to
accept this claim rather than accepting it for superficial reasons, out of some tradition, without any realization of the awesome and mysterious nature of this
claim and of the potential scandal which it contains.

Yet while this is Kierkegaard's greatness, he did less to elucidate the luminous reason for the sake of which the leap of faith can be taken with utmost confidence.

3. The Uninventable Glory of God as the Deepest Reason
for Our Faith in Jesus Christ

Let us now turn to this deepest reason for our faith in Jesus Christ. We are
not speaking at this point of the hidden mystery of divine grace which gives us
an inner conviction beyond all human reason: an inexplicable and mysterious
firmness of conviction of faith which is a gift of the Holy Spirit. Rather, we speak
of a reason which appeals to human understanding and makes of faith simultaneously a reasonable act, although reason can never fathom or exhaust this reason of faith nor could any man be led through this reason, by its own sole force,
to faith. Nevertheless, the datum which we seek lends itself, in its intelligibility,
also to philosophy of religion and to reason. Saint Paul himself speaks of this in
his letter to the Romans when he blames the pagans and calls them inexcusable
for not having recognized God, whose glory has been known from eternity
through the world:

> Because that which may be known of God is manifest in them; for God hath
> shewed it unto them. For the invisible things of him from the creation of the
> world are clearly seen, being understood by the things that are made, even his
> eternal power and Godhead; so that they are without excuse: Because that, when
> they knew God, they glorified him not as God, neither were thankful; but
> became vain in their imaginations, and their foolish heart was darkened.
> (*Romans* 1: 1921).

> Therefore, also those who had to search God only with the help of their reason
> have sinned not recognizing God's glory because they: changed the glory of the
> uncorruptible God into an image made like to corruptible man, and to birds, and
> fourfooted beasts, and creeping things. (*Romans* 1:23).

But then what in Jesus Christ is the ultimate ground on the basis of which
our unwavering faith in Him is justified and on the basis of which also the fulfillment of prophecies, the signs and miracles Jesus performs, and His words and

life themselves do indeed instill faith? What is it in His words and deeds which lets us recognize that He is truly the Son of God himself and not a mere man like us, or even an evil or mad man? There must be something in the words and deeds, and in fact in the very being and life of Jesus Christ, which strikes us and lets us, like the blind man who was cured, fall on our knees in adoration before Jesus Christ and before Him alone of all men.

Indeed, there is such a deeper reason in the words and teachings, in the miracles and life of Christ which grounds our faith. There is a sublime light, and reason for faith, in Jesus which is difficult to speak about and which is yet overwhelmingly clear for the believer:

It is as if the uninventable eternal glory of God, the necessary sacred holiness of God which no mortal man could ever have invented, is encountered in an incarnate/ visible form in Jesus Christ. This is "the new light" which appears to us in Christ, from the announcement of the angels to the shepherds and the new born babe in the crib on to the glory of Easter. Far beyond anything we can grasp of the glory of God by means of philosophical reasons, this glory of God moves us and shines through the incarnate word of God in Jesus Christ. In the miracles and words of Christ we are struck by this glory of God. It is the inner holiness and glory of the words and teachings of Christ which lets Peter say: "Lord, to whom shall we go? You have words of eternal life" (*John* 6;68). It is the divine beauty and the uninventable glory of God's mercy beyond all telling which shines through the parable of the prodigal son, however simple this story is. In spite of, nay, in all its simplicity it reveals a light which no other purely human fairy tale or story contains. Again, it is a sacred love beyond all human dreams of love which moves the listener when he hears the parable of the good shepherd and its interpretation given by Christ. It is a truly divine mercy and forgiveness which shines forth here and which puts to shame human, all-too human or pharisaic reasoning about sinners and evildoers. All our natural rejection of adulterers and sinners is transcended and even shattered when we witness Christ's words to the adulterous woman or when we see Jesus pardon Mary Magdalen. And yet also the horror of sin appears more clearly to us through Christ's words: "But whoso shall offend one of these little ones which believe in me, it were better for him that a millstone were hanged about his neck, and that he were drowned in the depth of the sea." (*Matt* 16:8)[7]

Only on the background of the horror of sin also the glory of God's mercy can shine forth. Jesus' words to and about Mary Magdalen, on the power of love to prompt divine forgiveness, and so many other words of Christ and incidents in the Gospels reveal this divine splendor of mercy and infinite charity:

> "37And, behold, a woman in the city, which was a sinner, when she knew that Jesus sat at meat in the Pharisee's house, brought an alabaster box of ointment, 38 And stood at his feet behind him weeping, and began to wash his feet with

tears, and did wipe them with the hairs of her head, and kissed his feet, and anointed them with the ointment. 39 Now when the Pharisee which had bidden him saw it, he spake within himself, saying, This man, if he were a prophet, would have known who and what manner of woman this is that toucheth him: for she is a sinner. 40 And Jesus answering said unto him, Simon, I have somewhat to say unto thee. And he saith, Master, say, 41 There was a certain creditor which had two debtors: the one owed five hundred pence, and the other fifty. 42 And when they had nothing to pay, he frankly forgave them both. Tell me therefore, which of them will love him most? 43 Simon answered and said, I suppose that he, to whom he forgave most. And he said unto him, Thou hast rightly judged. 44 And he turned to the woman, and said unto Simon, Seest thou this woman? I entered into thine house, thou gavest me no water for my feet: but she hath washed my feet with tears, and wiped them with the hairs of her head. 45 Thou gavest me no kiss: but this woman since the time I came in hath not ceased to kiss my feet. 46 My head with oil thou didst not anoint: but this woman hath anointed my feet with ointment. 47 Wherefore I say unto thee, Her sins, which are many, are forgiven; for she loved much: but to whom little is forgiven, the same loveth little. 48 And he said unto her, Thy sins are forgiven. 49 And they that sat at meat with him began to say within themselves, Who is this that forgiveth sins also? 50 And he said to the woman, Thy faith hath saved thee; go in peace. (*Luke* 7:3750)

It is the inner beauty and truth of the words and deeds of Christ which moves us when Jesus says that the little children shall possess the kingdom of God and that we will possess heaven only if we become spiritually humble like one of them. It is the same beauty of the "world" of God, of the sacredness of God, which touches us when Jesus enjoins us: "See that you do not despise one of these little ones, for I say to you, that their angels in heaven continually behold the face of My Father who is in heaven." (*Matt* 18:10). But this sacred divinity shines also on us when the sword of divine justice reveals itself in Christ, as it moved Him to cleanse the temple and filled Him with the zeal for the House of the Lord.

With all the miracles and words of Christ, it is most of all His very being and His life which manifest God to us. His passion and crucifixion and the words which He spoke from the cross, although the passion of Jesus first scandalized even His Apostles, reveal in a hidden form behind all humiliation this unspeakable divine glory which no mere man could ever have invented or made up. In the crucified Christ and His open heart the abysses of divine love opened. When the believer contemplates the unheard of forgiveness of His murderers, the love with which He entrusted on the cross St. John, and with him humanity, to Mary and Mary to John, and all the other last words which He spoke, these words and the divine charity expressed in this love, of which no one has a greater love than the one who laid down his life for his friends, reveal this same immense "breath" of the Eternal which constitutes the deepest reason for our faith in Christ. When we see the hands and the feet of Jesus crucified and His heart opened, of the same Jesus who had a short time before, by the mere power of His word, thrown unto the ground all those who had come to imprison Him, we witness the mystery of God becoming flesh, of the divine glory manifesting itself concretely in history and in such uniqueness in one man only in history: in Jesus Christ, the incarnate Word of God.

In the image of the crucified Lord himself, in Jesus Christ who was prompted by His love of sinners to give His life for us, is manifested the divine love and holiness, the breadth and width and depth of God's charity, of God himself WHO IS CHARITY which shatters our unbelief and which reveals to us such a light as to allow us to make, in a justified manner, the leap beyond all the darkness and incomprehension which we have always to overcome in the act of faith. It is therefore the reality of the whole Gospel and not only an abstract word which St. John expresses when he puts the core of Christianity into the stupendous words: "For God is Love." (*John* 4:8), a teaching inconceivable for the Greeks.

The divine glory and uninventable holiness of charity which permeates the words and miracles and the life and death of Jesus Christ, do not only justify faith but make it radically different from mere probable opinion. These luminous reasons make of the act of faith not a mere act of belief "that probably Jesus is God" or that it may be believed because it has not (yet) been shown false that Jesus rose from the dead. No, the act of religious faith is *essentially different from all such acts of belief* and of "probable opinions." We do not believe in Christ in the sense in which we believe that with a certain probability the weather will stay good if all the signs for that are given. Rather the act of faith is characterized by an inner certainty and by an absolute, unconditioned "yes" which makes even the weakest and most tempted faith radically distinct from a mere act of speculation or of belief based on probability or on hypotheses.

The rationality of faith could never be explained in the theory of Popper, through the fact that the Christian hypotheses are not "yet" falsified.[8] Such a faith could never be the rock upon which the Christian life is built.

The act of faith, however, in spite of its absoluteness and of the unconditioned yes which the believer speaks to Jesus Christ, in whom he believes, is not irrational nor is it an enemy of an "open, rational society," as some members of the German philosophical movement of critical rationalism[9] have claimed to the point of demanding the extermination of dogmatic Christians in the name of the "open society." No, the act of faith in Christ, and of unconditional belief that His words are true, is the supreme act of reason. To confess that "Truly this man was the Son of God" (*Mark* 15:39) is entirely justified, and is so ultimately on account of the splendor of divine holiness which manifests itself in Christ, in His teachings, parables, and deeds. This divine holiness permeates the whole being of Christ.

Also the greatest of all the miracles reported in the Gospel, the resurrection of our Lord Jesus Christ, moves us not only by the fact that it is well established by witnesses, that many saw the risen Lord, that women and men, Romans and Jews, single persons, and a group of hundreds of disciples—assembled at the same time and in the same place—testified to having seen Jesus risen from the dead. This miracle inspires our faith not only because later generations of saints have witnessed appearances of Jesus Christ and have fulfilled the words of Christ that his disciples would perform, in His power, "the same or even greater signs" than He Himself. We do not believe in the resurrection of Christ merely because, from St. Paul until this day, followers of Christ, in the power of God, also raised the dead, as Christ has raised Lazarus.[10]

We would certainly not believe in the resurrection, and on the basis of the resurrection in the divinity of Christ, if similar things had been ever so well established about any other man besides Jesus Christ. For what prompts our faith is far beyond the suspension of the laws of nature by the resurrection: the uninventable nature of God and the divine goodness and wisdom and love and glory which shine through the words, miracles, and the resurrection of Jesus Christ. It is, furthermore, the wisdom of the Holy Spirit, through which the Apostle Peter explains the miracle of the resurrection and the divine reasons for it, to the multitude who hear him speak, each in his own language, on the day of Pentecost, it is this "Wisdom of God" in the passion and resurrection of Christ which truly "forces us," without doing violence to our freedom, to believe in the resurrection of Jesus Christ.[11]

It is, in the last analysis, only because the invisible glory of God became visible in Jesus Christ and the holiness of God became flesh and manifested itself to us in Him, that Jesus can say to Philip, what would be blasphemous if any man besides Jesus had spoken these words: "He who has seen Me has seen the Father; how do you say, 'Show us the Father?'"(*John* 14;9). It is only because Jesus Christ is not merely objectively the Son of God but the uninventable beauty and holiness of God is experienced in him, that St. John can say: "And we beheld His glory, glory as of the only begotten from the Father, full of grace and truth." (*John* 1:14).

For this reason ultimately also we believe in Christ and say "Rabboni" (*John* 20:16) to Him when He calls us as He did call Mary Magdalen, because we, too, have "seen the divine glory through the Gospels in the very figure and voice of Christ."

The glory we mean here is not only the splendor of visible or audible forms that also Christ calls "glory,"[12] which in some mysterious fashion, beautifully described by Newman,[13] are able to carry a highly spiritual beauty which transcends their bearer entirely.[14] The glory we mean here is a beauty which is not only entirely objective[15] but which intelligibly proceeds from the being and goodness of that which possesses this glory that is the spiritual emanation and splendor of justice or of a great love of a person who gives his life for his friends.

More specifically still, the glory we mean here, and which is the deepest root of our faith, is not only the splendor of truth in general or of moral truth in particular, the *veritatis splendor*, but the *divine* glory, a spiritual splendor which can only proceed from the inner holiness of God,[16] and which presupposes the uninventable inner perfection and truth of the divine nature.[17] This uninventable inner goodness and necessity and glory also constitutes the basis of the so-called ontological argument for the existence of God (of Anselm, Bonaventure, Descartes, and others).[18] It is this unique *glory of the Holy* and of the *divine* Holiness which alone can motivate religious acts of faith and adoration and which constitutes our deepest reason for believing in Jesus Christ. For it is as if the irreducible and unique glory of God, which in philosophy we can come to understand only in a fragmented and distant way as if in a mirror, had become visible in Christ[19], in the newborn Savior announced to the shepherds, in the Sermon on the Mount, in the forgiveness of the adulterous woman, in Jesus's heart pierced for our sins on the Cross[20], and in the gloriously risen Christ. Thus this unique aesthetic value, the glory of God, this ontological beauty which reflects the holiness of God and proceeds from it, is the deepest reason for our faith in Jesus Christ. In spite of its spiritual nature, this glory of God can become visible in the flesh, in the face of Christ[21], and also finds its expression in the greatest works of visual art and of music.[22]

We also see a similitude of this glory in the true followers of Christ, the saints. The glory of God which became flesh in Jesus Christ also shines, as it were, through a smaller light in the Apostles or in Stephen the Archmartyr who, "falling on his knees, cried out with a loud voice; 'Lord, do not hold this sin against them'." (*Acts* 8;60) In this imitation of Christ's own forgiveness of those who crucified Him, St. Stephen fulfilled the words of Christ: "You are to be perfect, as your heavenly Father is perfect." (*Matt* 5;48). It is also the countless other men and women who live through their faith and according to the doctrines of the Church, it is these Edith Steins or Maximilian Kolbes who, in the midst of the hell of concentration camps and hatred, which would move most men to bitter resentment and retaliation, show sublime charity: it is all of them who give witness to the glory of Him whom they imitate. And countless heroic Christians of the different confessions gave witness to Him in their steadfast love and faith.

Think especially of St. Francis who sent back his friars, who had justly scolded and chased away villainous murderers who begged them for alms and wished to devour what had been given by the faithful to the poor. But Francis chided them severely because they had forgotten the charity by which they had been redeemed, and he demanded that they should follow the villains and ask pardon from these murderers for not having treated them with the charity of Christians. Francis sent the friars back a long way. He ordered that they should bring the murderers food and drink. They should tell them that "their brother Francis" implores them to change their lives and that he asks them with tears not to offend God. When the friars did this, the glorious charity of Christ touched and changed these criminals. It is because of this glory of God in Christ that the man who is desirous, like Daniel, of wisdom and truth and beauty, and who thirsts for the well of life, like the Samaritan woman, will come to believe in Jesus Christ.

Not even in the greatest men and women in history, not even in the noblest men of the pagan world, such as in a Socrates, in no patriarch and in no prophet, not even in the Apostles who reflect Christ, and not even in Mary, the Queen of all Saints, however, we will find that very fount of divine holiness which made the blind man fall on his knees and worship Christ after having been cured and after having asked Jesus to show him the Son of Man. When Jesus answered him: "He is the one who is talking with you" (*John* 9:37), he adored Him. It took the unique holiness of Jesus Christ to motivate this.

Yet the uninventable glory of God, while nowhere visible with the unique force and incarnation in which it lives in Jesus Christ alone, becomes also visible not merely in Christ's followers, but also in the doctrines of Jesus and of the Church. The extraordinary inner truth and unity and beauty, and the divine depth, of this doctrine reveal, too, the glory of God. For it is God's eternal and uninventable nature which the Gospels and holy doctrines describe, just as they reveal to us also the unspeakable mystery of God's free choice to become man and to redeem sinners, spelling out the implications of God's love, of man's sin and freedom, and of God's redemption and our justification. Indeed, this glory of God in Christ can also shine forth in a unique way in classical liturgical texts and in music, in the Gregorian chant, in Mozart's *Ave Verum* or *Laudate Dominum*, in Fra Angelico's paintings, in Zosima in *The Brothers Karamasoff* or in Leonardo's *Last Supper* or the Mosaics of Ravenna.

Let us conclude by repeating: we see in the words of St. John: "we beheld His glory, a glory as of the only begotten from the Father, full of grace and truth."(John 1:14) not only the witness of the Apostle who has actually lived with Jesus. Rather, we see in these words also the expression of the deepest reason for the faith of all of us who believe in Jesus Christ. We too have "witnessed" and "seen" in the life, in the doctrines, in the miracles, in the very "face" of Christ the unspeakable glory of God, its uninventable beauty and inner truth which cannot be the work of a madman, or the invention of historians or of liars.

Not so much the scholarship of Scripture scholars as the inner divine truth of the Bible gives witness of its authenticity, and it alone proves the divine origin of Scripture which no positive Scripture-scholarship can demonstrate. Thus the mode of knowledge which delves in the glory of God in Christ and in the inner spiritual meaning of the divine texts, in their "divine form," should be the basis of "Scripture-scholarship." Historical scholarship should only be secondary, a mere means and instrument of that wisdom of expounding the very Wisdom of God and the glory of Christ which we expect from an "Exegesis" worthy of its name.[23] One could show something similar for Christian Ethics and moral theology.[24]

One could expound here also the specifically Christian virtues of humility, charity, etc. as absolutely uninventable and intelligible in their inner necessity and goodness: and yet as based on faith in revealed truth. Kierkegaard[25], Bergson, Scheler, and Hildebrand[26] have explained this specifically Christian morality as the fulfillment of natural morality and as containing a sublime beauty which we can also perceive by reason and philosophy

Thus the uninventable glory of God, as it is revealed to us and yet gives light to our understanding, is the supreme object of theological knowledge, the only firm basis of a true *theology* of Revelation, and the deepest reason for our faith. For the incarnate glory of God in Christ contains already in this life some of that splendor and beauty of which Isaias and St. Paul say that "eye has not seen, and ear has not heard, and which have not entered the heart of man," (1 *Cor.* 2:9) of the splendor of God Himself which strikes us and moves us on earth in and through Jesus Christ. And Him, the incarnate glory of God, whose divine beauty instills faith, hope, and charity in us, we hope to see face to face in the unspeakable eternal bliss of heaven, so that His prayer may be fulfilled:

> "Father, I will that they also, whom thou hast given me, be with me where I am; that they may behold my glory, which thou hast given me: for thou lovedst me before the foundation of the world. O righteous Father, the world hath not known thee: but I have known thee, and these have known that thou hast sent me. And I have declared unto them thy name, and will declare it: that the love wherewith thou hast loved me may be in them, and I in them." (*John* 17:2426).

NOTES

[1] Or, in the beautiful Latin translation of Saint Jerome: "Et verbum caro factum est et habitavit in nobis. Et vidimus gloriam cius, gloriun quasi unigeniti a Patre, plenum gratiae et veritatis."

[2] We are reminded here of the famous distinction of John Cardinal Newman between "notional" and "real assent," John Henry Cardinal Newman, *An Essav in Aid of A Grammar of Assent* Md.: Christian Classics Inc.,1973).

[3] The scholastics distinguished aptly between three acts involved in faith: *credere Deum* (belief that God exists and that it is He, and His Son Jesus Christ, Who reveals Himself to us); *credere in Deum* (belief *in* God, surrendering ourselves to Him in trust and following Him); and *credere Deo* (believing *that* what He reveals to us is true). The second and third of these acts of faith are necessarily interconnected and rest on the first.

[4] Soeren Kierkegaard, in his *Fear and Trembling*, and in his *Book Adler*, and elsewhere, has spoken of the mystery and paradox of the object of faith and of the tremendous leap into the darkness of mystery it requires. Even if we see traces of irrationalism in Kierkegaard's notion of the leap of faith and take issue with some of his opinions, we must recognize in him the honest and profound aware-

ness of the abyss of mystery which we accept in faith when we believe that a man like us is the eternal and uncreated God. We agree with Soeren Kierkegaard also when he insists that we must feel the "scandal" we might take in Jesus's claim to be God, a scandal which we would rightfully have to experience if any other human person, making a similar claim, would blaspheme. Before we reach this potential sense of scandal, our faith in Jesus Christ really is not mature and authentic. As Jesus Christ Himself says: "And blessed is he, whosoever shall not be offended in me." (*Matt* 11:6). And again: "And blessed is he, whosoever shall find no occasion of stumbling in me." (*Luke* 7:23).

[5] Simon Peter answered and said, "Thou art the Christ, the Son of the living God." (*Matt* 16:16) and "Then Simon Peter answered him, Lord to whom shall we go? thou hast the words of eternal life. And we believe and are sure that thou art that Christ the Son of the living God," (*John* 6:68).

[6] Compare to this 2 *Corinthians* 4:6 and also the sublime "Praefatio" of Christmas of the Catholic liturgy, as well as the mystical and poetic explanation, in text and melody, of the theme of the light of Christ in the *Exsultet*, the Holy Saturday Night liturgical "Ambrosian Hymn," in which this "new light" of the invisible God becoming visible is praised.

[7] Cf. also: "Woe to him through whom they (scandals) come! It would be better for him if a millstone were hung around his neck and he were thrown into the sea." (*Luke* 17:1–2).

[8] I see it as the greatest problem in the theology of the very impressive German theologian Wolfgang Pannenberg that he interprets faith along the lines of this Popperian way as an "unfalsified hypothesis," which thus far resisted all trials to prove it wrong.

[9] Especially Hans Albert and his school which again derives from the philosophy of Sir Karl Popper. See my discussion of this in Josef Seifert, "Objektivismus in der Wissenschaft und Grundlagen philosophischer Rationalitaet. Kritische Ueberlegungen zu Karl Poppers Wissenschafts-, Erkenntnis- und Wahrheitstheorie," in: N. Leser, J. Seifert, K. Plitzner (Hrsg.), *Die Gedankenwelt Sir Karl Poppers*: Kritischer Rationalismus im Dialog (Heidelberg: Universitaetsverlag C. Winter, 1991), pp. 31–74; und "Diskussion", pp. 75–82. See likewise the whole discussion in this volume, and also my "Wissen und Wahrheit in Naturwissenschaft und Glauben" in Naturwissenschaft und Weltbild. Mathematik und Quantenphysik in unserem Denk- und Wertesystem, eds. H-C. Reichel and E. Prat de Ia Riba (Vienna: Verlag Hoelder-Pichler-Tempsky, 1992).

[10] Such extremely well-documented miracles from the time of the Gospels until today—of the dead having been raised—have been recorded carefully and scientifically. See Wilhelm Schamoni, *Auferweckungen vom Tode. Aus Heiligsprechungsakten uebersetzt*, 5th ed. (Stein am Rhein: Christiana Verlag, 1996).

[11] Let us record the Apostle's magnificent sermon on the meaning of Jesus's res-

urrection:

> But Peter, standing up with the eleven, lifted up his voice, and said unto them,
> Ye men of Judaea, and all ye that dwell at Jerusalem, be this known unto you,
> and hearken to my words: For these are not drunken, as ye suppose, seeing it is
> *but* the third hour of the day. But this is that which was spoken by the prophet
> Joel; And it shall come to pass in the last days, saith God, I will pour out of my
> Spirit upon all flesh: and your sons and your daughters shall prophesy, and your
> young men shall see visions, and your old men shall dream dreams: And on my
> servants and on my handmaidens I will pour out in those days of my Spirit; and
> they shall prophesy: And I will shew wonders in heaven above, and signs in the
> earth beneath; blood, and fire, and vapour of smoke: The sun shall be turned into
> darkness, and the moon into blood, before that great and notable day of the Lord
> come: And it shall come to pass, *that* whosoever shall call on the name of the
> Lord shall be saved. Ye men of Israel, hear these words; Jesus of Nazareth, a
> man approved of God among you by miracles and wonders and signs, which
> God did by him in the midst of you, as ye yourselves also know: Him, being
> delivered by the determinate counsel and foreknowledge of God, ye have taken,
> and by wicked hands have crucified and slain: Whom God hath raised up, hav-
> ing loosed the pains of death: because it was not possible that he should be hold-
> en of it. For David speaketh concerning him, I foresaw the Lord always before
> my face, for he is on my right hand, that I should not be moved: Therefore did
> my heart rejoice, and my tongue was glad; moreover also my flesh shall rest in
> hope: Because thou wilt not leave my soul in hell, neither wilt thou suffer thine
> Holy One to see corruption. Thou hast made known to me the ways of life; thou
> shalt make me full of joy with thy countenance. Men *and* brethren, let me freely
> speak unto you of the patriarch David, that he is both dead and buried, and his
> sepulchre is with us unto this day. Therefore being a prophet, and knowing that
> God had sworn with an oath to him, that of the fruit of his loins, according to
> the flesh, he would raise up Christ to sit on his throne; He seeing this before
> spake of the resurrection of Christ, that his soul was not left in hell, neither his
> flesh did see corruption. This Jesus hath God raised up, whereof we all are wit-
> nesses. Therefore being by the right hand of God exalted, and having received
> of the Father the promise of the Holy Ghost, he hath shed forth this, which ye
> now see and hear. For David is not ascended into the heavens: but he saith him-
> self, The LORD said unto my Lord, Sit thou on my right hand, Until I make thy
> foes thy footstool. Therefore let all the house of Israel know assuredly, that God
> hath made that same Jesus, whom ye have crucified, both Lord and Christ. (*Acts*
> 2:14–36).

[12] "And yet I say unto you, That even Solomon in all his glory was not arrayed
like one of these. Wherefore, if God so clothe the grass of the field, which today
is, and tomorrow is cast into the oven, shall he not much more clothe you, O ye
of little faith?" (Matt 6:29–30).

[13]   There are seven notes in the scale; make them fourteen; yet what a slender

outfit for so vast an enterprise! What science brings forth so much out of so little? Out of what poor elements does some great master in it create his new
world? Shall we say that all this exuberant intensiveness is a mere ingenuity or
trick of art like some game or fashion of the day without reality, without meaning? Or is it possible that that inexhaustible evolution and disposition of notes,
so rich yet so simple, so intricate yet so regulated, so various yet so majestic,
should be a mere sound which is gone and perishes? Can it be that those mysterious stirrings of the heart, and keen emotions, and strange yearnings after we
know not what, and awful impressions from we know not whence, should be
brought in us by what is unsubstantial, and comes and goes, and begins and ends
in itself? It is not so; it cannot be. No; they have escaped from some higher
sphere, they are the outpourings of eternal harmony in the medium of created
sound; they are echoes of our home; they are the voice of angels, or the
Magnificat of the Saints, or the Living Laws of Divine Governance, or Divine
Attributes; something they are besides themselves, which we cannot encompass, which we cannot utter, though mortal man, and he perhaps not otherwise
distinguished above his fellows, has the gift of eliciting them.

John Henry Cardinal Newman, *University Sermons*, xv. See also Hildebrand, *The
New Tower of Babel. Manifestations of Man's Escape from God* (Chicago:
Franciscan Herald Press, 1977), p.202.
[14] See on this Dietrich von Hildebrand, *Asthetik*. 1. Teil. Gesammelte Werke,
Band V (Stuttgart: Kohlhammer, 1977), 492 S. (1989 uebernommen vom Eos
Verlag, St. Ottilien). See also Josef Seifert, "Beauty of Higher Forms (Second
Potency) in Art and Nature" in *Annales dEsthetiques*, vol. 21–22 (1982–83).
[15] See Dietrich von Hildebrand, *Asthetik*. I. Teil. Gesammelte Werke, Band V
(Stuttgart: Kohihammer, 1977), 492 S. (1989 Eos Verlag, St. Ottilien), ch. 1. See
also Josef Seifert, "The Objectivity of Beauty in Music and a Critique of
Aesthetic Subjectivism", *XRONIKA AISQUETIKHS Annales d'Esthethique* Tom.
31–32/1992–1993, 3361.
16See the classic work by Rudolf Otto. *Das Heilige,Ueber das Irrationale in der
Idee des Goettlichen und sein Verhaeltnis zum Rationalen*, Sonderauflage
(Munich: Verlag C.H. Beck, 1962). See also Max Scheler, "Probleme der
Religion", in: Max Scheler, *Vom Ewigen im Menschen*, 5 Aufl. (Bern und
Muenchen: Francke Verlag, 1968), S.101–354.
17To this glory of God Jesus refers often, for example: "And now, O Father, glorify thou me with thine own self with the glory which I had with thee before the
world was." (*John* 17:5), or when he speaks to the Samaritan woman: "Jesus saith
unto her, Said I not unto thee, that, if thou wouldest believe, thou shouldest see
the glory of God?" (*John* 11:40); "For the Son of man shall come in the glory of
his Father with his angels; and then he shall reward every man according to his
works." *Matt* 16:27), or in: "When the Son of man shall come in his glory, and
all the holy angels with him, then shall he sit upon the throne of his glory..."
(*Matt* 25:31).

[18] I just published a new defense of this argument which I take to be the deepest of all proofs for the existence of God, whose foundation is also presupposed for all other proofs for the existence of God: the objective necessity and uninventable character of the unique divine nature which differs from all other natures and could never have been produced by human subjectivity but is found and discovered by our mind in its inner truth. See Josef Seifert, *Gott als Gottesbeweis. Eine phaenomenologische Neubegruendung des ontologischen Arguments* (Heidelberg: Universitaetsverlag C. Winter, 1996); and also my *Sein und Wesen* (Heidelberg: Universitaetsverlag C. Winter, 1996).

[19] "For now we see through a glass, darkly; but then face to face: now I know in part; but then shall I know even as also I am known." I *Corinthians* 13:12.

[20] One of the greatest masterworks of visual art in which this becomes, as it were "visible" is the painting of the Crucifixion in the *Isenheimer Altar* of Matthias Gruenewald in Colmar.

[21] Also as portrayed in art. See on this also a beautiful philosophical and theological explanation in D.S. Mereschkowskij, "Das Antlitz Jesu" in: D.S. Mereschkowskij. *Jesus der Kommende*, ch. 1, pp.7–34; and ibid., "Das Antlitz des Herrn im Evangelium," ibid., ch. 2, pp.35–59.

[22] I think here especially of the stunning incarnation of this specifically divine glory in the works of Fra Angelico, but also in such masterworks as Beethoven's or Mozart's. See the following description of this phenomenon in Beethoven's *Missa solemnis* by Dietrich von Hildebrand:

> ...For no other (composer) was so great and ultimate as artist that he would have been able to give so adequate an artistic expression as Beethoven to the greatest thing that exists between heaven and earth, ...this event in which the ultimate fate of humanity and of each individual man is in the balance. No one was so comprehensive and in this sense "Catholic" that he could have served as spokesman for humanity as such. When the violin resounds at the beginning of the Benedictus, it is as if heaven descended from on high, when the "Dona nobis Pacem" is heard, as if mankind looked up in prayer to God from its absolute metaphysical position. Truly, if anywhere in art we may say this, we must say it here: "It is the face of the Lord."

See Hildebrand, *Mozart Beethoven Schubert* (Regensburg: J. Habbel, 1964), p.75–76 (my own translation).

23See Hans Urs von Balthasar's *Glory* (*Herrlichkeit*) or theological aesthetics, but also his *Theodramatik II; Die Personen des Spiels,1: Der Mensch in Gott.* (Einsiedeln: Johannes Verlag, 1976). *Theodramatik II: Die Personen des Spiels, 2: Die Personen in Christus*, (Einsiedeln: Johannes Verlag, l978).

[24] See the Encyclical *Veritatis Splendor*

[25] I think here especially of the many volumes of Soeren Kierkegaard's magnificent *Edifying Discourses* but also of such works as *Fear and Trembling* in which

he analyses Abraham's unshakable faith and trust in God.

[26] This was the purpose of Dietrich von Hildebrand, *Transformation in Christ. Our Path to Holiness*. Reprint of 1948 (New Hampshire: Sophia Institute Press. 1989). See also Dietrich von Hildebrand, *Ethics*, 2nd ed. (Chicago: Franciscan Herald Press, 1978); see, likewise, by the same author, his treatment of the new quality of Christian charity in his *Das Wesen der Liebe; Dietrich von Hildebrand. Gesammelte Werke III* (Regensburg, 1971), Chapter 11.

21

Christ, Christianity and the World Religions

Hörst Bürkle

Jesus Christ—God and Man—this creed has received its explanation and differentation whenever a heretic cause challenged the Church to do so. Our common Christian creeds as for instance the Nicenum and the Nicenum-Constantinopolitanum are the result of such challenges. The basic Christian faith in Jesus Christ as Son of God and Saviour (J.Chr. huios sotar = ISXUS) had to be defended against misinterpretations and against any abolishment of the mystery 'God in Christ.' The sentences of the Christian creed were supposed to meet such errors. They are the result of a long process during which time the Church—guided by the Holy Spirit—had reasons to define the proper relation between the persons within the Trinity and between the divine and the human nature in Christ. Our creeds as the outcome of those early processes during which the Church had been forced to safeguard the biblical fundaments of faith are today all too much a given fact to us which is understood by itself. We forget that they have been developed as most necessary tools for the preservation of the Christian truth and even more: We overlook quite easily that this same faith of our fathers needs to be protected again in our time against depravations and errors. Each time and age has its own specific approaches toward the Christian message. But within each of such actualisations lies the tendency to overlook other essential parts of the whole Christian doctrine or even to estrange it using means of interpreting it which are strange to the Gospel. Onesidedness and estrangement are the two tendencies which are relevant when and wherever the spirit of the age meets the Spirit of Christ—present in His Word in the Church as His Body. We hear not only the demand that we have to be up to date with our Christian message and to speak the language of our time. This is a never ending necessary hermeneutic task in bringing the message to the people. But something else might happen— and many of us realize that it happens..Jesus Christ no longer remains to be the measure and the criteria for the demands and for the expectations of our society. But the opposite takes place: The dreams, the demands and the expectations of our time provide the frame for what is still relevant in Christ's message to us. The human horizon defines the Divine horizon. Man and his society of today know already beforehand what is desirable and therefore good for man and mankind. All what is needed then is to break single elements out from the treasure of God's Word and to transform them into a 'new theology'. It is this type of 'Genetive-theologies' which swallow the whole Gospel and digest it in the form of a pre-produced ideological or philosophical ideology: "Theology of feminism", "Theology of revolution", Theology of hope" (concrete: hoping for what is already in our minds), "Theology of liberation" etc. p.p.

Our faith as expressed in the Church's Creed in Jesus Christ as God and Man excludes every attempt to reduce the Gospel to a single preselected element of it. In this respect all heresies had been 'right'. They all have taken up one specific aspect out of the whole Christian truth of which they had been convinced that it had been neglected by the Church. Here lies the particle of truth in each heresy. But by isolating this partial element and singling it out of the whole Christian truth by making it a new 'confession' they misused it and turned it into an error.

The temptation of singling out specific elements of the Gospel is most of all relevant in the encounter of the Christian faith with other religions. In their advanced speakers we meet today not only a language which seems familiar to us. In their writings they quite often refer to the Bible. Their ethical and moral standards seem to be linked with basic Christian values. Some of their out-standing theologians and philosophers call for a new universal religion which is related to the basic concepts of their own traditions. The mission of the Church and the theology which has to serve this mission meets here a new challenge and task. By entering into this field of the encounter with other religions we are able to sharpen our eyes for the heresies of our time. For this kind of a 'missionary dialogue' and its consequences for finding the necessary corrections of our faith in our situation some selected examples will be given in this paper.

Jesus Christ and the kingdom of this world

Mohammed regarded himself "prophet and statesman" (Montgomery Watt). In his message to his Arabic folksmen he was convinced to go beyond the Jewish faith in the covenant with God and beyond the Christian expectation of the king-dom of heaven. His prophecy sounded like the final fulfilment of what had been prophesied in earlier ages. His message in the beginning of its proclamation was focussed on an eschatological event: the forth-coming final judgement of God.

But already during his time at Medina the perspective of the eternal fulfilment in the end of this time and history disappeared. It had to give way to a fulfilment 'here and now'. The will of Allah was prepresented by the power and the reign of his prophet Mohammed and his successors. There was a final identity of the victorious campaign of Mohammed's fighters and of Allah's triumph over the non-believers. The Holy Koran therefore is at once the book of Allah's revelation and the new state law. God's own city is now at hand. The *umma* as the community of believers is also the society as such. In it the non-believers have to live according to the law of the Koran which constitutes the state as Allah's revealed will.

It is this identity of religion and politics which marks one of the fundamental differences between the Koran and the New Testament. They have their roots in the difference between Mohammed—as prophet and statesman—and Jesus Christ—the incarnated son of God. It is the difference between a new powerful regime in the name of Allah and the mystery of the presence of the risen Christ in his body, the Church. "My kingship is not of this world" (Joh. 18,36) does not mean that there is nothing but inwardness and pure spirituality. But it refers to the very center of the New Being in Christ. Man is going to be changed and renewed in participating in the Christ-event. The new man is the one who has died and risen with Christ (Ro 6,8). 'Rebirth' qualifies the new life in Christ. Our true life is hidden in Him, as the Apostle describes this secret (Col.3,3) Therefore this new reality can never become manifest in or identical with any human organisation or social structure in this world. In the power of Christ's presence the Church finally has 'defeated' the pagan state in its sacralized absolute role. But this happened not through replacing it by another timely political power and by a sacred structure of the state. It was the finality of the communion with Jesus Christ which gave freedom to the Christians for 'de-mythologizing' the state. The function of the State became from now on to provide the necessary lawful conditions for a life according to God's will so that Christians might live and proclaim Christ's Lordship of all (1 Tim. 1,2).

In various ways we find today among Christian theologians a kind of "Islamic" approach toward the Christian message. To develop strategies for political actions in form of a theology of liberation or of revolution means to turn the New Being in Christ into a political program. Christ's grace working through man has been turned in this way into a human law. Such a law needs to be put into existence by force and power-struggle. Christ's message of the liberation and the renewal of man is going to be misused in the struggle for a change in the organisation in this society. There is just one dimension left: this earthly time man lives in and the limitations of this life. The call to action does not leave room anymore for the sacramental and hidden presence of Christ among his people in every nation, class or political system. 'Faith' in Christ and a certain political conviction become identical. The new 'islamized' theological message now proclaims: His kingdom is of this world. We are the fully instructed and committed fighters for the new kingdom of this world—but it is the world of Him who once refused to ask his heavenly father to send him angels to rescue him.

But even different from the Koranic message of the identity of Allah's will with the powerful action of his believers the new Christian political theology must pay a higher price: The action and the new political struggle replace the necessity of strengthening our faith in the invisible reality of Christ's reign by prayer, spirituality and in sacramental union. There seems to be no need for this any longer since the 'heavenly' reality has been replaced by the visible and 'makable' new reality of man's direct autonomous saving action and its finality.

Hinduistic inclusiveness and Jesus Christ the one way

Hinduism offers a pluralistic spectrum of religious practices, cults and philosophies. Throughout its history it has absorbed various traditions. It arose from the integration of the ancient Indian Dravidic cults into the Arian religion represented in the Vedic tradition. The worship of idols of various gods and goddesses in temples stands beside sophisticated methods of meditation or comprehensive systems of high philosophical calibre. This all embracing 'inclusiveness' (Paul Hacker) as the most significant characteristic phenomenon in Hinduism has its root in the very center of this religion itself. The eternal *brahma* is just a hidden reality in this world. In endless circles of return it 'plays' with itself by bringing the phenomena of the visible world into being. 'Rebirth' is the symbol of every being. All imagination and ways of understanding and of worshipping this absolute divine *brahman* participate in this illusionary situation. Therefore they all are just attempts of conceiving the Divine which is hidden in every being. According to his lifecondition, to his capacity and to his social and cultural context man chooses his way of religious devotion and of his discovery of this secret of life. Hinduism offers a whole variety of methods, means and religious practices. They all lead to the same goal. For it there are names and symbols. In practice they might exclude each other, but they all are just means serving the same aim. Within Hinduism we therefore find side by side the most extreme and opposite religious practices. They range from the highest ascetic ideal of a *sanyasi* in his removed loneliness in the Himalaya mountains down to the sexual rituals in the *tantric* and *shakti* tradition. In modern times also Jesus Christ had been included into this Hindu-pantheon. He is regarded as one of the outstanding *avatara*. Such manifestations of the highest *brahman* we find in Hinduism in various persons and at different times.

India's inclusive religious pluralism has found its expression in a number of narrative example stories. One of them is the story of the various paths which according to the ability and to the specific conditions of a hiker lead to the same top of the mountain. Modern Hindu thinkers interpret this Hinduistic pluralism as the base for all true tolerance and religious freedom. Every society and every man chooses their specific way of putting their religion into practice. Only Hinduism—they proclaim—knows about the hidden purpose which they all have to serve.

The Christian faith is based on the contrary on another fundament. It is the uniqueness and the exclusiveness of one single event in history and in time. Jesus Christ—God and Man—is the event through which God has finally made himself known to mankind. This event is unique in the sense that there have been no other occasions before and after in which this happened. The New Testament therefore calls this event the *kairos*. That means a time singled out by God in a unique way. There are many ways in nature and in history where man might meet God's actions and his omnipotence. But there is just one time and place when he revealed his very being and his Fatherly face in his begotten Son.

The message of this event has been transmitted to us, of course, in various texts and interpreted in a variety of testimonies through out the history of the Church. And here again we look into the heart of Christianity:The Church does not live just with her reminiscence of this event. Jesus Christ—God and man— is the risen Lord. He is present in this Church as in His mystic Body as well as sitting at the right hand of the Father.

It is not just by accident that this new reality of the unique relation of man through the Son to the Father has become fundamental for true humanity and personal freedom. The individualistic and liberalistic attitude of modern secular man has taken advantage of this root of freedom but has estranged it from itself. The religious 'menu-card' according to which everybody could choose religious practices and cults including the imports from ancient countries, and even mix his own religious 'cocktail' was already the latest 'fashion-cry' in the Roman empire. But the new reality of the risen Christ—God and man—had to overcome this religious pluralism in order to bring true freedom and response to God in faith and service. "So if the son makes you free, you will be free indeed" (Joh. 8,36).

It is not surprising that in our time the Hinduistic principle of religious pluralism has influence even among theologians and with the Church. There is almost no action or program in our societies with which the Church should not declare her solidarity. What is good and desirable man seems to know by himself. Christ has become an alien—the fellowman in action for purposes and means which not seldom are controversial even among Christians. The agenda of the day with its controversies and debates in parliaments and in the public seems to occupy Church-synods and the sermons of our preachers.

There is on the one hand a strong invasion of preproduced convictions and personal standpoints. They claim to be the 'message for the day'. But they are not the voice of the Good Shepherd. Because they do not confirm our faith in Him as God and man by building and strengthening our unity in His body, the Church. They much more disintegrate and weaken and dissolve this unique relation by a centrifugal pluralism.

No wonder if the victory of secular messages and aims in the voice of the Church is accompanied by a variety of practices and methods. Sacramental disciplines like confession and spiritual exercises centred in deepening our Christ-relation are replaced by a mixture of alien practices. They range from *yoga* and Zen to group-dynamics and concentration-training. Man moves into the centre with his unconscious and unsolved conflicts. The dialogue of man with man takes the place of the devotion and inner experience of Jesus Christ—God and man. We do not have to go into the details of this (socalled) 'Markt der Moglichkeiten' (market of everything possible) as the official program of the Evangelische Kirchentag in Germany quite significantly calls this proposal.

For the Church in India—who has to testify to her faith within the pluralism of Hindu religious ways and practices—there is no question that the Christian message and the faith of the Church has only one inexchangeable and exclusive content. Here we might learn anew why religous pluralism and the uniqueness of our New Being in Christ—God and man—are exclusive to each other. The variety of our expressions of faith according to our historic and cultural conditions is quite another thing than shifting from the unique centre to the peripheries of our pluralistic intentions. If this process should continue—but Christ's promise that he will be with His Church at all times stands against it—the principle of 'Hinduism' will have overcome the Christian 'principle' which is based and centred in Jesus Christ—God and man.

Jesus Christ—our guru or our Lord

Most of the modern approaches of representatives of other religions toward selected elements of the Christian truth go back to an outstanding Indian: Ram Mohan Roy (1772–1833). He was convinced that it was the ethics of the sermon on the mountain what India facing modern developments needed most. He still had experiences of the old Hindu society. He was convinced that burning widows (Sati) , the caste-system or the marriage of children were not just abuses and deprivations, but had their roots within the Hindu religion itself. When he came into contact with the Christian message he was overwhelmed by the ethics and moral standards of Jesus as expressed in the sermon of the mountain. Here he found the key for a new Indian society and its orientation toward human values and social justice. Jesus became for him the great *guru*—the spiritual leader Who was able to lead the way to this goal. It was a first attempt of integrating the Christian message into the Indian context. If Paul Tillich is right with his 'method of correlation' that the answer has to correspond to the existing question, then here we have a brillant example. The question for a new moral fundament was at hand. But Ram Mohan Roy and all those Hindu reformers who came after him did not go beyond the frame of their existential question. It was not Jesus

Christ—God and man—whom they found, but Jesus the divine inspired leader and example. Maybe for Ram Mohan Roy and for some of the others like Keshub Chandra Sen, Gandhi and others he was even more: He was an *avatara*—a manifestation of the divine absolute *brahman* in a human person. This still was an element of their Hindu tradition. There are many others of such divine manifestations according to Hindu faith. It is not God, the Father, revealing himself in his begotten Son, but it happens within the circle of repeated occasions of selfmanifestation of the Divine within the sphere of human appearances.

'Jesus—the guide to peace and happiness'—so the title of the important book in which Ram Mohan Roy broke through the boundaries of Hindu morals and customs—finally became a reformer of Hindu society. The later period of this reform took up those impulses which had been received from the New Testament message. But the way did not lead to Jesus Christ—God and man— and therefore not to His Church. It served the 'rebirth' of India as a nation. It opened up the door toward a development of a modern society within Hinduism. It gave way toward new civic rights and to the dignity of the individual.

One is reminded of this development toward the modern Indian society of today if one looks at similar tendencies within theology and within the Christian Church of our time. 'Peace and happiness' have lost even for many Christians their basic spiritual dimension. It is then no longer the peace which the Son has established between man and God: His peacemaking mission, His sufferings and His cross, Jesus Christ—man and God—as the mediator between an estranged creation and its creator. That the great and fundamental change refers to man and his own renewal and not just to the circumstances of his life and his preconditions—this very central and basic aspect of the Christian message seems to have lost interest for theology in these days. Hand in hand with this goes a decline and a loss of the pious and spiritual traditions and practices in the life of the Church and of the individual. When the reality of God's forgiving love and care is not seen anymore, why should man ask and pray for it? If men of our time think that 'peace and happiness' are just a question of making people aware of the necessary structural changes in society and to develop his social awareness and his sense for fellowship and international relationship—why should they refer first to Jesus Christ and his renewal of man? In such a situation it is hardly understood that the devotional life and the continous prayer of a monasterial community is an essential contribution towards more 'peace and happiness' of man in this world. The investment of hope which can be realized by political actions has become so big that the investment into the daily prayer, into the sacramental participation in his presence in his Church or any kind of spiritual discipline which deepens our relation to Him appear to be a lost investment on a blind account. "Exercising oneself into Christendom" ("Einübung ins Christentum", S. Kierkegaard) in this way seems to be a lost time. The fundament and the periphery, the root and fruit, *causa* (*efficiens*) and *causa causata* all this seems to have been turned around. What has to follow comes first. What is the precondition has become in this way a secondary matter.

Everybody seems to know already the conditions for peace and happiness. The "brave new world" (Huxley) has to be just the development of what is now already in the vision of an enlightening ideology: All men will live without conflicts and sorrows. Diseases are supposed to disappear by new inventions. New techniques will set man free from the need of work. The individual's first and basic right becomes to realize oneself ('Selbstverwirklichung').

And this means that a man has the right to decide whether a new life will be born or not, to finish his marriage when the next chance of 'self-realization' looks around the corner or to finish his life when it seems to be not worthwhile any longer. The dream of a coming 'golden age'—the great competition for the only and true revolutionary message of 'dying and living with Christ' in the days of the Roman Empire—is the secular horizon swallowing the eschatological hope in Christ—God and man.

The missionary encounter with modern Hindu philosophy can open our eyes to this development within the Church and theology. This reform leads to a pluralistic, synthetical combination and therefore alienation from the very roots it had risen from. It became a kind of religious philosophy with a humanitarian outlook. Its main forces helped to build up the new nation and to give her selfrespect and a stand within the international family. So far the "salt" of the Gospel has contributed its "saltiness" to the need of the many. But the source—Jesus Christ—God and man—where this salt came and still comes from—had been lost. According to the Hindu tradition the *guru* and the teacher has fulfilled his task and mission when the pupil has become 'adult' to practice his selfrealization for himself. The vessel which brought him across the stream of life to the other shore should be left behind, to use a well-known parable of Buddha himself.

Modern trends in "progressive" Christian theological thinking may be seen to be similar: Jesus and his mission once laid the foundations for a better mankind and its life. He gave basic orientations in regard to our relations to our fellowmen and towards social justice, freedom of the person and peaceful international relations. Others have developed those throughout history. But history itself became the great revelation of this divine blueprint. Hegel, Marx, Freud and others have become the new 'Church-fathers" who have turned the realities of this world and society into what for Jesus still was the other kingdom in its eschatological framework. The new gospel therefore sounds different: Let us join those revolutionary forces who are ready to change the historic conditions right now. Man has to bring the kingdom of heaven into this world. And Jesus Christ our *guru* receives the shape of an exemplary existence for any progressive innerworldly action: Jesus Christ—God and man—soon becomes just 'man', more exactly: the man of the day. Even more: He must have been already the type of revolutionary who wanted to over-throw imperialism and foreign rule. He already was the new 'proletarian' who fought for the rights of the oppressed and underprivileged classes. He was not only the fighter for women's rights, but his call 'Come to me, all who labour and are heavy laden ... (Mt. 11,28) has been misinterpreted as an encouragement for men of all times and in every situation toward any kind of emancipation.

Where the very character of the Christian faith has been estranged from its divine ground in Jesus Christ—God and man—the Church also received a new function. She no longer is the mysterium in which the union with the living and present Christ is realized, where man is brought into life giving union with Him and where this community is understood as the new nation of God reborn and called into a new life in Christ. No wonder when the Church loses her members where such secular theology becomes influential. Since it proclaims the dispensation from all unnecessary pious and transcendental orientation by calling into any kind of public affairs of today, the sermons, the prayers and the community events also receive a different new character. The sermon then has to inform man, to give him the correct picture of the situation which needs action for change. It has to motivate and to mobilize man's lazy bourgois reluctance and undecisiveness. It is no longer praise of God's saving action in Jesus Christ and a call for man's obedience and thanksgiving in answer to it. Prayers become lists of proposals what the expected change should bring. It might range from a new government for Nicaragua to the controversial demand that a highway in the vicinity of Munich should not be constructed. Prayer originally part of a Christian liturgy through which honour, thanks and intercession are brought before God's face for the whole Church and for all nations becomes in this way the useful occasion for proclaiming specific interests within the controversies of the day.

If breathtaking statistics of those who have cancelled their membership in the Church in my homecountry and elsewhere are revealed, it is mainly this reason why they leave the Christian Church. Many of them wanted to meet Jesus Christ—God and man—and to be in His presence during those hours in a Christian community. But continously they feel disappointed: instead they had been confronted with the preacher's own message of a strange issue and of political onesidedness which they cannot share. Seeking refuge in the communion of the saints, sharing in confession and looking for forgiveness and renewal through God's gracious presence, they got disturbed and confused. Instead of the peace which "passes all understanding" (Phil. 4,7) , they became peaceless through their mind and thoughts of this world and its daily affairs.

Search for the hidden relations and for the mystery of Jesus Christ: God and man.

Man is created to give response to his creator. In other words: he is a *homo religiosus*—bound again to and searching for the final reality of which he is part and to which he belongs. Jesus Christ—God and man—has made known to us this final destiny of man as well as his unknown origin. The New Testament uses the most universal term which Greek thinking had prepared at its time in order to express this. He is called the LOGOS. This does not mean less than every being in this kosmos has its origin and his final destiny in Him. Through the person by the name of Jesus of Nazareth man has entrance into the mystery of his and of any other being in this world. That means: There are no secrets left anymore beside this revealing act of God himself. All the secrets of man's life here and after are related to and rooted in this very *mysterion* "God in Christ"—the eternal absolute divine reality under the condition of being, named and in a personal relation—the uncreated being in the role of the created being. Here lies the deepest mystery of all mysteries in human life. It is the mystery *katexochan* which includes all the others and makes them part of this mysterious event: Jesus Christ—God in man. Therefore the dimensions in which man meets the secrets of life and of the kosmos have been consequently related to this event in the life of the historic Jesus as well as in his sacramental union in his Church.

We are used to interpreting the miracle stories of the New Testament as proof for the divine power and authority of Jesus Christ. But they are also expressions of this relation between the hidden realities in this world and in the kosmos and the revelation of God's own concealment in the Christ-event. It is the fulfilment of whatsoever was a previous answer to the unsolved experiences in the religions of mankind. When Jesus and later his apostles drove out demons and satanic spirits they took up an experience which underlies all types of exorcism. The healing power in his divine mission was the visible exegesis of the proclamation that to him had been given all authority in heaven and on earth (Matth. 18,18). Multiplying the food for the hungry was not just a social action. It was the demonstration of the newly revealed reality: In him, who is the satisfying food for every need of man, also the material (*res extensa*—Descartes) has its foundation. When storm and waves had to obey him, the hidden laws of nature revealed their divine center and base. Letters like the one to the Colossians and to the Ephesians show us the "cosmic Christ". The same who had raised Lazarus from death is now sitting beside the Father and ruling the kosmos. He is *pantokrator*—Lord of all. What is inbetween heaven and earth and what belongs to the unlimited universe and its hidden spheres is 'in his hands'. *Ta panta*—the universe—has its being in Him (*ta pana en auto*—Col. 1,17). The unknown, hidden powers (*dunameis, kürioted*) which are experienced in the religions of mankind as spirits and demons, as supernatural forces and human dependencies are 'under his feet' (Eph. 1,21).

Modern man in his autonomous independent attitude has done away with those supernatural powers and experiences. They have been explained as projections of his own misery. Finally Marx and Engels declared this kind of 'opium' necessary as long as man is "enslaved" in a capitalistic class-society. But with the "enlightenment" of modern secular existence also theology has lost this biblical dimension where Christ—God and man—rules and reveals his universal reign. "De-mythologisation" is just one aspect of this process of an a-religious interpretation of man and world. The splendid isolation of a nude existential concept of man remains. But the price for the emptiness is the loss of the divine secret of Christ in its universal dimensions.

As always when man withdraws from his divine father-house the rooms which became empty are not left empty. Since man is not a naked existential being, but experiences his dependency as a timely created being, he had to find other answers to this reality. Is it therefore surprising that the need of discovering the hidden, supranatural dimension of life is being met elsewhere? Not just members of our young generation celebrate the rituals of eastern religious experiences. Rigorously they undergo strong spiritual disciplines. Many discover true existence—apart from what seemed to be the real one so far—by taking the sevenfold path of Buddhism. In Christian sermons and Church proclamations they did not find this necessary religious element which is *contra speciem* (against that what can be seen). Among the pilgrims to the eastern sacred traditions we find today representatives of the academic elite in natural sciences. They find a correspondence between the relativity of the reality which they try to describe in terms of physical and mathematical figures and the mystic approach which seems to transcend the empirical world. What they may have denied and rejected in regard to the mystery and to the sacramental reality of the New Being in Jesus Christ—God and man—they easily admit to the mystic experiences of *moksha* (enlightenment) or believe in rebirth. Jesus Christ had to leave heaven as a mythological construction and a childish imagination. But the stars without Christ's reign become now dominant and decisive 'powers'. As new sovereigns they decide human fortune and destiny. Astrological speculations take the place of former trust in God.

For some years now we experience even a rebirth of Shamanism and animism among western authors. Their message sounds like this: The wisdom of the primal cultures and religions knew more about the reality of a human soul than a modern theology which has nothing to say anymore about a soul after death. Central Christian ways of describing the new life in and with Jesus Christ are now used to define their new religious message. Initiation into this Shaman religion means a ritual death and resurrection of a new man. The soul which has gone through this renewal of existence lives now beyond suffering and death. It has communication with the dead, and is able to see what no natural eye ever has seen. The new post-Christian message for secular man is even an invitation and a call for repentance: 'Come and see and you will find comfort' 'Set aside and forget a Christian message which has given up its sacramental, ritual and mysterious dimensions of reality and has lost itself in the affairs of the day'.

The Christ universal

What is going on around us is a call for repentance and for renewal in Church and theology. The dimensions and realms which have been lost by the Church because they have been left empty without Jesus Christ need to be included again in our theological work and in the life of the Church. The Christians of the Church in Asia, Africa and Latin America are ready to help us in this necessary task. They have never selected from the biblical testimony and from the tradition of the Church according to a onesided and secular concept of man. Jesus Christ for them was the victorious Lord who like in the New Testament has conquered heaven and earth, the visible and the invisible worlds, body, soul and mind, the conscious and the unconscious realm, the past and the future. They are able to introduce us again into the treasures of the Church which we find in her rich traditions. Age after age has contributed to the true exegesis of who Jesus Christ as God and man truly is. Before 'confessionalistic' separations had led to the departmentalisation of those treasures there was no room for substitutional religious interests in non-Christian religious experiences. Every time is tempted to reduce Christ's universal sovereignty by making him just the 'companion of the day'. But he does not fit into our self-made frame-work of our interests and purposes of our so-called "society". He breaks through such limitations and remains with his bride, the Church—even if we do not know anymore her secret and her mysterious glory. But all is preserved. Nothing in this treasure has been lost forever. Repentance in our time means to rediscover who He really is in His Body—the Church—beyond and apart from all the presumed renewals of mankind and of our society which we make Him responsible for. He provides for us what he ever has been. GOD's New Creation hidden in His mysterious Body: the Church universal and eternal.